W9-ANR-252

Zondervan Illustrated Bible Backgrounds Commentary

ABOUT THE AUTHORS

General Editor:

Clinton E. Arnold (Ph.D., University of Aberdeen), professor and chairman, department of New Testament, Talbot School of Theology, Biola University, Los Angeles, California

Gospel of Matthew:

Michael J. Wilkins (Ph.D., Fuller Theological Seminary), professor of New Testament and dean of the faculty, Talbot School of Theology, Biola University, Los Angeles, California

Gospel of Mark:

David E. Garland (Ph.D., Southern Baptist Theological Seminary), associate dean for academic affairs and professor of Christian Scriptures, George W. Truett Theological Seminary, Baylor University, Waco, Texas

Gospel of Luke:

Mark L. Strauss (Ph.D., University of Aberdeen), associate professor of New Testament, Bethel Seminary, San Diego, California

Volume 1

Matthew, Mark, Luke

Zondervan Illustrated Bible Backgrounds Commentary

Clinton E. Arnold
GENERAL EDITOR

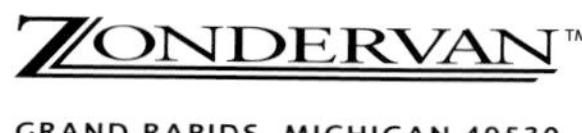

GRAND RAPIDS, MICHIGAN 49530

ZONDERVAN™

Zondervan Illustrated Bible Backgrounds Commentary: Volume 1, *Matthew, Mark, Luke*

Requests for information should be addressed to:

Zondervan, *Grand Rapids, Michigan 49530*

Library of Congress Cataloging-in-Publication Data
Zondervan illustrated Bible backgrounds commentary / Clinton E. Arnold, general editor.
p.cm.
Includes bibliographical references.
Contents: v. 1. Matthew, Mark, Luke—v. 2. John, Acts—v. 3. Romans to Philemon—v. 4. Hebrews to Revelation.
ISBN 0-310-21806-3 (v. 1)—ISBN 0-310-21807-1 (v. 2)—ISBN 0-310-21808-X (v. 3)—ISBN 0-310-21809-8 (v. 4)
1. Bible. N.T.—Commentaries. I. Arnold, Clinton E.
BS2341.52.Z66 2001
225.7—dc21 2001046801
CIP

This edition printed on acid-free paper.

Printed in China

Interior design by Sherri L. Hoffman

02 03 04 05 06 07 08 /❖ HK/ 10 9 8 7 6 5 4 3 2 1

CONTENTS

INTRODUCTION

All readers of the Bible have a tendency to view what it says it through their own culture and life circumstances. This can happen almost subconsiously as we read the pages of the text.

When most people in the church read about the thief on the cross, for instance, they immediately think of a burglar that held up a store or broke into a home. They may be rather shocked to find out that the guy was actually a Jewish revolutionary figure who was part of a growing movement in Palestine eager to throw off Roman rule.

It also comes as something of a surprise to contemporary Christians that "cursing" in the New Testament era had little or nothing to do with cussing somebody out. It had far more to do with the invocation of spirits to cause someone harm.

No doubt there is a need in the church for learning more about the world of the New Testament to avoid erroneous interpretations of the text of Scripture. But relevant historical and cultural insights also provide an added dimension of perspective to the words of the Bible. This kind of information often functions in the same way as watching a movie in color rather than in black and white. Finding out, for instance, how Paul compared Christ's victory on the cross to a joyous celebration parade in honor of a Roman general after winning an extraordinary battle brings does indeed magnify the profundity and implications of Jesus' work on the cross. Discovering that the factions at Corinth ("I follow Paul . . . I follow Apollos . . .") had plenty of precedent in the local cults ("I follow Aphrodite; I follow Apollo . . .") helps us understand the "why" of a particular problem. Learning about the water supply from the springs of Hierapolis that flowed into Laodicea as "lukewarm" water enables us to appreciate the relevance of the metaphor Jesus used when he addressed the spiritual laxity of this church.

My sense is that most Christians are eager to learn more about the real life setting of the New Testament. In the preaching and teaching of the Bible in the church, congregants are always grateful when they learn something of the background and historical context of the text. It not only helps them understand the text more accurately, but often enables them to identify with the people and circumstances of the Bible. I have been asked on countless occasions by Christians, "Where can I get access to good historical background information about this passage?" Earnest Christians are hungry for information that makes their Bibles come alive.

The stimulus for this commentary came from the church and the aim is to serve the church. The contributors to this series have sought to provide illuminating and interesting historical/cultural background information. The intent was to draw upon relevant papyri, inscriptions, archaeological discoveries, and the numerous studies of Judaism, Roman culture, Hellenism, and other features of the world of the New Testament and to make the results accessible to people in the church. We recognize that some readers of the commentary will want to go further, and so the sources of the information have been carefully documented in endnotes.

The written information has been supplemented with hundreds of photographs, maps, charts, artwork, and other graphics that help the reader better understand the world of the New Testament. Each of the writers was given an opportunity to dream up a "wish list" of illustrations that he thought would help to illustrate the passages in the New Testament book for which he was writing commentary. Although we were not able to obtain everything they were looking for, we came close.

The team of commentators are writing for the benefit of the broad array of Christians who simply want to better understand their Bibles from the vantage point of the historical context. This is an installment in a new genre of "Bible background" commentaries that was kicked off by Craig Keener's fine volume. Consequently, this is not an "exegetical" commentary that provides linguistic insight and background into Greek constructions and verb tenses. Neither is this work an "expository" commentary that provides a verse-by-verse exposition of the text; for in-depth philological or theological insight, readers will need to have other more specialized or comprehensive commentaries available. Nor is this an "historical-critical" commentary, although the contributors are all scholars and have already made substantial academic contributions on the New Testament books they are writing on for this set. The team intentionally does not engage all of the issues that are discussed in the scholarly guild.

Rather, our goal is to offer a reading and interpretation of the text informed by what we regard as the most relevant historical information. For many in the church, this commentary will serve as an important entry point into the interpretation and appreciation of the text. For other more serious students of the Word, these volumes will provide an important supplement to many of the fine exegetical, expository, and critical available.

The contributors represent a group of scholars who embrace the Bible as the Word of God and believe that the message of its pages has life-changing relevance for faith and practice today. Accordingly, we offer "Reflections" on the relevance of the Scripture to life for every chapter of the New Testament.

I pray that this commentary brings you both delight and insight in digging deeper into the Word of God.

Clinton E. Arnold
General Editor

LIST OF SIDEBARS

Matthew

Mark

Luke

LIST OF CHARTS

INDEX OF PHOTOS AND MAPS

ABBREVIATIONS

1. Books of the Bible and Apocrypha

1 Chron.	1 Chronicles
2 Chron.	2 Chronicles
1 Cor.	1 Corinthians
2 Cor.	2 Corinthians
1 Esd.	1 Esdras
2 Esd.	2 Esdras
1 John	1 John
2 John	2 John
3 John	3 John
1 Kings	1 Kings
2 Kings	2 Kings
1 Macc.	1 Maccabees
2 Macc.	2 Maccabees
1 Peter	1 Peter
2 Peter	2 Peter
1 Sam.	1 Samuel
2 Sam.	2 Samuel
1 Thess.	1 Thessalonians
2 Thess.	2 Thessalonians
1 Tim.	1 Timothy
2 Tim.	2 Timothy
Acts	Acts
Amos	Amos
Bar.	Baruch
Bel	Bel and the Dragon
Col.	Colossians
Dan.	Daniel
Deut.	Deuteronomy
Eccl.	Ecclesiastes
Ep. Jer.	Epistle of Jeremiah
Eph.	Ephesians
Est.	Esther
Ezek.	Ezekiel
Ex.	Exodus
Ezra	Ezra
Gal.	Galatians
Gen.	Genesis
Hab.	Habakkuk
Hag.	Haggai
Heb.	Hebrews
Hos.	Hosea
Isa.	Isaiah
James	James
Jer.	Jeremiah
Job	Job
Joel	Joel
John	John
Jonah	Jonah
Josh.	Joshua
Jude	Jude
Judg.	Judges
Judith	Judith
Lam.	Lamentations
Lev.	Leviticus
Luke	Luke
Mal.	Malachi
Mark	Mark
Matt.	Matthew
Mic.	Micah
Nah.	Nahum
Neh.	Nehemiah
Num.	Numbers
Obad.	Obadiah
Phil.	Philippians
Philem.	Philemon
Pr. Man.	Prayer of Manassah
Prov.	Proverbs
Ps.	Psalm
Rest. of Est.	The Rest of Esther
Rev.	Revelation
Rom.	Romans
Ruth	Ruth
S. of III Ch.	The Song of the Three Holy Children
Sir.	Sirach/Ecclesiasticus
Song	Song of Songs

Sus.	Susanna
Titus	Titus
Tobit	Tobit
Wisd. Sol.	The Wisdom of Solomon
Zech.	Zechariah
Zeph.	Zephaniah

2. Old and New Testament Pseudepigrapha and Rabbinic Literature

Individual tractates of rabbinic literature follow the abbreviations of the *SBL Handbook of Style*, pp. 79–80. Qumran documents follow standard Dead Sea Scroll conventions.

2 Bar.	*2 Baruch*
3 Bar.	*3 Baruch*
4 Bar.	*4 Baruch*
1 En.	*1 Enoch*
2 En.	*2 Enoch*
3 En.	*3 Enoch*
4 Ezra	*4 Ezra*
3 Macc.	*3 Maccabees*
4 Macc.	*4 Maccabees*
5 Macc.	*5 Maccabees*
Acts Phil.	*Acts of Philip*
Acts Pet.	*Acts of Peter and the 12 Apostles*
Apoc. Elijah	*Apocalypse of Elijah*
As. Mos.	*Assumption of Moses*
b.	*Babylonian Talmud* (+ tractate)
Gos. Thom.	*Gospel of Thomas*
Jos. Asen.	*Joseph and Aseneth*
Jub.	*Jubilees*
Let. Aris.	*Letter of Aristeas*
m.	*Mishnah* (+ tractate)
Mek.	*Mekilta*
Midr.	*Midrash I* (+ biblical book)
Odes Sol.	*Odes of Solomon*
Pesiq. Rab.	*Pesiqta Rabbati*
Pirqe. R. El.	*Pirqe Rabbi Eliezer*
Pss. Sol.	*Psalms of Solomon*
Rab.	*Rabbah* (+biblical book); (e.g., *Gen. Rab.=Genesis Rabbah)*
S. ᶜOlam Rab.	*Seder ᶜOlam Rabbah*
Sem.	*Semahot*
Sib. Or.	*Sibylline Oracles*
T. Ab.	*Testament of Abraham*
T. Adam	*Testament of Adam*
T. Ash.	*Testament of Asher*
T. Benj.	*Testament of Benjamin*
T. Dan	*Testament of Dan*
T. Gad	*Testament of Gad*
T. Hez.	*Testament of Hezekiah*
T. Isaac	*Testament of Isaac*
T. Iss.	*Testament of Issachar*
T. Jac.	*Testament of Jacob*
T. Job	*Testament of Job*
T. Jos.	*Testament of Joseph*
T. Jud.	*Testament of Judah*
T. Levi	*Testament of Levi*
T. Mos.	*Testament of Moses*
T. Naph.	*Testament of Naphtali*
T. Reu.	*Testament of Reuben*
T. Sim.	*Testament of Simeon*
T. Sol.	*Testament of Solomon*
T. Zeb.	*Testament of Zebulum*
Tanh.	*Tanhuma*
Tg. Isa.	*Targum of Isaiah*
Tg. Lam.	*Targum of Lamentations*
Tg. Neof.	*Targum Neofiti*
Tg. Onq.	*Targum Onqelos*
Tg. Ps.-J	*Targum Pseudo-Jonathan*
y.	*Jerusalem Talmud* (+ tractate)

3. Classical Historians

For an extended list of classical historians and church fathers, see *SBL Handbook of Style*, pp. 84–87. For many works of classical antiquity, the abbreviations have been subjected to the author's discretion; the names of these works should be obvious upon consulting entries of the classical writers in classical dictionaries or encyclopedias.

Eusebius

Eccl. Hist.	*Ecclesiastical History*

Josephus

Ag. Ap.	*Against Apion*
Ant.	*Jewish Antiquities*
J.W.	*Jewish War*
Life	*The Life*

Philo

Abraham	On the Life of Abraham
Agriculture	On Agriculture
Alleg. Interp	*Allegorical Interpretation*
Animals	*Whether Animals Have Reason*
Cherubim	*On the Cherubim*
Confusion	*On the Confusion of Thomas*
Contempl. Life	*On the Contemplative Life*
Creation	*On the Creation of the World*
Curses	*On Curses*
Decalogue	*On the Decalogue*
Dreams	*On Dreams*
Drunkenness	*On Drunkenness*
Embassy	*On the Embassy to Gaius*
Eternity	*On the Eternity of the World*
Flaccus	*Against Flaccus*
Flight	*On Flight and Finding*
Giants	*On Giants*
God	*On God*
Heir	*Who Is the Heir?*
Hypothetica	*Hypothetica*
Joseph	*On the Life of Joseph*
Migration	*On the Migration of Abraham*
Moses	*On the Life of Moses*
Names	*On the Change of Names*
Person	*That Every Good Person Is Free*
Planting	*On Planting*
Posterity	*On the Posterity of Cain*
Prelim. Studies	*On the Preliminary Studies*
Providence	*On Providence*
QE	*Questions and Answers on Exodus*
QG	*Questions and Answers on Genesis*
Rewards	*On Rewards and Punishments*
Sacrifices	*On the Sacrifices of Cain and Abel*
Sobriety	*On Sobriety*
Spec. Laws	*On the Special Laws*
Unchangeable	*That God Is Unchangeable*
Virtues	*On the Virtues*
Worse	*That the Worse Attacks the Better*

Apostolic Fathers

1 Clem.	*First Letter of Clement*
Barn.	*Epistle of Barnabas*
Clem. Hom.	*Ancient Homily of Clement* (also called *2 Clement*)
Did.	*Didache*
Herm. Vis.; Sim.	*Shepherd of Hermas, Visions; Similitudes*
Ignatius	*Epistles of Ignatius* (followed by the letter's name)
Mart. Pol.	*Martyrdom of Polycarp*

4. Modern Abbreviations

AASOR	Annual of the American Schools of Oriental Research
AB	Anchor Bible
ABD	*Anchor Bible Dictionary*
ABRL	Anchor Bible Reference Library
AGJU	Arbeiten zur Geschichte des antiken Judentums und des Urchristentums
AH	*Agricultural History*
ALGHJ	Arbeiten zur Literatur und Geschichte des Hellenistischen Judentums
AnBib	Analecta biblica
ANRW	*Aufstieg und Niedergang der römischen Welt*

ANTC	Abingdon New Testament Commentaries
BAGD	Bauer, W., W. F. Arndt, F. W. Gingrich, and F. W. Danker. *Greek-English Lexicon of the New Testament and Other Early Christina Literature* (2d. ed.)
BA	*Biblical Archaeologist*
BAFCS	Book of Acts in Its First Century Setting
BAR	*Biblical Archaeology Review*
BASOR	*Bulletin of the American Schools of Oriental Research*
BBC	*Bible Background Commentary*
BBR	*Bulletin for Biblical Research*
BDB	Brown, F., S. R. Driver, and C. A. Briggs. *A Hebrew and English Lexicon of the Old Testament*
BDF	Blass, F., A. Debrunner, and R. W. Funk. *A Greek Grammar of the New Testament and Other Early Christian Literature*
BECNT	Baker Exegetical Commentary on the New Testament
BI	*Biblical Illustrator*
Bib	*Biblica*
BibSac	*Bibliotheca Sacra*
BLT	Brethren Life and Thought
BNTC	Black's New Testament Commentary
BRev	*Bible Review*
BSHJ	Baltimore Studies in the History of Judaism
BST	The Bible Speaks Today
BSV	Biblical Social Values
BT	*The Bible Translator*
BTB	*Biblical Theology Bulletin*
BZ	*Biblische Zeitschrift*
CBQ	*Catholic Biblical Quarterly*
CBTJ	*Calvary Baptist Theological Journal*
CGTC	Cambridge Greek Testament Commentary
CH	*Church History*
CIL	*Corpus inscriptionum latinarum*
CPJ	*Corpus papyrorum judaicorum*
CRINT	*Compendia rerum iudaicarum ad Novum Testamentum*
CTJ	*Calvin Theological Journal*
CTM	*Concordia Theological Monthly*
CTT	Contours of Christian Theology
DBI	*Dictionary of Biblical Imagery*
DCM	*Dictionary of Classical Mythology.*
DDD	*Dictionary of Deities and Demons in the Bible*
DJBP	*Dictionary of Judaism in the Biblical Period*
DJG	*Dictionary of Jesus and the Gospels*
DLNT	*Dictionary of the Later New Testament and Its Developments*
DNTB	*Dictionary of New Testament Background*
DPL	*Dictionary of Paul and His Letters*
EBC	*Expositor's Bible Commentary*
EDBT	*Evangelical Dictionary of Biblical Theology*
EDNT	*Exegetical Dictionary of the New Testament*

EJR	*Encyclopedia of the Jewish Religion*
EPRO	Études préliminaires aux religions orientales dans l'empire romain
EvQ	*Evangelical Quarterly*
ExpTim	*Expository Times*
FRLANT	Forsuchungen zur Religion und Literatur des Alten und Neuen Testament
GNC	Good News Commentary
GNS	Good News Studies
HCNT	*Hellenistic Commentary to the New Testament*
HDB	*Hastings Dictionary of the Bible*
HJP	*History of the Jewish People in the Age of Jesus Christ,* by E. Schürer
HTR	*Harvard Theological Review*
HTS	Harvard Theological Studies
HUCA	*Hebrew Union College Annual*
IBD	*Illustrated Bible Dictionary*
IBS	*Irish Biblical Studies*
ICC	International Critical Commentary
IDB	*The Interpreter's Dictionary of the Bible*
IEJ	*Israel Exploration Journal*
IG	*Inscriptiones graecae*
IGRR	*Inscriptiones graecae ad res romanas pertinentes*
ILS	*Inscriptiones Latinae Selectae*
Imm	*Immanuel*
ISBE	*International Standard Bible Encyclopedia*
Int	*Interpretation*
IvE	*Inschriften von Ephesos*
IVPNTC	InterVarsity Press New Testament Commentary
JAC	*Jahrbuch fur Antike und Christentum*
JBL	*Journal of Biblical Literature*
JETS	*Journal of the Evangelical Theological Society*
JHS	*Journal of Hellenic Studies*
JJS	*Journal of Jewish Studies*
JOAIW	*Jahreshefte des Osterreeichischen Archaologischen Instites in Wien*
JSJ	*Journal for the Study of Judaism in the Persian, Hellenistic, and Roman Periods*
JRS	*Journal of Roman Studies*
JSNT	*Journal for the Study of the New Testament*
JSNTSup	Journal for the Study of the New Testament: Supplement Series
JSOT	*Journal for the Study of the Old Testament*
JSOTSup	Journal for the Study of the Old Testament: Supplement Series
JTS	*Journal of Theological Studies*
KTR	*Kings Theological Review*
LCL	Loeb Classical Library
LEC	Library of Early Christianity
LSJ	Liddell, H. G., R. Scott, H. S. Jones. *A Greek-English Lexicon*
MM	Moulton, J. H., and G. Milligan. *The Vocabulary of the Greek Testament*
MNTC	Moffatt New Testament Commentary
NBD	*New Bible Dictionary*
NC	Narrative Commentaries
NCBC	New Century Bible Commentary Eerdmans

NEAE *New Encyclopedia of Archaeological Excavations in the Holy Land*
NEASB *Near East Archaeological Society Bulletin*
New Docs *New Documents Illustrating Early Christianity*
NIBC New International Biblical Commentary
NICNT New International Commentary on the New Testament
NIDNTT *New International Dictionary of New Testament Theology*
NIGTC New International Greek Testament Commentary
NIVAC NIV Application Commentary
NorTT *Norsk Teologisk Tidsskrift*
NoT *Notes on Translation*
NovT *Novum Testamentum*
NovTSup Novum Testamentum Supplements
NTAbh Neutestamentliche Abhandlungen
NTS *New Testament Studies*
NTT New Testament Theology
NTTS New Testament Tools and Studies
OAG *Oxford Archaeological Guides*
OCCC *Oxford Companion to Classical Civilization*
OCD *Oxford Classical Dictionary*
ODCC *The Oxford Dictionary of the Christian Church*
OGIS *Orientis graeci inscriptiones selectae*
OHCW *The Oxford History of the Classical World*
OHRW *Oxford History of the Roman World*
OTP *Old Testament Pseudepigrapha*, ed. by J. H. Charlesworth
PEQ *Palestine Exploration Quarterly*
PG *Patrologia graeca*
PGM *Papyri graecae magicae: Die griechischen Zauberpapyri*
PL *Patrologia latina*
PNTC Pelican New Testament Commentaries
Rb *Revista biblica*
RB *Revue biblique*
RivB *Rivista biblica italiana*
RTR *Reformed Theological Review*
SB Sources bibliques
SBL Society of Biblical Literature
SBLDS Society of Biblical Literature Dissertation Series
SBLMS Society of Biblical Literature Monograph Series
SBLSP *Society of Biblical Literature Seminar Papers*
SBS Stuttgarter Bibelstudien
SBT Studies in Biblical Theology
SCJ *Stone-Campbell Journal*
Scr *Scripture*
SE *Studia Evangelica*
SEG *Supplementum epigraphicum graecum*
SJLA Studies in Judaism in Late Antiquity
SJT *Scottish Journal of Theology*
SNTSMS Society for New Testament Studies Monograph Series
SSC Social Science Commentary

SSCSSG	Social-Science Commentary on the Synoptic Gospels
Str-B	Strack, H. L., and P. Billerbeck. *Kommentar zum Neuen Testament aus Talmud und Midrasch*
TC	Thornapple Commentaries
TDNT	*Theological Dictionary of the New Testament*
TDOT	*Theological Dictionary of the Old Testament*
TLNT	*Theological Lexicon of the New Testament*
TLZ	*Theologische Literaturzeitung*
TNTC	Tyndale New Testament Commentary
TrinJ	*Trinity Journal*
TS	*Theological Studies*
TSAJ	Texte und Studien zum antiken Judentum
TWNT	*Theologische Wörterbuch zum Neuen Testament*
TynBul	*Tyndale Bulletin*
WBC	Word Biblical Commentary Waco: Word, 1982
WMANT	Wissenschaftliche Monographien zum Alten und Neuen Testament
WUNT	Wissenschaftliche Untersuchungen zum Neuen Testament
YJS	Yale Judaica Series
ZNW	*Zeitschrift fur die neutestamentliche Wissenschaft und die Junde der alteren Kirche*
ZPE	*Zeischrift der Papyrolgie und Epigraphkik*
ZPEB	*Zondervan Pictorial Encyclopedia of the Bible*

5. General Abbreviations

ad. loc.	in the place cited
b.	born
c., ca.	circa
cf.	compare
d.	died
ed(s).	editors(s), edited by
e.g.	for example
ET	English translation
frg.	fragment
i.e.	that is
ibid.	in the same place
idem	the same (author)
lit.	literally
l(l)	line(s)
MSS	manuscripts
n.d.	no date
NS	New Series
par.	parallel
passim	here and there
repr.	reprint
ser.	series
s.v.	*sub verbo*, under the word
trans.	translator, translated by; transitive

Zondervan Illustrated Bible Backgrounds Commentary

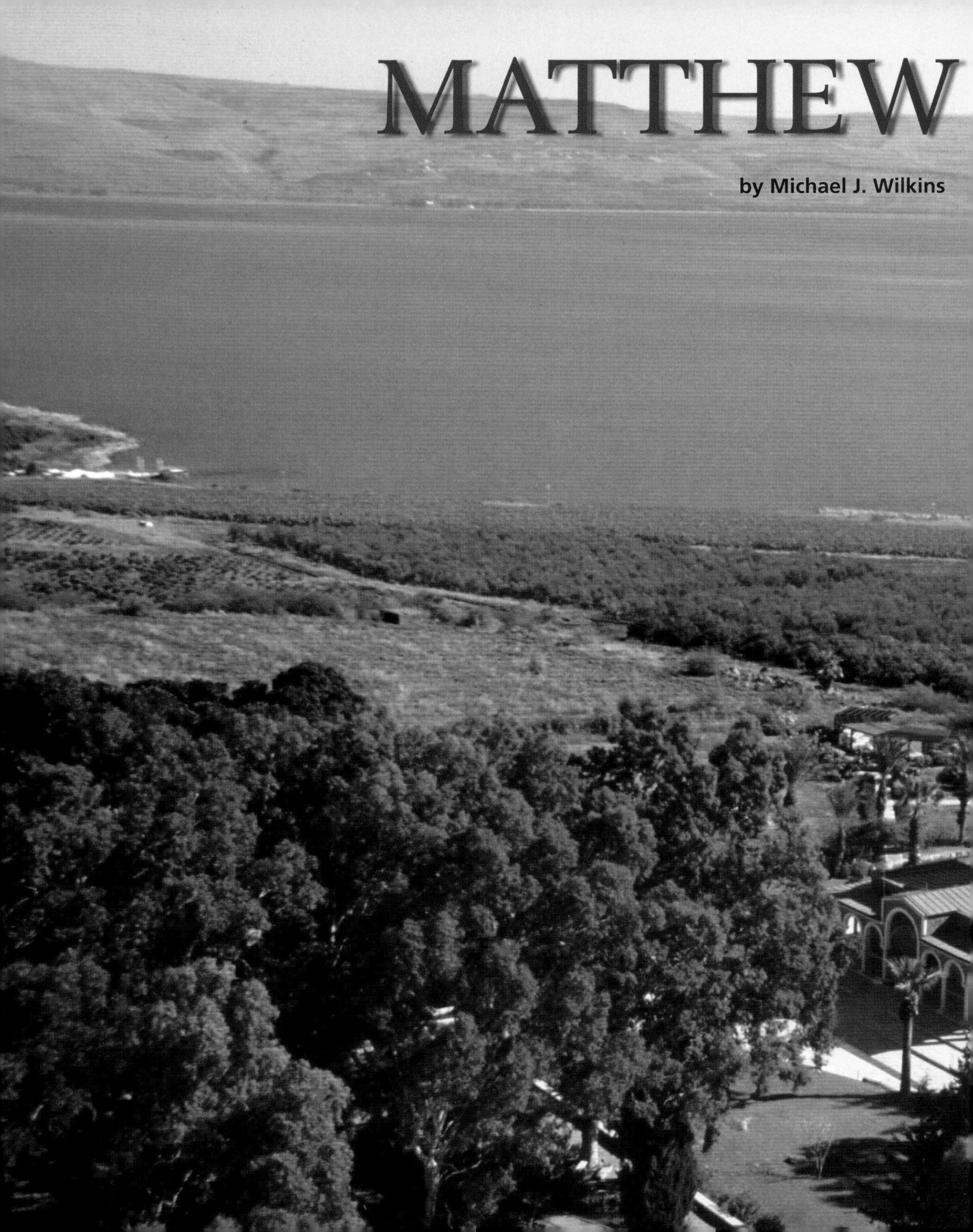

MATTHEW

by Michael J. Wilkins

Introduction to The Gospel According to Matthew

On the surface of the Mediterranean world lay the famed *pax Romana,* "the peace of Rome," which the Roman historian Tacitus attributes almost solely to the immense powers of Caesar Augustus. But as Tacitus observes, the "peace" that Augustus inaugurated did not bring with it freedom for all of his subjects; many continued to hope for change.[1] Tides of revolution swirled just below the surface and periodically rose to disturb the so-called peace of the Roman empire.

In one of the remote regions of the empire, where a variety of disturbances repeatedly surfaced, the hoped for freedom finally arrived in a most unexpected way. A rival to Augustus was born in Israel. But this rival did not appear with fanfare, nor would he challenge directly the military and political might of Rome. Even many of his own people would become disappointed with

MOUNT OF BEATITUDES

Overlooking the Sea of Galilee

Matthew IMPORTANT FACTS:

- **AUTHOR:** While technically anonymous, the first book of the New Testament canon was unanimously attributed by the early church to Matthew-Levi, one of the Twelve apostles of Jesus Christ.
- **DATE:** A.D. 60–61 (Paul imprisoned in Rome).
- **OCCASION:** Matthew addresses a church that is representative of the emerging Christian community of faith—it transcends ethnic, economic, and religious barriers to find oneness in its adherence to Jesus Messiah. His Gospel becomes a manual on discipleship to Jesus, as Jew and Gentile alike form a new community in an increasingly hostile world.
- **PORTRAIT OF CHRIST:** Jesus is the true Messiah, Immanuel, God-incarnate with his people.
- **KEY THEMES:**
  1. The bridge between Old and New Testaments.
  2. Salvation-historical "particularism" and "universalism."
  3. The new community of faith.
  4. The church built and maintained by Jesus' continuing presence.
  5. A "great commission" for evangelism and mission.
  6. The structure of five discourses contributes to a manual on discipleship.

the revolution that he would bring, because it was a revolution of the heart, not of swords or chariots.

This is the story of the arrival of Jesus of Nazareth, recorded by the apostle Matthew as a compelling witness that Jesus was the long-anticipated Messiah, the prophesied fulfillment of God's promise of true peace and deliverance for both Jew and Gentile.

Author

All of the four Gospels are technically anonymous, since the names of the authors are not stated explicitly. This is natural since the authors were not writing letters to which are attached the names of the addressees and senders. Rather, the evangelists were compiling stories of Jesus for churches of which they were active participants and leaders. They likely stood among the assembly and first read their Gospel account themselves. To attach their names as authors would have been unnecessary, because their audiences knew their identity, or perhaps even inappropriate, since the primary intention was not to assert their own leadership authority, but to record for their audiences the matchless story of the life and ministry of Jesus.

Therefore we must look to the records of church history to find evidence for the authorship of the Gospels. The earliest church tradition unanimously ascribes the first Gospel to Matthew, the tax-collector who was called to be one of the original twelve disciples of Jesus. The earliest and most important of these traditions come from Papias, bishop of Hierapolis in Asia Minor (c. 135), and from Irenaeus, bishop of Lyons in Gaul (c. 175). These church leaders either knew the apostolic community directly or were taught by those associated with the apostles; thus, they were directly aware of the origins of the Gospels. While the full meaning of their statements is still open to discussion, no competing tradition assigning the first Gospel to any other author has survived, if any ever existed. False ascription to a relatively obscure apostle such as Matthew seems unlikely until a later date, when canonization of apostles was common.

Matthew, the Person

The list of the twelve disciples in Matthew's gospel refers to "Matthew the tax collector" (10:3), which harks back to the incident when Jesus called Matthew

▸ Early Church Testimony to Matthean Authorship

Papias, bishop of Hierapolis in Asia Minor, lived approximately A.D. 60–130. It is claimed that Papias was a hearer of the apostle John and later was a companion of Polycarp.[A-1] He was quoted and endorsed by the church historian Eusebius (c. A.D. 325) as saying: "Matthew for his part compiled/collected the oracles in the Hebrew [Aramaic] dialect and every person translated/interpreted them as he was able" (Eusebius, *Eccl. Hist.* 3.39.16).

Irenaeus, bishop of Lyons in Gaul, was born in Asia Minor in approximately A.D. 135, studied under Polycarp, bishop of Smyrna, and according to tradition died as a martyr around A.D. 200. In one of his five monumental books against the Gnostic heresies, Irenaeus states, "Matthew also issued a written Gospel among the Hebrews in their own dialect, while Peter and Paul were preaching at Rome, and laying the foundations of the Church."[A-2] while he was sitting in the tax office (cf. 9:9). When recounting the call, the first Gospel refers to him as "Matthew" (9:9), while Mark's Gospel refers to him as "Levi son of Alphaeus" (Mark 2:14), and Luke's Gospel refers to him as "Levi" (Luke 5:27). Speculation surrounds the reason for the variation, but most scholars suggest that this tax collector had two names, Matthew Levi, either from birth or from the time of his conversion.

The name Levi may be an indication that he was from the tribe of Levi and therefore was familiar with Levitical practices. Mark's record of the calling refers to him as the "son of Alphaeus" (Mark 2:14), which some have understood to mean that he was the brother of the apostle "James son of Alphaeus" (cf. Mark 3:18). But since the other pairs of brothers are specified as such and linked together, it is unlikely that Matthew-Levi and James were brothers.

Matthew-Levi was called to follow Jesus while he was sitting in the tax collector's booth. This booth was probably located on one of the main trade highways near Capernaum, collecting tolls for Herod Antipas from the commercial traffic traveling through this area. Matthew immediately followed Jesus and arranged a banquet for Jesus at his home, to which were invited a large crowd of tax collectors and sinners (9:10–11; Luke 5:29–30). Since tax collectors generally were fairly wealthy and were despised by the local populace (cf. Zacchaeus, Luke 19:1–10), Matthew's calling and response were completely out of the ordinary and required nothing short of a miraculous turn-around in this tax collector's life.

Little else is known of Matthew-Levi, except for the widely attested tradition that he is the author of this Gospel that now bears his name. As a tax collector he would have been trained in secular scribal techniques, and as a Galilean Jewish Christian he would have been able to interpret the life of Jesus from the perspective of the Old Testament expectations. Eusebius said that Matthew first preached to "Hebrews" and then to "others," including places such as Persia, Parthia, and Syria (Eusebius, *Eccl. Hist.* 3.24.6). The traditions are mixed regarding Matthew's death, with some saying that he died a martyr's death, while others saying that he died a natural death.

Date and Destination

No precise date for the writing of Matthew is known, although Jesus' prophecy of the overthrow of Jerusalem (24:1–28), has recently been used to indicate that this Gospel must have been written after A.D. 70. However, such a conclusion is necessary only if one denies Jesus the

PAPYRUS MANUSCRIPT OF MATTHEW 26:19–52

This is a third-century A.D. fragment known as *p*37 now housed at the University of Michigan.

JERUSALEM DURING THE MINISTRY OF JESUS

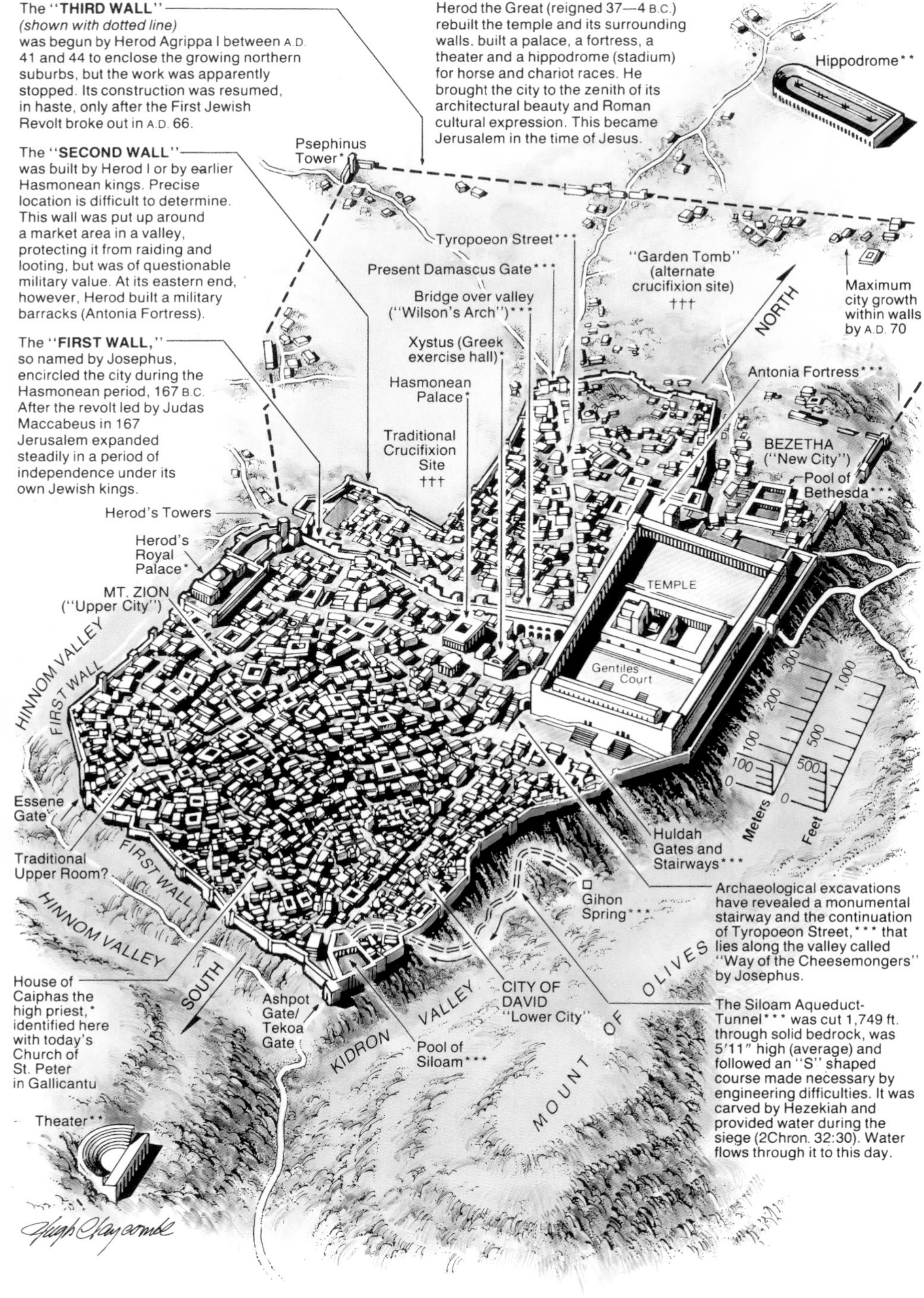

* Location generally known, but style of architecture is unknown; artist's concept only, and Roman architecture is assumed.

** Location and architecture unknown, but referred to in written history; shown here for illustrative purposes.

*** Ancient feature has remained, or appearance has been determined from evidence.

Buildings, streets and roads shown here are artist's concept only unless otherwise named and located. Wall heights remain generally unknown, except for those surrounding the Temple Mount.

ability to predict the future. Since the early church father Irenaeus (c. A.D. 175) indicates that Matthew wrote his Gospel while Paul and Peter were still alive,[2] the traditional dating has usually settled on the late 50s or early 60s.

The highly influential church at Antioch in Syria, with its large Jewish-Christian and Gentile contingents (cf. Acts 11:19–26; 13:1–3), has often been recognized as the original recipients of this Gospel. This is confirmed in part because of its influence on Ignatius, the bishop of Antioch, and on the *Didache*. But Matthew's message was equally relevant for the fledgling church throughout the ancient world, and appears to have been disseminated fairly quickly.

Purpose in Writing

Matthew's first verse gives the direction to his purpose for writing: It is a book that establishes Jesus' identity as the Messiah, the heir to the promises of Israel's throne through King David and to the promises of blessing to all the nations through the patriarch Abraham. Against the backdrop of a world increasingly hostile to Christianity, Matthew solidifies his church's identity as God's true people, who transcend ethnic, economic, and religious barriers to find oneness in their adherence to Jesus Messiah. His gospel becomes a manual on discipleship, as Jew and Gentile become disciples of Jesus who learn to obey all he commanded his original disciples.

Matthew's Story of Jesus Messiah

Matthew's Gospel, according to citations found in early Christian writers, was the most widely used and influential of any of the Gospels.[3] It has retained its appeal throughout the centuries and has exerted a powerful influence on the church. Its popularity is explained at least in part because of the following distinctives that are found throughout this gospel.

(1) The bridge between Old and New Testaments. From the opening lines of his story, Matthew provides a natural bridge between the Old Testament and New Testament. He demonstrates repeatedly that Old Testament hopes, prophecies, and promises have now been fulfilled in the person and ministry of Jesus, beginning with the "fulfillment" of the messianic genealogy (1:1), the fulfillment of various Old Testament prophecies and themes, and the fulfillment of the Old Testament law.[4] The early church likely placed Matthew first in the New Testament canon precisely because of its value as a bridge between the Testaments.

(2) Salvation-historical "particularism" and "universalism." These terms emphasize that Matthew's Gospel lays striking emphasis on both the fulfillment of the promises of salvation to a particular people, Israel, and also the fulfillment of the universal promise of salvation to all the peoples of the earth. Matthew's Gospel alone points explicitly to Jesus' intention to go first to the lost sheep of the house of Israel (10:5–6; 15:24), showing historically how God's promise of salvation to Israel was indeed fulfilled. Yet the promises made to Abraham that he would be a blessing to all the nations are also fulfilled as Jesus extends salvation to the Gentiles (cf. 21:44; 28:19). The church throughout the ages has found assurance in Matthew's Gospel that God truly keeps his promises to his people.

(3) The new community of faith. Facing the threat of gathering Roman persecution within a pagan world, Matthew addresses a church that is representative of the emerging community of faith. The community apparently has a large membership of Jewish Christians, familiar with temple activities and the Jewish religious system. But it also has a large contingent of Gentile Christians, who are discovering their heritage of faith in God's universal promise of salvation. The church has consistently found in Matthew's Gospel a call to a new community that transcends ethnic and religious barriers to find oneness in its adherence to Jesus Messiah.

(4) The church is built and maintained by Jesus' continuing presence. Matthew alone among the evangelists uses the term *ekklēsia*, which later became the common term to designate the church. He emphasizes explicitly that God's program of salvation-history will find its continuation in the present age as Jesus builds his church and maintains his presence within its assembly.[5] Whoever responds to his invitation (22:10)—whether Jew or Gentile, male or female, rich or poor, slave or free—are brought within the church to enjoy his fellowship and demonstrate the true community of faith.

THE COURT OF THE PRIESTS IN HEROD'S TEMPLE

This model shows the altar and the bronze laver.

(5) A "great commission" for evangelism and mission. The form of Jesus' commission to "make disciples of all the nations" (28:19) is unique to Matthew's Gospel, providing continuity between Jesus' ministry of making disciples in his earthly ministry and the ongoing ministry of making disciples to which the church has been called. This "great commission" has been at the heart of evangelistic and missionary endeavor throughout church history.

(6) The structure of five discourses contributes to a manual on discipleship. The concluding element of the commission, in which Jesus states that new disciples are to be taught "to obey everything I have commanded you" (28:20), gives a hint to one overall purpose for Matthew's Gospel. The presentation of five of Jesus' major discourses, all of which are addressed at least in part to Jesus' disciples (chs. 5–7, 10, 13, 18, 24–25), forms the most comprehensive collection of Jesus' earthly instructional ministry found in the Gospels. They provide a wholistic presentation on the kind of discipleship that was to be taught to disciples as the basis for full-orbed obedience to Christ and became the basis for Christian catechesis within the church throughout its history.

The Geneaology of Jesus Messiah (1:1–17)

This is the story of the arrival of Jesus of Nazareth, recorded as a compelling witness that Jesus was the long-anticipated Messiah, the prophesied fulfillment of

God's promise of deliverance for both Jew and Gentile.

A record of the genealogy of Jesus Christ (1:1). The Greek word translated "genealogy" in 1:1 is *genesis*, "beginning," which is the title of the Greek translation (LXX) of Genesis, where it implies that it is a book of beginnings. Genesis gave the story of one beginning—God's creation and covenant relations with Israel—while Matthew gives the story of a new beginning—the arrival of Jesus the Messiah and the kingdom of God.

Jesus Christ the son of David, the son of Abraham (1:1). Matthew's opening had special importance to a Jewish audience, which traced their ancestry through the covenants God made with Israel. "Jesus" (*Iēsous*) was the name normally used in the Gospels,[6] derived from the Hebrew *Yeshua*, "Yahweh saves" (Neh. 7:7), which is a shortened form of Joshua, "Yahweh is salvation" (Ex. 24:13). "Christ" is a title, the transliteration of the Greek *Christos*,[7] which harks back to David as the anointed king of Israel. The term came to be associated with the promise of a Messiah or "anointed one" who would be the hope for the people of Israel. God had promised David through Nathan the prophet that the house and throne of David would be established forever (2 Sam.7:11b–16), a promise now fulfilled in Jesus as the "son of David." But Jesus is also the "son of Abraham." The covenant God made with Abraham established Israel as a chosen people, but it was also a promise that his line would be a blessing to all the nations (Gen. 12:1–3; 22:18).

Abraham the father of Isaac (1:2). The Jews kept extensive genealogies, which served generally as a record of a family's descendants, but which were also used for practical and legal purposes to establish a person's heritage, inheritance, legitimacy, and rights.[8]

Matthew most likely draws on some of the genealogies found in the Old Testament[9] and uses similar wording (cf. 1:2 with 2 Chron. 1:34). For the listing of the individuals after Zerubbabel, when the Old Testament ceases, he probably uses records that have since been lost. Other sources indicate that extensive genealogical records were extant during the first century,[10] with some of the more important political and priestly families' records kept in the temple.[11] The official extrabiblical genealogies were lost with the destruction of the temple and

REFLECTIONS

THE GENUINENESS, AND UN-likeliness, of this genealogy must have stunned Matthew's readers. Jesus' descendants were humans with all of the foibles, yet potentials, of everyday people. God worked through them to bring about his salvation. There is no pattern of righteousness in the lineage of Jesus. We find adulterers, harlots, heroes, and Gentiles. Wicked Rehoboam was the father of wicked Abijah, who was the father of good King Asa. Asa was the father of the good King Jehoshaphat (v. 8), who was the father of wicked King Joram. God was working throughout the generations, both good and evil, to bring about his purposes. Matthew shows that God can use anyone—however marginalized or despised—to bring about his purposes. These are the very types of people Jesus came to save.

Jerusalem in A.D. 70, yet private genealogies were retained elsewhere.

Matthew gives a descending genealogy of Jesus in the order of succession, with the earliest ancestor placed at the head and later generations placed in lines of descent. This is the more common form of genealogy in the Old Testament (e.g., Gen. 5:1–32). Luke gives an ascending form of genealogy that reverses the order, starting with Jesus and tracing it to Adam (Luke 3:23–38; cf. Ezra 7:1–5). This reverse order is found more commonly in Greco-Roman genealogies.

Jesse [was] the father of King David. David was the father of Solomon (1:6). David is not simply the son of Jesse (Luke 3:31–32), but "King" (Matt. 1:6). Matthew traces Jesus' genealogy through David's son Solomon, who had succeeded his father as king of Israel, while Luke traces the line through David's son Nathan, who had not actually reigned as king.[12] David's greater Son, the anticipated Davidic messianic king, has arrived with the birth of Jesus.[13]

Tamar ... Rahab ... Ruth ... whose mother had been Uriah's wife ... Mary (1:3, 5, 6, 16). Women were not always included in Old Testament genealogies since descent was traced through men as the head of the family. When women were included, there was usually some particular reason.[14] Matthew seems to emphasize that these women, some of whom were Gentiles, others disreputable, and others wrongfully treated because of their gender, each had a role to play in the line of Messiah. By including them in this genealogy Matthew shows that God is reversing the gender marginalization of women found in some circles in Judaism to bring about his purposes.

Jacob the father of Joseph, the husband of Mary, of whom was born Jesus, who is called Christ (1:16). While the genealogy establishes that Joseph is the legal father of Jesus, Matthew emphasizes that Mary is the biological parent "of whom" Jesus was born, preparing for the virgin birth by shifting attention from Joseph to Mary.

Thus there were fourteen generations (1:17). Matthew skips some generations in Jesus' family tree so that the structure can be made uniform for memorization, while other members are given prominence to make a particular point. The number fourteen may be a subtle reference to David, because the numerical value of the Hebrew consonants of his name is fourteen (d w d = 4+6+4). The Jewish practice of counting the numerical value for letters is called *gematria*. Some forms of Jewish mysticism took the practice to extremes,[15] but its most basic form helped in memorization and for encoding theological meaning.

The Angelic Announcement of the Conception of Jesus Messiah (1:18–25)

Joseph her husband was a righteous man (1:19). Joseph first learns of Mary's condition without knowing of the concep-

right ▶

THE ANGEL APPEARING TO JOSEPH

A painting in the Church of St. Joseph in Nazareth.

tion's supernatural origin, and therefore, as a righteous man, it is appropriate to obtain a certificate of divorce because he thinks that she has committed adultery. Once Joseph discovers that Mary is pregnant, he experiences a personal dilemma. Divorce for adultery was not optional, but mandatory, among many groups in ancient Judaism, because adultery produced a state of impurity that, as a matter of legal fact, dissolved the marriage.

He had in mind to divorce her quietly (1:19). Joseph cannot follow through and marry her, because that would condone what he thinks is her sin of adultery. Therefore Joseph has only two options open to him. He can make Mary's condition known publicly—but then she will be subject to widespread disgrace as an adulteress, and it can make her liable to be stoned as an adulteress according to the demands of the law.[16] Or he can divorce her quietly—the only option that allows him to retain his righteousness and yet save Mary from public disgrace and possible death. Since the law did not require the deed to be made public, it

Jewish Marriage Customs: Betrothal and Wedding

The marriage customs of Jewish culture at that time usually included two basic stages of the relationship, the betrothal and the wedding.[A-3]

(1) Betrothal (or engagement). The first stage of betrothal[A-4] was the choosing of a spouse. The family in ancient Near Eastern culture usually initiated the arrangements. Although we find in the Old Testament examples of young men and women making their preferences known (Ruth 2–4), customarily the parents of a young man chose a young woman to be engaged to their son (e.g., Gen. 21:21; 38:6). Young men and women were often pledged between twelve and thirteen years of age, although later rabbinic texts suggest that men in Jesus' day often married around the age of eighteen.[A-5]

The second stage of betrothal involved the official arrangements. In a formal prenuptial agreement before witnesses, the young man and woman entered into the state of betrothal or engagement. This was a legally binding contract, giving the man legal rights over the woman. It could only be broken by a formal process of divorce.[A-6] The terminology "husband" and "wife" were now used to refer to the betrothed partners (see 1:16, 19, 20, 24). While there is some evidence in Judea of the betrothed couple being alone during this interval at the man's father's home,[A-7] in Galilee sexual relations between the betrothed partners were not tolerated, and the girl did not leave her own family to live with the man. Sexual unfaithfulness during this stage was considered adultery, the penalty for which was death by stoning (cf. Lev. 20:10; Deut. 22:23–24), although by New Testament times stoning was rare. If one of the partners died during the betrothal period, the one remaining alive was a "widow" or "widower."[A-8]

(2) Wedding. In a formal ceremony about a year after the betrothal, the marriage proper was initiated.[A-9] Dressed in special wedding garments, the bridegroom and companions went in procession to the bride's home and escorted the bride and bridesmaids back to the groom's home, where a wedding supper was held (Matt. 22:1–14; Ps. 45:14–15). Parents and friends blessed the couple (Gen. 24:60; Tobit 7:13), and the father of the bride drew up a written marriage contract.[A-10] Soon afterward in a specially prepared nuptial chamber[A-11] the couple prayed and consummated sexually the marriage, after which a bloodstained cloth was exhibited as proof of the bride's virginity (Deut. 22:13–21). The wedding festivities continued sometimes for a week or more (Gen. 29:27; Tobit 8:20). Afterward the couple established their own household, although they usually lived with the extended family.

made allowance for a relatively private divorce (two to three witnesses).

An angel of the Lord appeared to him (1:20). Sometimes in the Old Testament God himself is represented by the phrase "angel of the Lord,"[17] but here the angel is one of God's created spirit beings.[18] The word "angel" (Gk. *angelos*; "messenger") speaks of one of an angel's primary roles as a messenger from God to humanity. Nothing is said of this angel's appearance, but they sometimes took the form of humans (Gen. 18). Gabriel appears in the book of Daniel as an agent of eschatological revelation (Dan. 8:15–26; 9:20–27), and in Luke's Gospel he is "the angel of the Lord," who announces both the birth of John the Baptist to Zechariah and the birth of Jesus to Mary (Luke 1:11, 19, 26ff.). The unnamed "angel of the Lord" who announced the birth of Jesus to the shepherds (Luke 2:9) and here the conception of Jesus to Joseph may also be Gabriel, who seems to have a special role in announcements.[19]

In a dream (1:20). Dreams were commonly believed in the Greco-Roman world not only to be of natural origin, but also to be a medium of divine communication.[20] In the Old Testament, dreams were believed to derive from natural, divine, and evil sources,[21] but primarily point to a message from God about present activities or future events.[22] The expression "in a dream" is more restricted in its New Testament use, found only in Matthew's Gospel. In each case the dream is related to Jesus,[23] providing supernatural guidance.

What is conceived in her is from the Holy Spirit (1:20). The Old Testament writers repeatedly refer to the Spirit of God as the agency of God's power (e.g., Gen. 1:2; Judg. 3:10), but it is not until here in the incarnation that the Spirit is clearly understood as a person distinct from the Father and Son.

Give him the name Jesus, because he will save his people from their sins (1:21). The name "Jesus" was popular in Judaism of the first century (see comments on 1:1), being given to sons as a symbolic hope for Yahweh's anticipated sending of salvation. A highly popular expression of this salvation was the expectation of a Messiah who would save Israel from Roman oppression and purify his people (e.g., *Pss. Sol.* 17). But the angel draws on a less popular, although perhaps more important theme: Salvation from sin is the basic need of Israel.[24]

All this took place to fulfill what the Lord had said through the prophet (1:22). The events surrounding the conception of Jesus fulfill Isaiah's prophecy

REFLECTIONS

MATTHEW COMBINES THE REMARKABLE FACTS OF Jesus' human nature in the genealogy and his divine nature in the conception narrative. Without giving details, the angelic announcement makes clear that the conception is not of ordinary human means, but by a totally unparalleled action of the Holy Spirit. Matthew does not theorize how such a conception can take place but merely presents it as historically authentic.

There is something both natural and supernatural about Jesus in his conception, birth, and development. Matthew presents the virgin conception and birth of Jesus as an accepted reality, thus accounting for the astounding truth that God has taken on human nature and is now with his people. It is only this God-man who can atone for the sin of humanity, which should cause us to pause in unending gratitude and worship him as Jesus, "God saves," and Immanuel, "God with us."

made during the dark days of national threat under Ahaz, king of Judah. Isaiah declared that God would not allow an invasion to happen, reassuring the king that God would maintain his promise that a descendent of David would sit on his throne forever (2 Sam. 7:11–17).

The virgin will be with child (1:23). There are two primary words for "virgin" in Hebrew. The term *ʿalmah*, which occurs in the prophecy of Isaiah 7:14, means "maiden, young girl" and never refers to a married woman.[25] The other primary term is *bᵉṭulah*, which can indicate a "virgin" (Gen. 24:16; Lev. 21:3), but also "old widow" (Joel 1:8). The Jewish translators of Isaiah 7:14 (LXX) rendered the Hebrew term *ʿalmah* with the Greek term *parthenos*, which almost without exception specifies a sexually mature, unmarried woman who is a virgin.

"They will call him Immanuel"—which means, "God with us" (1:23). Earlier the angel instructs Joseph to name the child Jesus (1:21)—the name by which he was called through his earthly life and by the early church. We have no record of Jesus being called "Immanuel" by his family or followers. Instead, as Matthew translates it, the name indicates Jesus' identity—"God with us." The name *Jesus* specifies *what he does* ("God saves"), while the name *Immanuel* specifies *who he is* ("God with us").

But he had no union with her until she gave birth to a son (1:25). Matthew's phrase (lit., "he was not knowing her") is a delicate way in both Hebrew and Greek to refer to sexual intercourse. Sexual abstinence during pregnancy was widely observed in Judaism of the first century; e.g., "Do not lay your hand upon your wife when she is pregnant."[26] Josephus writes, "For the same reason none who has intercourse with a woman who is with child can be considered pure."[27] Abstinence maintains Joseph and Mary's ritual

The Fulfillment of "The Virgin Will Be with Child. . ."

Isaiah prophesied that a woman who was a virgin at the time of Ahaz (734 B.C.) would bear a son named Immanuel. Since neither the queen nor Isaiah's wife was a virgin, this most likely was some unmarried young woman within the royal house with whom Ahaz was familiar. The woman would soon marry and conceive a child, and when it was born give it the name Immanuel—perhaps as a symbolic hope of God's presence in these dark times of national difficulty. Before the child was old enough to know the difference between right and wrong, Judah would be delivered from the threat of invasion from King Pekah of Israel and King Rezin of Aram (Isa. 7:14–17). The northern alliance was broken in 732 B.C., when Tiglath-Pileser III of Assyria destroyed Damascus, conquered Aram, and put Rezin to death. All this was within the time-frame miraculously predicted as the sign to Ahaz, plenty of time for the virgin to be married and to carry the child for the nine months of pregnancy, and for the approximately two years it would take until the boy knew the difference between good and evil. Thus there was immediate fulfillment of a miraculous prediction.

The sign given to Ahaz and the house of Judah was also a prediction of a future messianic figure who would provide spiritual salvation from sin. A future messianic age would honor Galilee of the Gentiles (Isa. 9:1–2), with a child born who would be called " Wonderful Counselor, Mighty God, Everlasting Father, Prince of Peace" (9:6). Of this one to whom Isaiah points, only Jesus can be the fulfillment.

purification during the pregnancy as well as ensures that Jesus is virgin born. But this is not a hint of continued celibacy after Jesus' birth. The expression "until" most naturally means that Mary and Joseph have normal marital sexual relations after Jesus' birth (cf. 12:46; 13:55).

The Magi Visit the Infant Jesus (2:1–12)

After Jesus was born in Bethlehem in Judea (2:1). As chapter 2 opens, the time frame has jumped ahead upwards of two years (see comments on 2:16). The baby is now a "child" (2:8, 10), and the family lives in a house "in Bethlehem in Judea" (2:1), six miles south/southwest of Jerusalem.

Magi (2:1). The term "Magi" (*magoi*) was originally used in early records to refer to a priestly caste in ancient Persia, perhaps followers of Zoroaster, the Persian teacher and prophet. Babylonian elements were also introduced. These Magi were leading figures in the religious court

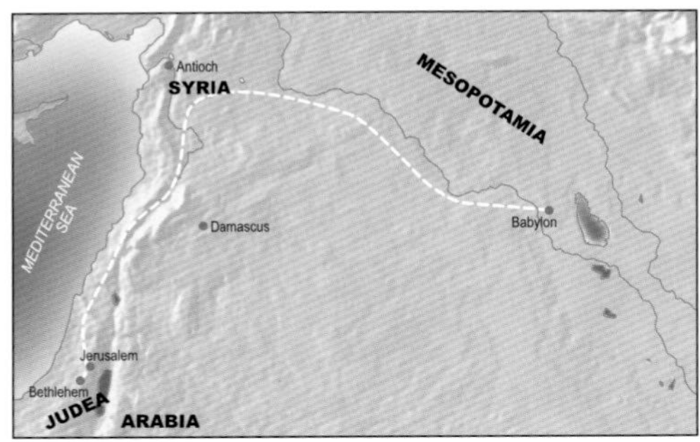

THE NEAR EAST

Possible route of the Magi.

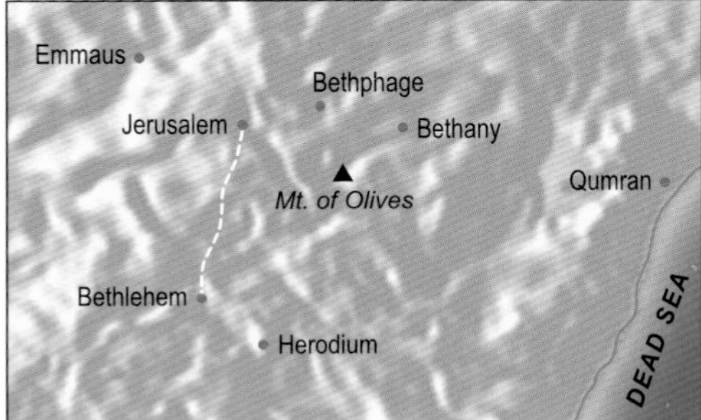

ROUTE TO BETHLEHEM

The Magi arrived at Jerusalem and travelled to Bethlehem.

life of their country of origin, employing a variety of scientific (astrology), diplomatic (wisdom), and religious (magical incantations) means to try to understand present and future life. This is in distinction from a more common type of "magician" (e.g., Acts 13:6, 8).

Magi from the east came to Jerusalem (2:1). Since a large colony of Jews remained in the east after the Exile, especially in Babylon, Parthia, and Arabia, these Magi apparently had been exposed to Judaism from those Jewish colonies. Pagan leaders, both political and religious, were well aware of Jewish religious distinctives, such as the Sabbath observance and marital restrictions.[28] If the Magi came from the environs of Babylon, they would have traveled approximately nine hundred miles. Since they would have had to make arrangements for the journey and gather a traveling party, it could have taken several months from the time they first saw the star until they arrived in Jerusalem (cf. Ezra and the returning exiles in Ezra 7:9).

Where is the one who has been born king of the Jews? (2:2). In the world of the first century an expectation circulated that a ruler would arise from Judea. Suetonius writes, "Throughout the whole of the East there had spread an old and persistent belief: destiny had decreed that at that time men coming forth from Judea would seize power [and rule the world]."[29] Israel's prophets had long spoken of a period of world peace and prosperity that was to be instituted by a future Davidic deliverer (e.g., Ezek. 34:23–31).[30]

We saw his star in the east (2:2). Through the Jewish community in their homeland,

MODERN BETHLEHEM

the Magi may have become familiar with Balaam's prophecy, "A star will come out of Jacob; a scepter will rise out of Israel" (Num. 24:17). In many quarters within Judaism this prophecy was understood to point to a messianic deliverer.[31] In the book of Revelation Jesus refers to himself in similar language: "I am the Root and the Offspring of David, and the bright Morning Star."[32]

Have come to worship him (2:2). Suetonius describes the homage that the princely *magos* Tiridates of Armenia paid to Emperor Nero: "As Tiridates approached along a sloping platform, the emperor first let him fall at his feet, but raised him with his right hand and kissed him."[33] Tiridates even addressed Nero as "god." Similarly, the Magi in Matthew's infancy narrative worship Jesus, but with their mixture of influence from paganism, astrology, and the Jewish Scriptures, it is doubtful that the Magi knowingly worshiped Jesus in recognition of his incarnate nature as God-man.

When King Herod heard this he was disturbed (2:3). Herod had developed a profound fear of attack from the east, especially because of prior invasions of Parthinians and Trachonites. So he built a series of fortress/palaces all along the eastern border, including Masada, Hyrcanium, Machaerus, and the Herodium, to ensure safety from invading forces.[34] Since the Magi most likely travel with servants and possibly guards or a military escort to protect themselves and the gifts they are to present to the child, this sizeable company prompts Herod to think that invading forces from the east are joining forces within Israel to oust him.

The people's chief priests and teachers of the law (2:4). The chief priests were members of the Sanhedrin (cf. 26:57), joining the high priest in giving oversight to the temple activities, treasury, and priestly orders. The term "teacher of the law" (*grammateus*, "scribe") was once most closely associated with reading, writing, and making copies of the Scriptures. But by New Testament times it came to signify an expert in interpreting the Law and was used interchangeably with the term "lawyer" or "expert in the law."[35]

In Bethlehem in Judea (2:5). The prophet Micah had referred to Bethlehem as the birthplace of the future Messiah (Mic. 5:2), which had become a fairly widespread expectation (cf. John 7:42). Although a small and seemingly insignificant village, Bethlehem was noted as the home of Ruth and Boaz, the ancestors of King David, and the birthplace of David himself.[36]

On coming to the house (2:11). Houses built on level ground often formed a series of rooms built around a courtyard. Included in these rooms were living spaces, which doubled as sleeping quarters, cooking area, stables, and storage rooms. Houses built in hilly areas might find two-story homes. The lower floor had a courtyard surrounded by stables, while the upper floor had the living/sleeping rooms. In rocky cavernous areas, the lower floor might incorporate caves or grottos into the structure as underground stables.[37]

They opened their treasures and presented him with gifts of gold and of incense and of myrrh (2:11). When approaching royalty or persons of high

▸ The Christmas Star

Several possibilities have been proposed as to the nature of the star.

(1) Many suggest that it was a natural phenomenon that can be traced back to some known periodically occurring astronomical event, whether a comet (e.g., Halley's Comet was visible in 12 and 11 B.C.), a supernova, or a conjunction of planets. One widely discussed possibility is an unusual conjunction of planets that occurred on May 27, 7 B.C.[A-12] According to this theory, Jupiter represented the primary deity in the Babylonian astrology. When Jupiter came close to Saturn (representing the Jews) in the constellation Pisces (representing Palestine), the Magi referred to Jupiter as the star of the king they were seeking, and the association with Saturn and Pisces showed them among which nation (the Jews) and where (Palestine) to look for him. Jupiter rose on March 11, 7 B.C., so this would have been the date when his star rose. A related suggestion draws on this conjunction, but links the specific star to a supernova that Chinese and Korean astronomers recorded in March-April 5 B.C. One astronomer concludes that the conjunction alerted the Magi to some supernatural appearance, but the supernova triggered their journey to Jerusalem.[A-13]

(2) Others suggest that the "star" was a supernatural astral phenomenon that God used to herald Jesus' birth. Note how it appears and reappears as well as moves to direct the Magi to the house Jesus and his family are occupying (2:9), not the normal activity of stars. Some conclude that this was a star-like phenomenon that may have only been seen by the Magi.

(3) Another plausible suggestion is that the supernatural phenomenon was an angel sent to the Magi to announce the birth of Messiah and to guide them to Jesus so they would be a witness to his birth through their worship. Good angels are commonly referred to as stars,[A-14] as are fallen angels and Satan.[A-15] Angels were used to guide and protect Israel to the Promised Land (Ex. 14:19; 23:20), and often appear in Jewish and Christian literature as guides.[A-16] The apocryphal Arabic *Gospel of the Infancy* (ch. 7) relates Matthew's account of the Magi but expands it to say, "In the same hour there appeared to them an angel in the form of that star which had before guided them on their journey; and they went away, following the guidance of its light, until they arrived in their own country." One scholar concludes, "This, I believe, only makes explicit what is implicit in Matthew, namely, that the guiding star was a guiding angel."[A-17]

religious, political, or social status, gifts were often brought to demonstrate obeisance.[38] "Gold" was valued throughout the ancient world as a medium of exchange as well as a precious metal for making jewelry, ornaments, and dining instruments for royalty. "Incense" or frankincense[39] is derived from an amber resin, which produced a sweet odor when burned. It was used as a perfume (Song 3:6; 4:6, 14), but in Israel it was used ceremonially for the only incense permitted on the altar (Ex. 30:9, 34–38).[40] "Myrrh" consists of a mixture of resin, gum, and the oil myrrhol and was used in incense (Ex. 30:23), as a perfume for garments or for a lover's couch,[41] as a stimulant (cf. Mark 15:23), and to pack in the wrappings of the clothing of a deceased person to stifle the smell of the body decaying (cf. John 19:39).[42]

They returned to their country by another route (2:12). The Magi may have gone south around the lower extremity of the Dead Sea to link up with the trade route north through Nabatea and Philadelphia in the Decapolis east of the Jordan River to Damascus and then east. Or they may have traveled south to Hebron and then west to the Mediterranean coast to link up with the trade route traveling north on the coastal plain, then through Sepphoris and Capernaum to Damascus and then east.

The Escape to Egypt and the Bethlehem Massacre (2:13–18)

Take the child and his mother and escape to Egypt (2:13). During the turn of the first century, Egypt was a Roman province outside of Herod's jurisdiction, so Joseph and his family would have found a natural hiding place there among their fellow dispersed Jews. As far back as

FRANKINCENSE

Abraham, Egypt had become a haven of refuge for the people of Israel when they faced difficulties or danger.[43] Perhaps the largest, most significant, and culturally creative center of the Jewish Diaspora ("dispersion") in the first century flourished in Alexandria. According to the Jewish philosopher Philo (15 B.C.-A.D. 50), who lived there, its population included about a million Jews.

So he got up, took the child and his mother during the night and left for Egypt (2:14). The border lies approximately eighty miles from Bethlehem. If they took the primary route, Joseph and the family would have traveled south to Hebron, west to the coast at Gaza, and then south again to the Nabatean border. From there, it is about fifty miles to the Egyptian border and over two hundred miles to the main Jewish community in Egypt at Alexandria.

"Out of Egypt I called my son" (2:15). The nation of Israel was consistently reminded by Old Testament authors to

COINS

These were minted in Israel during the reign of Herod the Great.

Herod, King of the Jews

Birth to kingship (73–39 B.C.). Herod (c. 73–4 B.C.) was born of noble stock from Idumean and Nabatean heritage.[A-18] His grandfather on his father's side, Antipas, converted to Judaism during the reign of Hyrcanus I. His father, Antipater II, was appointed adviser to Hyrcanus II. After the Roman general Pompey invaded Judea and deposed the Hasmonaean dynasty (63 B.C.), Antipater was made procurator of Judea by Julius Caesar (47 B.C.).[A-19] Antipater appointed his son Herod governor of Galilee when he was twenty-five years old (c. 47 B.C.). After his father's death by poisoning, Herod was appointed king of Judea by Emperor Augustus and the Roman Senate (39 B.C.).[A-20]

Solidification (38–25 B.C.). Herod's rule was troubled in the early years by lingering bitterness from surviving members of the Hasmonaean house, and he sought to solidify his position by marrying Mariamne I, a princess of the Hasmonaean line. He later had her executed, thinking that she would rouse popular opposition to him. This had a profound effect on Herod; he became seriously ill, almost to the point of death, and it instilled in him a paranoia that lasted throughout his lifetime.

Prosperity (25–14 B.C.). Herod is regarded as one of the greatest builders in antiquity. These projects often benefited his Jewish subjects, such as the rebuilding of the temple in Jerusalem. The rabbinic saying, "whoever has not beheld Herod's building [i.e., the temple] has not seen anything beautiful in his life,"[A-21] attests to the magnificence of this undertaking. Herod built or restored a chain of fortress/palaces all along the eastern border, which later aided the Jews in their rebellion against Rome. But Herod also alienated the Jews by some of his projects. He built a new city on the ancient site of hated Samaria, naming it Sebaste in honor of Emperor Augustus, and he built a temple dedicated to his worship. The creation of the port city of Caesarea Maritima is considered one of the marvels of antiquity, but it had many Gentile reminders. In Jerusalem, Jericho, and Caesarea, Herod built theaters, amphitheaters, and hippodromes for the Greek games inaugurated in honor of Augustus.

Intrigue and decline (14–4 B.C.). Herod's ten wives produced offspring who contended against each other for his throne.[A-22] As Herod became older he grew increasingly paranoid, and he had a number of his own relatives imprisoned and executed, including two of his favorite sons, Alexander and Aristobulus, his sons by Miramne I, whom he had executed earlier.[A-23] He had his eldest son, Antipater III, by his first wife Doris, executed just five days before his own death.[A-24] After several incidents of this sort, Caesar Augustus supposedly made the famous pun that he would rather be Herod's pig (*hus*) than his son (*huios*).[A-25]

Herod died at his palace in Jericho in March, 4 B.C.[A-26] Deathly ill with a painful terminal disease,[A-27] Herod commanded that many influential Jews should be executed when he died so that the people would mourn at the time of his death instead of rejoicing. But the order was countermanded after he died by his sister Salome.[A-28] An extensive burial procession of national dignitaries and military units marched with Herod's body on a golden bier studded with precious stones with a purple cover to where he was buried at or near the Herodium.[A-29]

Although he had been raised with the beliefs and practices of the Jews, and despite his attempts to win their favor, the Jewish people hated Herod as a foreigner and a friend of the Romans. Even the solicitous Josephus says of him, "He was a man who was cruel to all alike and one who easily gave in to anger and was contemptuous of justice."[A-30] look back to the way in which God redeemed Israel by bringing them out of Egypt.[44] The yearly Passover was a reminder, but also a promise, that God had provided a sacrificial lamb for his people Israel. Jesus' infancy corresponds analogically to Israel's history (cf. Hos. 11:1).

He gave orders to kill all the boys in Bethlehem (2:16). Only 123 men returned to Bethlehem from the Babylonian deportation (Ezra 2:21), and it appears not to have grown beyond a small village of perhaps a thousand people at the birth of Jesus. Herod's forces kill all the infant boys under the age of two years, which would calculate to between ten to thirty boys. Although this number of infant boys massacred would be a huge loss for the village of Bethlehem, it is not an incident that stands out significantly when seen in the light of other horrific events in Herod's infamous career, and historians would have easily bypassed it.

"A voice is heard in Ramah, weeping and great mourning" (2:18). Centuries earlier, Nebuchadnezzar's army had gathered the captives from Judah in the town of Ramah before they were taken into exile to Babylon (Jer. 40:1–2). Jeremiah depicts Rachel, who is the personification of the mothers of Israel, mourning for her children as they are being carried away. However, there was hope for their future because God would restore Rachel's children to their own land (31:16–17), and messianic joy would come in the future establishment of the new covenant with Israel (31:31–34).

The Return to Nazareth (2:19–23)

After Herod died (2:19). The family stays in Egypt until after Herod's death (March/April 4 B.C.), when the angel tells them to return to Israel (2:20). They probably stay in Egypt no more than a year.

Archelaus was reigning in Judea in place of his father Herod (2:22). After remaking his will at least seven times, Herod finally settled on dividing the kingdom between three of his remaining sons, Archelaus, Herod Antipas (14:1ff.), and Herod Philip (16:13).[45] Archelaus, a nineteen-year-old son by Malthace, was appointed successor to Herod's throne with power over Judea (including Samaria and Idumaea). Archelaus quickly displayed the same kind of cruelty that marked his father's reign. He overreacted to an uprising in the temple at Passover after his father's death, sending in troops and a cavalry who killed about three thousand pilgrims.[46] He was notorious for his cruel treatment of both Jews and Samaritans,[47] continually using oppressive measures to quell uprisings of the people. Augustus feared a revolution from the people, so he deposed Archelaus from

EGYPT AND JUDEA

The map traces the possible route Joseph took on the flight to Egypt.

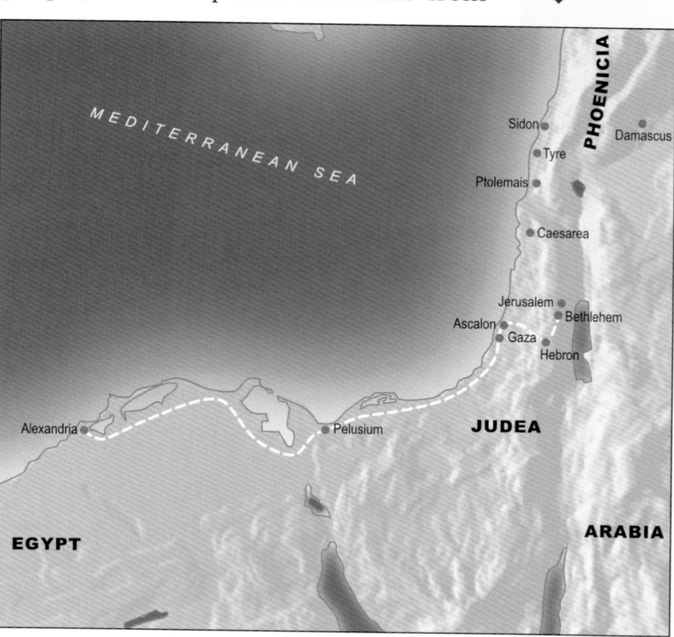

office and banished him to Gaul in A.D. 6. The rule over Judea was thereafter passed to Roman prefects.

Having been warned in a dream, he withdrew to the district of Galilee (2:22). Joseph led the family to the region of Galilee, which was not under the jurisdiction of Archelaus. Galilee was governed by another of Herod the Great's sons, Herod Antipas, who did not yet have the same bloodthirsty reputation as did his older brother.

COIN OF HEROD ARCHELAUS, SON OF HEROD THE GREAT

He went and lived in a town called Nazareth (2:23). Nazareth was occupied early in Israel's history, but was apparently deserted in 733 B.C. during the Assyrian invasion of the northern kingdom and appears to have been uninhabited from the eighth to third centuries B.C. Modern archaeological excavations have uncovered the remains of houses and a tomb from the Herodian period, indicating that Nazareth was reestablished as a small agricultural village around the third century B.C., perhaps founded and named by exiles returning from the Babylonian captivity. The town

Modern Calendars and the Date of Jesus' Birth

Modern calendars begin the present era, often called the "Christian era," with Jesus' birth. Dates after his birth are designated A.D. (Latin *anno domini*, "in the year of our Lord"). The birth of Jesus marks the beginning point of modern chronologies. The first person to develop this system was the Christian monk Dionysius Exiguus, in A.D. 525. Prior to him the Romans had developed the dating system used throughout the Western world. They commenced all dating with the establishment of the city of Rome, using the designation "AUC" (*ab urbe condita*—"from the foundation of the city [of Rome]"—or *anno urbis conditae*—"in the year of the foundation of the city").

Dionysius believed that it would be more reverent for calendrical dating to begin with Jesus' birth rather than the foundation of Rome. So with the historical records available to him, he reckoned the birth of Jesus to have occurred on December 25, 753 AUC. That placed the commencement of the Christian era at January 1, AUC (allowing for lunar adjustment), or under the new reckoning, January 1, A.D. 1. However, Dionysius did not have all of the historical data now available to scholars to make a more precise dating. We now know that Herod died in March/April 750 AUC. Since Jesus was born while Herod was still alive, he was actually born according to the Roman calendar between 748–750 AUC, four to six years earlier than Dionysius's calculations. Dionysius's dating was questioned by the English saint Bede in the eighth century and rejected outright by the German monk Regino of Prüm at the end of the ninth century. But Gregory XIII, pope from 1572 to 1585, using largely the dating of Dionysius, produced the system currently in use throughout the Western world and in parts of Asia (the Gregorian calendar).

Therefore, more accurate dating of the birth of Jesus places it before the start of the Christian Era, in 4–6 B.C. This has nothing to do with the accuracy of the biblical records, only the historical accuracy of the well-intentioned, but misguided Dionysius Exiguus.

is located in the hills in lower Galilee, twenty miles from the Mediterranean Sea to the west and fifteen miles from the Sea of Galilee to the east. Nazareth was not a strategic town politically, militarily, or religiously in Jesus' day, so it is largely left out of documents of the first century.[48] However, it was not isolated. A ten minute walk up to the ridge north of Nazareth provided villagers with a magnificent view of the trade routes a thousand feet below on the valley floor and of Herod Antipas's capital city, Sepphoris. In Jesus' day, this humble agricultural village probably had a relatively small population of around five hundred people.[49]

So was fulfilled what was said through the prophets: "He will be called a Nazarene" (2:23). The term "Nazarene" (Gk. *Nazōraios*) derives from "Nazareth" (Gk. *Nazaret*) to indicate a person from that town.[50] The returning founders of the village were apparently from the line of David and gave the settlement a consciously messianic name. They connected the establishment of the town with the hope of the coming messianic *neṣer*, "branch" (Isa. 11:1), and the believing remnant of Israel (Isa. 60:21; NIV "shoot"). The "Branch" or "Shoot" had became an important designation of the Messiah in Jewish literature.[51] One text from Qumran says, "This refers to the 'branch of David,' who will arise with the Interpreter of the law who will rise up in Zion in the last days."[52] Matthew also points to "Nazarene" as a slang term for an individual from a remote, despised area. He draws a connection between the divinely arranged association of Jesus with Nazareth and various Old Testament prophets who foretold that the Messiah would be despised.[53]

John the Baptist Prepares the Way (3:1–6)

Matthew now jumps from Jesus' infancy to his adulthood. More than twenty-five

HEROD'S FORTRESS

The remains of the Herodium, Herod's citadel built near Bethlehem.

years elapse from the time Joseph takes his family to Nazareth to the time that John the Baptist appears in the Judean desert.

In those days John the Baptist came, preaching in the Desert of Judea (3:1). John probably appears in the barren desert area in the lower Jordan River valley and hills to the west of the Dead Sea. The desert wilderness was an important place in Israel's history for the giving of the Law, revelation of the prophets, Maccabean guerilla warfare, and expected messianic deliverance.[54] Although there are several points of similarity between John the Baptist and the Qumran community near the Dead Sea, the significant dissimilarities lead most scholars to the conclusion that John had not been a member of the Qumran community.[55] Most notably, John's message calls the entire nation to repentance, not isolationism, which makes him more like the Old Testament prophets than Qumran. While it is a matter of conjecture as to whether John may have ever been connected with Qumran, the Gospels' portrait of John makes it doubtful.

Repent (3:2). "Repentance" in the Old Testament prophets called for a change in a person's attitude toward God, which

NAZARETH

The church of the Annunciation. The cave underneath the church contains the remains of a fourth-century church and possibly an earlier synagogue.

would impact one's actions and one's overall direction in life. External signs of repentance regularly included confession of sin, prayers of remorse, and abandonment of sin.

The kingdom of heaven is near (3:2). "Kingdom of heaven" is interchangeable with the expression "kingdom of God."[56] "Kingdom of heaven" reflects the Hebrew expression *malkut šamayim*, found abundantly in Jewish literature.[57] A feeling of reverence and not wishing inadvertently to blaspheme the name of God (Ex. 20:7) led the Jews at an early date to avoid as far as possible all mention of the name of God. "Heaven" is one of the usual substitutions.[58]

John's clothes were made of camel's hair, and he had a leather belt around his waist (3:4). John's description is strikingly similar to the prophet Elijah (2 Kings 1:8). Goat or camel hair was often woven into a thick, rough, dark cloth, which was used as an outer garment or cloak, particularly by nomadic desert dwellers. It was so dense that it was waterproof. It was proverbially the garb of poorer people, in distinction from the finery worn by those in the royal court.[59] Since sackcloth symbolized distress or self-affliction,[60] John the Baptist's garment of camel hair visualizes the repentance to which he calls the people.[61]

His food was locusts and wild honey (3:4). Locusts and wild honey were not an unusual diet for people living in the desert.[62] The locust is the migratory phase of the grasshopper and was allowable food for the people of Israel to eat, as opposed to other kinds of crawling and flying insects (Lev. 11:20–23). They are an important food source in many areas of the world, especially as a source of protein, because even in the most desolate areas they are abundant. They are often collected, dried, and ground into flour. Protein and fat were derived from locusts, while sugar came from the honey of wild bees.[63]

The Impact of the Kingdom of Heaven (3:7–12)

He saw many of the Pharisees and Sadducees coming (3:7). The Pharisees and Sadducees were distinct and often opposed to each other. John recognizes immediately that they are not coming to validate his ministry; they come with

bottom left

JUDEAN WILDERNESS

The rugged terrain where John the Baptist spent much time.

bottom right

LOCUST

A food source for John the Baptist.

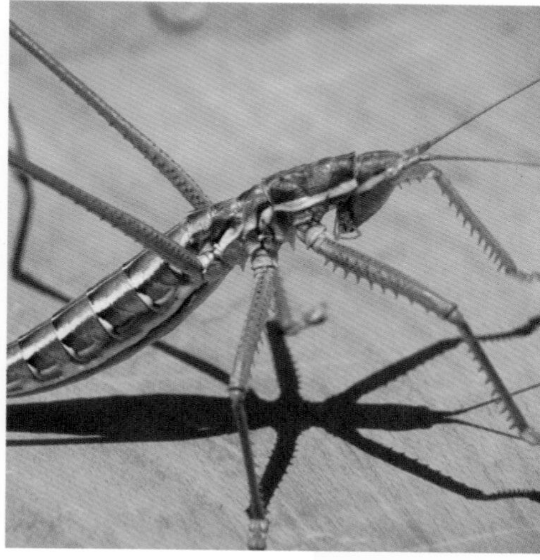

Baptism in the Ancient World

Various kinds of "washings" were commonly known and practiced throughout much of Israel's history, always as a symbol of some deeper meaning.

- The Old Testament prescribed various forms of water rituals for different types of symbolic purification.[A-31] These cleansings were understood to be ongoing symbols of God's inner cleansing (e.g., Ps. 51:2, 7) and were practiced into the New Testament era.
- Widespread voluntary forms of water rituals were primarily symbolic of purification, such as the table fellowship of the Pharisees[A-32] or commitment to the community at Qumran.[A-33] Ceremonial *mikveh* ("immersion pool") baths have been discovered by archaeologists throughout Israel, indicating regular washings by immersion and by pouring flowing water over oneself. Ritual water purifications were repeated, sometimes more than once a day.
- By the time of John it was possible that Gentile proselytes were required to undergo baptism as an act of initiation into Judaism. This was a one-time baptism signifying the conversion of adults from a Gentile background to Judaism.
- John's baptism was also symbolic of purification, but it was a one-time baptism, whereas groups such as those at Qumran and the Pharisees had highly structured regulations for regular, repeated washings. John's baptism had some similarity to proselyte one-time baptism, but it was far different since John was baptizing Jews, not Gentiles. Those responding were heeding the call to the presence of the kingdom and the "Coming One" whom John announced.

JORDAN RIVER

Near the outlet at the Sea of Galilee.

ulterior motives. Matthew notes two other occasions when the Pharisees and Sadducees are listed together in their opposition to Jesus (16:1–4; 16:5–12).

You brood of vipers (3:7). "Brood of vipers" (cf. 12:34; 23:33) is a reference to the dozen or more small, dangerous snakes that can emerge at birth from a mother snake. Vipers are proverbial for their subtle approach and attack, as was the original serpent (Gen. 3).

I baptize you. . . . He will baptize you (3:11). The Coming One will baptize the repentant with the blessing of the Holy Spirit. But the unrepentant, those who are not receptive to the Coming One, will be baptized with the judgment of eternal fire (cf. Joel 2:28–29).

Pharisees and Sadducees

Josephus refers to the Pharisees, Sadducees, and Essenes as "schools of thought,"[A-34] something of a mix between a religious faction and a political affiliation.

1. The name *Pharisee* is probably derived from the Hebrew/Aramaic *perušim*, the separated ones, alluding to both their origin and their characteristic practices. They tended to be politically conservative and religiously liberal and held the minority membership on the Sanhedrin:[A-35]

- They held to the supreme place of Torah, with a rigorous scribal interpretation of it.
- Their most pronounced characteristic was their adherence to the oral tradition, which they obeyed rigorously as an attempt to make the written law relevant to daily life.
- They had a well-developed belief in angelic beings.
- They had concrete messianic hopes, as they looked for the coming Davidic messianic kingdom. The Messiah would overthrow the Gentiles and restore the fortunes of Israel with Jerusalem as capital.
- They believed in the resurrection of the righteous when the messianic kingdom arrived, with the accompanying punishment of the wicked.
- They viewed Rome as an illegitimate force that was preventing Israel from experiencing its divinely ordained role in the outworking of the covenants.
- They held strongly to divine providence, yet viewed humans as having freedom of choice, which ensures their responsibility.
- As a lay fellowship or brotherhood connected with local synagogues, the Pharisees were popular with the common people.

2. The *Sadducees* were a small group with aristocratic and priestly influence, who derived their authority from the activities of the temple. They tended to be politically liberal and religiously conservative and held the majority membership on the Sanhedrin:

- They held a conservative attitude toward the Scriptures, accepting nothing as authoritative except the written word, literally interpreted.
- They accepted only Torah (the five books of Moses) as authoritative, rejecting any beliefs not found there.
- For that reason they denied the resurrection from the dead, the reality of angels, and spirit life.
- They produced no literature of which we are aware.
- They had no expressed messianic expectation, which tended to make them satisfied with their wealth and political power.
- They were open to aspects of Hellenism and often collaborated with the Romans.
- They tended to be removed from the common people by economic and political status.

His winnowing fork is in his hand (3:12). At the end of the season the farmer brought the harvested wheat into the threshing floor, a stone or hard-packed dirt surface, often with a short wall around the perimeter. He then took a large pitchfork and tossed the wheat into the air, where the wind blew the lighter chaff away, leaving only the good wheat heads in the threshing floor. The wheat would be stored in the granary for later grinding into flour to make bread, but the chaff would be raked into piles and burned.[64]

WINNOWING GRAIN

A modern winnowing fork.

John Baptizes Jesus (3:13–17)

Heaven was opened (3:16). As Jesus comes up from the water, the heavens are opened, not an uncommon expression in Scripture to refer to significant times of God's revealing something important to his people.[65]

The Spirit of God descending like a dove (3:16). The descent of the Spirit alludes to the anointing of the Servant of the Lord by the Spirit (Isa. 42:1) and the anointing of the Davidic Branch by the Spirit (Isa. 11:2). Jesus' anointing by the Spirit is both the coronation of Israel's Messiah and the commissioning of God's righteous Servant for the work that he will now carry out in the power and presence of the Spirit.

right

DOVE

A symbol of the coming of the Spirit upon Jesus

This is my Son, whom I love (3:17). The phrase calls to mind the well-known messianic image of Father and Son in Psalm 2:7. The title "Son of God" had clear messianic significance prior to Jesus' ministry.[66]

With him I am well pleased (3:17). Jesus, the divine Son, is the triumphant messianic King (Ps. 2) and the humble, suffering Servant (Isa. 43), a pronouncement repeated by the voice in the Transfiguration (Matt. 17:5). Through the anointing of the Spirit, the Father has placed into the hands of his beloved Son the mission of the Servant to bring salvation to the nations (Isa. 42:1, 4; cf. *Tg. Isa.* 42:1).

Temptations of the Messiah (4:1–11)

Then Jesus was led by the Spirit into the desert (4:1). Jesus' ministry, like John the Baptist's, begins in the desert. Early Christian tradition placed Jesus' forty-day-and-night fast on the mountain site of Jebel Quarantal in the Jericho area. Emperor Justinian in the sixth century erected a church on the summit to commemorate Jesus' vigil. While it is possible that this is the actual site, one cannot be certain. The desert stretches west for a dozen miles as it rises from the Jordan River valley to the heights of Jerusalem, a virtual no-man's-land.

To be tempted by the devil (4:1). Entering for the first time on the scene of Matthew's story is "the devil," or, as he will be called later, Satan (4:10; 12:26; 16:23). The devil leads a host of other powerful spiritual beings that assist him in trying to thwart God's purposes. Paul calls him "the ruler of the kingdom of the air" (Eph. 2:2). The word "tempted" is the verb *peirazō*, which can mean either "I tempt" or "I test."[67] A *temptation* is an enticement to get a person to go contrary to the will of God, as Satan will try to do to Jesus. A *test* tries to get a person to prove oneself faithful to God's will, with the good intention that the person pass the test.

After fasting forty days and forty nights, he was hungry (4:2). Fasting was often used as a means of focusing one's attention in prayer, disciplining oneself to unite body and soul. Jesus has been readying himself for his public ministry. Forty days of hardship often indicated preparation for a particularly significant involvement in God's activities, such as Moses, Elijah, Ezekiel, and here, Jesus.[68]

If you are the Son of God (4:3, 6). Satan does not doubt Jesus' identity as the Son of God, nor is he trying to get Jesus to

REFLECTIONS

JOHN AND JESUS GIVE US A POWERful example of humility as they carry out their roles as the prophet and the Savior. Neither got carried away with appearances. They demonstrated strength in carrying out their roles in the plan of salvation, yet that strength also included diminishing the appearance of their own importance. The key word here is humility, a term that does not get much good press in our day, since we hear much more of rights. But the picture John and Jesus give to every age is the incongruity of their humility relative to the significance of their roles.

We don't like to give up our appearance of importance. But knowing God's purposes for our lives and not allowing our self-promotion to get in the way will enable us to accomplish God's calling for our lives as well.

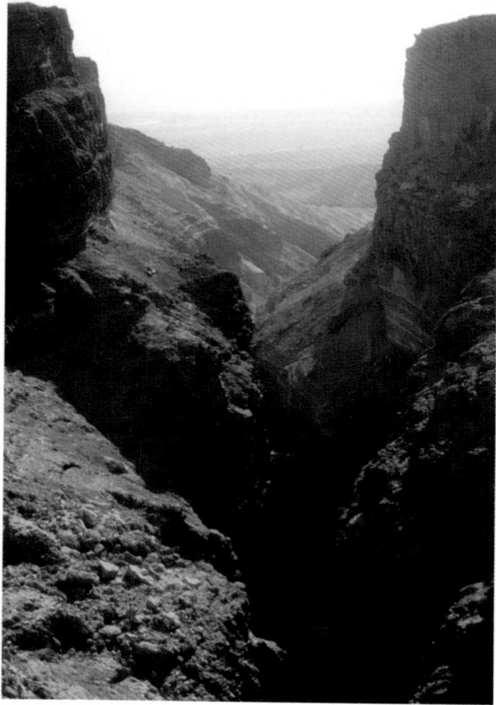

MASADA AREA

In the wilderness of Judea.

doubt it; rather, he is trying to get Jesus to misuse his prerogatives as the Son of God.

The highest point of the temple (4:5). The identification of this "highest point" is debated, but it may refer either to the southeast corner of the temple area, where it looms some 450 feet high over the Kidron Valley,[69] or to a high gate of the temple.

Throw yourself down (4:6). Satan quotes from Psalm 91, where the psalmist asserts God's protecting care for the faithful in Israel (vv. 11–12). This is a blatant misuse of Scripture to try to manipulate Jesus.

Do not put the Lord your God to the test (4:7). In the first century many believed that the Messiah would descend the Mount of Olives, enter the holy city through the Shushan gate, which was left ajar in this expectation, and then triumphantly enter the temple. This is a very devilish temptation for Jesus to gain the following of the nation Israel by a spectacular display at the central place of Israel's religion, the temple.

If you will bow down and worship me (4:9). The pictures of the king of Tyre (Ezek. 28:2, 11–19) and the king of Babylon (Isa. 14:12–14) epitomize this obsession and have often been understood as pointing beyond those earthly diabolical rulers to Satan.

REFLECTIONS

THREE IMPORTANT IMPLICATIONS surface in reflecting on Jesus' temptations:

(1) Satan's power. Satan does have significant influence over the people and powers of this world,[A-36] but his influence is limited.

(2) The Scripture's power. Temptations involve the twisting of reality, so the antidote comes from the truth of Scripture.

(3) The Spirit's power. Jesus was guided and empowered by the Spirit in his temptations. He was never alone in his struggle, even at the most difficult moments. Jesus relied on the power of the Spirit to enable him to resist the devil's temptations.

Throughout his life Jesus gives the ultimate example of how Christians today can also overcome the temptations that will come our way: Resist the devil in the power of the Spirit through the guidance of the Word to accomplish the will of God.

Jesus Messiah Begins His Galilean Ministry (4:12–17)

When Jesus heard that John had been put in prison (4:12). Josephus tells us that John was imprisoned by Herod Antipas for political reasons; that is, Herod Antipas feared that John's popularity with the people and his preaching and baptism might lead the people to some form of sedition.[70] Matthew will fill in later that there was an additional moral reason behind John's arrest (see on 14:1–12).

He went and lived in Capernaum (4:13). Jesus makes Capernaum in Galilee his base of operations and his new hometown for the length of his ministry in Galilee. Capernaum is the Greek form of the Hebrew *Kefar Nahum*, which means the "village of Nahum." Josephus gives one of the earliest Greek renderings as

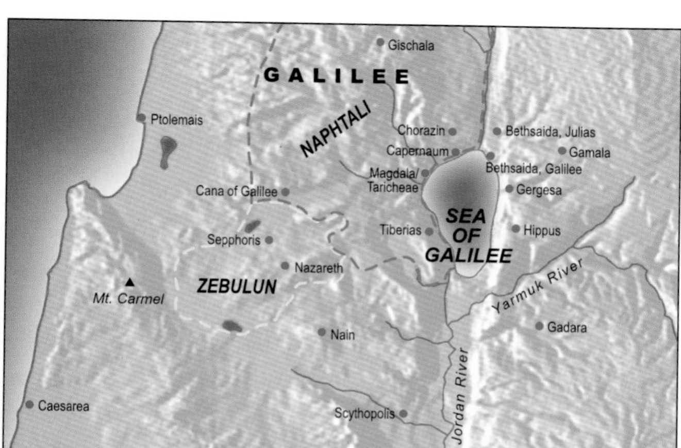

◀ *left*

GALILEE

The land of Zebulun and Naphtali.

Kapharnaoum,[71] for what is most likely the site today called by Arabs Tell-Hum on the northwest shore of the Sea of Galilee. Capernaum was a Galilean frontier town, with around a thousand inhabitants.[72] What may have been a 2,500-foot promenade with several piers extending out into the water made for a bustling fishing trade and transportation center at Capernaum for crossing the Sea of Galilee.[73] Capernaum, Chorazin, and Bethsaida are the cities in which most of Jesus' miracles are performed, an area of gospel operation referred to as the "Evangelical Triangle."[74]

"Land of Zebulun and land of Naphtali, the way to the sea, along the Jordan" (4:15). Zebulun and Naphtali were the two tribes of Israel that settled in the northernmost region near the Sea of Galilee. Nazareth was in the territory of Zebulun in the lower Galilee region, while Capernaum was in Naphtali in the upper Galilee region. The trade route that ran through this region to the Mediterranean Sea was called the "Via Maris" or "way to the sea." Jesus' ministry will extend far beyond the physical confines of Jewish Galilee, influencing those traveling through the region.

"Galilee of the Gentiles" (4:15). The tribes of Israel in the north were surrounded on three sides by non-Jewish populations. Ever since the Assyrian campaign that reduced it to a province under an Assyrian governor in 732 B.C. (2 Kings 15:29), this region had long experienced

CAPERNAUM

Remains of the synagogue at Capernaum.

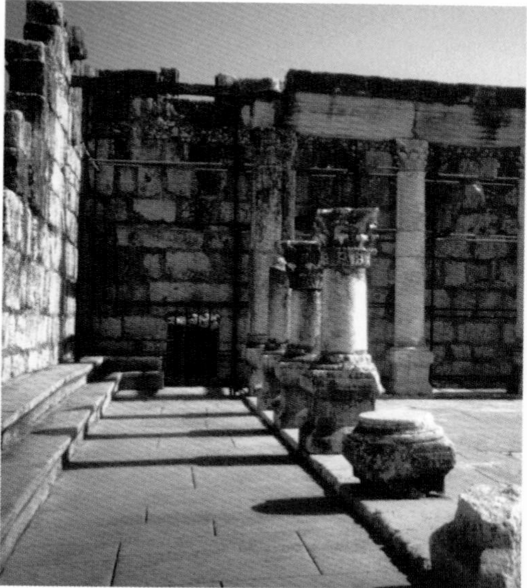

turmoil and forced infiltration of Gentile influence.

"The people living in darkness" (4:16) The term "people" (*laos*) in Matthew regularly refers to Israel (cf. 1:21), so this is a description of Jewish people awaiting deliverance while living among the hopelessness of the Gentiles.

Jesus Calls Fishers of Men (4:18–22)

They were casting a net into the lake (4:18). The fishing industry was an important contributor to Capernaum's prosperity. "Casting a net" describes a customary form of fishing on the lake, even up to recent times. The "cast net" (*amphiblēstron*) was used by a single fisherman, either while standing in a boat or in shallow water. It was circular, about 20–25 feet in diameter, with lead sinkers attached to the outer edge. The net was pulled down by the sinkers on the outer ring (like a parachute), finally sinking to the bottom with fish trapped inside. The fisherman would dive to the bottom and pull the trapped fish through the net one by one, placing them in a pouch, or he would carefully pull together the edges of the net and carry it to the surface with the catch inside.[75]

Come, follow me (4:19). The normal pattern in Israel was for a prospective disciple to approach a rabbi and ask to study with him (e.g., 8:19). Joshua b. Perahyah said, "Provide thyself with a teacher and get thee a fellow disciple," which Rabban Gamaliel echoed, "Provide thyself with a teacher and remove thyself from doubt."[76] At the inauguration of his kingdom mission Jesus establishes a new pattern, because he is the one who takes the initiative to seek out and give a call for these brothers to enter into a permanent relationship with him.[77]

They were in a boat (4:21). Fishing boats were a common sight on the Sea of Galilee. Josephus indicates that they were so plentiful that on one occasion he ordered 230 available boats to be assem-

▸ The Sea of Galilee

The "Sea of Galilee," located about sixty miles north of Jerusalem, is a 12.5 by 7 mile lake. In the Old Testament it is called "Sea of Kinnereth,"[A-37] the name by which it is known today in Israel. It is also called the "Sea of Tiberias,"[A-38] because Herod Antipas's capital city Tiberias lay on the west shore. Luke calls it the "Lake of Gennesaret or Gennesar," derived from a town and plain by that name situated above the west/northwest shore.[A-39] Josephus implies that this was the oldest and most common name used by the local people.[A-40]

The lake is located in the great Jordan rift valley, at least 636 feet (212 meters) below sea level. The Jordan River enters the lake in the north and exits to the south, where it finally terminates in the Dead Sea about 65 miles to the south. Ancient writers all acclaim the Sea of Galilee for its fresh waters and pleasant temperatures, unlike the Dead Sea. It had clear sandy beaches rather than swampy marshes along the seashore, and all remarked that it was well stocked with fish.[A-41] The lake's low elevation provides it with relatively mild year-round temperatures, permitting sleeping outdoors in the surrounding areas as a common practice.[A-42] However, encompassed as it is with mountain ranges to the east and west that rise over 2,650 feet from the level of the lake, the low-lying setting results in sudden violent downdrafts and storms.[A-43]

◀ *left*

KINNERET BOAT

A first-century fishing boat recently discovered in the Sea of Galilee.

bled to form a naval armada.[78] The recent (1986) extraordinary discovery of an ancient fishing boat at Galilee from the time of Jesus gives us an idea of the kind of boat the Zebedees may have owned. The wooden vessel, called the "Kinneret boat," is approximately 26.5 feet long, 7.5 feet wide, and 4.5 feet high, and equipped for both sailing and rowing. A crew of at least five was needed to handle the boat (four rowers and one rudder man), but it was able to carry as many as eight to sixteen.[79] It was equipped for cooking during nightlong commercial fishing expeditions on the lake.[80]

Preparing their nets (4:21). These nets may have been the larger *seine* or "dragnet,"[81] but more likely the *trammel* net, the only net used in ancient times that is still widely used commercially on the lake today. It is a compound net of three layers, five units each over a hundred feet long, used by at least two crews of boats throughout the night when the fish cannot see the entangling nets.[82] Probably after a long night of fishing with their father and others of their hired crew (cf. Mark 1:20), James and John are mending or preparing their nets for the next commercial excursion on the lake.

◀

MODERN FISHERMEN ON THE SEA OF GALILEE

Jesus Unfolds the Gospel of the Kingdom (4:23–25)

Jesus went throughout Galilee (4:23). Approximately forty-five miles from north to south and twenty-five miles from east to west, Galilee must have been intensively cultivated and extensively populated in Jesus' day. Conservative estimates place the population at around 300,000 people in the two hundred or more villages and towns in Galilee, which make for a large citizenry to whom Jesus presents the message of the kingdom.[83]

Teaching in their synagogues (4:23). Teaching (*didaskōn*) is often related to explanation of truth to those already familiar with the content (see comments on 5:1–2). In the Jewish synagogues Jesus clarifies the nature of his message from the Old Testament Scriptures, demonstrating that he is the expected messianic deliverer (cf. Luke 4:16–30).

SYRIA, GALILEE, THE DECAPOLIS, AND JUDEA

Preaching (4:23). "Preaching" (*kēryssōn*) is generally related to the proclamation of truth to those unfamiliar with the content (cf. 24:14). When he is in the countryside, where many are most likely not proficient in the Old Testament Scriptures, Jesus gives a straightforward proclamation of the message.

The good news of the kingdom (4:23). Matthew uses the noun "gospel" (*euangelion*) only four times, three of which occur in the phrase, "gospel of the kingdom," found only in Matthew.[84] The real "good news" is that the age of the kingdom of God has finally dawned in the ministry of Jesus.

Healing every disease and sickness among the people (4:23). This good news is also demonstrated as Jesus is "healing" every disease and sickness among the people. Healing signals that Jesus has authority over the powers of this world and confirms the reality of the arrival of the kingdom of God (11:4–6).

Those suffering severe pain, the demon-possessed, those having seizures, and the paralyzed, and he healed them (4:24). As news of Jesus' ministry spreads outside the borders of Galilee, even to the Gentile region of Syria in the north (4:24), people bring those suffering "severe pain" or "torment" (cf. Luke 16:23, 28). The "demon-possessed" are also brought, indicating Jesus' continuing power over the devil's realm. Jesus also heals "epileptics" (lit., "moonstruck"), an illness associated with demon-possession (17:14–21), and "paralytics," a distressing affliction at a time when foot-travel is the most common.

Large crowds from Galilee, the Decapolis, Jerusalem, Judea and the region across the Jordan followed him (4:25). The Decapolis ("ten cities") is the generally Gentile district to the south and east of the Sea of Galilee. The region known as "across the Jordan" is a common expression to designate the area of Perea,[85] presupposing a typical Jewish point of view west of the Jordan River. Those coming to Jesus are still primarily Jews, but they come from all of the surrounding regions.

The Beatitudes of the Kingdom of Heaven (5:1–12)

He went up on a mountainside (5:1). This first major discourse gets its name from the geographical setting, "on a mountain" somewhere in Galilee. The traditional site, as well as the most recent consensus, identifies it above Tabghah, near Capernaum. The local mountain of Capernaum is actually a ridge of hills just to the west of the town. Ancient tradition named this hillcrest "Eremos," a transliteration of the Greek word for "lonely" or "solitary" (*erēmos*). At the foot of Eremos lies the area of "seven springs," *Heptapegon*, later roughly transliterated into Arabic as *et-Tabgha*.[86]

He . . . sat down. His disciples came to him, and he began to teach them (5:1–2). Sitting down is the typical position from which a teacher in Judaism taught (cf. 23:2), a position Jesus takes regularly.[87] Since Jesus' teaching in this setting is directed primarily to the disciples, not the crowds, it can be designated in large part as training in discipleship. Yet the response at the conclusion of the message indicates that the crowds are being offered an invitation to discipleship in the kingdom (7:28–29).

HILL OF THE BEATITUDES

Marking the traditional site of the Sermon on the Mount. The Sea of Galilee is in the background.

Blessed are . . . (5:3). The name "beatitude" is derived from the Latin noun *beatitudo*, because the first word of each statement in the Latin *Vulgate* is *beati* (adj. related to the noun), which translates the Greek word *makarios* (traditionally rendered in English as "blessed").

Theirs is . . . they will be . . . (cf. 5:3, 10 with 5:4–9). In the first and last beatitude, an identical phrase in the present tense gives the reason for the blessing: "for theirs *is* the kingdom of heaven" (5:3, 10). This creates "bookends" to the beatitudes—an example of the common literary device called an *inclusio*, indicating that kingdom life is a present possession of Jesus' disciples. The third through seventh beatitudes (5:4–9) have a future tense (e.g., "for they *will be* comforted," 5:4), indicating that the blessings will not be experienced completely until the future when the kingdom is established completely on the earth.

Blessed are the poor in spirit (5:3). The poor are not only those who have encountered unfortunate circumstances from an economic point of view (19:21; 26:11), but also those who are spiritually and emotionally oppressed and disillusioned and in need of God's help.

REFLECTIONS

***MAKARIOS* IS A STATE OF EXISTENCE IN RELATIONSHIP** to God in which a person is "blessed" from God's perspective even when he or she doesn't feel happy or isn't presently experiencing good fortune. This does not mean a conferral of blessing or an exhortation to live a life worthy of blessing, but rather is an acknowledgment that the ones indicated are blessed. Negative feelings, absence of feelings, or adverse conditions cannot take away the blessedness of the one who exists in relationship with God.

For theirs is the kingdom of heaven (5:3). The kingdom of God belongs to those who see themselves, and are seen by others, as having no resources, material or spiritual, to help them before God. These are the "poor" to whom Jesus has come to announce "good news" (11:5), and to whom the kingdom of heaven belongs.

Blessed are those who mourn (5:4). The loss of anything that a person counts valuable will produce mourning, whether it is one's financial support, loved ones, status in society, or even one's spiritual standing before God (Ps. 119:136).

For they will be comforted (5:4). The arrival of the kingdom in Jesus' ministry brings the first taste of God's comforting blessing on those in Israel who have realized their loss and who mourn over it (cf. Isa. 40:1; 61:1–3), but they will receive final comforting in the presence of the heavenly Lamb (Rev. 7:17).

Blessed are the meek (5:5). The "meek" (or better, "gentle") are those who do not assert themselves over others in order to advance their own causes. That this does not imply weakness becomes plain when we see this same term applied to Jesus (11:29; 21:5).

For they will inherit the earth (5:5). This perhaps recalls the lowly position before others found in the reference in Isaiah 61:1, 3. Ultimately this points to the reign of Christ on this earth (25:35), but even now Jesus' disciples have entered into their spiritual inheritance.[88]

Blessed are those who hunger and thirst for righteousness (5:6). Those who "hunger and thirst" are in dire need. In the context of the preceding beatitudes, righteousness here includes several facets: (1) "justice" for those who have been downtrodden or who have experienced injustice; (2) personal ethical righteousness for those who desire a deeper purity in their own lives; (3) God's promised salvation come to the earth.

For they will be filled (5:6). The ultimate source of this righteousness is found only in God himself (cf. Ps. 42:1–2; 63:1). His gift of kingdom life is the only true satisfaction for those who long to see and experience true justice, personal righteousness, and salvation. God's enablement is the only satisfaction for those who long for his standard of righteousness written in his law (e.g., Ps. 119:10–11, 20).

Blessed are the merciful (5:7). In God's great mercy he does not give humans what they deserve; rather, he gives to them what they do not deserve (cf. Ps. 25:6–7; Prov. 14:21). In like manner, the merciful are those who demonstrate forgiveness toward the guilty and kindness for the hurting and needy.

Blessed are the pure in heart (5:8). The rabbis were developing a complex system of laws for maintaining ceremonial purification, which later comprised *Tohoroth* ("Cleannesses"), one of the divisions of the Mishnah. But all of those laws could bypass the most important purity of all, purity of the heart. A pure heart produces external purity, not vice versa (e.g., 15:1–19). A pure heart describes a person whose single-minded loyalty to God has affected every area of life.[89]

For they will see God (5:8). While no human can look fully at the glorious face of God (Ex. 33:20), the hope that culminates this age is that "they will see his face, and his name will be on their foreheads" (Rev. 22:4).

Blessed are the peacemakers (5:9). The theme of "peace," known by the grand Hebrew term *šâlôm* and the Greek term *eirēnē*, permeates the biblical record. It indicates completeness and wholeness in every area of life, including one's relationship with God, neighbors, and nations.[90] Making peace has messianic overtones (cf. "Prince of Peace" in Isa. 9:6–7), and true peacemakers are those who wait and work for God, who makes whole the division created by humans.

For they will be called sons of God (5:9). Those who have waited for God's messianic peace can now respond to Jesus' invitation and will receive the ultimate reward: They will be called "sons of God," fulfilling the role Israel assumed but takes for granted (Deut. 14:1; Hos. 1:10).

Salt and Light: True Disciples Witness to the Kingdom of Heaven (5:13–16)

You are the salt of the earth (5:13). The variety of important uses for salt as a preservative, as an important element of one's diet, and as a fertilizer leads to different interpretations of what Jesus means to communicate with the analogy.[91] Jesus may not be pointing to one specific application but using it in a broad, inclusive sense to refer to something that is vitally necessary for everyday life. One ancient Jewish writer listed salt as one of the basic necessities of life (Sir. 39:26), and an ancient Roman official commented, "There is nothing more useful than salt and sunshine."[92] Taken in this way, the metaphor indicates that by their very presence Jesus' disciples are necessary for the welfare of the world.

OIL LAMPS

Two of these Roman-era lamps depict the Jewish menorah (candelabrum).

A city on a hill cannot be hidden (5:14). The city may be Jerusalem, which sits on Mount Zion, since Israel with Jerusalem as the holy city were considered the light to the world (Isa. 2:2–5; 42:6; 49:6). Or Jesus may have used a local Galilean city for an illustration, such as Hippos, one of the Greek cities of the Decapolis. It was situated on a rounded hill above the southeastern shore and detached from its background, so it was clearly visible from the Capernaum area, especially when it was lit up at night.[93]

Light a lamp (5:15). The lamp (*lychnos*) that was used in a typical Palestinian home was usually a partially closed reservoir made of clay. It had a hole on top in which

If the Salt Loses Its Saltiness

Strictly speaking, salt cannot lose its saltiness, because sodium chloride is a stable compound. What then does Jesus mean in 5:13?

- Jesus may be alluding to rock formations that contained deposits of sodium chloride. Meat and fish were packed in these rocks to preserve them. After a period of time the salt leached out of the rocks, so the rocks were not good for anything and so thrown out.
- Jesus may be referring to the salt collected from the Dead Sea by evaporation, which often includes crystals of another mineral, gypsum, formed by the precipitation of calcium sulfate from seawater. Salt and gypsum were often mixed in various saline deposits. This impure mixture of salt and gypsum could easily be mistaken for pure salt, but the mixture was not usable for either preservation or seasoning and so was regarded as having lost its taste.
- Jesus may be alluding to salt blocks used by Arab bakers to line the floor of their ovens. After some time the intense heat eventually caused the blocks to crystallize and undergo a change in chemical composition, finally being thrown out as unserviceable.
- Jesus may be citing a well-known proverbial saying. When rebuffing a trick question, Rabbi Joshua ben Haniniah (c. A.D. 90) apparently alludes to a proverbial saying when he asks, "Can salt lose its flavor?" The context of the saying implies that it is impossible for salt to lose its flavor, because he parallels the saying by asking, "Does the mule (being sterile) bear young?" (*b. Bek.* 8b). Sterile mules can no more bear young than can salt lose its flavor.

Thus, Jesus may be using this expression to describe an equally impossible characteristic of his disciples. As they go out into the world as salt, the proof of the reality of their profession is in the nature of their lives. True disciples cannot lose what makes them disciples because they have become changed persons, made new by the life of the kingdom of heaven. However, imposter disciples have only an external flavoring. They cannot be made salty again, because they never had that kingdom life in the first place.

to pour oil, and a spout on one end into which a wick of flax or cotton was set. It was a fairly small lamp, giving off only a modest light, so it was placed on a lampstand to give maximum illumination. Since Jewish homes were often humble one-room structures, such an elevated lamp could give light to everyone in the house.

Put it under a bowl (5:15). The word for "bowl" (*modios*)[94] comes from the Latin *modius*, the basic unit of measure for dry goods, equaling 16 sextarii, or about 2 gallons (7.5 liters). Lamps were essential for finding one's way in enclosed areas during the night and would be placed under a measuring bowl only to extinguish the light.[95]

Jesus and the Kingdom as Fulfillment of the Law (5:17–20)

Do not think that I have come to abolish the Law or the Prophets (5:17). The "Law" or "Torah" refers to the first five books of the Old Testament, called the books of Moses or the Pentateuch. The "Prophets" includes the major and minor prophets of the Old Testament as well as the historical books from Joshua to 2 Kings. The expression "the Law and the Prophets" is a way of referring to the entire Hebrew Scriptures.[96]

I have not come to abolish them but to fulfill them (5:17). The term "fulfill" (*plēroō*) is more than obedience. Jesus not only fulfills certain anticipated roles, but his interpretation and application of the Old Testament Scriptures completes and clarifies God's intent and meaning through it. All that the Old Testament intended to communicate about God's will and hopes for humanity find their full meaning and accomplishment in Jesus' teaching and ministry.

Anyone who breaks one of the least of these commandments (5:19). The rabbis recognized a distinction between "light" and "weighty" Old Testament commandments and advocated obedience to both.[97] Light commandments are those such as the requirement to tithe on produce (cf. Lev. 27:30; Deut. 14:22), while weighty commandments are those such as profaning the name of God or the Sabbath or matters of social justice (Ex. 20:2–8; Mic. 6:8). Rabbi Simlai stated that "613 commandments were revealed to Moses at Sinai, 365 being prohibitions equal in number to the solar days of the year, and 248 being commands corresponding in number to the parts of the human body."[98]

Unless your righteousness surpasses that of the Pharisees (5:20). This may have been Jesus' most shocking statement, because the Pharisees and teachers of the law were the epitome of righteousness

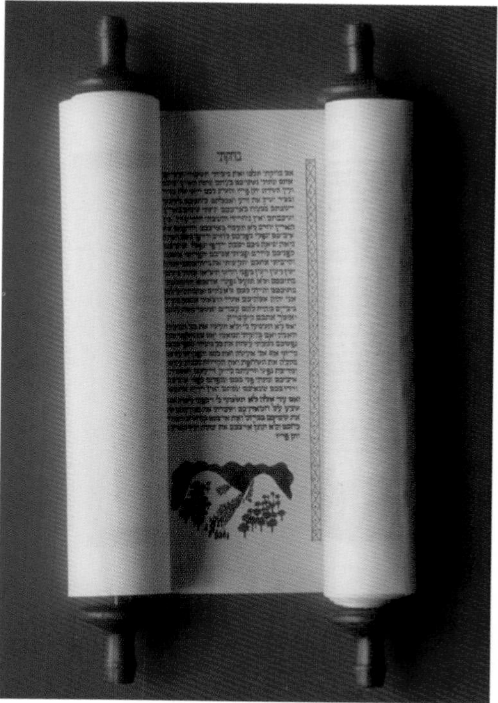

THE LAW

Replica of an ancient Torah scroll.

(*dikaiosynē*). The Pharisees (see "Pharisees and Sadducees" at 3:7) were members of the sect that was committed to fulfilling the demands of the Old Testament through their elaborate oral tradition. Their scrupulous adherence to the written and oral law was legendary in Israel; yet Jesus says it did not gain them entrance to the kingdom of heaven.

You will certainly not enter the kingdom of heaven (5:20). Kingdom righteousness operates from the inside-out, not the outside-in, a principle fully in line with Old Testament understandings of righteousness and purification (e.g., Ps. 51:2, 7, 10, 16–17). Jesus' disciples are called to a different *kind* and *quality* of righteousness than that of the current religious leaders.

Jesus Fulfills the Law (5:21–48)

Do not murder (5:21). Although Hebrew possesses seven words for killing, the verb used in Exodus 20:13 (*rāṣaḥ*) carries the idea of murder with premeditation and deliberateness: self-murder (i.e., suicide), accessory to murder (2 Sam. 12:9), or those who have responsibility to punish known murderers but fail to do so (1 Kings 21:19). Penalty for murder, as against manslaughter (Num. 35:22ff.), was death; it was not reducible to a lesser sentence (Num. 35:31).

Anyone who says to his brother, "Raca" (5:22). "Raca" ("empty-headed") was a term of contempt used as a personal, public affront. Name-calling was highly insulting in Jewish culture, because the significance attached to one's name was thereby stripped from him or her.

Is answerable to the Sanhedrin (5:22). The Sanhedrin was the official adjudicating body of the Jews (similar to a supreme court), which was allowed by the Roman authorities to handle Jewish cases unless they impinged on Roman rule.

Anyone who says, "You fool" (5:22). Calling a person *mōre* ("fool") likewise was highly insulting, because moral connotations were attached to the term (e.g., Prov. 10:23). The Hebrew word *mōreh* means "rebel," indicating a person who was a persistent rebel against God. More likely, however, this expression comes from the Greek term *mōros* (the origin of the English word "moron"), indicating a person who consistently acted moronically.

▸ Not the Smallest Letter, Not the Least Stroke of a Pen (5:18)

Jesus confirms the full authority of the Old Testament as Scripture for all ages (2 Tim. 3:15-16), even down to the smallest components of the written text. (1) The "smallest letter" (Gk. *iōta*; KJV "jot") of the Hebrew alphabet is the *yôd*. (2) "The least stroke of a pen" (Gk. *keraia*; KJV "tittle") most likely refers to a *serif*, a small hook or projection that differentiates one Hebrew letter from a similar one (such as the letters ב bêt/ כ kap, the letters ד dalet/ ר rêš, and the letters ה he/ ח–hiêt).

ב – bêt ד – dalet ה – he י – yôd
כ – kap ר – rêš ח – hêt

According to this statement, Jesus indicates that the inspiration and authority of the Old Testament Scripture extends to the actual words, even to the smallest of letters and the least parts of words. Scripture does not simply contain the Word of God; the words of Scripture are the very words of God.

VALLEY OF HINNOM

"Gehenna" was located along the west and south sides of Jerusalem.

 *left*

ALTAR OF BURNT SACRIFICE

A model of the altar in the Court of Priests in the Jerusalem Temple.

Will be in danger of the fire of hell (5:22). "Fire of hell" comes from the term *geenna*, "Gehenna." It referred to the "valley of the son of Hinnom," an area west and southwest of Jerusalem. Here Ahaz and Manasseh sacrificed their sons to Molech,[99] which caused Josiah to defile the place (2 Kings 23:10). Later the valley was used to burn refuse from Jerusalem, so the constant burning made the valley an appropriate reference to fires of punishment. Jewish apocalyptic writers began to call the Valley of Hinnom the entrance to hell, later hell itself (*4 Ezra* 7:36).

Your adversary who is taking you to court (5:25). This probably assumes a Gentile legal setting, since there is no record in Jewish law of imprisonment for debt. Before the legal process is put into action, Jesus' disciples are to "settle matters quickly," that is, to "make friends quickly" with their adversaries.

Until you have paid the last penny (5:26). The "penny" (*kodrantēs*) is the Roman bronze/copper coin *quadrans*, the smallest of the Roman coins at approximately 18 mm. A *quadrans* was the least in value of Roman coins, equal to approximately 1/64 of a *denarius* (the *denarius* was equal to approximately a day's wage; cf. 18:28; 20:1–16).[100]

QUADRANS

A Roman "penny."

You have heard that it was said, "Do not commit adultery" (5:27). Adultery (Ex. 20:14) involved sexual intercourse with mutual consent between a man, married or unmarried, and the wife of another man. The term and the penalty (death) applied equally to both man and woman, and a betrothed woman was counted as a wife.[101] Joseph recognized that adultery not only would have been an offense to Potiphar, but is especially a "sin against God" (Gen. 39:9; cf. Ps. 51:4).

But I tell you that anyone who looks at a woman lustfully (5:28). God graphically condemns the people of Israel for spiritual adultery not just when they actually worship pagan idols, but when Israel's heart and eyes desired other gods (Ezek. 6:9).

If your right eye causes you to sin, gouge it out (5:29). Jesus uses hyperbole (deliberate exaggeration) for the sake of emphasizing the seriousness of single-minded, single-eyed, single-handed spouse commitment.

"Anyone who divorces his wife must give her a certificate of divorce" (5:31). See comments on 19:3–12.

But I tell you that anyone who divorces his wife (5:32). Jesus states categorically that divorce creates adultery, the despicable nature of which he has just declared (5:27–30), because an illicit divorce turns the woman into an adulteress when she remarries.

Except for marital unfaithfulness (5:32). See comments on 19:3–12.

"Do not break your oath" (5:33). In the Old Testament, God often guarantees the fulfillment of his promises with an oath. In the same way, the Old Testament permitted a person to swear by the name of God to substantiate an important affirmation or promise. The Pharisees developed a complicated series of rulings regarding *Shebuoth* ("oaths"), which were of two kinds: a positive oath was a promise to do something, while a negative oath was a promise not to do something (*m. Šeb*, 1:1, passim). There was a tendency among some interpreters to make this permission mean that only oaths made by invoking the name of the Lord were binding. If they weren't really serious about their oath they would say, "I swear by heaven," and since they didn't invoke the literal name of God, it wasn't binding. The increasing tendency to try to find loopholes in one's oath included swearing by "less sacred" things (e.g., "earth," "Jerusalem," etc.; cf. Matt. 23:16–22), which in turn led to the devaluation of vows. This caused some Jewish groups to warn against using any kind of oath too often.[102]

Let your "Yes" be "Yes," and your "No," "No" (5:37). A simple "yes" or "no" is enough for a trustworthy person (cf. 2 Cor. 1:15–24), a saying of Jesus that James seemingly reproduces and passes on (James 5:12). A disciple's word should be considered as trustworthy as a signed document or contract. When Jesus goes further to suggest that "anything beyond this is evil," he indicates that swearing by something with the intent to deceive can only have one source, the evil one, Satan (cf. 6:13; 13:19, 38).

"Eye for eye, and tooth for tooth" (5:38). Among some ancient societies punishment was handed out without real regard for individual cases, and often the penalty greatly exceeded the crime. The law of revenge (*lex talionis*) was originally intended as a means of providing justice and of purging evil from among God's people (Deut. 19:20–21). It was established as a check to inappropriate punishment and was not to be administered by individuals, but only by civil authorities and civil courts to protect the public, to punish offenders, and to deter crime.[103]

But I tell you, Do not resist an evil person (5:39). It is not the disciple's personal responsibility to "resist [the] evil." That is the responsibility of society's governing authorities. On the personal level, the disciple's first responsibility is to reverse the dynamic of the situation from taking to giving. Jesus uses four illustrations from the everyday affairs of a people under oppression (cf. Deut. 19:16–21).

If someone strikes you on the right cheek (5:39). To strike a person on the right cheek implied giving someone the back of the hand from a right-handed person. It is not so much the hurt as the *insult* that is here in mind, because it was a symbolic way of insulting a person's honor.[104]

CLOAK

Representation of a Roman woman wearing a cloak *(top)*; an Egyptian (Coptic) tunic.

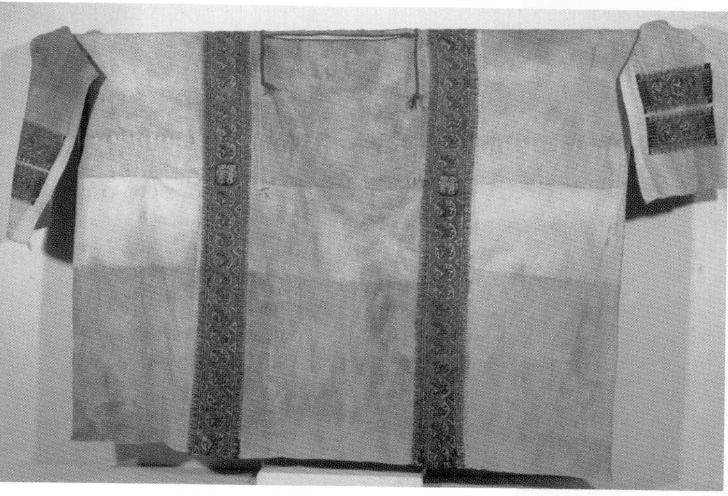

If someone wants to sue you and take your tunic, let him have your cloak as well (5:40). The tunic was the basic garment, a long-sleeved inner robe similar to a nightshirt that a person wore next to the skin. It was often worn short by men and ankle length by the women. The "cloak" was the outer robe (cf. 27:35; John 19:23–24), which was an indispensable piece of clothing. When it was given as a pledge, it had to be returned before sunset, because it was used by the poor as a sleeping cover.[105]

If someone forces you to go one mile, go with him two miles (5:41). Persian royal post officers could force a civilian to carry official correspondence, and Roman military personnel could organize bands of unpaid laborers from the common people to construct roads, fortifications, and public buildings. The most familiar New Testament scene is when Simon of Cyrene was forced into service by the Roman guards to carry Jesus' cross (27:32; Mark 15:21). The Greek term *milion* means a "thousand paces," which measures approximately 4,854 feet (just under the distance of a modern U.S. "mile").[106]

Give to the one who asks you (5:42). Giving alms and loaning to the poor was a central exercise of Jewish piety (Deut. 15:7–11). However, Jesus widens the obligation by admonishing his disciples generally not to turn away the one who wants to borrow. This is a powerful image of generosity, because the one seeking a loan could be unscrupulous, even one's enemy, who might not repay the loan (cf. Luke 6:34–35). The Old Testament gives a low status to people who consistently seek loans and do not repay them (Ps. 37:21),[107] but to give freely to whoever seeks assistance, especially to those from whom there is little chance of repayment, is the height of generosity.

"Love your neighbor" (5:43). Love for one's neighbor was commanded by God through Moses (Lev. 19:18) and was one of the central truths of the Old Testament. When answering the legal test of a Pharisaic legal expert about the greatest commandment in the law, Jesus replied with love for God and love for one's neighbor (Matt. 22:36–40).

"Hate your enemy" (5:43). This command is not found in the Old Testament. In fact, Moses directed the people to assist an enemy in need (Ex. 23:4–5). But God's hatred of evil is a central theme that runs through the Old Testament.[108] Those who desired to be righteous learned to adopt God's hatred of evil, so that the Psalmist could say in another place, "Do I not hate those who hate you, O LORD, and abhor those who rise up against you? I have nothing but hatred for them; I count them my enemies" (Ps. 139:21–22; cf. 26:4–5). Later groups within Israel took this further. The starkest extreme may be found at Qumran, which gave in the *Rule of the Community* explicit directions to "hate" those against God: "that they may love all the sons of light, each according to his lot in God's design, and hate all the sons of darkness, each according to his guilt in God's vengeance" (1QS 1.9–11).[109]

That you may be sons of your Father in heaven (5:45). The children of Israel were God's sons by his calling, and that calling included the obligation to carry out God's will. Now anyone who does the will of the Father is a "son" or "daughter" (cf. 12:48–50). If a person responds to God's will in the ministry of Jesus, he or she has God as heavenly Father. That includes the obligation to act like a son or daughter, which means loving as the Father loves.

Be perfect, therefore, as your heavenly Father is perfect (5:48). Jesus' disciples are to pursue the perfection of God himself: "Be holy because I, the LORD your God, am holy" (Lev. 19:2). The word "perfect" (*teleios*) reflects the Hebrew *tâmîm*, which is used for the complete commitment of a person to God, involving ethical blamelessness.[110] *Teleios* is used in the LXX in Deuteronomy 18:13: "You shall be perfect before the LORD your God." It can be used to indicate a person who has attained spiritual "maturity,"[111] but in Matthew 5:48, with the Father as the goal, disciples are to pursue the Father's perfection as the goal of their lives.

The Giving of Alms (6:1–4)

Be careful not to do your "acts of righteousness" before men (6:1). "Acts of righteousness" are the public demonstration of one's piety, which in Judaism often centered on giving alms, praying, and fasting, three issues that Jesus now addresses (6:2–4, 5–15, 16–18). A statement in the apocryphal book of Tobit highlights their interdependence within Judaism:

> Prayer with fasting is good, but better than both is almsgiving with righteousness. A little with righteousness is better than wealth with wrongdoing. It is better to give alms than to lay up gold. For almsgiving saves from death and purges away every sin. Those who give alms will enjoy a full life, but those who commit sin and do wrong are their own worst enemies. (Tobit 12:8–10)

If you do, you will have no reward from your Father in heaven (6:1). The two-ways texts of the Qumran *Rule of the Community* present lists of virtues and vices with their corresponding present world and future life rewards and punishments (1QS 4:2–14). The reward for walking in obedience to the covenant was a profound visitation of God's blessing:

> And the visitation of those who walk in it will be for healing, plentiful peace in a long life, fruitful offspring with all everlasting blessings, eternal enjoyment with endless life, and a crown of glory with majestic raiment in eternal light. (1QS 4:6–8)

Similar notions permeated much of Judaism at the time of Jesus. But Jesus shows here that legalistic obedience does not guarantee reward from God since motive is more important than simple activity.

So when you give to the needy (6:2). Performing deeds of mercy or lovingkindness was one of the pillars of religious life in Israel. Simeon the Just said, "By three things is the world sustained: by the Law, by the [temple-]service, and by deeds of loving-kindness" (*m. ʾAbot* 1.2). Poverty was widespread in ancient agrarian societies, and the people of Israel took seriously the obligation to provide for the poor (cf. Deut. 15:11). By the time of Jesus the phrase "to do mercy" had become a technical expression for doing mercy to the poor by giving alms.[112]

Do not announce it with trumpets (6:2). Some suggest a literal trumpet is in mind, either to call the people to fasts with accompanying almsgiving or to signal an especially large gift being given. Perhaps what is called to mind is the sound of

SHOFAR WITH MENORAH

The ram's horn and candelabrum engraved on a basalt stone at Gamla in Galilee.

coins being tossed into the trumpet-shaped money chests ("shofar-chests") in the temple used for collecting alms.[113] But more likely Jesus is drawing on a vivid piece of typical irony. In our day the same metaphor is well known as a person who wants to "toot his/her own horn."

SHOFAR

A Jewish man blowing the ram's horn on New Year's Eve.

As the hypocrites do in the synagogues and on the streets, to be honored by men (6:2). The term "hypocrite" (*hypokritēs*) originally was used for actors on a Greek stage who put on various masks to play different roles.[114] Modern usage normally designates a hypocrite to be a person who says one thing and lives a different way. But the religious leaders are indicted by Jesus for a particular form of hypocrisy: They were carrying out external acts of righteousness that masked, even from themselves, their own inner corruption. Their hypocrisy, especially here, means doing *right things* for the *wrong reasons*.

Model Prayer: "The Lord's Prayer" (6:5–13)

When you pray (6:5). Although individual prayer was appropriate at any time, pious Jews prayed publicly at set times: morning, afternoon, and evening (Ps. 55:17; Dan. 6:10; Acts 3:1). Josephus indicates that sacrifices, including prayers, were offered "twice a day, in the early morning and at the ninth hour."[115]

For they love to pray standing in the synagogues and on the street corners to be seen by men (6:5). When the set time of prayer arrived, pious Jews would stop what they were doing and pray. This could be done discreetly or with a great deal of display.

But when you pray, go into your room (6:6). Since common people did not often have separate, private quarters in their homes, the meaning is intended metaphorically to emphasize privacy, or it may refer to a storeroom for grain and foodstuffs. Jesus does not condemn public prayer, because he prayed publicly himself (14:19; 15:36).

right ▶

STOREROOM

The remains of a storeroom from a fourth-century rural house in northern Israel.

Do not keep on babbling like pagans (6:7). The priests of Baal continued from morning until noon to cry, "O Baal, answer us" (1 Kings 18:26), and the multitude in the theater at Ephesus shouted for two hours "Great is Artemis of the Ephesians" (Acts 19:34).

This, then, is how you should pray (6:9). Jesus doesn't necessitate verbatim repetition of these words, because frequent repetitive use may lead to the sin of formalism condemned here. However, following Jewish custom, some Christians recited the Lord's Prayer three times a day toward the end of the first century (e.g., *Did.* 8.2–3).

Our Father in heaven (6:9). The term for "Father" is *ʾabba*, a term used by children for their earthly fathers to express the warmth and intimacy a child experiences when in the security of a loving father's care. The motif of the "heavenly Father" occurs throughout the Old Testament,[116] growing increasingly popular during the Second Temple period in prayers for protection and forgiveness.[117] The Jewish *Ahabah Rabbah* begins, "Our Father, merciful Father," and the first-century *Eighteen Benedictions* includes the petitions, "Graciously favor us, our Father, with understanding from you," and "Forgive us, our Father, for we have sinned against you."[118] The way Jesus uses "heavenly Father" to address God is unique because Jesus is the unique Son (cf. 3:17), but by calling his disciples to share in the kingdom of heaven, they now have entered into a relationship with his Father as well.[119]

Hallowed be your name (6:9). The first petition is directed toward God's name. The purpose of hallowing that name (the name signifies the person) is that God will be "sanctified" or set apart as holy among all people and in all actions. The Jewish *Qaddish* ("holy") prayer of the synagogue, which likely goes back to Jesus' time, begins similarly: "Exalted and hallowed be his great name in the world which He created according to his will."[120] This affirms the typical Jewish expectation that God is to be treated with the highest honor.

Your kingdom come (6:10). The *Qaddish* continues similarly: "May he establish his kingdom in your lifetime and in your days, and in the lifetime of the whole household of Israel, speedily and at a near time." The Old Testament looked for God to send his anointed one to rule the earth. Now that Jesus has inaugurated that kingdom, his disciples live with the anticipation of the completion of that program. This petition is reflected in a prayer expressed in the early church in *marana tha*, "Come, O Lord!"[121]

Your will be done on earth as it is in heaven (6:10). God reigns in heaven absolutely, which means that all of heaven experiences his perfect will. Jesus prays that earth will experience that same rule of God.

Give us today our daily bread (6:11). "Bread" is an example of synecdoche, a part-whole figure of speech for "food" (4:4), but especially referring to all of the believer's needs, physical and spiritual.[122] The word translated "daily" (*epiousios*) in connection with "bread" has been broadly debated, but the wording seems to recall Israel's daily reliance on God for manna in the desert (Ex. 16). In the same way as manna was only given one day at a time, disciples are to rely on daily provision for life from God, helping them to develop a continuing, conscious dependence on him (cf. Matt. 6:34; Phil. 4:6).

Forgive us our debts, as we also have forgiven our debtors (6:12). Sin creates an obligation or "debt" to God that humans cannot possibly repay. The evidence that a person has truly been forgiven of his or her debt of sin is the willingness to forgive others (cf. 18:21–35), a sentiment found commonly in Judaism: "Forgive your neighbor the wrong he has done, and then your sins will be pardoned when you pray" (Sir. 28:2).

Lead us not into temptation, but deliver us from the evil one (6:13). Since God is not one who tempts his people to do evil (James 1:13) and the word rendered "temptation" can be used for either temptation or test (cf. 1:12–13; see comments on Matt. 4:1), this petition indicates that the disciples should pray either that God removes tests of their faith, such as when manna was given to test Israel,[123] or else they should pray that their testing will not become an occasion for temptation. This is similar to a standardized Jewish morning and evening prayer:

> *Bring me not into the power of sin,*
> *And not into the power of guilt,*
> *And not into the power of temptation,*
> *And not into the power of anything shameful.*[124]

Satan's influence is behind every attempt to turn a testing into a temptation to evil, so Jesus teaches his disciples that they need to rely on God, not only for physical sustenance, but also for moral triumph and spiritual victory.[125]

Fasting (6:16–18)

When you fast (6:16). The law required only one fast a year—on the Day of Atonement.[126] The expression used there is "deny yourselves" (NIV) or "humble your souls" (NASB), indicating that in addition to fasting, the people were to demonstrate a humbling of their souls by wearing sackcloth, mourning, and praying on the Day of Atonement (cf. Ps. 35:13; Isa. 58:3).[127] As time passed, fasts multiplied for legitimate purposes, such as a sign of repentance and seeking God's mercy (e.g., Ezra 8:21–23), and certain days of the year became regular days of fasting (Neh. 9:1; Zech. 8:19).

Do not look somber as the hypocrites do (6:16). Fasting also became legalized among some sectarians to twice a week (cf. Luke 18:12), usually on Monday and Thursday, because Moses is said to have gone up on Sinai on those days. Jesus condemns the practice of hypocritical fasting by the religious leaders, since they were fasting with the intention of getting recognition from the people.

But when you fast, put oil on your head and wash your face (6:17). This kind of anointing and washing is not religious, but is to signify preparation to enjoy life, similar to the expression in Ecclesiastes, "Go, eat your food with gladness, and drink your wine with a joyful heart, for it is now that God favors what you do. Always be clothed in white, and always anoint your head with oil" (Eccl. 9:7–8).

Choose Your Master: God or Wealth (6:19–24)

Do not store up for yourselves treasures on earth (6:19). Material wealth was important to the people of Israel, because wealth was often seen as a sign of God's blessing and the reward for obedience to him (see comments on 6:1). One ancient rabbi said:

> A man should always teach his son a cleanly [or easy] craft, and let him pray to him to whom riches and possessions belong, for there is no craft

wherein there is not both poverty and wealth; for poverty comes not from a man's craft, nor riches from a man's craft, but all is according to his merit. (*m. Qidd.* 4.14)

But the accumulation of wealth for its own sake was deceptive, because one could find a false sense of security or an inaccurate assessment of one's spirituality in material treasure.

Where moth and rust destroy, and where thieves break in and steal (6:19). Jewish writers regularly warned the people that wealth is not the final determination of one's spiritual standing before God. Wealth could be acquired illegitimately, and it also was subject to the destructive effects of life in a fallen world.[128]

But store up for yourselves treasures in heaven (6:20). The idea of storing up good works before God was prominent in Israel's history. Sirach 29:10–11 exhorts, "Lose your silver for the sake of a brother or a friend, and do not let it rust under a stone and be lost. Lay up your treasure according to the commandments of the Most High, and it will profit you more than gold."

The eye is the lamp of the body. If your eyes are good, your whole body will be full of light (6:22). Some Greek and Jewish writers spoke of the eye as a lamp that contained its own source of light that shone outward to illuminate objects, which was the indication of the vitality of life in a person.[129] But here Jesus seems to use the eye in a different metaphorical sense, as a lamp that will illumine a person's inner life. The "evil eye" in the ancient world is an eye that enviously covets what belongs to another. It is a greedy or avaricious eye.[130] A "good eye" speaks of singleness of purpose, undivided loyalty. It will let into the body that which its sight is fixed upon. If the eye is good, it is fixed on good treasure, the things of God; then the heart will be filled with the light of God's treasure (e.g., *T. Iss.* 4.4–6).

Either he will hate the one and love the other, or he will be devoted to the one and despise the other (6:24). The biblical notion of "hate" and "love" understands them to be patterns of life, not simply emotional reactions. "Do I not hate those who hate you, O LORD, and abhor those who rise up against you? I have nothing but hatred for them; I count them my enemies" (Ps. 139:21–22; cf. Matt. 5:43; 1QS 1.9–11).

You cannot serve both God and Money (6:24). Jesus personifies wealth or possessions of all kinds as a rival god, "Money" (Gk. *mamōnas*). The temptation to worship the god of materialism was well known in Judaism. A heartrending confession from the second-century. B.C. *Testament of Judah* 19:1–2 states: "My children, love of money leads to idolatry, because once they are led astray by money, they designate as gods

MAMMON

First-century bronze coins found in an oil lamp at En Gedi.

REFLECTIONS

A WELL-KNOWN BUMPER STICKER expresses the idolatry of the modern world: "He who dies with the most toys wins." That is, life and the afterlife have no real meaning, so make it your ambition to play hard and find your worth in the materialism and pleasure of this world. One primary way to avoid this form of idolatry is to put God at the center of our lives and love him with all that we have. Money, wealth, and possessions have three primary purposes in Scripture:

- to give appropriate care for one's own family and prevent them from becoming a burden to others.[A-44]
- to help those who are in need, especially the church.[A-45]
- to encourage and support the work of the gospel both at home and around the world.[A-46]

those who are not gods. It makes anyone who has it go out of his mind. On account of money I utterly lost my children." The writer goes on to say, "The prince of error blinded me" (19:4), pointing to Satan's activity in using material idolatry to lead astray the children of God.

Provider of the Disciples' Needs (6:25–34)

Do not worry about your life (6:25). Worry is inappropriate when it is misdirected or in wrong proportion, or when it indicates lack of trust in God. Appropriate concern and work are connected with trusting God and working within the pattern of his creation.

What you will eat or drink; or about your body, what you will wear (6:25). Jesus is speaking to people familiar with life's daily struggle. Much of their daily routine was spent trying to get enough supplies for day-to-day existence. The poor especially did not have extensive supplies, so the question of what one would eat tomorrow was very real, especially with the vagaries of seasonal famine, fire, or flood.

Look at the birds of the air; they do not sow or reap or store away in barns, and yet your heavenly Father feeds them (6:26). Birds expend energy in doing what is their natural way, such as building nests and collecting food for their young, yet it is actually God who feeds and clothes them. A first-century Jewish text states, "For if I am hungry, I will cry out to you, O God, and you will give me (something). You feed the birds and the fish, as you send rain to the wilderness that the grass may sprout to provide pasture in the wilderness for every living thing, and if they are hungry, they will lift up their face to you" (*Pss. Sol.* 5.8–10).

Are you not much more valuable than they? (6:26). This is a typical rabbinic style of arguing "from the lesser to the greater." The point is that when disciples are properly responsible to carry out the ways of life as ordained by God, God is faithful to carry out his responsible care of the order. Humans are the crown and ruler of God's creation (Ps. 8:3–8), and their needs will receive appropriate attention from God.

Who of you by worrying can add a single hour to his life? (6:27). The NIV translation is a good rendering of a curious expression in Greek, which reads, "add one forearm length (*pēchys*) to his age/stature (*hēlikia*)." The term *pēchys* is a standardized unit of measure, the typical length of a forearm, or about eighteen inches, called a "cubit."[131] The term *hēlikia* usually designates a measure of age or maturity (e.g., Heb. 11:11), but occasionally is used for physical stature (e.g., Luke 2:52; 19:3). The present context instead indicates a measure of duration of life. Worrying can't extend one's life.

See how the lilies of the field grow (6:28). "Lilies [*krina*] of the field" draw to mind God's provision in nature for flowers growing wild, which probably surround Jesus, the disciples, and the crowd. Even today, red and purple anemone (*anemone coronaria*) crowning ten-inch stalks, along with blue iris, grow wild on the hillside above the Sea of Galilee.[132]

Not even Solomon in all his splendor was dressed like one of these (6:29). The beautiful flowers growing wild on the Galilean hillside surrounding Jesus elicit a striking contrast to Solomon's royal robes, whose wealth prompted a visit from the Queen of Sheba and whose life became a proverbial success story.[133]

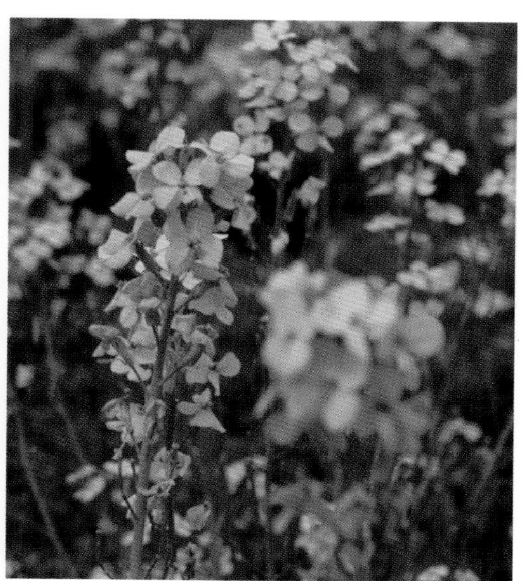

The grass of the field, which is here today and tomorrow is thrown into the fire (6:30). The green grass of spring when cut, dried, and bundled was a natural source of fuel for fire ovens (6:28) and a common biblical metaphor for dramatic changes of fortune as well as for human frailty and transience.[134]

For the pagans run after all these things, and your heavenly Father knows that you need them (6:32). "Pagans" (*ta ethnē*), rendered elsewhere in Matthew as "the nations" (12:21; 25:32; 28:19), commonly designates non-Jews or Gentiles. Here the emphasis is on those who operate outside of God's values. Those with faith in God's provision will not worry and will reject the pursuits and values of unbelievers.

But seek first his kingdom and his righteousness (6:33). This climactic admonition draws the listeners back to the key verse of the sermon, where Jesus declared,

▲

GRASS OF THE FIELD

Grass is being carried by women to feed animals in Samaria.

◀ *left*

"NOT EVEN SOLOMON IN ALL HIS SPLENDOR"

Spring wildflowers in the Middle East

"Unless your righteousness surpasses that of the Pharisees and the teachers of the law, you will certainly not enter the kingdom of heaven" (5:20).

Each day has enough trouble of its own (6:34). Since no exact parallel to this maxim exists,[135] Jesus' saying apparently became proverbial, because James gives an admonition that apparently draws on this truth (James 4:13–15).

The Kingdom Life in Relation to Others (7:1–6)

Do not judge, or you too will be judged (7:1). A similar sentiment is found in an earlier Jewish writing, "Before judgment comes, examine yourself; and at the time of scrutiny you will find forgiveness" (Sir. 18:20).

With the measure you use, it will be measured to you (7:2). A similar warning is found in a rabbinic ruling on adultery: "With what measure a man metes it shall be measured to him again" (*m. Soṭah* 1.7). The "measure" could be a scale, or a vessel or rod used for calculating weight or distance, but was often used figuratively, as here (cf. 23:32).

Why do you look at the speck of sawdust in your brother's eye and pay no attention to the plank in your own eye? (7:3). Jesus now uses hyperbole (intentional exaggeration) as an illustration to make his point. The "speck" refers to a small twig or stalk, in contrast to a "plank" or large beam. The contrast may reflect Jesus' own background as a carpenter's son (13:55). The extreme that Jesus condemns is passing judgment on another person while having a similar problem oneself.

Do not give dogs what is sacred (7:6). "Dog" came to be a derogatory label for a person who was apart from, or an enemy of, Israel's covenant community (see "Dogs and Pigs in the Ancient World"). "What is sacred" in this context most likely refers to the message of the gospel of the kingdom, indicating that this holy message must not be defiled by those who are unreceptive to, or have rejected, Jesus' invitation.

Do not throw your pearls to pigs (7:6). The image of the dog is reinforced by the

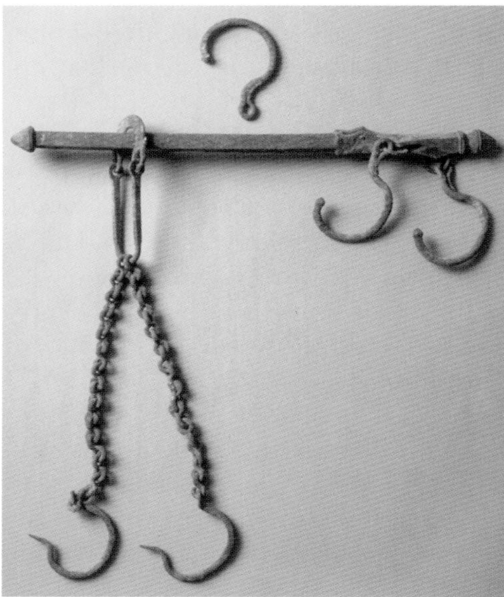

ROMAN SCALES

Dogs and Pigs in the Ancient World

Dogs. To modern readers the mention of "dogs" conjures up images of well-groomed household pets, but in the ancient world dogs lived in squalor, running the streets and scavenging for food (Ps. 59:14–15). To refer to a person as a dog was a grave insult, reducing the person's status to among the lowest on the social scale (2 Sam. 16:9). Jews had a particular revulsion for dogs because they alone among domesticated animals were willing to eat human corpses (1 Kings 21:19, 24; 22:38). As a metaphor, "dog" was a humiliating label for those apart from, or enemies of, Israel's covenant community.[A-47] Although dogs were often trained for guarding flocks (Job 30:1) and humans (Isa. 56:10; Tobit 6:2; 11:4), they were not normally brought into the home (see comments on 15:26–28). Jesus' statement means that his disciples are not to treat the gospel message as discarded food thrown to scavengers who are outside the kingdom.

Pigs. Although pork was a highly prized food among many people in the ancient Mediterranean world, it was rejected by Jews (and perhaps some ancient priestly Egyptians), perhaps because pigs, like dogs, were scavenging animals. Their omnivorous habits occasionally led pigs to feed on decaying flesh, a practice deplorable to Jews. The rejection of pork came to symbolize the Jews' separation from the unclean Gentile world. When the martyr Eleazar was forced to eat pork, he refused and was executed by the Greek tyrant Antiochus IV Epiphanes (2 Macc. 6:18–20; *4 Macc.* 5:1–6:30). Pigs were often dangerous because they ravaged fields (Ps. 80:13) and, while running wild in city streets, were sometimes responsible for the death of little children.[A-48]

parallel image of a pig, because pigs, like dogs, were usually wild, scavenging animals. "Pearls" symbolize the value of the message of the kingdom of heaven (see comments on 13:45–46). Something so valuable should not be given to those who have no appreciation for such precious truths, whose nature is demonstrated by their rejection of the message of the gospel.

If you do, they may trample them under their feet, and then turn and tear you to pieces (7:6). Dogs and pigs are linked elsewhere in Scripture (Isa. 66:3; 2 Peter 2:22) as dangerously wild and ritually unclean animals. The bizarre behavior of wild animals produced fear because their often-intense hunger could cause them to attack humans (cf. Ps. 22:16–17). Pigs and dogs were symbols of filth and paganism (cf. Isa. 65:4; 66:3, 17), and the image warns disciples about the danger of those who have rejected the message of the kingdom of heaven.

Prayer and the Disciples' Kingdom Life (7:7–12)

Ask . . . seek . . . knock and the door will be opened to you (7:7). "Ask" means to pray with humility and consciousness of need. "Seek" means to pray and to be active in pursuing God's will. "Knock" seems to point toward persistence. Jesus uses "knocking" here as a metaphor for prayer; in the apostle John's vision the risen Jesus "knocks" so that the church will hear and open themselves to the intimacy of his fellowship (Rev. 3:20).[136]

Bread . . . stone . . . fish . . . snake (7:9–10). Staple food in a Jewish daily diet included bread and fish. A responsible father would not be mean and trick his children with stones that resembled bread (cf. Jesus' first temptation, 4:1–4), now would he trick them with snakes that resembled fish? Jews were prohibited from eating fish that lacked fins and scales (Lev. 11), perhaps because of their resemblance to snakes (e.g., eel, catfish).[137]

True Discipleship: With Jesus or Against Him? (7:13–29)

Enter through the narrow gate (7:13). The image of two roads in life is fairly common, whether speaking of separate roads that lead either to paradise or to Gehenna (*b. Ber.* 28b), or of a narrow road of life's hardships that ultimately leads to a broad path of eternal blessing (e.g., 2 Esd. 7:3–9).

Watch out for false prophets (7:15). Jesus warns against revolutionary leaders who can lead the people astray with their false form of prophecy, a common Old Testament warning.[138] These are general warnings against those who attempt to

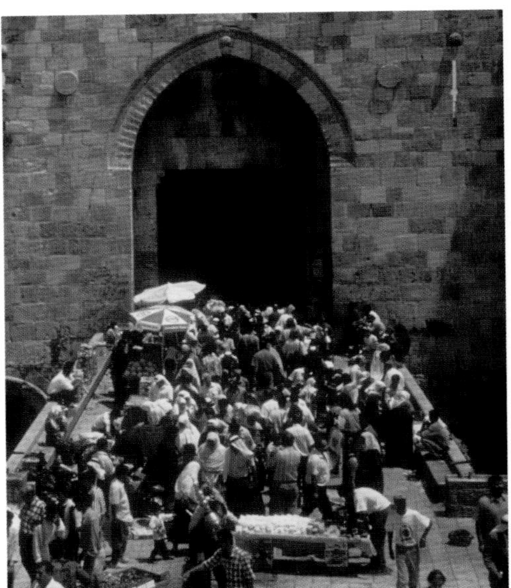

right ▸

ENTER THROUGH THE NARROW GATE

A crowd enters modern Jerusalem through the wide Damascus Gate.

▸ The Golden Rule

The moral maxim that has come to be known as the "Golden Rule" is one of the commonly accepted bases of human civilization. It occurs in both positive and negative forms. The ancient Roman philosopher and statesman Seneca (4 B.C.–A.D. 65) expressed the principle positively, "Let us show our generosity in the same manner that we would wish to have it bestowed on us" (*De Beneficiis* 2.1.1), while the Chinese philosopher Confucius (551–479 B.C.) stated it negatively, "Do not do unto others what you would not want others to do unto you!" (*Analects* 15:23).[A-49]

The precept appears to have been a common theme in Judaism of the time of Jesus. Tobit gives a negative form of the principle, "Watch yourself, my son, in everything you do, and discipline yourself in all your conduct. And what you hate, do not do to anyone" (Tobit 4:14b–15). Hillel the Elder (c. 70 B.C.–A.D. 10) supposedly had as his motto, "What is hateful to you, do not do to your neighbor." In the only text in the whole of rabbinic literature that attributes the saying to Hillel, the Elder goes on to say, "That is the whole Torah. The rest is commentary. Go and learn!" (*b. Šabb.* 31a).[A-50]

For Jesus, the kingdom life that he is inaugurating fulfills the deepest inclination of humans, who are created in the image of God. Kingdom life now enables his disciples to live life the way God intends it to be lived. As such it "sums up the Law and the Prophets" (cf. 5:17–20).

lead the people of Israel by falsely speaking for God. Josephus tells of a variety of popular prophets who led the people to insurrection: "Deceivers and imposters, under the pretense of divine inspiration fostering revolutionary changes, they persuaded the multitude to act like madmen, and led them out into the desert under the belief that God would there give them tokens of deliverance."[139] Among the more popular of these leaders of movements were Theudas (c. A.D. 45), the prophet from Egypt (c. A.D. 56), and Jesus son of Hananiah (c. A.D. 62–69).[140]

They come to you in sheep's clothing (7:15). This proverbial expression draws on the natural enmity of sheep and wolves (e.g., Isa. 11:6; 65:25) and will be the basis of Paul's later warning to the Ephesian elders (Acts 20:29) and the early church father Ignatius's warning to the church at Philadelphia (Ign. *Phil.* 2:1–2).

Thus, by their fruit you will recognize them (7:20). False prophets will produce bad fruit, which from an Old Testament perspective includes leading the people away from God to follow false gods (Deut. 13:1–18) or whose prophecies are not fulfilled (18:21–22).

Therefore everyone who hears these words of mine and puts them into practice (7:24). This is typical Jewish figurative language, as is reflected in the Qumran literature (1QH 6:26 [14:26]; 7:8–9 [15:8–9]) and in an early second century Tannaitic saying: "A man of good deeds who has studied much Torah, to what may he be likened? To someone who first lays stones and then bricks. Even when much water rises and lies against them, it does not dislodge them."[141] But Jesus' saying reflects a more specific reference to his surroundings and the object of his criticism.

Like a wise man who built his house on the rock . . . like a foolish man who built his house on sand (7:24, 26). Jesus demonstrates familiarity with building techniques in this parable, perhaps a reflection of his own training in his father's trade as a carpenter (*tektōn*; see comments on 13:54). The alluvial sand ringing the seashore on the Sea of Galilee was hard on the surface during the hot summer months. But a wise builder would not be fooled by such surface conditions. He would dig down sometimes ten feet below the surface sand to the bedrock below, and there establish the foundation for his house. When the winter rains came, overflowing the banks of the Jordan River flowing into the sea,

REFLECTIONS

THE RELIGIOUS ESTABLISHMENT OF JESUS' DAY advocated a form of surface righteousness that masked an unstable foundation of religious hypocrisy. Jesus gives the bedrock invitation to true life in the kingdom of heaven, but it will be the unpopular way, the hard way, because those who follow him will leave behind the way of comfort found in identifying with the popular religious establishment.

As always, the wise person shows he or she has carefully viewed the shifting sands of life's teachings and understands that Jesus is the only secure truth in life. The wise person thinks ahead to when there will be storms, and he sacrifices the enjoyment of the present good weather for the sake of building his or her life on the rock of Jesus' words about reality. The foolish man thinks only of the present convenient situation and does not plan for storms of life or eternity. The choice is no less stark in our own day. Wise men and women build their lives on Jesus, regardless of cultural weather.

houses built on the alluvial sand surface would have an unstable foundation layer; but houses built on bedrock would be able to withstand the floods. Excavations in the late 1970s in the region uncovered basalt stone bedrock that was apparently used for the foundation of buildings in antiquity.[142]

Cleansing the Leper (8:1–4)

Large crowds followed him (8:1). The people will see that Jesus is not only Messiah in word (chs. 5–7) but is also Messiah in deed (chs. 8–9). Jesus' miracles may be divided into three general classes: healings, exorcisms, and nature miracles, with raisings of the dead as a subcategory of the last. Matthew will focus on each of these types of miracles here as a demonstration that the kingdom of God truly has arrived (cf. 12:28).

A man with leprosy came and knelt before him (8:2). The word "leprosy" is a transliteration of the Greek word *lepros*. In the ancient world leprosy was associated with a variety of skin diseases and suspicious skin disorders. The Old Testament provided specific guidelines for the examination and treatment of those with skin diseases (see Lev. 13–14), since many of the disorders were considered highly contagious. The line between medical and spiritual impurity was often blurred, however, because of the uncertainty of diagnosis.

All those with leprosy were required to be examined by the priest, who after examination could pronounce a person clean or unclean (Lev. 13:2ff.). If found leprous, the diseased individual was to be isolated from the rest of the community, required to wear torn clothes, cover the lower part of his or her face, and cry out "Unclean! Unclean!" (Lev. 13:45–46; Num. 5:2–4). The rabbinic tractate *Negaᶜim* distinguishes two categories of two types each of leprosy: the Bright Spot, which is bright-white like snow, the second shade of which is the white like the lime of the temple; the Rising, which is white like the skin in an egg, the second shade of which is the white like white wool (*m. Neg.* 1:1). The modern conception of leprosy brings to mind the dreaded and debilitating illness known as Hansen's disease, caused by the *Mycobac-*

Military Units of the Roman Army

In the Roman army at the time of Jesus there were twenty-five legions spread throughout the empire—eight on the Rhine, six in the Danube provinces, three in Spain, two in Africa, two in Egypt, and four in Syria (Tacitus, *Ann.* 4.5). The tactical strength called for the following numbers, but each unit often operated with fewer.

- *Legion* = normally 6,000 men (5,300 infantry and 700 cavalry).
- *Cohort* = Each legion was divided into 10 cohorts.
- *Centuria* = Each cohort had 6 *centuria* (century), 100 men, the smallest unit of the Roman legion. Each *centuria* was commanded by a centurion.
- *Centurion* = The centurion was the principal professional officer in the armies of ancient Rome. Most centurions were of plebeian origin and were promoted from the ranks of the common soldiers. They formed the backbone of the legion and were responsible for enforcing discipline. They received much higher pay and a greater share of the spoils than did common soldiers (as much as fifteen times more).[A-51]

terium leprae bacillus. It is most prevalent in low, humid, tropical or subtropical areas of the world, most cases being found in Asia, Africa, South America, and the Pacific Islands.

See that you don't tell anyone. But go, show yourself to the priest (8:4). Lepers had to be reexamined by the priest and declared "clean," and then had to offer a sacrifice on his behalf (Lev. 14:1–32). The sacrifice offered by the cleansed leper was in the category of *ʾāšam* offering, offered as payment for either purification or reparation.

Healing the Centurion's Servant (8:5–13)

When Jesus had entered Capernaum, a centurion came to him (8:5). The centurion was a Roman military officer. Although there is little tangible evidence of a centurion being stationed in Galilee until A.D. 44,[143] recent excavations reveal a military garrison at Capernaum with quarters to the east of the Jewish village. The troops lived in better houses than the local population. To the surprise of archaeologists, the excavations reveal that these soldiers had a typical Roman bath at their disposal.

My servant lies at home paralyzed and in terrible suffering (8:6). The descriptions have led some to suggest that the cause was poliomyelitis (i.e., polio), a scourge of many ancient societies.

Lord, I do not deserve to have you come under my roof (8:8). The centurion displays a sensitivity for the Jewish populace when he considers himself unworthy to receive the Jewish teacher Jesus into his Gentile home, because entering the home of a Gentile rendered a Jew ceremonially unclean (see Acts 10:28). A rabbinic saying states, "The dwelling places of gentiles are unclean" (*m. ʾOhal.* 18:7).

Rabbi Hanina Ben Dosa and Healing from a Distance

Much-discussed accounts of healing over distance appear in the rabbinic literature, among them a story of Rabbi Hanina ben Dosa that occurs in the Babylonian Talmud (*b. Ber.* 34b). It reads:

> It happened that when Rabban Gamaliel's son fell ill, he sent two of his pupils to R. Hanina ben Dosa that he might pray for him. When he saw them, he went to the upper room and prayed. When he came down, he said to them, "Go, for the fever has left him." They said to him, "Are you a prophet?" He said to them, "I am no prophet, neither am I a prophet's son, but this is how I am blessed: if my prayer is fluent in my mouth, I know that the sick man is favored; if not, I know that the disease is fatal." They sat down, and wrote and noted the hour. When they came to Rabban Gamaliel, he said to them, "By heaven! You have neither detracted from it, nor added to it, but this is how it happened. It was at that hour that the fever left him and he asked us for water to drink."

Such accounts within Judaism are rare and were considered extraordinary, so Jesus' healing in this manner would have been regarded as astonishing. Rabbi Hanina ben Dosa knew that he was only a prayer intermediary and that he did not have even the stature of a prophet. In striking contrast, Jesus knew that he was himself the source of the healing (8:7, "I will go and heal him"), which the centurion knew as well (8:8, "But just say the word, and my servant will be healed"), a prerogative that only a divine Messiah could claim and validate.

Many will come from the east and the west and will take their places at the feast (8:11). "East and west" points to the breadth of peoples who will come from the ends of the earth. The Old Testament anticipated the inclusion of all the peoples of the earth in the eschatological banquet (Isa. 25:6–9; 56:3–8).

But the subjects of the kingdom will be thrown outside (8:12). The expression "subjects of the kingdom" (lit., "*sons* of the kingdom") is a Semitism pointing to national Israel,[144] whose leaders have taken exclusive claim to God's kingdom through their Abrahamic heritage (3:8–9). Jesus paints a woeful picture of the future of unrepentant Israel with terms common to descriptions of hell, or Gehenna.[145] These themes are not much different from the Old Testament prophets, who consistently called Israel back to God.

And his servant was healed at that very hour (8:13). Different from other stories of healing that circulated in Judaism, this account of Jesus' authority as the one who himself heals, not as an intermediary, sets him apart from all others (see "Rabbi Hanina Ben Dosa and Healing from a Distance").

Healing Peter's Mother-In-Law (8:14–17)

Jesus came into Peter's house (8:14). In 1968 excavations were undertaken that have convinced most archaeologists that they have found the actual site of Peter's house in Capernaum. Sifting down through the remains of centuries-old

Excavating the House of Simon Peter

Much of church history has venerated a location that is said to be the actual site of Peter's house. The majority of scholars now believe that excavations undertaken in 1968 have basically confirmed the authenticity of the claim.[A-52]

The building was used as a typical home for an extended family from approximately 63 B.C. until A.D. 50. Peter and Andrew apparently moved the family fishing business from Bethsaida to Capernaum and established their residence in this house, large enough for an extended family. Mark tells us it was the home of both Peter and Andrew (cf. Mark 1:29).

During the second half of the first century A.D. the use of the house changed. Domestic pottery ceased to be used and the walls of the large center room were plastered—quite unusual for the region except for where groups of people gathered. Graffiti that mention Jesus as "Lord" and "Christ" in Greek are found. These pieces of evidence indicate that during this time the house became a center of Christian worship.

The house-church continued in existence for nearly three hundred years, as is evidenced from over a hundred Greek, Aramaic, Syriac, Latin, and Hebrew graffiti scratched on the plastered walls, along with numerous forms of crosses, a boat, and other letters. Among the graffiti are at least two possible occurrences of Peter's name.

In the fifth century an octagonal church was built precisely over the original plastered house-church, with the same area and dimensions, a type of architecture used to venerate earlier sacred sites.

Princeton Seminary New Testament scholar James Charlesworth exclaims, "Since there are no rival options for Peter's house, and since it was clearly where the house has been discovered or somewhere close to it, it seems valid to conclude that Peter's house may have been excavated and identified. The discovery is virtually unbelievable and sensational. Despite the sensational nature of the find, learned archaeologists and historians have slowly come to the same conclusion."[A-53]

◀
SYNAGOGUE AT CAPERNAUM

An aerial view of the remains.

"HOUSE OF PETER" EXCAVATIONS

The remains of this first-century home are located adjacent to the synagogue.
▼

churches, excavators came to what was originally a house, built in approximately 63 B.C. The house was originally one story, with the walls of black basalt stones and an original roof made from beams and branches of trees covered with a mixture of earth and straw. Pottery shards, oil lamps, and coins discovered in the ruins date back to the first century, along with artifacts that included several fishhooks in the earliest layers of the floor. The house was organized as several rooms built around two interior courtyards. The dimensions were fairly large by ancient standards, but it was similar to other houses in the area.

He saw Peter's mother-in-law (8:14). Mark informs us that this is both Peter and Andrew's house (Mark 1:29). Perhaps it had been a home of Peter and Andrew's parents, but was now occupied by the sons and their larger extended families, including on Peter's side at least his wife and her parent(s). Paul also alludes to Peter's marriage (cf. 1 Cor. 9:5).

Lying in bed with a fever (8:14). Matthew's expression (*beblēmenos*; lit., "having been thrown on a bed") indicates that Peter's mother-in-law is in the throes of severe feverish illness, perhaps malarial. Fever was considered by the populace to be a disease, not a symptom (cf. John 4:52; Acts 28:8).

This was to fulfill what was spoken through the prophet Isaiah: "He took up our infirmities and carried our diseases" (8:17). This is another allusion by Matthew to the Servant of Isaiah's prophecy (Isa. 53:4),[146] here focusing on the Servant's role of bringing healing. The Servant bears the sicknesses of others through his suffering and death. Many modern scholars doubt that first-century Jews would have interpreted Isaiah 53:4 messianically,[147] but some later rabbinic texts knew a messianic interpretation of the passage.[148]

Expected Discipleship Disappointed (8:18–22)

Then a teacher of the law came to him (8:19). Although the Jews had a high percentage of the population trained in the rudiments of reading and writing, only a small segment of people regularly worked with writing materials, and even fewer had access to books or Scriptures. Therefore, the skills of writing and reading were highly valued. Throughout the ancient world a class of people arose called "scribes" (Gk. *grammateus*), people trained in reading, writing, and transcribing. Because of the importance of that trade, their role often went far beyond simple secretarial skills to include teaching, interpretation, and regulation of laws found in official documents. In Judaism a class of scribes had developed who were experts in interpreting and teaching Scripture (hence the NIV "teacher of the law").

SEA OF GALILEE
The northern shore near Capernaum.

Teacher, I will follow you wherever you go (8:19). This teacher of the law has in mind the kind of master-disciple relationship in which the would-be disciple examines various masters and then enlists himself in following the most popular or the best-equipped teacher.[149]

Foxes have holes and birds of the air have nests, but the Son of Man has no place to lay his head (8:20). Jesus draws on a familiar metaphor to explain the uniqueness of his form of master-disciple relationship.

The Son of Man has no place to lay his head (8:20). Jesus' stern reply checks this enthusiastic recruit, because his form of discipleship is a different sort from what he has experienced in his prior training. Teachers of the law enjoyed a relatively high status within Judaism, but Jesus has no school or synagogue or prestigious place of honor among the religious establishment. Jesus apparently stayed at the home of friends, relatives, and disciples through most of his ministry, such as the home of Peter and Andrew while in Capernaum. The expression "no place to lay his head" does not indicate he is a homeless Cynic-type philosopher, but rather that his ministry will not result in an institutional establishment with comfortable benefits.

Jesus as the "Son of Man"

The expression "Son of Man" would strike a relatively ambiguous chord with the scribal teacher of the law. In Ezekiel, God refers to the prophet with the expression "son of man" over ninety times,[A-54] pointing to Ezekiel's frailty as a human before the mighty God revealed in the vision. But "Son of Man" is also used in Daniel's prophecy to refer to a glorified Sovereign, the apocalyptic messianic figure who rules forever with the Ancient of Days (Dan. 7:13–14). This latter sense of the expression found its way into use in Judaism, in the pseudepigraphal writings *1 Enoch* and 2 Esdras 13 (or *4 Ezra* 13). The reference in *1 Enoch* is particularly interesting because it precedes the time of Jesus: "...pain shall seize them when they see that Son of Man sitting on the throne of his glory. [These] kings, governors, and all the landlords shall [try to] bless, glorify, extol him who rules over everything, him who has been concealed. For the Son of Man was concealed from the beginning, and the Most High One preserved him in the presence of his power; then he revealed him to the holy and the elect ones" (*1 En.* 62:5–7).[A-55]

With such a general ambiguity, "Son of Man" is convenient for Jesus to use to give instruction about his true identity. It does not have popular associations attached to it, such as were attached to titles like "Messiah," "Son of David," or even "Son of God." Instead, he can teach the meaning of his true identity by referring to himself with the expression, which indeed is his favorite self-designation. With a general threefold progression, Jesus uses the expression to clarify exactly who he is and what is his ministry.

- The Son of Man is the humble Servant, who has come to forgive sins of common sinners in his earthly ministry.[A-56]
- The Son of Man is the suffering Servant, whose atoning death and resurrection will redeem his people.[A-57]
- The Son of Man is the glorious King and Judge, who will return to bring the kingdom of heaven to earth.[A-58]

Jesus' mission is not always understood because of the misperceptions and faulty expectations of the people, the religious leaders, and even his own disciples. But at the end, it is perfectly clear that he is claiming to be the divine Messiah of Israel (cf. 26:63–68).

Another disciple said to him (8:21). This is not one of the Twelve, but one of the broader circle of followers who gather around Jesus, not yet fully understanding what his form of discipleship will entail. Like the teacher of the law, this person desires to be a disciple of Jesus and is even perceived to be one in the loose sense of the term.[150]

Lord, first let me go and bury my father (8:21). Burial of the dead supersedes other religious obligations in Israel, even for the priests, who were allowed to be defiled by touching the dead if it was for a family member (Lev. 21:2). The obligation to care for the dead comes implicitly from the command to "honor your father and mother," which is among the greatest commandments[151]; this was made explicit in later Jewish practice.[152] Surprisingly, the practice began to supersede other religious obligations: "He whose dead lies unburied before him is exempt from reciting the *Shema*, from saying the *Tefillah* and from wearing phylacteries" (*m. Ber.* 3:1). The Talmudic interpretation carries it even one step further: "He who is confronted by a dead relative is freed from reciting the *Shema*, from the Eighteen Benedictions, and from all the commandments stated in the Torah" (*b. Ber.* 31a).

BURIAL TOMBS

These date from the Maccabean era.

Follow me, and let the dead bury their own dead (8:22). Jesus will later rebuke the Pharisees and teachers of the law for not rightly honoring father and mother (15:1–9), so he is not advocating the contravening of the Old Testament prescription. Trying to understand Jesus' response has led to a number of explanations. Some think that the person's father has not yet died and that he wants to stay with him until then. Or perhaps he is returning to fulfill the second stage of burial by the transfer of the bones of his father a year after death to an ossuary. Others look for explanation in a metaphorical allusion in Jesus' language, so that he intends to mean something like "let those who are *spiritually* dead bury the *physically* dead." In any case, Jesus perceives the real problem with this disciple: He had not yet understood clearly the place that Jesus must have as the primary allegiance of his life.

Calming a Storm (8:23–27)

Without warning, a furious storm came up on the lake (8:24). The lake's low elevation (at least 636 feet [212 meters] below sea level) provides it with relatively mild year-round temperatures. However, encompassed with mountain ranges to the east and west that rise over 2,650 feet from the level of the lake, especially infamous is an east wind that blows in over the mountains, particularly during the spring and fall (cf. 14:19, 24; John 6:1–4). The lake's low-lying setting results in sudden violent downdrafts and storms (cf. Mark 4:37; Luke 8:23; John 6:18) that can produce waves seven feet and more, easily able to swamp a boat.[153]

But Jesus was sleeping (8:24). Traversing the Sea of Galilee by night was a common experience for fishermen, where trammel nets were used throughout the night (cf. 4:16–20; on the type of boat used, see comments on 4:21).[154] The boat was equipped for cooking during nightlong commercial fishing expeditions on the lake, with enough room for a person to lie down in the stern and sleep when not on duty, with perhaps a ballast sandbag for a pillow (cf. Mark 4:38).[155]

Then he got up and rebuked the winds and the waves, and it was completely calm (8:26). To "rebuke" indicates that Jesus is able to command even the forces of nature, in the same way that in the Old Testament God "rebukes" the sea, a demonstration of his sovereign control over all of nature.[156]

A GALILEAN FISHING BOAT

This mosaic depiction was found at Bethsaida and dates to the late Roman period.

REFLECTIONS

"WHO REALLY IS THIS JESUS?" the disciples are wondering. As a man Jesus was extremely tired after the exhausting day, but with divine power he quieted the storm by a mere word of command. He is far more than they ever could have understood. And Jesus is far more than what we have often understood. It is a challenge for all of us to look clearly at Jesus as the divine-human Messiah and allow him to amaze us and move us to follow him as his true disciples. And it won't hurt to humble ourselves to call on him at our time of need, as self-sufficient as we might think that we are!

Exorcising the Demoniacs (8:28–34)

When he arrived at the other side in the region of the Gadarenes (8:28). The "other side" is often a reference to the movement from a Jewish to a Gentile region. "Gadarenes" refers to both the village of Gadara, located about five miles southeast of the Sea of Galilee, and to the surrounding region,[157] which probably included a little village that lay on the eastern shore of the Sea of Galilee called Gerasa (modern Khersa or Kursi), the traditional site of the exorcism.[158]

Two demon-possessed men coming from the tombs (8:28). Contact with the dead rendered a Jew ceremonially unclean,[159] which may have been the reason for the demon-possessed men to accost this Jewish contingent. The book of *Jubilees* views Gentiles as unclean because they "slaughter their sacrifices to the dead, and to demons they bow down. And they eat in tombs" (*Jub.* 22:16–17).

Matthew apparently has independent knowledge of a second demonized man, because Mark (5:1–20) and Luke

(8:26–39) specify only one such person. Matthew is often concerned only with giving general details of the narrative, so he merely mentions that there are two demoniacs; Mark and Luke, giving a more detailed account, single out the spokesman of the two and describe him in more detail. This is similar to the incident where Matthew describes the healing of two blind men (20:29–34), but Mark (10:46–52) and Luke (18:35–43) mention only one. Again, they go into more detail in the incident, with Mark even explicitly identifying the blind man as Bartimaeus, the son of Timaeus (Mark 10:46).

Have you come here to torture us before the appointed time? (8:29). The author of *1 Enoch* 16:1 says graphically that evil spirits "will corrupt until the day of the great conclusion, until the great age is consummated, until everything is concluded (upon) the Watchers[160] and the wicked ones."[161] The demons question whether Jesus has come to torment them before that appointed time arrives.

Some distance from them a large herd of pigs was feeding (8:30). The east shore of the Sea of Galilee is a Gentile region.

SEA OF GALILEE REGION

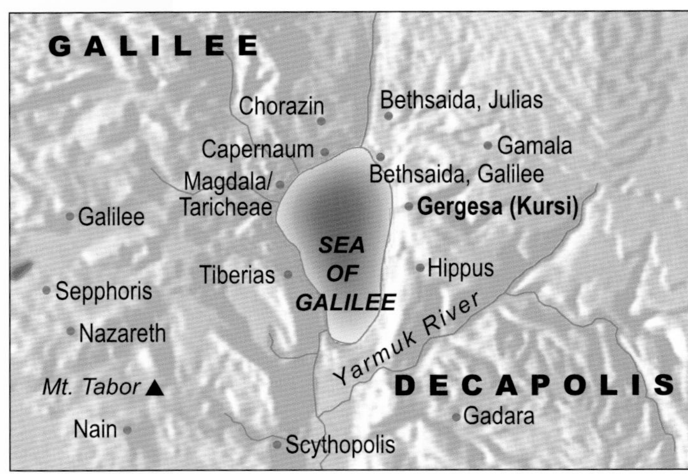

Jews would not be raising pigs, since they were unclean (Lev. 11:7; Deut. 14:8).

The whole town . . . pleaded with him to leave their region (8:34). Jesus has given a special witness to the Gentiles of this region, but there is a terrible perversion of values. Instead of rejoicing at the release and restoration of two human beings, the townspeople weep over the loss of pigs.

Healing the Paralytic (9:1–8)

Jesus stepped into a boat, crossed over and came to his own town (9:1). Jesus "crosses over," which marks the transition from the Gentile to the Jewish regions surrounding the Sea of Galilee. He comes back to the town explicitly named Capernaum in Mark's narrative (cf. Mark 2:1; 5:18), which is now "his own town," the home base of Jesus' ministry in the Galilee region (cf. 4:17; 8:5; 11:23).

Take heart, son; your sins are forgiven (9:2). Individual sin is not always the direct cause of a person's disease or illness (John 9:2–3), but at the heart of humanity's problem is sin. Healing has confirmed Jesus' authority to announce the arrival of the kingdom of heaven (4:23–25), and healing now confirms that forgiveness of sin accompanies the arrival of the kingdom. Once sin is forgiven and redemption has occurred, all sickness and death will ultimately be abolished (cf. Isa. 25:8–9).

This fellow is blaspheming! (9:3). Blasphemy is an act in which a human insults the honor of God. This extends to misusing the name of God, which is cursed or reviled instead of being honored, the penalty for which is death by stoning (Lev. 24:10–23; 1 Kings 21:9ff.). The teachers of the law charge Jesus with blasphemy because they believe that he is dishonoring God by taking to himself the prerogative to forgive sins, something that only God can do (cf. Mark 2:7; Luke 5:21).

Matthew Called (9:9–13)

A man named Matthew sitting at the tax collector's booth (9:9). Taxes in ancient Rome were collected by persons who were the highest bidders for a collection contract (*ordo publicanorum*, Livy, *History* 25.3.8–19). But in Palestine, tax collectors were employed as representatives of the Roman governing authorities, collecting the prescribed duties and generally seeing to public order. They usually were enlisted from the native population, because they needed to know local people and local customs to avoid being deceived. They were expected to collect a certain amount of tax money for the Roman authorities, and whatever extra they collected constituted their own commission. A tendency to resort to excessive extortion made them despised and hated by their own people (cf. Luke 19:8), and they became proverbial of a person with a self-seeking outlook (Matt. 5:46).

Matthew's tax collection booth must have stood at some place where the Via Maris passed close by the lakeshore on the outskirts of Capernaum (cf. 4:13).[162] He may have been collecting tolls from the commercial traffic traveling through the area or collecting taxes for the fish caught on the Sea of Galilee, for both of which Herod Antipas was responsible. Josephus says that Herod Antipas received annual revenue of two hundred talents from Galilee and Perea, his taxation region[163]—approximately five million dollars a year.

"Follow me," he told him, and Matthew got up and followed him (9:9). The wording implies following Jesus as his disciple. Like the two sets of brothers called earlier (cf. comments on 4:18–22; see also John 1:35–51), Matthew had been under the influence of Jesus' preaching for some time prior to this and is now ready to join him as one of his disciples. Little is known of Matthew Levi, except for the widely attested tradition from the second century on that he is the author of the Gospel that now bears his name. As a tax collector he has been trained in secular scribal techniques, and as a Galilean Jewish Christian he would have been able to interpret the life of Jesus from the perspective of the Old Testament expectations.[164]

Why does your teacher eat with tax collectors and "sinners"? (9:11). Table fellowship was an important social and religious convention among many groups in the ancient world. Boundaries were established that designated who was included and excluded from the meal, and also served to delineate religious and ethical obligations toward the participants. Within Judaism, the Therapeutae, Essenes, and Pharisees were especially known for the role that table fellowship played in defining their group identities.[165] The shared meal was a formal occasion when group members consumed food made sacred through various ritual practices such as ceremonial washings or tithing. Participants were often marked out by a prior required initiation.[166]

The derision that many felt generally for tax collectors was aggravated because they were regarded as ceremonially unclean because of their continual contact with Gentiles and because of their compromise of the Sabbath by working on it.[167] The term "sinner" (*hamartōlos*) was often used by the Pharisees to point to an identifiable segment of the people who were opposed to God's will as reflected in their understanding of proper obedience to the law and their *halakah*. But "sinner" is normally used more generally to designate the person who commits acts of sin defined by the law (e.g., Luke 7:36–50; cf. Matt. 26:45).[168] In the minds of the Pharisees, for Jesus to share a meal with these types of persons indicates that he includes them within his own fellowship; it also suggests that he condones their behavior. Jesus must now clarify who he is and what his mission entails.

It is not the healthy who need a doctor, but the sick (9:12). The Pharisees considered themselves to be righteously healthy before God, because they defined righteousness by their observance of the law—their "sacrifice." But they are blind to their real sinfulness before God. Jesus' offer of salvation to sinners apart from sectarian observances threatens the foundation and way of life of the Pharisees, yet is at the heart of the gospel he has come announcing.[169]

Discipleship and Religious Traditions (9:14–17)

Then John's disciples came (9:14). The "disciples of John" are committed followers of the prophet John the Baptist. They gathered around him as the prophet who would usher in the messianic age. They have assisted John in baptizing those who came to him and engaged in strict religious practices John taught, such as fasting and prayer (Luke 5:33; 11:1). The "disciples of the Pharisees" (see Mark 2:18; cf. Matt. 22:16) are most likely those in training to become full initiates to their brotherhood. They have been immersed in the Pharisaic commitment of the oral law and rigorous practice of their traditions.

How is it that we and the Pharisees fast, but your disciples do not fast? (9:14). For fasting in the Old Testament and in Jewish tradition, see comments on 6:16–18. John's disciples do not understand why Jesus' disciples do not regularly fast as a sign of repentance.

How can the guests of the bridegroom mourn while he is with them? (9:15). Jesus now alludes to himself as the "bridegroom," who in the Old Testament is Yahweh (cf. Isa. 62:5; Hos. 2:19–20). The arrival of the kingdom of heaven has brought to fulfillment the promises of Israel, which should cause a time of rejoicing, like what would be experienced during marriage ceremonies (cf. Matt. 25:12–13).

No one sews a patch of unshrunk cloth on an old garment (9:16). Using two examples from everyday life, Jesus emphasizes that he has not come simply to provide a corrective to the traditional practices of the Jews. Rather, he has come to offer an entirely new approach to God, which will be incompatible with rigid traditionalism. Jesus' kingdom life is an entirely new garment and entirely new wine, which must have appropriate traditional practices.

Healing the Ruler's Daughter and the Hemorrhaging Woman (9:18–26)

A ruler came and knelt before him (9:18). Mark 5:22 and Luke 8:41 give the man's name as Jairus; Matthew simply calls him a "ruler" (*archōn*), which can

◀ *left*

GOATSKINS

Skins such as these were used as wine containers in the first century.

be used of either a community leader or a head of a synagogue board. Mark and Luke specify him as the latter, though Jairus may in fact function as both a community and a synagogue leader.[170] By kneeling before Jesus he indicates the extreme honor he gives to him, for kneeling is the appropriate position one takes before God[171] or a king or superior.[172]

Just then a woman who had been subject to bleeding for twelve years (9:20). The woman's bleeding could have been from some sort of internal disease or hemophilia, although the latter is mostly a male disorder. The term *haimorroeō*, "subject to bleeding," was used in Greek medical writings and in Leviticus 15:33 (LXX) to mean "menstruous." This most likely indicates that the woman had menorrhagia, a disease in which the menstrual flow is abnormally prolonged, usually producing anemia as well.[173] The condition was all the more difficult because she would have been considered ritually unclean and excluded from normal social and religious relations, since others making contact with her would become unclean as well (Lev. 15:25–30).

Came up behind him and touched the edge of his cloak (9:20). The expression "edge of his cloak" is *kraspeda*, which in some contexts can refer to the outer fringe (decorated or plain) of a garment (cf. 14:26). However, the term is rendered "tassel" in 23:5, which may be the meaning here as well. Attached to the four corners of a garment worn by men were "tassels" (Heb. *ṣîṣît*) that had a blue cord. The tassels reminded an individual to obey God's commands and to be holy to God (Num. 15:40).

When Jesus entered the ruler's house and saw the flute players and the noisy crowd (9:23). Music was long considered an important element at both times of mourning and at times of gladness. The music of the dirge (*qînâ*); David's lament over Saul and Jonathan (2 Sam. 1:18–27) is an example of the music that accompanied a time of mourning. Professional mourners were customarily hired to assist at funerals, usually including flautists and wailing women. Rabbi Judah later said, "Even the poorest in Israel should hire not less than two flutes and one wailing woman."[174] In the family of a prominent person like the ruler, many professional mourners would have joined the family and friends in expressing their grief. Mourning was considered an important way of dealing with the reality of death, and various rites encompassed the mourner's clothing, diet, relationships, and religious activities, usually for a period of seven days.[175]

After the crowd had been put outside, he went in and took the girl by the hand, and she got up (9:25). Touching a corpse renders a person unclean for a period of seven days (Num. 19:11–21), but Jesus brings the girl to life, which transforms uncleanness to purity.

The Messiah at Work (9:27–38)

Two blind men followed him, calling out, "Have mercy on us, Son of David!" (9:27). The blind men understand Jesus to be the "Son of David," a reference to the promise of the messianic deliverer from the line of David whose kingdom would have no end (2 Sam. 7:12–16; cf. *Pss. Sol.* 17:23). The messianic age promised to bring healing to the blind (Isa. 29:18; 35:5; 42:7), which Jesus told John the Baptist was one of the signs that he indeed was the Expected One (11:2–6).

REFLECTIONS

THE BASIC MEANING OF COMPASSION is "to be moved in the inward parts," which usually indicates the heart and affections. But Jesus is not simply "emotional." He is moved by the profound needs of the crowd and motivated to send out workers who will bring healing to sin-sick humanity. As we see the needs of people all around us, we must allow our heart to feel deeply for them. But we cannot stop there. We must get close enough to them to see how it is that we can bring the healing touch of the gospel of the kingdom to their deepest needs. Humanity is dying without the Great Physician, and we are the ones who must go next door or around the world carrying his healing touch, because they will either be gathered in this harvest of grace or face the next harvest of judgment.

A man who was demon-possessed and could not talk was brought to Jesus (9:32). Demon-possession took a variety of external forms. In the case of those in 8:28, it produced violent behavior that threatened people. Here the phenomenon prohibits a man from speaking (see also 12:22). The term for "could not talk" is *kōphos*, "dull," which can be used of dull of hearing (i.e., deaf, 11:1) or dull of speech (i.e., mute, as here).

He had compassion on them, because they were harassed and helpless, like sheep without a shepherd (9:36). The leaders in Israel's history had been likened to shepherds. Joshua was appointed as leader after Moses, so that "the LORD's people will not be like sheep without a shepherd" (Num. 27:17).[176] That is what Israel is like in Jesus' day. The leaders have not fulfilled their responsibility to guide and protect the people, so the crowds are harassed (*skyllō*) and helpless (*rhiptō*), descriptions that indicate that they are experiencing distressing difficulties and are unable to care for themselves.

The harvest is plentiful but the workers are few (9:37). The theme of harvest was

right ▶
WHEAT HARVEST
Women gathering wheat in the hills of Judea.

common in Judaism. A rabbinic saying from around A.D. 130 gives a similar emphasis: "R. Tarfon said: The day is short and the task is great and the labourers are idle and the wage is abundant and the master of the house is urgent" (*m. ʾAbot* 2.15). Jesus will draw on the harvest metaphor elsewhere in an eschatological context, but there it is harvest time of judgment (13:30, 39; cf. Isa. 17:11; Joel 3:13; Rev. 14:14–20).

Instructions for the Short Term Mission to Israel (10:1–15)

He called his twelve disciples to him (10:1). The number "twelve" has obvious salvation-historical significance, corresponding with the twelve patriarchs of Israel, the sons of Jacob, from whom the tribes of Israel descended. The twelve disciples symbolize the continuity of salvation-history in God's program, as Jesus now sends out the Twelve to proclaim to the lost sheep of the house of Israel that the kingdom of heaven has arrived (cf. 10:5–6).[177] In the future age, the twelve apostles will sit on twelve thrones judging the house of Israel (cf. 19:28).

These are the names of the twelve apostles (10:2). "Apostle" has narrow and wide meanings in the New Testament. The narrow sense, as here, is the usual meaning, signifying the special authoritative representatives chosen by Jesus to play a foundational role in the establishment of the church.[178] Paul normally used the term to refer to the Twelve, but includes himself among them as a special apostle to the Gentiles (1 Cor. 15:8–10). The wide sense of apostle derives from the common verb *apostellō*, "I send" (e.g., 10:5), and therefore can mean merely "messenger" (John 13:16), refer to Jesus as "the apostle and high priest whom we confess" (Heb. 3:1), or designate an individual such as Barnabas, Titus, or Epaphroditus within the group of missionaries that is larger than the Twelve and Paul.[179]

Do not go among the Gentiles or enter any town of the Samaritans. Go rather to the lost sheep of Israel (10:5–6). Jesus goes first to Israel (cf. 15:21–28) to fulfill the salvation-historical order that God established with Israel, who was the tool that God intended to use to bring blessing to the world.[180] The Twelve symbolize the continuity of salvation-history in God's program. According to Paul, God's offer of salvation to the world was "first for the Jew, then for the Gentile" (Rom. 1:16). Once Israel has had her chance to receive the offer of the kingdom, the offer is proclaimed equally to all the nations, including both Jew and Gentile (see 28:19–20).

ISRAEL

Samaria was excluded from this mission.

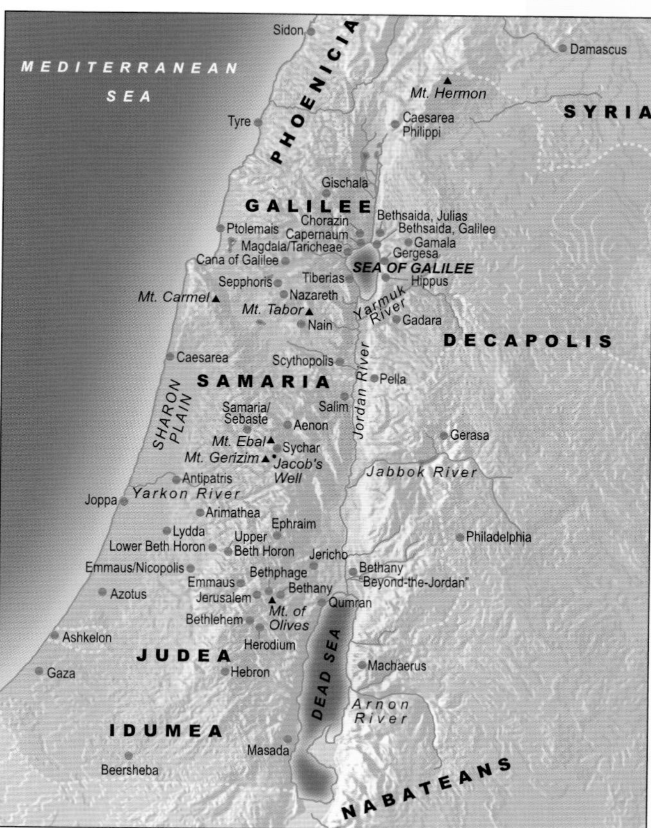

REFLECTIONS

THE TWELVE DISCIPLES/APOSTLES ARE NOT TO BE idealized. When we look at these men, and the many other men and women who were Jesus' followers, we find that they are not much different from you or me. Look at the brief description of each and see if you can identify with one or more. If Jesus could transform their lives, he can transform ours as well. That is the overwhelming story of Jesus' ministry. He came to change lives.

Simon (who is called Peter)—a successful businessman in the fishing industry, who was regularly in a leadership position.

His brother Andrew—a person highly sensitive to God's leading, but overshadowed by his brother Peter.

James son of Zebedee—left a successful family business to follow Jesus, but was the first apostle martyred.

His brother John—had a fiery temper but also a profound love for God.

Philip—never quite one of the inner circle, yet took a leadership role among the lesser-known apostles.

Bartholomew—known for his outspoken honesty (he is probably the one called Nathaniel in John 1:43–51).

Thomas—a skeptical rationalist, but eventually had one of the most profound theological understandings of Jesus' identity as the God-man.

Matthew the tax collector—formerly a traitor to his own people to save his neck and make money; became a missionary to them by writing his Gospel.

James son of Alphaeus—either younger, shorter, or less well-known than the other James; was faithful throughout his life, but never given much recognition for it.

Thaddaeus (or, Lebbaeus)—also called Judas son of James, often confused with Judas Iscariot and didn't develop much of his own reputation.

Simon the Zealot—before accepting Jesus as Messiah, a guerrilla warfare fighter who wanted to bring in God's kingdom by force.

Judas Iscariot, who betrayed him—his love of money and power may have drawn him to abandon and betray even his closest friends.

As you go, preach this message: "The kingdom of heaven is near" (10:7). The disciples are to go with the same message that both John the Baptist and Jesus preached (see comments on 3:2; 4:17).

Heal the sick, raise the dead, cleanse those who have leprosy, drive out demons (10:8). Not only do they go with the same message, but they also go with the same authority as Jesus (10:1), who performed each of these miracles (cf. chs. 8–9).

For the worker is worth his keep (10:10). The apostle Paul will call on this principle as a rationale for the support of full-time Christian workers (1 Cor. 9:14; cf. *Did.* 13:1–2). In 1 Timothy 5:18 he quotes the parallel passage in Luke 10:7, giving it the stature of "Scripture." Although the disciples are not to charge for their ministry, they are to accept the hospitality extended to them as traveling missionaries (10:11), so they will have no need to take along money ("gold or silver or copper") or extra clothing or typical traveling equipment (10:9–10). It is the responsibility of those to whom they minister to support their mission (10:10).

Search for some worthy person there and stay at his house until you leave (10:11). If a household does not receive God's messenger, then they are to shake the dust off of their feet when they leave, a sign used by Jews when leaving Gentile regions that they have removed completely unclean elements (*b. Sanh.* 12a). Paul practiced this symbol when leaving regions where his message was rejected (Acts 13:51).

Instructions for the Long-Term Mission to the World (10:16–23)

I am sending you out like sheep among wolves (10:16). Jesus reverses the metaphor. Before this the disciples were to go to the sheep (9:36; 10:6), but now they themselves are the sheep going out among wolves. In 10:5–15, Jesus gave instructions to the disciples about their short-term mission to Israel during Jesus' earthly ministry. In 10:16–23, Jesus gives instructions to the disciple/apostles about their long-term mission throughout the world until his return.

They will hand you over to the local councils and flog you in their synagogues (10:17). The synagogue was not only the place of assembly for worship, but was also an assembly of justice where discipline was exercised (cf. John 9:35).

All men will hate you because of me (10:22). The phrase "because of me" is literally "because of my name" and is an important Christological expression (cf. 5:11; 24:9) that harks back to the Old Testament significance of God's name as the representation of his person as the sole focus of Israel's worship and allegiance (e.g., Ex. 3:15; 6:3; 9:16; 20:7). Jesus' disciples will have the privilege of carrying his name, but that also brings with it suffering insofar as the antagonism and hatred directed to him will naturally fall on his followers.[181]

▸ Flogging in the Synagogue

The Old Testament gave prescriptions for exercising discipline and punishment (Deut. 25:1–3), which later Judaism applied to the responsibility of the synagogue. Flogging (*mastigoō*) was prescribed as a punishment for various sins, such as slandering a woman, incest, or entering the temple while unclean.[A-59] The lifting of the ban upon eating certain meats (e.g., Acts 10:9–16) would make a Jewish convert to Christ unclean in the eyes of the synagogue officials and subject to flogging (*m. Mak.* 3:2). After a decision by the court of judges the person was made to lie down in front of the judge and be whipped. The standard number of lashes was forty, although the number could be adjusted to make it appropriate for the crime. But no more than forty lashes could be given, because more than forty would be inhumane (Deut. 25:1–3). The number normally applied was forty less one, in case they miscounted (*m. Mak.* 3:2, 10; cf. 2 Cor. 11:24).

The Mishnah tractates *Sanhedrin* and *Makkot* ("stripes"), originally one book, give later rabbinic prescriptions for flogging. Three judges rendered the decision, although as many as twenty-three may be needed (*m. Sanh.* 1:2). The person's hands were tied to a pillar and the *ḥazzan* (administrator) of the synagogue removed the garments of the accused to bare his chest and back. The *ḥazzan* stood on a stone and gave him one-third of the prescribed stripes on the chest, and two-thirds on the back, while the person neither stood nor sat, but bent low to the ground. During the flogging the reader read Deuteronomy 28:58–9, a second person counted the blows, and a third gave the commands. The instrument of flogging was a whip (*mastix*), a strap of calf leather divided into four thongs through which smaller thongs were plaited to make it stronger, and the handle contained a device to make the strap longer or shorter. Flogging could be administered to either a man or a woman. If the accused appeared to be near death, the flogging was stopped, although there are records of people dying (*m. Mak.* 3:14).[A-60]

You will not finish going through the cities of Israel before the Son of Man comes (10:23). This is a reference, similar to the admonitions of the Olivet Discourse, that the mission to Israel will not be completed until Jesus returns to establish his kingdom on the earth (see comments on 24:1–31).

Characteristics of Missionary Disciples (10:24–42)

It is enough for the student to be like his teacher, and the servant like his master (10:25). The word "student" (*mathētēs*) is the common word for "disciple." The ultimate goal of a disciple is to be like the master—a general principle of master-disciple relations in Judaism and the Greco-Roman world. The harsh treatment that Jesus is now beginning to receive from the religious leaders will be the lot of his disciples as well.

If the head of the house has been called Beelzebub, how much more the members of his household! (10:25). The Pharisees have accused Jesus of casting out demons by the "prince of demons" (9:34), another name for Satan. That identity is further revealed to be "Beelzebub"[182] or better, "*Beelzeboul*"[183] (see comments on 12:24, 27), meaning "master of the house," as Jesus' translation and play on words with "head of the house" (*oikodespotēs*) indicates.[184] The term most likely comes from an identification of the chief of the evil spirits with Baal Shamayim, whose worship was installed in the temple by Antiochus IV Epiphanes.[185]

Do not be afraid of those who kill the body but cannot kill the soul (10:28). A Jewish parallel may be found in the saying, "With all our hearts let us consecrate ourselves unto God, who gave us our souls. . . . Let us have no fear of him who thinks he kills" (*4 Macc.* 13:13–14). This was a call to courage in the face of persecution from humans.

I did not come to bring peace, but a sword (10:34). This is a metaphorical sword, as is indicated by Jesus' rebuke of those who take up a sword to defend him in the Garden of Gethsemane (26:52). The sword can be a metaphor of God's divine judgment (Ps. 7:12) and, as here, a metaphor of separation between those who believe and those who do not, even if it is in one's family.

right ▶

SWORD AND LANCE

Anyone who loves his father or mother . . . his son or daughter . . . more than me is not worthy of me (10:37). This saying reminds one of Jesus' statement to the disciple who wanted to return to bury his father (see comments on 8:21–22). Jesus' form of discipleship calls for giving him ultimate supremacy beyond parents or children, something that not even the most esteemed rabbi would demand. Therefore, this is an implicit declaration of his deity, because only God deserves a higher place of honor than one's father and mother. A precedent for giving supremacy to God, even over parents, is found in the commendation to the tribe of Levi: "He said of his father and mother, 'I have no regard for them.' He did not recognize his brothers or acknowledge his own children, but he watched over your word and guarded your covenant" (Deut. 33:9–10).

Anyone who does not take his cross and follow me is not worthy of me (10:38). See comments on 16:24–26.

Anyone who receives a prophet . . . and anyone who receives a righteous man (10:41). The "prophets" and the "righteous" are linked elsewhere, indicating Old Testament luminaries (13:17; 23:29), but here they refer to Christian prophets (cf. 23:34) and righteous persons (cf. 13:43, 49; 25:37, 46). These distinctions are not mutually exclusive. "Prophet" refers to those who speak for God and for those with whom Jesus' followers are aligned (cf. 5:10–12; 7:15–23), and "righteous man" is a generic category that refers to all who are righteous in Christ Jesus (cf. 5:20), including the righteous people of earlier generations.

If anyone gives even a cup of cold water to one of these little ones because he is my disciple (10:42). "Little ones" points explicitly to needy disciples, which may include prophets and the righteous who are in need. As in 25:40, 45, the expression helps to emphasize that needy disciples are often the ones who are excluded from care, while attention is given to the prominent members of the discipleship community (see 18:1–5).

John the Baptist Questions Jesus (11:1–6)

After Jesus had finished instructing his twelve disciples (11:1). Matthew uses the familiar stylized conclusion to the missionary discourse (cf. 7:28; 13:53; 19:1; 26:1) as he transitions to the next section of narrative (chs. 11–12). The narrative draws attention to the gathering opposition to Jesus, which comes innocently enough from John the Baptist (11:2–19) but with outright hostility from the Jewish religious leaders (12:1–45).

When John heard in prison what Christ was doing (11:2). John has been imprisoned by Herod Antipas at the fortress Machaerus, where ultimately he was put to death (see 14:1–14). Imprisoned for upwards of a year or more, John sends his disciples to query Jesus about the messianic program.

He sent his disciples (11:2). John's disciples (see comments on 9:14) apparently stay as close to John as they can while he

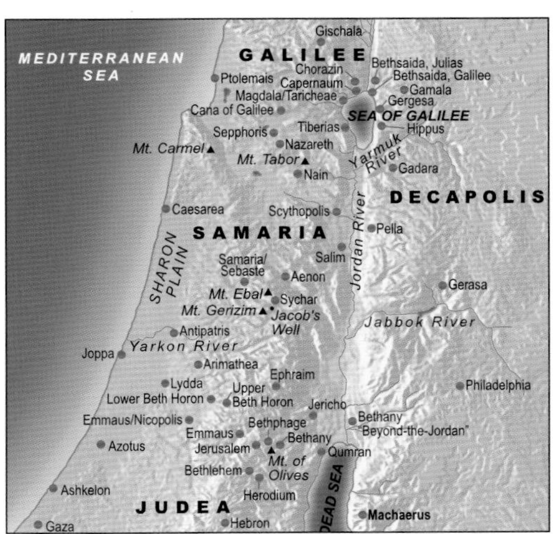

ISRAEL

Machaerus is located near the east shore of the Dead Sea.

is in prison. They probably travel from the fortress Machaerus north through Perea along the Jordan River, crossing into Galilee where Jesus is ministering.

Are you the one who was to come, or should we expect someone else? (11:3). The expression "the one who was to come" is an allusion to the Messiah, the Coming One, the expression John used to refer to Jesus at the beginning of his public ministry (3:11). The expression recalls Zechariah's prophecy, which is the prophecy fulfilled at Jesus' entry to Jerusalem (cf. Zech. 9:9; Matt. 21:4). It would be natural for John to experience some perplexity as he languishes in prison, much as had earlier prophets such as Elijah (e.g., 1 Kings 19:1–18).

Go back and report to John what you hear and see (11:4). The way that Jesus' ministry has unfolded (chs. 8–9) is in line with the prophetic promises. Isaiah's Coming One was described in these very terms: "The blind receive sight (Isa. 29:18; 35:5), the lame walk (35:6), those who have leprosy are cured (cf. 53:4; Matt. 8:1–4), the deaf hear (Isa. 29:18–19; 35:5), the dead are raised (26:18–19), and the good news is preached to the poor" (61:1).

Jesus' Tribute to John (11:7–19)

What did you go out into the desert to see? A reed swayed by the wind? (11:7). The metaphor of tall reed grasses growing along the shores of the Jordan suggests weakness and vacillation with every changing wind of opportunity or challenge.

right ▶

REEDS

Papyrus reeds growing along the Nile river.

▶ The Fortress Machaerus

Machaerus[A-61] was an important fortress east of the Dead Sea, near the southern frontier of the region of Perea. It was originally built by the Hasmonean ruler Alexander Jannaeus[A-62] around 90 B.C., destroyed by the Roman commander Gabinius in 57 B.C., and then rebuilt by Herod the Great[A-63] around 30 B.C. as one of the series of fortresses guarding the eastern frontier of Palestine (Masada, the Herodium, etc.). Pliny the Elder called Machaerus "the most important Jewish stone fortress immediately after Jerusalem."[A-64] The name of the fortress probably derives from *machaira*, "dagger," and it sits perched atop a rocky mountain with steep sides rising to an elevation seven hundred meters (1,600 feet) above sea level, protected by deep ravines on three sides.[A-65]

After the death of Herod the Great the fortress was assigned to the tetrarch of his son Herod Antipas. Here, according to Josephus,[A-66] Herod Antipas imprisoned John the Baptist and later had him put to death (see comments on 14:1–12). When Perea was added to the province of Judea (A.D. 44), Machaerus was occupied by a Roman garrison and remained in Roman control until the Jewish revolt in A.D. 66. The Jewish insurgents occupied Machaerus until A.D. 71–72, when they were besieged and finally surrendered to the Roman forces under governor Lucilius Bassus.[A-67]

Among those born of women there has not risen anyone greater than John the Baptist (11:11). "Among those born of women" is a Jewish idiom that contrasts ordinary human birth (Job 14:1; 15:14; 25:4) with the birth of those into the kingdom of heaven. The contrast is not between human accomplishments but between eras. The arrival of the kingdom of heaven ushers in an incomparably greater era than any preceding it.

The kingdom of heaven has been forcefully advancing, and forceful men lay hold of it (11:12). Since the announcement of the kingdom of heaven in John's ministry, it has received opposition from the religious establishment of Israel. Now John has received opposition from Herod Antipas, a violent man who will put John to death violently.

If you are willing to accept it, he is the Elijah who was to come (11:14). Malachi prophesied that Elijah would prepare the way for the Messiah (Mal. 3:1; 4:5). Malachi did not imply a reincarnation of Elijah or a return to life in a whirlwind (in the way he left). Rather, at John the Baptist's conception he was designated as the one who ministers in the "spirit and power of Elijah" (Luke 1:17). For those who receive John's ministry, he is the fulfillment of Malachi's prophecy (see Matt. 17:10–13).

But wisdom is proved right by her actions (11:19). Wisdom was often personified in Judaism (Prov. 8; Wisd. Sol. 7–8) to exemplify the way in which those who are guided by God's practical approach to life will make right decisions. This saying appears to be proverbial.

The Privileged Unrepentant Cities (11:20–24)

Woe to you, Korazin! Woe to you, Bethsaida! (11:21). Capernaum, Korazin (or Chorazin), and Bethsaida were the cities in which most of Jesus' miracles had been performed (11:20). The people there have had the greatest privilege and opportunity to meet Jesus, but with that comes greater accountability and responsibility.

If the miracles that were performed in you had been performed in Tyre and Sidon (11:21). Tyre and Sidon were Gentile cities in northwest Philistia/Phoenicia, an ancient region that bordered Galilee to the west along the coast of the Mediterranean Sea. These two cities were known throughout the ancient world as powerful maritime commercial centers. In Israel they became proverbial for pagan peoples, often linked as the

NORTHERN PALESTINE

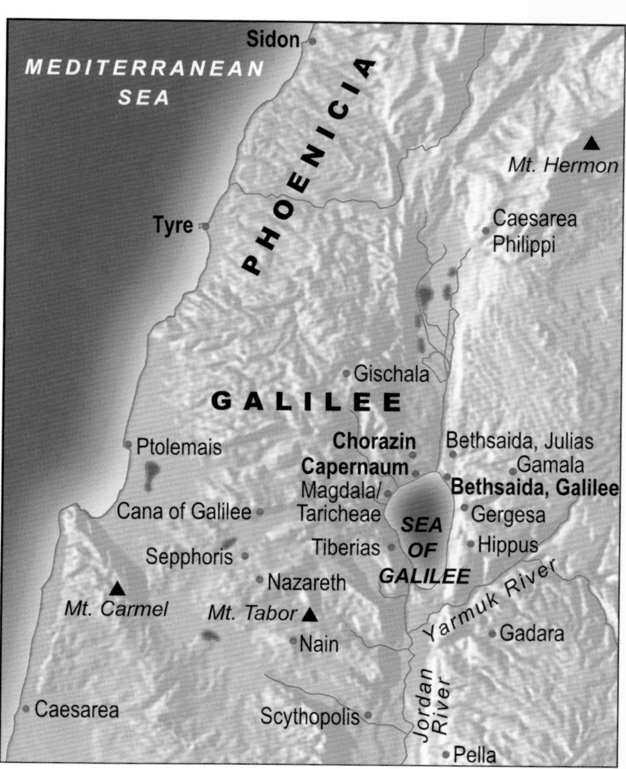

Korazin and Bethsaida

Jesus' public ministry has centered in the region surrounding the towns of Capernaum, Korazin, and Bethsaida, what some call the "Evangelical Triangle" (for Capernaum see comments on 4:17; 8:5; 9:1).

Korazin (Khirbet Kerazeh) is only 2-1/2 miles (4 kilometers) north of Capernaum. Little evidence from the time of Jesus remains, but by the third to fourth centuries it was described in rabbinic literature as a "medium-size town."[A-68] The black basalt ruins of a large synagogue from that later era have been excavated, with the famous "seat of Moses" (cf. 23:2) discovered in the ruins. The city was destroyed by an earthquake and rebuilt in the fifth century, only to be destroyed again in the seventh or eighth century.[A-69]

Bethsaida (Aram. "house of fishermen") was the birthplace of Peter, Andrew, and Philip (John 1:44; 12:21), and possibly others of the disciples including James and John, the sons of Zebedee. It is mentioned more often in the New Testament than any city except Jerusalem and Capernaum. It is located four miles northeast of Capernaum at the northernmost tip of the Sea of Galilee at the place where the Jordan River enters the sea. The city was built by Herod Philip (cf. 16:13), son of Herod the Great and half-brother of Herod Antipas, and lay in the region under Philip's governance. During Jesus' time the Jordan delta extended further inland at that point (perhaps as much as 1-1/2 miles further than presently[A-70]), giving it one of the largest harbors on the Sea of Galilee and making it an important fishing center.[A-71]

object of condemnation from Old Testament prophets for their Baal worship and arrogant pride in their power and wealth, and therefore deserving of judgment.[186]

They would have repented long ago in sackcloth and ashes (11:21). "Sackcloth and ashes" were familiar symbols of repentance. The rough cloth woven from camel or goat's hair was worn close to the skin as a symbolic rejection of comfort and ease in cases of mourning, national disaster, or repentance (e.g., Jonah 3:5–8). Ashes symbolized loss, whether sprinkled over one's head or lying in them (Est. 4:1–3; *Jos. Asen.* 10:8–15).

You, Capernaum, will you be lifted up to the skies? No, you will go down to the depths (11:23). Jesus uses a strikingly familiar reference to prideful ancient Babylon (Isa. 14:12–15) to emphasize the consequence of Capernaum's satanically stimulated refusal to repent.

If the miracles that were performed in you had been performed in Sodom, it would have remained to this day (11:23). If Tyre and Sidon are stereotypes of pagan worship and prideful arrogance, Sodom is the consummately proverbial city of sin.[187]

The Invitation to an Easy Yoke (11:25–30)

I praise you, Father, Lord of heaven and earth (11:25). The intimacy of Jesus' relationship with God is again revealed as he addresses him as "Father" (6:9; cf.

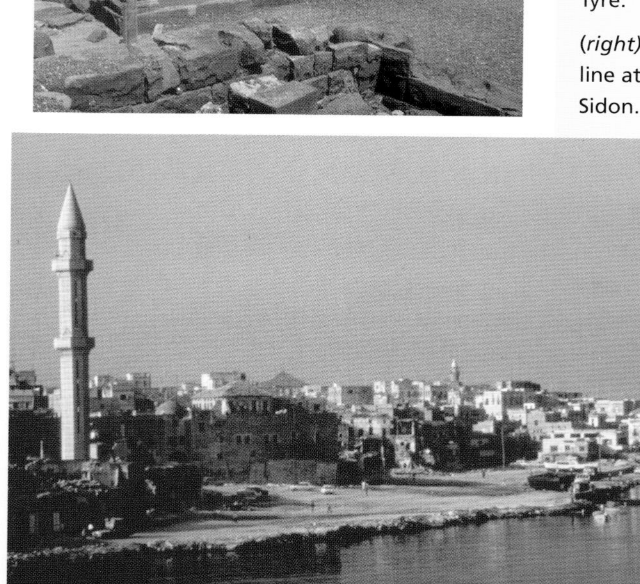

top left

BETHSAIDA

The site of Bethsaida.

top right

SODOM

The salt pans south of the Dead Sea.

 *middle*

CHORAZIN

Ruins of the synagogue.

bottom

TYRE AND SIDON

(left) Remains of the Roman hippodrome at Tyre.

(right) The shoreline at the site of Sidon.

Sir. 51:10). "Lord of heaven and earth" is a title of sovereignty that brings comfort and security, as is expressed in Jewish literature, "Take courage, my daughter; the Lord of heaven grant you joy in place of your sorrow" (Tobit 7:16).

You have hidden these things from the wise and learned, and revealed them to little children (11:25). "The wise and learned" are not just academic specialists, but those who stubbornly and arrogantly refuse to repent and learn from Jesus the true way to God (cf. 13:10–16). "Little children" are those who innocently (not naively) receive Jesus' revelation from the Father.

Take my yoke upon you and learn from me. . . . For my yoke is easy (11:29–30). Yoke (*zygos*) can be used literally for the wooden frame joining two animals (usually oxen), or it can be used metaphorically to describe one individual's subjection to another. In that latter sense, yoke was a common metaphor in Judaism for the law: "He that takes upon himself the yoke of the Law, from him shall be taken away the yoke of the kingdom [troubles from those in power] and the yoke of worldly care; but he that throws off the yoke of the Law, upon him shall be laid the yoke of the kingdom and the yoke of worldly care" (*m. ʾAbot* 3:5; cf. *m. Ber.* 2:2). Sirach invited people to the yoke of studying Torah to gain wisdom: "Acquire wisdom for yourselves without money. Put your neck under her yoke, and let your souls receive instruction; it is to be found close by" (Sir. 51:25–26; cf. 6:23–31). The New Testament refers to the yoke of legalism (Acts 15:10; Gal. 5:1). But Jesus' yoke is none other than commitment to him, gaining his authoritative understanding of God's truth. To learn from Jesus is to receive his revelation of what the law truly intends (cf. Matt. 5:17–48).

REFLECTIONS

JESUS' EASY YOKE IS IN STARK CONTRAST TO THE burden of Pharisaic Judaism. The Pharisees spoke of 613 commandments, and their *halakot* (binding interpretations) produced an overwhelmingly complicated approach to life. In our quest to know God's Word it is good to remember that we can turn Jesus' yoke into an equally unbearable burden unless we consciously recognize that discipleship to Jesus is not essentially a religious obligation. Rather, ours is an intimate relationship with the One who calls, "Come to me" and "learn from me." As complicated as life may become, discipleship at heart simply means walking with Jesus in the real world and having him teach us moment by moment how to live life his way.

Lord of the Sabbath (12:1–21)

God had given the Sabbath as a day of rest and holiness to God. The fourth commandment specified that no work be performed on the Sabbath, so that the day would be kept holy to God. Over time the Sabbath became one of the most distinctive characteristics of the Jewish people, along with circumcision and dietary laws. The legal mandate not to work had to be interpreted for the people, so the Pharisees developed an extensive set of laws to guide them so that they would not violate the Sabbath.

At that time Jesus went through the grainfields on the Sabbath (12:1). Exodus 16:29 set a standard for travel on the Sabbath, admonishing people not to go out in order to observe the Sabbath rest. The Qumran community interpreted the admonition to mean that a person could not walk more than one thousand cubits outside the city" (CD 10:21), while the rabbis allowed a combination of a thousand cubits to travel a distance of two thousand cubits (e.g., *m. Soṭah* 5:3)—approximately three thousand feet or a little over half of a mile.[188]

His disciples were hungry and began to pick some heads of grain and eat them (12:1). The law made provision for people who were hungry to eat from a neighbor's field: "If you enter your neighbor's vineyard, you may eat all the grapes you want, but do not put any in your basket. If you enter your neighbor's grainfield, you may pick kernels with your hands, but you must not put a sickle to his standing grain" (Deut. 23:24–25). Similarly, the edges of a field were not normally harvested, so that the poor and hungry, the foreign travelers, the orphans, and the widows would have grain available to them. This also included olives and grapes left after the first harvest (24:19–22; cf. Ruth 2:2–3).

Look! Your disciples are doing what is unlawful on the Sabbath (12:2). A later ruling stated that there were thirty-nine ("forty less one") main classes of work prohibited on the Sabbath, among them "sowing, ploughing, reaping, binding sheaves, threshing, winnowing, cleansing crops, grinding, sifting" (*m. Šabb.* 7:2). The disciples could have been guilty of several of these in the eyes of the Pharisees as they plucked the grain heads, separated the chaff from the grain, and ground the grain in their hands to prepare it to eat.

I tell you that one greater than the temple is here (12:6). The Old Testament priests regularly violated the Sabbath when they performed their duties on the Sabbath, yet they were considered guiltless. Using typical rabbinic logic, *qal wāḥômer* (lit., "light and weighty," usually trans. "how much more"), Jesus emphasizes that if the guardians of the temple are allowed to violate the Sabbath for the greater good of conducting priestly rituals, how much more should Jesus and his disciples be considered guiltless when doing God's work. After all, someone greater than the temple is here. The "greater" points either to the ministry of Jesus and his disciples in proclaiming the arrival of the kingdom of heaven or to Jesus himself.

For the Son of Man is Lord of the Sabbath (12:8). As Messiah, Jesus has supremacy over the temple, and he has the authority to give the true interpretation of the law (5:17–48), including the role of the Sabbath. Jesus does not challenge the Sabbath law itself, but the prevailing Pharisaic interpretation of it.

Is it lawful to heal on the Sabbath? (12:10). Rabbinic teaching allowed that only in extreme cases of life and death could the Sabbath be violated: "If a man has a pain in his throat they may drop medicine into his mouth on the Sabbath, since there is doubt whether life is in danger, and whenever there is doubt whether life is in danger this overrides the Sabbath" (*m. Yoma* 8:6). The person with a withered hand has quite likely had the condition for some time; thus, his life certainly is not in danger, so he can wait until the next day.

If any of you has a sheep and it falls into a pit on the Sabbath, will you not take hold of it and lift it out? (12:11). There was active debate in Judaism at the time on just such a point. In many ways the debate centered on how much a person was willing to sacrifice to give honor to

HEROD'S TEMPLE

20 B.C. – A.D. 70

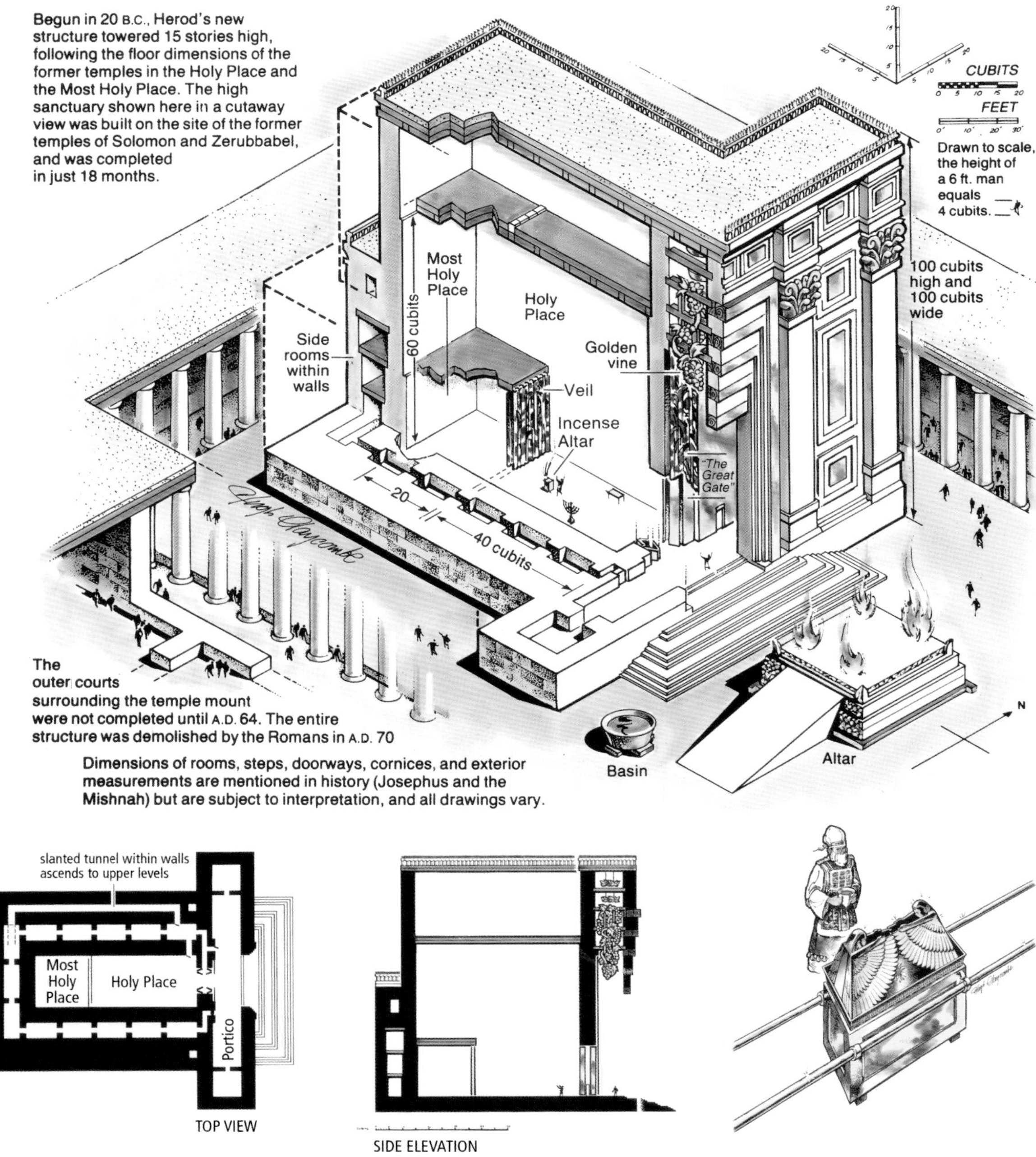

Was the Ark still present during the Roman period? Josephus describes the Most Holy Place as having "nothing at all" which was accurate on the day he wrote it. Yet the Mishnah hints that the Ark was hidden (Shekalim 6:12). Fearing Roman intervention, it could have been secretly moved into the Temple interior for use only on the Day of Atonement. It may be hidden underground to this day.

God and his holy day. The Qumran community was more rigorous on this matter than most others: "No one should help an animal give birth on the Sabbath day. And if he makes it fall into a well or a pit, he should not take it out on the Sabbath" (CD 11:13–14). In the same document the community contends that even if a living man fell into water, they were not to take him out by using a ladder or a rope or a utensil (CD 11:16–17).

The Pharisees went out and plotted how they might kill Jesus (12:14). The law prescribed the death penalty to be carried out in cases of extreme Sabbath desecration (Ex. 31:14; 35:2), but under the Roman occupation the Jews did not have arbitrary power to impose or to carry out a death penalty (cf. John 18:31). The collaboration and plotting of the Pharisees with Caiaphas, the chief priests, and the rest of the Sanhedrin was sufficient to persuade the Romans to put Jesus to death for them.

Here is my servant whom I have chosen, the one I love, in whom I delight (12:18). Matthew identifies Jesus with the messianic Servant of Isaiah 42:1–4. The identity of the Servant in Isaiah is perplexing, because it vacillates between the nation Israel as the Servant[189] and an individual who leads the nation.[190] Jesus emerges as the Servant Messiah who has a ministry and mission both to Israel and the nations and who is the gentle Spirit-endowed Servant with a mission of justice to the nations.

Beelzebul and the Blasphemy Against the Spirit (12:22–37)

All the people were astonished and said, "Could this be the Son of David?" (12:23). The different sectarian groups had difficulty putting together all of the varied messianic promises of the Old Testament, so the common people especially seemed to focus on one strand of the prophecies. In their mind, because King David was a warrior, the messianic son of David would be a liberator. Although David is the only person recorded to have exorcised a demon in the Old Testament, he was not considered a miracle worker. Yet the Son of David would bring a time of eschatological fulfillment, including the healing of all illnesses. It is astonishing to recognize that the gentle healing Servant Messiah (8:17; 12:18–21) is indeed the Son of David who will shepherd his people and bring the time of covenantal peace (Ezek. 34:23–31; 37:24–28).

It is only by Beelzebub, the prince of demons, that this fellow drives out demons (12:24). The ancient world regularly drew on magical incantations to manipulate the spirit world. The Pharisees accuse Jesus of drawing on the power of "the prince of demons," *Beelzebub*, or better, *Beelzeboul*, "master of the house," to cast out the demon from the blind and mute man (12:22). *Beelzeboul* most likely comes from an identification of the chief of the evil spirits with Baal Shamayim, whose worship was installed in the temple by Antiochus IV Epiphanes[191] and came to be another title for Satan in Judaism: "I am Beelzeboul, the ruler of the demons" (*T. Sol.* 3:6). The Pharisees do not deny the miracle but instead attribute Jesus' power to Satan. Judaism continued this charge into the early centuries of the church era, branding him a sorcerer (e.g., *b. Sanh.* 107b; *b. Šabb.* 104b).

If I drive out demons by Beelzebub, by whom do your people drive them out? So then, they will be your judges (12:27).

Some of those exorcisms were well known among the Jews. Josephus gives a peculiar perspective of Solomon developing the art of incantations for healing and exorcism. That art was passed down to Eleazar, a Jewish exorcist of Josephus's day. Eleazar used a signet ring with part of a root to draw out a demon through the nostrils of a possessed man and then commanded the demon to overturn a cup of water to demonstrate the reality of the exorcism.[192] The legendary Tobias exorcised the demon Asmodeus from his wife, Sarah, on their wedding night by forcing the demon to smell a fish's liver and heart (Tobit 8:1–3). These accounts are obvious clashes of God's power against Satan's.

How can anyone enter a strong man's house and carry off his possessions unless he first ties up the strong man? (12:29). *Testament of Levi* 18:12 refers to the eschatological priest-king who inaugurates the age of blessing as he binds Satan, "And Beliar [Satan; cf. 2 Cor. 6:15] shall be bound by him. And he shall grant to his children the authority to trample on wicked spirits."[193] The analogy refers to Jesus' "binding" Satan and then releasing those held captive by demons through his exorcisms.

Anyone who speaks against the Holy Spirit will not be forgiven (12:32). The Old Testament regarded deliberate, defiant sin against God and his ordinances to be blasphemy, the guilt of which remained (Num. 15:30–31). Such defiant sin was considered within Judaism to be unforgivable: "And there is therefore for them no forgiveness or pardon so that they might be pardoned and forgiven from all of the sins of this eternal error" (*Jub.* 15:34). Rejection of Jesus' ministry as validated by the Spirit is the same sort of defiant, deliberate sin. Thus the only "unpardonable sin" occurs when a person consciously and willfully rejects the operation of the Spirit bearing witness to the reality of Jesus as the Savior and rejects the convicting power of the Spirit in his or her life. The person who does not receive this work of the Spirit cannot come to Jesus and therefore cannot receive forgiveness.

You brood of vipers, how can you who are evil say anything good? (12:34). Jesus uses the same harsh title that John used for the Pharisees and Sadducees, "brood of vipers" (cf. 3:7; 23:33). Vipers are proverbial for their subtle approach and attack, as was the original serpent (Gen. 3).

The Sign of Jonah (12:38–42)

Teacher, we want to see a miraculous sign from you (12:38). A "sign" (*sēmeion*) is some kind of visible mark or action that conveys an unmistakable message, such as the mark of Cain that warned people not to kill him (Gen. 4:15) or that act of speaking in tongues that is a sign to unbelievers of the reality of the gospel message (1 Cor. 14:22). Jesus' return as the glorious Son of Man is the sign that announces the eschatological consummation of the age (see Matt. 24:29; cf. 16:27; 26:64), but Judas's kiss of death is the sign that marks out Jesus' identity to the arresting forces (26:48). "Signs and wonders" will be the proof of God's activity in the proclamation of the gospel in the early church (Acts 2:22, 43; 4:30; Rom. 15:19).

The problem with a sign is that it can be interpreted different ways.[194] The Pharisees are asking Jesus to perform some kind of on-demand spectacular display of power that will irrefutably convince them that his power is from God, not from Satan. Although their request appears innocent enough, they are not asking in good faith. They are asking for a sign they can use against him.

None will be given it except the sign of the prophet Jonah (12:39). The sign of Jonah is not some kind of sign that Jonah brings. Rather, Jonah *is* the sign.[195] When Jonah himself appeared among the people of Nineveh, he was the sign to the people of Nineveh that his message was from the God who had rescued him from death (Jonah 3:1–5). The generation that has heard Jesus' message and seen his ministry has enough validating proof in his miracles that he is the Messiah. Instead of repenting when they see his miracles (cf. Matt. 12:9–14, 22), however, they attempt to use them as the basis of the charge that he is in league with Satan (12:24). Because of their evil intention, the only other sign Jesus will give to them will be a sign of God's coming judgment on them, as Jonah was to the people of Nineveh.

As Jonah . . . so the Son of Man will be three days and three nights in the heart of the earth (12:40). The Old Testament regularly reckoned a part of a day as a whole day[196]; in rabbinic thought, a part of a day was considered to be a whole day: "A day and a night constitute an *ōnâh* (a full day), and part of an *ōnâh* counts as a whole."[197] Three days and three nights is a proverbial expression and means no more than three days or the combination of any part of three separate days. See "The Days of the Lord's Supper and Crucifixion During the Passion Week" at 26:16.

The Queen of the South will rise at the judgment with this generation and condemn it (12:42). The Queen of the South is the queen of Sheba (1 Kings 10:1–29). Sheba is most likely the home of the Sabaeans in southwestern Arabia in present-day Yemen. It was known for its strong agricultural base, but even more for being one of the most important trade centers involving Africa, India, and the Mediterranean countries. Solomon's wisdom was so widely renowned that the queen went to question him and found his wisdom to be more than she had anticipated. She and the people of Nineveh had allowed the revelation of God to penetrate to their pagan hearts and so will be God's eternal witnesses against the Jewish religious leaders that they have not opened their heart to Jesus, the preeminent revelation of God.

The Return of the Unclean Spirit (12:43–45)

An evil spirit . . . goes through arid places seeking rest and does not find it (12:43). Demons are often associated with desert (waterless) places as their home.[198] These spirits are evil, and their intent is to find a suitable place to work even greater evil. The demon seeks ownership of the person, which he calls, literally, "*my* house." That is why it is called demon *possession*.

Takes with it seven other spirits more wicked than itself, and they go in and live there (12:45). The number seven is linked in Scripture with completion, fulfillment, and perfection.[199] Here it may point to the completeness of demon-possession once the demon returns.

Jesus' Disciples Are His True Family (12:46–50)

His mother and brothers stood outside, wanting to speak to him (12:46). The omission of "father" may indicate that

Joseph has died by this time. No reason is given for why his family wishes to speak to him. Mark indicates that his family wants to take control of Jesus and alter his ministry, because people think he is crazy (Mark 3:21; cf. John 7:5).

Pointing to his disciples, he said, "Here are my mother and my brothers" (12:49). Jesus has already accentuated to his disciples the inevitable separation that will occur between family members because of the decision to make a commitment to him (10:34–39; cf. 8:21–22). Jesus did not come to abolish the family, because he will continue to uphold the law that demands children to honor their father and mother (15:4). Instead, he stresses preeminence of a person's commitment to Jesus and the kingdom of heaven above all other commitments. This will form a new spiritual family of disciples of Jesus.

Whoever does the will of my Father in heaven is my brother and sister and mother (12:50). Jesus intentionally broadens the gender reference to include women as disciples by stating "sister." This was a unique form of discipleship in Judaism at that time, especially among the rabbis, because only men could become a disciple of a rabbi and study Torah. A later passage in the Mishnah gives what probably was a general feature during Jesus' time. It discourages too much conversation between men and women, even one's own wife, because it distracts the rabbinic disciple from studying Torah: "He that talks much with womankind brings evil upon himself and neglects the study of the Law and at the last will inherit Gehenna" (*m. ʾAbot* 1:5). But with Jesus, any person—woman or man, young or old, Gentile or Jew—who responds to the gospel of the kingdom and believes on him for eternal life is his disciple and will be taught to obey all that Jesus commands (cf. 28:19–20).

REFLECTIONS

EXORCISM WAS CONVINCING EVIDENCE THAT JESUS had brought the kingdom of heaven to Israel (12:28). Experiencing an exorcism was important enough, but the exorcised person must then respond to Jesus' invitation to believe and enter the kingdom of God and experience its new life in Christ through his Spirit. If not, the exorcised person is more vulnerable to the renewed and persistent attack of the demon world to take back ownership of him or her. No fundamental change has taken place in the person that prevents the return of the demon. This is truly spiritual warfare, and the battle is over the lives of people. An exorcised person when repossessed will be worse off because of the persistent battle to take full control of him or her. Exorcism is the first step, but the most important step is to enter the kingdom of heaven and receive the resources necessary to resist the devil, including a regenerated heart, the presence of Jesus, and the power of the Spirit.

The Parable of the Soils (13:1–23)

He got into a boat and sat in it, while all the people stood on the shore (13:2). Local tradition locates the place of this discourse at a distinctive inlet called the "Cove of the Parables." It lies approximately a mile (1.5 km) southwest of Capernaum, halfway to the traditional site of the Sermon on the Mount near Tabgha. The land slopes down like a natural, horseshoe-shaped amphitheater around the cove, providing environmental acoustics for Jesus' voice to have carried over one hundred meters from the boat to a crowd of perhaps hundreds gathered on the shore. Israeli scientists have tested the acoustics in modern times and found them to be realistic for Jesus' parables to have been heard.[200]

Then he told them many things in parables (13:3). Jesus speaks (*laleō*, not "teaches") to the crowd (*ochlos*, not "people" as NIV) many things in parables. Later, Jesus will explain the parables to his disciples (13:10–23, 36–43). Parables have distinctively different purposes for the crowd and for the disciples. Jesus has already given several parables,[201] but this is the first time that Matthew uses the term "parable" (*parabolē*). Underlying the term *parable* is the Hebrew *māšāl*, which refers to a wide spectrum of ideas based on comparison or analogy, including byword, proverb, wisdom sayings, and story.[202] As used by Jesus, the parable is a way of communicating truth through a narrative analogy in the service of moral or spiritual argument. They are often deeply, even frustratingly, perplexing.[203] The analogies or comparisons Jesus uses to make his point come from everyday experiences, but they press the listener to search for the intended meaning. That is why in popular preaching Jesus' parables are often referred to as "an earthly story with a heavenly meaning."

A farmer went out to sow his seed (13:3). Jesus' listeners are well aware of farming techniques, because most everyone took care of his own fields and gardens or worked the fields of his landlord. We are not certain of the type of seed that the sower (NIV "farmer") was sowing, but we may think of wheat to help illustrate the scene, since wheat was one of the most important crops in Israel,[204] and it appears as the subject of a later parable (13:24–30).

Some fell along the path, and the birds came and ate it up (13:4). Seed was sown "broadcast" style by scattering it in all directions by hand while walking up and down the field. The average rate of sowing wheat varies from twenty pounds

GALILEAN SHORELINE

Looking northwest toward Tiberias.

per acre (22.5 kilograms per hectare) upward, which allowed for wasted seed. Fields were apparently plowed both before the seed was sown and after, plowing across the original furrows to cover the seeds with soil. The desired depth of plowing under wheat seed was usually one to three inches (2.5 to 7.5 centimetres), but it could be less in certain areas where the topsoil was shallow. In the rabbinic listing of the thirty-nine main classes of work, plowing follows sowing (*m. Šabb.* 7:2). It was common for seed to be scattered on the hard paths that surrounded the fields. Birds would swoop down as the farmer walked on and eat the seed.

FARMING IMPLEMENTS

Roman era iron hoe discovered in the Jerusalem area. ▶

Iron sickle, scraper, and hoe found in Samaria dated to 6th–4th century B.C. ▼

Some fell on rocky places, where it did not have much soil (13:5). Conditions for farming in many areas of Israel were not favorable. The hardships that many people experienced included insufficient amounts of water and soil. The terrain in most cases was uneven and rocky, with only thin layers of soil covering the rock. Seed that landed on this shallow soil could begin to germinate, but it couldn't put down deep roots to collect what little moisture was in that parched thin layer of earth.[205] Sprouting seed would soon wither and die in the hot sun (13:6). James gives a fitting commentary: "For the sun rises with scorching heat and withers the plant; its blossom falls and its beauty is destroyed" (James 1:11).

Still other seed fell on good soil, where it produced a crop—a hundred, sixty or thirty times what was sown (13:8). In the fourth example, seed falls on what is described as "good soil." As the seeds germinate and mature, they keep on yielding a range of a hundred, sixty, or thirty times what is sown, signifying a good harvest, typical of what a harvest blessed by God would yield,[206] such as Isaac's harvest: "Isaac planted crops in that land and the same year reaped a hundredfold, because the LORD blessed him" (Gen. 26:12).

The knowledge of the secrets of the kingdom of heaven has been given to you, but not to them (13:11). Jesus speaks to the crowd in parables because God has given (cf. the divine passive "has been given") the secrets of the kingdom of heaven to the disciples, not to the crowd, to know. "Secrets" (NIV) is the Greek *mystēria* (lit., "mysteries"), which draws on a Semitic background of an eschatological secret passed on in veiled speech to God's chosen. The term is found explicitly in Daniel: "During the night the mystery was revealed to Daniel in a vision" (Dan. 2:18–19; cf. 2:27–30, 47; 4:9). The idea of God revealing his secrets is also found as a powerful theme elsewhere in the Old Testament.[207]

Though seeing, they do not see; though hearing, they do not hear or understand (13:13). The crowd in Jesus' ministry mirrors the people of Israel to whom the prophet Isaiah ministered (Isa. 6:9–10). They reject the message because they are spiritually deadened.

Listen then to what the parable of the sower means (13:18). To his disciples, not to the crowd, Jesus gives the intended meaning behind the parable of the soils and sower. A similar parable, but with a different emphasis, is found in Jewish literature: "For just as the farmer sows many seeds upon the ground and plants a multitude of seedlings, and yet not all that have been sown will come up in due season, and not all that were planted will take root; so all those who have been sown in the world will not be saved" (*4 Ezra* 8:41). In this parable the chief character is the farmer; that is, God. The fate of the seed depends on his action, especially his distributing the right amount of water at the correct time (*4 Ezra* 8:42–45). Jesus' emphasis is on the spiritual responsiveness and responsibility of the types of soil that represent the lives of those who hear the message of the kingdom.

The evil one comes and snatches away what was sown in his heart (13:19). Satan is the prince of demons (12:24–27), the prince of the power of the air (Eph. 2:2). *Jubilees* refers to him as "Prince Mastema," likening him to a swooping bird leading a pack of other birds: "Prince Mastema sent crows and birds so that they might eat the seed which was being sown in the earth in order to spoil the earth so that they might rob mankind of their labors. Before they plowed in the seed, the crows picked it off the surface of the earth" (*Jub.* 11:10–11; cf. *b. Sanh.* 107a).

Further Parables (13:24–58)

The kingdom of heaven is like a man who sowed good seed in his field (13:24). Satan operates in this world both as a swooping bird (13:19) and as the enemy farmer attempting to disrupt the growth of good wheat (disciples) by sowing among it *zizanion* (*Lolium temulentum*), a kind of weed referred to also as "darnel" or "tares." It is a weedy rye grass with poisonous seeds, which in early stages of growth looks like wheat, but can

REFLECTIONS

A "CROP" WILL BE PRODUCED IN THE LIFE OF THE person who is "good soil" for the kingdom of heaven to operate. Many think that this "crop" refers to converts won to Christ through the believer. This no doubt is partially correct, but in this context it refers to something more fundamental—the transformation of a person who has encountered the kingdom of heaven. In the fourth soil the crop represents the outworking of the life of the divine seed (cf. 1 John 3:9), with special reference to the production of the fruit of the Spirit (cf. Gal. 5:22–23), and the outworking of the Spirit in the gifts of the Spirit in the believer's life (1 Cor. 12). This results in personal characteristics produced by the Spirit (Gal. 5:22–23), the external creation of Spirit-produced righteousness and good works (e.g., Col. 1:10), and indeed, new converts won through the believer's testimony (e.g., Rom. 1:13). The "crop" produced is the outward evidence of the reality of inward life of the kingdom of heaven.

be distinguished easily in its mature state at the time of harvesting.

The kingdom of heaven is like a mustard seed (13:31). The seed of the mustard plant was proverbially small (cf. 17:20). Rabbinic literature gives similar contrasting metaphors using the mustard seed. The mustard seed exemplifies the smallest quantity of blood (*y. Ber.* 5:8d; *b. Ber.* 31a), while the Galilean Rabbi Simeon ben Halafta (2d cent. A.D.) asserts that he climbed a mustard bush that was as tall as a fig tree (*y. Peʾah* 7:20b).[208] The metaphor contrasts the small beginnings of the kingdom of heaven with its growth.

So that the birds of the air come and perch in its branches (13:32). The image of a large tree with birds alighting on its branches recalls several Old Testament references to a great kingdom (cf. Ezek. 17:22–24; 31:2–18; Dan. 4:9–27).

The kingdom of heaven is like yeast (13:33). Yeast is any number of different forms of fungi that multiply rapidly. Homemade bread required a bakers' yeast (*saccharomyces cerevisiae*) to cause it to rise, also called "leaven." Therefore, a small piece of fermenting, acidic dough, set aside from a former baking, was called a "leaven." It was "mixed" (lit., "hidden") in the flour and kneaded. A typical lump of leaven might have been no more than 2 percent of the dough weight.[209] Bread made with yeast was known as "leavened," as distinct from "unleavened" bread (Ex. 12:15).

Scripture uses leaven almost exclusively as a negative metaphor, probably because fermentation implied disintegration and corruption (Ex. 12:8, 15–20), as in the Feast of Unleavened Bread, which reminded the Israelites of their hurried departure from Egypt (Ex. 12:31–39; Deut. 16:3). But Jesus seems to reverse the connotation here to symbolize the hidden permeation of the kingdom of heaven in this world. The mustard seed emphasizes growth, while the yeast suggests permeation and transformation. In spite of its small, inauspicious beginnings, the kingdom of heaven will permeate the world.

"I will open my mouth in parables, I will utter things hidden since the creation of the world" (13:35). The psalmist Asaph reflected on Israel's history and clarified through parables the meaning of past events so that the people would learn from their history and would not be a stubborn and rebellious people with hearts hard to God (Ps. 78:2, 8). Matthew's standard fulfillment formula says that Jesus has done a similar service to Israel in his day, revealing in his parables the mysteries of the kingdom of heaven that have been hidden since the beginning. Once again, the difference is in the response of the audience. Those spiritually alive will come to Jesus for further clarification and understanding, while those spiritually deadened will turn away.

LEAVENED AND UNLEAVENED BREAD

Also depicting a container of yeast.

◀ *left*

A PEARL OF GREAT PRICE

Pearls of various size.

The kingdom of heaven is like treasure hidden in a field (13:44). Treasures were often hidden in fields, because there were no formal banks as we know them today. The intriguing Copper Scroll found at Qumran lists sixty-four places in Palestine where treasures were supposed to be hidden: e.g., "In the ruin which is in the valley, pass under the steps leading to the East forty cubits . . . [there is] a chest of money and its total: the weight of seventeen talents" (3QCopper Scroll 1:1–3). Jesus speaks of a treasure hidden in a field. If the field is the world (cf. 13:38), then the treasure is the kingdom of heaven that lies unnoticed because of its small, inconsequential nature. The emphasis is on the supreme worth of that treasure unseen by others; it is worth far more than any sacrifice one might make to acquire it.

Once again, the kingdom of heaven is like a net (13:47). The net (*sagēnē*) is the large *seine* or "dragnet," the oldest type of net used and until recently the most important fishing method on the Sea of Galilee. It was shaped like a long 750 to 1,000 foot wall, upwards of twenty-five feet high at the center and five feet high at the ends. The foot-rope was weighted with sinkers, while the head-rope floated with attached corks, enabling the net wall to be dragged toward shore by both ends, trapping fish inside.[210] Bad fish would have included those without fins and scales, which were unclean (Lev. 11:9–12).

Like a large dragnet, the kingdom of heaven has all sorts respond to it in the preaching of "fishers of men" (4:19). The true nature of those who are gathered in will not always be readily apparent, as Judas Iscariot will so sadly exemplify. Only at the judgment will the full implication be known.

Brings out of his storeroom new treasures as well as old (13:52). The Torah-trained teacher of law has studied under a great rabbi, but for the one who has been made a disciple[211] of the kingdom of heaven, Jesus is the great Teacher (cf. 28:20). The true disciple knows how to draw spiritual truths from the parables properly, to balance the new teachings of Christ with the fulfilled promises of the messianic kingdom, and to understand how Jesus truly fulfills the Law and the Prophets (5:17).

He began teaching the people in their synagogue, and they were amazed (13:54). Although Capernaum had become Jesus' "own city" during his

FISHING WITH A NET

The man is fishing in the Sea of Galilee.

▼

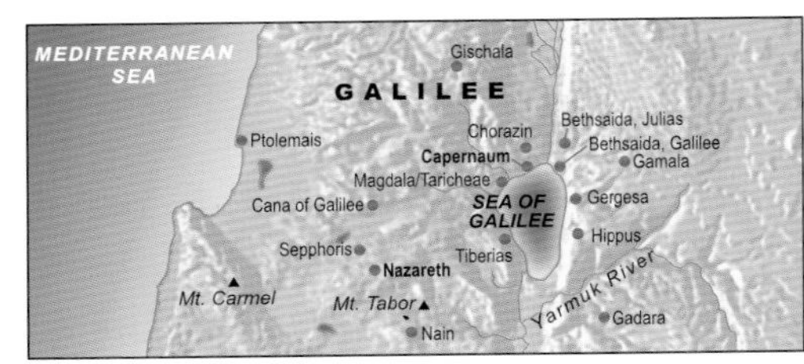

CAPERNAUM AND NAZARETH

Galilean ministry (9:1), Nazareth was his "hometown" (*patris*), the land of his father and family (13:54; cf. 2:23). Most scholars see this as a thematic abridgment of the same incident recorded much more fully in Luke 4:14–30, although it is possible that this is a later return to Galilee for a second visit (cf. Mark 6:1–6). The later may be implied by the reference to wisdom and miracles, which are not a significant part of Jesus' ministry until after the visit to Nazareth as recorded in Luke.

John the Baptist Beheaded by Herod (14:1–12)

At that time Herod the tetrarch heard the reports about Jesus (14:1). Herod Antipas was the Roman client-ruler over the region where Jesus ministered. He was only seventeen years old when his father, Herod the Great, died. Herod's kingdom was divided among three of his sons, Archelaus, Philip, and Antipas (see comments on 2:19ff.; 16:13). Herod Antipas had a long rule (4 B.C.-A.D. 39) and was the most prominent of Herod's sons in the four Gospels because he ruled the area of Galilee, the region of Jesus' primary ministry. His chief infamy comes from his execution of John the Baptist and his interview of Jesus prior to his crucifixion (cf. Luke 23:6–12).

Herod Antipas's capital city, Tiberias, was only eight miles down the coast of the Sea of Galilee from Capernaum. The news of Jesus' ministry has reached him possibly through Cuza, his steward, whose wife is part of the group of women who on occasion support and travel with the apostolic band (cf. Luke 8:1–3).

right EXCAVATIONS AT SEPPHORIS

MODERN NAZARETH

This is John the Baptist; he has risen from the dead! (14:2). Herod Antipas was a Jew by religion, although he had an Idumean background. His reaction reveals a curious blend of emotion, theology, and superstition. His guilty fear for having executed John combines with a confused notion of resurrection, probably based in part on Pharisaic beliefs along with semi-pagan superstitious ideas of returning spirits. As a Roman client-ruler, he has been well versed in Roman mythology. The Herodian family had long been notorious for this syncretistic mixture of beliefs.

Now Herod had arrested John and . . . put him in prison because of Herodias, his brother Philip's wife (14:3). Herod Antipas had married the daughter of King Aretas IV of Nabataea, probably a political marriage arranged by Emperor Augustus to keep peace in the region. The marriage lasted for several years, until Antipas fell in love with Herodias, the wife of his brother Herod Philip I (not the better known half-brother, Herod Philip the tetrarch), another of Antipas's half-brothers (by Mariamne II; Mark 6:17). Herod Philip was a private citizen who lived in Rome. On a trip to Rome, Antipas stayed at the home of his half-brother and fell in love with Herodias. They determined to marry, but Herodias demanded that Antipas divorce his wife of over fifteen years.[212] Some years later (A.D. 36), King Aretas IV attacked and conquered Antipas's military forces, at least in part to seek revenge for repudiating his daughter.[213]

John had been saying to him: "It is not lawful for you to have her" (14:4). When Antipas married Herodias, the highly popular John the Baptist publicly con-

COINS OF HEROD ANTIPAS

demned him for marrying his half-brother's wife, who was also his half-niece (14:3–4; Mark 6:18; Luke 3:19). This would have been considered an incestuous affront to God's law (Lev. 18:16; 20:21).

On Herod's birthday the daughter of Herodias danced for them (14:6). Herod the Great built a royal palace at the fortress Machaerus, in part because he prized the hot springs at Calirrhoe not far away. The remains of a majestic peristyle court that rose to an ornate triclinium (banquet room) have been excavated, an indication of the lavish entertaining that

MAP SHOWING MACHAERUS

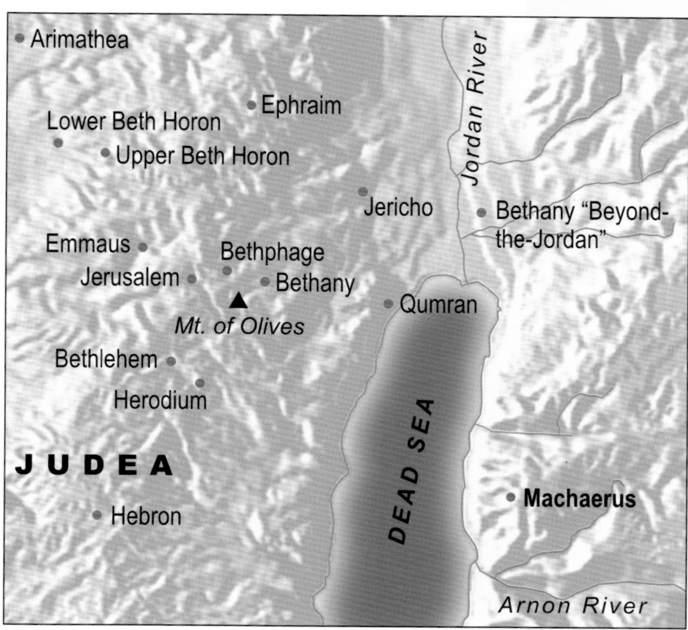

was held at the palatial fortress.[214] After the death of Herod the Great the fortress was assigned to the tetrarch of his son Herod Antipas. Here, according to Josephus,[215] Herod Antipas imprisoned John the Baptist and later had him put to death[216] (see "Machaerus" at 11:1–6).

Herodias had her daughter (named Salome in Josephus, *Ant.* 18.5.4 §136) perform a dance for Antipas. She was probably only twelve to fourteen years old,[217] but in that kind of degraded, deceptive setting it likely was a sensual dance.

Give me here on a platter the head of John the Baptist (14:8). Behind the scenes of the majority of the intrigues in Antipas's life was his second wife, Herodias. She had demanded that Antipas divorce his first wife, the daughter of Aretas IV. Here she manipulates Antipas to execute John the Baptist. Later she will persuade Antipas to go to Emperor Gaius Caligula to denounce her brother Agrippa I, because she is envious of his success at being named "king" over Herod Philip's former region northeast of Antipas.[218] She finally got her own due on that incident, however, because the emperor was a close friend of her brother. Gaius turned the tables and banished Antipas to Gaul, where Herodius accompanied him.

During the Hasmonean reign more than a century earlier, Alexander Jannaeus performed an even more heinous

John the Baptist's Execution by Herod Antipas as Recorded by Josephus

Josephus took a soldier's and politician's perspective on the arrest and execution of John the Baptist, while the evangelists tended to take more of a moral and spiritual perspective. Both accounts are necessary in order to get the full impact that John the Baptist had on Israel as he prepared the way for Jesus Messiah. Josephus's perspective follows his description of Herod Antipas's defeat at the hands of Aretas IV, his former father-in-law, who had waged war in part to seek revenge for the repudiation of his daughter by Antipas.

> To some of the Jews the destruction of Herod's army seemed to be divine vengeance, and certainly a just vengeance, for his treatment of John, surnamed the Baptist. For Herod had put him to death, though he was a good man and had exhorted the Jews to lead righteous lives, to practice justice towards their fellows and piety toward God, and so doing to join in baptism. In his view this was a necessary preliminary if baptism was to be acceptable to God. They must not employ it to gain pardon for whatever sins they committed, but as a consecration of the body implying that the soul was already thoroughly cleansed by right behaviour. When others too joined the crowds about him, because they were aroused to the highest degree by his sermons, Herod became alarmed. Eloquence that had so great an effect on mankind might lead to some form of sedition, for it looked as if they would be guided by John in everything that they did. Herod decided therefore that it would be much better to strike first and be rid of him before his work led to an uprising, than to wait for an upheaval, get involved in a difficult situation and see his mistake. Though John, because of Herod's suspicions, was brought in chains to Machaerus, the stronghold that we have previously mentioned, and there put to death, yet the verdict of the Jews was that the destruction visited upon Herod's army was a vindication of John, since God saw fit to inflict such a blow on Herod. (Josephus, *Ant.* 18.5.2 §116–119)

act of cruelty while engaged in a riotous party: "While he feasted with his concubines in a conspicuous place, he ordered some eight hundred of the Jews to be crucified, and slaughtered their children and wives before the eyes of the still living wretches."[219]

John's disciples came and took his body and buried it. Then they went and told Jesus (14:12). John's disciples had remained loyal to the prophet throughout his imprisonment; now they perform the duties of loyal followers, since John's family are likely all deceased by this time. We hear of other disciples of John throughout the next few decades, although they are increasingly separated from his true message (Acts 19:1–7). The natural transition should have been to follow Jesus.[220]

Feeding the Five Thousand (14:13–21)

The crowds followed him on foot from the towns (14:13). The traditional site of the feeding of the five thousand is west of Capernaum, past the traditional site of the Sermon on the Mount, above the Heptapegon ("Seven Springs"), at present-day Tabgha,[221] just a mile or so beyond the "Cove of Parables" (cf. 13:1–3). This area was a favorite hideaway for Jesus. The site is supported by an ancient report from the pilgrim Egeria (c. A.D. 383–395):

> Above the Lake there is also a field of grass with much hay and several palms. By it are the Seven Springs, each of which supplies a huge quantity of water. In the field the Lord fed the people with the seven loaves of bread. . . . The Stone on which the Lord placed the bread has been made into an altar. Visitors take small pieces of rock from this stone for their welfare and it brings benefit to everyone.[222]

Crowds could easily have followed Jesus from the Capernaum region to Tabgha (about two miles) or to Bethsaida (about four miles).

We have here only five loaves of bread and two fish (14:17). Bread and dried or pickled fish were food suitable for taking on a short journey into the hills. John tells us that a young boy had supplied them, indicating that they were small cakes sufficient for one person's afternoon meal, not full "loaves" found on modern grocery store shelves (John 6:9). John further reports that the bread cakes were made of barley, the chief component of the staple food in Israel, especially of the poorer people.[223]

Taking the five loaves and the two fish and looking up to heaven, he gave thanks and broke the loaves (14:19). An old tradition recounts that Jesus placed the five loaves and two fish on a large piece of rock and then gave the common Jewish *Berakah*: "Blessed art thou, O Lord our God, King of the universe, who bringest forth bread from the earth" (*m. Ber.* 6:1). The rock is visible today beneath the altar of the Church of the Multiplication

FIVE LOAVES AND TWO FISH

A mosaic in the church at Tabgha (Heptapegon)

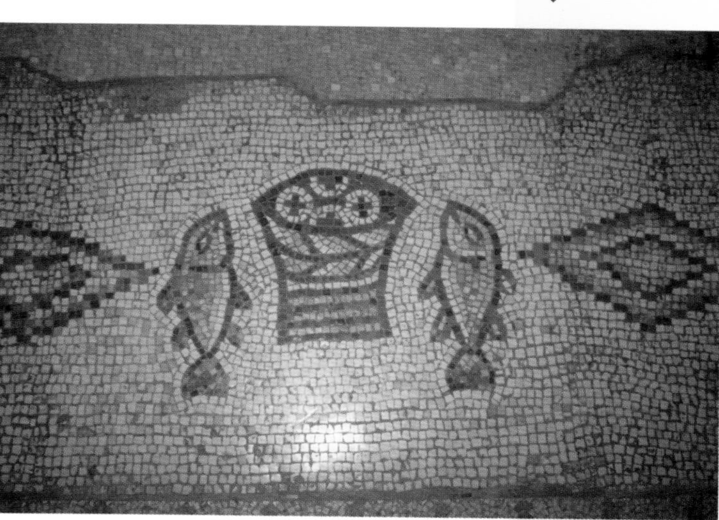

at Tabgha. A mosaic of fishes and bread cakes covers the floor in the basilica next to the rock. If Tabgha was the location of the feeding, this area is probably close.[224]

The disciples picked up twelve basketfuls of broken pieces (14:20). The "basket" (*kophinos*) is a small woven container that occurs in Jewish contexts to denote a hamper for carrying kosher foods. In the feeding of the four thousand a different word for basket (*spyris*) occurs (see comments on 15:37).

Five thousand men, besides women and children (14:21). The total number may have stretched to 10,000 or more, far larger than the populations of most villages surrounding the Sea of Galilee.

The Son of God Walks on the Water (14:22–36)

After he had dismissed them, he went up on a mountainside by himself to pray (14:23). If the feeding was in the Tabgha area, Jesus may have stayed in a grotto below a hanging cliff, which tradition today calls the Eremos Cave, named after Jesus' lonely prayer vigil. For "mountainside," see comments on 28:16.

right ▶

A GALILEAN FISHING BOAT

A mosaic in the floor of the fifth-century Byzantine church at Beth Loya in the southern foothills of Judea.

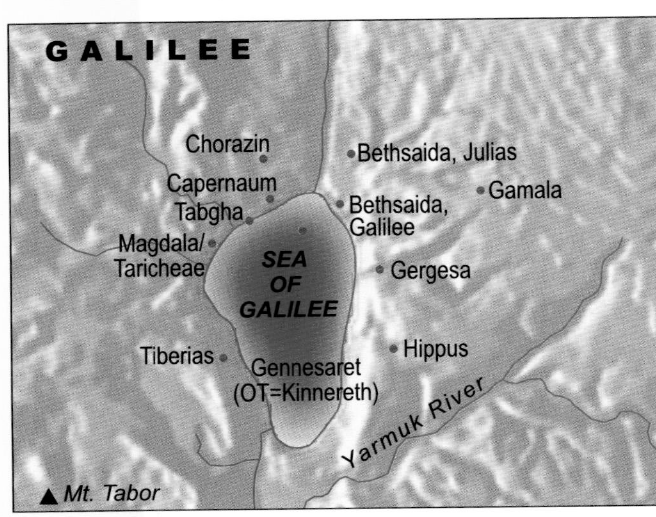

SEA OF GALILEE ▼

The boat was ... buffeted by the waves because the wind was against it (14:24). The winds against the boat probably indicate that they are moving from west to east, because the most severe storms come down the mountains to the east. "A considerable distance" out on the lake in Greek is literally "many stadia." A *stadion* is 185 meters (approximately 600 feet), which would have put the disciples anywhere from a mile to even two or three miles out on the lake, which is seven miles at its widest point. The lake's low elevation (see comments on 8:24) leads it to be subject to a powerful east wind ("Sharkiyeh") that blows in over the mountains.

During the fourth watch of the night Jesus went out to them, walking on the lake (14:25). The Roman military divided the night into four "watches," based on the need to provide rotating guards throughout the night. At three hours each, the fourth watch was from 3:00 A.M. to 6:00 A.M.

The disciples ... were terrified. "It's a ghost," they said, and cried out in fear (14:26). In Greek literature the term "ghost" (*phantasma*) is used for dream appearances or spirit appearances or apparitions, but in the Old Testament it means a "deception" (Job 20:8 LXX; Isa. 28:7; cf. Wisd. Sol. 17:14).[225] It only occurs in the New Testament here and in

REFLECTIONS

PETER'S WALKING ON THE WATER is a story that is surpassed only by the perfect walk of our Lord Jesus on the lake. Peter is often unfairly criticized by modern readers for being presumptuous to ask to go out on the lake. But Jesus does not criticize him for that request; he only mildly chides him for his ineffective faith once he gets out there. It took much courage to follow Jesus on the water, and Peter does fine until he looks at his circumstances ("seeing the wind," 14:30) and takes his eyes off of Jesus; then he finds himself afraid and in trouble. We will face many circumstances for which we are completely unprepared, and the circumstances we face from day to day will change. But the one constancy we have in this life is Jesus. As we go through life focused on an intimate walk with Jesus through each and every circumstance, we learn how to apply his consistency to our circumstances.

the parallel in Mark 6:49. The disciples may be thinking that some evil spirit is attempting to deceive them.

Take courage! It is I. Don't be afraid (14:27). The meaning behind the expression "It is I" (lit., "I am") may allude to the voice of Yahweh from the bush (Ex. 3:14) and the voice of assurance to Israel of the Lord's identity and presence as their Savior (Isa. 43:10–13).

"Lord, if it's you," Peter replied, "tell me to come to you on the water" (14:28). Peter will play an increasingly important role as a leader and spokesman for the disciples in the next several incidents (14:28–31; 15:15; 16:17–19; 17:24–27; 18:21). Matthew emphasizes Peter's leadership role, but also shows how Peter is an imperfect leader who is in process of development, as Jesus prepares him for the early days of the church ahead.[226]

Then those who were in the boat worshiped him, saying, "Truly you are the Son of God" (14:33). All of the events evoked from the disciples an act of worship (*proskyneō*), which in Scripture is nearly always reserved for God. One may prostrate oneself before other esteemed personages as a symbol of respect, such as David before King Saul (1 Sam. 24:8) or Abigail before David (25:23). But in this context of miracles of divine significance, the disciples are gripped with the reality that Jesus is much, much more; he is the "Son of God," and so they worship him.

When they had crossed over, they landed at Gennesaret (14:34). Either coming from Bethsaida or having been blown back to the west shore (cf. 14:13), the disciples with Jesus now land at Gennesaret. This site may refer to the Old Testament town of Kinnereth, for which the Sea was named,[227] but the more usual use of the

GENNESARET

The site of Tel Kinnereth near the Sea of Galilee.

Gennesaret

The region of Gennesaret did not figure prominently in Jesus' ministry as recorded in the Gospels, but the response to Jesus on this occasion was remarkable. Josephus's description captures not only the beauty of the region, but also indicates the exquisiteness of the lands surrounding the Sea of Galilee.

Skirting the Lake of Gennesar [Galilee], and also bearing that name, lies a region whose natural properties and beauty are very remarkable. There is not a plant which its fertile soil refuses to produce, and its cultivators in fact grow every species; the air is so well-tempered that it suits the most opposite varieties. The walnut, a tree which delights in the most wintry climate, grows luxuriantly, beside palm-trees, which thrive on heat, and figs and olives, which require a milder climate. One might say that nature had taken pride in this assembling, by *tour de force*, the most discordant species in a single spot, and that, by a happy rivalry, each of the seasons wished to claim this region for her own.[A-72]

name is to refer to a plain extending about 3.5 miles (5 km.) by 1.5 miles (2.5 km.) along the northwest shore of the Sea of Galilee. The plain of Gennesaret is the only easily tillable land bordering the Sea of Galilee (for Josephus's description see "Gennesaret"). It was heavily populated during Jesus' day and included the urban centers of Tiberias, Herod Antipas' elaborate and bustling capital city, and Tarichaeae/Magdala, the hometown of Mary Magdalene.[228]

Jesus and the Tradition of the Elders (15:1–20)

Why do your disciples break the tradition of the elders? (15:2). The primary point of contention between Jesus and the Pharisees was that Jesus did not recognize the binding authority of the Pharisees' oral law, here called the "tradition of the elders."

The term "tradition" comes from a noun that refers to something that has been "handed over" or "passed on" (*paradosis*). The "tradition of the elders" (15:1) became a technical expression among the Pharisees for the interpretation of Scripture made by past esteemed rabbis that was "passed on" to later generations. This generally was connected later with Mishnah's *halakah*, "walking," that sets forth law to guide the faithful in their walking, or living, in consistency with Scripture.[229] The traditions of the elders, therefore, came to refer to "rules of Jewish life and religion which in the course of centuries had come to possess a validity and sanctity equal to that of the Written Law and which, as the 'Oral Law,' were deemed, equally with the Written Law, to be of divine origin and therefore consonant with and, for the most part, deducible from the Written Law."[230]

The tractate ʾ*Abot*, "The Fathers," in one of the most famous of rabbinic sayings, traces the traditions of the elders back to the giving of the oral law to Moses, who in turn passed it on to succeeding generations: "Moses received the Law ["Oral Law"] from Sinai and committed it to Joshua, and Joshua to the elders, and the elders to the Prophets; and the Prophets committed it to the men of the Great Synagogue" (*m. ʾAbot* 1.1). The Great Synagogue was the body of 120 elders that came up from the Exile with Ezra and committed themselves to making Scripture practically relevant by developing new rules and restrictions for its observance.[231] The saying goes on, "They said three things: Be deliberate in judgment, raise up many disciples, and make a fence around the Law" (*m. ʾAbot* 1.1).

At the time of Jesus the "traditions of the elders" was a developing system of interpretation that was the distinctive characteristic of the Pharisees.[232] It had not yet been written and codified. That was the accomplishment of post-A.D. 70 Judaism, which finally resulted in the Mishnah, promulgated by Judah the Prince around 200.

They don't wash their hands before they eat! (15:2). Bodily cleanliness was valued highly in the ancient world. The heat and dust made frequent washing necessary for both health and refreshment. Within ancient Israel, a host provided travelers with water for their feet so that they would be refreshed and cleansed from their journey and ready for a meal.[233] The hands were a particular concern for cleanliness, as something unclean could be transmitted to oneself and others, so the priests were required to wash their hands and feet prior to offering their ritual service (Ex. 30:18–21). The Pharisees and later rabbis adapted this concern for ceremonial cleanness to common Israelites, with the purpose that they would consume everyday food as though it were a sacrifice to God at the temple altar. Mishnah *Yadayim* ("hands") describes the procedure: "[To render the hands clean] a quarter-*log* or more [of water] must be poured over the hands [to suffice] for one person or even for two."[234] A quarter-log of water is equal in bulk to an egg and a half,[235] which was poured over the hands up to the wrists prior to the consumption of food. Such a small amount of water demonstrates that the concern for washing was ceremonial, not hygenic (see "Purity" at Mark 7).[236]

bottom left

LARGE STORAGE JARS

These third-century B.C. containers—for water, oil, or wine—were discovered at Dor.

bottom right

EATING UTENSILS

A model of a table with eating utensils typical of the Roman period.

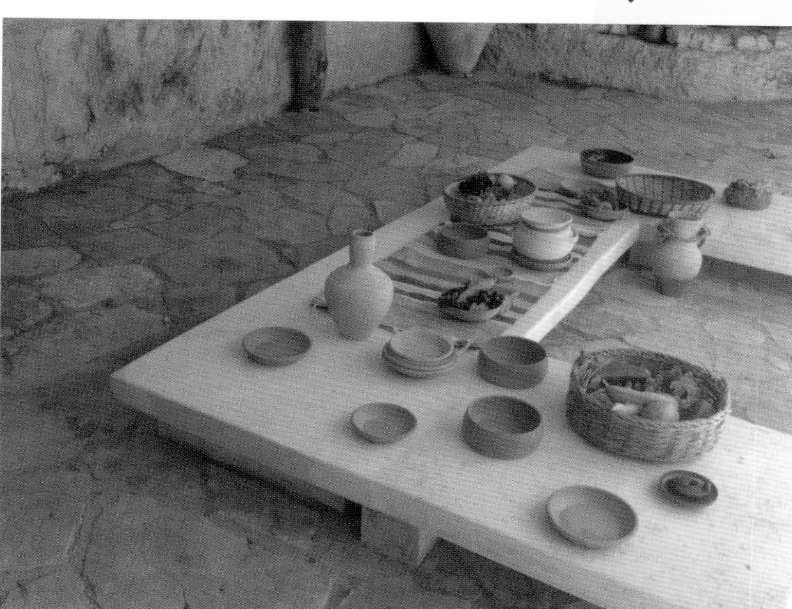

And why do you break the command of God for the sake of your tradition? (15:3). The traditions of the elders were not simply preferred ways of living, but were equal in authority to the written Law. Jesus contrasts what God has given with what the elders pronounced.

Whatever help you might otherwise have received from me is a gift devoted to God (15:5). The expression "gift devoted to God" reflects the Hebrew term "Corban" (Mark 7:11), a technical term designating a formal vow made to God. Such a formal vow allowed a person to be exempt from one's other responsibilities. The Pharisees developed a complicated series of rulings regarding vows and oaths that were eventually compiled in the rabbinic Mishnaic tractates *Nedarim* ("vows") and *Šebuᶜot* ("oaths"). Summarized, the difference is that "a vow forbids a certain thing to be used ('Let such-a-thing be forbidden to me, or to you!'), while an oath forbids the swearer to do a certain thing although it is not a thing forbidden itself ('I swear that I will not eat such-a-thing!')."[237] Jesus addresses oaths in 5:34–37 and 23:16–22, but addresses vows here in 15:1–9. Vows are of two kinds: vows of dedication, which render a thing to be forbidden in the future for common use (as the vow in 15:5), and vows of abstention, which render forbidden those things or acts that are ordinarily permissible (*m. Ned.* 1.1).[238] The situation Jesus raises is a gift vowed for the support of the temple, which takes precedence over the support of one's parents.

REFLECTIONS

TRADITIONS DEVELOPED BY HUMANS CAN BE DAN-gerous when they supplant God's revelation. But tradition is not wrong per se. Paul uses the same term (*paradosis*) to refer to the gospel truths and doctrines that he passed to the churches (1 Cor. 11:2; 2 Thess. 2:15; 3:6), and a related verb (*paradidōmi*) to refer to the fundamental creedal truths of the cross and resurrection that he had received and passed on to the church (1 Cor. 15:1). The essential difference between these forms of tradition and those developed within Judaism rests on the fact of Jesus' incarnation. Jesus is the revelation of God embodied, and Paul declares therefore that the traditions he received and passed on to the church have derived from God himself through the revelation of Jesus the Messiah. That is a crucial dissimilarity for us to reflect upon.

Thus you nullify the word of God for the sake of your tradition (15:6). The Pharisees would not have disagreed with Jesus' emphasis on honoring parents, but their human traditions of allowing certain vows actually supplanted Scripture. They would have considered anyone who broke a vow (human law) in order to help needy parents (God's law) to have committed a serious sin.

Do you know that the Pharisees were offended when they heard this? (15:12). The Pharisees, in contrast to the Sadducees (see "Pharisees and Sadducees" at 3:7), were increasingly influential in Israel as the authoritative interpreters of Scripture and the most righteous in their daily behavior. Jesus with one swipe undercuts both of those distinctives, and his disciples report that Jesus has "offended" or "scandalized" (*skandalizō*) the Pharisees. They rightly understand that Jesus has elevated himself as critic of their entire religious tradition, which would undercut their influence with the people.

The things that come out of the mouth come from the heart, and these make a man "unclean" (15:18). Clean or unclean is ultimately God's judgment. Jesus gives

God's perspective by rendering superfluous the Pharisees' fastidious and obsessive preoccupation with dietary purity laws, especially those at the center of the controversy, the washing of hands. God's evaluative judgment concerns behavior that originates in the heart of a person. The implication is that the heart is evil (cf. 7:11), and all of the sinful activity in the world around them, and even in their own lives, cannot be cleansed through the religious traditions of the elders.

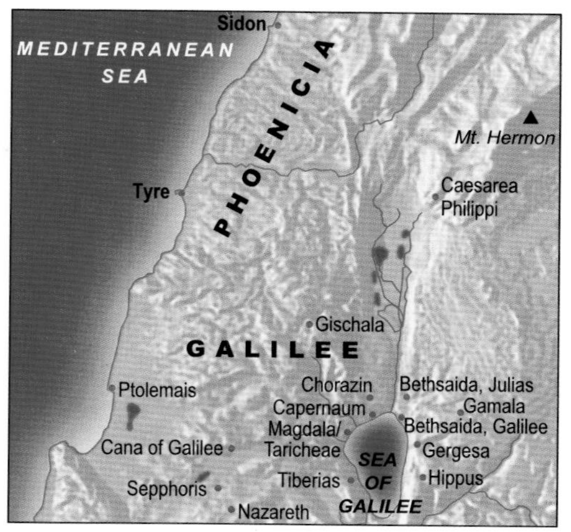

GALILEE, TYRE, AND SIDON

Phoenicia belonged to the Roman province of Syria.

Gentiles Acknowledge Jesus as the Son of David (15:21–31)

Jesus withdrew to the region of Tyre and Sidon (15:21). Tyre and Sidon were Gentile cities in northwest Philistia/ Phoenicia, an ancient region that bordered Galilee to the west along the coast of the Mediterranean Sea. They were known throughout the ancient world as powerful maritime commercial centers. In Israel they became proverbial for pagan peoples, often linked as the object of condemnation from Old Testament prophets for their Baal worship and arrogant pride in their power and wealth, and therefore deserving of judgment.[239] In his denunciation of the Jewish cities of Korazin and Bethsaida, Jesus had said that if the miracles performed in them had been performed in Tyre and Sidon, they would have repented (11:21). Now they get their chance.

A Canaanite woman from that vicinity came to him, crying out, "Lord, Son of David, have mercy on me!" (15:22). The expression "Canaanite" (*Chananaia*) indicates a woman from the region that was a virtual stereotype in the Old Testament and rabbinic literature of pagan non-Jews.[240] Mark calls her "a Greek, born in Syrian Phoenicia," which may indicate she was from a higher, more affluent class (see comments on Mark 7:26). Intriguingly, she demonstrates familiarity with Jewish messianic tradition by calling Jesus "Son of David" and calling for his merciful, miraculous ministry of exorcism for her daughter. Her use of "Lord" three times in the interaction (15:22, 25, 27) is probably for her a title of great respect, but she is saying more than she realizes.

I was sent only to the lost sheep of Israel (15:24). "Lost sheep of Israel" (cf. 10:5–6) does not mean the lost sheep *among* Israel, as though some are lost and others not. The expression indicates the lost sheep *who are* the house of Israel. Jesus comes as the Suffering Servant to save all of Israel. The prophet Isaiah laments, "We all, like sheep, have gone astray, each of us has turned to his own way; and the LORD has laid on him the iniquity of us all" (Isa. 53:6). Jesus must first go to Israel with the fulfillment of the promises made to the nation (cf. 53:6–8), so that the Gentiles themselves will glorify God for his promises made to his people (cf. Rom. 15:8–9).

"Lord, help me!" she said (15:25). This recalls a prior Gentile woman from Sidon (1 Kings 17:7–24) who was persistent in her desire for the prophet Elijah to heal her son.

It is not right to take the children's bread and toss it to their dogs (15:26). The "children's bread" emphasizes the care that God promised to provide for his covenant children, Israel: "You are the children of the LORD your God . . . for you are a people holy to the LORD your God. Out of all the peoples on the face of the earth, the LORD has chosen you to be his treasured possession" (Deut. 14:1–2; Hos. 11:1). As a metaphor, "dogs" is a humiliating label for those apart from, or enemies of, Israel's covenant community (cf. 7:6).[241] Some suggest that the diminutive form for dog used here (*kynarion*) conjures up an image of a little puppy dog, so that Jesus is using the term as an endearing metaphor. More likely, the diminutive form parallels "children's bread" and suggests a dog that has been domesticated, but is nonetheless still a dog. Jesus is contrasting God's care for those of his family with those who are not. He is not condoning the use of a derogatory title, as the response of the woman indicates.

Even the dogs eat the crumbs that fall from their masters' table (15:27). The woman continues the metaphor but uses it to emphasize that dogs too have a caring relationship with "their master." Most dogs were not domesticated, living in squalor, running the streets, and scavenging for food (Ps. 59:14–15). Some dogs were trained for guarding flocks (Job 30:1) and humans (Isa. 56:10; Tobit 6:2; 11:4), but were not normally brought into the home. However, some dogs were domesticated and trained as household watchdogs; they were fed in the house (cf. *Jos. Asen.* 10:13). This perceptive woman, who had already confessed Jesus as the messianic Son of David, presses Jesus by calling on the extended blessings promised to the Gentiles. Although Israel receives the primary blessings of the covenant, Gentiles also were to be the recipient of blessing through them, a promise central to the Abrahamic covenant.[242]

TYRE

Remains of a colonnaded street.

Feeding the Four Thousand (15:32–39)

This is now the second time that Jesus feeds a crowd of thousands miraculously, although now he is in the primarily Gentile region of Decapolis. For comments on the feeding of the five thousand see 14:13–21.

Went up on a mountainside (15:29). See comments on 28:16 for the meaning of this phrase.

"How many loaves do you have?" Jesus asked. "Seven," they replied, "and a few small fish" (15:34). In this feeding the

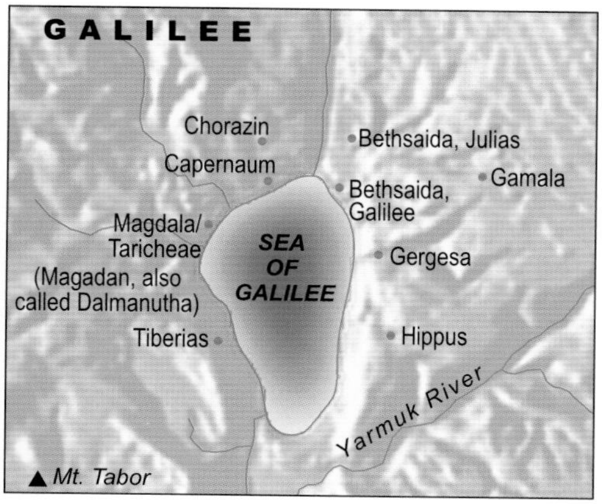

◀ *left*

GALILEE

Showing Magadan, or Dalmanutha.

number of small bread cakes is seven, and there are seven baskets left over (15:37). If the number of twelve baskets left over in the feeding of the five thousand is symbolic of Israel, as most suppose, then the number seven here—normally symbolic of perfection or completion—may symbolize the completion or fullness of God meeting the needs of all peoples, now including Gentiles. The word for basket in 15:37 is *spyris*, a large, flexible basket, often with handles, used for carrying provisions. This word contrasts with the smaller "basket" (*kophinos*) in the feeding of the five thousand (see comments on 14:20).[243]

Jesus . . . got into the boat and went to the vicinity of Magadan (15:39). The name Magadan occurs only here in the New Testament, while the parallel in Mark 8:10 has Dalmanutha. The identity of the town or region is puzzling, because there are no historical or archaeological records to confirm the identity. One suggestion is that it is an ancient Canaanite name, "ma-gadan" or "may-gad," which may have meant "the Waters of (the Canaanite god of springs) Gad,"[244] or perhaps "Waters of Good Luck." This identification links it with the place called in Greek, Heptapegon, "the Seven Springs," later shortened into the Arabic, Tabgah.[245] A more promising proposal is that Magadan is actually a variant spelling for Magdala, the home of Mary, called Magdalene (27:55; cf. Luke 8:2).[246]

Magdala is generally identified with Migdal Nunya ("Tower of Fish") of Talmudic times (*b. Pesaḥ.* 46b), located about three miles north of Tiberias on the Gennesaret plain, which is usually connected with the town about which Josephus writes, the Greek name of which was Taricheae, roughly translated "the place where fish were salted."[247] During Jesus' day and up to Talmudic times, Magdala-Taricheae was the center of Galilee's fish-processing industry, making it one of the most important fishing centers on the Sea of Galilee and the administrative seat of the surrounding region.[248] Archaeologists uncovered in Magdala a decorative mosaic depicting a boat with a mast for sailing and oars for rowing in the ruins of a first century A.D. home,[249] and discovered about a mile north of the town the remains of the famous first-century A.D. "Kinneret boat" (see comments on 4:21). These discoveries have been invaluable for recreating life in first-century A.D. Galilee.

Another Request for a Sign Denied (16:1–4)

Tested him by asking him to show them a sign from heaven (16:1). For "sign," see comments on 12:38ff. "Heaven" is often used as a circumlocution for the name of God, as in the expression "kingdom of heaven" (cf. 3:2; 4:17). The problem with a sign is that it can be interpreted different ways.[250] The Pharisees and Sadducees want a sign from God, but most likely want one that will be displayed in the skies.[251] They are looking to "test" or "tempt" Jesus, the same word used for

Jesus' temptations by Satan (*peirazō*; see comments on 4:1). That is, they are asking for a sign they can use against him.

When evening comes, you say, "It will be fair weather, for the sky is red," and in the morning, "Today it will be stormy, for the sky is red and overcast" (16:2–3). People who live close to nature are aware of daily patterns and irregularities in those patterns that may portend future natural phenomena. There are numerous proverbial expressions that capture signals from nature. Mariners are famous for maxims that predict the patterns of weather, which they must heed daily, if not hourly, in order to conduct safe passage on the seas, such as the well-known saying, "Red skies at night, sailor's delight; red skies in the morning, sailor's warning."

The sign of Jonah (16:4). See comments on 12:39–41.

Spiritual Leaven (16:5–12)

Be on your guard against the yeast of the Pharisees and Sadducees (16:6). Jesus earlier used yeast in a positive metaphorical sense to point to the permeating nature of the kingdom of heaven (cf. 13:33). Now he returns to the more consistent use of yeast in Scripture as a negative metaphor to indicate the evil of disintegration and corruption that can permeate what is good (e.g., Ex. 12:8, 15–20).

JONAH AND THE FISH

Roman catacomb painting depicting the sailors throwing Jonah overboard.

Against the teaching of the Pharisees and Sadducees (16:12). Josephus testifies to the "controversies and serious differences" between the Pharisees and Sadducees.[252] Jesus does not suggest that these two religious groups share the same overall theological teaching, but emphasizes that they have a united opposition to Jesus.

The Christ, the Son of the Living God (16:13–20)

Jesus came to the region of Caesarea Philippi (16:13). Jesus continues to move away from Galilee, extending his ministry into a predominantly Gentile area to the north-northeast of the Sea of Galilee. This region was governed by Philip the Tetrarch, one of Herod the Great's three sons (see "Herod Philip the Tetrarch and Caesarea Philippi").

"Who do people say the Son of Man is?" . . . "Some say John the Baptist; others say Elijah; and still others, Jeremiah or one of the prophets" (16:13–14). Each response to Jesus' question indicates a prophet, in line with one of the popular messianic expectations held in Israel. This goes back to the strand of Old Testament predictions about a great prophet that would arise. Included in this strand are the eschatological Prophet of Moses' prophecy (Deut. 18:15–18),[253] the return of Elijah (Mal. 4:5), and the hope of the return of great Old Testament prophetic figures such as Isaiah and Jeremiah (*4 Ezra* 2:18).

You are the Christ (16:16). *Christ* as a title (cf. 1:1) draws on the promise to

◀ left

GALILEE AND CAESAREA PHILIPPI

David of a perpetual heir to his throne (2 Sam. 7:14), which became a fixture of the hope of a coming age of blessing for the nation (e.g., Isa. 26–29, 40), inaugurated by a figure who would bring to reality the promise of the end-time reign of David's line (cf. Ps. 2:2; Dan. 9:25–26). By the first century, many Jews referred the term *Messiah* or *Christ*, although understood in a variety of ways,[254] to a kingly figure who, like David, would triumph in the last days over Israel's enemies.[255]

The Son of the living God (16:16). "Son of the living God" also points back to the profound prophecy of David's line, "I will be his father, and he will be my son" (2 Sam. 7:14). This spoke immediately of Solomon, but also of the future messianic line. The successor to the line was to be God's Son, as the Old Testament and later Jewish writings reveal. One of the magnificent Royal Psalms that speaks of the anointing and coronation of the Lord's Anointed, the Davidic King, declares, "I will proclaim the decree of the LORD: He said to me, 'You are my Son; today I have become your Father'" (Ps. 2:7; cf. 89:27). The first-century B.C. *Psalms of Solomon* express a combined hope of son and king, "Behold, O Lord, and raise up unto them their king, the son of David, at the time you have foreseen, O God, to rule over Israel your servant."[256] The *Florilegium* from the Qumran community, in commenting on 2 Samuel 7:12–14, says, "This refers to the 'branch of David,' who will arise with the Interpreter of the law who will rise up in Zion in the last days."[257] The expression "living God" would have special significance in the area of Caesarea Phillippi with its ancient Baal, Pan, and Caesar worship.

CAESAREA PHILIPPI

(bottom left) Aerial view of the Jordan river near Caesarea Philippi (modern Banias).

(bottom right) Niches in the stone for the worship of the god Pan at Caesarea Philippi.

▼

Blessed are you, Simon son of Jonah, for this was not revealed to you by man, but by my Father in heaven (16:17). "Blessed" (*makarios*) is the same word found in the Beatitudes of the Sermon on the Mount (cf. 5:3ff.); as there, this is not a *conferral* of blessing but an *acknowledgment* that Peter has been blessed personally by a revelation from God, Jesus' Father (cf. 5:3–11; 11:6; 13:16; 24:46).

You are Peter, and on this rock I will build my church (16:18). In Aramaic, almost certainly the language Jesus spoke on this occasion, the same word, *kēpha'*, would have been used for both "Peter" and "rock." Translating the wordplay into Greek, Matthew most naturally uses the feminine noun *petra*, because it is the closest equivalent to *kēpha'*, a common noun in Aramaic texts found in the Qumran caves, meaning "rock" or "crag" or "a part of a mountainous or hilly region."[258] But when it comes to making the wordplay, Matthew has to use the less common *petros* in the first half because it is a masculine noun, for he would not refer to Peter with a feminine noun. But the use of the two different Greek words does not change the meaning of the wordplay, because *petros* and *petra* were at times used interchangeably.

Herod Philip the Tetrarch and Caesarea Philippi

Philip was the son of Herod by his fifth wife, Cleopatra of Jerusalem, and half-brother of Archelaus and Antipas. When Caesar Augustus settled Herod's will, he gave to sixteen-year-old Philip the title of tetrarch over the region north-northeast of the Sea of Galilee.[A-73] Philip ruled for thirty-seven years (4 B.C.–A.D. 33/34) and was a conscientious ruler. Josephus says, "In his conduct of the government he showed a moderate and easy-going disposition."[A-74] He married Salome, the daughter of Herodias, who had married Herod Antipas. She was the one who had danced at the infamous scene in which Herod Antipas beheaded John the Baptist.[A-75]

Although Philip was not as ambitious a builder as was his father, he did rebuild and enlarge the cities of Bethsaida-Julias, on the northern shore of the sea of Galilee (cf. 11:21), and Panion (or Paneas, the modern city of Banias), a scenic town at the foot of Mount Hermon, twenty-five miles north of the Sea of Galilee and thirty miles inland from the Mediterranean Sea. This town originally may have been the Old Testament Baal-Gad or Baal-Hermon,[A-76] a place of worship to the pagan god Baal, near the tribal area of Dan, the northern boundary of ancient Israel. During the Hellenistic occupation following the conquest of the region by Alexander the Great, a sanctuary to the god Pan was built in a grotto on the main source of the Jordan River, with the nearby town taking the name Paneas, and the shrine being called Panion. Pan is the god of fields, forests, mountains, flocks, and shepherds, keeping watch over this lush setting looking over the northern Galilean valley countryside.

After the Roman conquest, Caesar Augustus gave the region to Herod the Great, who built near the site of the Pan sanctuary a white marble temple to honor his patron Augustus.[A-77] Later, Philip developed near the site a sizeable town, which he renamed Caesarea-Philippi[A-78] in honor of Caesar Augustus, but carrying his own name (Philippi, i.e., "of Philip") to distinguish it from the larger and more influential Caesarea Maritima on the Mediterranean coast (Acts 8:40).[A-79]

At the time Jesus and his disciples traveled there, Caesarea Philippi was an important Greco-Roman city, whose population was primarily pagan. This region becomes the site where Jesus calls for a decision about his own identity and where it is revealed by the Father to Peter that Jesus is truly the prophesied divine Messiah.

The wordplay points to Peter as a leader among the apostles, who will play a foundational role in the early church. Once he has fulfilled that role, he will pass off the scene. He does not hold a permanent position that is passed on to others.

I will build my church (16:18). Matthew is the only evangelist to use the word "church" (*ekklēsia*; cf. 18:18), which brings to mind the "community/assembly (*qāhāl*) of the LORD" (Deut. 23:3; cf. 5:22). In selecting the twelve disciples/apostles to go with his message of fulfillment to Israel (Matt. 10:1–6), who will judge the tribes of Israel (19:28), Jesus points ahead to the time when his disciples, his family of faith (12:48–50), will be called "my church." Jesus will build his church, but it will come about through the foundational activity of the apostles and prophets (Eph. 2:20).

The gates of Hades will not overcome it (16:18). Hades, or Sheol, is the realm of the dead. "Gates," which were essential to the security and might of a city, indicate power. So the expression "gates of Hades" in the Old Testament and later Jewish literature,[259] which is basically the same as the "gates of death,"[260] refer to the realm and power of death. "For a moment my soul was poured out to death; I was near the gates of Hades with the sinner. Thus my soul was drawn away from the Lord God of Israel, unless the Lord had come to my aid with his everlasting mercy" (*Pss. Sol.* 16:2). Jesus thus promises that death will not overpower the church, his own family of faith (cf. Matt. 12:48–50).

I will give you the keys of the kingdom of heaven (16:19). The metaphor points most clearly to the authority given to Peter to admit entrance into the kingdom. In this way Peter is contrasted to the teachers of the law and Pharisees, who shut off entrance to the kingdom and do not enter in themselves (23:13). Peter, as the representative disciple who gives the first personal declaration of the Messiah's identity, is the one in the book of Acts who opens the door of the kingdom to all peoples (Acts 1:8). On each of three occasions, it is Peter's authoritative preaching and presence that opens the door to the kingdom—first to Jews (ch. 2), then to Samaritans (ch. 8), and finally to Gentiles (ch. 10).

Whatever you bind on earth will be bound in heaven, and whatever you loose on earth will be loosed in heaven (16:19).

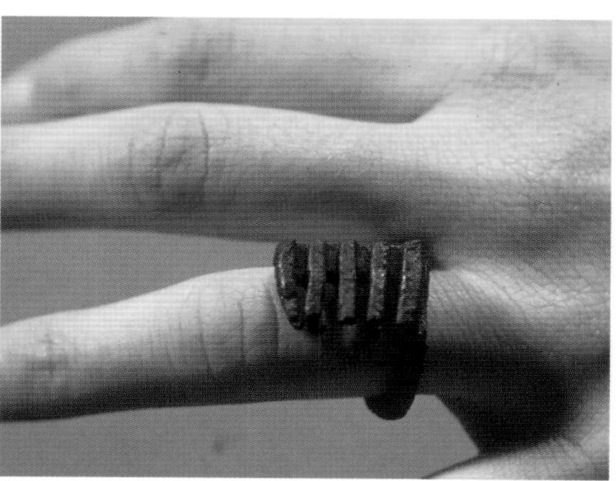

ANCIENT KEYS

(left) A key worn on the finger as a ring (discovered in Herodian-era Jerusalem).

(right) Door key to a house found in Tiberias (late Roman era).

Since the keys metaphor suggests that Peter is the one given authority to open the door to the kingdom of heaven, the binding and loosing metaphor continues that theme by indicating that Peter is the one who is given authority to declare the terms of forgiveness of sins under which God grants entrance to, and exclusion from, the kingdom. But Peter's role of binding and loosing is representative of what all disciples will experience, because all disciples share in the authority of "binding and loosing" (cf. 18:18; John 20:22b–23).

The Suffering Sacrifice (16:21–28)

Jesus began to explain to his disciples that he must go to Jerusalem and suffer many things (16:21). Martyrdom is the act of choosing death rather than renouncing one's religious principles.[261] Hebrews recounts the tragedies that befell many Old Testament heroes (Heb. 11:32–38), and Jewish literature abounds with stories of the gruesome treatment suffered by many who stood up for their faith. During the early stages of the Maccabean revolt the Jewish rebels refused to fight on the Sabbath day, even if attacked, choosing to die rather than to violate the commandment. When the enemy attacked, they said, "'Let us all die in our innocence; heaven and earth testify for us that you are killing us unjustly.' So they attacked them on the Sabbath, and they died, with their wives and children and livestock, to the number of a thousand persons" (1 Macc. 2:36–38).

Although others throughout Jewish history had experienced martyrdom, it was for them a *consequence* of their convictions. But for Jesus, his death is the *purpose* of his entrance to history (cf. 20:28). This is the first of four times that Jesus will predict his arrest and crucifixion (16:21; 17:22–23; 20:17–19; 26:2).

Suffer many things at the hands of the elders, chief priests and teachers of the law (16:21). The single article "the" with the three groups—the elders, chief priests, and teachers of the law—indicates the combined leadership of Jerusalem. "Elders" (*presbyteroi*) is a somewhat generic title for a person whose age, experience, and character have resulted in a position of leadership within groups such as the Pharisees and Saduccees. The "chief priests" (*archiereis*) were part of the ruling aristocracy over Judea during the reigns of the Hasmoneans, Herod, and the Roman governors. They came from four prominent families of chief priests who dominated Jewish affairs in Jerusalem at the time of Jesus up to A.D. 70, alternately supplying the offices of the high priest, captain, and treasurers of the temple and making up an intermediary layer of aristocracy above the general priestly line. The "teachers of the law" (*grammateis*) were professional interpreters of the law, especially associated with the Pharisees in the Gospels.[262]

Peter . . . began to rebuke him (16:22). Within Jewish master-disciple relationships, it was unthinkable for a disciple to correct his master, let alone "rebuke" him, as Peter does here.[263]

Get behind me, Satan! You are a stumbling block to me (16:23). "Satan" is not a proper name, but rather is a common Hebrew noun meaning "adversary." But when it occurs with the definite article, it means "the adversary." Satan had tried to tempt Jesus away from carrying out his

Father's will at the start of his earthly ministry (see comments on 4:1–11); he now uses a different strategy to accomplish the same goal: through Peter. A "stumbling block" (*skandalon*) was an obstacle in one's path, but it became a metaphor to indicate something that caused a person to sin or falter in his or her faith.[264]

If anyone would come after me, he must deny himself and take up his cross and follow me (16:24). In the first century, crucifixion was one of the most feared forms of execution, used effectively by the Romans as one of the strongest forms of deterrence against insurrection or rebellion. It was a dreadful way to die. Condemned victims were often forced to carry a cross-beam to the scene of crucifixion.[265] There they were nailed to it, which in turn was nailed to the upright beam, which was then hoisted into place. The horror of the cross will be Jesus' own tragic fate, but in what must have been to the disciples a shocking shift of emphasis, Jesus uses the cross and crucifixion as an image of discipleship. Although the image is often understood as bearing up under some personal hardship or life's cruel fate, as used here by Jesus the cross has a much more profound significance: One must die to his or her own will and take up God's will (cf. 16:25–26). Jesus' path of suffering and death on the cross is the ultimate example of obedience to the Father's will.[266]

What can a man give in exchange for his soul? (16:26). The word "exchange" (*antallagma*), found only in the New Testament here and in the parallel in Mark 8:37, occurs twice in Sirach, both times expressing something beyond comparative value: "Faithful friends are *beyond price* [*antallagma*]; no amount can balance their worth" (Sir. 6:15); "a wife's charm delights her husband, and her skill puts flesh on his bones. A silent wife is a gift from the Lord, and *nothing is so precious* [*antallagma*] as her self-discipline" (26:13–14).

For the Son of Man is going to come in his Father's glory with his angels, and then he will reward each person according to what he has done (16:27). Whether at the end of one's life or at the unexpected time of the return of the Son of Man in glory, each person must give an accounting of the choices made with his or her life. Although he will die (v. 21), the Son of Man will also come in glory, an allusion to the prophecy of Daniel 7:13–14, a theme Jesus takes up more fully later (cf. 19:28; 24:30–31; 25:31). The juxtaposition of dying and coming in glory provoked misunderstanding in at least some of the disciples (cf. 20:17–22).

Some who are standing here will not taste death before they see the Son of Man coming in his kingdom (16:28).

REFLECTIONS

PETER HAD HIS OWN IDEAS ABOUT THE PATH OF the Messiah, but he needed to know God's plans. God's ways are often different from our human ways. Peter partially understands Jesus' messiahship, but when it comes to an aspect of God's program that he does not understand, he tries to force it into his own understanding. He tries to stop Jesus from going to the cross, whereupon Jesus refers to Peter as a stumbling block. The word "stumbling block" is sadly significant, because it shows that without consistency of character, Peter the rock becomes Peter the stumbling stone. This disciple has perhaps been carried away with his importance as the "rock-man" and oversteps his responsibilities. We can each display a rock-like consistency in our lifestyle if we will know who we are as created by God (and no more!!), and if we will then commit ourselves to maximizing all God wants to do through us as his uniquely gifted vessels.

The expression "taste death" was an idiom for "die." The most natural reading of context concludes that Jesus refers to the Transfiguration that follows. Taking up the cross in discipleship is not something a person can put off, because death or the coming of the Son of Man will bring with it certain accountability and judgment.

The Transfiguration of Jesus (17:1–8)

Jesus took with him Peter, James and John the brother of James, and led them up a high mountain by themselves (17:1). The inner circle of disciples sometimes included the three found here (cf. 26:37; Mark 5:37), while other times Andrew was included (e.g., Mark 13:3).

There he was transfigured before them (17:2). Jesus was transfigured (*metemorphōthē*), a word Paul uses to describe the spiritual transformation that believers experience as a result of regeneration (Rom. 12:2; 2 Cor. 3:18). Here this word points to a physical transformation visible to the disciples that is a reminder of Jesus' preincarnate glory (John 1:14; 17:5; Phil. 2:6–7) and a preview of his coming exaltation (2 Peter 1:16–18; Rev. 1:16), revealing his divine nature and glory as God. Those in the presence of God often experience a radiant countenance, like Moses on Mount Sinai,[267] but here Jesus radiates from his own glory. In Scripture clothes that are "white as the light" indicate purity, like the angel at Jesus' resurrection (Matt. 28:3).

The "High Mountain" of Jesus' Transfiguration

The "high mountain" (17:1) of Jesus' transfiguration is not identified, but since Jesus and the disciples have been in the region of Caesarea Philippi (16:13), many scholars suggest nearby Mount Hermon. It is the most majestic summit in the region and is snow-capped much of the year. Its primary peak rises 9,166 feet above sea level, with a series of two other peaks rising somewhat less in altitude. If this is the location, Jesus and the disciples probably do not ascend to the top, but go up the mountainside to a secluded spot. The primary difficulty of identifying Mount Hermon as the site of the Transfiguration is that the following scene favors, although does not demand, a Jewish setting.

Mount Tabor is the site most favored by church tradition. It is a relatively small summit, only 1,800 feet above sea level, but rising prominently 1,200 feet above the northeast corner of the plain of Jezreel. It is only six miles from Nazareth and twelve miles from the Sea of Galilee. As early as Emperor Constantine in A.D. 326, a church was built there, with three small sanctuaries later erected in honor of Jesus, Moses, and Elijah. But a fortress had been occupying the relatively flat summit for centuries prior to Jesus' time, since it was located at one of the most important crossroads of travel in the region. Consequently, it seems unlikely that Jesus would be on this mountain for the Transfiguration; moreover, it would have required an unusually roundabout route from Caesarea Philippi. Few today contend for Mount Tabor as the Mount of Transfiguration.

Another possible location is Mount Meiron (or Meron; *Jebel Jarmak*) in the upper Galilee region, eight miles northwest of the Sea of Galilee but still within the ancient boundaries of Israel. It is the highest peak within Palestine proper, at an altitude of approximately 3,960 feet; the towns at its base were Jewish. It is located on an easily accessible route back to Capernaum from Caesarea Philippi, yet in a more remote area than Mount Tabor. Matthew seems to suggest that the Transfiguration occurs outside Galilee (cf. 17:22), which Mount Meiron isn't. If so, Mount Hermon is the most likely spot.

Moses and Elijah (17:3). The arrival of two of the greatest Old Testament figures, Moses and Elijah, probably represents how Jesus is the fulfillment of the Law and the Prophets (5:17), and how Moses, the model prophet (Deut. 18:18), and Elijah, the forerunner of the Messiah (Mal. 4:5–6; cf. Matt. 3:1–3; 11:7–10), are witnesses to Jesus' eschatological role of initiating the kingdom of heaven. Both Moses and Elijah had unique endings: Elijah was taken directly to heaven (2 Kings 2:11–12), and Moses, whose grave was never found (Deut. 34:6), was said by rabbinic tradition to also have been taken directly to heaven.[268]

Peter said to Jesus, "Lord . . . if you wish, I will put up three shelters—one for you, one for Moses and one for Elijah." (17:4). This is the fourth of five incidents found only in Matthew in which Peter figures prominently.[269] He may here be indicating the tremendous privilege for the three disciples to witness the event, although "good" seems rather weak. Or is he here perhaps posing a question: "Is it good for us to be here?" voicing their fear at this frightening event? The offer to build three "shelters" may recall the tabernacle, since the same word (*skēnē*) is used in the LXX for the tabernacle (Ex. 25:9), though the same word is also used for the shelters erected during the Old Testament Feast of Tabernacles (Lev. 23:42). Peter, trying to make sense of this overwhelming transfiguration of Jesus and the appearance of these great Old Testament figures, apparently wishes to make some sort of memorial.

A bright cloud enveloped them (17:5). The bright cloud is reminiscent of the way God often appeared in the Old Testament—to Moses on Mount Sinai (Ex. 34:29–35); God's Shekinah glory filling the tabernacle (40:34–35); the cloud guiding the Israelites during their wandering in the desert (13: 21–22; 40:36–38); the cloud of the glory of the Lord filling Solomon's temple (1 Kings 8:10–13); and the Branch of the Lord bringing restoration to Jerusalem, as the cloud of the glory of the Lord shelters Zion (Isa. 4:1–6). Jewish literature recognized the cloud of God's glory as the time when the Lord would gather his people and reveal the location of the ark of the covenant (2 Macc. 2:4–8).

This is my Son, whom I love; with him I am well pleased. Listen to him! (17:5). The voice of God from the cloud gives the same public endorsement of Jesus as was given at his baptism (3:17), combining elements prophesied in Psalm 2:7

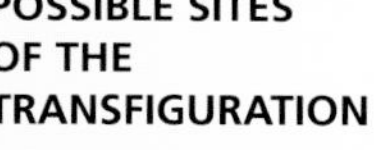

POSSIBLE SITES OF THE TRANSFIGURATION

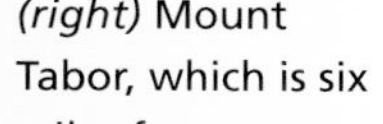

(left) Mount Meron in the upper Galilee region.

(right) Mount Tabor, which is six miles from Nazareth.

("this is my Son") and Isaiah 42:1 ("with whom I am well pleased"). Jesus is both Son and Suffering Servant. He is superior to both Moses and Elijah, so the disciples must listen to him to understand his messianic mission, which directs him to the cross.

The disciples ... fell facedown to the ground, terrified (17:6). To experience the awesome reality of God's presence God commonly produced fear, whether by observing a cloud or hearing his voice.[270]

Elijah Has Come (17:9–13)

Don't tell anyone what you have seen, until the Son of Man has been raised from the dead (17:9). The disciples (and the crowd) could think that Jesus' transfiguration and the meeting with Moses and Elijah indicate that the time has come to effect national and military liberation, but this would misunderstand his mission. Thus, once again Jesus directs them to be silent (cf. 8:4; 9:30; 12:16; 16:20). Jesus' message must be understood to focus on forgiveness of sins through his suffering on the cross. It will be at the resurrection that Jesus will clearly be declared to be Son of God (cf. Rom. 1:3); then they will finally understand who Jesus is, and what he had come to accomplish (for Son of Man, see "Son of Man" at 8:20).

Why then do the teachers of the law say that Elijah must come first? (17:10). The need for silence is immediately illustrated in the question the disciples ask. After having seen Elijah and Jesus transfigured, they don't understand how Malachi's prophecy of Elijah as the forerunner can be fulfilled in Jesus if he truly is the Messiah who has inaugurated the messianic age. The Jewish teachers of the law at that time variously interpreted Malachi's prophecy, as is reflected in later rabbinic passages: "Elijah will not come to declare unclean or clean, to remove afar or to bring nigh, but to remove afar those [families] that were brought nigh by violence and to bring nigh those [families] that were removed afar by violence."[271]

Elijah has already come, and they did not recognize him, but have done to him everything they wished (17:12). John the Baptist was a partial fulfillment of Malachi's Elijah prophecy. He came "in the spirit and power of Elijah" (Luke 1:17), but he was not a reincarnated Elijah, as some of the religious leaders may have expected (John 1:19–27). John prepared the way for Jesus Messiah (Matt. 3:1–3), and if the people and religious leadership would have repented fully and accepted Jesus' message of the gospel of the kingdom, John would have been the complete fulfillment of Malachi's prophecy (11:14). But since the people rejected John and he was executed, and will reject Jesus, who will also be executed, another Elijah-type figure will yet have to come in the future (17:11), again preparing the way—but then for the final consummation of the wrathful Day of the Lord prophesied in Malachi.[272]

The Healing and Exorcism of an Epileptic Boy (17:14–23)

He has seizures and is suffering greatly. He often falls into the fire or into the water (17:15). "Seizures" is most likely the word for epilepsy (*selēniazomai*; lit. "moonstruck"), which occurred for the only other time in Matthew at the beginning of Jesus' ministry (4:24), when he also healed the demon-possessed and paralytics. The lack of control over motor skills causes the boy to suffer greatly.

REFLECTIONS

FAITH IS EITHER EXISTENT OR nonexistent, but it can also either function effectively or be defective. Jesus says that even the littlest faith (like a mustard seed, the smallest of seeds) can move a mountain. It is not the *amount* of faith that is in question, but rather the *focus* of faith. Faith is not a particular substance, so that the more we have of it the more we can accomplish. Rather, faith is confidence that God will do through us what he calls us to do—"taking God at his word." Jesus' point is that anyone with any amount of faith can do the most unthinkable things if that is what God has called him or her to do. Therefore, we should not place confidence in what we have, but rather have confidence that if God calls us to do something, we can do it in his strength, even the most absurdly impossible sounding things from the world's point of view.

Because you have so little faith (17:20). The people of Israel who have witnessed Jesus' miracles and heard his message should have believed on him as the long-anticipated Messiah, but instead he calls this generation "unbelieving" (*apistos;* 17:17). By contrast, he refers to his disciples who could not heal the boy as having "little faith" (*oligopistia*). That is, the crowd does not have faith in Jesus as Messiah; the disciples do have faith, but it is defective.

Paying the Temple Tax (17:24–27)

Doesn't your teacher pay the temple tax? (17:24). The Old Testament gave a directive that at the annual census each person over the age of twenty was to give a half-shekel (*beka*ᶜ) offering to the Lord for the support of the tabernacle (Ex. 30:11–16). A half-shekel was approximately one-fifth of an ounce of silver (cf. Ex. 38:26), which after the Exile, with devaluation, equaled one-third of a shekel for temple support (Neh. 10:32). The half-shekel is the equivalent of two days of work wages.[273] At first the shekel was likely not a coin but a measure of weight, usually silver.[274] By Jesus' day, coins minted among the Romans, Greeks, and Phoenicians were used interchangeably. The half-shekel temple tax was the

SHEKELS

(left) A horde of silver shekels dated to A.D. 66–70 with an oil lamp.

(right) Silver shekels *(top)* and half shekels *(bottom)*, which were used for the temple tax.

equivalent of the Greek silver *didrachma*, a "two-drachma" coin. But the most common coin used among the people was the *denarius*, equivalent to a day's wage, so a person would pay two denarii, the equivalent of the *didrachma*, since the latter was seldom minted (see "Equivalence Table of Weights and Coinage at the Time of Jesus" at 18:25).

These collectors of the temple tax are not "tax collectors" as Matthew had been, who had worked for the Roman occupying forces (cf. 9:9); rather, they are representatives of the Jewish religious establishment in Jerusalem overseeing the temple. The high priest was usually in charge of collecting the temple offering. In the Diaspora on the 15th of Adar, local community leaders collected the half-shekel tax by installing in conspicuous community centers containers similar to those found in the temple, shaped like trumpets.[275] In Palestine, representatives of the Jerusalem priesthood went throughout the land collecting the temple tax.[276]

The grammatical structure of the question indicates that these temple tax agents are attempting to elicit an affirmative response: "He does pay the tax, doesn't he?"[277] This may mask an attempt to embroil Jesus in a contemporary debate among the religious leaders about who should pay the tax. Some within the Qumran community declared that the census tax needed to be paid only once in a person's lifetime (4QOrdinances 1.6–7). Within the developing rabbinic tradition were some who questioned who exactly was liable for the tax (cf. *m. Šeqal.* 1:3–7). These representatives from the temple establishment may have been attempting, with duplicity, to confirm charges of Jesus' disloyalty to the temple.

From whom do the kings of the earth collect duty and taxes—from their own sons or from others? (17:25). The "duty and tax" are civil tolls and poll taxes that a ruler exacted from his subjects, not from his own sons.

Then the sons are exempt (17:26). Jesus is the Son of God, which makes him exempt from the tax, and Jesus' disciples, who are now part of the Father's family (12:48–50), are likewise exempt. This is a profound Christological statement, indicating not only Jesus' relationship by analogy to his Father, the ultimate King, but also the way in which he is the fulfillment of the law. As there will be no temple sacrifice in the heavenly kingdom because of Jesus' sacrifice (cf. Heb. 7:26–28), so there will be no temple tax for Jesus' disciples.

Go to the lake and throw out your line (17:27). All other references to fishing in the New Testament indicate the use of a net, not a hook. Interestingly, fishhooks were found beneath one of the upper pavements in the floor at the site of the ancient excavation believed to be Peter's home in Capernaum (see "Excavating the House of Simon Peter" at 8:14).[278] Although line and hook were used regularly for fishing on the Sea of Galilee, nets were the most effective means of commercial fishing (see comments on 4:18–22).

Take the first fish you catch (17:27). The miracle is both of foreknowledge (cf. 21:2) and of divine provision. God may have arranged providentially for a fish to swallow a shiny coin at the lake's bottom, which is not an unknown phenomenon, or this may have been a uniquely arranged miracle. The fish known popularly, but probably inaccurately, as "Saint Peter's Fish" is the *musht*. The reason why it probably is not the type of fish Peter caught is that it feeds only on plankton and is not attracted by bait on a hook. More likely Peter caught the *barbel*, a voracious predator of the carp family that feeds on small fry like sardines, but also on mollusks and snails at the lake bottom. Peter may have baited the hook with a *sardine*, the most numerous fish in the Sea of Galilee, to which the *barbel* would have readily been attracted[279] (see "Common Fish in the Sea of Galilee").

Open its mouth and you will find a four-drachma coin. Take it and give it to them for my tax and yours (17:27). The coin found in the fish's mouth was the *statēr*, a common coin minted in Tyre or Antioch. It was the equivalent of the *tetradrachma* or two *didrachma*, hence, one shekel (see "Equivalence Table of Weights and Coinage at the Time of Jesus" at 18:25). A treasure jar found at Qumran dating to around 10 B.C. was filled with Tyrian *staters* (*shekels*), which bore the laureate head of Baal Melkart portrayed as a Grecian Heracles; on the other side the Seleucid eagle strode fiercely toward the left with a palm of victory and the Greek legend: "Of Tyre the Holy City-of-Refuge." This is one of many indications that Herod the Great originally had these coins minted in Jerusalem for use in paying the temple tax. It is estimated that the temple tax drew in silver alone the equivalent of 14.5 tons every year. Silver *statērs* were most likely the coins paid to Judas for his betrayal of Jesus (cf. 26:16).[280]

FISH FROM THE SEA OF GALILEE

(left) The Musht fish, also known as "Saint Peter's Fish."

(right) Various fish from the Sea of Galilee.

Common Fish in the Sea of Galilee

- The Kinneret Sardine (*Acanthobrama terrae sanctae*) was the most important for commercial fishing on the lake.[A-80]
- The Barbel group of biny ("hair") Carp family (*Cyprinideae*) included three primary types, the first two of which were popular as fish dishes. (1) The Long-headed Barbel (*Barbus longiceps*), (2) the Kishri ("scaley") (*Barbus Canis*), and (3) the Hafafi (*Varicorhinus*) (a distasteful bottom feeder). One of the first two was probably caught by Peter with the line and hook.
- The Musht (*Tilapia Galilea*) means "comb" in Arabic, because of the long dorsal fin that looks like a comb found on each of the species. It is a surface fish that moves in shoals, easily caught in nets. It has been named "Saint Peter's Fish," erroneously assuming that this was the fish Peter caught. The misnomer probably came from an attempt to capitalize on its tourism value because it is easily caught, fried, and sold at lakeside tourist sites.
- The Catfish (*Claries Lazera*) or *sfamnun* ("the mustached fish" in Hebrew) lack scales, so it was prohibited for consumption by Jews (Lev. 11:10; Deut. 14:11).

The Greatest in the Kingdom (18:1–9)

He called a little child and had him stand among them (18:2). Children in ancient society were often valued for the benefit that they brought to the family by enhancing the work force, adding to the defensive power, and guaranteeing the future glory of the house. In some cultures babies and young children were left exposed to the elements to die as a means of weeding out cripples and the unfit, often focusing on eliminating weak females.[281] Jewish tradition regarded children as a blessing and gift from God.[282] Josephus extols the joy and thankfulness that parents experience through the birth and upbringing of children, but he also emphasizes the necessity for children to be obedient and submissive to their parents in order to experience God's blessing. Rebellious children were subject to being stoned to death.[283]

Unless you change and become like little children, you will never enter the kingdom of heaven (18:3). Jesus does not commend an inherent innocence of children. The Old Testament has a balanced view of both the sinfulness and the value of children from birth. The psalmist acknowledges his sinfulness from conception (Ps. 51:5), yet he also knows that he is a wonderful creation of God (139:13–14). Children were without right or significance apart from their future value to the family and were among the most powerless in society. Yet Jesus celebrates the weakness, defenselessness, and humility of children in contrast to the self-advancement displayed in the Twelve. If persons wish to enter the kingdom, they must turn away from their own power, aggressiveness, and self-seeking and call on God's mercy to allow them to enter the kingdom of heaven. The child thus becomes a metaphor of the values of discipleship.

Whoever humbles himself like this child is the greatest in the kingdom of heaven (18:4). The humility of a child consists of the inability to advance his or her own cause apart from the help, direction, and resources of a parent. The child who tries to take care of himself is destined for disaster. Childlikeness is a primary characteristic of discipleship, making for a reversal of the typical conception of "greatness."

Whoever welcomes a little child like this in my name welcomes me (18:5). Although the rabbis fell prey to the common human condition of seeking their

REFLECTIONS

CHILDLIKENESS IS A CHARACTERISTIC of all true disciples. Some of those who called themselves Jesus' disciples attached themselves to him according to their own agendas, not Jesus'—most noticeably Judas among the Twelve and many others who did not truly believe in his true identity and mission (cf. John 6:60–66). This encounter between Jesus and his disciples is an important time for them to check themselves. If they do not truly believe, even though they may be "disciples" in name, they must repent, be converted, and enter the kingdom of heaven. This is an important reminder for us as well. Not all who call themselves disciples of Jesus are so truly. The proof will be, at least in part, in our character of childlike discipleship, which is solely a product of the new life produced through entrance to new life in Christ.

own advancement (cf. Jesus' condemnation in 23:5–7), humility toward others, including children, was highly valued. "R. Ishmael says: Be swift to do service to a superior, and kindly to the young, and receive men cheerfully" (*m. ᵓAbot* 3:13). For Jesus, the "child" is anyone who has humbled himself or herself to receive God's enabling mercy to enter the kingdom of heaven and become Jesus' disciple.

It would be better for him to have a large millstone hung around his neck and to be drowned in the depths of the sea (18:6). The normal millstone that people used in everyday life was the "hand mill" (*mylos*; cf. 24:41), which refers to the stones found in the home for grinding smaller portions of grain. This type of common millstone weighed from a few ounces to a few pounds and wouldn't be much of an anchor. Instead, Jesus refers here to the "large millstone" (*mylos onikos*), which means "donkey-driven millstone," the large stone rotary quern turned by donkeys or by prisoners (e.g., Samson in Judg. 16:21). This type of millstone, weighing dozens, if not hundreds of pounds, rotated in a cone-shaped interior piece of stone socket, propelled by a donkey walking in circles on a track and often guided by two men. It was used in areas where large amounts of grain were ground to make flour. The fires of the hell of Gehenna await those who receive God's judgment (cf. 3:12; 5:32; 25:42).

The Parable of the Lost Sheep (18:10–14)

Their angels in heaven always see the face of my Father in heaven (18:10). "Little ones" are disciples who have humbled themselves to be like powerless children (cf. 18:2–6). Angels are known to be active in the affairs of humans, but in a strikingly personal way, Jesus refers to "*their* angels." Scripture speaks of angelic care for individual persons (Gen. 48:16; cf. Ps. 34:7; 91:11), individual churches (Rev. 1:20), and nations (Dan. 10:13), while Jewish literature has a fairly consistent emphasis on angels who are guardians of individual persons.[284] The Old Testament story of Jacob, who had angelic protection, is often picked up in later Jewish literature as an example of an individual with a guardian angel: "So the angel said to him, 'Do not fear, O Jacob; I am the angel who has been walking with you and guarding you from your infancy'" (*T. Jac.* 2:5–6).

Whether or not Jesus' statement should be interpreted to imply guardian angels who watch over individual believers on an ongoing basis, it nonetheless confirms that the heavenly Father uses angels to care for childlike disciples. The thought is similar to the role of angels mentioned in Hebrews 1:14, "Are not all angels ministering spirits sent to serve those who will inherit salvation?" Although some Jewish literature pictures only the higher echelons of the angelic orders who can approach God (cf. *1 En.* 14:21; 40:1–10), Jesus' statement "always see the face of my Father" speaks of the

SHEEP

Sheep resting in the shade of a tree near Jotapata, Galilee.

constant access and communication of the disciples' angels with God, which implies the access of all angels to the Father.

If a man owns a hundred sheep, and one of them wanders away (18:12). The secure image of God's people as his sheep is replete throughout the Old Testament,[285] as is the distressful image of some who stray.[286] Since shepherds often worked with one another while their sheep grazed the hillsides, to leave the ninety-nine was of no real concern, since other shepherds would keep an eye on them. A hundred sheep is an average size for a flock, easily cared for by a shepherd.[287]

Discipline of a Sinning Brother (18:15–20)

If your brother sins against you, go and show him his fault, just between the two of you (18:15). "Brother" harks back to the scene where Jesus emphasizes that his disciples, who have obeyed the will of the Father by following him, are his mother and brother and sister (cf. 12:46–50). Jesus addresses in a practical manner what the community of disciples must do if one in the family commits a sin. The ultimate objective of the encounter is not punishment but *restoration*, winning over a brother so that he would be restored to the faithful path of discipleship. The basis of the process is rooted in Leviticus 19:15–18. This passage also stands behind a three-stage process of discipline found in the Qumran community, which includes individual confrontation, witnesses, and if necessary, final judgment by the leaders.[288]

But if he will not listen, take one or two others along (18:16). Deuteronomy 19:15 says, "One witness is not enough to convict a man accused of any crime or offense he may have committed. A matter must be established by the testimony of two or three witnesses."

If he refuses to listen to them, tell it to the church (18:17). This is the second time that the word "church" (*ekklēsia*) occurs in Matthew's Gospel, both times used by Jesus (see comments on 16:18). Jesus looks to the future functioning of his family of faithful disciples.

Treat him as you would a pagan or a tax collector (18:17). The fourth step of discipline is to treat the sinning brother like a pagan (lit., "Gentile," *ethnikos*) or a tax collector, the common titles for those who are consciously rebellious against God and his people. The Old Testament prescriptions for exercising punishment (Deut. 25:1–3) were later applied by Judaism to the responsibility of the synagogue. The synagogue was not only the place of worship, instruction, and fellowship, but also the place of discipline. Extreme discipline included flogging and expulsion (*m. Makk.* 3:1–2; cf. Matt. 10:17). Jesus does not reiterate physical punishment but instead focuses on spiritual exclusion from the fellowship of the church, which is symbolic of spiritual death.

Whatever you bind on earth will be bound in heaven, and whatever you loose on earth will be loosed in heaven (18:18). The same authority earlier given to Peter is here given to the church (see comments on 16:19).

If two of you on earth agree about anything you ask for, it will be done for you by my Father in heaven (18:19). Jewish councils required a minimum of three judges to come to a decision regarding minor cases in the local community, assuming that the Shekinah remains with a just court.[289] Likewise, when two men gathered to discuss the law, the Shekinah was present: "But if two sit together and words of the Law are spoken between them, the Divine Presence rests between them" (*m. ʾAbot* 3:2). Jesus assumes the place of the divine presence among his disciples, guaranteeing that when his followers have consensus when asking in prayer for guidance in matters of discipline, his Father in heaven will guide them as they carry it out.

Parable of the Unforgiving Servant (18:21–35)

Lord, how many times shall I forgive my brother when he sins against me? Up to seven times? (18:21). Forgiveness in the Old Testament came from the God of grace, who instituted sacrifices that gave benefit only because he had given the means of making atonement through the shedding of blood (Lev. 17:11). But the same God of grace "does not leave the guilty unpunished; he punishes the children and their children for the sin of the fathers to the third and fourth generation" (Ex. 34:6–7). Judaism recognized that repeat offenders might not be repenting at all and drew the line at how many times a person could seek restoration and forgiveness: "If a man commits a transgression, the first, second and third time he is forgiven, the fourth time he is not" (*b. Yoma* 86b, 87a). Another case is even less forgiving: "If a man said, 'I will sin and repent, and sin again and repent,' he will be given no chance to repent . . . for transgressions that are between a man and his fellow the Day of Atonement effects atonement only if he has appeased his fellow" (*m. Yoma* 8:9). Peter's offer to forgive a person seven times is magnanimous, reflecting a desire for completeness that the number seven usually evokes. But he wonders where the limit should be drawn on his generosity of spirit.

I tell you, not seven times, but seventy-seven times (18:22). Whether one reads "seventy-seven times," which is the same wording found in the LXX of Genesis 4:24, or the less likely "seventy times seven,"[290] the meaning is that the number doesn't matter.

A man who owed him ten thousand talents was brought to him (18:24). The man must have been a significant figure since he owed the king ten thousand talents. The word for "ten thousand" is *myrioi*, "countless" (cf. Heb. 12:22; Jude 14). Perhaps in view is a governor of a region who collected taxes for the king but who had squandered the amount. The *talanton* was not a coin but a unit of monetary reckoning, valued at approximately seventy-five pounds or six thousand denarii. Today's equivalent would be at least two and a half billion dollars.

Josephus recounts the taxes that were collected at the death of Herod the Great by his sons. Antipas collected two hundred talents from Perea and Galilee, Philip received an income of one hundred talents from Batanaea, Trachonitis, and Auranitis, and Archelaus received

SILVER DENARIUS

A denarius from Tyre with an image of Alexander the Great.

from Judea, Idumea, and Samaria six hundred talents.[291] The total collected from the region was nine hundred talents (over two hundred twenty million dollars in modern currency). The man in the parable owed over ten times as much, an unthinkable amount. The hyperbole of the parable is dramatic.

The master ordered that he and his wife and his children and all that he had be sold to repay the debt (18:25). Debtors were often forced to sell their children as slaves, or their children were seized as slaves by the creditor (cf. 1 Kings 4:1; Neh. 5:4–8). A Hebrew slave had to work for six years as an attempt to recoup the loss.[292] Debtor's slavery was designed as much for punishment as for rerepayment. The rabbinic tradition forbad selling a woman into slavery (e.g., *m. Soṭah* 3.8), but the situation of the parable may assume a pagan king, who would have ignored these kinds of sensitivities.

He grabbed him and began to choke him. "Pay back what you owe me!" he demanded (18:28). Using the same figures to compare the amount owed, the second slave owed just a little over four thousand dollars, a pittance in comparison to the billions owed by the first slave (see "Equivalence Table of Weights and Coinage at the Time of Jesus").

In anger his master turned him over to the jailers to be tortured, until he should pay back all he owed (18:34). Until modern times, prisons were commonly used for the confinement of debtors who could not meet their obligations. Debtor-prisoners were required to perform hard labor until the debt was repaid. Retribution in the form of corporal punishment was common among pagan nations (2 Kings 17:3–5; 25:7), although not unknown in Israel (Deut. 25:1–3; *m. Makk.* 3:1–2).[293] Since it was impossible for the servant in this parable to repay the vast amounts he owed, the scene concludes with the grim certainty that he will experience that punishment forever, a harsh allusion to his eternal destiny (cf. Matt. 8:12; 10:28; 13:42, 49–50; 18:34; 22:13; 24:51).

Equivalence Table of Weights and Coinage at the Time of Jesus[A-81]

Jewish weight	Greek coin or equivalent	Roman coin or equivalent	Phoenician (Tyrian) coin	Modern U.S. approximate equivalent
	Drachma (Luke 15:8-9)	*Denarius* (Matt. 18:28; 20:2, 9, 13; 22:19; et al.)		Approximately $41.20[A-82]
Half-Shekel	*Diadrachma* (seldom minted) (Matt. 17:24)	Equivalent to two *Denarii*	*Diadrachma* (seldom minted) (Matt. 17:24)	Approximately $84.20
Shekel	*Tetradrachma* (not in the New Testament)	Equivalent to four *Denarii*	*Stater* or Shekels (Matt. 17:27; cf. 26:16)	Approximately $164.80
	Talent (Matt. 18:24; 25:15-28)	Equivalent to approximately 6,000 *Denarii*		Approximately $247,200.00

PRISON

A small room in the church of the Holy Sepulchre identified as "the prison of Christ" on the basis of an eighth century A.D. legend.

This is how my heavenly Father will treat each of you unless you forgive your brother from your heart (18:35). "Mercy" is *not giving* to a person what *he deserves*, while "grace" is *giving* to a person what *he doesn't deserve*. A person who has truly experienced the mercy and grace of God by responding to the presence of the kingdom of God will be transformed into Jesus' disciple, which, in a most fundamental way, means to experience a transformed heart that produces a changed life of mercy and grace (cf. Isa. 40:2).

Marriage and Divorce (19:1–15)

Is it lawful for a man to divorce his wife for any and every reason? (19:3). A hotbed of discussion surrounded the various interpretations of Moses' divorce regulations. The leading Pharisaic scholars of Jesus' day debated the grounds for divorce that Moses established, who allowed a man to divorce his wife because he "finds something indecent about her" (Deut. 24:1). The debate focused on the meaning of "indecent." The Mishnah tractate *Gittin* ("Bills of Divorce") reflects back on the debate between different schools of thought among the Pharisees at Jesus' time and records the differing interpretations (*m. Giṭ.* 9:10). The more conservative school of Shammai held to the letter of the Mosaic law and said, "A man may not divorce his wife unless he has found unchastity in her." The more liberal school of Hillel interpreted "indecency" to mean that "he may divorce her even if she spoiled a dish for him." The esteemed Rabbi Akiba, who belonged to the school of Hillel, later added, "Even if he found another fairer than she," demonstrating that divorce be granted for even the most superficial reasons (see also comments on Matt. 5:31–32).

"For this reason a man will leave his father and mother and be united to his wife, and the two will become one flesh" (19:5). God designed his human creatures to be male and female, with marriage to be a permanent union of a man and woman into one new, lasting union (Gen. 2:24). God "hates" divorce because it tears apart what should have been considered permanent (cf. Mal. 2:16).

Moses permitted you to divorce your wives because your hearts were hard. But it was not this way from the beginning (19:8). Since sinful abuse of a marriage partner was a harsh reality in the ancient world, Moses instituted a regulation designed to do three things (cf. Deut. 24:1): (1) protect the sanctity of marriage from something "indecent" defiling the relationship; (2) protect the woman from a husband who might simply send her away without any cause; (3) document her status as a legitimately divorced woman, so that she was not thought to be a prostitute or a runaway adulteress. Although this was allowed, divorce had never been God's intention.

Anyone who divorces his wife, except for marital unfaithfulness, and marries another woman commits adultery (19:9). As did Moses, Jesus allows for an exception to protect the non-offending partner and the institution of marriage from being an indecent sham. Such an occasion is when a person has committed *porneia*, "marital unfaithfulness" (NIV). The semantic range of *porneia* includes whatever intentionally divides the marital relationship, possibly including, but not limited to, sexual sins such as incest, homosexuality, prostitution, molestation, or indecent exposure. Later rabbis declared that divorce was the requirement when adultery was committed, because adultery produced a state of impurity that, as a matter of legal fact, dissolved the marriage.[294]

For some are eunuchs (19:12). Singleness is an appropriate exception for those for whom it has been given as their lot in life, whether they are literal (either born or man-made; *m. Zabim* 2:1) or figurative eunuchs. Some eunuchs have been born impotent, especially those without the capacity for sexual relations, such as those born without properly developed genitalia, like hermaphrodites. Others have been castrated for official functions, especially those in some cultures, like the Ethiopian eunuch, who was castrated because he was an official in a court among royal women (e.g., Acts 8:27ff.). Others adopted abstinence because God made an exception for their particular work in the kingdom of heaven, such as John the Baptist and Jesus himself (cf. 1 Cor. 7:7–9). Some groups in Judaism went to the extreme of saying that celibacy was a higher spiritual order. There is fairly substantial evidence that at least some groups of Essenes practiced celibacy as a part of the ritual order.[295] On the other extreme, some excluded literal eunuchs from their worship assemblies as being unclean.[296]

GALILEE AND THE AREA EAST OF THE JORDAN

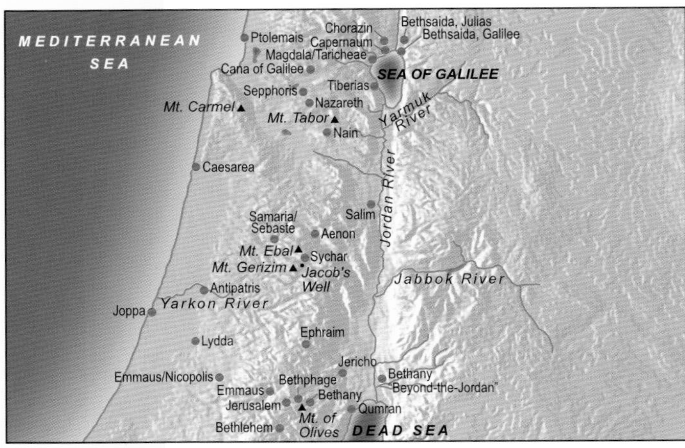

Celibacy *is* an acceptable position, although it is the exception, and it is certainly not a higher calling than God's original order for men and women.

Let the little children come to me, and do not hinder them, for the kingdom of heaven belongs to such as these (19:14). Placing hands on children for blessing had a long history in Israel, primarily when passing on a blessing from one generation to another (cf. Gen. 48:14; Num. 27:18). Bringing children to Jesus for his blessing was an irritation to the disciples, probably because they had an insignificant societal status. Jesus once again turns prevailing societal values on their head (see comments on 18:1–5; also on Mark 10:13–16).

Valuing the Kingdom: The Tragedy of the Rich Young Man (19:16–22)

A man came up to Jesus (19:16). This young man (*neaniskos* in v. 22, which indicates that he is somewhere between twenty and forty years of age) is some kind of religious layleader, possibly a Pharisee (note his scrupulous adherence to the law), among the religious elite in the land. Such people often were well off because they were among the retainer class, well above the common people. In the political situation in first-century Palestine, the Roman occupiers allowed a form of self-rule, and within Judaism the religious leaders exercised much of that leadership.

Teacher, what good thing must I do to get eternal life? (19:16). Addressing Jesus with a title of respect that acknowledges the help he could receive from his learning and mastery of Scripture, the young man has evidently experienced a need in his life to perform some kind of righteous deed in order to assure him of having eternal life.

There is only One who is good (19:17). Among the many ways a person should bless God, Jewish writings exhorted each person to bless God as the truly Good: "For rain and good tidings he should say, 'Blessed is he, the good and the doer of good'" (*m. Ber.* 9:3). By looking at God as Good, Jesus takes the young back to obeying the law as the exprèssion of the truly Good One. The truly Good God's law is the written good will of God for his people. The law is also equated with good in the rabbinic writings: "It is written, *The wise shall inherit honour*, and *The perfect shall inherit good*; and 'good' is naught else than 'the Law'" (*m. ʾAbot* 6:3).

Do not murder . . . (19:18–19). Jesus gives a representative listing of the law, including five of the ten commandments that come primarily from the second table of the Decalogue (sixth, seventh, eighth, ninth, and then fifth; cf. Ex. 20:1–17; Deut. 5:7–21) and the second of the two greatest commandments (Lev. 19:18; cf. Matt. 22:36–40).

All these I have kept (19:20). Although the man may seem presumptuous to say he has kept all the commandments, he was not alone in Israel. When Sirach calls his readers to acknowledge their responsibility for obedience to the law and the power of their own free choice, he challenges them, "If you choose, you can keep the commandments, and to act faithfully is a matter of your own choice" (Sir. 15:15). When the apostle Paul recounted his former life as a Pharisee, he said that, when viewing himself then

REFLECTIONS

THE "GOD" OF A PERSON'S LIFE is whatever rules his or her values, priorities, and ambitions. The lack this young man sensed could not be filled with his wealth or his own religious efforts. It could only be filled with the perfection that comes through entering the kingdom of heaven and experiencing the inner transformation of heart; those two things will set him on the path to be perfect as the heavenly Father is perfect (see comments on 5:48). The inner change will produce a transformation from the inside out.

and his obedience to the law, he considered himself, "as to righteousness under the law, blameless" (Phil. 3:6 NRSV).

If you want to be perfect, go, sell your possessions and give to the poor, and you will have treasure in heaven. Then come, follow me (19:21). The young man has almost certainly given to the poor in the past, because giving alms was one of the pillars of piety within Judaism, especially among the Pharisees (see comments on 6:1–4). But giving to the poor can be done out of the abundance of a person's life. It can give a person an even greater sense of power and pride.

He went away sad, because he had great wealth (19:22). The young man knows that Jesus has correctly pinpointed what is lacking in his life. His "great wealth" (lit., "many possessions"), which include money, but also his houses, land, animals, and so on, has captivated his heart, and he cannot exchange this god of his life for Jesus (cf. 6:21–24). So he goes away with great distress (cf. 26:22, 37), because he knows deep in his heart that he has made a decision that will have eternal consequences.

Grace and Reward in the Kingdom for Those Who Follow Jesus (19:23–30)

It is easier for a camel to go through the eye of a needle than for a rich man to enter the kingdom of God (19:24). To illustrate the difficulty of a rich person entering the kingdom of God, Jesus draws on an analogy using a camel, the largest land animal in Palestine, and the eye of a needle, the smallest aperture found in the home. This may have been drawn from a pool of similar circulating analogies, for an illustration of "an elephant passing through a needle's eye" is found in the Talmud from Babylon, where elephants were the largest land-animal.[297] If not for the seriousness of the issue, the analogy would bring a chuckle to Jesus' listeners as they envision the impossibility of the huge, humped, hairy, snorting, spitting beast squeezing through the tiny eye of a common sewing needle.

Who then can be saved? (19:25). Wealth was often equated with the blessing of divine favor (Deut. 28:1–14). Abraham's wealth is assumed to be a reward for his obedience as a God-fearing man (Gen. 13:2), and the psalmist declares of the person who fears the Lord, "His children

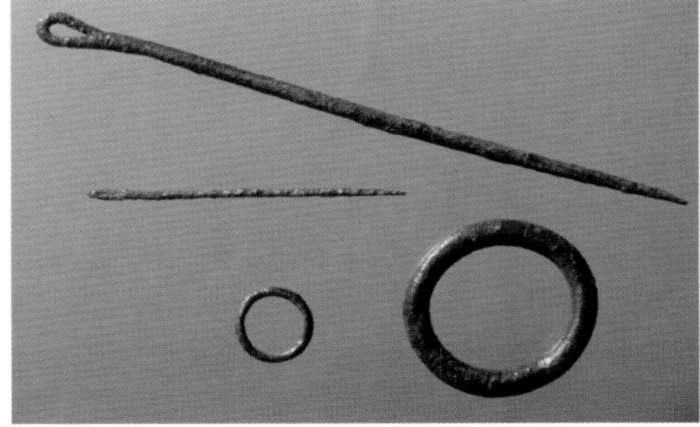

right ▶

EXCAVATED SEWING NEEDLES

The needles and two rings were found in Jerusalem and date to the Roman period.

will be mighty in the land; the generation of the upright will be blessed. Wealth and riches are in his house, and his righteousness endures forever (Ps. 112:2–3). If those who seemingly are the most blessed of God cannot be saved, then who can be? Note that the disciples understand that "entering the kingdom of heaven/God" (19:23–24) is equivalent to being "saved" (19:25), which in turn is equivalent to entering life and obtaining eternal life (19:16–17).

With man this is impossible, but with God all things are possible (19:26). Other rich persons, like Joseph of Arimathea (27:57), found salvation by becoming Jesus' disciple. Even the despicable little tax collector Zacchaeus, who had accumulated great wealth at the expense of his fellow Jews, found salvation at Jesus' invitation (Luke 19:9–10). It is possible when one opens oneself to God.

At the renewal of all things, when the Son of Man sits on his glorious throne, you . . . will also sit on twelve thrones, judging the twelve tribes of Israel (19:28). The word "renewal" or "regeneration" renders the Greek noun *palingenesia,* which occurs in the New Testament only here and in Titus 3:5. Here Jesus refers to the future time of renewal, a hope basic to the Jewish expectation of Israel's future national restoration. Although "judging" can indicate condemnation of Israel for rejecting Jesus as national Messiah, the idea of ruling or governing is paramount (cf. Rev. 3:21; 20:6). Jesus indicates a time of renewal when the Twelve will participate in the final establishment of God's kingdom on the earth, that is, when Israel is restored to the land and the Twelve will rule with Jesus Messiah over all things.

The Parable of the Workers (20:1–16)

For the kingdom of heaven is like a landowner who went out early in the morning to hire men to work in his vineyard (20:1). Grapes were one of the most important crops in ancient Israel, leading to one of the most important metaphors to describe Israel as the "vine" or "vineyard" of God (e.g., Jer. 2:21; Hos. 10:1).[298] Jesus pictures harvest time, when a landowner hired seasonal workers to help with an abundant harvest. In the parable, he goes early to the marketplace (20:3), where laborers have gathered waiting for landowners to hire daily laborers. The agreed-on sum of a denarius was expected, because a denarius was the equivalent of a day's wage for a common laborer.[299]

About the third hour he went out and saw others standing in the marketplace (20:3). The work day was typically divided into three-hour increments, running from approximately 6:00 A.M. to 6:00 P.M. The landowner hired the first workers at the beginning of the day, probably at about 6:00 A.M., to work in the vineyard at the coolest time of the day. Families in the ancient world usually went day to day, often earning only enough for the food for that particular day (cf. 6:11). If they didn't find work, they wouldn't have enough to eat, so these workers continued to wait in the marketplace for someone to hire them. In the parable, the laborers agree to work for the landowner for "whatever is right," expecting most likely to receive a proportional reduction from the day's regular denarius. The abundance of the harvest was such that he went again at the third (9:00 A.M.), sixth (noon), and the ninth hours (3:00 P.M.).

About the eleventh hour he went out and found still others standing around (20:6). Needing still more laborers, the landowner goes back to the town marketplace and finds workers who are desperate enough to remain waiting for work. It is the eleventh hour (i.e., 5:00 P.M.), close to the end of the work day. They would expect only one-twelfth of the amount of those who worked for the denarius, or only about $3.50 in modern equivalents, which probably indicates their desperate need.

Call the workers and pay them their wages (20:8–12). At the end of the day when the foreman or steward of his property[300] gives the day's wages, a shocking development unfolds. The laborers hired last are paid a full denarius, the wages expected for a full day's work. This builds up the expectation that those who worked longer would receive a proportional increase in their wages. But, no! Those who worked the entire long, hot day receive the same wage as those who worked only an hour, which quite expectedly causes the laborers hired first to protest that the others don't deserve equal treatment.

Are you envious because I am generous? (20:15). The expression "are you envious" (20:14) can be rendered literally, "Is your eye evil?" (cf. 6:23), indicating that the laborer cannot be thankful because he is so blinded with self-centered envy.

So the last will be first, and the first will be last (20:16). The parable is a lesson on gratitude and motivation in service, not about salvation or gaining eternal life, because salvation is not earned by works (Eph. 2:8–9; Titus 3:5–6). That would be more similar to a saying found in the rabbinic literature: "Some obtain and enter the kingdom in an hour, while others reach it only after an lifetime" (*b. ʿAbod. Zar.* 17a). Nor is the parable about rewards for service, because God will reward believers differently according to their service (John 4:36; 1 Cor. 3:8).

VINEYARD

A view of a vineyard from the remains of an ancient gate at Lachish.

Suffering and Service (20:17–28)

We are going up to Jerusalem, and the Son of Man will be betrayed to the chief priests and the teachers of the law (20:18). This is the third of four times that Jesus predicts his arrest and crucifixion, but the drama is heightened by the reference to Jerusalem for the first time, the religious leaders' condemnation of Jesus to death, and the Gentiles' carrying out the execution (see further details at 16:21; cf. 17:22–23; 20:17–19; 26:2).

Then the mother of Zebedee's sons came to Jesus with her sons and . . . asked a favor of him (20:20). The sons of Zebedee, James and John, were one of two sets of brothers called to follow Jesus (4:19–20). Their mother was a faithful follower of Jesus, but also evidently a relative of Jesus. She was among the women who attended Jesus at the cross and later witnessed the empty tomb, which would identify her as Salome (cf. 27:56; Mark 15:40; 16:1), the sister of Mary, Jesus' mother. Therefore, Jesus is the cousin of James and John on his mother's side. The mother apparently comes to exercise her kinship advantage. A mother seeking the advancement of her sons through direct petition to a person in authority was a fairly well-known phenomenon, such as Bathsheba's seeking the throne for her son Solomon from the aging King David (1 Kings 1:15–21; cf. 2 Sam. 14:2–20).

Grant that one of these two sons of mine may sit at your right and the other at your left in your kingdom (20:21). Since "judging" indicates ruling more than condemnation, the mother desires for her sons to have the highest positions of importance when Jesus inaugurates his kingdom reign. Seated at the right hand side is the most typical place of honor, whether the king's mother at the king's right side (Judg. 2:19), King David at God's right hand side (Ps. 16:11), or the Messiah at God's right side (Ps. 110:1, 5; cf. Matt. 22:44). The left side is reserved for the second highest position of importance to the monarch. Josephus records that King Saul reserved those two places for his son and general: "The next day, which was the new moon, the king, after purifying himself as the custom was, came to the feast; and ... his son Jonathan had seated himself on his right side and Abener, the commander of the army, on his left."[301] Relegating a person to the left hand side instead of the right side can be a place of disfavor symbolically (e.g., Matt. 25:33ff.), but typically it is a place of high importance.

Can you drink the cup I am going to drink? (20:22). The "cup" throughout Scripture refers figuratively to one's divinely appointed destiny, whether it was one of blessing and salvation (Ps. 16:5; 116:13) or of wrath and disaster (Isa. 51:17; Jer. 25:15–29). Jesus is referring to his forthcoming cup of suffering of the cross (Matt. 26:39), to which he has just given his third prediction (20:17–19).

"We can," they answered (20:22). Perhaps the brothers think of other heroes in Israel's history who boldly stepped forward in times of crisis and volunteered to fight for God. David had volunteered to fight Goliath to defend the honor of the living God, though he knew the one who killed Goliath was to be rewarded with wealth and the king's daughter in marriage (1 Sam. 17:25–37).

You will indeed drink from my cup (20:23). Jesus has seen down the corridor of time to when the brothers will suffer for the kingdom of heaven. James became a martyr (Acts 12:2), and John experienced persecution and exile (Rev. 1:9), although apparently not martyrdom.

The ten ... were indignant with the two brothers (20:24). The other disciples are probably indignant not so much because of the immodesty of the request, but because Salome, James, and John have attempted to use the family relationship to Jesus as an unfair advantage to get what they themselves wanted. The disciples had already been arguing about who would be the greatest in the kingdom of heaven (cf. 18:1), and they had already been promised to sit on thrones in Jesus' eschatological rule over Israel (19:28).

You know that the rulers of the Gentiles lord it over them (20:25). Greatness among the Gentiles was measured by being able to be in a position to "lord it over" others and "exercise authority over" them. What may have first come to the minds of the disciples was the harsh Roman occupation under which Israel had suffered for decades, which meant repressive government, exploitive taxation, and tyrannical military rule. For oppressed people who have experienced such hardships, capturing positions of power and authority is the only way they can think of gaining any measure of self-respect and significance in their lives.

Whoever wants to become great among you must be your servant (20:26–27). The prevailing dictum in the ancient world was that ruling, not serving, is proper to the status of a human. The ancient Greek Sophists declared, "How can a man be happy when he has to serve someone?"[302] The servant (*diakonos*) worked for hire to maintain the master's home and property, and the slave (*doulos*) had been forced into service. These were two of the lowest positions in society's scale. The ideal servant or slave lived to care for, protect, and make better the lives of those over him or her.

Jesus' disciples have the ambition to be great (18:1), to be in the first and highest positions (20:21). Thus, Jesus gives them the means by which they can do so according to the values of the kingdom of God, not the kingdoms of the world. They must arrange their lives with the ambition to give themselves for the benefit of others. It is no coincidence that Paul adopts these titles to describe himself[303] and others[304] who would give their lives for the welfare of humanity and the church. John will later call himself a slave of Jesus (Rev. 1:1), as will Peter (2 Peter 1:1) and Jesus' own brothers, James (James 1:1) and Jude (Jude 1).

The Son of Man did not come to be served, but to serve, and to give his life as a ransom for many (20:28). Jesus gives for the first time an indication of his self-understanding of the purpose of the crucifixion that he has been predicting he will soon suffer (16:21; 17:22–23; 20:17–19). Jesus will give his life as a "ransom" (*lytron*), which means "the price of release,"[305] often used of the money paid for the release of slaves, but in the New Testament means "redemption" or "release" as a theological concept based on the experience of Israel's release from the slavery of Egypt. The term may also

REFLECTIONS

SACRIFICE IS A READILY UNDERstood concept when we think of it in terms of our own benefit. "No pain, no gain" is an old adage that communicates a well-known and appreciated value among those who must sacrifice the present pleasure for personal gain, whether that means experiencing the pain of exercise for the gain of a healthy physical heart or the pain of sacrificing a periodic night at the movies to save enough for that long-anticipated skiing vacation. Jesus would not overturn that principle completely, but he would reverse the focus to say, "My pain, others' gain." Jesus' sacrificial servanthood was not directed toward his own personal gain, but for the gain of all those who would believe on his atoning work on the cross and gain forgiveness of their sins. As such his servanthood provides us with the example we now must display toward one another. We sacrifice for the sake of empowering others.

contain an allusion to the Suffering Servant passage of Isaiah 53 (esp. v. 6b: "The LORD has laid on him the iniquity of us all"). The phrase "for many," which does not mean "on behalf of many" but "in place of many," signifies the notion of exchange substitution for all those who will accept his payment for their sins. This saying of Jesus is the basis of the doctrine of substitutionary atonement as the work of his sacrifice on the cross, which involves the greatest cost of all, the life of the Son of Man.[306]

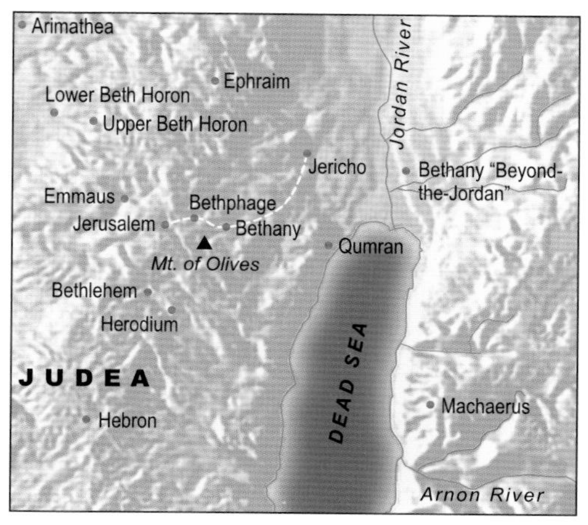

JUDEA

The route from Jericho to Jerusalem.

Healing Two Blind Men (20:29–34)

As Jesus and his disciples were leaving Jericho, a large crowd followed him (20:29). Jesus leaves Jericho for the final approach to Jerusalem, which lies ahead on a winding road for fifteen miles as it ascends three thousand feet through dry desert. It would take some six to eight hours of uphill walking, so he and the disciples are naturally eager to make it to their destination before nightfall, because the road was infamous for highway robberies (cf. Luke 10:30ff.).

Two blind men . . . shouted, "Lord, Son of David, have mercy on us!" (20:30). The blind men understand Jesus to be the "Son of David," a reference to the promise of the messianic deliverer from the line of David whose kingdom would

Jericho: Ancient and Herodian

In New Testament times the city of Jericho was not the ancient city of Old Testament fame (e.g., Josh. 5:13ff.), which was still inhabited, but whose days of glory were long past. It survived primarily because of the fresh water from the nearby spring, making it to this day perhaps "the oldest continually inhabited oasis in the world."[A-83]

The more prominent Jericho in Jesus' day refers to the developments surrounding a huge palace complex first built by the Hasmoneans on a three-acre site about a mile south of the ancient city mound. Much of this palace was destroyed in 31 B.C. by the same earthquake that destroyed much of the original Qumran community's buildings. The Hasmonean palace was greatly expanded by Herod the Great to include three contiguous palaces on an area of twenty-five acres. One part of the final palace had gardens, porticos, and a swimming pool, connected to the main building by a flight of stairs and a bridge across the Wadi Qelt, where there was a reception hall, colonnaded courtyards, and a large, lavish bathhouse.

On the spacious grounds, Herod also built a complex that was unique in the ancient world, consisting of an integrated horse- and chariot-racing course, a huge theater, and a large building that served either as a reception hall or gymnasium. The combined building project accommodated horse races, athletics, boxing, theater, and musical shows. Herod and later governors escaped the cold Jerusalem winters to this extravagant desert oasis.[A-84] have no end (2 Sam. 7:12–16; cf. *Pss. Sol.* 17:23). The messianic age promised to bring healing to the blind (Isa. 29:18; 35:5; 42:7), which Jesus told John the Baptist was one of the signs that he indeed was the Expected One (Matt. 11:2–6), so these blind men ask for the gift of messianic mercy that will heal their blindness.

The Climactic Entry into Jerusalem (21:1–11)

The crescendo of Jesus' messianic ministry occurs as he enters Jerusalem, the city of the great King (Ps. 48:1–2), the center of Israel's spiritual life and messianic hope. This initiates the "Holy Week" or "Passion Week." "Passion" comes from the Latin *passio* ("suffering"), which originally meant the suffering of a martyr. Early Latin translations of the New Testament adopted the term *passio* to point to the Gospel narratives of Jesus' suffering and its attending events. The earliest message about Jesus given by the apostolic band was the Passion, as we can see from the earliest preaching accounts in Acts. If we look at percentages of the Gospels given over to the Passion Week, it comprises from 25–48 percent of their materials.

As they approached Jerusalem (21:1). On the road from Jericho to Jerusalem, see comments on 20:29. Close to Jerusalem, the road approached the back (east) side of the Mount of Olives, passing through Bethany, the place where Jesus stayed during his final week,[307] about two miles (3 km.) southeast of Jerusalem (John 11:18). The road continued over the Mount of Olives, down through the Kidron Valley, and entered Jerusalem.

Bethphage (21:1). Near Bethany was the town of Bethphage, today called el-Azariyeh, named in honor of Lazarus, who was raised in this proximity (cf. John 11:1, 17ff.). The traditional site of the village is on the southeast slope of the Mount of Olives, less than a mile east of Jerusalem. The name Bethphage (Heb. *bet pagê*) means "house of unripe young figs" (cf. linked with Bethany in Mark 11:1; Luke 19:29).[308] The name is men-

JERICHO

(top left) The tel of ancient Jericho.

(bottom left) Aerial view of King Herod's winter palace at Herodian Jericho.

(bottom right) Aerial view of the tel of ancient Jericho.

tioned in a number of rabbinic passages, sometimes as a village on its own and sometimes as part of Jerusalem, since Bethphage marked the limit of the confines of Jerusalem.[309]

On the Mount of Olives (21:1). Rising 2,660 feet above sea level, the Mount of Olives lies to the east of Jerusalem, directly overlooking the temple area. It is a flattened, rounded ridge with four identifiable summits. The name derived from the olive groves that covered it in ancient times. The traditional site of the Garden of Gethsemane lies near the foot of the Mount of Olives, on the western slope above the Kidron Valley.

The Lord needs them (21:3). The term "Lord" (*kyrios*) can be taken in a common

Walking With Jesus Through the Holy (Passion) Week
A Harmony of the Events of the Week[A-85]

Modern Calendar Days	Event
	• Arrival in Bethany (John 12:1)
Saturday	• Evening celebration, Mary anoints Jesus (Matt. 26:6-13; John 12:2-8)
Sunday	• Triumphal entry into Jerusalem (Matt. 21:1-9; John 12:12-18) • Jesus surveys the temple area (Mark 11:11) • Return to Bethany (Mark 11:11)
Monday	• Cursing the fig tree on the way to Jerusalem (Mark 11:12-14; cf. Matt. 21:18-22) • Cleansing the temple (Matt. 21:12-13; Mark 11:15-17) • Return to Bethany (Mark 11:19)
Tuesday	• Debates with religious leaders in Jerusalem and teaching in the temple (Matt. 21:23–23:39; Mark 11:27–12:44) • Olivet Discourse (Matt. 24:1–25:46; Mark 13:1-37)
Wednesday	• "Silent Wednesday"—Jesus and his disciples remain in Bethany • Judas makes arrangements for the betrayal (Matt. 26:14-16; Mark 14:10-11)
Thursday	• Preparations for Passover (Matt. 26:17-19; Mark 14:12-16) • Passover meal and Last Supper (Matt. 26:20-25; Mark 12:17-25) • Upper Room discourses (John 13–17) • Prayers in Garden of Gethsemane (Matt. 26:36-46; Mark 14:32-42)
Friday	• Betrayal and arrest (Matt. 26:47-56; Mark 14:43-50) • Jewish trial Annas—John 18:13-24 Caiaphas—Matt. 26:57-68; Mark 14:53-65 Sanhedrin—Matt. 27:1-2; Mark 15:1 • Roman trial (three phases) Pilate—Matt. 27:2-14; Mark 15:2-5 Herod Antipas—Luke 23:6-12 Pilate—Matt. 27:15-23; Mark 15:6-14 • Crucifixion (approx. 9:00 A.M. to 3:00 P.M.; Matt. 27:27-54; Mark 15:16-39)
Sunday	• Resurrection witnesses (Matt. 28:1-8; Mark 16:1-8; Luke 24:1-12) • Jesus' resurrection appearances (Matt. 28:9-20; Luke 24:13-53; John 20-21)

sense to mean one's earthly "master," or it can be taken to refer to deity. Jesus, at this climactic time of his earthly ministry, reveals himself with increasing clarity.[310]

"Your king comes to you, gentle and riding on a donkey" (21:5). The prophecy of Zechariah 9:9 indicates the nature of Jesus' arrival: He comes as the righteous one who offers salvation, not as a conquering military leader, and with reconciliation, as did rulers who sometimes rode a donkey in times of peace (Judg. 5:10; 1 Kings 1:33).

They brought the donkey and the colt (21:7). Zechariah's prophecy specified in synonymous parallelism that a young colt, the unbroken foal of a donkey, was the animal on which the peace-bringing king of Israel would enter Jerusalem. Matthew alone mentions two animals (cf. Mark 11:4, 7; Luke 19:33, 35), which adds a touch of historical reminiscence. An unbroken young colt would be controlled best by having its mother ride alongside to calm it in the midst of the tumult of entering Jerusalem.[311]

DONKEY

Egyptian boy riding on a donkey.

Spread their cloaks on the road, while others cut branches from the trees and spread them on the road (21:8). Throwing garments in the path of a king to walk on was a symbol of submission (cf. 2 Kings 9:13). Palms symbolized Jewish nationalism and victory, such as when Judas Maccabeus and his followers recovered Jerusalem and the temple was desecrated by Antiochus: "Therefore, carrying ivy-wreathed wands and beautiful branches and also fronds of palm, they offered hymns of thanksgiving to him who had given success to the purifying of his own holy place" (2 Macc. 10:7; cf. 1 Macc. 13:51). Palms are seen on many coins of that time, expressive of nationalism generally, both Jewish and Roman.

right

COIN WITH PALM BRANCHES

Jewish coin minted during the Bar-Kochba revolt against Rome.

Hosanna to the Son of David! (21:9). "Hosanna" is the transliteration of a Hebrew expression that means "O save."[312] This draws the crowd to make a connection to the Egyptian Hallel (Ps. 113–118) sung during the Passover season, especially expressing the messianic hopes of Israel as voiced in Psalm 118:19–29 (see esp. v. 25). Linked with Hosanna, "Son of David" is unmistakably messianic. The crowd acknowledges what Jesus has already stated in his fulfillment of Zechariah 9:9: He is the Davidic Messiah (see comments on 1:1), whom they call on to save them out of their oppression.

This is Jesus, the prophet from Nazareth in Galilee (21:11). Some in the crowd preceding Jesus call him a prophet, which

JERUSALEM TEMPLE

The East Gate of the temple viewed from the east (the model of the Temple at the Holyland Hotel).

many in his ministry saw him to be (16:14; 21:46). This does not seem to imply that they understand Jesus to be *the* eschatological Prophet of Moses' prophecy (Deut. 18:15–18),[313] but rather the prophet who had been creating such a stir in Galilee, whose hometown was Nazareth. Others who call out "Hosanna" seem to expect Jesus to bring liberation, as had the kings of ancient Israel and the Maccabees of more recent times.

Jesus Challenges the Temple Establishment (21:12–17)

Jesus goes to the temple and drives out those selling and buying and overturns the money changers' tables. This has often been called a "cleansing" of the temple, implying that he is trying to purify the temple from corrupt practices and restore it to proper usage as intended by God. While corrupt practices are certainly being rebuked, Jesus goes beyond cleansing to perform intentionally a symbolic act of judgment against the religious leadership of Israel.

Jesus entered the temple area (21:12). Climbing the imposing steps on the southern end of the temple mount, Jesus enters the temple through the Huldah Gates located on the southern wall. The Huldah Gates, named after the prophetess Huldah (2 Kings 22:14; 2 Chron. 34:22) were a double and triple gate.[314] He then climbs another series of steps to enter the Royal Stoa, a long hall with four rows of forty thick columns each. The northern side opened into the temple courts, but within the Stoa was a market where commercial activity enabled pilgrims from the Diaspora to participate in temple activities. Here they exchanged their currency for temple currency, the Tyrian shekel, which was used to pay the required temple tax (17:24–27; cf. Ex. 30:11–16) and purchase animals and other products for their sacrifices.[315]

Drove out all who were buying and selling there (21:12). Both those buying and selling, as well as the money changers, were making this simply a commercial operation, and the temptation for abuse was real, since surplus tax was consigned to the temple fund (*m. Šeqal.* 2:5). Doves were the sacrifice made by the poor, who could not afford animal sacrifices, and by those making a variety of types of personal offerings (cf. Lev. 5:7; 12:6; 15:14, 29). Temple commerce was at times notorious for exploiting the disadvantaged (*m. Ker.* 1:7). As a spokesman for God, a prophet sometimes performed acts that were pronouncements of judgment, even in the temple precincts (cf. Jeremiah's smashing the clay pot; Jer. 19).

"My house will be called a house of prayer, but you are making it a 'den of robbers'" (21:13). The religious leaders were treating the temple as robbers do their dens—a place of refuge for both accumulating illicitly gained wealth and for plotting future illegal activities. Caves in Palestine were regularly used as robbers' dens, so the metaphor was clear to Jesus' hearers.[316] The temple's primary purpose, as a house for communing with God, was lost in the frenzy of temple activity.

The blind and the lame came to him at the temple, and he healed them (21:14). The blind and lame were restricted from

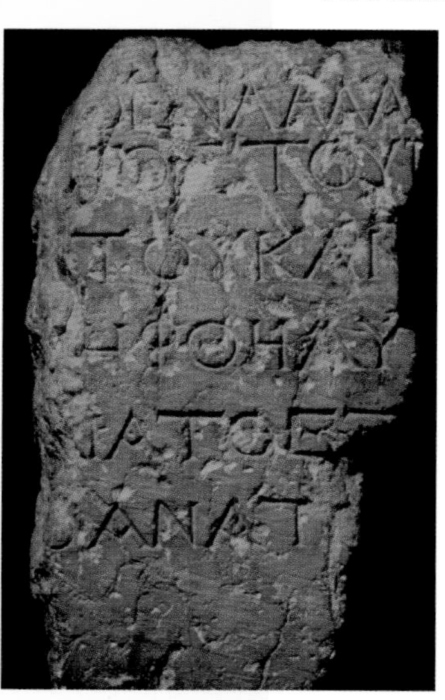

TEMPLE WARNING INSCRIPTION

The sign restricts Gentiles from entering the inner courts of the temple or face death. ▼

full access to temple activities, to symbolize purity in those approaching God (cf. Lev. 21:18–19). The Qumran community employed these restrictions for admission to their covenantal fellowship.

> And no-one stupid or deranged should enter; and anyone feeble [-minded and insane,] those with sightless [eyes, the lame or one who stumbles, or a deaf person, or an under-age boy, none of these] should enter [the congregation, since the holy angels are in its midst]. (CD 15:15–17)

He . . . went out of the city to Bethany (21:17). Jesus first arrived in Bethany prior to his climactic entry to Jerusalem (cf. John 12:1) and returned to Bethany throughout the week. His close association with Lazarus, whom he raised from the dead, and with Lazarus's sisters, Mary and Martha (Luke 10:38–42; John 11:1–44), leads many to assume Jesus spends each night at their home.

right ▶

MODERN BETHANY

Cursing the Fig Tree: Judgment of the Nation (21:18–22)

Seeing a fig tree by the road (21:19). Known for its abundant produce of early figs (Bethphage means "house of the early fig"), the appearance of leaves on a fig tree in this region was a promise of the especially sweet early fig, which also was a promise of later fruitfulness when the normal crop of figs was produced. The fig tree without the early fig was an appropriate object for Jesus to use to indicate that Israel, which should have been producing the sweetest of all figs, was unproductive and so was being judged. This had just been demonstrated by Jesus in the temple (cf. Hos. 9:10).[317]

You can say to this mountain, "Go, throw yourself into the sea," and it will be done (21:21). Using the handy object of either the Mount of Olives or perhaps even the temple mount across the Kidron Valley, Jesus says that one with faith could throw the mountain into the sea. If they are on the western slope of the Mount of Olives moving into the city, it is doubtful that they could see the Dead Sea. Jesus is more likely using a general figure of speech.

left

A WELL-KNOWN MOUNTAIN

The Herodion, location of a citadel built by Herod the Great.

Controversies in the Temple Court over Jesus' "Authority" (21:23–27)

Jesus now enters into a series of interactions with the religious leaders. After they question his authority, he gives three extended parables (21:28–22:14) that reveal God's judgment on them for not fulfilling their responsibility among the people to respond to his invitation to the kingdom of God. Then there is a series of four interactions with the religious leaders (22:15–46) as they attempt to entrap him, in which he turns the tables to reveal his true identity as the Son of God.

The chief priests and the elders of the people came to him (21:23). The "chief priests" were high-ranking members of the priestly line who joined the high priest in giving oversight to the temple activities, treasury, and priestly orders (cf. 2:4). Linked here with the "elders" (so also in 26:3, 47; 27:1), they were members of the Sanhedrin, the ruling body (although Matthew doesn't refer to this body; cf. 26:57; Mark 14:53). The elders were representatives from the Sadducees and Pharisees.

By what authority are you doing these things? (21:23). The religious leaders question Jesus' "authority" to do "these things," most likely referring to his cleansing the temple on the day before (21:12–13), but also questioning his authority to heal (21:14–16) and to preach and teach in the temple (21:23). Jesus was, after all, neither an official priest nor a scribal authority. He engages in a series of rabbinic-type debates that follow a typical pattern: a hostile question, a counterquestion, admission, and final rejoinder.[318]

John's baptism—where did it come from? Was it from heaven, or from men? (21:25). Jesus counters by asking whether

REFLECTIONS

THE FIG TREE PROVIDED A STRIKING LESSON FOR the disciples. Just as its fruitfulness was a sign of its health, so fruitfulness was a sign of Israel's faithfulness to the covenantal standards. Now that Israel, especially represented by its religious leadership, had perverted temple practices and had not repented at the appearance of Jesus Messiah proclaiming the arrival of the kingdom of heaven, Israel was being judged by God.

Jesus' cursing the fig tree was not a fit of temper but a symbolic act, demonstrating that God's creatures must produce that for which they were created. Even so we humans have been created by God to carry out his will, which means first of all entering into a relationship with him, which will then allow us to bear the fruit of that relationship, found especially in the fruit of the Spirit produced in our lives (cf. Gal. 4:6–7; 5:13–26). With the empowering of God's Spirit, whatever he calls for us to do we can accomplish in his power, if we only will submit to his will.

SCALE MODEL OF THE JERUSALEM TEMPLE

the religious leaders think John the Baptist had divine or human authority. By shifting the questioning back to the religious leaders, Jesus lays a logical trap (21:25b–26). They cannot alienate the people by saying that the highly popular John's prophetic ministry was not from God, but they cannot endorse the prophet who had condemned them for not repenting (cf. 3:7–10).

The Parable of the Two Sons (21:28–32)

Son, go and work today in the vineyard (21:28). The grapevine and the vineyard were one of the most important crops in ancient Israel and became one of the most important metaphors to describe Israel, God's vineyard (e.g., Jer. 2:21; Hos. 10:1; cf. *2 Bar.* 36–40).[319]

Which of the two did what his father wanted? (21:31). The son that originally refused but then obeyed is like those in Israel who were disobedient to the law, such as the tax collectors and prostitutes. But when John came with the message of true righteousness through the announcement of the arrival of the kingdom of God, they obeyed God's call and repented. By contrast, the religious leaders are like the son who agreed but did nothing. They were externally obedient to the law, but when God sent his messenger John the Baptist, they did not obey God's message through him.

The Parable of the Wicked Tenants (21:33–46)

A landowner . . . planted a vineyard (21:33). Clearly alluding to Isaiah 5:1–7, Jesus intensifies his rebuke of the religious leadership by pronouncing God's judgment. Stone walls were built around vineyards to protect them from thieves and wild animals, and some larger vineyards had watchtowers built for added security. It was common to have large farming estates in Palestine, which were owned either by foreigners or wealthy Jews and rented out to poor Jewish farmers. A wealthy landowner might employ a farmer or rent out his vineyard to tenants, if he had other preoccupations.[320]

SELAH COIN

This coin, minted during the Bar Kochba revolt (A.D. 134), depicts the front of the Jerusalem temple.

The tenants seized his servants; they beat one, killed another, and stoned a third (21:35). Many absentee landowners were notorious for harsh treatment of their tenants. Here, the scene is reversed, and the landowner's servants are abused when they come to collect a portion of the harvest. The treatment of these "servants" calls to mind the same fate that befell God's prophets throughout Old Testament history (e.g., 1 Kings 18:4; Jer. 20:1–2).

Last of all, he sent his son to them (21:37). This is an unmistakable allusion to the Father's sending his Son, Jesus (cf. 10:40–41; cf. 3:17; 11:27; 15:24; 17:5), which is further evidence of Jesus' self-consciousness of his identity as God's unique Son (cf. 3:17; 11:27).

They . . . threw him out of the vineyard and killed him (21:39). Jesus has been telling his disciples of his crucifixion at the hands of the religious leaders for several months (16:21; 17:23; 20:18), and now he tells the rulers themselves in parabolic form.

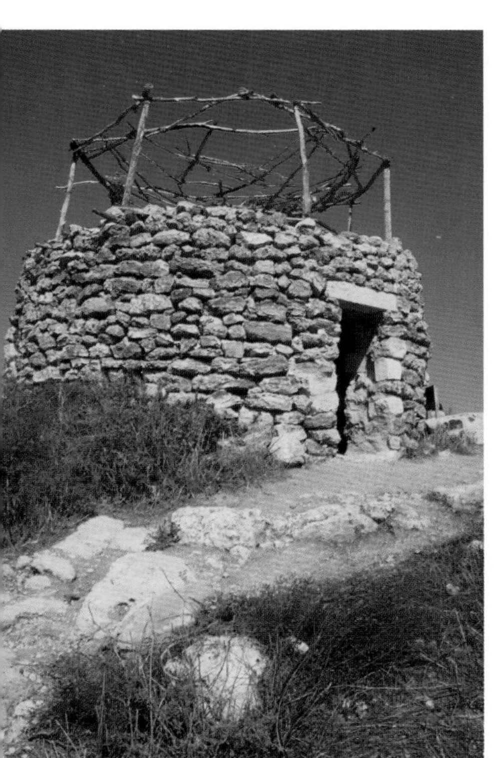

◀ *left*

VINEYARD WATCHTOWER

Located in the hills of Samaria.

"The stone the builders rejected has become the capstone" (21:42). The crowds at Jesus' entrance into Jerusalem had sung out a portion of the last of the Egyptian Hallel psalms, "O Lord, save us," a quotation of Psalm 118:25 (cf. Matt. 21:9). Now Jesus draws on Psalm 118:22 to point to his rejection and future vindication. God has given prominence to his suffering servant like a "capstone" (lit., "head of the corner"), either the stone that held two rows of stones together in a corner ("cornerstone") or the wedge-shaped stone placed at the pinnacle of an arch that locked the ascending stones together. The suffering of the Son will be turned into the position of ultimate prominence and importance.

The kingdom of God will be taken away from you and given to a people who will produce its fruit (21:43). In the context of the parable this means that the privileged role of the religious leaders in caring for God's "vineyard" is now being taken away. But this is also a hint that Israel's privileged role in the establishment of God's kingdom will be taken away and given to another people. "People" is the singular *ethnos*, which prepares for the time when the church, a nation of gathered people, will include both Jew and Gentile in the outworking of God's kingdom in the present age (cf. 1 Peter 2:9).

He who falls on this stone will be broken to pieces, but he on whom it falls will be crushed (21:44). Not only will the rulers' privileged position and role in the outworking of the kingdom of God be taken away, but judgment also will come on those rejecting the Son. Those who stumble over the stone and try to destroy it, such as the religious leaders who reject Jesus and will later condemn him, will be destroyed. In the end Jesus will come as judge and fall on those who have rejected him (cf. chs. 24–25).

The Parable of the Wedding Banquet (22:1–14)

The kingdom of heaven is like a king who prepared a wedding banquet for his son (22:2). A Jewish wedding (Heb. *ḥatunnâ*) was a sacred affair, in which the wife was separated to the husband through the wedding ceremony (*qiddušin*, "sanctification"), which in later Talmudic times was formalized when the groom recited to the bride: "You are sanctified to me in accordance with the law of Moses and Israel (*b. Qidd.* 5b).[321] In the case of a king's son's wedding, this would be a country-wide celebration that would go on for several days.

He sent some more servants (22:4). Although one might overlook a first invitation, the refusal of the invitation from the king to the wedding would be unthinkable, a terrible and dangerous affront to the monarch. Yet his graciousness wins the day, and he reissues the invitation, elaborating on the bounty of the celebration.

The rest seized his servants, mistreated them and killed them (22:6). The allusion to the vineyard of Isaiah's prophecy in the preceding parables is continued, as Jesus points to the destruction of the vineyard and judgment on Israel for despising the Holy One of Israel (cf. Isa. 5:3–12; 24–25).[322] Not only do the invitees reject the king's second invitation with trivial substitutes of everyday affairs (e.g., farming and business); others actually abuse and kill the king's messengers. This is an unthinkable insult to the king, who now finally brings judgment on his insubordinate subjects for the most serious treason and revolt against the monarch. While this may predict the destruction of Jerusalem and the judgment of the religious establishment in A.D. 70, the destruction of the rebellious subjects and their city parallels other rebellions in Jewish history.[323]

Go to the street corners and invite to the banquet anyone you find (22:9). The second part of the parable draws on another unthinkable development. Instead of the privileged few, now the undeserving and unworthy many are invited to the wedding.

He noticed a man there who was not wearing wedding clothes (22:11). The third part of the parable focuses on one of the guests who has gained entrance to the wedding, but who did not have the appropriate wedding garment. Although the invitation was given to all, both good and bad, proper attire is expected. Drawing on some evidence for a king in the ancient world supplying festal garments for guests (Gen. 45:22; Est. 6:8–9), some have understood this as an allusion to the imputed righteousness that Jesus hinted at early in his ministry (Matt. 5:20), and which Paul will later enunciate (e.g., Rom. 3:21–31; 4:22–25). Others suggest this refers to clean garments as opposed to dirty ones, symbolizing not works meriting salvation but evidential works of righteousness.[324] In any case, since the individual is addressed as "friend" and is left speechless when confronted by the king (22:12), the implication is left that the guest had proper clothing available, but declined to wear it. This once again points to the culpability of both the privileged religious leaders, the populace in Israel, and even Jesus' professing disciples such as Judas (called "friend" in 26:50), which is the point of all these parables. The man is bound and cast into the outer place of weeping and gnashing of teeth—language that commonly refers to eternal judgment (cf. 8:12; 13:42, 50; 24:51; 25:26, 30).[325]

For many are invited (22:14). This pithy statement gives a concluding pronouncement to the parable of the wedding feast, but also to the preceding parable. "Many" (*polloi*) without the article is a common Semitic universalizing expression, which is normally translated "everyone" or "all" (cf. 20:28). This is seen in the use of the Hebrew *rabbim* in Psalm 109:30, which the LXX translates with the Greek *pollōn*, indicating an inclusive reference for "all" in the congregation. The Hebrew parallel also occurs in the Qumran literature, especially in 1QS as a fixed inclusive title for "the many," whether all those in the Congregation (1QS 6:8–11) or all those who exercise jurisdiction as leaders in the Congregation (e.g., 1QS 6:1).[326] By the expression "many are invited," Jesus points to a universal invitation to the kingdom of heaven.

But few are chosen (22:14). The counterbalancing point in the second half of the saying emphasizes that not all those who are called are chosen. This does not specify the actual amount, but rather points to the divine perspective of the preceding parables. Those chosen are "the elect," which for Jesus is an alternative expression for his true disciples (cf. 11:27; 24:22, 24, 31). Israel and her leadership had been known as the "chosen," but even their privilege is lost through unresponsiveness to Jesus' invitation to the kingdom of heaven.

Tribute in the Kingdom: Paying Taxes to Caesar (22:15–22)

They sent their disciples to him (22:16). As the controversies continue to unfold between Jesus and Israel's religious leadership, the Pharisees send their disciples to entrap Jesus.[327] The "disciples" of the Pharisees are mentioned in the New Testament only here and in Mark 2:18. Josephus refers to John Hyrcanus, the Jewish Hasmonean high priest and prince, as a disciple of the Pharisees, indicating that he was an adherent of the sect's way of life and thinking. The disciples of the Pharisees are most likely those in training to become full initiates to their brotherhood and would be fully engaged in the Pharisaic commitment of the oral law and rigorous practice of their traditions.

The Herodians (22:16). The Herodians are noted only here, in the parallel (Mark 12:13), and in an earlier incident where they also join the Pharisees in an attempt to destroy Jesus (Mark 3:6).

COIN WITH A PORTRAIT OF CAESAR

This coin depicts Caesar Augustus.

The Herodians were supporters of the Herodian family—most immediately Herod Antipas, the Roman client tetrarch—and they were unhappy that he had not gained control over all of his father's former territory. Thus, the Herodians joined Antipas in an attempt to regain Judea, which Pilate now governed for Rome. Although the Herodians and the Pharisees were normally at odds on many political and religious issues, here they combine to combat the common threat to their respective power bases.

Teacher . . . we know you are a man of integrity (22:16). "Teacher" (*didaskalos*) is a title of respect, equivalent to the Hebrew title "rabbi." "Teacher" can be used generically (13:52; 23:8) or it can be used positively to refer to Jesus (10:24–25; 23:10; 26:18; cf. 8:19). In Matthew it is the normal title used when non-disciples approach Jesus.[328]

Is it right to pay taxes to Caesar or not? (22:17). Either answer Jesus might give could be used against him. At question was the legal requirement of paying taxes to Caesar, the family name of Julius Caesar, which had become a title for the Roman emperors who followed him. Currently, Tiberius Claudius Caesar Augustus was emperor of Rome.

The tax mentioned here was the *kēnsos* (Lat. *census*), which was either the annual head tax or one of the more general taxes, such as the poll-tax.[329] The people of Israel, indeed all of Rome's subjects, labored under heavy taxation that kept the empire operating. The Herods had long collected taxes in the name of Rome to support their own military ventures, building projects, and lavish lifestyles. The Herods paid a tribute to Rome directly, so they exacted heavier taxes to compensate. The prefect of Judea and Samaria collected the land and poll

The Roman Emperors Called "Caesar" During New Testament Times and Later

Caesar was the family name of Julius Caesar (assassinated in 44 B.C.), which became a title for the Roman emperors who followed him.[A-86]

Roman Emperor	New Testament Reference or Incident
Augustus (31 B.C.—A.D.14)	Birth of Jesus (Luke 2:1).
Tiberius (A.D. 14-37)	Jesus' public ministry; birth of the church (Luke 3:1; cf. Matt. 22:17, 21, par.; Luke 23:2).
Gaius (Caligula) (A.D. 37-41)	Not mentioned in the New Testament. Demanded worship of himself, ordered a statue of himself placed in the temple in Jerusalem, but died before carried out.
Claudius (A.D. 41-54)	Expelled Jews from Rome (Acts 17:7; 18:2; cf. 11:28).
Nero (A.D. 54-68)	First major persecution of Christians. Peter and Paul martyred. (Acts 25:8-12, 21; 28:18; Phil. 4:22)
Galba (A.D. 68)	
Otho (A.D. 69)	
Vitellius (A.D. 69)	Siege of Jerusalem (civil war in Rome).
Vespasian (A.D. 69-79)	Siege of Jerusalem (ended civil war in Rome).

taxes directly for Rome. The Jewish religious authorities exacted their own taxes for the temple and their other institutional expenses (cf. 17:24–27), so the people were seething at the exhausting taxation. Some estimate that a Jewish family paid approximately 49 percent of its annual income to these various taxes: 32 percent to the Romans (19 percent on crops; 13 percent on sales, income, and other taxes), 12 percent to Jewish taxes (8 percent on crops and 4 percent on temple and sacrifice taxes), and 5 percent on forced extractions from corrupt officials.[330]

Show me the coin used for paying the tax (22:19). The smallest silver coin of the day in circulation in Palestine was the denarius. It was the equivalent of a day's wage for an agricultural worker, so it was widely circulated and readily available in the pouches of those testing Jesus.

Whose portrait is this? And whose inscription? (22:20). On the obverse side of the silver denarius was a profile of the head of Tiberius Caesar, with the Latin inscription on the perimeter of the coin, "Tiberius Caesar, son of the divine Augustus." On the reverse of the coin was a picture of the seated Pax, the Roman goddess of peace, with the Latin inscription "High Priest." The coins were issued by Herod Antipas in Tiberius, his new capital on the Sea of Galilee named in honor of Tiberius Caesar, where Herod had established a mint.[331]

Give to Caesar what is Caesar's, and to God what is God's (22:21). Those who respond to the invitation to the kingdom of heaven will continue to have obligations to the governing authorities of this world, a fact that later New Testament writers emphasize while living under oppressive authorities (Rom. 13:1–7; 1 Peter 2:13–17). God as Creator has sovereign right over all creation and everything in it, however, which implies that even what belongs to Caesar is only his in a secondary way. Allegiance to God takes precedence over allegiance to Caesar, especially when Caesar attempts to usurp allegiance to God's will (cf. Acts 4:19; 5:29). Jesus may have implied further that while the "image" (*eikōn*) of Caesar was stamped on coins, humans bear the image of God from creation (Gen. 1:26–27), and therefore God has claim on all that any person has or is.

Marriage at the Resurrection (22:23–33)

The Sadducees, who say there is no resurrection (22:23). The Sadducees (see "Pharisees and Sadducees" at 3:7) did not believe in the resurrection since they drew only on the Pentateuch for doctrine. Resurrection as a doctrine is developed more clearly in the latter books of the Old Testament (Isa. 26:19; Dan. 12:2). It occurred regularly in Jewish literature[332] and became a central belief in later rabbinic thought[333] (see "The Resurrection of the Dead in Judaism and in Jesus" at 28:6–8).

Moses told us that if a man dies without having children, his brother must marry the widow and have children for him (22:24). The Sadducees cite the Old Testament law of "levirite marriage," in which the "levir," the surviving brother of a childless, deceased man, was required to marry his sister-in-law (also called the "rite of removing the shoe"). The law was designed to provide care for the widow as well as an attempt to preserve the deceased brother's genealogical line if they should bear children (Deut. 25:5–10).

At the resurrection people will neither marry nor be given in marriage (22:30). Jesus accuses the Sadducees of developing faulty doctrine, such as denying the resurrection, because "you do not know the Scriptures or the power of God" (22:29). They should recognize that the rest of the Old Testament is also truly Scripture, where the doctrine of resurrection is clearer. He also chides them for denying the reality of the resurrection, because what lies behind any thought of resurrection is the power of God to do so.

They will be like the angels in heaven (22:30). Jesus draws a parallel to angels to note that resurrected humans will not continue the practice of marriage. This line of argumentation holds a double edge, since the Sadducees also denied the existence of angels (cf. Acts 23:8).

He is not the God of the dead but of the living (22:32). Drawing on the present tense in Exodus 3:6, "I *am* the God of Abraham, the God of Isaac, and the God of Jacob" (LXX, *eimi*, "I am"), Jesus states that the logical implication is that even though the patriarchs died physically, they were still alive at the writing of the book of Exodus, since God continues in a relationship with them as their God, which could not be sustained with them if they were dead. If they were still alive, and if the rest of Scripture points to resurrection, the Sadducees should believe the power of God to raise them to enjoy his continued purposes for humanity.[334]

The Greatest Commandment (22:34–40)

One of them, an expert in the law, tested him (22:35). This "expert in the law" (*nomikos*), another expression for the scribe of the Pharisees, also "tests" Jesus (*peirazō*; cf. 22:18). But Mark tells us that at the end of the interchange Jesus commends him (Mark 12:34), which may indicate that he approaches Jesus with more sincerity than the previous questioners.

Love the Lord your God with all your heart and with all your soul and with all your mind (22:37). The twice-daily repeated Shema was well-known as an overarching obligation of each individual Jew, which included the duty of obedience to the other commandments given by God (see the similar logic in 5:16–20). Love for God was not understood as simply emotion, but as the entire person—heart, soul, and mind—given over to God.

The second is like it: "Love your neighbor as yourself" (22:39). The venerable Rabbi Akibah declared Leviticus 19:18 to be a "great principle in the Torah" (*Gen. Rab.* 24:7), an opinion that was likely expressed also in Jesus' day, with which this expert in the law would be familiar. "Love" indicates a concrete responsibility, the act of being useful and beneficial to God and to one's neighbors, both Jew and Gentile (cf. Lev. 19:18, 34).[335] In this light, these commandments are similar to the responsibility of the Golden Rule, which Jesus said is a summary of the Law and the Prophets (7:12).

The Son of David (22:41–46)

The Christ . . .whose son is he? (22:42). This must have seemed like a simple question to the Pharisees. The automatic reply is that the Messiah is the Son of David, based on common knowledge that the prophesied Messiah was from the line of David.[336] This is confirmed by common practice, with the recurring declarations of Jesus' messianic identity as "Son of David."[337]

If then David calls him "Lord," how can he be his son? (22:45). Jesus takes the Pharisees to Psalm 110:1, the most quoted Old Testament passage in the New Testament, which they recognized as a messianic prophecy by David under the inspiration of the Holy Spirit. David refers to the coming messianic ruler, his son, as *kyrios*, "lord." The LXX has *kyrios* in both instances of the word "Lord." The underlying Hebrew has *Yahweh* for the first and *Adon* for the second occurrence of "Lord." Jews would not read the term *Yahweh*, but instead would substitute *Adonai* when they read it, thus making Psalm 110:1 read, "The *Adonai* says to my *Adon*. . . ."[338] Familial respect would not expect an older person, such as David, to refer to his offspring as "lord"; rather the offspring, "son," would refer to David, his "father," as "lord." The coming Messiah is not just his descendant, but his "Lord."

REFLECTIONS

IF JESUS IS TRULY WHO HE DECLARES himself to be, then we have a most unique message to proclaim. Jesus is unlike any figure ever to walk the earth, because he claims not to be simply a messenger of God, but the unique Son of God. The religious leaders' silence (22:46) is outspoken testimony that the straightforward implication of the text cannot be avoided. Their silence is also outspoken testimony of their own hypocritical avoidance of the implications for themselves. They should acknowledge Jesus as their own Lord and Messiah. But ultimately, none of us, Christian or non-Christian, can ignore the implications of Jesus for our personal lives.

Judgment on the Teachers of the Law and Pharisees (23:1–12)

The series of "woes" Jesus pronounces on the religious leadership of Israel follow closely from the preceding parables and debates that have revealed the culpability of these Jewish authorities for not leading the nation in repentance with the arrival of the kingdom of heaven.

So you must obey them and do everything they tell you (23:3). Jesus' statement follows from the religious leaders' position as expounders of Moses' teaching (23:1). He gives a scathing denunciation of the teachers of the law and the Pharisees, yet he recognized their official capacity when exercised in the proper manner.

They tie up heavy loads and put them on men's shoulders (23:4). "Heavy loads" denotes the rabbinic oral tradition that was a distinctive feature of the Pharisaic branch of Judaism. It was intended as a means of making the Old Testament relevant to life situations where it seemed irrelevant, such as the complex sacrificial system in life contexts removed from the temple, both in time and in locale (for more on this, see "The Tradition of the Elders" at 15:2). Since the oral law was considered to be of divine origin, its massive obligations became far more burdensome than Scripture itself, and with the passing of years and the addition of more and more prescriptions, the rabbis could not lessen the burden without overthrowing the whole system.

They make their phylacteries wide (23:5). Phylacteries (only here in the New Testament) or *tefillin* (from the Heb. *tefillah*, "prayer") are small leather cubical cases containing passages of Scripture written on parchment. They were worn as an attempt to obey literally the Old Testament admonition, "Fix these words of mine in your hearts and minds; tie them as symbols on your hands and bind them on your foreheads" (Deut. 11:18; cf. Ex. 13:9, 13; Deut. 6:8). The phylacteries were fastened to the left arm and forehead and worn by adult males in the morning service.

Tassels on their garments long (23:5). On the four corners of a garment worn by men were attached "tassels" (*kraspeda*) that had a blue cord, conforming to the

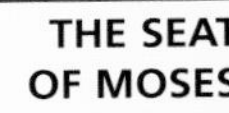

THE SEAT OF MOSES

(left) From the synagogue at Chorazin.

(right) From the synagogue on the island of Delos.

The Seat of Moses

Jesus' allusion to the "seat [*kathedra*] of Moses" in Matthew 23:2 is the earliest known reference to this expression.[A-87] A later Jewish midrash (c. 5th to 6th century) also refers to a "seat of Moses" (*Pesiqta de-Rab Kahana* 1:7). Other references in rabbinic literature speak more generally of a synagogue chair on which an esteemed rabbi sits when teaching (e.g., "R. Huna in the name of R. Yose said: 'Everywhere that this Jerusalemite goes they offer him a cathedra and they seat him on it so that they can listen to his wisdom'"; *t. Sukkah* 4:6).

This "seat" was often viewed as a figurative expression, referring to the authority of Moses. However, recent archaeological evidence points to a literal chair found in early synagogues. A magnificent marble chair was excavated in a synagogue dating to as early as the first century B.C. on the Aegean island of Delos. A stone chair was found attached to the synagogue structure at Dura Europas in western Syria (c. 3d cent. A.D.). Stone chairs, dating to the third or fourth centuries A.D. have been found at excavations of synagogues in Palestine, at Hammat Tiberias, Chorazim, and En Gedi.

The purpose of the seat has been debated. Some view it as the place where the Torah scroll was placed after being read. Most scholars, however, view it as the seat for a leader in the synagogue, although the role of that leader is questioned. Some suggest it was the place from which the ruler of the synagogue presided, others suggest it was the place from which the person interpreting would sit after reading a portion of Scripture, while still others suggest that it was a place where an honored guest or speaker would sit.[A-88] Jesus' statement confirms the use of the "seat of Moses" as a place from which experts in the law would teach.

Phylacteries at Qumran

Two intact phylactery cases of leather and parts of others were found in Qumran Cave 1 (1Q). One type was about two centimeters long (approximately one inch), with four small inner compartments for holding four tiny scrolls on which would have been written in tiny script, Exodus 13:9, 16; Deuteronomy 6:8; 11:18, respectively. This type was worn on the forehead. The second type of phylactery discovered measured nine by seven millimeters (approximately 1/3 inch) and had only one compartment formed of a single piece of leather folded in half to contain a single minute scroll with all four verses. This type was worn on the left arm.[A-89]

The rabbis had regulations about wearing phylacteries because of the temptation to wear them too large or inappropriately to draw attention to one's piety: "If a man made his phylacteries round, it is a danger and is no fulfilling of the commandment. If he put them on his forehead [too low down] or on the palm of his hand [instead of above the inside of the elbow], this is the way of heresy. If he overlaid them with gold or put them over his sleeve [to make conspicuous], this is the way of the sectaries" (*m. Meg.* 4:8).

admonitions of Numbers 15:37–42 (*ṣîṣît*; LXX *kraspeda*) and Deuteronomy 22:12 (*gedilîm*; LXX *kraspeda*). Tassels were to be a reminder to obey God's commandment and to be holy to God (Num. 15:40). Jesus himself wore these tassels on his garment (Matt. 9:20; 14:36), although the term in these contexts could refer to the outer fringe (decorated or plain) of the garment. Jesus chides these religious leaders for extending the tassels as a display of their piety, another way to try to gain the admiration of the people.

They love the place of honor at banquets (23:6). Seating at special occasions such as banquets required that the most honored guests were on either side of the host. The other guests were seated in descending order of importance.[339]

The most important seats in the synagogues (23:6). Seating in the synagogue varied from location to location, with some synagogues having stone benches along one, two, three or four of the walls, with removable benches or mats brought in for the majority of the congregation. There is ample evidence that the elders and other synagogue leaders, including the *ḥazzan* (the synagogue administrator), had places of prominence. A later rabbinic passage may be representative: "How did the elders sit? Facing the congregation and with their backs to the holy [i.e., Jerusalem and the temple] . . . the *ḥazzan* of the synagogue faces the holy and the entire congregation faces the holy" (e.g., *t. Meg.* 3:21). Benches or chairs may have been reserved on special occasions for important personages, and if a regular part of each synagogue, the seat of Moses (Matt. 23:2) was reserved for the one expounding on Scripture.[340]

They love to be greeted in the marketplaces and to have men call them "Rabbi" (23:7). The rabbi was generally a master of the Torah, and the title was used most frequently to refer to the head of a rabbinical school (*bet midrash*), such as the leader of the school of Shammai or Hillel. Association with these schools tended to set a person aside somewhat from the populace. The school was a holy community, and the people regarded the members with great deference.[341] The rabbinic tradition indicates that these academic institutions were distinguished from the synagogue, with the academy a place to promote Torah study and the synagogue a place to promote prayer (e.g., *b. Meg.* 27a).[342]

But you are not to be called "Rabbi," for you have only one Master and you are all brothers (23:8). The ultimate goal of a disciple of a rabbi was to become a rabbi himself at the end of his course of study and initiation. Later rabbinic literature is insightful to the aspirations of students, who would traverse the levels from the basic "disciple" (*talmîd*), to "distinguished student" (*talmîd watîq*), to "disciple associate" (*talmîd hābēr*), to "disciple of the wise" (*talmîd ḥākām*). At the later stages a disciple became a rabbi himself, the ultimate goal being to become a master of Torah with disciples studying under him.[343] With Jesus a new form of discipleship emerged. A disciple of his would always and forever be only a disciple, because Jesus alone is Teacher (*didaskalos*; "Master" is better for 23:10, where *kathēgētēs* occurs; see comments).

Do not call anyone on earth "father" (23:9). "Fathers" is a term used to refer to esteemed patriarchs, such as in the Mishnah tractate *Pirqe ʾAbot*, the "Sayings or Chapters of the Fathers." *ʾAbba* was used regularly in rabbinic sources as a title for esteemed scholars and rabbis, such as Rabbi Abba Arikha (cf. *b. Ketub.* 8a; *t. Beṣah* 1:7).[344] The expression "father of the synagogue" (*patēr synagōgēs*) was used in rabbinic times of an individual holding a place of honor and leadership within the synagogue affairs generally. This continuation of the use of the term "father" as a title of honor, respect, and authority had deep roots in ancient Judaism, including its use by Elisha to cry to Elijah who was ascending to heaven (2 Kings 2:12; 6:21), its reference to the Maccabean martyr Razis as "father of his people" (2 Macc. 14:37), and its later use to denote the head of a rabbinic court (*'ab bet din*).[345]

You have one Father, and he is in heaven (23:9). The motif of the heavenly "Father," occurring throughout the Old Testament,[346] grew increasingly popular during the Second Temple period in prayers for protection and forgiveness.[347] Jesus brought his disciples into a unique relationship with God as Father, since he is the unique Son of God and they are his brothers and sisters (cf. 6:9; 12:48–50).

Nor are you to be called "teacher," for you have one Teacher, the Christ (23:10). Matthew uses a word found only here in the New Testament to describe the third title that Jesus' disciples are to avoid. The word is *kathēgētēs*, which is a near synonym for *didaskalos* (23:8), but it carries an additional sense of "leader" (NASB). Some have suggested that Jesus may have originally used the term *môreh*, "guide," which was used to refer to the Teacher of Righteousness at Qumran,[348] although a direct allusion by Jesus to the sect is unlikely.[349] The term *kathēgētēs* does not occur in the LXX, but does occur in Greek literature to designate a teacher, especially a private tutor.[350] Since Jesus seems to be alluding to various titles that one might take, perhaps a better rendering might be "master."[351] Jesus' disciples are not to seek out personal authority as "master" over other disciples, because as "the Christ," Jesus alone is Master.

The Seven Woes (23:13–36)

Woe to you, teachers of the law and Pharisees, you hypocrites! (23:13). Now begin a series of seven woes on the religious leaders, which flesh out the condemnation Jesus has directed to them throughout his ministry. The first "woe" establishes the strong language, "Woe to you" that is reminiscent of Old Testament prophetic series of pronouncements of judgment.[352]

You travel over land and sea to win a single convert (23:15). In the second woe, Jesus addresses the extent of Jewish activity of making proselytes. Jewish history records an active propaganda that was directed toward gaining proselytes, because some of the rabbis declared that this was actually the divine purpose for the dispersion of the Jewish people (cf. *b. Pesaḥ.* 87b).[353] Josephus indicates that immediately before and after the destruction of the Second Temple many proselytes were made both among the masses and the upper classes in the Gentile cities surrounding Israel. He states that the men of Damascus set out to kill the Jews among them, because their own wives "had all become converts to the Jewish religion."[354] Josephus also tells of Queen Helena and her son King Izates of Adiabene (possibly a region on the Armenian border east of the sources of the Tigris River), who were converted independently to Judaism.[355]

Some advocate that the extant evidence does not indicate that Judaism was a proselytizing religion.[356] Others, however, while recognizing that Judaism never had professional missionaries, counter that the evidence in Josephus and the strong Gentile criticism of conversions to Judaism[357] suggest that common Jews zealous for their faith carried out an active attempt at bringing Gentiles to their faith through their everyday occupations and lifestyles.[358]

You make him twice as much a son of hell as you are (23:15). Jesus criticizes the way in which the Pharisees, zealous to win people (whether pagan Gentiles or "God-fearers") to their ways succeed only in placing them under their particular burdensome code of conduct in the oral law (cf. 23:4). On "son of hell" (lit., "child of Gehenna"), see comments on 5:22.

If anyone swears by the temple (23:16). The Pharisees developed a complicated

REFLECTIONS

THREE TIMES IN 23:8–10 JESUS GIVES AN ADMONITION to his disciples that they are not to be called by a certain title. The warning is not so simple as to suggest that titles are always inappropriate. No, the warning is directed against three issues that can stifle our discipleship to Jesus.

- *Rabbi* (23:8)—In our desire to teach and provide others with insight into the Word of God, we should be careful to avoid *academic arrogance*. We should never seek to supplant Jesus as the Teacher who will guide his disciples into all truth through the Spirit-guided Word of God (cf. John 16:13–14).
- *Father* (23:9)—In our desire to protect and nurture others, we should be careful to avoid *religious elitism*. All Jesus' disciples are his brothers and sisters, and we should never elevate ourselves to where we supplant our heavenly Father.
- *Master* (23:10)—In our desire to guide and lead others into the fullness of discipleship, we should be careful to avoid *authoritarian dominance*. Jesus is the Master, the one with all authority, the Lord and Head of the church.

series of rulings regarding vows and oaths (see comments on 15:5). The Pharisees distinguished between oaths made "by the temple" and those made "by the gold of the temple," and oaths made "by the altar" and those made "by the gift on it" (23:18). A person who lives in moment-by-moment accountability to the presence of the living God will need only to give a simple "yes" or "no" as a binding oath (cf. 5:23, 34–37).

You give a tenth of your spices—mint, dill and cummin (23:23). The Mosaic law specified that a tenth of all that one had was to be given to the Lord for the ongoing work of God through the Levites and the priests.[359] The Pharisees were so scrupulous about attending to this requirement that they measured out the smallest of crops—such as the spices mint, dill (cf. *b. ʿAbod. Zar.* 7b), and cummin (cf. *Demai* 2:1)—and paid a tenth out of these.

You blind guides! You strain out a gnat but swallow a camel (23:24). With sardonic humor Jesus shows through what may have been a well-known proverbial saying that the Pharisees and teachers of the law have indeed overlooked the obviously important issues while focusing on minute regulations. The law declared that many winged creatures were unclean (Lev. 11:23, 41), which the rabbis applied by straining wine to keep out small insects that made wine unclean (cf. *m. Šabb.* 20:2; *b. Ḥul.* 67a). While attending to the minutia of legal matters, they overlooked the largest land animal in Palestine, the camel, which was also ceremonially unclean (Lev. 11:4).

You are like whitewashed tombs (23:27). The term for tomb (*taphos*) probably indicates a burial ground rather than an individual monument or coffin. It was the custom to mark tombs with white chalk to make them publicly conspicuous so that passersby unfamiliar with the terrain would not come in contact with a tomb and so be rendered unclean for seven days (Num. 19:16; cf. Luke 11:44). This whitewashing practice was especially carried out in Jerusalem on the 15th of Adar, lest those pilgrims who

right ▶

WHITEWASHED TOMB

A tomb with ossuaries on the grounds of the Dominus Flevit chapel.

▶

CUPS AND DISHES

Pottery excavated east of Jerusalem at the Monastery of St. Martyrius.

made the trek to the holy land inadvertently walked over tombs and so incurred pollution before the Passover (cf. John 11:55; 18:28).[360]

You build tombs for the prophets and decorate the graves of the righteous (23:29). Matthew alternates here between the "tombs" (*taphoi*) of the prophets and the "graves" (*mnēmeia*) of the righteous. This may indicate a difference between these two terms, the former indicating "burial grounds" for prophets, the latter indicating "monuments" (RSV) adorned for "righteous" religious leaders. The "prophets" and the "righteous" are linked elsewhere (10:41; 13:17), indicating Old Testament prophets and others renowned for their righteous lives lived out before God. During the second century B.C., Simon Macabbee built an elaborate memorial in Modin for his family that was well-known for its uniqueness (1 Macc. 13:27–30). In the first century A.D., burial customs underwent a transformation. Secondary burials were commonly practiced, in which a person's decomposed bones were removed from a burial tomb and placed in ossuaries (cf. comments on 27:57–61). Funerary art became rich and varied, with widespread ornamentation of tomb facades, ossuaries, and sarcophagi, as well as wall paintings and graffiti.[361] The well-known tombs of esteemed figures from Israel's history (cf. Acts 2:29) benefited from this development of funerary beautification.

Final Invective and Lament Over Jerusalem (23:33–36)

You snakes! You brood of vipers! (23:33). The wording is reminiscent of John the Baptist's pronouncement against the religious leaders earlier (see comments on 3:7), as well as Jesus' (see comments on 12:34). Snakes (*opheis*; only here in Matthew) and "brood of vipers" are virtually synonymous, thus heaping up the culpability of these religious leaders.

Some of them you will kill and crucify (23:34). The Jewish leaders could not take on capital punishment without support from the Roman occupying forces, so with their backing they were able to unfurl their wrath first on Stephen (Acts 7:54–60). Crucifixion of Christians would have been at the hands of the Romans but likely instigated by jealous Jewish officials.

From the blood of righteous Abel to the blood of Zechariah son of Berekiah (23:35). The first righteous person in human history to be killed was Abel, slain by his brother Cain in an act of unrighteous jealousy, whose innocent blood cried out from the ground (cf. Gen. 4:8–11). The last murder recorded in the Old Testament in the canonical order of the Hebrew Bible (Law, Prophets, Writings) was Zechariah, a son of the high priest (2 Chron. 24:20–22). The language there fits closely with Jesus' statement, because he was murdered in the courtyard of the temple. Like Abel, his death called for revenge from the Lord. Zechariah's death was either identified by a developing tradition with the prophet Zechariah,[362] or he was named in Chronicles from his grandfather rather than his father, a common practice (see comments on Matt. 1:1–16).[363]

O Jerusalem, Jerusalem (23:37). Jerusalem has stood for the leadership of the nation (cf. 2:3), but the lament now seems to include a reference to the whole nation of Israel for whom Jesus was deeply burdened.

AERIAL VIEW OF MODERN JERUSALEM

The temple mount is on the bottom left.

He is especially burdened in light of her coming judgment.

"Blessed is he who comes in the name of the Lord" (23:39). The Christological implications of Jesus' quotation of Psalm 118:26 are profound. The same words were cited in 21:9 at Jesus' entrance to Jerusalem, shouted by those identifying him as the messianic Son of David. Now as Jesus cites the same passage, he identifies himself with God, Israel's Savior, the Coming One, who will once again come to his people after a time of great judgment, when they will have no other choice but to acknowledge him as Lord, either in great joy or in great sorrow.

MOUNT OF OLIVES

A slope of the mount just below the Pater Noster church.

The Setting of the Olivet Discourse (24:1–3)

The series of "woes" Jesus has pronounced on the religious leadership of Israel stem from their culpability for not leading the nation in repentance with the arrival of the kingdom of heaven. The woes transition Jesus' attention to the events of judgment that will befall the nation with the destruction of the temple, but also beyond that to prepare them for the interval before his return in glory and triumph. This is the fifth and final major discourse in Matthew's Gospel.

His disciples came up to him to call his attention to its buildings (24:1). The rabbinic saying, "Whoever has not beheld Herod's building [i.e., the temple] has not seen anything beautiful in his life,"[364] attests to the magnificence of the temple as rebuilt by Herod the Great. Josephus likewise gushes,

> The exterior of the building wanted nothing that could astound either mind or eye. For, being covered on all sides with massive plates of gold, the sun was no sooner up than it radiated so fiery a flash that persons straining to look at it were compelled to avert their eyes, as from the solar rays. To approaching strangers it appeared from a distance like a snow-clad mountain; for all that was not overlaid with gold was of purest white.[365]

Not one stone here will be left on another (24:2). Herod the Great had ascended to power in 37 B.C. when he recaptured Jerusalem from the Hasmoneans and took over ruling for the Romans. He began the rebuilding of the temple in 20/19 B.C., and most of the major renovations were completed within a decade. However, additional details and ornamentation continued to be added to it up to the outbreak of the Jewish revolt in A.D. 66 (cf. John 2:20).[366] Now Jesus is giving a prophecy of its destruction, which will occur in A.D. 70!

The Birth Pains (24:4–14)

Many will come in my name, claiming, "I am the Christ" (24:5). Prophetic figures and messianic deliverers had long attempted to incite revolution against occupying forces in the Second Temple period, and they continued into the years after the foundation of the church. Simon Bar Kokhba ("son of a star") was so named by Rabbi Akiba, proclaiming him Messiah on the basis of the star from Jacob in Numbers 24:17. Later rabbis rejected this identification and referred to him as Bar Kosiba ("son of a lie"), a pejorative epithet reflecting the rabbinic rejection of him as Messiah.[367] Throughout the ages since Christ, many have attempted to claim messianic identity.

You will hear of wars and rumors of wars . . . but the end is still to come (24:6). The Old Testament linked wars, cosmic battles, famines, earthquakes, and other catastrophic events with the end of the age, as did the apocalyptic vision of *4 Ezra* 9:1–6. Note also the catastrophic events recorded in Revelation. But Jesus emphasizes that throughout this age these activities will be a regular and recurring part of the suffering of this life until the coming of Christ begins the redemption of all creation. The end is not near even though calamities may seem to indicate it is.

EARTHQUAKES

Ground deformation following a major quake

All these are the beginning of birth pains (24:8). "Birth pains" is a common metaphor from the Old Testament prophets to depict terrible human suffering generally,[368] but it also points to the suffering that Israel specifically will endure prior to her deliverance.[369] The imagery points to an expected time of suffering that would characterize the period prior to the messianic age.

Then you will be handed over to be persecuted and put to death (24:9). The disciples will be handed over to *thlipsis* ("persecution, distress, tribulation"), a word that occurs four times in Matthew, three of which are found in this chapter (13:21; 24:9, 21, 29). In 24:21, 29, *thlipsis* points to a specific future period of unparalleled "distress" (NIV) or "tribulation" (NASB); here, as in 13:21, the use of the term indicates a general kind of trouble or persecution.

He who stands firm to the end will be saved (24:13). The disciple who endures to the end, which points to the end of the persecution with the advent of the Parousia, or perhaps to the end of a person's life, will be saved. "Saved" does not speak of rescue from death, because many true disciples have experienced martyrdom, but to the full blessing and peace of salvation with Jesus' arrival.

This gospel of the kingdom will be preached in the whole world . . . then the end will come (24:14). Although the increase of events in 24:9–13 are some indication that the Parousia is near, the only explicit condition to be met is the proclamation of the gospel of the kingdom to all the nations. After this proclamation has occurred, the end will come.

The Abomination that Causes Desolation (24:15–28)

"The abomination that causes desolation," spoken of through the prophet Daniel (24:15). The prophecy in Daniel refers to a period of "seven," during which in the middle of the seven a ruler will set up "an abomination that causes desolation."[370] During the days of the Maccabees this expression was used to describe the sacrilege of Antiochus IV Epiphanes, the Seleucid king who decreed that an altar to Olympian Zeus and perhaps a statue of himself were to be erected in the temple on 15 Chislev, 167 B.C.: "They erected a desolating sacrilege on the altar of burnt offering. They also built altars in the surrounding towns of Judah."[371] Antiochus further decreed that the Sabbath and other festal observances were to be profaned, that circumcision was to be abolished, and that swine and other unclean animals were to be sacrificed in the temple (cf. 1 Macc. 1:41–50). This was one of the lowest points of Jewish history and was considered by many the primary focus of Daniel's prophecy.

But the Daniel references were also brought to mind in A.D. 26 when Pontius Pilate arrived as prefect in Judea and

right ▶

STANDARD OF THE 10TH ROMAN LEGION

This legion attacked and destroyed Jerusalem in the Jewish War (A.D. 70).

introduced to Jerusalem military standards bearing idolatrous symbols of the emperor.[372] Others believed Daniel's prophecy was about to be fulfilled when Emperor Gaius (Caligula) ordered a gigantic statue of himself be set up in the temple, although he was dissuaded by King Herod Agrippa I and died in A.D. 41 before the order could be carried out.[373]

Jesus now quotes Daniel directly to clarify that the fulfillment of the "abomination that causes desolation" is yet future.[374] Paul harks back to Jesus' and Daniel's prophecy as he gives his own prophetic statement of the Antichrist who is yet to come (2 Thess. 2:3–4), which prefigures the Antichrist (the first beast) who will be set up by the false prophet (the second beast) as a god in the temple (Rev. 13:11–18).

Let the reader understand (24:15). This phrase is an aside intended to get the reader of Matthew to see that in Jesus' words one will find the true fulfillment of Daniel's prophecy. With the onset of the abomination of desolation as spoken of by Daniel (Dan. 9:27), the period of "great tribulation" begins (Matt. 24:21). This desolating sacrilege is the predominant event of the period of tribulation, which corresponds to Daniel's period of "seven" (see previous comment). When we look closely at Daniel (esp. Dan. 9:25–27) and the events recorded in Revelation (see the 1,260 days, Rev. 12:6 = 3-1/2 years), this marks the second half of the seven years of tribulation, the time of "great tribulation." Apparently the first three and a half years is a time of relative peace and quiet.

Let those who are in Judea flee to the mountains (24:16). The Christian historian Eusebius reported that Jesus' warning to flee to the mountains was fulfilled during the Jewish revolt when Christians fled to Pella.[375] But Jesus' warning is more general, for mountains have always been a place of refuge for those beleaguered by invading armies; thus, they must find refuge there at this future time of great danger.

One on the roof (24:17). Likewise, there will not be time to gather provisions in the home. The flat rooftops on many homes in Israel were places to find a cool breeze in the evening and were considered part of the living quarters.

One in the field (24:18). The outer coat was an essential garment for traveling, often used as a blanket when sleeping outdoors, and only those in the greatest hurry would think of leaving it behind.

How dreadful it will be in those days for pregnant women and nursing mothers! (24:19). The danger of travel in this perilous time is greatest for those most at risk, especially pregnant mothers and their infants. Jesus describes their fate with a cry of "woe," emphasizing that those who are most vulnerable and who normally can rely on the help of others, may not find any help and thus will suffer the most.

Pray that your flight will not take place in winter or on the Sabbath (24:20). Flight in winter, when roads are washed out and rivers are swollen, presents even more difficulty for those fleeing the horrors of the coming desolation. In prayer the disciples must cling to God's presence and ever-ready help, even though they may have to disrupt even the most devoutly held religious traditions, such as the Jewish Sabbath.

Great distress, unequaled from the beginning of the world until now—and never to be equaled again (24:21). In his *Jewish War* 5–6, Josephus describes in great detail the horrors that fell on Jerusalem during the siege of A.D. 70. But the description here in Matthew indicates a time of tribulation that did not occur during the fall of Jerusalem. The horrors that fell on the Jewish people and on the entire world with the two World Wars of the twentieth century are a somber warning that the desolation that comes from humanity's unleashed depravity will yet be unequaled. The vision Jesus paints must yet be ahead (e.g., Rev. 7–19).

For the sake of the elect those days will be shortened (24:22). This is not a shortening of twenty-four hours, but rather is a proverbial way of indicating that God is in control even of these days of horror. If the wickedness of humanity and the wrath of God were allowed to run unchecked, there would be no end to the horror and no one would survive. This is a promise that the time of tribulation will not last indefinitely, because God is in control. The people of Israel are often referred to as "the elect" (e.g., Isa. 45:4; *1 En.* 1:1), but in the New Testament it refers to believing Christians (e.g., Rom. 11:7). In the time of future great tribulation, when Israel will once again be used of God for witness (e.g., Rev. 7:3–8) to bring in a multitude of believers from all the nations who worship God and the Lamb (7:9–12), the expression "the elect" includes all those who believe on Christ during this period (cf. Matt. 24:22, 24, 31).

If anyone tells you, "There he is, out in the desert," do not go out (24:26). The desert had messianic overtones for diverse groups within Israel, who associated the desert with God's forthcoming deliverance (e.g., Essenes of the Qumran community), and messianic pretenders often gathered their followers in the desert prior to their public appearance.[376] Josephus narrates the story of Simon, son of Gioras, who joined the brigands of Masada in the desert, but then withdrew to the hills of the desert where, "by proclaiming liberty for slaves and rewards for the free, he gathered around him the villains from every quarter." As his success and reputation grew, many other men of higher standing went to the desert to join him, "and his was no longer an army of mere serfs or brigands, but one including numerous citizen recruits, subservient to his command as to a king." Josephus calculates Simon's army at over 20,000 men.[377]

"Here he is, in the inner rooms," do not believe it (24:26). Josephus also recounts how John of Gischala, with an army of six thousand men, seized the temple during the Jewish rebellion, and how 2,400 Zealots joined him there in the inner quarters of the temple.[378]

Wherever there is a carcass, there the vultures will gather (24:28). The term *aetos* can be used to refer to an "eagle" (Rev. 4:7; 8:13), but where a carcass is mentioned, it is best to render it as "vultures" (NIV; contra RSV, KJV) since eagles do not gather as a group and do not normally feed on dead meat. This saying is proverbial, either quoted by Jesus or created by him to make a macabre point (cf. Luke 17:37; cf. Job 39:26–30). This saying either connects with the appearance of false messiahs and prophets or else illustrates the coming of the Son of Man.

Description of the Coming of the Son of Man (24:29–31)

Immediately after the distress of those days (24:29). Here "distress" (*thlipsis*) connects with 24:21 to point to a specific period of great tribulation, not with 24:9, where it is used to point to general distress. Once again, the mixture of prophecy referring to both the fall of Jerusalem and the end of the age must be acknowledged. Although the judgment that was to fall on Israel in A.D. 70 with the destruction of Jerusalem does seem to be in Jesus' mind (cf. 23:37–39; Luke 21:20–24), the primary emphasis must rest on the end of the age, when he will come as the Son of Man in great universal power.

"The sun will be darkened, and the moon will not give its light; the stars will fall from the sky, and the heavenly bodies will be shaken" (24:29). Jesus uses typical apocalyptic imagery as he alludes to passages such as Isaiah 13:10 and 34:4[379] to describe his coming with a mixture of literal and figurative language. God will cause the skies to be darkened and the heavenly bodies to be disturbed. Such language may point both to physical phenomena and to political and spiritual disruptions. The darkness at Jesus' crucifixion indicated that Jesus had conquered the forces of evil on the cross, and the darkness during the second coming of the Son of Man is an indication that he will now exert his rule over all forces, especially those of the demonic prince of the powers of the air.

The sign of the Son of Man will appear in the sky (24:30). Many have connected the "sign" with the "banner" that the Messiah will raise as he gathers the nations and Israel (Isa. 11:10–12; 18:3), or the type of "banners" noted in the War Scroll that the battle formations of the congregation at Qumran will raise at the final battle (cf. 1QM 3:13–4:17). However, since the rest of the verse points to the coming of the Son of Man himself as that which promotes mourning, the apparent reference to Daniel 7:13 ("one like the son of man") indicates that Christ himself is the sign of the eschatological consummation of the age (see Matt. 16:27; 26:64).

All the nations of the earth will mourn (24:30). This language would have held special meaning to a Jewish audience, since the prophecy of Zechariah 12:10 speaks of the people of Israel mourning when they look on the one whom they have pierced. The apostle John applies this prophecy to those Jews who mourned the crucifixion (John 19:37), and he quotes the prophecy at the beginning of his revelation of the end times (Rev. 1:7). Those events had great import for the people of Israel, and John uses the same term for "nations" (*phylē*) as he does to refer to each individual tribe of the twelve of Israel (Rev. 7:4–8).

The Son of Man coming on the clouds of the sky, with power and great glory (24:30). Jesus completes his self-identity

COMING OF THE SON OF MAN

The return of Christ will be accompanied by signs in the heavens.

through the use of the relatively ambiguous title "Son of Man" (see "Jesus as the 'Son of Man'" at 8:20). He is the Son of Man who displays humiliation with nowhere to lay his head (8:20), who experiences suffering as the Servant who gives his life for many (20:17–19, 28), and who is now revealed as the One who will come in glorious power as the majestic sovereign designated by the Ancient of Days to receive worship as the divine King of the kingdom of God (cf. Dan. 7:13–14).

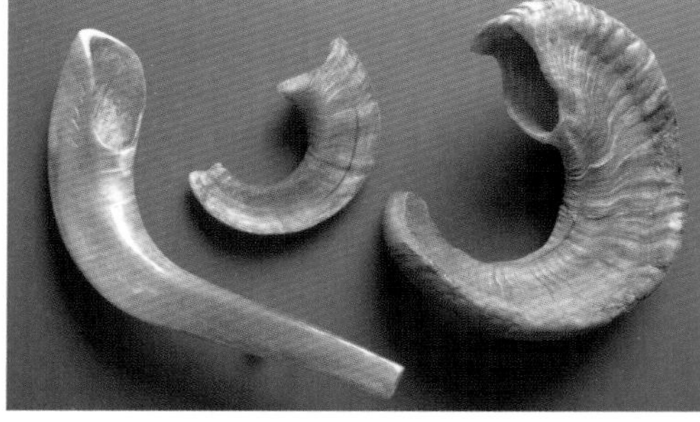

TRUMPETS

"Shofar" trumpets made from rams' horns.

He will send his angels with a loud trumpet call (24:31). Both banners and trumpets were associated in Jewish eschatological thought with the majestic arrival of the Messiah.[380]

They will gather his elect from the four winds, from one end of the heavens to the other (24:31). This gathering has been taken to refer to the four points of the compass (cf. Ezek 37:9; Dan. 8:8; 11:4) to indicate the gathering of all believers who are on the entire earth at the time. Others have taken the expression "from one end of the heavens to the other" to refer to Jesus' angels gathering and bringing with him all of the redeemed already in heaven to join living believers on the earth (cf. Rev. 19:11–16). It probably should include both, so that as Jesus returns, he both brings with him those who have died and are with him in heaven (e.g., 1 Thess. 4:14) and gathers those believers alive on the earth (e.g., 1 Thess. 4:17).

The Lesson of the Fig Tree (24:32–35)

Jesus now deals with attitudes that should characterize those who live during this age and await his coming. He gives several lessons in order to equip people during this age in preparation for the end: The first is the parabolic lesson from the fig tree.

As soon as its twigs get tender and its leaves come out (24:32). In the winter months figs lose their leaves, so even as the buds on a branch and new leaves in spring indicate that summer is near, so also when the events in the preceding context occur, the disciples are to be prepared for the coming of the Son of Man. Jesus stated in 24:1–8 that the general distressful events of this age must not be interpreted to mean that the Lord is near. However, as the end does grow nearer, subtle increases of difficulty begin to mark the end (24:9–14).

right FIG TREE

This generation will certainly not pass away until all these things have happened (24:34). The identity of "this generation" has vexed interpreters. Perhaps it is easiest to see a twofold reference, as Jesus has done throughout the discourse. The disciples to whom Jesus is speaking on the Mount of Olives is most naturally "this generation" who sees the events of the destruction of the temple, which shows the applicability of the discourse to A.D. 70. Yet within the context of Jesus' statements about the coming of the Son of Man at the end of the age, there must be primary applicability to those at the end of the age who see the events surrounding the abomination of desolation occurring. When these signs of the end of the age appear, those waiting for his arrival are to recognize that their redemption is drawing near (Luke 21:28). The generation that sees these things occurring will be the generation that sees the Lord appear.

The "Time" of Jesus' Coming (24:36–41)

No one knows about that day or hour, not even the angels in heaven (24:36). Now Jesus gives a direct answer to the question about the time of his coming: No one knows! The expression "day or hour" is used throughout Scripture to indicate a general reference to time (cf. 7:22; 10:19; 24:42, etc.). This includes not only a literal day or time of day, but also the year or month.

As it was in the days of Noah, so it will be at the coming of the Son of Man (24:37). The people in the days of Noah did not heed the warnings given. They continued to carry along their activities as normal. They were caught off-guard because they were so wrapped up in the everyday events of life that they had no concern for the warnings Noah had given about spiritual realities. By contrast, Noah and his family went about with preparations for the future deluge even though they saw no specific signs of its coming and did not know the time of its arrival until it came.

Two women will be grinding with a hand mill (24:41). For "hand mill" see comments on 18:6.

One will be taken and the other left (24:40, 41). The "taking" and "leaving" probably indicates that one is taken away to safety to enjoy the blessing of the arrival of the Son of Man (like Noah and his family in the ark) and the other is left to experience the wrath of the Son of Man (like those who died with the arrival of the Flood). This view has in its favor that it corresponds in some sense with the angels who gather the elect at the coming of the Son of Man (24:31) and seems to be more consistent with the following parables.

The Homeowner and the Thief (24:42–44)

Jesus has stressed the deep division between those who are prepared and those who are not. He now tells four parables that give variations on the theme, each teaching a particular point about how and why people should be prepared: the homeowner and the thief in the night (24:43–44), the good and wicked servant (24:45–51), the ten virgins (25:1–13), and the talents (25:14–30).

Keep watch, because you do not know on what day your Lord will come (24:42). "Watch" implies not only looking out, but also includes the active dimension of being prepared.

If the owner of the house had known at what time of night the thief was coming (24:43). Jesus used the image of a thief digging through to break in, in the Sermon on the Mount (see comments on 6:19–20). This parable is consistent with the roofing materials and clay walls of common homes.

He would have kept watch and would not have let his house be broken into (24:43). The responsibility for the safety of each home lay on the master of the house, since modern conceptions of police force were nonexistent. Some protection was provided by military forces for rulers and for the upper classes, but not for individual homes. If a homeowner knew that a thief was coming, he would do whatever was necessary to be prepared, whether that meant staying up all night, or patrolling each opening, or even enlisting the help of neighbors.

So you also must be ready, because the Son of Man will come at an hour when you do not expect him (24:44). The point of comparison between the thief and the Son of Man is the unexpectedness of his coming (cf. 1 Thess. 5:2; 2 Peter 3:10; Rev. 3:3; 16:15); it will be at an unknown hour. Thus, they are to watch all through the age because he can come at any time.

REFLECTIONS

ACTIONS REVEAL OUR NATURE. IN THE PARABLE OF the two servants, Jesus indicates that a person's faithfulness is the external evidence of whether or not he or she is truly one of Jesus' own. We should therefore examine ourselves to determine whether we are true believers, which will be evidenced by the way we think, the way we treat others, and our righteousness or unrighteousness. We must be careful not to imply that one can earn one's salvation by watchfulness or preparedness, but rather that a person who truly is a disciple of Jesus will watch and be prepared, because it is their good new nature to do so. The point for non-disciples is that they should not delay repenting too long, thinking they will have time. Rather, their own death or Jesus' return may find them to be unrepentant sinners.

The Two Servants (24:45–51)

Who then is the faithful and wise servant, whom the master has put in charge of the servants in his household? (24:45). The servant placed in a position of responsibility to oversee and care for other servants in the master's household was often called a "steward" (*oikonomos*), which is the term used in a similar parable in Luke 12:41–46. He was the chief servant, head over the master's household affairs and staff, and he was often responsible for caring for the master's personal affairs. The more responsibly the chief servant carried out those affairs, the more responsibility he was given.

He will cut him to pieces and assign him a place with the hypocrites, where there will be weeping and gnashing of teeth (24:51). The wickedness of the chief servant comes because the master's long absence allows him to abuse his authority, mistreat his fellow servants, and consort drunkenly with bad acquaintances—all activities characteristic of idolaters, pagans, and unbelievers.[381] When the master does return, the servant is caught unawares. He is therefore cut in pieces and given treatment that is proverbial for hell (cf. 8:12).

The Ten Virgins (25:1–13)

The kingdom of heaven will be like ten virgins who took their lamps and went out to meet the bridegroom (25:1). "Virgins" is *parthenoi*, the same term used of Mary, Jesus' mother, at the time when she was discovered to be with child (1:23). These ten virgins are bridesmaids,

◀ *left*

OIL LAMP

and the description of them as virgins emphasizes that they also have not yet married. Following typical Jewish marriage customs[382] (see also comments on 1:18), the groom left his parents' home with a contingent of friends to go to the home of his bride, where nuptial ceremonies were carried out. After this the entire wedding party formed a processional to a wedding banquet at the home of the bridegroom. The wedding feast was usually held at the house of the groom (22:1–10; John 2:9) and often at night (Matt. 22:13; 25:6), although sometimes the banquet was held at the home of the bride following the nuptial ceremonies. The Old Testament portrayed Yahweh as the "husband" of his people Israel,[383] which paves the way for Jesus as the messianic Son of Man to be pictured as a bridegroom (cf. 9:14–17).

The foolish ones said to the wise, "Give us some of your oil; our lamps are going out" (25:8). The word for lamp is *lampas*, different from the lamp in 5:15 (*lychnos*), which was used in a typical Palestinian home. Both lamps were similar in makeup, basically a clay basin filled with oil with a wick attached, but the *lampas* in 25:8 has more of the connotation of a torch. It was a larger dome-shaped container with rags soaked in the oil to light the way while a person was walking outside.[384] These outdoor torches could last for several hours when extra containers of oil were brought for replenishing the lamp (25:2), as the wise virgins had done.

The virgins who were ready went in with him to the wedding banquet. And the door was shut (25:10). The previous parable (24:50–51) and the following one (25:29–30) both speak of hell as the destiny for those who do not "watch" correctly by being properly "prepared" with salvation. Therefore, the shut door would appear to point to hell here as well, especially with the comment from the bridegroom: "I tell you the truth, I don't know you" (25:12), a stark, straightforward statement of rejection of a person who does not have a true relationship with Jesus (7:23). Throughout the Old Testament God is said to "know" those whom he has chosen to be his people (Jer. 1:5; Hos. 13:5; Amos 3:2), a theme reiterated throughout the New Testament to speak of a saving relationship found with God through Jesus Christ (cf. Gal. 4:8–9; 2 Tim. 2:19).

The Talents (25:14–30)

A man going on a journey . . . called his servants and entrusted his property to them (25:14). Wealthy landowners often entrusted their property and affairs to trustworthy servants (*doulos*, as in 24:45) when they went away on business or for personal dealings.

To one he gave five talents of money, to another two talents, and to another one talent (25:15). The landowner in the parable is portrayed as wealthy, for he has liquid disposability of eight talents. The exact monetary value is difficult to determine, because the *talanton* was not a coin but a unit of monetary reckoning. Silver was the most common precious metal available in Palestine, so a talent was usually of silver—which is confirmed here by the use of the term *argyrion* ("silver, silver coin") in 25:18. A silver talent weighed approximately seventy-five pounds and had a value of six thousand denarii. It therefore was worth approximately $247,200 (see chart at 18:24). Altogether, the landowner dispersed nearly two million dollars to the three servants. Comparisons are difficult to appreciate, however, because such a sum in first-century Palestine would have been far more disproportionate to the average worker than in modern times.

The man who had received the five talents . . . put his money to work and gained five more (25:16). The first and second servants "at once" made effective use of their entrusted amounts, probably setting up some kind of business and making a capital return on the original investment.

Well done, good and faithful servant! (25:21, 23). The identical statement of praise to both servants, even though they received different amounts of talents and earned different amounts, indicates that the point of the parable is not on amount earned, but on faithful responsibility in living up to one's potential and giftedness.

You wicked, lazy servant! (25:26). The wickedness of the third servant primarily stems from his attitude about his master, which in turn led to laziness and bad stewardship. The way he conceives of him ("you are a hard man") causes him to fear him and then to hide away the talent and not seek to advance the master's capital. The servant's misperception of the master produces alienation, mistrust, fear, and then personal sloth. Had he truly loved his master, he would not have attempted to place the blame on the master, but would have operated out of love.

You should have put my money on deposit with the bankers (25:27). The word "banker" comes from *trapeza* ("table"), most often used to refer to the money changer's table (cf. 21:12). The reference here is most likely to money changers who charged a fee for their services. Investment houses or banks as we know them, in the sense of an establishment for the safekeeping of private money or the granting of commercial credit, were basically nonexistent in Judaism. For safe-keeping a private person would either bury valuables (see 13:44; cf. Josh. 7:21) or entrust them with a neighbor (Ex. 22:7).

So that when I returned I would have received it back with interest (25:27). The Old Testament prohibited charging interest from other Jews,[385] but not from Gentiles (Deut. 23:20). While contemporary usage distinguishes interest from usury, which is a higher rate of interest charged for a loan than is allowed by law or common practice, ancient Judaism and later rabbinic practice made no such distinction and consistently avoided all appearance of charging interest from each other.[386] Jesus may be referring to the investment of the talent with money changers who performed a valuable service of exchanging a variety of forms of currency for those traveling through Palestine from the Diaspora. This is different from the money changers who were perverting temple practice (see comments on 21:12).

Judgment at the End (25:31–46)

Each of the preceding four parables included statements of judgment, but the emphasis has been on getting one's life prepared. Now the emphasis is squarely on the judgment of those who are excluded and on the reward for those who are admitted to the kingdom (25:34).

All the nations will be gathered before him (25:32). All the nations are gathered before the ruling Son of Man. This debated expression has been interpreted to mean the church, all humanity, and all unbelievers, among other things, but within the Matthean context it is most likely intended to mean both Jews and Gentiles, who throughout this age are the combined object of the Great Commission (see comments on 24:14; 28:18–20).

He will separate the people one from another as a shepherd separates the sheep from the goats (25:32). The nations as entities are not judged, but rather the people within them, who are separated one from another. The shepherd metaphor softens the judgment image, but does not diminish the foreboding consequences of separating the sheep from the goats. "Sheep" is a consistent image of God's people, whether the reference is specifically to Israel[387] or to Jesus' disciples.[388] Goats do not occur often in the New Testament,[389] but in the Old Testament seventy percent of the references concern their use as animals for sacrifice, such as the goat offered for sin sacrifice and the scapegoat, where in a symbolic way sin was removed from the community and sent to the region of desert or death (Lev. 16:8–10, 26).

In most areas of the world the problem of separating the sheep from the goats would never arise, since such flocks are unlikely to mix. But in the lands surrounding Palestine they often run together, and native breeds can look alike in size, color, and shape.[390] There does not appear to be any significant reason why the goat was selected to contrast with the sheep, except for the symbolism that will be attached to both in a surprising manner.

He will put the sheep on his right and the goats on his left (25:33). For the significance of the right hand side, see comments on 20:21. The left hand side is not typically a place of disfavor (cf. 20:21, 23), although the context signifies it to be so here.

The King will say to those on his right, "Come, you who are blessed by my Father; take your inheritance, the kingdom" (25:34). The King is understood to be the Son of Man sitting on the throne (25:31), bringing to mind Daniel 7:13–14, where the Son of Man receives the kingdom from the Ancient of Days. This is one of the rare times that Jesus refers to himself as King, although the theme

GOATS AND SHEEP

has been there throughout Matthew's Gospel. The King addresses the sheep on his right as "blessed by my Father." The blessing consists of their inheritance, which is the kingdom that they now receive, not because they have earned it through their own efforts, but because it is a gift of their relationship with the Father and the Son.

I was hungry and you gave me something to eat (25:35). The explanation for why the sheep receive the inheritance of the kingdom is that they cared for Jesus when he was hungry, thirsty, a stranger, naked, sick, or imprisoned. The precedent is found in those Old Testament admonitions where God rejects Israel's external displays of religiosity (e.g., fasting) as a sham and declares that true righteousness is displayed in caring for the needy (e.g., Isa. 58:6–10).

Whatever you did for one of the least of these brothers of mine, you did for me (25:40). Solving the question of the identification of these "brothers" is important, and four primary solutions have been offered: all needy persons in humanity, all Christians, Jewish Christians, Christian missionaries. The use of "brothers" by Jesus in Matthew's narrative to refer to his disciples is the most convincing argument, suggesting that Jesus is referring to his disciples. But the expression "least of these my brothers" points to needy disciples. This helps make some distinction from the sheep (disciples generally), to emphasize that needy disciples are often the ones excluded from care, while attention is given to prominent members of the discipleship community.

Then they will go away to eternal punishment, but the righteous to eternal life (25:46). Daniel's prophecy of a future time of great tribulation that will come on the earth leads to a prophecy of eternal life and punishment: "Multitudes who sleep in the dust of the earth will awake: some to everlasting life, others to shame and everlasting contempt. Those who are wise will shine like the brightness of the heavens, and those who lead many to righteousness, like the stars for ever and ever" (Dan. 12:2–3; cf. *2 Bar.* 51:5–6). Daniel's prophecy is echoed here in the final words of Jesus' discourse. As has been the emphasis throughout this discourse and ultimately throughout this Gospel, there are only two types of people: Those who have not followed Jesus are actually against him and will endure separation from him in their eternal punishment, while his disciples are with him and will enjoy with him life that is eternal.

REFLECTIONS

THOSE ON JESUS' LEFT ARE AS surprised as the others. The five foolish virgins and the wicked servant who did not invest his talent in the preceding parables (25:1–30) were condemned to eternal punishment, not for some externally heinous sin but for their failure to do the right thing. Here too "sins of omission" are also worthy of eternal damnation because they are an evidence that a person has not been made righteous by the work of the Spirit. Righteous acts spring from a heart made righteous by the Spirit of God, while unrighteous acts, even of omission, indicate a heart lacking in the Spirit's work of transformation (cf. 15:19; Titus 3:1–8).

Jesus' Prediction and The Plot of the Religious Leaders (26:1–5)

The Passover is two days away (26:2). The Passover Feast was celebrated annually to commemorate Israel's escape from Egypt under Moses' leadership (Ex. 12). The month of Passover (Abib/Nisan) was to be the first month of the religious year for the Israelites (12:2), which corresponds to the current calendar of late March to the beginning of April (Neh. 2:1). The Passover lamb was selected on the tenth day of the month and sacrificed at twilight on the fourteenth day. "Twilight" was interpreted by the Pharisees to be between the decline of the sun (3:00–5:00 P.M.) and sunset.[391] By New Testament times the custom moved the time up so that the Levites could help the large crowds assembled at the temple with their sacrifices. After dark (Nisan 15) the Passover meal itself was eaten (Ex. 12:2–11), which commenced the seven-day Feast of Unleavened Bread.[392]

The NIV rightly follows the traditional order of the events, with the conclusion of the Olivet Discourse (26:1) and the plot to arrest Jesus (26:3–5) on late Tuesday afternoon, two days before the Passover. Jesus is pointing ahead to Thursday evening at sundown when he and the disciples will celebrate the Passover together, at which he initiates the "Lord's Supper."

The chief priests and the elders of the people (26:3). The chief priests and elders (cf. 21:23; 26:47; 27:1) are probably representatives of the Sanhedrin, the ruling body in Jerusalem, but not here the full assembly (see comments on 26:59).[393]

Assembled in the palace of the high priest, whose name was Caiaphas (26:3). The "palace" (Gk. *aulē*, "courtyard") in

SITE OF THE HOME OF CAIAPHAS?

Some traditions suggest this location north of the church of Dormition on Mount Zion as the site of Caiaphas's home.

The High Priest, Caiaphas

Caiaphas was appointed high priest in A.D. 18 by the Roman prefect Valerius Gratus, Pontius Pilate's predecessor.[A-90] He maintained the office until he was deposed in A.D. 36 by Vitellius, the Roman consular legate of Syria.[A-91] Because the Roman governor appointed and deposed the high priest, he made the office into a political office, which apparently Caiaphas knew how to manipulate well. He reigned as high priest for around eighteen years, whereas from the time he was deposed until the destruction of the temple in A.D. 70, Josephus counts no less than twenty-five high priests appointed and removed from office.[A-92] This points to the close cooperation between Caiaphas and the Roman government, especially at that time with the Roman prefect, Pontius Pilate. Because the high priest's office had been more of a political office than a place of religious leadership ever since the Hasmonean period, the reputation of the office was ruined (cf. the Dead Sea Scrolls in their criticism of the high priestly leadership, which they subsumed early under the title "Wicked Priest," declaring that the judgment of God would fall on the priesthood for plundering the people of Israel[A-93]).

this context must mean the private home of the high priest (see 27:56), Caiaphas, whom Josephus calls "Joseph surnamed Caiaphas."[394] "Caiaphas" is probably a family nickname that was passed on from generation to generation and may derive from a word meaning "basket" or "wooden rod." The original family patriarch who introduced the name may have been a basketmaker, a person who used pack-animals to move goods, or a person who worked in the vineyard business.

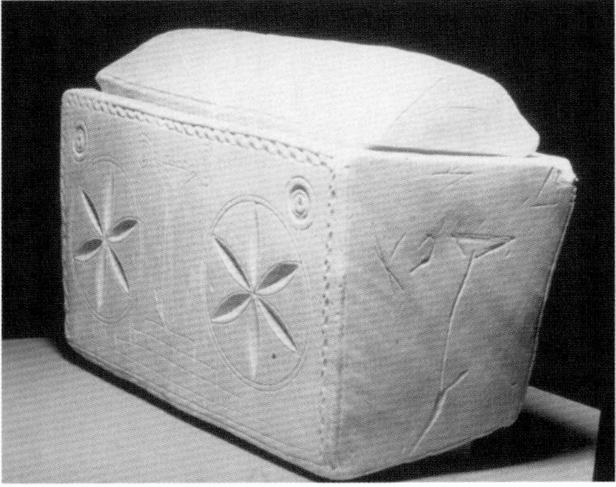

OSSUARY OF CAIAPHAS

Not during the Feast . . . or there may be a riot among the people (26:5). Popular uprisings were increasingly common in first-century Palestine as the people grew weary under the oppression of the Romans and the duplicity of their own religious leaders. These religious leaders may well have remembered the uprising in the temple at Passover after the death of Herod the Great in 4 B.C. His son Archelaus quickly displayed the same

The Ossuary of Caiaphas

In November 1990, while constructing a children's recreational water park in Jerusalem's Peace Park, workmen using bulldozers unearthed an ancient burial cave. When Israeli archaeologists arrived, they found a dozen ossuaries or burial bone boxes. The most elaborate ossuary had an exquisitely decorated façade featuring two large circles, each composed of five rosettes surrounding a center rosette. The sides and top were framed with stylized branches. On the back and on one side were slightly varied inscriptions that read, "Yehosef bar Qafa" ("Joseph son of Caiaphas"). Excavators discovered the bones of six different people inside the ossuary, which were determined to be the bones of two infants, a child between two and five years, a boy between thirteen and eighteen years, an adult woman, and a man about sixty years old. The remains of the man very well could be those of the high priest Caiaphas, who directed the Sanhedrin's trial of Jesus. The tomb therefore was determined to be the burial cave of Caiaphas's family or clan, typical of tombs that were reserved for temple aristocracy, landed gentry, and wealthy merchants. This is a remarkable find, because, as Jewish scholar David Flusser remarks, "Caiaphas is the most prominent Jewish personality of the Second Temple period whose ossuary and remains have been discovered."[A-94]

The Jews for about a hundred years ending in A.D. 70 had developed a practice chiefly in Jerusalem of regathering from a burial chamber the bones of a decayed corpse and placing them with the bones of family members in a depository called an ossuary, a small, rectangular coffin-like box made of a single block of limestone (approx. two feet long, one foot wide, and a little more than one foot high). The ossuary lids varied, some flat, others triangular (gabled) or curved (vaulted). The ossuaries were often decorated with geometric designs; many were inscribed with graffiti-like inscriptions to commemorate and preserve the deceased.[A-95]

This discovery gives remarkable insight into burial practices of the Jewish aristocracy and offers an electrifying archaeological link to real-life persons involved in the events of Jesus' final days before going to the cross.

kind of cruelty that had marked his father when he sent in troops and cavalry who killed about three thousand pilgrims who had taken part in the riots.[395]

Jesus Anointed at Bethany (26:6–13)

Matthew (and Mark 14:3–9) recounts the story of Jesus' anointing thematically, placing it in the context of the conspiracy to arrest Jesus, whereas John (12:1–8) narrates the story chronologically, showing that it occurred on the Saturday night before the triumphal entry into Jerusalem. This sort of thematic arrangement is typical of Matthew's style (see comments on 8:1ff).

In the home of a man known as Simon the Leper (26:6). On Saturday evening, just after the end of the Sabbath at sunset, Jesus and the disciples attend a dinner at the home of Simon the leper in Bethany. Since Simon is hosting a meal in his own home, Jesus has probably healed him of his leprosy, since lepers were required to live away from the common population. John fills in important details when he tells us that Lazarus and his sisters, Mary and Martha, were there.

A woman ... with an alabaster jar of very expensive perfume ... poured on his head (26:7). At a Jewish banquet, small amounts of oil were poured on a guest's head, which would remain on the hair and clothing, enhancing the fragrance of the feast for the guest. At this dinner, Mary is the woman who brings an alabaster jar filled with very expensive perfume (John 12:3). The vessel is likely a long-necked flask made of translucent, finely carved stone standing some five to ten inches high. The perfume is pure nard (see Mark 14:3; John 12:3), an oil extracted from the root of the nard plant grown in India.[396] This is not a typical household oil for anointing, but an expensive perfume oil used for a solemn and special act of devotion. By breaking the flask Mary shows that she is not just pouring a few drops to enhance the aroma of the feast but is performing the highest act of consecration to Jesus, even to the anointing of his feet (cf. John 12:3).

The poor you will always have with you, but you will not always have me (26:11). The perfume had cost at least three hundred denarii (Mark 14:5), equivalent to about a year's wages for the average worker, or the equivalent of over $12,000 (cf. 18:28; 20:9). Jesus is not relieving the disciples of caring for the poor, but instead is drawing on the law, which emphasized that precisely because there are always the poor among them, giving to the poor is a duty of ideal conduct (cf. Deut. 15:11). The last scene of the preceding discourse has left the disciples with a dramatic scene of reward and punishment related to caring for the needy (25:31–46). In other words, Jesus is here emphasizing that the woman is performing an act of homage to him that can only be done at this time while he is with them.

She did it to prepare me for burial (26:12). Whatever her motivation, Jesus tells his disciples that unknowingly she

PERFUME JARS

Cosmetic jars and other instruments found in the excavations at Masada.

has begun the preparations for his burial, which will come sooner than any of them conceive possible.

Judas Arranges the Betrayal (26:14–16)

So they counted out for him thirty silver coins (26:15). The counting out of thirty silver coins calls to mind Zechariah 11:12. This amount was the price of a slave accidentally gored to death by an ox (Ex. 21:32). The identity of the coin is not specified, but a manuscript variant reading has *statēr*, the most common coin used for paying the temple tax (see com-

right ▶

SILVER COINS

A handful of silver Tyrean drachmas.

▶ The Day of the Lord's Supper and Crucifixion During the Passion Week

The traditional understanding of the day of the week on which the Passover and the celebration of the Lord's Supper occurs, and thereafter the day of the week of Jesus' death, derives from a basic comment from all the Gospels, namely, that Jesus was crucified on the "day of Preparation": "It was Preparation Day (that is, the day before the Sabbath)" (Mark 15:42).[A-96] This expression points to Friday, the day preceding the Sabbath, when the Jews would prepare everything for the beginning of the Sabbath. When Sabbath began, all work was to cease. This indicates that Jesus died on Friday afternoon.[A-97]

However, several passages in John's Gospel seem to indicate that when Jesus was led away to trial and crucifixion, the Passover meal had not yet been eaten by the Jews, which would imply that Jesus' final meal with his disciples was not a Passover meal.[A-98]

Explanations for the Differences between the Synoptics and John

There have been several attempted explanations of the differences between the Synoptics and John, but the two most promising are as follows:

1. One view suggests that Jesus and the disciples celebrated the Passover according to a solar calendar known from *Jubilees* and possibly used by the Qumran community.[A-99] The rationale for this position is as follows: (a) The Synoptic Gospels followed the method of the Galileans and the Pharisees, by whose reckoning the day was measured from sunrise to sunrise. Jesus and his disciples had their Paschal lamb slaughtered in the late afternoon of Thursday, Nisan 14, and ate the Passover with unleavened bread later that evening. (b) John's Gospel followed the method of the Judeans, especially the Jerusalem Sadducees, in reckoning the day from sunset to sunset. Therefore the Judean Jews had the Paschal lamb slaughtered in the late afternoon of Friday Nisan 14 and ate the Passover with the unleavened bread that night, which by then had become Nisan 15. (c) Thus, Jesus had eaten the Passover meal when his enemies, who had not yet celebrated the Passover, arrested him.[A-100]

2. Another view suggests that the passages in John that seem to contradict the Synoptics all point to a use of the expression "Passover" for the week-long series of events, not just the Passover meal itself. Therefore, Jesus and his disciples ate the Passover meal on Thursday, the beginning of Nisan 15, at the same time that the rest of those assembled in Jerusalem.[A-101]

ments on 17:27). It was the equivalent of four denarii, so that a total amount is equivalent to four months' wages, or about $5,000.

The Lord's Supper (26:17–30)

Where do you want us to make preparations for you to eat the Passover? (26:17). Since the Passover lamb was actually sacrificed on the afternoon of Nisan 14, just prior to the Passover meal after sundown, this seems to imply that the day of Unleavened Bread was prior to the Passover. However, although the lambs were slain on the afternoon of Nisan 14 and the Passover meal, initiating the Feast of Unleavened Bread, was eaten after sundown, initiating Nisan 15, popular usage viewed the slaughter of the lambs as initiating the Passover. This is in part attributable to the wording in Exodus 12:6, where animals were to be slaughtered at "twilight." Popular usage saw the beginning of Passover with the slaughtering of the animals, whereas technically the Passover itself was the meal, which began after sundown. Josephus uses this popular reckoning often when he refers to the Passover beginning on Nisan 14.[397]

I am going to celebrate the Passover with my disciples at your house (26:18). The famous Church of the Apostles, now incorporated within the Crusader Church of Saint Mary on Mount Zion, has a long tradition that claims it is the site of the home containing the Upper Room, in which Jesus celebrated the Last Supper with his disciples (Mark 14:15; Luke 22:11). The tradition further claims that this is the same home where the disciples gathered after Jesus' crucifixion when he appeared to them, where the apostles and other disciples gathered after Jesus' ascension (Acts 1:13), and where the Spirit was poured out on Pentecost. Recent archaeological work has convinced many that after the destruction of Jerusalem in A.D. 70, Jewish-Christians returned to the city and built a Judeo-Christian house of worship on the site to commemorate the Last Supper and the headquarters of the early church. Although it has been enhanced, destroyed, and rebuilt several times throughout the centuries, it still marks the site revered by early Christians as the place of the home of the Upper Room.[398]

Jesus was reclining at the table with the Twelve (26:20). The most widespread style of formal dining in the Greco-Roman world was the *triclinium*, which is demonstrated in the "House of the Faun," an exquisite, luxurious home in the city of Pompeii, which was captured for later centuries' enlightenment in the violent eruption of Mount Vesuvius in A.D. 79.[399] Common also in the Jewish world, the *triclinium* was a dining room in which

UPPER ROOM

An historical tradition locates the last supper in the Cenacle on Mount Zion. This present structure was reconstructed by Franciscans in 1335.

the guests reclined on a couch that extended around three sides of the room. The host was seated in the center of the U-shaped series of tables, with the most honored guests on either side, their heads reclining toward the tables and their feet toward the wall.[400]

The one who has dipped his hand into the bowl with me will betray me (26:23). Each of those around the room dipped their bread into bowls that served the group around the table, so this saying implies no more than one of those who was at the meal, rather than specifying any one particular person.

"Surely not I, Lord?" . . . "Surely not I, Rabbi?" Jesus answered, "Yes, it is you" (26:22, 25). Although "Lord" (*kyrios*) can be used as a formal address (7:21), when addressing Jesus it has come to designate discipleship. It is interesting to note that Judas is never recorded to have addressed Jesus as "Lord," only as "Rabbi" (cf. 26:49), perhaps a clue to the fact that Jesus knew all along those who did not truly believe in him and who would betray him (cf. John 6:60–65).

The Institution of the Lord's Supper (26:26–30)

Jesus took bread, gave thanks and broke it, and gave it to his disciples, saying, "Take and eat; this is my body" (26:26). The "Haggadah of Passover" was the set form in which the Exodus story was told on the first two nights of Passover as part of the ritual *Seder* ("order"). The expression "Haggadah of Passover" then came to be used for the entire *Seder* ritual as well as for the book containing the liturgy and ritual narration of the events of Deuteronomy 26:5–9 (first referred to in *m. Pesaḥ.* 10). Central to the meal were three foods—unleavened bread, bitter herbs, and the Passover offering (lamb in temple days)—along with the four (traditional) cups of wine. Since the Old Testament prescribed that the paschal sacrifice was to be consumed by a company previously invited (Ex. 12:4), Jewish practice has always focused on the corporate character of the *Seder*.[401] Jesus uses the bread as a stunning illustration that his body will be the fulfillment of the ceremonies surrounding the Passover lamb, as he will become the sacrificial atonement for the "passing over" of the sins of the people.

He took the cup, gave thanks and offered it to them, saying, "Drink from it, all of you" (26:27). The traditional four cups of wine consumed at a Passover celebration each had special significance: (1) The first cup initiated the ceremony with the Kiddush, the cup of benediction, a blessing over wine that introduces all festivals. (2) The second cup just before the meal and after the Haggadah of the Passover concluded with the singing of the first part of the Hallel (Ps. 113–114). (3) The third cup was drunk after the meal and the saying of grace. (4) The fourth cup followed the conclusion of the Hallel (Ps. 115–118) (*m. Pesaḥ* 10:1–7).[402]

This is my blood of the covenant, which is poured out for many for the forgiveness of sins (26:28). The traditional cups of the Passover celebration now offer another stunning illustration for Jesus to show that his sacrificial life is the fulfillment of all that for which the historical ritual had hoped. This is the new covenant that was promised to the people of Israel: "'The time is coming,' declares the LORD, 'when I will make a new covenant with the house of Israel and with the house of Judah. . . . For I will forgive their wickedness and will remember their sins no more" (Jer. 31:31, 34).

I will not drink of this fruit of the vine from now on until that day when I drink it anew with you in my Father's kingdom (26:29). In later Judaism a dispute arose as to whether a fifth cup was obligatory during the Passover celebration. This led to the custom of filling, but not drinking, still another cup of wine, subsequently called the cup of Elijah. This is the cup kept in readiness for the advent of the prophet Elijah, who the Jews believed would come on the Festival of Redemption from Egypt to herald the messianic redemption of the future.[403]

Prediction of the Falling Away and Denial (26:31–35)

"I will strike the shepherd, and the sheep of the flock will be scattered" (26:31). The shepherd who is struck by the sword is the one described as pierced (Zech. 12:10; cf. Matt. 24:30) and rejected (Zech. 11). But the scene shifts in Zechariah 13:7, as this time Yahweh strikes the shepherd. This shepherd is identified as Yahweh's companion, who is side-by-side with Yahweh as his equal. As this messianic Shepherd is smitten, the sheep are scattered, which in the Zechariah context speaks to the dispersion of the Jews,[404] but as applied by Jesus refers to the hardship that will also fall on Jesus' disciples.

This very night, before the rooster crows, you will disown me three times (26:34). Roman military guards were organized around various "watches" (see comments on 14:25). The crowing of the rooster is proverbial for the arrival of the day. Thus, the denial will take place before the end of the fourth watch.

Gethsemane: Jesus' Agonizing Prayers (26:36–46)

Jesus went with his disciples to a place called Gethsemane (26:36). Gethsemane is only mentioned twice in the Bible—here and in Mark 14:32. Luke's parallel account only notes that they went to the Mount of Olives (Luke 22:39). In neither place is Gethsemane called a "garden," but John locates Jesus' arrest in a *kēpos* (John 18:1, 26), a term that indicates a cultivated area or garden.[405] The Greek word

REFLECTIONS

JESUS, THE "PRINCE OF PEACE." MATTHEW HAS demonstrated that Jesus' life is the fulfillment of the prophecies of Isaiah concerning a messianic deliverer. But what about the "peace" that was prophesied to come when the "Prince of Peace" established his kingdom (Isa. 9:6–7)? Many Jews today disregard Jesus as the true Messiah, because he did not destroy the enemies of Israel and establish a time of worldwide peace and prosperity. Shalom is integral to the anticipated eschatological time (cf. Ps. 85:8–10; Isa. 55:12), and Ezekiel speaks of the Davidic messianic shepherd, who will make a covenant of peace, shalom, that will usher in a time of blessing and security (Ezek. 34:23–30).

Christians also live in the anticipation of the establishment of the kingdom, when Jesus will return to bring worldwide peace. But Christians also live in the reality of the new covenant peace that Jesus, the Passover lamb (1 Cor. 5:7), has brought through his work on the cross. The new covenant brings personal peace as a disciple's alienation from God is solved through the forgiveness of sin (Rom. 5:1; Col. 1:20), but it also brought, and brings, peace between Jew and Gentile as the two become one new person in the church of Jesus Christ (Eph. 2:11–18). The new covenant enables Jesus' disciples to be instruments of peace in this world through their message (Acts 10:36) and their lives (Rom. 12:17–21; 14:19) and enables them to have personal inward peace regardless of the circumstances of this world (Phil. 4:7).

Gethsemane (*Gethsēmani*) comes from the Hebrew/ Aramaic *gat šemanîm*, which most likely means "oil-press." Therefore, Gethsemane was a garden area among the olive tree groves on the Mount of Olives where a place for the preparation of olive oil was located, which Jesus and his disciples often frequented (John 18:2).

GARDEN OF GETHSEMANE

The traditional site of the garden on the Mount of Olives.

THE ROCK OF AGONY

The patch of bedrock in the chancel floor of the Church of All Nations next to the Franciscan Garden of Gethsemane is the traditional location of where Jesus sweat drops of blood as he prayed.

Two primary sites for the actual location of Gethsemane have claimed scholars' attention.[406] The first site now houses the Church of All Nations (or the Franciscan Basilica of the Agony), which is adjacent to an olive grove about fifty-five yards square, with olive trees perhaps more than a thousand years old. Josephus indicates that Titus cut down the original trees in the siege of Jerusalem.[407] This site corresponds to the area specified by Eusebius and Jerome.

The second site is perhaps more promising, which is located a few hundred feet north of the traditional garden, slightly lower on the Mount of Olives. The cave is quite large, measuring approximately 36 by 60 feet (11 by 18 meters), with interior caves cut into the walls for locating oil presses. Some suggest that a cultivated garden area originally surrounded the cave within the olive groves on the hill. After an extensive archaeological reconstruction, one archaeologist suggests that the disciples went to the cultivated garden area to sleep in the cave that they had frequented on other occasions. Once there, Jesus asked the inner group of disciples to stay awake with him while he prayed. The soldiers came to the garden area and found Jesus praying there, with the disciples asleep in the cave.[408]

The Arrest (26:47–56)

A large crowd armed with swords and clubs, sent from the chief priests and the elders of the people (26:47). The most heavily armed would have been a contingent of Roman soldiers assigned by governor Pilate to the temple for security,[409] who were authorized to carry swords (*machaira*), the short double-edged sword preferred in hand-to-hand combat (cf. 26:51; Eph. 6:17). Levitical temple police and personal security of the chief priests and Sanhedrin carrying clubs would have made up another large detachment in the arresting crowd.

Judas said, "Greetings, Rabbi!" and kissed him (26:48–49). Men in ancient (and modern) Palestine customarily greeted one another with a kiss on the cheek. This was the customary way of greeting a venerable rabbi and would have seemed to the other disciples as a greeting of peace, but it was only shameless hypocrisy.[410]

One of Jesus' companions reached for his sword . . . and struck the servant of the high priest, cutting off his ear (26:51). It is likely that Judas brought such a heavily armed contingent because they expected Jesus' disciples to resist arrest, which indeed was the reaction of at least one, whom John tells us was Simon Peter (John 18:10–11). Peter tries to defend Jesus by taking the sword he is carrying and striking Malchus, the high priest's servant. At least some of the disciples regularly carried swords, most likely for self-defense from robbers as they traveled (cf. Luke 22:36). Essenes were known to carry arms as protection against thieves.[411]

◀ *left*

SWORD

A Roman soldier holding his sword.

He will at once put at my disposal more than twelve legions of angels (26:53). A Roman legion had six thousand soldiers, which means Jesus could have called on 72,000 angels. The number may have symbolic value, but more importantly it points to the enormous resources at Jesus' disposal, should he desire. This is similar to the angelic host that surrounded Elisha, ready to come to his aide, even though his servant could not see them until his eyes were opened (1 Kings 6:17).

Jesus Before the Sanhedrin (26:57–68)

The courtyard of the high priest (26:58). The "courtyard of the high priest" harks back to the same phrase in 26:3, where it is rendered "palace of the high priest" in the NIV. Jesus is taken to the home of the high priest, Caiaphas, which was a large enough complex to be used for the business of the Sanhedrin.

The chief priests and the whole Sanhedrin were looking for false evidence against Jesus so that they could put him to death (26:59). "Sanhedrin" means a gathered council, rendered loosely in Judaism to indicate a local Jewish tribunal, but also, as here, the supreme ecclesiastical court of the Jews. Later, "Sanhedrin" became a title for the Mishnah tractate dedicated to the organization of the Israelite government and court system. Although the Sanhedrin had seventy members plus the high priest, cases concerning theft or personal injury could be decided by as few as three members. When a capital case was

THE HOUSE OF CAIAPHAS?
(left) The Church of St. Peter Gallicantu. *(top right)* A wealthy Herodian era home discovered in excavations of the Jewish quarter in Jerusalem. *(bottom right)* This area north of the Dormition Church on Mount Zion is another possible location for Caiaphas's home. This is a portico of an Armenian shrine under restoration.

The Trial of Jesus and the House of Caiaphas

Apparently Jesus is taken after his arrest at Gethsemane to the palatial mansion home of the high priest, Caiaphas. Tradition has identified a site at the Church of St. Peter Gallicantu (Latin for "Cock-crow") as the home of Caiaphas, but most scholars now reject that proposal. Archaeologists have recently focused on a nearby area on the eastern slope of the Upper City of Jerusalem, where large homes of the upper class in the Herodian era were located. This district, immediately overlooking the temple mount across from the south end of the western wall, was known to be the location of the homes of the high priestly families[A-102] and accords with some of the earliest known records.[A-103]

In this district a team of modern archaeologists have excavated a large palatial type mansion that covered an area of over six hundred square meters, laid out with a large, central paved courtyard reaching through a secluded gateway and forecourt. Around the courtyard was a series of living quarters, some with second floors, indicating that more than one family occupied the quarters. There was also a large room decorated with elaborate plaster design and an elegantly adorned vaulted ceiling, as well as rooms for ritual *mikveh* baths. By all standards this was the home of a very wealthy family, matched in size and affluence with the wealthiest of homes uncovered at the ruins of Pompeii, Herculaneum, Delos, and Ephesus.

All of this evidence has led many to postulate that this is a home similar to the home (if not the very one) that Caiaphas owned. His home was likely the quarters for both Caiaphas's family and the family of his father-in-law, Annas, the former high priest. Jesus was shuffled through the complex, appearing first to Annas, then to Caiaphas, then to the assembled Sanhedrin (cf. 26:57–58; 27:1–2; John 18:12–28). Peter appears to have remained in the same courtyard, moving from the entryway to the main courtyard.[A-104] involved, the sages required that twenty-three members made up a quorum (*m. Sanh.* 1:1). The composition of the Sanhedrin at the time of Jesus would have been a mixture of the priestly nobility, the aristocratic elders of Jerusalem, especially dominated by Sadducee influence, but with some elements of Pharisee influence through their scribal legal experts, the "teachers of the law" (26:57).[412]

I charge you under oath by the living God: Tell us if you are the Christ, the Son of God (26:63b). In the minds of the common people the title *Christ* (Heb. *Messiah*) probably implied the hope of a deliverer out of the house of David, who would liberate the people of Israel. By leading Jesus this way, Caiaphas is trying to get him to pit himself against the Roman rule, so that Caiaphas can rightly take Jesus to Pilate with charges of insurrection. "Messiah" and "Son of God" are basically equivalent expressions in this context, emphasizing that the expected Messiah is both Son of David and Son of God.[413] Caiaphas draws on the Jewish conception of the Messiah as the Davidic king, God's Anointed, who will rule his people forever (cf. Ps. 2:7).

In the future you will see the Son of Man sitting at the right hand of the Mighty One and coming on the clouds of heaven (26:64). Jesus declares that he is not just a human messianic deliverer, but he is the divine Son of Man foretold earlier in Daniel's prophecy (Dan. 7:13–14) and the object of the psalmist's reference to the divine figure who sits at the right hand of God (Ps. 110:1–2), cited earlier in his debates with the Pharisees (Matt. 22:41–46). The very title that Jesus has used throughout his ministry to clarify his identity, *Son of Man*, now unmistakably clarifies for Caiaphas and the Sanhedrin that the next time they see him, he will come as the everlasting King, who will be worshiped and will reign for ever. He is the Messiah, the Son of God, but in an exalted way that they cannot possibly conceive. Jesus is making himself equal with God.

Then the high priest tore his clothes and said, "He has spoken blasphemy!" (26:65). Caiaphas does not miss Jesus' point. Blasphemy is to act or, more specifically, to speak contemptuously against God.[414] The Old Testament tells of the stoning of a man who "blasphemed the Name with a curse" (Lev. 24:11; cf. Dan. 3:29; 2 Macc. 15:22–24). The Mishnah gave guidelines for blasphemy, which specified that a person "is not culpable unless he pronounces the Name itself"; witnesses were needed to confirm the pronouncement. After confirmation, "the judges stand up on their feet and rend their garments, and they may not mend them again" (*m. Sanh.* 7.5). The culpable act of blasphemy in Jesus' case is not his claim to be the Messiah, but his assertion that he has divine status as the Son of Man. Caiaphas tears his clothing and pronounces that there are witnesses enough to the blasphemy. Later Barnabas and Paul will tear their clothes in horror when the people at Lystra try to assign them divine status (Acts 14:14).

He is worthy of death (26:66). From the standpoint of the law (Lev. 24:10–23), as interpreted by the rabbis as well (*m. Sanh.* 7:5), Jesus now deserves death because he has made himself to be of divine status by taking to himself the Name of God. But from the standpoint of Roman law blasphemy is not a crime deserving of death. Therefore, the Jewish leaders will have to manipulate the charges and focus on Jesus as a common messianic pretender, one who is dangerous to Rome as an insurrectionist, gathering around himself men whom he will lead in an uprising against the military government.

Peter's Denial of Jesus (26:69–75)

You also were with Jesus of Galilee (26:69). Peter's three denials are all compressed into one passage (26:69–75), which makes their impact on the reader all the more striking. At the same time, it supports the theory that the three phases of Jesus' Jewish trial (Annas, Caiaphas and partial Sanhedrin, the official Sanhedrin) take place in the palatial compound that is home to the familes of Caiaphas and Annas and also acts as the meeting place for the Sanhedrin.

Surely you are one of them, for your accent gives you away (26:73). The accent in the pronunciation of "shibboleth" by the Ephraimites gave them away to the men of Gilead (Judg. 12:1–6). There is some evidence that people from Galilee had difficulty distinguishing their gutturals. Judeans were contemptuous of the way Galileans pronounced certain words, not certain whether a Galilean meant "wool," "a lamb," "an ass," or "wine" (*b. ʿErub.* 53a, 53b).[415]

Judas's Remorse and Death (27:1–10)

Early in the morning, all the chief priests and the elders of the people came to the decision to put Jesus to death (27:1). At daybreak on Friday morning, probably a larger number of the Sanhedrin assemble to form a quorum so that they can give

ST. PETER'S CHURCH IN GALLICANTU

The courtyard and various chambers. The rock cut structures, cellars, and chambers date to the Herodian period (37 B.C.- A.D. 70).

Pilate, the Governor (A.D. 26–36)

Pilate was the Roman prefect and governor of Judea under Emperor Tiberius. He was a Roman equestrian (knight) of the Pontii clan (hence the name Pontius[A-105]). He was appointed prefect of Judea through the intervention of Lucius Aelius Sejanus, who was prefect of the emperor's household troops, the Praetorian Guard. Sejanus became one of the most powerful men in Rome, when he ruled as de facto emperor in Tiberius's absence.

Under the protection of Sejanus, Pilate was secure and carried out an attempt to impose Roman superiority throughout Israel. He hung worship images of the emperor throughout Jerusalem and had coins bearing pagan religious symbols minted. However, Sejanus's thirst for power caused him to fall under the suspicion of Tiberius, who had him arrested and executed (A.D. 31). During the time of his demise, Pilate was exposed to increasing criticism from the Jews. This may have encouraged the religious leaders to capitalize on Pilate's vulnerability, leading them to align themselves with him in his attempt to maintain peace. Their demand for a legal death sentence on Jesus, a falsely accused rival to Caesar (27:11–14; John 19:12), would have been a welcome way of putting down a popular uprising.

Several years later (A.D. 36), during a religious prophetic revival among the Samaritans on Mount Gerizim, Pilate's military forces suspected political and military insurgency, so they attacked the supposed uprising with great severity. Vitellius, legate of Syria, reported the attack to Tiberius, and Pilate was ordered back to Rome to give account for the actions of his soldiers. Pilate is not heard from again, but according to an uncertain fourth-century tradition, he killed himself on orders from Emperor Caligula in A.D. 39.

The New Testament, Josephus,[A-106] Philo,[A-107] and later historians[A-108] all record the rule of Pilate as prefect over Judea during the time of Jesus. In 1962 a stone slab was discovered at Caesarea Maritima that provides archaeological evidence as well. Caesarea Maritima was an architectural and engineering marvel built by Herod the Great (see discussion in Acts), which was used as the residence for the Roman governors in Palestine, including Pilate. When archaeologists excavated the ancient Roman theater that had been destroyed and rebuilt, a two-by-three foot stone slab was discovered that had been reused as one of the steps of a stairway. The stone bore an inscription, though several letters are obliterated or marred:

S TIBERIÉVM
NTIVS PILATVS
ECTVS IVDA E
É

The best reconstruction renders the basic words to be: ". . .this Tiberium, Pontius Pilate, prefect of Judea, did (or erected)." The full text and meaning of the inscription is still debated, but scholars are vitually unanimous that this stone is an authentic contemporary witness of Pilate's existence and the only extant archaeological evidence that he was prefect of Judea at the time of Jesus. This provides solid support for the consistent New Testament record.[A-109]

THE PONTIUS PILATE INSCRIPTION

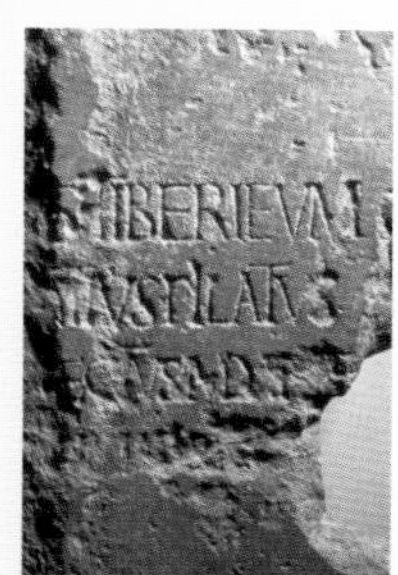

a more formal ratification of the earlier pronouncement (see comments on 26:59). The ruling is still not legal by Mishnaic criteria, but those are later idealized standards for the Jewish judicial system. They may not have been fully in force at this time.

They . . . handed him over to Pilate, the governor (27:2). Since the Jewish religious leaders at this time do not have the liberty under the Roman occupation to perform capital punishment at will, they take Jesus to Pilate to have the deed carried out. Handing over a Jewish citizen to a foreign power was considered a horrible deed in Jewish practice.[416] The Qumran *Temple Scroll* declares, "If there were to be a spy against his people who betrays his people to a foreign nation or causes evil against his people, you shall hang him from a tree and he will die."[417]

Returned the thirty silver coins to the chief priests and the elders (27:3). It is unlikely that Judas could have gotten near the inner sanctuary, so the scene may indicate his getting as near as he can to the restricted area of the priests, and he throws the coins over a separator.

He went away and hanged himself (27:5). This is the only example of suicide in the New Testament. The Old Testament records the cases of Saul and his armor-bearer (1 Sam. 31:4–5), Ahithophel (2 Sam. 17:23), and Zimri (1 Kings 16:18). The death of Samson (Judg. 16:28–31) may be seen as either a heroic suicide or an acceptance of an inevitable consequence of his life's actions. Rabbinic Judaism considered suicide morally wrong, as a rebellion against God who gave life and who alone may choose to take it (*b. ʿAbod. Zar.* 18a).

The potter's field as a burial place for foreigners. That is why it has been called the Field of Blood to this day (27:7–8). As early as the third and fourth centuries, Christian travelers visiting Jerusalem identified the place to be about a half mile south of the Old City of Jerusalem—at the southeast end of the Hinnom Valley, near where it joins the Kidron Valley. This was based on the fact that the area contains about eighty burial caves, most of which date to the time of Jesus. However, most scholars consider this a faulty identification. This section is indeed an ancient burial ground, some dating to the First Temple era, but restored in its second phase as a tomb complex for the wealthy aristocracy of Jerusalem. One elegant tomb may well be the burial place of the family of Annas, who was high priest from A.D. 6–15 and who was the father-in-law of Caiaphas, the high priest at Jesus' trial. Later Christians mistakenly identified this tomb complex as the "field of blood," even though there is no evidence to link it to any prior "potter's field."[418]

POTTER'S FIELD

The traditional site of Hakeldama, the "field of blood," in the Hinnom Valley near the monastery of St. Onuphrius.

The Roman Trial of Jesus (27:11–26)

Jesus stood before the governor (27:11). Pilate carried the title "procurator," which in Roman imperial administration indicated the financial officer of a province, but it was also used as the title of the "governor" (27:11) of a Roman province of the third class, such as in Judea. A governor was a "legate" with control over the military legions. Pilate also originally carried the title "prefect," which is used to designate various high officials or magistrates of differing functions and ranks in ancient Rome. It carried with it administrative, financial, military, and judicial functions, and included responsibilities as final judge in a region, under the emperor, with power to pronounce death sentences. Tiberius had created a hybrid of responsibilities in Judea in Jesus' time, so that Pilate had a combination of responsibilities as prefect and procurator/governor.

Are you the king of the Jews? (27:11). Pilate's question probably reflects the change of charges brought to him, making it a more politically subversive allegation. Pilate would not be concerned with the religious implications of the Sanhedrin's charge of blasphemy, so the Jewish leaders focus their allegation on challenges to Roman rule.

It was the governor's custom at the Feast to release a prisoner chosen by the crowd (27:15). There is no extrabiblical historical verification for this Passover pardon custom, but there is evidence of widespread customs of prisoner releases at festivals in the ancient world. The Gospel account of such a custom echoes the practice of the ancient world. Some scholars find reflections of this custom in a rabbinic ruling on killing a paschal lamb for those in need, including an imprisoned person: "They may slaughter for one that mourns his near kindred, or for one that clears away a ruin; so, too, for one whom they have promised to bring out of prison, for a sick man, or for an aged man that is able to eat an olive's bulk" (*m. Pesaḥ.* 8:6). Apparently this custom originated in Judea with Pilate as a way of creating good will with the people.

A notorious prisoner, called Barabbas (27:16). Barabbas does not occur elsewhere in the New Testament, and there is no extrabiblical account of his activities leading up to the biblical account or of his subsequent history. An interesting

▸ Barabbas and the Thieves

Barabbas is called "one of those among the rebels who had committed murder in the insurrection,"[A-110] a "notorious prisoner" (Matt. 27:16), and a "bandit" (John 18:40 NRSV). These terms closely resemble the characteristics of social banditry common in first-century Palestine.[A-111] As a "bandit" (*lēstēs*), Barabbas may have belonged to one of the rural brigands who instigated social unrest. The two criminals between whom Jesus is crucified are also called by this same term.[A-112] These bandits were popular with the common people because they preyed on the wealthy establishment of Israel and created havoc for the Roman government.

Barabbas is being held prisoner by the Roman authorities at the time of Jesus' trial and is released by Pontius Pilate to carry out the customary Paschal pardon (27:15–26; Mark 15:6–15). The reason given for the crowd's choosing Barabbas over Jesus is said to be the instigation of the chief priests and elders (Matt. 27:20; Mark 15:11). Likely the Jerusalem crowds also have come to recognize that Jesus is not going to be the military and political liberator that they want, preferring Barabbas's active methods of Roman resistance to Jesus' way of nonresistance.[A-113] manuscript variant occurs in 27:16–17, where he is called "Jesus Barabbas." While manuscript evidence is weak, Origen implies that most manuscripts in his day (c. A.D. 240) included the full name. Many scholars today accept this name as original and suggest that it was probably omitted by later scribes because of the repugnance of having Jesus Christ's name being shared by Barabbas.[419] It is not improbable for Barabbas to have the common name Jesus. Matthew's text reads more dramatically with two holders of the same name: "Which Jesus do you want; the son of Abba, or the self-styled Messiah?"[420]

While Pilate was sitting on the judge's seat (27:19). The judge's seat or tribunal is the *bēma* (Acts 18:12ff.), the platform on which a Roman magistrate sat, flanked by counselors, to administer justice. The *bēma* could be located in an auditorium (Acts 25:23), but was traditionally in some public place—as apparently is the case here, because Pilate is able to address the assembled crowd. The location where Pilate adjudicates Jesus' case is debated, but a good candidate is the magnificent palace of Herod the Great, built on the western edge of the Upper City, described by Josephus as "baffling all description: indeed, in extravagance and equipment no building surpassed it."[421] After the demise of Herod's son Archelaus, the palace was the Jerusalem residence of the Roman prefect. Therefore, when Pilate was in Jerusalem, he may have taken up residence there and held court there. The palace had been built to double as a fortress, so a large military contingent accompanied Pilate.

Others suggest that Pilate stayed at the old palace/fortress Antonia that is adjacent to the northwest corner of the outer temple, since this would put him in a more strategic location to keep an eye on the religious leaders of Jerusalem and to have his troops readily available for any uprisings.[422] Still others suggest that he resided at the old Hasmonean royal palace on the west slope of the Tyropoean Valley, opposite the southwest corner of the Temple.[423]

"ANTONIA PAVEMENT"

Roman period pavement where the Antonia Fortress once stood but now in the monastery of the Sisters of Zion.

Don't have anything to do with that innocent man, for I have suffered a great deal today in a dream because of him (27:19). Dreams have figured prominently in Matthew's narrative, especially since supernatural dreams guided Joseph to protect the innocent infant Jesus from social rejection and from the cruelty of Herod the King (cf. chs. 1–2). It is possible that the dream of Pilate's wife is a supernatural dream used by God to make clear to Pilate that Jesus is innocent of any crime. On the other hand, the Romans often took dreams as omens. Dio Cassius tells the story of Caesar's wife, who, "the night before he was slain his wife dreamed that their house had fallen in ruins and that her husband had been wounded."[424] There is no indication that Pilate's wife is either a God-fearer or a disciple of Jesus, which may lead to the conjecture that this is a natural, although profound premonition.

Pilate . . . took water and washed his hands in front of the crowd. "I am innocent of this man's blood," he said (27:24). There is abundant background for the practice of washing one's hands as a way of showing public innocence,[425] not an attempt to purge oneself of sin, as is practiced elsewhere.[426] When asked why the Jewish translators of the LXX washed their hands in the sea while saying their prayers to God, the response was: "It is evidence that they have done no evil, for all activity takes place by means of the hands."[427]

All the people answered, "Let his blood be on us and on our children!" (27:25). The term "crowd" (*ochlos*) has been the normal word Matthew uses to designate the masses of people who have been witnessing the trial, and then ask for Jesus' crucifixion (27:20–24). But now Matthew switches to "people" (*laos*), the term normally used to designate Israel.[428] The Jewish leaders and the crowds whom they have manipulated are responsible for Jesus' death, as they now claim in the expression, "Let his blood be on us and on our children!" Blood on a person (or "on the head") is a common idiom to indicate responsibility for someone's death[429]; "on our children" indicates the familial solidarity of generations within Israel (e.g., Gen. 31:16).

Then he released Barabbas to them. But he had Jesus flogged (27:26). Flogging or scourging was a beating administered with a whip or rod, usually on the person's back. It was a common method of punishing criminals and preserving discipline. In the Old Testament, flogging was a punishment for crime (Deut. 25:1–3), and later rabbinic tradition gave extensive prescriptions for flogging offenders in the synagogue[430] (cf. Matt. 10:17; 23:34, *mastigoō*). But the Roman flogging (*phragelloō*) mentioned here is quite different. It is a Latin loan word used to designate the Roman *verberatio*, a horrific

REFLECTIONS

ANTI-SEMITISM IS A CANCER THAT HAS PLAGUED humanity for much of history. Unfortunately, Matthew's narration of the people's statement—"Let his blood be on us and on our children!"—has been wrongly interpreted to condone, and even promote, anti-Semitism. But we must clearly understand that Matthew's statement is not the invoking of a self-curse by the Jews, nor an oblique reference to God's curse on Israel. Matthew records the statement to show how the religious leaders and some of the people of Israel claimed responsibility for Jesus' death. They believe him to be a blasphemer and want him executed for it. The words reflect the same accusatory statements elsewhere in the narrative when Jesus places the blame squarely on the religious leaders for not receiving him as the Messiah of Israel, and for their role in turning the people away from him (e.g., 23:13ff.). But this certainly does not mean that later Jews should be labeled with racist titles like "Christ-killer," or that Christians should abuse Jews in the name of seeking revenge for God.

The sad and painful tragedy of this verse is that Israel has rejected its Messiah. But God's love for Israel continues, and he will remain loyal to the covenants with the nation (23:39; Rom. 11:25–32). Now each individual Jew must consider the claims of Jesus and the message the apostles bring. Thousands of Jews only days later will repent at Peter's preaching about the Jesus whom they have put to death (Acts 2:23, 37–41), and even many of the priests will become believers (6:7). Those who reject Jesus, whether Jew or Gentile, will suffer the consequences.

The responsibility of Christians today is to love Jews as God does, recognize the special place that they enjoy in God's plan for the ages, and share the gospel with them as they would any other people. No one can support racial bigotry toward Jews by appealing to Matthew's record.[A-114]

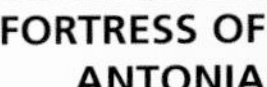

FLOGGING STRAP

Wooden handle with six leather straps.

form of flogging. Roman law required that the *verberatio* always accompany a capital sentence, preceding the execution. Flogging in the Jewish synagogue was limited to forty lashes by the law (Deut. 25:3), but no such restrictions limited Roman flogging. In many cases the flogging itself was fatal. When the condemned man (women were not flogged) was tied to a post, he was flogged with the cruel *flagellum*, a leather strap interwoven with pieces of bone and metal that cut through the skin, leaving the skin hanging in shreds. The repeated flaying often left the bones and intestines showing, and the person was not infrequently near to the point of death when he was taken to be executed.

The Soldiers' Treatment of Jesus (27:27–31)

The governor's soldiers took Jesus into the Praetorium (27:27). The Praetorium was the official residence of the Roman governor, but the term was also used of the camp of the troops that served him. The location of Pilate's residence in Jerusalem is debated (see comments on 27:19). Each of the three possible palaces had been built to double as a fortress, so a large military contingent was right there at Pilate's residence.[431]

Gathered the whole company of soldiers around him (27:27). The "whole company of soldiers" probably indicates a Roman military cohort, from 420 to 600 soldiers, which is the tenth part of a legion. But the term was also used of a *maniple* (a third part of a cohort), which was from 120 to 200 soldiers. Josephus says that a large contingent (Gk. *tagma*, "cohort") of Roman soldiers was permanently quartered at the Antonia palace,[432] which would support Antonia being Pilate's residence. Yet the wording "the governor's soldiers" may indicate that in addition to the cohort at the Antonia, a smaller *maniple* was housed at Herod the Great's palace, which attended Pilate as his personal guard.[433]

FORTRESS OF ANTONIA

A model of the Roman fortress, which was located in the northwest corner of the temple mount.

They stripped him and put a scarlet robe on him (27:28). Roman soldiers in Jerusalem at the time were known to play a cruel game with condemned prisoners, especially revolu-

◀ left

THE KING'S GAME

A Roman era pavement on the Via Dolorosa inscribed with images related to "the king's game."

tionary bandits. The prisoner was dressed up like a burlesque king and used as a game piece. With each roll of "dice" the prisoner "king" was moved around a game board etched in the floor. All for the entertainment of the troops, they hurled verbal and physical abuse at the mock king.[434] One of the red cloaks worn by the Roman soldiers became a mock royal robe. Plaited branches with thorns became a mimic crown, perhaps inflicting wounds to his head, but certainly becoming a malicious imitation of a Roman emperor's crown. A common wooden staff was a nasty hoax for a ruler's scepter. This staff is used to beat Jesus again and again around the head, as they spit at him and mock him.

The Journey to Golgotha and the Mocking (27:32–44)

A man from Cyrene, named Simon, and they forced him to carry the cross (27:32). Criminals condemned to die were customarily required to carry to the scene of crucifixion the heavy wooden crosspiece (*patibulum*), on which they were to be nailed. Plutarch writes, "Every criminal condemned to death bears his

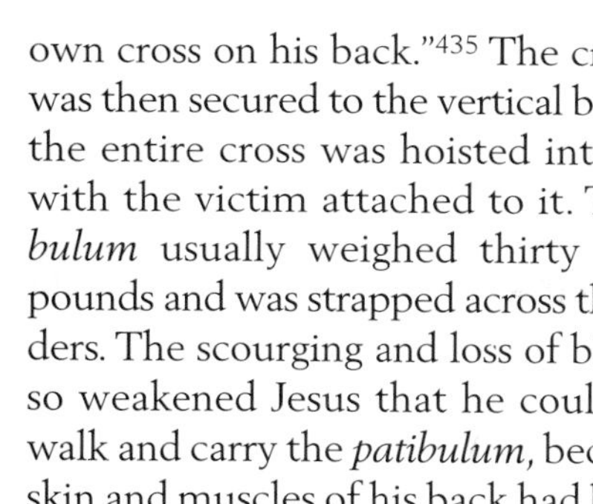

own cross on his back."[435] The crosspiece was then secured to the vertical beam, and the entire cross was hoisted into the air with the victim attached to it. The *patibulum* usually weighed thirty or forty pounds and was strapped across the shoulders. The scourging and loss of blood had so weakened Jesus that he could hardly walk and carry the *patibulum*, because the skin and muscles of his back had been lacerated. Apparently at random the Roman soldiers forced Simon of Cyrene into service to carry Jesus' cross. Cyrene was a town in North Africa that had a large Jewish population. Simon is likely a Jew who had made a pilgrimage to Jerusalem for the Passover. Mark says that Simon was the father of Alexander and Rufus (Mark 15:21). Many suggest that Rufus is the one named in Romans 16:13 (cf. Alexander in Acts 19:33). The connection is strong when we consider that earliest tradition declares that Mark wrote his Gospel while in Rome, to the Roman church.

Golgotha (which means The Place of the Skull) (27:33). On the name "Golgotha," see "Golgotha." The common designation "Calvary" comes from the Latin word for skull, *calvaria*.

VIA DOLOROSA

The Via Dolorosa ("the way of the cross") as it appears today.

They offered Jesus wine to drink, mixed with gall; but after tasting it, he refused to drink it (27:34). A rabbinic tradition indicates that when a prisoner was led out to execution, he was to be given a goblet of wine containing a grain of frankincense to numb his senses.[436] The practice was done out of sympathy and was performed by Jewish sympathizers. More likely the present drink is another attempt at cruelty by the Roman soldiers, who are hardly sympathetic. Feigning that they are offering Jesus a cup of refreshment, the wine has instead been mixed with "gall," a bitter herb that could even be poisonous. When Jesus tastes the bitter drink, he knows it is not for refreshment but is only another way of

Golgotha

Golgotha is the name attached to the place where Jesus was crucified. The identity and location of the place has been given considerable attention throughout history.

Proposals for the name Golgotha: No known place in ancient Jerusalem has ever been found that is called Golgotha, but three primary reasons for the name have been proposed: (1) it was a place of execution; (2) it was an area known for having a number of tombs; or (3) the site in some way resembled a skull. That leads to the following discussion.

Clues to the location of Golgotha: The most important clues to the identity and location of Golgotha are as follows. (1) The place must have been outside of Jerusalem, because Roman law (and Jewish law, Lev. 24:14) directed crucifixion to take place outside the city. (2) It must have been a fairly conspicuous spot, probably not far from a city gate and a highway, because the Romans used crucifixion as a deterrent and wanted the gruesome scene to be witnessed by as many people as possible. (3) A garden containing a tomb was nearby. The tomb belongs to Joseph of Arimathea, who claims Jesus' body and places him there (John 19:41–42).

Two primary locations have been proposed:

(1) "Gordon's Hill" and the "Garden Tomb" are named after General Charles George Gordon, a renowned British military hero. During his brief service in Israel (1883) he identified a hill that looked similar to a skull. The hill was located north of the northern wall of the Old City of Jerusalem. Underneath the hill is a vast underground cemetery, including one tomb that he identified as Jesus' burial tomb. Scholars agree that this Garden Tomb was part of a vast series of tombs that date to the eighth or seventh centuries B.C.; it was reused for burial purposes in the Byzantine period (fifth to seventh centuries A.D.). Therefore, it cannot be identified as the newly hewn tomb of Joseph of Arimathea.[A-115]

(2) "The Church of the Holy Sepulchre" was built in the fourth century by Emperor Constantine as a memorial to Jesus' crucifixion and burial. Three Christian religious communities—Armenian, Greek, and Latin—have long traditions that point to this site, west of the city of Jerusalem, as both the place of Jesus' crucifixion and burial. Scholars agree with these traditions for the following reasons: (a) During the time of Jesus this location was located outside of the city walls. Another wall was built later by Herod Agrippa between A.D. 41 and 44, which enclosed the site within the city. (b) The area was likely near a thoroughfare, since it was adjacent to a working stone quarry. (c) The site is an ancient limestone quarry, which had been exhausted of its useable stone by the first century B.C. At that time the quarry was filled and used as a garden or orchard. The area also began to be used as a cemetery, and by the turn of the era contained a large burial ground. A number of tombs have been discovered that are consistent with the type of tombs long associated with Jesus' first-century burial.[A-116]

torturing him. The bitterness will only intensify his parched thirst, so he refuses (see Ps. 69:20–21).

The Crucifixion (27:35–44)

Crucified him (27:35). Recent historical and archaeological studies have helped bring a more realistic sense of crucifixion's horrors.[437] The bones of a crucified man named Jehohanan were discovered in Jerusalem in 1968 at Giv'at ha-Mivtar in a group of cave tombs. He had been crucified sometime between A.D. 7–66.[438] His arms were evidently tied to the crossbeam, and he had apparently straddled the upright beam with each foot nailed laterally to the beam. Likewise, once at the crucifixion site, the soldiers may have tied and nailed Jesus' hands to the crossbeam he carried[439] and nailed his ankles to the upright beam, possibly with a spike driven through the bones and into the beam between them (see comments on Mark 15:24; "Crucifixion" at Luke 23:33).

They divided up his clothes by casting lots (27:35). The readers know that as the soldiers divide up his clothing by casting lots, this fulfills what Scripture anticipated (Ps. 22:18). The lot was cast in the Old Testament to discover God's will on various matters, such as the goat to be sacrificed on the Day of Atonement (Lev. 16). But here the lot is used as a form of gambling by the Roman guards as they divide up whatever is left of Jesus' clothes. By so doing they take away his final external dignity and protection from the flies and elements that torture his beaten body.

Two robbers were crucified with him (27:38). The two robbers between whom Jesus is crucified likely were political insurrectionists like Barabbas, since the same term (*lēstēs*) is used of them and Barabbas (see "Barabbas and the Thieves" at 27:16).

Those who passed by hurled insults at him, shaking their heads (27:39). Golgotha must have been a fairly conspicuous spot, probably not far from a city gate and a highway (see "Golgotha" at 27:33). Quintilian states, "Whenever we crucify the guilty, the most crowded roads are chosen, where the most people can see and be moved by this fear. For penalties relate not so much to retribution as to their exemplary effect."[440]

The Death of Jesus (27:45–46)

From the sixth hour until the ninth hour (27:45). The most widely accepted method of calculating the time of the day throughout much of the ancient world began with sunrise, generally 6:00 A.M. (cf. *Let. Aris.* 303). Therefore, the sixth hour is 12:00 noon and the ninth hour is 3:00 P.M. According to Mark, Jesus has already been on the cross for about three hours, because he was crucified at the third hour (Mark 15:25).

CHURCH OF THE HOLY SEPULCHRE

A courtyard by the entrance of the church. Ancient tradition associates the location of this church with both the crucifixion and burial of Jesus.

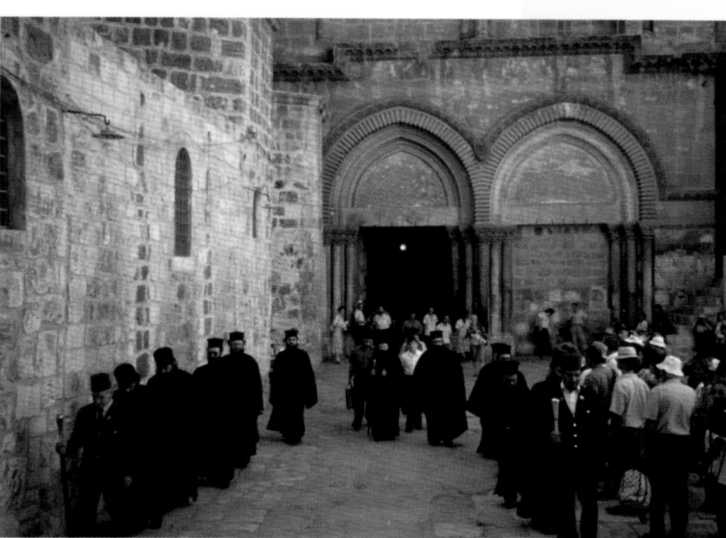

Darkness came over all the land (27:45). If light symbolizes God, darkness evokes everything that is anti-God: the wicked, judgment, death.[441] Salvation brings light to those in darkness (Isa. 9:1; Matt. 4:16). The time of God's ultimate judgment, the Day of the Lord, is portrayed in both Old and New Testaments as a day of darkness.[442] While darkness often accompanies the concept of death in Scripture (cf. Job 10:21–22), darkness at the crucifixion scene displays the temporary power of Satan (cf. Luke 2:53), God's displeasure on humanity for crucifying his Son, and most importantly God's judgment on evil.[443] This was not an eclipse, for the Passover was at the full moon, but was some unknown act of God indicating his judgment on the sins of the world.

***"Eloi, Eloi, lama sabachthani?"*—which means, "My God, my God, why have you forsaken me?" (27:46).** Once again the crucifixion scene is reminiscent of Psalm 22.[444] Jesus is experiencing the separation from the Father that must accompany bearing the sin of his people (1:21; 20:28; 26:28). He now bears the divine retribution and punishment for sin, as the Father's cup of wrath is poured out on him in divine judgment of sin. In the apostle Paul's words, "God made him who had no sin to be sin for us, so that in him we might become the righteousness of God" (2 Cor. 5:21), and, "Christ redeemed us from the curse of the law by becoming a curse for us, for it is written: 'Cursed is everyone who is hung on a tree'" (Gal. 3:13).

The Bystanders Think of Elijah (27:47–50)

He's calling Elijah (27:47). Jesus' citation of Psalm 22:1 is misunderstood by the bystanders to imply that he is calling Elijah. According to a tradition in later Judaism, since Elijah did not die but was taken by God in a whirlwind (2 Kings 2:1–12), he would return in an equally instantaneous way to help those in distress (*b. Ned.* 50a).[445]

He filled it with wine vinegar, put it on a stick, and offered it to Jesus to drink (27:48). The drink offered Jesus is *oxos*, from the word for "sharp, sharpness," which was used to refer to a sour wine used by common people and soldiers as a daily drink with meals. The same drink was given to Jesus by the soldiers in mockery (cf. Luke 23:36), and nothing indicates that the earlier mockery of the crowds has ceased.[446]

The Immediate Impact of the Death (27:51–56)

The curtain of the temple was torn in two from top to bottom (27:51). The word for curtain (*katapetasma*) is used in the LXX sometimes of the curtain between the Holy Place and the Most Holy Place,[447] and sometimes of the curtain over the entrance to the Holy Place.[448] The former is more likely meant here. The curtain was an elaborately woven fabric of seventy-two twisted plaits of twenty-four threads each and the veil was sixty feet long and thirty wide (cf. *m. Šeqal.* 8:5).[449] Being split from top to bottom is a sign that God has done this, signifying that the new and living way is now open into the presence of God through the sacrifice of Christ.[450]

The tombs broke open and the bodies of many holy people who had died were raised to life (27:52). The expression "holy people" probably refers to pious Old Testament figures selected to bear testimony to the resurrection of Jesus. We might think of the way in which Moses and Elijah were selected to appear with Jesus on the Mount of Transfiguration (17:1–8). But in this case it is a resurrection of their bodies. The best implication of the text is that they are not raised until after Jesus is raised, which anticipates Paul's teaching on Jesus being the firstfruits of the dead (1 Cor. 15:20–23).

The Women Followers of Jesus

Women and men were originally created by God as equal human beings, who were complementary coworkers in ruling God's creation for him (Gen. 1:26–28). But in some circles within Judaism, because of misinterpretation of Scripture and cultural bias, women had lost their dignity, value, and worth.

Josephus states, "The woman, says the Law, is in all things inferior to the man,"[A-117] apparently interpreting Genesis 3:16 to indicate that women are not only under the authority of men, but also have a lower personal status. Women are categorized in the repeated rabbinic formula, "women, slaves and minors,"[A-118] demonstrating that a woman, like a Gentile slave and a minor child, is under the authority of a man and has limited participation in religious activity. One of the most widely cited rabbinic sayings from the days after the formation of the Mishnah, but prior to the formation of the Talmud, reflects at least among some of the rabbis an inferior position of women. This attitude was echoed in a threefold daily prayer: "Praised be God that he has not created me a gentile! Praised be God that he has not created me a woman! Praised be God that he has not created me an ignoramus!"[A-119]

Nevertheless, the rabbinic literature in other places reiterates the Old Testament directive that honor is to be given equally to the mother and father. One passage indicates that since the father is listed first in Exodus 20:12 and the mother is listed first in Leviticus 19:3, Scripture teaches that "both are equal."[A-120] One saying attributed to R. Joseph indicates his attitude toward the spiritual status of his mother. When he heard his mother's footsteps coming he said, "Let me arise before the approach of the Shekinah (Divine presence)."[A-121] The wife and mother were considered to be of substantial spiritual value.

One direct result of Jesus' ministry has been the restoration and affirmation of women that God intended from the beginning of creation, which we can see demonstrated in the following ways.

- Women were equally worthy of Jesus' saving activity (e.g., John 4:1–42).
- Women were called to be Jesus' disciples (Matt. 12:48–50).
- Women received instruction and nurture as Jesus' disciples (Luke 10:38–42).
- Women were part of his ministry team (Luke 8:1–3).
- Because of their courageous presence at the cross and the empty tomb, women were designated as the first to testify to the reality of Jesus' resurrection (Matt. 28:10; Mark 16:7; John 20:17).

For women to be disciples of a great master was certainly an unusual circumstance in Palestine in the first century. Yet here we find another instance of the unique form of discipleship Jesus instituted. While women were not part of the Twelve, several women disciples traveled with Jesus and had a significant part in his earthly ministry. Jesus restores and reaffirms to women their dignity and worth as persons fully equal to men as humans created in the image of God. He also preserves the male-female distinction of humans, so that they are restored and affirmed in the different roles that God intended from the beginning. Distinctions among Jesus' disciples relate to function, not spiritual standing or commitment or essential personal worth. Jesus restores and affirms to women the status of being coworkers with men in God's plan for working out his will on earth.[A-122]

Many women were there, watching from a distance. They had followed Jesus from Galilee (27:55). All of the evangelists mention a group of women who followed and served Jesus in Galilee and who also followed him to Jerusalem, witnessing the events of the final week, including the crucifixion[451] and the resurrection.[452] Their following means that they had been accompanying Jesus as his disciples.

To care for his needs (27:55). According to Luke 8:1–3 a group of women joined Jesus and the Twelve as a part of the mission team. The term behind the expression "care for his needs" (*diakoneō*) is better rendered "serve." Besides providing financial support for the missionary outreach (Luke 8:1–3), the women joined the Twelve as Jesus' companions and as witnesses of his ministry.

Among them were Mary Magdalene, Mary the mother of James and Joses, and the mother of Zebedee's sons (27:56). "Magdalene" implies that Mary was from Magdala (see comments on 15:39). The only information about Mary's personal life is that she is the woman "from whom seven demons had come out" (Luke 8:2). Her being listed first demonstrates her prominence in the days of Jesus' ministry, as she was likely a leader among the women. The other Mary may be the mother of James who is identified with one of the Twelve called James, the son of Alphaeus (cf. Matt. 10:3). The mother of Zebedee's sons is likely Salome, Jesus' mother's sister, or Jesus' aunt on his mother's side. This would mean that James and John, the sons of Zebedee, are Jesus' cousins on his mother's side (see comments on 20:20).

The Burial of Jesus by Faithful Followers (27:57–61)

As evening approached (27:57). Jewish custom dictated that bodies should be taken down before evening, especially with the Sabbath beginning at sundown (approx. 6:00 P.M.).[453]

A rich man from Arimathea, named Joseph (27:57). Joseph, one of the most common names for Jewish men, was from Arimathea. The location is in doubt, identified by some as Ramathaim, the birthplace of Samuel (1 Sam. 1:1, 19), and by others as Rathamein (1 Macc. 11:34) or Ramathain.[454] Extensive apoc-

GARDEN TOMB

An alternative (although unlikely) site of Jesus' tomb. The tomb is associated with the site that General Charles Gordon suggested as the location of Golgotha in 1883.

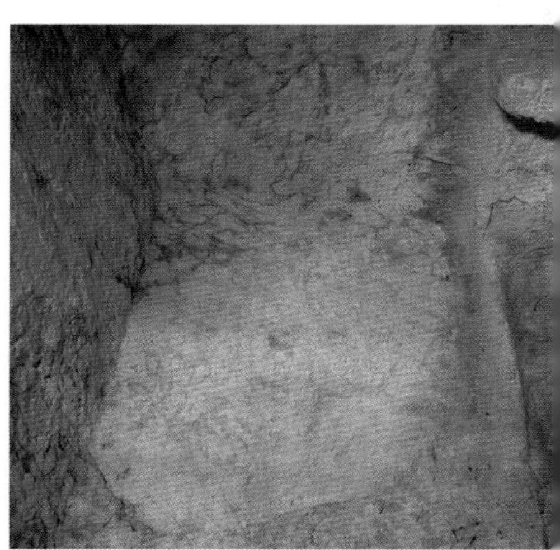

ryphal legends later circulated about Joseph of Arimathea, which have no scholarly historical support.

A disciple of Jesus (27:57). Joseph was a fellow member of the Sanhedrin with Nicodemus, both of whom appear as exemplary Jews anticipating the arrival of the kingdom of God (Mark 15:43; Luke 23:50–51; John 3:1–15; 19:38–42). Joseph is an example of a person who apparently did not follow Jesus around in his earthly ministry, but who was still considered a disciple, even as he continued to serve within the religious establishment of Israel.[455] Now is the turn for these two men to step forward and show their true colors.

Going to Pilate, he asked for Jesus' body (27:58). Because he is a rich man, Joseph's tomb becomes the fulfillment of the proper place for a burial for Jesus (Isa. 53:9). Not only is the Sabbath approaching, but Deuteronomy 21:22–23 instructs that a person hanged on a tree should be buried the same day so that the land will not be defiled, for the person hanged on a tree is under God's curse. Rabbinic interpretation insisted that burial should be completed if possible on the day of death: "Every one that suffers his dead to remain overnight transgresses a negative command."[456]

Joseph took the body, wrapped it in a clean linen cloth (27:59). The Jews did not practice cremation or embalming.[457] Coffins were not used; rather, the body was dressed in linen cloths.[458] Contact with corpses caused ritual impurity, so tombs were marked with whitewash (cf. 23:27) to warn passersby. Corpses were left in tombs until the flesh decayed (from one to three years), when the bones were collected and placed in ossuaries (see comments on 23:29).[459]

Placed it in his own new tomb that he had cut out of the rock (27:60). On the location of this tomb, see "Golgotha" at 27:33. Burial was generally in a cave, to which the body was carried on a bier in a funeral procession (*m. Ber.* 3:1). Family tombs predominated in first-century Judaism, which could be reused over several generations. The tomb was a rectangular underground chamber cut into rock, sometimes in abandoned quarries. It was accessed through a low entry chamber, normally closed with a stone. The dead were laid out on benches cut parallel into the rock and/or placed in perpendicular burial slots or recesses cut into the sides of the tomb chambers. Large family tombs were quite expensive, sometimes with several chambers connected together with tunnels.[460]

He rolled a big stone in front of the entrance to the tomb (27:60). Stones of various types were used to lodge against the entryway, which permitted repeated use of the tomb. Some were rolling disc-shaped stones, while others were more like plugs that were dislodged from the entry. The word for "rolled" (*proskyliō*) can be used of either "rolling away" or "dislodging."[461] The burial of bodies with some personal effects such as pottery, tools, or weapons was common, but the entrance to the tomb was not primarily to protect from grave robbers. Rather, it was used to protect the body from wild animals that would feed on carcasses.

Mary Magdalene and the other Mary (27:61). Prior to burial, out of respect and honor the corpse was watched over and washed.

Arrangements for a Guard at the Tomb (27:62–66)

The next day, the one after Preparation Day (27:62). The expression "Preparation Day" was a common expression for the day preceding the Sabbath (cf. Mark 15:42), that is, Friday, when the people made their preparations for the Sabbath. Therefore, the events Matthew now narrates occur on the day after the Preparation Day, another expression for "the Sabbath."

The chief priests and the Pharisees went to Pilate (27:62). As long as they did not travel more than a day's journey or enter the residence of the governor (John 18:28), the Jewish leaders would not defile the Sabbath (cf. Acts 1:12). Exodus 16:29 set a standard for travel on the Sabbath, admonishing people not to go out so that they would observe the Sabbath rest. The Qumran community interpreted the admonition to mean that a person "could not walk more than one thousand cubits outside the city" (CD 10:21), while the rabbis allowed a combination of a thousand cubits to travel a distance of two thousand cubits (*m. Soṭah* 5:3; see comments on 12:1).

Take a guard.... Go, make the tomb as secure as you know how" (27:65). An earlier contingent of Roman military had been assigned to the temple authorities for security, which had been used for the arrest of Jesus (cf. 27:47). This is the same guard troop Pilate indicates the Jewish officials are to use to make the tomb secure. The expression rendered as a charge, "Take a guard," may be a statement, "You have a guard" (NASB, NRSV), indicating that they are authorized to use the troops for this security assignment. The Jewish officials were not authorized to use the troops except for the purposes the Roman governor authorized.

They ... made the tomb secure by putting a seal on the stone and posting the guard (27:66). After a family placed the body of one of its members in a burial recess in the tomb, a stone was placed over the entrance, and it was often sealed with clay.[462] However, the "seal" here seems to be more of an official security device, so it is more likely an apparatus such as a cord attached to both the stone that blocks the entrance and to the rock face of the tomb, with wax imprinted with the Roman seal anchoring both ends, so that any tampering can be detected (cf. Dan. 6:17). The military contingent standing guard also acts as a security seal.

The Women Followers Discover an Empty Tomb (28:1–7)

Matthew's concluding chapter climaxes the amazing story of Jesus Messiah. He was conceived in a miraculous manner as the Savior of his people. He lived a sensational life in the power of the Spirit, announcing the arrival of the kingdom of heaven. But he was tragically betrayed by his own people and crucified by the Roman government. Will that be the end of the story? Indeed not! On the third day after his crucifixion, Jesus Messiah is found missing from his grave! Various explanations have been set forth, but Matthew tells in convincing fashion that the only explanation for the empty tomb is that Jesus has been raised, just as he predicted. The angels announce the resurrection, his women followers are the first to witness both the empty tomb and the risen Jesus, and all of his followers now have the commission to proclaim the invitation to enter into a relationship with the risen Jesus as his disciples.

Mary Magdalene and the other Mary went to look at the tomb (28:1). The same women who courageously witnessed Jesus' gruesome crucifixion and burial observe the Sabbath from sundown Friday until Saturday evening, after which they purchase materials to continue preparing Jesus' body for burial (cf. Mark 16:1). At sunrise they intend to visit the tomb. Although there was a practice in the ancient world for family members to visit a tomb three days after the funeral to make certain that the person was dead (*b. Sem.* 8:1), no mention is made of this expectation. The military had made certain of Jesus' death on the cross (John 19:32). Instead, consistent with Jewish burial practices, the women have come to assist the surviving family as they finalize preparing the body for burial.

Mary Magdalene once again takes a prominent role, but also accompanying her is "the other Mary," the mother of James the younger and Joses (cf. Mark 16:2). A comparison of the various Gospel accounts points to the following women who attended Jesus at the cross and those who visit the tomb: (1) Mary Magdalene, (2) the "other Mary" (the mother of James the younger and Joses), (3) Salome (the mother of James and John the sons of Zebedee), (4) Jesus' mother, Mary, (5) Joanna, wife of Chuza, (6) Susanna, and several other unnamed women.[463]

A violent earthquake (28:2). One of the chief geological characteristics of Palestine has been its proneness to earthquakes, especially because the Jordan Rift Valley is part of a large fault zone that stretches northward from the entrance of the Gulf of Aqaba for over 683 miles to the foot of the Taurus range.[464]

Rolled back the stone and sat on it (28:2). The entrances to burial tombs were sealed in a variety of ways, including a plug-like stone inserted into the tomb opening,[465] but also as here, a cylindrical stone rolled up a trough, which was wedged open while a body was being attended inside the tomb.

His appearance was like lightning, and his clothes were white as snow (28:3). The brilliance of the angel of the Lord is often associated with descriptions of lightning.[466] The white clothing is typical to indicate angelic brilliant purity. The appearance of a fiery angel often terrified people (Judg. 13:19–20; *4 Ezra* 10:25–27).

He is not here; he has risen, just as he said. Come and see the place where he lay (28:6). Judaism hoped for the bodily resurrection of all people; now Jesus is the dramatic firstfruits of that expectation (1 Cor. 15:20, 23).

Go quickly and tell his disciples (28:7). Several of the women witnessed the sealing of the tomb[467]; they are among the first witnesses of the empty tomb and the resurrected Jesus.[468] They are designated by both the angel and Jesus to be the

CHAMBER INSIDE THE CHURCH OF THE HOLY SEPULCHRE

Hadrian's Destruction and Constantine's Monuments

ORIGINAL TOMB CUT INTO SOLID BEDROCK

TOTAL DESTRUCTION BY THE ROMAN EMPEROR HADRIAN (After A.D. 135)
After suppressing the second Jewish Revolt Hadrian demolished the rock hillside down to about the level of the bench and built a temple to Venus over the area. Jerome stated that the sacred resurrection spot was occupied by a statue of Jupiter.

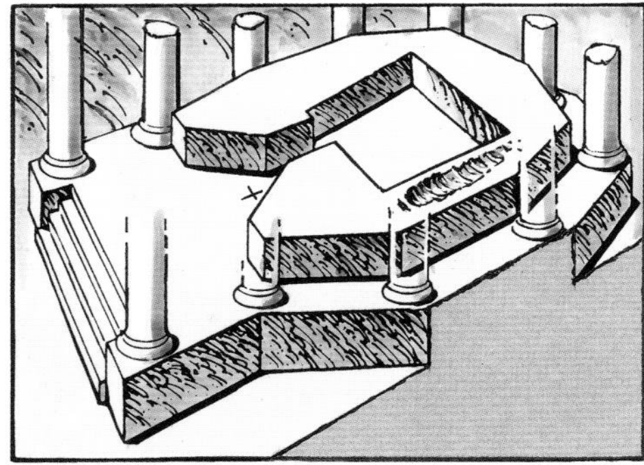

CONSTANTINE'S MONUMENTS
(After A.D. 326 when Christianity was official)
Following the Roman custom of building an "above ground" tomb for an important person, Constantine carved out all around the bench, lowered the floor and built a "small building" or "edicule". Around and above it he later erected a rotunda and dome. As reported by the traveler Egeria, by 395 pilgrims had chipped away pieces of the burial bench for souvenirs and it "began to resemble a trough". Marble slabs later covered it, as they do to this day.

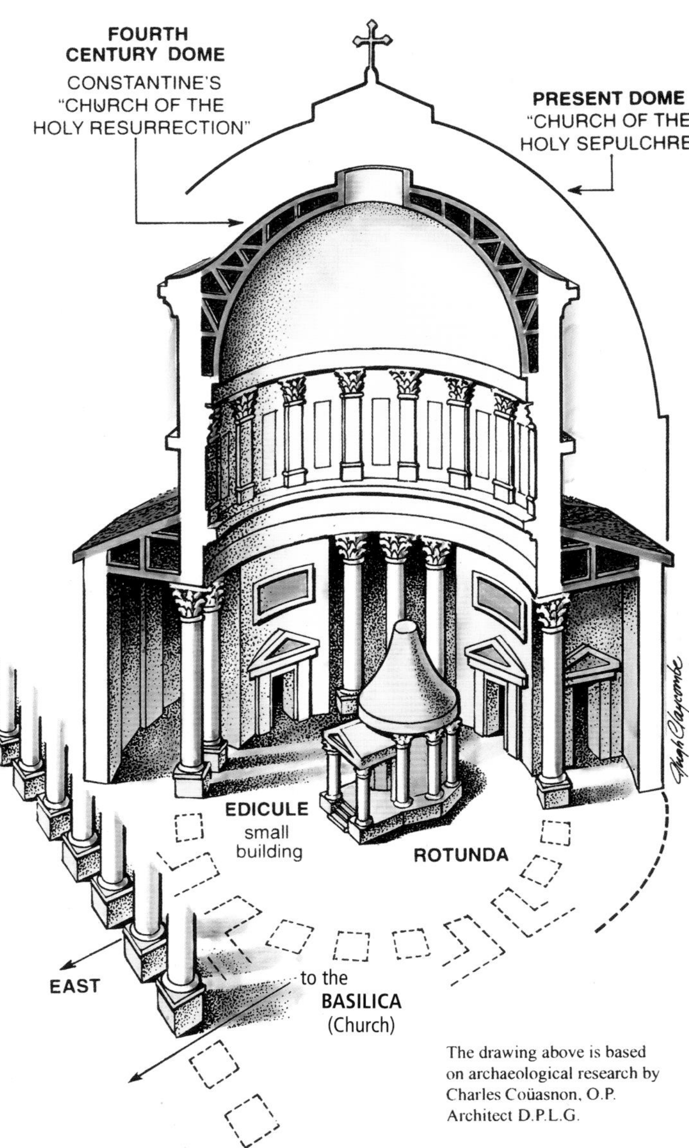

The drawing above is based on archaeological research by Charles Coüasnon, O.P. Architect D.P.L.G.

Constantine's architects did not erect the dome exactly over the burial bench where Jesus' body had lain, but rather 48" to the South and 20" to the East. The focus point of the rotunda (the exact center) and centered under the dome was the outer edge of the entrance, precisely where the risen Christ first stepped out of the tomb into the world of the living. Thus the entire building complex commemorated the resurrection. Eastern churches still celebrate Easter at midnight, when closed doors are opened and pastors step out into the congregation proclaiming "Christ has Risen.

ones to carry their witness to the other disciples as the first to testify to the reality of the resurrection (28:10; Mark 16:7; John 20:17).

The Risen Jesus Appears to the Women (28:8–10)

They . . . clasped his feet and worshiped him (28:9). "Worship" can either indicate kneeling before an esteemed religious figure (e.g., 8:2) or, when linked with the action of grasping feet, indicate actual worship. By allowing this act of worship here and in 28:17, something that neither angels nor apostles allow,[469] Jesus accepts the acknowledgment of his deity. Only God is to be worshiped.

Go and tell my brothers to go to Galilee; there they will see me (28:10). Elsewhere Jesus' disciples are called his 'brother, and sister, and mother" (12:49–50), indicating not only their relationship to him but also their relationship to each other. They are now brothers and sisters of one family of faith. Galilee was the location of his boyhood, but even more important the central location of Jesus' earthly ministry (cf. 4:12ff.). Now Galilee continues as a central place of his earthly ministry, which will last forty days until his ascension (Acts 1:3).

The Conspiracy to Deny Jesus' Resurrection (28:11–15)

Some of the guards . . . reported to the chief priests everything that had happened (28:11). These Roman military personnel were assigned by Pilate to the temple authorities for security, which is why they report to them and not to Pilate (see 26:48; 27:65).

You are to say, "His disciples came during the night and stole him away while we were asleep" (28:13). It is unlikely

▸ The Resurrection of the Dead in Judaism and in Jesus

The expectation of a resurrection of the righteous to new life and the wicked to punishment is well attested in the Old Testament and Second Temple Jewish literature.[A-123] Resurrection in rabbinic Judaism refers to the concept of all the dead being brought back to life by God on the Day of Judgment, giving eternal life to the righteous and consigning the wicked to Gehenna. This was a central part of rabbinic belief from the first century after the destruction of the temple in A.D. 70, with the decline of the Sadducees, who rejected the notion of resurrection (Matt. 22:23; Acts 23:8) and the ascendance of Pharisaism, which placed resurrection as a central blessed hope.[A-124] Belief in the resurrection plays a prominent role in synagogue liturgy, including *Amidah* (Standing Prayer), with the *Shemoneh Esre* or *Tefillah* (Eighteen Benedictions, Prayers), which are recited in all worship services. The prayer of the second benediction praises God as one who resurrects the dead: "Who is like You, almighty, and who is compared to you, King, who kills and gives life and brings salvation to spring up? And You are reliable to give life to the dead. Praised are You, Lord, who gives life to the dead."[A-125]

But the resurrection of Jesus Messiah has even more far-reaching implications. With his resurrection Jesus is declared with power to be the Son of God (Rom. 1:2–6), through whom all peoples of the world now gain access to salvation through his sacrifice on the cross. With his resurrection, the age of the gospel of salvation is inaugurated with the sending of the Spirit of God at Pentecost. In his life, death, and resurrection, Jesus is the exemplar of the new people who will be regenerated and transformed into his image.[A-126] that all of the guards would have been asleep on guard duty, because the penalty for falling asleep while on duty could be execution.[470] Further, rolling the stone away would surely have awakened at least some of the guards. And how did they know what had happened to the body if they were asleep? Besides these factors, the disciples had not had sufficient courage to attend the crucifixion and had even denied him, which makes it most unlikely that they would have mounted up a plot to steal Jesus' body from a well-guarded tomb. To concoct such a dubious story indicates the desperation of the religious leaders, but the religious leaders were desperate to hide what really happened.

The soldiers took the money and did as they were instructed (28:15). Military personnel are trained to do as ordered without asking questions of their superiors. These soldiers knew well enough the truth, but they could not have known the deep significance of the threat to the religious establishment, nor of the deep religious significance of the empty tomb.

This story has been widely circulated among the Jews to this very day (28:15). Matthew writes upwards of thirty years after these events, which indicates an active attempt to counteract the increasingly widespread declaration that Jesus had been raised from the dead in vindication of his claim to be the Messiah. Nearly a century later the rumor was still circulating among the Jews, as is evident in the writings of Justin Martyr (*Dialogue with Trypho* 108.2). The famous "Nazareth Decree," a stone slab with a decree from Caesar (Claudius?) warning of capital punishment for those violating tombs, points to the seriousness with which disturbing graves and moving dead bodies was held in the ancient world. It may also give some insight to the events in Matthew's narrative, if it was erected (as some propose) in A.D. 50 in Nazareth in response to the controversy between Jews and Christians about Jesus' empty tomb.[471]

REFLECTIONS

MANY SCHOLARS CONSIDER GOD'S CHOICE OF WOMEN as the first witnesses of Jesus' resurrection to be one of the bedrock truths of the resurrection narratives and the historicity of the resurrection itself. It is unlikely that any Jew would have created such a story as fiction, for a variety of reasons.

(1) Because of the debated status of a woman in Judaism at the time, there was disagreement among some of the rabbis as to the acceptability of a woman giving testimony in a court of law. This would make it much less likely that a Jew would fictionalize a woman's testimony in the case of Jesus' resurrection.[A-127]

(2) The cowardly picture painted of the men hiding away in Jerusalem, while the women boldly carry out their responsibilities to prepare Jesus' body for burial, would certainly offend the sensibilities of Jewish readers and doubtless would not have been recorded unless it were true.

(3) The listing of the names of the women weighs against being fiction, because these women were known in early Christian fellowship and would not have easily been associated with a false account.

(4) Jesus' appearances to these women with debated status lend credibility to the account, because again, they would be unlikely selections for a fictionalized account trying to be understood as believable.

For these reasons and more, the selection of women as the first witnesses yields high credibility to the resurrection narratives and to the resurrection itself.[A-128] It is vitally important for us to build our faith on the solid foundation of the historically verifiable truth of the resurrection of Jesus Christ.

The Galilean Appearance and Great Commission (28:16–20)

The eleven disciples went to Galilee, to the mountain where Jesus had told them to go (28:16). Jesus' and the disciples' familiarity with Galilee and their regular retreat to the hills[472] to escape the press of the crowds implies that there had been a prearranged meeting place. Mount Tabor has been the traditional site associated with this appearance, but for the same reasons that it was likely not the site of the Transfiguration (see comments on 17:1ff.), it is likely not the scene of this resurrection appearance. Rather, Jesus has arranged to meet with the disciples at some spot known to them in the many hills surrounding the Sea of Galilee.

When they saw him, they worshiped him; but some doubted (28:17). The Eleven, who had received at least two or three appearances from the risen Jesus prior to this in Jerusalem, are prepared to worship him. However, those disciples in Galilee who have not yet seen the risen Jesus (cf. "brothers" in 28:10), much like Thomas prior to his experience with the risen Jesus (John 20:24–29), doubt until Jesus appears to them bodily. This historical reminiscence by Matthew stresses the historicity of Jesus' resurrection, which was not met by gullible enthusiasm, but by logical hesitancy until people were convinced by facts. This may well be an allusion to the group of more than five hundred persons to whom the apostle Paul states Jesus appeared, most of whom were still alive when he wrote (1 Cor. 15:6).

All authority in heaven and on earth has been given to me (28:18). In his earthly ministry Jesus had declared his authority as the Son of Man to forgive sin (9:6) and to reveal the Father (11:27). Now as the risen Messiah he has been given all authority, glory, and power, who is rightly worshiped by all peoples and nations and whose dominion and kingdom last forever (Dan. 7:13–14).

Therefore go and make disciples of all nations (28:19). Disciples of a significant master were a common phenomenon in the ancient world, but throughout his ministry Jesus had developed a unique form of discipleship for those who would follow him. He breaks through a variety of barriers—gender, ethnic, religious, social, economic, and so on—by calling all peoples into a personal discipleship relationship with himself. Being a disciple of Jesus is not primarily an academic endeavor like the Pharisees (e.g., 22:16), nor even a commitment to a great prophet like John the Baptist (e.g., 9:14). A disciple of Jesus has come to him for salvation and eternal life and will always be only a disciple.

Baptizing them (28:19). Purity washings were common among the various sects in Israel, whether for entrance to the temple or for daily rituals. Proselyte baptism increasingly indicated conversion from paganism to Judaism. But Jesus' form of baptism is unique. It is the symbol of conversion of discipleship, indicating a union and new identity with Jesus Messiah, who had died and been raised to new life (cf. Rom. 6:1–4).

In the name of the Father and of the Son and of the Holy Spirit (28:19). Jews were

MIQVEH

The pools were used for Jewish ritual purity washings. This miqveh was discovered in the excavations near Herod's palace in Roman Jericho.

not baptized in the name of a person. Baptism in the "name" (note the singular) of the Father, Son, and Holy Spirit associates the three as personal distinctions, an early indication of the Trinitarian Godhead and an overt proclamation of Jesus' deity.

Teaching them to obey everything I have commanded you (28:20). Access to education under an esteemed rabbi was normally reserved for privileged men in rabbinic Judaism. Some rabbis denied young girls even the basics of Torah instruction, such as Eliezer who said: "If any man gives his daughter a knowledge of the Law it is as though he taught her lechery" (*m. Soṭah* 3:4). But Jesus once again breaks down barriers to indicate that *all* of his disciples—women and men, Gentile and Jew, poor and rich—are to be taught to obey everything he has commanded. But the emphasis is not simply on acquisition of knowledge. The goal of instructing new disciples of Jesus is obedience to what he has commanded, so that their lives increasingly become like their Master (10:24–25). What Jesus has done

ANNOTATED BIBLIOGRAPHY

Blomberg, Craig L. *Matthew: An Exegetical and Theological Exposition of Holy Scripture, NIV Text*. NAC 22. Nashville: Broadman, 1992.

This commentary serves a valuable purpose for pastors and lay teachers because it is brief, yet based on sound scholarship.

Carson, Donald A. "Matthew." Pages. 3–599 in vol. 8, *EBC*. Grand Rapids: Zondervan, 1984.

For many years this was the best evangelical, exegetical commentary on Matthew. While it is somewhat dated, it deserves a prominent place of reference for study, teaching, and preaching on Matthew.

Davies, W. D., and Dale C. Allison Jr. *A Critical and Exegetical Commentary on the Gospel According to Saint Matthew*. ICC. 3 vols., rev. ed. Edinburgh: T. & T. Clark, 1988, 1991, 1997.

This 3-volume set surfaces all possible interpretations of the text from a historical-critical perspective. It discusses the Jewish cultural and historical issues, but one must weigh carefully its critical orientation.

Hagner, Donald A. *Matthew*. WBC 33 A-B. 2 vols. Dallas: Word, 1993, 1995.

Hagner has provided the most comprehensive exegetical commentary on Matthew from a professedly evangelical perspective. The commentary requires the basic use of Greek, but is not burdensome. His discussion of background issues is broadly informed.

Keener, Craig S. *A Commentary on the Gospel of Matthew*. Grand Rapids: Eerdmans, 1999.

This is a valuable commentary for discussing historical, social/cultural backgrounds to Matthew's Gospel. Keener comments on the text from a theological perspective, adding many helpful devotional insights. Additionally, he has many extensive excurses that go into depth on background issues.

Morris, Leon. *The Gospel According to Matthew*. Pillar Commentaries. Grand Rapids: Eerdmans, 1992.

Morris has a classic, genuine grasp of the meaning of the text and communicates in a warm, pastoral fashion. Recommended for pastors and teachers.

Rousseau, John J. K., and Rami Arav. *Jesus and His World: An Archaeological and Cultural Dictionary*. Minneapolis: Fortress, 1995.

The authors have compiled a wealth of valuable material, although at many points are unduly critical of conservative conclusions.

Wilkins, Michael J. *Matthew*. NIVAC. Grand Rapids: Zondervan, forthcoming.

This is a commentary for pastors and informed laypersons that combines analysis of the original meaning of the text with discussion of biblical theology and suggestions for contemporary application.

_____. *Following the Master: A Biblical Theology of Discipleship*. Grand Rapids: Zondervan, 1992.

This is an extensive discussion of the Hellenistic and Jewish backgrounds to discipleship, leading to a full discussion of a biblical theology of discipleship to Jesus.

in making disciples of his first followers, succeeding generations of the church will do in the making of new disciples of Jesus.

Surely I am with you always, to the very end of the age (28:20). Jesus' entrance into history is encapsulated in the name Immanuel, "God with us" (1:23), and his abiding presence with his disciples throughout history is pronounced in his concluding assurance, "I am with you always." A true Israelite would proclaim only God to be eternal and omnipresent, so here Matthew records a concluding claim by Jesus to his deity, as he is with his disciples forever.

CHAPTER NOTES

Main Text Notes

1. Tacitus, *Annals* 1.4.
2. Ibid.
3. A study that is still valuable for establishing this thesis is Édouard Massaux, *The Influence of the Gospel of Saint Matthew on Christian Literature before Saint Irenaeus, Book 1: The First Ecclesiastical Writers*, trans. Norman J. Belval and Suzanne Hecht; ed. Arthur J. Bellinzoni (New Gospel Studies 5/1; 1950; Macon, Ga.: Mercer, 1990).
4. E.g., 1:22–23; 2:4–5, 15, 17, 23; 5:17–20.
5. See 16:18; 18:15–20; cf. 28:20.
6. E.g., Luke 1:31; 3:21, 23; Matt. 1:21.
7. Heb. *māšîah.*; Aram. *mĕšîḥam*, "anointed."
8. See Marshall D. Johnson, *The Purpose of Biblical Genealogies*, 2d. ed. (SNTSMS 8; Cambridge: Cambridge Univ. Press, 1988).
9. E.g., Ruth 4:12–22;1 Chron. 1:34; 2:1–15; 3:1–24.
10. E.g., Josephus, *Life* 1 §6; idem, *Ag. Ap.* 1.6–10 §§28–56.
11. *Gen. Rab.* 98:8; *y. Taʿan.* 4:2.
12. Cf. 2 Sam. 5:14; Matt. 1:6; Luke 3:32.
13. Cf. 22:41–46; 2 Sam. 7:12–16; Ps. 89:19–29, 35–37; 110:1–7; 132:11–12.
14. E.g., 1 Chron. 1:39; 2:3–4, 16, 18, 24, 26, 29, 48–49; 3:9, etc.
15. See Moshe Idel, *Kabbalah: New Perspectives* (New Haven, Conn.: Yale Univ. Press, 1990).
16. Cf. Lev. 20:10; 22:23ff.; Deut. 22:13–21.
17. Gen. 21:17; 22:15–18; Ex. 3:2ff.; Judg. 6:11ff.
18. Cf. Zech. 1:8–17; Luke 1:26; *1 En.* 6:7; 8:3–4; 69:1.
19. See Larry W. Hurtado, *One God, One Lord: Early Christian Devotion and Ancient Jewish Monotheism* (Philadelphia: Fortress, 1988), 71–92; Carol A. Newsom, "Gabriel," *ABD*, 2:863; also Carol A. Newsom and Duane F. Watson, "Angel," *ABD*, 1:248–55.
20. Ovid, *Metam.* 9.685–701; Tacitus, *Annals* 2.14.
21. Natural (Eccl. 5:3), divine (Gen. 28:12; Dan. 2:19), evil (Deut. 13:1, 2; Jer. 23:32).
22. Gen. 37:5–11; Num. 12:6; Job 33:15–17; Dan. 7:1–28.
23. Cf. 1:20; 2:12, 13, 19, 22; 27:19.
24. Cf. Ps. 130:8; *Pss. Sol.* 18:3–5.
25. Gen. 24:43; Ex. 2:8; Ps. 68:25.
26. *Pseudo-Phocylides* 186 (c. 100 B.C.–A.D. 100).
27. Josephus, *Ag. Ap.* 2.25 §§202–203.
28. Josephus *Ant.* 18.9.2, 5, §§318–19, 340.
29. Suetonius, *Vesp.* 5.
30. Josephus (*J.W.* 3.8.9 §§399–408; 6.5.4 §§310–15) and Tacitus (*Hist.* 5:13) make similar mention of this widespread expectation (the debate includes whether these Roman historians read Josephus).
31. E.g., CD 7:18–26; 4QTest. 9–13.
32. 2 Peter 1:19; Rev. 22:16; cf. 2:28.
33. Suetonius, *Nero* 13; cf. Dio Cassius, *Rom. Hist.* 63.1.7.
34. See Josephus, *Ant.* 14.13.3–10 §§335–69; 17.2.1 §23.
35. *Nomikos*; cf. 23:4, Luke 11:45–46.
36. Ruth 4:11–21; 1 Sam. 17:12.
37. John S. Holladay, Jr., "House, Israelite," *ABD*, 3:313; Rousseau and Arav, "House," *Jesus and His World*, 128–31.
38. Gen. 43:11–15; 1 Sam. 9:7–8; 1 Kings 10:1–2.
39. *Libanos*; Lev. 2:1; 14:7; Neh. 13:9.
40. W. E. Shewell-Cooper, "Frankincense," *ZPEB*, 2:606–7.
41. Est. 2:13; Ps. 45:8; Prov. 7:17; Song 3:6.
42. Kjeld Nielsen, "Incense," *ABD*, 3:404–9; Victor H. Matthews, "Perfumes and Spices," *ABD*, 5:226–28; Joel Green, "Burial of Jesus," *DJG*, 88–92.
43. Gen. 12:10; 42:1–2; 1 Kings 11:40; 2 Kings 25:26; Zech. 10:10.
44. E.g., Ps. 78; 81; 105–106; Jer. 2:6; 7:22–25; Ezek. 20:1–20; Mic. 6:1–4.
45. Josephus, *Ant.* 17.8.1 §§188–89. Herod's grandson, Agrippa I (10 B.C.–A.D. 44; Acts 12, called Herod) and great-grandson Agrippa II (c. A.D. 28–93; Acts 25–26) continued Herod's influence in Palestine through much of the first century.

46. Josephus, *Ant.* 17.9.3 §§213–18; idem, *J.W.* 2.6.2 §§88–90.
47. Josephus, *J.W.* 2.7.3 §111.
48. The earliest extant reference is by Julius Africanus (A.D. 170–240), as cited by Eusebius (*Eccl. Hist.* 1.7.14).
49. James F. Strange, "Nazareth (Place)," *ABD*, 4.1050–51.
50. Cf. 21:11; 26:71. For a good general overview of the terms and various other interpretations, see A. F. Walls, "Nazarene," *Illustrated Bible Dictionary*, 2:1060–61, and J. W. Charley, "Nazareth," *Illustrated Bible Dictionary*, 2:1061–63.
51. E.g., Isa. 4:2; 53:2; Jer. 23:5; 33:15; Zech. 3:8; 6:12; 1QH 14:15; 15:19; 16:5–10 [=1QH 6:15; 7:19; 8:5–10]; 4QIsa[a] 3:15–26 (some of these use *ṣemaḥ*, not *neṣer*, though the meaning is essentially the same). See Marinus de Jonge, "Messiah," *ABD*, 4:777–88.
52. 4QFlor 1:10–12.
53. Ps. 22:6–8, 13; 69:8, 20–21; Isa. 11:1; 49:7; 53:2–3, 8; Dan. 9:26; the theme especially culminates in Isa. 52–53.
54. E.g., Ex. 19:1ff.; 1 Kings 17:2–3; 19:3–18; 1 Macc. 5. See Joseph Patrich, "Hideouts in the Judean Wilderness," *BAR* 15.5 (Sept./Oct. 1989): 32–42. For an overview of these groups, see Richard A. Horsley and John S. Hanson, *Bandits, Prophets, and Messiahs: Popular Movements at the Time of Jesus* (Minneapolis: Winston, 1985).
55. See Ben Witherington III, "John the Baptist," *DJG*, 384; John P. Meier, *A Marginal Jew: Rethinking the Historical Jesus* (ABRL; New York: Doubleday, 1994), 2:49–52; Darrell L. Bock, *Luke* (BECNT; Grand Rapids: Baker, 1994), 1:198; Rousseau and Arav, *Jesus and His World*, 80–82, 262; Todd S. Beall, *Josephus' Description of the Essenes Illustrated by the Dead Sea Scrolls* (SNTSMS 58; Cambridge: Cambridge Univ. Press, 1988).
56. Cf. 12:28; 19:24; 21:31, 43; Mark 10:24–25; Luke 18:24–25.
57. E.g., *m. Ber.* 2:2, 5.
58. E.g., 1 Macc. 3:18–19; 4:10; 12:15; *m. ʾAbot* 1:3, 11.
59. Cf. Josephus, *J.W.* 1.24.3 §480.
60. Cf. Gen. 37:34; 2 Sam. 3:31; 2 Kings 6:30; Heb. 11:37.
61. Cf. Neh. 9:1; Jer. 6:26.
62. CD 12:13–15.
63. See the interesting presentations by G. S. Cansdale, "Locust," *ZPEB*, 3.948–50; Edwin Firmage, "Zoology (Animal Profiles): Locusts; Bees," *ABD*, 6:1150.
64. For a discussion of the religious and social dynamic addressed to the general audience, see Robert L. Webb, *John the Baptizer and Prophet: A Socio-Historical Study* (JSNTSup 62; Sheffield: JSOT, 1991), 289–300.
65. Cf. Isa. 64:1; Ezek. 1:1; John 1:51; Acts 7:56; 10:11.
66. Cf. 4QFlor 1:10–13; 4QpsDan[a]. See Ben Witherington III, *The Christology of Jesus* (Minneapolis: Fortress, 1990), 148–55.
67. BAGD, 646. This is true as well for the noun *peirasmos*, which can mean either "temptation" or "test."
68. Ex. 24:18; Deut. 9:25; 1 Kings 19:8; Ezek. 4:6. See Horst Balz, "τεσσεράκοντα," *TDNT*, 8:135–39; R. A. H. Gunner, "Number," *IBD*, 2:1098–1100.
69. Cf. Josephus, *Ant.* 15.11.5 §§411–13.
70. Josephus, *Ant.* 18.5.2 §§116–19.
71. Josephus, *J.W.* 3.10.8 §520.
72. For an excellent archaeological overview of the history of Capernaum, see John C. H. Laughlin, "Capernaum: From Jesus' Time and After," *BAR* 19.4 (May 1993): 55–61, 70; Bargil Pixner, *With Jesus Through Galilee According to the Fifth Gospel* (Israel: Corazin, 1992), 35.
73. Mendel Num, "Ports of Galilee: Modern Drought Reveals Harbors from Jesus' Time," *BAR* 25.4 (July/August 1999): 19–31, 64.
74. E.g., Pixner, *With Jesus Through Galilee*, 33–35.
75. For full description and illustrations, see Mendel Nun, *The Sea of Galilee and Its Fishermen in the New Testament* (Kibbutz Ein Gev: Kinneret Sailing Co., 1989), 23–37; idem, "Cast Your Net Upon the Waters: Fish and Fishermen in Jesus' Time," *BAR* 19.4 (July/August 1993): 52–53.
76. *m. ʾAbot* 1:6, 16
77. See Martin Hengel, *The Charismatic Leader and His Followers* (1968; ET; New York: Crossroad, 1981), 42–57; Wilkins, *Following the Master*, 100–109, 124–25.
78. Josephus, *J.W.* 2.11.10 §645.
79. Accounts that Josephus gives of traversing the lake with soldiers confirm these numbers: Josephus, *Life* 9 §32; idem, *J.W.* 2.21.8–9 §§636–641.
80. For the fascinating story of the discovery and excavation of the boat by the lead excavator, see Shelley Wachsmann, *The Sea of Galilee Boat: An Extraordinary 2000 Year Old Discovery* (New York: Plenum, 1995).
81. *Sagēnē*; cf. 13:47–48.
82. This most likely was the kind that Peter and his men use in Luke 5:1–11 and John 21:1–14 (Nun, *The Sea of Gaililee and its Fishermen*, 16–44). The general term for net, *diktyon*, is used in all of the fishing accounts (Matt. 4:20, 21; Mark 1:18, 19; Luke 5:2, 4–6; John 21:6, 8, 11). Matthew used a different term (*sagemnem*) for the "dragnet" in 13:47.

83. See Carl G. Rasmussen, *Zondervan NIV Atlas of the Bible* (Grand Rapids: Zondervan, 1989), 166–67. Josephus' statistic of 15,000 people living in even the smallest of the 204 cities and villages (Josephus, *J.W.* 3.3.2 §43; cf. idem, *Life* 45 §235), implying that Galilee has three million people, is probably an exaggeration.
84. Matt. 4:23; 9:35; 24:14.
85. Josephus, *Ant.* 12.4.9 §222; idem, *J.W.* 3.3.3 §§46–47.
86. Pixner, *With Jesus Through Galilee,* 34. Pixner also equates the place with Magadan (see comments on 15:39).
87. Cf. 13:1–2; 15:29; 24:3–4; 26:55.
88. E.g., Eph. 1:18; Col. 1:12; Heb. 9:15.
89. Ps. 24:3–6; 73:1; Prov. 22:11.
90. Cf. Ps. 28:3; Eccl. 3:8; Isa. 26:3.
91. See the interesting discussion of this view by a soils professor, Eugene P. Deatrick, "Salt, Soil, Savior," *BA* 25 (1962): 41–48.
92. Pliny, *Nat. Hist.* 31.102.
93. See K. M. Campbell, "The New Jerusalem in Matt. 5:14," *SJT* 31 (1978): 335–63; Rousseau and Arav, *Jesus and His World,* 127–28.
94. Cf. Mark 4:21; Luke 11:33.
95. Cf. *m. Šabb.* 16:1. See John Rea, "Lamp," *ZPEB,* 3:865–66, for pictures of excavated lamps from patriarchal times to the New Testament era; cf. Carol Meyers, "Lampstand," *ABD,* 4:141–43.
96. Cf. Matt. 7:12; 11:13; 22:40; Luke 24:27, 44; Rom. 3:21.
97. *m. ʾAbot* 2:1; 4:2.
98. *b. Mak.* 23b.
99. 2 Kings 16:3; 21:6; Jer. 32:35; cf. 7:31–32; 19:1–13.
100. For a fine discussion and numerous illustrations of various coinage see D. H. Wheaton, "Money," *IBD,* 2:1018–23; John W. Betlyon, "Coinage," *ABD,* 1:1076–89; Rousseau and Arav, *Jesus and His World,* 55–61.
101. Lev. 20:10; cf. Deut. 22:22–24.
102. See the attitude of the Essenes toward oaths recorded in Josephus, *J.W.* 28.6 §135; see also Sir. 23:9, 11; Philo, *Decalogue* 84–95.
103. See Ex. 21:24; Lev. 24:20; Deut. 19:21.
104. Cf. *m. B. Qam.* 8:6.
105. Ex. 22:26–7; Deut. 24:12; Ezek. 18:7; Amos 2:8. For a good overview of ancient wardrobes, see Douglas R. Edwards, "Dress and Ornamentation," *ABD,* 2:232–38.
106. BAGD. For a helpful chart showing equivalent distances, see H. Wayne House, *Chronological and Background Charts of the New Testament* (Grand Rapids: Zondervan, 1981), 26.
107. See "Lend, Lending," *DBI,* 506–7.
108. See Ps. 5:4–5; cf. 45:7; Deut. 7:2; 30:7.
109. Using the translation of Geza Vermes, *The Dead Sea Scrolls in English* (2d ed.; New York: Penguin, 1975), 72. Note also 1QS 1.3–4.
110. Gen. 6:9; 17:1; Deut. 18:13; 2 Sam. 22:24–27.
111. E.g., 1 Cor. 14:20; Eph. 4:13; Heb. 5:14; 6:1.
112. See Acts 9:36; 10:2; 24:17; cf. Tobit 1:3, 16; 4:7–8; Sir. 7:10.
113. *m. Šeqal.* 2:1.
114. E.g., Diogenes Laertius, *Lives of Eminent Philosophers* 7.160.
115. Josephus, *Ant.* 14.4.3 §65.
116. Deut. 14:1; 32:6; Ps. 103:13; Jer. 3:4; 31:9; Hos. 11:1.
117. E.g., *Jub.* 1:24, 28; 19:29; *Jos. Asen.* 12:14; Sir. 23:1, 4; Wisd. Sol. 2:16–20; 14:3; Tobit 13:4; 4Q372; 1QH 9:35 [17:35]. See Geza Vermes, *The Religion of Jesus the Jew* (Minneapolis: Fortress, 1993), 152–83; see "Father, God as," *DJBP,* 224.
118. Cited in James H. Charlesworth, "A Caveat on Textual Transmission and the Meaning of *Abba*: A Study of the Lord's Prayer," in *The Lord's Prayer and other Prayer Texts from the Greco-Roman Era,* ed. James H. Charlesworth with Mark Harding and Mark Kiley (Valley Forge, Pa.: Trinity, 1994), 7.
119. Cf. 5:16, 45, 48; 6:26, 33; 7:11.
120. Cited in James D. G. Dunn, "Prayer," *DJG,* 617.
121. 1 Cor. 16:22; *Did.* 10.6; cf. Rev. 22:20.
122. See Grant R. Osborne, *The Hermeneutical Spiral: A Comprehensive Introduction to Biblical Interpretation* (Downers Grove, Ill.: InterVarsity, 1991), 100–101, 108.
123. Ex. 16:4; Deut. 8:16; 1 Peter 1:7.
124. *b. Ber.* 60b, cited in Joachim Jeremias, *New Testament Theology: The Proclamation of Jesus* (New York: Scribner's, 1971), 202.
125. The ending that many Christians are accustomed to pray—"For yours is the kingdom, and the power, and the glory forever, Amen"—is not included in the oldest manuscripts, but it is found in many old ones. The earliest probably dates back to the late second century. Although it was not originally included in Matthew's Gospel, it is in line with many other scriptural concepts (e.g., 1 Chron. 29:11).
126. Lev. 16:29–34; 23:26–32.
127. BDB, 776, 847; see John E. Hartley, *Leviticus* (WBC 4; Dallas: Word, 1992), 242; R. Laird Harris, "Leviticus," *EBC,* 2:591.
128. E.g., 1QS 10:18–19; Sir. 31:8–11.
129. E.g., eyes become dimmed; Gen. 27:1; 48:18. See D. C. Allison Jr., "The Eye Is the Lamp of the Body (Matthew 6.22–23 = Luke 11.34–36)," *NTS* 33 (1987), 61–83.
130. This expression occurs similarly in Matt. 20:15, where the literal expression "evil eye"

indicates envy (cf. NIV; see G. Harder, "πονηρός," *TDNT*, 6:555–56. So also Donald A. Hagner, *Matthew* (WBC 33; Dallas: Word, 1993), 1:158.

131. Marvin A. Powell, "Weights and Measures," *ABD*, 4:899.
132. Irene and Walter Jacob, "Flora," *ABD*, 2:813; Pixner, *With Jesus Through Galilee*, 37.
133. See 1 Kings 10:1–29; 2 Chron. 9:1–28.
134. Ps. 37:2; 102:4, 11; 129:6; Isa. 40:6–8, quoted in 1 Peter 1:24–25; James 1:10; see "Grass," *DBI*, 348–49.
135. But for similar sayings, see Prov. 27:1; *b. Sanh.* 100b; *b. Ber.* 9a; Hagner, *Matthew*, 166.
136. See Michael J. Wilkins, "Prayer," *DLNT*, 941–48.
137. For discussion, see Firmage, "Zoology (Animal Profiles: D. Fish," *ABD*, 6:1146–47.
138. Jer. 6:13–15; 8:10–12; Ezek. 13:1–23; 22:27–29; Zeph. 3:1–4.
139. Josephus, *J.W.* 2.13.4 §259.
140. Josephus recounts stories of each of these: Theudas (*Ant.* 20.5.5 §§97–98), the Egyptian false prophet (*Ant.* 20.9.6 §§169–71; *J.W.* 2.14.5 §§261–63), and Jesus son of Hananiah (*J.W.* 6.5.3 §§300–309). For an overview of these groups, see Horsley and Hanson, *Bandits, Prophets and Messiahs*, 160–89.
141. Attributed to Elisha ben Abuyah in *Abot de-Rabbi Nathan* A, 24, 77; cited in Vermes, *Religion of Jesus the Jew*, 102.
142. Gordon Franz, "The Parable of the Two Builders," *Archaeology in the Biblical World* 3.1 (1995): 6–11.
143. A. N. Sherwin-White, *Roman Society and Roman Law in the New Testament* (Oxford: Clarendon, 1963), 123–24.
144. E.g., Luke 16:8 refers to "sons of light," and 1QM 17.8 refers to "sons of his truth" and "sons of his covenant."
145. Matt. 22:13; 5:29; cf. *4 Ezra* 7:93; *1 En.* 63:10.
146. See comments on 2:23.
147. E.g., Morna D. Hooker, "Did the Use of Isaiah 53 to Interpret His Mission Begin with Jesus?" in *Jesus and the Suffering Servant: Isaiah 53 and Christian Origins*, eds. William H. Bellinger Jr. and William R. Farmer (Harrisburg, Pa.: Trinity, 1998), 88–103.
148. David Hill, *The Gospel of Matthew* (NCBC; London: Marshall, Morgan and Scott, 1972), 161; e.g., *b. Sanh.* 98b: "Surely he hath borne our griefs and carried our sins, yet we did esteem him stricken with leprosy, and smitten of God and afflicted."
149. See Hengel, *Charismatic Leader*, 3–15.
150. See Wilkins, *Following the Master*, ch. 6.
151. Ex. 20:12; Deut. 5:16.
152. Cf. Tobit 4:3; 6:15.
153. See Freyne, *Galilee from Alexander the Great to Hadrian*; idem, "Galilee, Sea of," *ABD*, 2:900; Riesner, "Archeology and Geography," 37.
154. Nun, *The Sea of Galilee*, 16–44.
155. Wachsmann, *The Sea of Galilee Boat*, 326–28.
156. 2 Sam. 22:16; Ps. 18:15; 104:7; 106:9; Isa. 50:2; Nah. 1:4.
157. Josephus, *Life* 9 §42.
158. See Vassilios Tzaferis, "A Pilgrimage to the Site of the Swine Miracle," *BAR* 15.2 (March/April 1989): 44–51. This location best accounts for the variant readings in Mark and Luke.
159. Num. 19:11, 14, 16; Ezek. 39:11–15.
160. Lit. "diligent guards," a reference to the fallen angels (cf. *1 En.* 1–36).
161. Cf. Jude 6; Rev 20:10; *Jub.* 10:8–9; *T. Levi* 18:12; 1QS 3:24–24; 4:18–20.
162. Pixner, *With Jesus Through Galilee*, 35.
163. Josephus, *Ant.* 17.11.4 §319.
164. Cf. R. T. France, *Matthew: Evangelist and Teacher* (Grand Rapids: Zondervan, 1989), 70–74.
165. E.g., Philo, *Contempl. Life* 40–89; 1QSa 2.
166. Dennis E. Smith, "Table Fellowship," *ABD*, 6:302–4; see "Table Fellowship," *DJBP*, 613.
167. J. H. Harrop, "Tax Collector," *IBD*, 3:1520–21.
168. For background to the various uses of "sinner" in the Gospels, see Michael J. Wilkins, "Sinner," *DJG*, 757–60.
169. Ibid., 760.
170. Lee I. Levine, *The Ancient Synagogue: The First Thousand Years* (New Haven, Conn.: Yale Univ. Press, 2000), 402–3.
171. E.g., Gen. 22:5; Ex. 4:31; Deut. 26:10; Ps. 5:7.
172. 1 Sam. 24:9; 1 Kings 1:16, 23.
173. D. H. Trapnell, "Health, Disease and Healing," *IBD*, 2:619.
174. *m. Ketub.* 4:4; cf. *b. Moʾed Qaṭ.* 22b–23a.
175. Gen. 50:10; 1 Sam. 31:13; Sir. 22:12.
176. "Sheep, Shepherd," *DBI*, 782–85.
177. Cf. Karl H. Rengstorf, "δώδεκα," *TDNT*, 2:326.
178. Cf. Gal. 1:17, 19; 1Cor. 9:1–5; 15:7; Eph. 2:19–22.
179. Barnabas in Acts 14:4, 14; Titus in 2 Cor. 8:23; Epaphroditus in Phil. 2:25; probably Timothy and Silas also in 1 Thess. 1:1 with 2:6; cf. Andronicus and Junias in Rom. 16:7. James the brother of Jesus seems to be included among the apostles in Jerusalem as a "pillar of the church" (Gal. 1:17; 2:9).
180. E.g., Gen. 12:2–3; 22:18.
181. Cf. John 15:21; 2 Tim. 3:12; 1 Peter 4:13–14.
182. *Baʿal zebub*, Heb. for "Lord of the flies."
183. βεελζεβούλ in most Greek MSS, βεεζεβούλ according to א and B, βεελζεβούβ or βεελζεβυβ read by many non-Greek MSS.

184. Reflecting the Semitic *zbl* (lord/exalted one; or [exalted] abode, i.e., heaven).
185. See "Beelzebul," *DJBP*, 84.
186. E.g., Isa. 23:1–17; Jer. 25:22; 27:3–7; Ezek. 26:2–9; Joel 3:4–8; Zech. 9:2–4.
187. Gen. 18:16–19:29; Ezek. 16:48; cf. *m. Sanh.* 10.3.
188. A cubit was 17–18 inches, or the common length from elbow to tip of fingers. The formalized Jewish cubit was 17.5 inches.
189. Isa. 41:8–10; 44:1–3, 21; 45:4 [49:3?].
190. Isa. 42:1–4; 49:5–7.
191. See "Beelzebul," *DJBP*, 84.
192. Josephus, *Ant.* 8.2.5 §45–49; cf. "roots" in *J.W.* 7.6.3 §185.
193. Cf. *T. Moses* 10:1; Rev. 20:2.
194. James D. G. Dunn, "Sign," *IBD*, 3:1450.
195. The genitive "of Jonah" is an epexegetic genitive.
196. Cf. Gen. 42:17–18; 1 Sam. 30:12–13; 1 Kings 20:29; 2 Chron. 10:5, 12; Esth. 4:16; 5:1.
197. *b. Naz.* 5b; *m. Pesaḥ.* 4:2; cf. *y. Šabb.* 12a, 15, 17; cited in Gerhard Delling, "ἡμέρα," *TDNT*, 2:949–50.
198. Isa. 13:21; 34:14; Tobit 8:3; *1 En.* 10:4.
199. From earliest times the number seven also had sacred associations (Gen. 2:2; 4:24; 21:28; Ex. 20:10; Lev. 25:2–6, 8).
200. Charles R. Page, *Jesus and the Land* (Nashville: Abingdon, 1995), 85; Pixner, *With Jesus Through Galilee*, 40.
201. E.g., Matt. 5:14–15; 7:24–27; 9:16–17; 12:27–29, 43–45.
202. For an overview of the relationship to Jewish usage, see Vermes, *Religion of Jesus the Jew*, 90–97.
203. John W. Sider, *Interpreting the Parables: A Hermeneutical Guide to Their Meaning* (Grand Rapids: Zondervan, 1995), 88–89.
204. Judg. 6:11; Ruth 2:23; 2 Sam. 4:6.
205. Oded Borowski, "Agriculture," *ABD*, 1:97–98; idem, *Agriculture in Ancient Israel* (Winona Lake, Ind.: Eisenbrauns, 1987).
206. Some understand this to imply an extraordinary, superabundant, perhaps even miraculous crop, because typical Palestinian harvests yielded only about five to ten times the quantity sown; e.g., Joachim Jeremias, *The Parables of Jesus* (2d ed; New York: Scribner's, 1972), 149–51.
207. E.g., Job 15:8; Ps. 25:14; Prov. 3:32; Amos 3:7.
208. Cited in Vermes, *The Religion of Jesus the Jew*, 100.
209. "Yeast," Encyclopædia Britannica Online; J. D. Douglas, "Leaven," *IBD*, 2:891.
210. Nun, *The Sea of Galilee and its Fishermen*, 16–44.
211. The term is *mathēteuō*, which the NIV renders "has been instructed." The same verb occurs elsewhere in Matthew at 27:57; 28:19, and only in Acts 14:21 elsewhere in the New Testament. Each case should be translated, "become a disciple." See Michael J. Wilkins, *Discipleship in the Ancient World and Matthew's Gospel* (2d ed.; Grand Rapids: Zondervan, 1995), 160–63.
212. Josephus, *Ant.* 18.5.1 §109–115.
213. For a brief overview, see Harold W. Hoehner, "Herodian Dynasty," *DJG*, 322–25. For the most extensive treatment of the era, see idem, *Herod Antipas: A Contemporary of Jesus* (Grand Rapids: Zondervan, 1972; repr. 1980).
214. Cf. Josephus, *J.W.* 7.6.2 §§172–76.
215. Josephus, *Ant.* 18.5.1–2 §§112, 119.
216. For brief overviews, see F. F. Bruce, "Machaerus," *IBD*, 2:928–29; Stanislao Loffreda, "Machaerus," *ABD*, 4:457–58.
217. The term *korasion* in 14:11 is the diminutive "little girl."
218. Josephus, *Ant.* 18.6.10 §§225–39; cf. Acts 12.
219. Ibid., 13.14.2 §380.
220. Wilkins, *Following the Master*, 86–88, 253–56.
221. The Arabic *Et-Tabgha* is a corruption of the Greek *Heptapegon*.
222. Cited in Pixner, *With Jesus Through Galilee*, 36; cf. Bargil Pixner, "The Miracle Church at Tabgha on the Sea of Galilee," *BA* 48 (1985): 196–206.
223. Cf. Deut. 8:8; Ruth 2:17; Ezek. 4:9; cf. Philo, *Spec. Laws* 3.57.
224. See Dodo Joseph Shenhav, "Loaves and Fishes Mosaic Near Sea of Galilee Restored," *BAR* 10 (1984): 22–31.
225. Rudolf Bultmann/Dieter Lührmann, "φάντασμα," *TDNT*, 9:6.
226. For Matthew's portrait of Peter and his developing leadership role, see Wilkins, *Discipleship in the Ancient World*, 173–216, 264.
227. See Num. 34:11; Deut. 3:17; Josh. 12:3; 13:27.
228. Douglas R. Edwards, "Gennesaret," *ABD*, 2:963.
229. Samuel Sandmel, *Judaism and Christian Beginnings* (New York: Oxford, 1978), 103.
230. Danby, ed., *The Mishnah*, 446 n. 4.
231. Ibid., 446 n. 5.
232. Cf. Josephus, *Ant.* 13.10.6 §297.
233. Gen. 18:4; 19:2; 1 Sam. 25:41; cf. John 13:1–10.
234. *m. Yad.* 1:1.
235. Danby, *The Mishnah*, 778 n. 9.
236. See "Washing of Hands," *DJBP*, 667.
237. Danby, *The Mishnah*, 264 n. 1.
238. Ibid.
239. E.g., Isa. 23:1–17; Jer. 25:22; 27:3–7; Ezek. 26:2–9; Joel 3:4–8; Zech. 9:2–4.
240. E.g., *m. Qidd.* 1:3.

241. 1 Sam. 17:43; Ps. 22:16; Prov. 26:11. See "Dog," *DJBP*, 172; "Animals," "Dogs," *DBI*, 29, 213–14.
242. Gen. 12:3; see comments on Matt. 1:1; 8:5–13.
243. A. R. Millard, "Basket," *IBD*, 1:177–78; Pixner, *With Jesus Through Galilee*, 83.
244. Rainer Riesner, "Archaeology and Geography," *DJG*, 38.
245. See Pixner, *With Jesus Through Galilee*, 29, 73, 84.
246. So Robert H. Gundry, *Matthew: A Commentary on His Handbook for a Mixed Church Under Persecution* (2d ed.; Grand Rapids: Eerdmans, 1994), 322; Craig S. Keener, *A Commentary on the Gospel of Matthew* (Grand Rapids: Eerdmans, 1999), 420; Rousseau and Arav, *Jesus and His World*, 189–90.
247. Josephus, *J.W.* 2.21.8–10 §634–641; 3.9.7–3.10.5 §§443–503.
248. James F. Strange, "Magdala," *ABD*, 4:463–64.
249. See Shenhav, "Loaves and Fishes Mosaic Near Sea of Galilee Restored," 22–31.
250. James D. G. Dunn, "Sign," *IBD*, 3:1450.
251. Josephus records signs that warned of the destruction of Jerusalem. He believed God brought a star resembling a sword that stood over the city of Jerusalem, a comet that continued for a year, and a brilliant light that shone around the altar for half an hour (*J.W.* 6.5.1 §§288–292).
252. Josephus, *Ant.* 13.10.6 §298.
253. Cf. John 6:14; 7:40, 52; Acts 3:22; 7:37.
254. E.g., priests (1QRule of the Community [1QS] 9:11) and prophets (CD 2:12; 5:21–6:1; 1QM 11:7–8).
255. E.g., 1QRule of the Congregation (1QSa) 2:14, 20. See, e.g., Lawrence H. Schiffman, *The Eschatological Community of the Dead Sea Scrolls: A Study of the Rule of the Congregation* (SBLMS 38; Atlanta: Scholars, 1989).
256. *Pss. Sol.* 17:21.
257. 4QFlor 1:10–12. For an overview, see Marinus de Jonge, "Messiah," *ABD*, 4:777–88.
258. Joseph Fitzmyer, "Aramaic *Kepha'* and Peter's Name in the New Testament," in *To Advance the Gospel* (New York: Crossroad, 1981), 115.
259. Isa. 38:10; Wisd. Sol. 16:13; *3 Macc.* 5:51.
260. Job 38:17; Ps. 9:13; 107:18; cf. 1QH 6:24–26 [14:24–26].
261. See James D. Tabor, "Martyr, Martyrdom," *ABD*, 4:574–579; Arthur J. Droge and James D. Tabor, *A Noble Death: Suicide and Martyrdom Among Greeks and Romans, Jews and Christians in the Ancient World* (San Francisco: HarperSanFrancisco, 1992).
262. See comments on 8:19; cf. 12:38; 21:15. For an overview of these groups, see Brown, *The Death of the Messiah*, 1425–29.
263. Wilkins, *Discipleship in the Ancient World*, 116–24.
264. Cf. Matt. 13:41; 18:7; the cognate verb occurs in 11:6.
265. Plutarch, *Moralia* 554A/B; cf. 554D: "Every criminal condemned to death bears his cross on his back" (see comments on 27:26, 35). See also Martin Hengel, *Crucifixion in the Ancient World and the Folly of the Message of the Cross* (Philadelphia: Fortress, 1977), 77.
266. Ryken, et. al., "Cross," *DBI*, 184.
267. Ex. 34:29–35; cf. Dan. 12:3; 2 Esdras 7:97.
268. Cf. *As. Mos.*; *b. Soṭah* 13b.
269. Matt. 14:28–31; 15:15; 16:17–19; 17:24–27; 18:21.
270. Ex. 19:16; 20:18; 34:30; Deut. 4:33; 5:5, 23–27; Hab. 3:2–6, 16.
271. *m.ʿEd.* 8:7; cf. *m. B. Meṣiʿa* 3:5.
272. Mal. 4:5–6 (possibly a reference to Rev. 11:3–13?).
273. Cf. Josephus, *Ant.* 3.8.2 §§194–96.
274. John I. Durham, *Exodus* (WBC 3; Waco, Tex.: Word, 1987), 402–3; John W. Betlyon, "Coinage," *ABD*, 1:1076–89; Marvin A. Powell, "Weights and Measures," *ABD*, 6:897–908 (esp. 905–8).
275. See *m. Šeqal.* 1:3; 2:1; *y. Šeqal.* 6:1, 5; Josephus, *J.W.* 5.5.2 §200; idem, *Ant.* 18.9.1 §312–313.
276. Cf. Josephus, *Life* 12 §§62–63. Betlyon, "Coinage," 1089; Powell, "Weights and Measures," 905–8; Rousseau and Arav, *Jesus and His World*, 309–11; see "Tax Collectors" and "Taxes," *DJBP*, 618–19.
277. The negative particle *ou* is used in a question when an affirmative answer is expected, while *mē* is used when a negative response is expected; BDF §427.2 (p. 220).
278. Strange and Shanks, "Has the House Where Jesus Stayed in Capernaum Been Found?" 196.
279. Nun, "Cast Your Net," 46–56, 70.
280. Rousseau and Arav, *Jesus and His World*, 56; Archer, "Coins," 906.
281. Cf. Albrecht Oepke, "παῖς, παιδίον," *TDNT*, 5:639–40.
282. Ps. 127:3–5; 128:3–4; *Pss. Sol.* 1:3.
283. Josephus, *Ant.* 4.8.24 §§260–265.
284. E.g., Tobit 12:13–22; *1 En.* 100:5; *Jub.* 35:1; *T. Levi* 5:3.
285. E.g., Ps. 23; Isa. 53:6; Jer. 13:17; Zech. 10:3; 13:7.
286. E.g., Ps. 119:176; Isa. 53:6; Jer. 23:1–4; 50:6; Ezek. 34:1–30.
287. Edwin Firmage, "Zoology (Animal Profiles): Sheep," *ABD*, 6:1126–27; Keener, *Matthew* (1999), 452.
288. See *Rule of the Community* (1QS 5:24–6:1); cf. also CD 9:2–4.
289. Cf. *m. Sanh.* 1:1; *b. Ber.* 6a.

290. BDF §248.2, 130.
291. Josephus, *Ant.* 17.11.4 §§317–320.
292. Ex. 21:2–6; 7–11; Deut. 15:12–18.
293. See Karel van der Toorn, "Prison," *ABD*, 5:468–69.
294. E.g., *m. Soṭah.* 5:1; *m. Yebam.* 2:8.
295. E.g., Josephus, *J.W.* 2.8.13 §§160–161; 2.8.2 §120; Pliny, *Nat. Hist.* 5.73. See James C. VanderKam, *The Dead Sea Scrolls Today* (Grand Rapids: Eerdmans, 1994), 90–91.
296. *m. Yebam.* 8:4–6; cf. Deut. 23:1.
297. *b. Ber.* 55b.
298. See "Vine and Vineyard," *DJBP*, 657–58.
299. See comments on 17:24–27; 18:24–28; 22:19. Using the current minimum wage of $5.15 an hour in the United States in 2000, a common laborer would receive the equivalent of $41.20 a day.
300. Cf. Luke 8:3; Gal. 4:2.
301. Josephus, *Ant.* 6.11.9 §235.
302. Plato, *Gorgias*, 491e; cf. 492b; cited in H. W. Beyer, "διακονέω, διακονία, διάκονος," *TDNT*, 2:82.
303. E.g., *diakonos*: 2 Cor. 3:6; Eph. 3:7; Col. 1:23; *doulos*: Rom. 1:1; Gal. 1:10.
304. E.g., *diakonos*: Phoebe, Rom. 16:1; Tychicus, Eph. 6:21; Epaphras, Col. 1:23; *doulos*: Epaphras, Col. 4:12.
305. Cf. BAGD.
306. Cf. Sydney Page, "Ransom Saying," *DJG*, 660–62.
307. Matt. 21:17; cf. John 12:1–10.
308. See Scott T. Carroll, "Bethphage," *ABD*, 1:715.
309. Cf. *m. Menaḥ.* 7:3 [n. 11 in Danby]; 11:2.
310. Cf. D. A. Carson, "Matthew" (*EBC* 8; Grand Rapids: Zondervan, 1984), 437; Gundry, *Matthew*, 593.
311. Cf. Gundry, *Matthew*, 409–10.
312. See 2 Sam. 14:4; 2 Kings 6:26.
313. Cf. John 6:14; 7:40, 52; Acts 3:22; 7:37.
314. See *m. Mid.* 1:3; Josephus, *Ant.* 15.11.5 §§410–11. For discussion, see Rousseau and Arav, *Jesus and His World*, 304–9; Kathleen and Leen Ritmeyer, "Reconstructing the Triple Gate," *BAR* 15.6 (Nov./Dec. 1989): 49–53.
315. See Kathleen Ritmeyer, "A Pilgrim's Journey," *BAR* 15.6 (Nov./Dec. 1989): 43–45, for an informative insight to a journey into the temple. Also in the same issue, see Kathleen and Leen Ritmeyer, "Reconstructing Herod's Temple Mount in Jerusalem," *BAR* 15.6 (Nov./Dec. 1989): 23–42, for a painstaking overview of the specifics of the temple architecture.
316. The term "robber" (*lēstēs*) was not used for a common thief, but for one who was an insurrectionist, such as Barabbas and the two robbers between whom Jesus was crucified, who fought against the Roman occupation; cf. Michael J. Wilkins, "Barabbas," *ABD*, 1:607. This may be a subtle use of the term to indicate that the Temple authorities were insurrectionists against God's intended plan for the Temple.
317. For a discussion of the symbolism of the fig tree and Israel, see "Fig, Fig Tree," *DBI*, 283–84.
318. See Keener, *Matthew*, 506, for background and literature.
319. See "Vine and Vineyard," *DJBP*, 657–58.
320. See Rousseau and Arav, *Jesus and His World*, 328–32.
321. See "*ḥatunnâ*," *DJBP*, 275.
322. See Gundry, *Matthew*, 436–37.
323. E.g., Judg. 1; 8; Isa. 5:24; 1 Macc. 5:28; *T. Jud.* 5:1–5.
324. Gundry, *Matthew*, 439; W. D. Davies and Dale C. Allison Jr., *A Critical and Exegetical Commentary on the Gospel According to Saint Matthew* (ICC; Edinburgh: T. & T. Clark, 1997), 3:204 n. 53; Keener, *Matthew*, 522 n. 189.
325. See Keener, *Matthew*, 523.
326. Joachim Jeremias, "πολλοί," *TDNT*, 6:536–45.
327. Cf. Mark 12:13–17; Luke 20:20–26.
328. See Matt. 9:11; 12:38; 17:24; 19:16; 22:16, 24, 36.
329. Colin Brown, Norman Hillyer, "Tax, Tax Collector," *NIDNTT*, 3:751–59.
330. See Rousseau and Arav, *Jesus and His World*, 278.
331. Rousseau and Arav, *Jesus and His World*, 55–61.
332. E.g., 2 Macc. 7; *1 En.* 102; *2 Bar.* 49–51.
333. E.g., *m. Sanh.* 10:1; *b. Roš Haš.* 16b–17a.
334. The patriarchs are assumed to continue to enjoy the blessings of the covenant, even though they had been long deceased; cf. Gen. 24:12, 27, 48; 26:24; 28:13; 32:9; 46:1, 3–4; 48:15–16; 49:25; Carson, "Matthew," 462.
335. See Abraham Malamat, "Love Your Neighbor As Yourself," *BAR* 16.4 (July/Aug. 1990): 50–51.
336. See comments on 1:1; cf. 2 Sam. 7:12–14; Ps. 89:4; Isa. 11:1, 10; Jer. 23:5: cf. *Pss. Sol.* 17:21.
337. See comments on 1:1, 20; 9:27; 12:23; 15:22; 20:30–31; 29:9.
338. See Hagner, *Matthew*, 651.
339. For more on meal customs and seating, see comments on 26:20.
340. Levine, *The Ancient Synagogue*, 313–17.
341. Neusner and Green, "Rabbi," *DJBP*, 516; Levine, "The Sages and the Synagogue," in *The Ancient Synagogue*, 440–70.
342. For discussion of this distinction, see Levine, *The Ancient Synagogue*, 449–51.
343. See Wilkins, *Discipleship in the Ancient World*, 116–24.

344. E.g., R. Abba Benjamin (*b. Ber.* 6a); R. Abba bar Ahda (*y. Ber.* 1.6.3d); R. Hdiyya bar Abba (*y. Ta*ᶜ*an.* 4.5.68b). See other examples in *DJBP*, 2–3.
345. See Levine, *The Ancient Synagogue*, 404–6.
346. Deut. 14:1; 32:6; Ps. 103:13; Hos. 11:1; Jer. 3:4; 31:9.
347. E.g., *Jub.* 1:24, 28; 19:29; *Jos. Asen.* 12:14; Sir. 23:1, 4; Wisd. Sol. 2:16–20; 14:3; Tobit 13:4; 4Q372 1:16; 1QH 9:35 [17:35]. See in "Father, God as," *DJBP*, 224.
348. A direct allusion to the original leader of the Qumran community was first suggested by C. Spicq, "Une allusion au docteur de justice dans Matthieu, XXIII, 10?," *RB* 66 (1959): 387–96, but followed recently by several others, including M. Eugene Boring, "The Gospel of Matthew: Introduction, Commentary, Reflections," *The New Interpreter's Bible* (Nashville: Abingdon, 1995), 3:432.
349. Most commentators doubt a direct allusion, including Davies and Allison, *Matthew*, 3:278; Carson, "Matthew," 476 n. 10.
350. E.g., Dionysius of Halicarnassus, *Jud. De Thuc.* 3, 4; Plutarch, *Moralia* 327; Vettius Valens 115, 18; PGiess. 80, 7; 11; POxy. 930, 6; 20 (BAGD). See Bruce W. Winter, "The Messiah as the Tutor: The Meaning of καθηγητής in Matthew 23:10," *TynBul* 42 (1991): 152–57.
351. E.g., Robertson, *Grammar*, 138.
352. E.g., six "woes" in Isa. 5:8–22; five in Hab. 2:6–20; cf. the two series of three in Rev. 8:13; 9:12; 11:14; 12:12; and 18:10, 16, 19.
353. See Werblowsky and Wigoder, "Proselytes," *EJR*, 312–13.
354. Josephus, *J.W.* 2.20.2 §§560–561.
355. Josephus, *Ant.* 20.2.2–4 §§24–48.
356. Especially suggested by the work of Scot McKnight, *A Light Among the Gentiles: Jewish Missionary Activity in the Second Temple Period* (Minneapolis: Fortress, 1991), esp, 106–8; followed by, among others, Blomberg, *Matthew*, 344; Hagner, *Matthew*, 669; Donald Senior, *Matthew* (ANTC; Nashville: Abingdon, 1998), 261.
357. E.g., Tacitus, *Hist.* 5.5.
358. See Louis H. Feldman, *Jew and Gentile in the Ancient World: Attitudes and Interactions from Alexander to Justinian* (Princeton, N.J.: Princeton Univ. Press, 1993); Werblowsky and Wigoder, "Proselytes," 312–13; Keener, *Matthew*, 548.
359. Lev. 27:30–33; Num. 18:21, 24; Deut. 12:5–19; etc.
360. Colin J. Hemer, "Bury, Grave, Tomb," *NIDNTT*, 1:265.
361. See Rachel Hachlili, "Burials," *ABD*, 1:789–94.
362. Hagner, *Matthew*, 677; Davies and Allison, *Matthew*, 3:319; Keener, *Matthew*, 556.
363. Morris, *Matthew*, 589 n. 45.
364. *b. B. Bat.* 4a.
365. Josephus, *J.W.* 5.5.6 §§222–223. The Mishnah tractate *Middot* ("Measurements") renders a description of the temple as it was before its destruction in A.D. 70. The tractate is traditionally assigned to Rabbi Eliezer ben Jacob, who was a young boy at the time of the first Jewish revolt in the A.D. 60s (cf. *m. Mid.* 1:2, 9; 2:6; 5:3).
366. For an overview, see Michael O. Wise, "Temple," *DJG*, 811–17.
367. Neusner and Green, "Bar Kosiba, Simon," *DJBP*, 77–78.
368. Isa. 13:8; 21:3; 42:14; Jer. 30:7–10; Hos. 13:13.
369. Isa. 26:17–19; 66:7–11; Jer. 22:23; Mic. 4:9–10.
370. See Dan. 9:27 NIV; cf. 12:11, which is similar to the expressions in 8:13; 11:31.
371. 1 Macc. 1:54; cf. 2 Macc. 6:2.
372. See Josephus, *Ant.* 18.3.1 §§55–59. For discussion see Paul Barnett, *Jesus and the Rise of Early Christianity: A History of New Testament Times* (Downers Grove, Ill.: InterVarsity, 1999), 144–48.
373. Philo, *Embassy* 200–203; Josephus, *Ant.* 18.8.1–9 §§257–309. See F. F. Bruce, *New Testament History* (New York: Doubleday, 1969), 253–57.
374. For discussion of related issues, see Gleason L. Archer Jr., "Daniel" (*EBC* 7; Grand Rapids: Zondervan, 1985), 111–21.
375. Eusebius, *Eccl. Hist.* 3.5.3.
376. See Joseph Patrich, "Hideouts in the Judean Wilderness," *BAR* 15.5 (Sept./Oct. 1989): 32–42. For an overview of these groups, see Horsley and Hanson, *Bandits, Prophets, and Messiahs*.
377. Josephus, *J.W.* 4.9.3–5, 7 §§508–515.
378. Ibid., 5.6.1 §§250–51.
379. Cf. Ezek. 32:7; Joel 2:31; 3:15; Amos 8:9; 2 Esd. 5:4–5; 7:39; *T. Mos.* 10:5.
380. Isa. 18:3; 27:13; Jer. 4:21; 6:1; 51:27; 1QM 3–4, 8, 16, 17–18; cf. 1 Cor. 15:51–52; 1 Thess. 4:16.
381. Ex. 32:6; Isa. 28:7; 56:12; 1 Cor. 10:7; Gal. 5:21.
382. See J. S. Wright and J. A. Thompson, "Marriage," *IBD*, 2:955–56; Victor P. Hamilton, "Marriage (OT and ANE)," *ABD*, 4:559–69; Jeremias, *Parables of Jesus*, 173–74.
383. Isa. 54:4–6; 62:4–5; Ezek. 16:7–34; Hos. 2:19.
384. For a good discussion of the different types of lamps, see R. E. Nixon, "Lamp, Lampstand, Lantern," *IBD*, 2:871–73.
385. Ex. 22:25; Lev. 25:35–37; Deut. 23:19.
386. For discussion, see "Interest," *DJBP*, 319.
387. Matt. 9:36; 10:6; 15:24; cf. Ezek. 34.

388. Matt. 10:16; cf. 26:31 quoting Zech. 13:7; John 10.
389. In the New Testament the form *eriphos* occurs only here and the diminutive *eriphion* in 10:33; Luke 15:29 has a textual variant between the two essentially synonymous forms.
390. George S. Cansdale, "Goats," *ZPEB*, 2:739–41.
391. Cf. *m. Pesaḥ* 5:1. This is the modern practice.
392. Nisan 15–21; cf. Ex. 12:1–20; 23:15; 34:18; Deut. 16:1–8; Luke 22:1, 7. See discussion of the original Passover in Walter C. Kaiser Jr., "Exodus" (*EBC* 1; Grand Rapids: Zondervan, 1990), 371–76.
393. See the helpful overview of the Sanhedrin in Keener, *Matthew*, 614–16.
394. E.g., Josephus, *Ant.* 18.4.3 §95.
395. Josephus, *Ant.* 17.9.3 §§213–18; *J.W.* 2.6.2 §§88–90.
396. Rousseau and Arav, *Jesus and His World*, 216–20.
397. Josephus *Ant.* 14.2.1 §21; 17.9.1 §213; 18.2.2 §29; idem, *J.W.* 2.1.3 §10. See Robert H. Stein, *Jesus the Messiah: A Survey of the Life of Christ* (Downers Grove, Ill.: InterVarsity, 1996), 200–201.
398. Bargil Pixner, "Church of the Apostles Found on Mt. Zion," *BAR* 16.3 (May/June 1990): 16–35, 60. Pixner contends that the reconstructed building was intended as a Judeo-Christian synagogue.
399. See the striking illustrations at "Pompeii," *Encyclopædia Britannica* Online.
400. For various customs, see Gene Schramm, "Meal Customs (Jewish)," and Dennis E. Smith, "Meal Customs (Greco-Roman)," *ABD*, 4:648–53.
401. For an overview of Second Temple Jewish practices, see "Haggadah of Passover," *DJBP*, 266–67; Joachim Jeremias, *The Eurcharistic Words of Jesus* (trans Norman Perrin; London: SCM, 1966), 84–88. For an overview of contemporary Passover rituals, see Werblowsky and Wigoder, "Haggadah, Passover," *EJR*, 166–67.
402. See Werblowsky and Wigoder, "Haggadah, Passover," for modern expressions of the cups.
403. Werblowsky and Wigoder, "Cups," *EJR*, 104; idem, "Haggadah, Passover," 166–67.
404. Walter C. Kaiser Jr., *The Messiah in the Old Testament* (Grand Rapids: Zondervan, 1995), 226–27.
405. Cf. Luke 13:19; John 19:41.
406. Joan E. Taylor, "The Garden of Gethsemane: NOT the Place of Jesus' Arrest," *BAR* 21.4 (July/Aug. 1995): 26–35, 62. See also Rousseau and Arav, *Jesus and His World*, 110–11.
407. Josephus, *J.W.* 5.12.4 §523.
408. Taylor, "The Garden of Gethsemane," 35.
409. Cf. John 18:3, 12; see comments on Matt. 27:65; 28:11.
410. Matt. 10:4; 26:25; 27:3; Mark 8:19; Luke 6:15–16; John 6:71; 12:4; 13:2; 18:2, 5. See Wilkins, *Following the Master*, 164ff.
411. Josephus, *J.W.* 2.8.4 §§125–26.
412. For an extensive discussion, see Brown, *Death of the Messiah*, 340–57.
413. Matt. 16:16; cf. 2 Sam. 7:14; Ps. 89:26–27.
414. Cf. "Blaspheme," *DJBP*, 97–98.
415. Keener, *Matthew*, 655, citing Martin Dibelius, *Jesus* (trans. C. B. Hedrick and F. C. Grant; Philadelphia: Westminster, 1949), 40. See also Morris, *Matthew*, 689 n. 123; Richard A. Horsley, *Archaeology, History, and Society in Galilee: The Social Context of Jesus and the Rabbis* (Valley Forge, Pa: Trinity, 1996), 162–71.
416. See Flusser, *Jesus*, 205–6.
417. 11QTemple Scroll 64:7–8; cf. also *t. Ter.* 7:20 and *y. Ter.* 7:46b.
418. See the extended discussion in Leen and Kathleen Ritmeyer, "Akeldama: Potter's Field or High Priest's Tomb?" *BAR* 20 (Nov./Dec. 1994): 22–35, 76–78; also in the same issue, Gideon Avni and Zvi Greenhut, "Akeldama: Resting Place of the Rich and Famous," *BAR* 20 (Nov./Dec. 1994): 36–46.
419. Bruce M. Metzger, *A Textual Commentary on the Greek New Testament* (2d ed.; New York: United Bible Societies, 1994), 56.
420. W. F. Albright and C. S. Mann, *Matthew* (AB 26; Garden City, N.Y.: Doubleday, 1971), 343–44.
421. Josephus, *J.W.* 5.4.4 §177ff.
422. Rousseau and Arav, *Jesus and His World*, 12–14.
423. Cf. Josephus, *Ant.* 20.8.11 §§1223–24; idem, *J.W.* 6.7.1 §358. See Rainer Riesner, "Archaeology and Geography," *DJG*, 42–43.
424. Dio Cassius 44.17.1; cited in Davies and Allison, *Matthew*, 3:587 n. 38.
425. Deut. 21:6–9; Ps. 26:6; 73:13.
426. Herodotus, *Hist.* 1:35; Virgil, *Aen.* 2.719; Sophocles, *Ajax* 654.
427. *Let. Aris.* 305–6.
428. E.g., Matt. 1:21; 2:6; 4:16; 15:8.
429. E.g., Lev. 20:9; Josh. 2:19; 2 Sam. 1:16; Ezek. 18:13; Acts 5:28; 18:6.
430. *m. Sanh.*; *m. Mak.*
431. Rousseau and Arav, *Jesus and His World*, 151–52.
432. Josephus, *J.W.* 5.5.8 §244.
433. For background to the Roman military contingents, see Ferguson, *Backgrounds of Early Christianity*, 46–52.
434. Page, *Jesus and the Land*, 149–51.

435. Plutarch, *Moralia* 554A/B; cf. 554D; *De sera numinis vindicta* (*On the Delays of Divine Vengeance*) 9.
436. *b. Sanh.* 43a, citing Prov. 31:6.
437. The most important study as it helps clarify Jesus' fate is Hengel, *Crucifixion*, 77.
438. Joe Zias and James H. Charlesworth, "Crucifixion: Archaeology, Jesus, and the Dead Sea Scrolls," in *Jesus and the Dead Sea Scrolls*, ed. J. H. Charlesworth (New York: Doubleday, 1992), 273–89; Joe Zias and E. Sekeles, "The Crucified Man from Giv'at ha-Mivtar—A Reappraisal," *IEJ* 35 (1985): 22–27; V. Tzaferis, "Jewish Tombs at and near Giv'at ha-Mivtar, Jerusalem," *IEJ* 20 (1970): 18–32; idem, "Crucifixion—the Archeological Evidence," *BAR* 11.1 (Jan./Feb. 1985): 44–53; N. Haas, "Anthropological Observations on the Skeletal Remains from Giv'at ha-Mivtar," *IEJ* 20 (1970): 38–59.
439. See Frederick T. Zugibe, "Two Questions About Crucifixion: Does the Victim Die of Asphyxiation? Would Nails in the Hands Hold the Weight of the Body?" *BRev* 5.2 (1989): 34–43.
440. Quintilian, *Declamationes* 274 (cited in Hengel, *Crucifixion*, 50 n. 14).
441. Ex. 10:21; Ps. 88:13; Prov. 2:13–14; Matt. 25:30; 1 Thess. 5:4–7.
442. Joel 2:2; Amos 5:18, 20; Zeph. 1:15; Matt. 24:29; Rev. 6:12–17.
443. Michael J. Wilkins, "Darkness," *EDBT*, 142–43; Hans Conzelmann, "σκότος, κτλ." *TDNT*, 7:423–45; H.-C Hahn, "Darkness," *NIDNTT*, 1:420–25.
444. The saying in Matthew's Gospel may be a transliteration that is partly from the Hebrew (*ēli ēli*) and partly from the Aramaic (*lema sebachthani*) (Metzger, *Textual Commentary*, 58–59, 99–100). The best MSS have "Eli, Eli, Lema Sabachthani?" although it is more likely that the entire saying is a variation of Aramaic, since the Aramaic Targum to Psalm 22:1 has *ēli ēli*. (See Davies and Allison, *Matthew*, 3:624.)
445. Joachim Jeremias, "Ἠλ(ε)ίας," *TDNT*, 2:930–31.
446. See Hans W. Heidland, "ὄξος," *TDNT*, 5:288–89.
447. E.g., Ex. 26:31–35; 27:21; 30:6; 2 Chron. 3:14; Heb. 6:19; 9:3; 10:20.
448. E.g., Ex. 27:37; Num. 3:26.
449. Josephus gives a detailed description of the curtain in *J.W.* 5.5.4 §212–13. (See comments on Mark 15:38.)
450. Eph. 2:11–22; Heb. 10:20.
451. Matt. 27:55–56, 61; cf. Mark 15:40–41; Luke 23:49, 55–56; John 19:25–27.
452. Matt. 28:1; cf. Mark 16:1; Luke 24:1, 10–11; John 20:1–18.
453. 11QTemple Scroll 64:11–12.
454. Cf. Josephus, *Ant.* 13.5.9 §127.
455. Michael J. Wilkins, "Named and Unnamed Disciples in Matthew: A Literary/Theological Study" (*SBLSP* 30; Atlanta: Scholars, 1991), 418–39.
456. *m. Sanh.* 6:5; cf. *b. Sanh.* 46b; 11QTemple Scroll 64:11–12. See Colin J. Hemer, "Bury, Grave, Tomb," *NIDNTT*, 1:263–66.
457. Joseph and Jacob were embalmed using Egyptian practice; cf. Gen. 50:2, 26.
458. Shemuel Safrai and Menahem Stern, eds., *The Jewish People in the First Century* (Philadelphia: Fortress, 1974–76), 2:776–77.
459. See "Burial," *DJBP*, 103–4.
460. For background, see Rousseau and Arav, *Jesus and His World*, 164–69.
461. See Amos Kloner, "Did a Rolling Stone Close Jesus' Tomb?" *BAR* 25.5 (Sept./Oct. 1999): 23–29, 76.
462. See citation of examples in "Burial Sites," *DJBP*, 104.
463. Cf. Matt. 27:56, 61; 28:1; Mark 15:40–41; 16:1; Luke 8:1–3; 23:55; 24:1, 10–11; John 19:25; 20:1ff.
464. See the drawings showing the primary faults in D. R. Bowes, "Earthquake," *ZPEB*, 2:178–80.
465. See Kloner, "Did a Rolling Stone Close Jesus' Tomb?" 22–29, 76.
466. Cf. Rev. 4:5; 16:17–18.
467. Cf. 27:60–61; Mark 15:46–47; Luke 23:55.
468. Matt. 28:1–6; Mark 16:1–6; Luke 24:1–8; John 20:1–16.
469. Matt. 4:9–10; 14:33; Acts 10:25–26; 14:11–15; Rev. 22:8–9.
470. Cf. Petronius, *Satyricon* 112; Acts 12:19.
471. Favoring a reconstruction that understands the Decree being given in response to Christian and Jewish disputes over the empty tomb is E. M. Blaiklock, "Nazareth Decree," *ZPEB*, 391–92; see also idem, *The Archaeology of the New Testament* (Nashville: Nelson, 1984). Doubting any association with the Christian-Jewish controversy is Raymond E. Brown, *The Death of the Messiah*, 2:1294.
472. See 4:8; 5:1–2; 14:23; 15:29; 17:1; 24:3; 26:30. The phrase used here (*eis to oros*) often carries a looser connotation of "hills" as opposed to a specific mountain.

Sidebar and Chart Notes

A-1. Irenaeus, *Against Heresies*, 5.33.4.
A-2. Ibid., 3.1.1.
A-3. See Joachim Jeremias, *Jerusalem in the Time of Jesus: An Investigation into Economic and Social Conditions During the New Testament Period* (1962; ET; Philadelphia: Fortress, 1969), 363–68; J. S. Wright and J. A. Thompson, "Marriage," *IBD*, 2:955–56;

Victor P. Hamilton, "Marriage (OT and ANE)," *ABD*, 4:559–69.

A-4. Heb. *ʾērûsîn* and *qîddûšâ*.

A-5. *m. ʾAbot.* 5:21; *b. Qidd.* 29b–30a.

A-6. See *m. Ketub.* 1:2; 4:2.

A-7. *m. Ketub.* 1:5; *b. Ketub.* 9b, 12a.

A-8. Cf. Josephus, *Ant.* 7.8.1 §168.

A-9. *m. Ketub.* 5:2; *m. Ned.* 10:5.

A-10. Heb. *keṭûbâ*.

A-11. *ḥuppâ* ("canopy"); cf. Ps. 19:5; Tobit 7:16.

A-12. See the work of the astronomer David Hughes, *The Star of Bethlehem: An Astronomer's Confirmation* (New York: Walker, 1979). Another astronomer discusses an alternative conjunction of Jupiter and Venus on June 17, 2 B.C. (John Mosley, *The Christmas Star* [Los Angeles: Griffith Observatory, 1988]), but that date is rejected by most because it is after the accepted dating of King Herod's death in 4 B.C.

A-13. Mark Kidger, *The Star of Bethlehem: An Astronomer's View* (Princeton, N.J.: Princeton Univ. Press, 1999).

A-14. E.g., Rev. 1:16, 20; 2:1; 3:1. See also Job 38:7; Dan. 8:10; *1 En.* 43:1–4, 90:20–27; *2 En.* 29; *3 En.* 46; *Pseudo Philo* 32:13–15; *Jos. Asen.* 14:1–14; *T. Sol.* 20:14–17; *b. ʿAbod. Zar.* 43a-b. Jesus is referred to as the "morning star" (Rev. 22:16; cf. 2:28; also 2 Peter 1:9).

A-15. Rev. 8:10, 11; 9:1. Cf. *1 En.* 86:1–6; 90:20–27; *2 En.* 29. Satan is referred to as a fallen morning star (Isa. 14:12–13).

A-16. E.g., *1 En.* 1:2 ff.; *T. Levi* 2–5; *History of the Rechabites* 1:3 and throughout.

A-17. Dale C. Allison, "What Was the Star that Guided the Magi?" *BRev* 9.6 (1993): 24.

A-18. For a thorough overview of Herod's life, see Harold W. Hoehner, "Herodian Dynasty," *DJG*, 317–26; Lee I. Levine, "Herod the Great," *ABD*, 3:161–69; Stewart Henry Perowne, "Herod," *Encyclopædia Britannica*. For the most extensive recent study, see Peter Richardson, *Herod: King of the Jews and Friend of the Romans* (rev. ed; Philadelphia: Fortress, 1999).

A-19. Josephus, *Ant.* 14.8.1–5 §§127–55.

A-20. Strabo, *Geog.* 16.2.46.

A-21. *b. B. Bat.* 4a.

A-22. Josephus, *Ant.* 17.1.3 §§19–22.

A-23. Ibid., 16.10.5–16.11.8 §§324–404.

A-24. Ibid., 17.10.1 §253.

A-25. Macrobius, *Saturnalia* 2.f.11.

A-26. Josephus calculates the length of Herod's reign as thirty-seven years from his accession or thirty-four from the time of his effective reign (Josephus, *Ant.* 17.8.1 §191; idem, *J.W.* 1.1.8 §665), and those years indicate that he died in 4 B.C. Therefore, Herod's death is placed by most scholars at the latter part of March, 4 B.C. For extensive discussion, see Harold W. Hoehner, *Chronological Aspects of the Life of Christ* (Grand Rapids: Zondervan, 1977), 11–27.

A-27. Josephus gives a most graphic description of Herod's terminal disease (*Ant.* 17.6.5 §§168–69), which some think was syphilis or arteriosclerosis (Richardson, *Herod*, 18).

A-28. Josephus, *Ant.* 17.6.5 §§174–79; 17.8.2 §193.

A-29. Ibid., 17.8.3 §§196–199.

A-30. Ibid., 17.8.1 §191.

A-31. E.g., the diseased person (Lev. 14:1–8); men with bodily discharges and menstruating women (ch. 15); the high priest before and after rites of atonement (16:4, 24).

A-32. Matt. 15:1–2; the later Mishnah has an entire tractate, *Miqwaʾot*, devoted to ritual washings.

A-33. 1QS 3:4–12.

A-34. Josephus, *Ant.* 13.5.9 §171.

A-35. The composition of the "Sanhedrin" is debated by modern scholars because the ancient sources (e.g., Josephus, New Testament, and the rabbinic literature) demonstrate a changing nature of this body. See comments on 26:59; cf. Anthony J. Saldarini, *Pharisees, Scribes, and Sadducees* (Wilmington, Del.: Michael Glazier, 1988).

A-36. 2 Cor. 4:4; Eph. 2:1–2; Rev. 13:1–2.

A-37. Num. 34:11; Deut. 3:17; Josh. 12:3; 13:27.

A-38. John 6:1; 21:1.

A-39. Luke 5:1, 2; 8:22, 23, 33. "Lake Gennesaret" is a grecized version of the Hebrew "Lake of Kinneret."

A-40. Josephus, *J.W.*, 2.20.6 §573; 3.10.1 §463; 3.10.7 §506; 3.10.7–8 §§515–16; idem, *Ant.* 5.1.22 §84; 13.5.7 §158; 18.2.1, 3 §28, 36; cf. 1 Macc. 11:67. Pliny assumes that the usual name is the "lake of Gennesaret" (*Nat. Hist.* 5.15, 71).

A-41. Strabo, *Geog.* 16.2; Pliny, *Nat. Hist.* 5.15, 71; Josephus, *J.W.* 3.10.7 §506.

A-42. E.g., Matt. 15:32; Mark 8:2.

A-43. Matt. 8:24; 14:19, 24; Mark 4:37; Luke 8:23; John 6: 1–4, 18. See Seán Freyne, *Galilee from Alexander the Great to Hadrian* (Wilmington, Del.: Michael Glazier, 1980); idem, "Galilee, Sea of," *ABD*, 2:900; Rainer Riesner, "Archeology and Geography," *DJG*, 37.

A-44. 1 Thess. 4:11–12; 2 Thess. 3:6–15; 1 Tim. 5:8.

A-45. Prov. 19:17; Acts 11:27–30; Rom. 15:25–27; 2 Cor. 8:1–15; Gal. 6:7–10; Eph. 4:28; 1 Tim. 5:3–7.

A-46. 1 Cor. 9:3–14; Phil. 4:14–19; 1 Tim. 5:17–18.

A-47. 1 Sam. 17:43; Ps. 22:16; Prov. 26:11.

A-48. See "Dog," "Pork," *DJBP*, 172; "Animals," "Dogs," "Swine," *DBI*, 29, 213–14; Edwin Firmage, "Zoology," *ABD*, 6:1130–35, 1143–44.

A-49. For other examples, see Hans Dieter Betz, *The Sermon on the Mount: A Commentary on the Sermon on the Mount, Including the Sermon on the Plain (Matthew 5:3—7:27 and Luke 6:20–49)* (Hermeneia; Minneapolis: Fortress, 1995), 509–16.

A-50. See P. S. Alexander, "Jesus and the Golden Rule," in *Hillel and Jesus: Comparative Studies of Two Major Religious Leaders*, ed. James H. Charlesworth and Loren L. Johns (Minneapolis: Fortress, 1997), 363–88.

A-51. Everett Ferguson, *Backgrounds of Early Christianity* (2d ed.; Grand Rapids: Eerdmans, 1993), 47–48.

A-52. For a popular recounting, see James F. Strange and Hershel Shanks, "Has the House Where Jesus Stayed in Capernaum Been Found?: Italian Archaeologists Believe They Have Uncovered St. Peter's Home," vol. 2 of *Archaeology in the World of Herod, Jesus and Paul, Archaeology and the Bible: The Best of BAR*; (Washington D.C.: Biblical Archaeological Society, 1990), 188–99.

A-53. James H. Charlesworth, *Jesus Within Judaism: New Light from Exciting Archaeological Discoveries* (ABRL; New York: Doubleday, 1988), 109–15.

A-54. E.g., Ezek. 2:1, 3, 6, 8, etc.; cf. Dan. 8:17.

A-55. Although the dating of this portion of *1 Enoch* is debated, current scholarly opinion dates it around the time of Herod the Great. Cf. E. Isaac, "1 (Ethiopic Apocalypse of) Enoch," in *The Old Testament Pseudepigrapha*, ed. James H. Charlesworth (Garden City, N.Y.: Doubleday, 1983), 1:7.

A-56. Matt. 8:20; 9:6; 11:19; 12:8; 12:32, 40.

A-57. Matt. 16:13, 27–28; 17:9, 12, 22; 20:18, 28; 26:2, 24, 45.

A-58. Matt. 10:23; 13:37, 41; 19:28; 24:27, 30, 37, 39, 44; 25:31; 26:64.

A-59. See, respectively, Deut. 22:13–19, Lev. 20:17–21, Num. 5:1–4. See also *m. Mak.* 3.1–2.

A-60. Levine, *The Ancient Synagogue*, 131–32, 417; Carl Schneider, "μαστιγόω, μάστιξ," *TDNT*, 4:515–19.

A-61. For brief overviews, see F. F. Bruce, "Machaerus," *IBD*, 2:928–29; Stanislao Loffreda, "Machaerus," *ABD*, 4:457–58.

A-62. Josephus, *J.W.* 7.6.2 §171.

A-63. Ibid., 7.6.2 §172.

A-64. Pliny, *Nat. Hist.* 5.15.72.

A-65. Cf. Josephus, *J.W.* 7.6.1 §§163–70.

A-66. Josephus, *Ant.* 18.5.1–2 §§112, 119.

A-67. Josephus, *J.W.* 7.6.1 §§163–64; 7.6.4 §§190–209.

A-68. *t. Mak.* 3:8; *b. Menaḥ.* 85a, 85b.

A-69. See "Chorazin," *DJBP*, 118–19; Rousseau and Arav, *Jesus and His World*, 52–54.

A-70. Most archaeologists today consider the site of ancient Bethsaida to be et-Tell. A minority position held by Mendel Nun contends for el-Araj to be the real Bethsaida. See Mendel Nun, "Has Bethsaida Finally Been Found?" *Jerusalem Perspective* (July/Aug. 1998).

A-71. Rami Arav, Richard A. Freund, and John F. Shroder, "Bethsaida Rediscovered: Long-Lost City Found North of Galilee Shore," *BAR* 26.1 (Jan./Feb. 2000): 45–56. See also "Bethsaida," *DJBP*, 89.

A-72. Josephus, *J.W.* 3.10.7–8 §§515–18.

A-73. Trachonitis, Gaulanitis, Auranitis, Batanaea, and Ituraea (cf. Luke 3:1; Josephus, *Ant.* 18.4.6 §106).

A-74. Josephus, *Ant.* 18.4.6 §106.

A-75. Cf. 14:6–11; Josephus, *Ant.* 18.5.4 §136–37.

A-76. Josh. 11:17; Judg. 3:3; 1 Chron. 5:23.

A-77. Josephus, *Ant.* 15.10.3 §360–64

A-78. Ibid., 18.2.1 §28; idem, *J.W.* 2.9.1 §168. Both names reflect Philip's Roman backing.

A-79. See Seán Freyne, *Galilee From Alexander the Great to Hadrian*, 13–14, 32, 43, 52 n. 28, 136–37, 272. Also, John Kutsko, "Caesarea Philippi," *ABD*, 1:803.

A-80. Nun, "Cast Your Net," 48–51.

A-81. Cf. Gleason L. Archer, "Coins," *ZPEB*, 1:902-11; Rousseau and Arav, *Jesus and His World*, 57.

A-82. A denarius was the equivalent of a day's wage for a common laborer (see comments on 17:24-27; 22:19). Using the minimum wage of $5.15 an hour in the United States in 2000, a common laborer would receive $41.20 a day. A talent, therefore, would be worth approximately $247,200 (cf. 25:15) by modern U.S. standards. The figure would be much lower in many areas of the world. The comparisons are only suggestive.

A-83. T. A. Holland, "Jericho," *ABD*, 3:737.

A-84. Cf. Ehud Netzer, "Jericho: Roman Period," *ABD*, 3:737–39; Rousseau and Arav, *Jesus and His World*, 132–36.

A-85. Cf. Matt. 21–28; Mark 11–16; Luke 19–24; John 12–21. See comments on 26:1 for a discussion of the chronological problems.

A-86. For background, dating and discussion, see Ferguson, *Backgrounds of Early Christianity*, 24-38. A convenient collection of charts of Roman (and other) organizational entities is found in House, *Chronological and Background Charts*, 64-65, etc.

A-87. For thorough discussion, see Levine, "Cathedra of Moses," *The Ancient Synagogue*, 323–27.
A-88. Levine, *The Ancient Synagogue*, 326.
A-89. See Neusner and Green, "Tefillin" and "Tefillin, Archaeology of," *DJBP*, 621.
A-90. Josephus, *Ant.* 18.2.2 §35.
A-91. Ibid., 18.4.3 §95.
A-92. Ibid., 20.10 §§224–251. See David Flusser, *Jesus* (2d ed.; Jerusalem: Magnes, 1998), 195–205; Bruce Chilton, "Caiaphas," *ABD*, 1:803–6.
A-93. Cf. 1QHabakkuk Pesher 1:13; 9:4–5.
A-94. Flusser, *Jesus*, 195.
A-95. For narrative on the discovery and the ancient burial practices, as well as drawings and pictures, see Hershel Shanks, *In the Temple of Solomon and the Tomb of Caiaphas* (Washington, D.C.: BAS, 1993), 35–45.
A-96. See also Matt. 27:62; Mark 15:42; Luke 23:54; John 19:14, 31, 42.
A-97. Matt. 27:62; Mark 15:42; Luke 23:54; John 19:14, 31, 42.
A-98. Cf. John 13:1–2; 13:27–29; 18:28; 19:14, 31.
A-99. Annie Jaubert, *The Date of the Last Supper*, trans. Isaac Rafferty (Staten Island, N.Y.: Alba, 1965).
A-100. Harold Hoehner, "Chronology," *DJG*, 121; so also Robert L. Thomas and Stanley N. Gundry, eds., *The NIV Harmony of the Gospels* (San Francisco: Harper & Row, 1988), 312–13.
A-101. D. A. Carson, *The Gospel According to John* (Grand Rapids: Eerdmans, 1991), 455–58; so also Blomberg, *Historical Reliability of the Gospels*, 175–78.
A-102. E.g., Josephus, *J.W.* 2.17.5 §422; 2.17.6 §§426–27, 429.
A-103. These accounts include the journal of the Bordeaux Pilgrim (c. A.D. 333), the account of Theodosius (A.D. 530), and the Madaba mosaic map, the earliest known map of Jerusalem (c. A.D. 560).
A-104. For a recounting of the excavation and the possible relationship to the Gospel accounts, see Arthur Rupprecht, "The House of Annas-Caiaphas," *Archaeology in the Biblical World* 1.1 (Spring 1991): 4–17. See also Rousseau and Arav, *Jesus and His World*, 136–39.
A-105. Pilate is called Pontius Pilate in the New Testament in Luke 3:1; 4:27; 1 Tim. 6:13.
A-106. Josephus, *Ant.* 18.2.2 §35; 18.3.1–2 §§55–62; 18.4.1–2 §§85–89; idem, *J.W.* 2.9.2–4 §§169–77.
A-107. Philo, *Embassy* 299–305.
A-108. Tacitus, *Annals* 15.44.
A-109. Barnett, *Jesus and the Rise of Early Christianity*, 144–49; cf. Daniel R. Schwartz, "Pontius Pilate," *ABD*, 5:395–401; Rousseau and Arav, *Jesus and His Times*, 225–27.
A-110. Mark 15:7; Luke 23:19; cf. Acts 3:14.
A-111. Horsley and Hanson, *Bandits, Prophets, and Messiahs*, 48–87.
A-112. See comments on 27:38; Mark 15:27.
A-113. Excerpt from Michael J. Wilkins, "Barabbas," *ABD*, 1:607.
A-114. "Despite the Christian use of Matthew for anti-Semitic attacks, the harsh polemics in the gospel do not attack Jews as a group but the leaders of the Jews (scribes, Pharisees, Sadducees, chief priest, elders) and those people who have been misled into hostility toward Jesus" ("Matthew, Jews in the Gospel of," *DJBP*, 416).
A-115. Gabriel Barkay, "The Garden Tomb: Was Jesus Buried Here?" *BAR* 12.2 (March/April 1986): 40–57; John McRay, "Tomb Typology and the Tomb of Jesus," *Archaeology in the Biblical World* 2.2 (Spring 1994): 34–44.
A-116. Dan Bahat, "Does the Holy Sepulchre Church Mark the Burial of Jesus?" *BAR* 12.3 (May/June 1986): 26–45; Joan E. Taylor, "Golgotha: A Reconsideration of the Evidence for the Sites of Jesus' Crucifixion and Burial," *NTS* 44 (1998): 180–203.
A-117. Josephus, *Ag. Ap.* 2.25 §201.
A-118. *m. Ber.* 3:3; *m. Sukkah* 2:8.
A-119. *t. Ber.* 7:18.
A-120. *m. Ker.* 6:9; cf. *m. Ned.* 9:1.
A-121. *b. Qidd.* 31b.
A-122. This material is developed more fully in Michael J. Wilkins, "Women in the Teaching and Example of Jesus," in *Complementarity in Church Ministry*, Robert L. Saucy and Judy TenElshof, eds. (Chicago: Moody, forthcoming).
A-123. E.g., Isa. 26:19; Dan. 12:2; 2 Macc. 7; *1 En.* 102; *2 Bar.* 49–51.
A-124. E.g., *m. Sanh.* 10:1; *b. Roš Haš.* 16b–17a.
A-125. See "Amidah," "Resurrection," *DJBP*, 30–31, 526–27.
A-126. Rom. 8:29; 1 Cor. 15; 2 Cor. 3:18.
A-127. E.g., Rabbi Akiba; *m. Yebam.* 16:7. See also *m. Šeb.* 4:1; Josephus, *Ant.* 4.8.15 §219. See Witherington, *Women in the Ministry of Jesus*, 9–10, for a discussion of the mixed rabbinic attitudes toward women's ability to give witness.
A-128. For discussion of the broader issues, see William L. Craig, "Did Jesus Rise From the Dead?" in *Jesus Under Fire: Modern Scholarship Reinvents the Historical Jesus*, Michael J. Wilkins and J. P. Moreland, eds. (Grand Rapids: Zondervan, 1995), 151, 155.

MARK

by David E. Garland

Authorship and Place of Origin

The writer of this Gospel wished only to give witness to Jesus Christ and not to identify himself, but ancient testimony has always attributed it to Mark. When the Gospels were shared with other communities, they needed titles so that hearers would know what was being read and readers would know what was on the shelf. Had they circulated anonymously, each community would have given them a different title. Why accredit a Gospel to someone not known as an apostle unless there was some basis for this in fact?

Ancient tradition also connects Mark to Peter. Some claim that this testimony is muddled, but the Gospel's relationship to Peter is likely. The author would certainly not have been an unknown upstart who decided independently to write a Gospel. He must have been a recognized teacher in the church who could appeal to an even greater authority—Peter. That Matthew and Luke allowed themselves to be guided by Mark in writing their Gospels testifies to this fact.

AREA OF CAESAREA PHILIPPI

The waterfall at Banias, near the source of the Jordan River.

Mark IMPORTANT FACTS:

- **AUTHOR:** John Mark, coworker of the apostle Peter.
- **DATE:** Between A.D. 68 and A.D. 70.
- **OCCASION:** There was terrible social upheaval in Palestine and throughout the Mediterranean world for the Jews. Life was also difficult for the early Christians. It was a time of suffering and martyrdom.
- **KEY THEMES:**
  1. To fortify the faith of believers who were suffering.
  2. To explain the current suffering of believers.
  3. To admonish "cross-bearing" as integral to discipleship.
  4. To encourage believers with hope—in spite of their failures.

Where Mark wrote his Gospel is difficult to decide. Tradition associates it with Rome, which may explain why Mark must interpret Palestinian customs for his audience (e.g., 7:3–5, washing of hands; 15:42, the "day of preparation" is the day before Sabbath).[1] A good case can also be made for the Palestinian origin of the Gospel, however.

Setting and Purpose

Wherever this Gospel was written, it addressed a setting of persecution and crisis, probably around A.D. 68–70. The Roman historian, Tacitus, described the period of the late 60s this way:

The history on which I am entering is that of a period rich in disasters, terrible with battles, torn by civil struggles, horrible even in peace. Four emperors fell by the sword; there were three civil wars, more foreign wars, and often both at the same time. . . . Italy was distressed by disasters unknown before or returning after the lapse of the ages. . . . Beside the manifold misfortunes that befell mankind there were prodigies in the sky and on the earth, warnings given by thunderbolts, and prophecies of the future, both joyful and gloomy, uncertain and clear.[2]

Jews faced even greater catastrophes. When Mark wrote, a Roman legion either was on the verge of or had recently sacked Jerusalem and demolished the temple. The discourse in Mark 13 suggests that Christians faced the full brunt of Satan's onslaught. In addition to the social upheaval created by wars and the desecration of what was once a revered and holy shrine (13:7–8, 14), Christians had to deal with inquisitions (13:9), betrayal (13:12), family crack-ups (13:12), and hatred because of their faith (13:13). False prophets proliferated, peddling false hope (13:5–6).

In a context of suffering and martyrdom, Mark wrote:

(1) *To fortify the faith of those in danger of being overwhelmed by fear (4:41; 10:32; 16:8)*. They may cry out in the midst of storms, "Don't you care if we drown?" (4:38). Mark seeks to lift the community's "eyes from the surging chaos that seems to engulf it and to fix them instead on the vision of the one enthroned in heaven, the monarch omnipotent in every storm."[3]

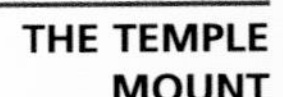

THE TEMPLE MOUNT

Leen Ritmeyer's classic reconstruction of the Jerusalem Temple.

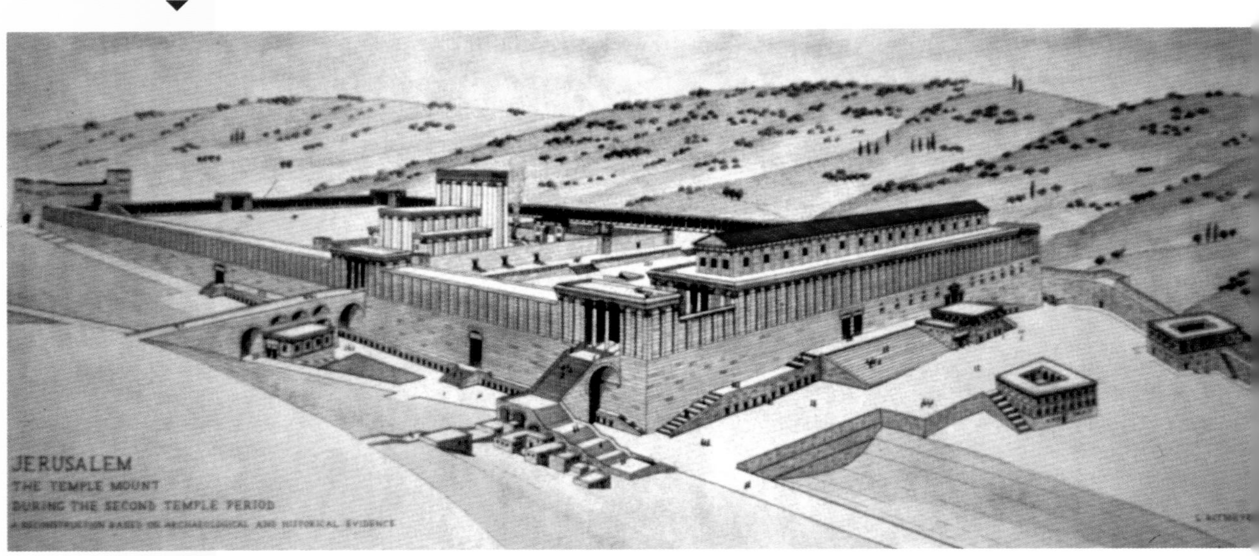

(2) *To account for the present circumstances of believers.* Jesus promises his followers rewards but only with persecutions (10:29–30). He warns that they will be salted with fire (9:49–50). Their suffering is all part of the mystery of how the kingdom of God advances in the world.

(3) *To admonish.* Cross-bearing is not optional but an integral requirement of discipleship (8:34–38). The disciples' sad performance provides a negative example of those who prefer glory to arduous hardship. Having no root in themselves, they endure awhile but fall away when affliction arises because of the word (4:17). Jesus' behavior under severe trial sets the standard the community must follow.

(4) *To encourage.* Despite their grievous failures, Jesus never disowns his disciples and promises a renewed relationship after his resurrection (16:7). Readers would know, for example, that Peter repented, was restored, and died a martyr for the faith. They learn from Mark that God overcomes human weakness and that Jesus' death and resurrection atones for even the worst sins.

(5) *To prevent believers from being deluded by end-time delirium.* Mark wants to fit readers with spiritual lenses that will allow them to see clearly heavenly realities through the blinding cloudbursts of earthly disasters.

(6) *To fit Christ's followers for mission to all the world (14:9).* They are not selected for special privileges but sent out to call others to repent and believe the gospel (6:12). They are to feed spiritually hungry masses (6:37).

(7) *To inform pious interest in Jesus their Lord.* Mark gives a human face to the one whom these people believe is the Christ, the Son of God. Jesus is a real person firmly planted in the soil of everyday Palestinian life.

Prologue (1:1–13)

Mark opens his Gospel with a prologue that provides the reader with privileged information unavailable to the characters in the story other than Jesus. A transcendent voice from offstage announces that John's ministry fulfills divine prophecy and then identifies Jesus as the beloved Son and the conveyor of the Spirit. Next, Mark shows Jesus confronting and defeating Satan, living at peace with the wild animals, and being served by angels.

The beginning of the gospel about Jesus Christ (1:1). "Gospel" refers to the story about Jesus narrated in the text, but it also includes the oral tradition that supplements the text. It comprises Jesus' words, deeds, death, and resurrection as God's direct intervention into history; it challenges an imperial cult propaganda that promotes a message of good tidings and a new age of peace through the Roman emperor.

This opening line may serve as the introduction to the opening segment of Mark (1:1–13) or may be the title Mark

JUDEA

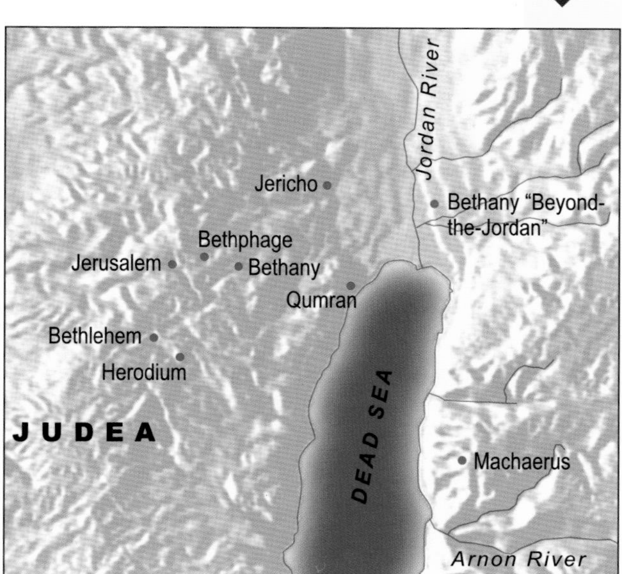

gives to his Gospel or the summary of its contents. If the latter, it explains why Mark abruptly ends the story with the women fleeing the tomb (16:8). The Gospel is open-ended. The reader knows that their flight and silence are not the end of the matter but is not given the details of how their fear was vanquished or their mouths opened. The end, therefore, serves as a beginning to a story to be continued (cf. Acts 1:1–2).

The Son of God (1:1). With the title "Son of God," Mark affirms that a profound relationship exists between Jesus and God, but this term's long history in the ancient Near East and the Old Testament meant it had a variety of associations. It would not necessarily have implied divinity or preexistence as it does for most today. The Old Testament applied the term to angelic figures[4] and to Israel as chosen and protected by God.[5] The expression was also used for the individual righteous Jew;[6] and in *Joseph and Asenath,* Joseph was called firstborn "son of God" because of his beauty.[7] Most relevant is God's declaration that the one who ascends the royal throne is "my son."[8] These enthronement passages invited the use of "son" as a title for the royal Messiah. Though it was only rarely employed in Palestinian Judaism, evidence exists for its usage as a messianic title in pre-Christian Judaism.[9] Clearly, the high priest's query, "Are you the Christ, the Son of the Blessed One?" (14:61), treats "Christ" and "Son of God" as equivalent.

The title had a variety of connotations in the Greco-Roman world. It was applied to figures such as Heracles, who shared the characteristics of a heroic mortal and of a god. The emperor Augustus received the title *divi filius,* the son of the deified one (Julius Caesar). The Roman emperors and members of their family were deified posthumously, while Gaius Caligula (and later Commodus) sought to emphasize his own divinity during his lifetime. The idea of bestowing divine honors and titles on human beings, however, was more accepted in the East, which was accustomed to ruler cults. An inscription on a stele in Pergamum identifies Augustus as "emperor Caesar, Son of God, God Augustus."[10] In this context, the expression would have been deemed fitting for a king or ruler as well as a divine figure (see Acts 14:11).

Mark's doubling of terms such as "Christ, the Son of God" serves as a two-step progression in which the second element has the effect of sharpening and heightening "the meaning of what precedes."[11] "Son of God" therefore means more than that Jesus is the Messiah or a royal ruler. Mark's narrative does not simply present Jesus as the long-awaited Messiah but as one who is God's Son in a unique way. The unclean spirits possess supernatural knowledge and recognize that Jesus is the Son of God who has come to destroy them (3:11; 5:7; see 1:24). They attest to his divine nature, authority, and power, not that he is Israel's Messiah. Mark also describes Jesus doing what only God can do. He battles Satan, calls disciples with the power of God, casts out demons, heals fever, cures leprosy, forgives sins, controls the sea, raises the dead, walks on the waves, and miraculously feeds thousands; and his death unleashes apocalyptic events. His coming signifies not the advent of some earthly messianic rule but the advent of the reign of God that will subjugate principalities and powers, things present and things to come, things above the earth and things beneath the earth, and even death.

It is written in Isaiah the prophet (1:2). The gospel message continues a longer story stretching back to Isaiah. Mark quotes from three texts: the law (Ex. 23:20 LXX), the greater prophets (Isa. 40:3), and the minor prophets (Mal. 3:1, the last of the prophets) to attest that God initiates the action.[12] Postbiblical Judaism tended to combine Old Testament texts in much the same way that modern hymnals conflate various texts in responsive readings. No simple device, such as footnotes, existed to identify all of the texts cited. By singling out Isaiah as the source, Mark informs the reader that the story "is to be understood against the backdrop of Isaian themes."[13]

John came, baptizing in the desert region (1:4). John chooses to preach and baptize in the desert for its symbolic associations. (1) For Israel, the desert was the place of new beginnings and renewal.[14] (2) It was also the place one went to elude persecution and to flee iniquity, since it was beyond the control of the cities.[15] According to the *Martyrdom of Isaiah* 2:7–11, the prophets Isaiah, Micah, Ananias, Joel, Habbakuk, and Josab, his son, abandoned the corruption of Judah for the desert. They clothed themselves in sackcloth, lamented straying Israel, and ate wild herbs as an act of symbolic judgment. The covenanters at Qumran cited Isaiah 40:3 as warrant for separating themselves from sinners "to walk to the desert in order to open there His path."[16] (3) The desert was also viewed as the mobilizing area for God's future victory over evil and the place where Elijah (Mal. 4:5) and the Messiah were thought to appear (Matt. 24:26). On the other side of the Jordan (John 1:28), John draws the people away from Jerusalem to the place where Israel had once stood prior to entering the Promised Land.

A baptism of repentance for the forgiveness of sins (1:4). John demands that everyone who comes for his baptism seal his or her pledge of repentance. A Jewish tradition claimed that Israel was prepared on Sinai for receiving salvation by means of immersion.[17] According to the prophets, Israel's cleansing was preparation for receiving God's Spirit.[18]

Ritual immersion was a common practice in Judaism, so common that the wealthier inhabitants of Jerusalem had their own immersion pools built in their houses. Nearly 150 of them have been found. Immersion pools had to contain

THE JUDEAN WILDERNESS

(left) Jebel Qaruntul, a mountain in the desert near Jericho associated with the temptation of Jesus.

(right) The monastery of the Mount of Temptation.

forty seahs of water (a *seah* equals a little less than two gallons). They were to be one cubit square and three cubits deep to enable people standing in it to immerse themselves completely by bending their knees.[19] This standard Jewish practice probably means that John did not immerse each person but served as the priestly mediator supervising the people as they submerged themselves by bending forward into the water.

John's baptism differs significantly from normal Jewish immersions for ceremonial purification because it is done only once and does not need repeating. It is not simply a rite of cleansing but an initiatory rite in which the one baptized repents and accepts God's offer of forgiveness to be saved from the coming fiery judgment. Josephus's description of John's baptism as only a purificatory rite and his statement that "they must not employ it to gain pardon for whatever sins they committed" suggests that he found this idea offensive.[20]

John wore clothing made of camel's hair, with a leather belt around his waist (1:6). John's clothing conjures up images of the prophet Elijah, who wore the same things.[21] According to 2 Kings 2:5–14, Elijah was taken up on the banks of the Jordan near Jericho. John may have deliberately chosen this site for his baptism because of its associations with Elijah and with Elisha's request for a double share of his spirit.

And he ate locusts and wild honey (1:6). The diet conveys asceticism and piety. Locusts were ritually clean and therefore permitted for Jews to eat (Lev. 11:20–23). They could "be cooked in salt-water, or roasted on coals, then dried, reduced to powder, and eaten with salt."[22] Josephus also refers to an abundance of bees in this region that would have produced ample honey.[23]

The thongs of whose sandals I am not worthy to stoop down and untie (1:7). John preaches that a more powerful person is coming who will baptize with the Spirit. The "strong one" is a name for God in the Greek Old Testament (LXX). John's water baptism is only preparatory as people plunge into the Jordan, signifying their repentance to ready themselves for God's coming kingdom. The Spirit's baptism will be definitive. John comes as a voice crying, a servant unworthy to perform even the demeaning task of stooping to loosen the sandals of the one who comes after him. A rabbinic commentary takes Leviticus 25:39, "do not make him work as a slave" to mean:

A Hebrew slave must not wash the feet of his master, nor put his shoes on him, nor carry his things before him when going to the bathhouse, nor support him by the hips when ascending steps, nor carry him in a litter or a sedan chair as slaves do. For it is said: "But over your brethren the children of Israel ye shall not rule, over one another, with rigor" (Lev. 25:46).[24]

He saw heaven being torn open (1:10). The heavens are usually described as "opening" as a sign that God is about to speak or act.[25] Mark says they are "torn" at Jesus' baptism, just as the temple veil is "torn" at his death (15:38). Joshua (Josh. 3:14–17), Elijah (2 Kings 2:8), and Elisha (2:14) each parted the Jordan river, and the false prophet Theudas promised to do it.[26] By contrast, when Jesus is baptized in the Jordan, the heavens are parted, recalling the longing expressed in Isaiah 64:1, "Oh, that you would rend the heavens and come down, that the mountains would tremble before you!"

The Spirit descending on him like a dove (1:10). This detail recalls the image of the Spirit's hovering over the waters at the beginning of creation (Gen. 1:2), as well as a rabbinic tradition that describes the Spirit's hovering like a dove.[27] God's Spirit swooping down on Jesus signifies the beginning of a new creation. The image confirms that Jesus' ministry will be Spirit directed (Isa. 11:2).

The rabbis relegated the Spirit's activity to the past because their authority was based on their ability to interpret previous revelation. To protect that authority, they undermined any who acted unconventionally and claimed more direct links to the divine through the Spirit.[28] A rabbinic tradition says that the Holy Spirit came to an end in Israel when the last prophets (Haggai, Zechariah, and Malachi) died. From then on, one could only hear the heavenly messages from an echo, the daughter of the voice (*bat qôl*). It continues that the sages were gathered in an upper room when the heavenly voice said, "There is a man among you who is worthy to receive the Holy Spirit, but his generation is unworthy of such an honor." They assumed that the person was Hillel the elder.[29] Significantly, Mark begins his gospel by featuring the work of the prophet John the Baptizer and the descent of the Spirit on Jesus. The Spirit has not come to an end in Israel but is breaking loose in a new, momentous way.

The Spirit sent him out into the desert (1:12). The Spirit does not induce a state of inner tranquility but drives Jesus deeper into the desolate desert, where wild beasts prowl, and into the clutches of Satan. The desert was also known as God's proving grounds for the people. Jesus emerges victorious over Satan, and his healing ministry continues his onslaught on Satan's realm.

▸ The Kingdom of God

The kingdom of God is not primarily a spatial or temporal category but refers to God's active reign. God approaches with strength (Isa. 40:10 LXX) to establish "his dominion over sin, sickness and hostile powers." In the ancient world, kingship conveyed power, sovereignty, dominion, and preeminence; but in the Old Testament kingship was also connected to ruling with justice and mercy. For Israel, God alone was King, who ruled over all creation, powers, and peoples.[A-1] In this period of oppression under pagan rulers, many pious Jews expected God to establish a transcendental kingdom greater than all the kingdoms of earth and to avenge injustice, destroy the wicked, and vanquish the host of Satan. God's reign claimed the people's absolute obedience. They must sever all other allegiances and completely submit to God's law.

For zealous militants, the rallying cry "God is King" became a call to arms and fierce resistance to the pagan encroachment in God's land. For the sect at Qumran, it meant withdrawing into the desert to await the final battle between God's angelic army and the forces of evil. For the Pharisees, it meant intensifying obedience to strict interpretations of the law, what they called building a fence around the law, to establish and preserve the holiness of the people in preparation.[A-2] For Jesus, the kingdom of God denotes something quite different. It signals a divine outbreak of mercy and forgiveness, of healing and restoration. It entails good news to the oppressed, the sick, the demon-possessed, the impure, and moral outcasts. Jesus' preaching challenges nationalistic expectations and ritual protocol.

Beginning of Jesus' Ministry (1:14–15)

After John was put in prison (1:14). The announcement that John was "delivered up" (the literal meaning of "put in prison") foreshadows how the fates of John and Jesus will be intertwined. Jesus also will be delivered up.[30] John is Jesus' forerunner in ministry, conflict with earthly authorities, and death (6:7–13; 9:11–13).

Jesus went into Galilee, proclaiming the good news of God. "The time has come," he said. "The kingdom of God is near" (1:14–15). With the forerunner's work completed, Jesus' work now begins as he returns victoriously from his battle with Satan. He announces God's timely intervention into the present. The time of waiting is over, and the decisive moment has arrived when God's rule will be established.[31]

Calling of the First Disciples (1:16–20)

Simon and his brother Andrew casting a net into the lake (1:16). Jesus calls Peter and Andrew as they are casting nets from the shoreline. Early church tradition suggests that this scene took place in the cove of Tabgha, west of Capernaum. Warm mineral springs flowed into the lake there, attracting schools of fish.[32] We should not presume that they were too poor to own a boat. In the winter, a type of fish called *musht* "move closer to the shore in schools to seek warmer waters." One expert notes that "twentieth-century fisherman continue to use this spring, now known as Ein Nur, for these purposes."[33] The throw net was eighteen to twenty-five feet in diameter, with a rope in its center and lead sinkers on its circumference. It was cast by one person standing in a boat or on a rock near the lakeshore. The net was laid on one arm and shoulder and was then thrown with a large swing of the other arm. The net sank to the bottom like an opened parachute capturing the fish. The fisherman then had to pull out the fish one by one or carefully draw all the lead weights together and haul the catch to shore or into a boat.

"Come, follow me" (1:17). Jesus' first act creates a community of followers by calling some to follow him. Prophets did not call people to follow them, but to follow God. The teachers of the law had disciples who came to them to be instructed in the law, but none ever said to anyone, "Come, follow me." The disciple, rather, always chose the master and moved on when he believed that he had learned as much from him as possible about the tradition. Jesus does not wait for volunteers but chooses his own disciples and requires absolute obedience. Mark shows Jesus calling disciples with divine authority, just as God called the prophets in the Old Testament and expected the relationship to be permanent. He also does not call them to a house of study but to an itinerant ministry.

I will make you fishers of men (1:17). In the Old Testament, the metaphor of fishing for men is associated with gathering people for judgment.[34] For Jesus, the imagery has to do with a messianic gathering of the people. In *Joseph and Asenath*, Joseph's new wife prays a psalm of thanksgiving after her conversion and says that her husband "grasped me like a fish on a hook."[35] The disciples are called to be agents who will bring a compelling message to others, one that will change their lives beyond recognition.

He saw James son of Zebedee and his brother John in a boat, preparing their nets (1:19). After each outing, fishing nets required mending, washing, drying, and folding, and Jesus finds John and James engaged in this task. Three types of nets were used in New Testament times: the seine net (Matt. 13:47–48), the cast net (Mark 1:16), and the trammel net, which could stretch to five hundred feet and required two boats working together. Owning a boat does not indicate that Zebedee and his sons are well-to-do, any more than owning a yoke of oxen or a flock of sheep indicates that a farmer is well-to-do. Note how both the boat owner and the hired laborers are pictured working side by side. Fish suppliers had to lease their fishing rights, and these fishermen are probably part of a fishing cooperative that has contracted to deliver fish to wealthier middlemen.

The Man with an Unclean Spirit (1:21–28)

When the Sabbath came, Jesus went into the synagogue and began to teach (1:21). The remains of a limestone synagogue visible today in Capernaum date from the late second to third century or perhaps as late as the fifth century. Religious structures were normally rebuilt in the same sacred area, and an earlier building made of rough black basalt stones has been discovered beneath it. It is probable that the synagogue in Jesus' day was located in the same spot, and its outline fits the plan of early synagogues found at Masada, Herodium, Gamla, and

▸ Capernaum

The village of Capernaum (*K^efar Nahum* in Hebrew) was located on the northwest shore of the Sea of Galilee, two miles west of the upper Jordan River, some 680 feet below sea level. It was the first town west of the border between the tetrarchy assigned to Herod Antipas and that assigned to Herod Philip (Gaulanitus) and sat east of the extension of the Via Maris highway to Damascus. The village's situation on this frontier gave it some importance. It had a customs office manned by Levi (Mark 2:13–15) and a detachment of soldiers under a centurion (Luke 7:1–10; Matt. 8:5–13). By the time of Josephus, however, it had apparently lost its significance. Josephus claimed to have organized the defense in Galilee in the war against Rome but gave Capernaum only incidental mention as the place where he fell off a horse and as a fertile district for grapes and figs with a "genial air" and watered by "a highly fertilizing spring."[A-3]

Capernaum's economy was based on fishing, agriculture, industry (manufacture of tools made from basalt stones and of glass vessels), and trade. This side of the lake was particularly rich for fishing, which may explain why Peter and his brother Andrew left their hometown Bethsaida and settled here. The coins and vessels uncovered by archaeologists suggest that the village was commercially linked to the northern regions of upper Galilee, Golan, Syria, Phoenicia, Asia Minor, and Cyprus.

Archaeologists estimate the population of the town to have been between 1,000 to 1,500. The private houses that have been excavated are unpretentious and average for the living standard of an ancient village. Local volcanic basalt stones in their natural state were used to build walls and pavements. The houses had a single door opening onto a public street and consisted of several roofed rooms clustered around a large open courtyard that served as the focal point where daily activities such as cooking and craft work took place. Houses of this kind were probably shared by two or more kindred families governed by a patriarchal structure.

Magdala. It measures 4,838 square feet and is the largest of the synagogues found from this era.[36]

The Palestinian synagogues dating from the third and fourth centuries with their external and internal ornamentation, Torah niches, and raised platforms may mislead us to expect first-century synagogues to look much the same. By contrast, the synagogues of the first century "were functional and plain."[37] Synagogues became more official institutions in the second and third centuries after the temple's destruction created a desire to create an organization for nonsacrificial worship.[38]

A man . . . possessed by an evil spirit (1:23). Mark uses the term "unclean [*akatharton*] spirit" rather than "evil [*ponēron*] spirit." This is not a medical diagnosis, but a religious term. In the Old Testament, that which is unclean has evaded the control of the divine holiness and causes humans to be banished from God's presence.[39] Jesus, endued with the Holy Spirit, has come to purify what is unclean.

Mark draws a distinction between those who are demonized and those who are sick (1:32, 34). Unlike the sick, those identified as controlled by demons have extraordinary strength (5:4) and suffer violently (5:5; 9:22). The demons, agitated by Jesus' presence, usually howl their alarm (1:24; 5:7) and often do some kind of harm when they depart. The possession is caused by an evil power that requires a greater power to expel it.

"I know who you are—the Holy One of God!" (1:24). The unclean spirit assumes that knowledge is power and tries to fend off its impending defeat with the exorcist's trick of pronouncing the name of the opponent. In the ancient magical papyri, names were used as incantations because it was believed that pronouncing the name of the power or enemy gave one a tactical advantage in manipulating and defeating it. The cry (lit.) "What between you and me?" (1:24) is the same cry used by the widow of Zarephath (1 Kings 17:18) and the king of the Ammonites (Judg. 11:12) as a defensive maneuver. A magical papyri drawn up to ward off demons illustrates the strategy: "I know your name which was received in heaven, I know your forms. . . . I know your foreign names and your true name. . . . I

CAPERNAUM

(left) Remains of basalt homes. The modern structure in the background is built over the top of the site identified as the home of Peter.

(right) Remains of the home of Peter in Capernaum. The property was converted into a church during the 2d–4th centuries A.D.

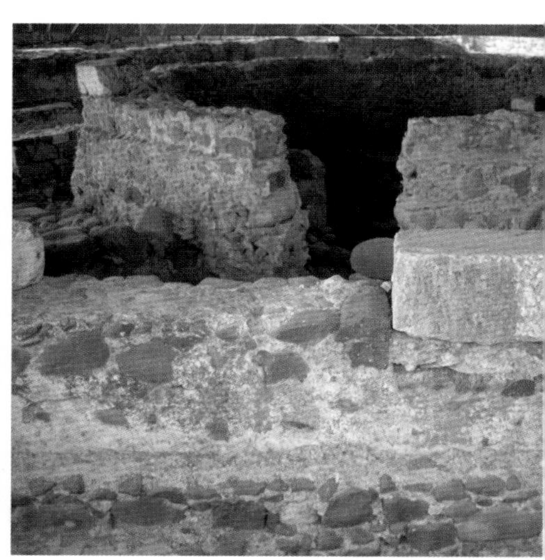

know you Hermes, who you are and whence you came."[40]

Unlike other exorcisms recorded in the ancient world, Jesus uses no incantations, chants, rites, noises, pharmaceutical recipes, knots, or other magical devices. In Tobit 8:2–3, for example, Sarah drives off the demon Asmodeus with the help of the angel Raphael by burning a fish's liver and heart, whose stench "repelled the demon . . . to the remotest parts of Egypt." Jesus makes no appeals to a supernatural power and does not rattle off a litany of powerful names. He simply commands, and the demons flee.

Healing Peter's Mother-in-Law (1:29–34)

They went . . . to the home of Simon and Andrew (1:29). Archaeologists have uncovered a house that may well have been Peter's home. Inside the building, numerous coins, pottery, and oil lamps dating to the first century have been discovered, along with artifacts that include several fish hooks. It is located only one hundred feet south of the city's synagogue on the main street of the town and consists of a large, circular cluster of rooms around a spacious courtyard. An open area between the street and the doorway leading to the courtyard would have allowed space for a large number of people to "gather at the door" (1:33; cf. 2:1–3).

This site was venerated by later Christians from the inscriptions and symbols found in the debris. In the late first century, it was changed into a house for religious gatherings; and in the fourth century, it was enlarged and set apart

The Synagogue

Synagogues could be found everywhere in this era, but we should not always envision a distinctive building.[A-4] They were primarily gatherings of people, not buildings. In Jesus' time, most village synagogues were probably modified rooms in private homes or public buildings. Josephus describes the impetus for such gatherings:

> He [Moses] appointed the Law to be the most excellent and necessary form of instruction, ordaining, not that it should be heard once for all or twice or on several occasions, but that every week men should desert their other occupations and assemble to listen to the Law and to obtain a thorough and accurate knowledge of it, a practice which all other legislators seem to have neglected.[A-5]

A synagogue inscription found in Jerusalem on Mount Ophel illumines the synagogue's purpose as the place where the law was read and heard, taught and learned, interpreted and applied to life:

> Theodotus [son of] Vettenus, priest and
> archisynagogos, son of the archisynago-
> gos and grandson of the archisynagogos con-
> structed the synagogue for the rea-
> ding of the Law and the study of the
> commandments
> and the guest-room and the (upper?) chambers and
> the instal-
> lations of the water for a hostelry for tho-
> se needing [them] from abroad, which was foun-
> ded by his fathers and the el-
> ders and Simonides.[A-6]

Philo gives us a picture of a group gathered around the study of the law. He describes an Egyptian in Alexandria arguing with Jews to break with their Sabbath customs: "And will you sit in your conventicles [synagogues] and assemble your regular company and read in security your holy books, expounding any obscure point and in leisurely comfort discussing at length your ancestral philosophy?"[A-7] from the rest of the town through an imposing enclosure wall. The pilgrim Egeria (ca. 383–95) wrote that "the house of the chief of the apostles has been turned into a church." In the second half of the fifth century, an octagonal church was built over the large room, probably to serve pilgrims, and remained in use until the seventh century, when Capernaum was conquered and destroyed by invading Muslim forces.

Simon's mother-in-law (1:30). When a woman married, she left her family and moved to the home and family of her husband. For this reason, daughters were not prized because they could not add to the family's wealth or honor. They were destined to become part of another's family, and a wife's blood relatives were not counted as kin by her new family. A mother-in-law would normally be living in her husband's house or, if he has died, in the home of a son. If she had no living sons, she would seek to return to her family. Otherwise, she would be destitute. Since Peter's mother-in-law has apparently moved to the home of her daughter, she has no living sons, and Peter has consented to accept responsibility for her. Another possibility, however, is that the home belongs to Peter's mother-in-law. Peter is said to come from Bethsaida (John 1:44), a few miles away; and he may have been visiting his mother-in-law.

An interesting ruling in the Mishnah insists that a man must tithe again any food that he gives his mother-in-law to prepare when he receives it back. It assumes that she will naturally want to exchange the produce given to her for something of better quality out of concern to improve the welfare of her daughter.[41]

In bed with a fever (1:30). A large segment of the ancient world considered fever to be an illness in and of itself caused by demons, divine beings, curses, or astrological phenomena.[42] In Leviticus 26:16 and Deuteronomy 28:22, fever is a divine chastisement. Many believed that it could only be cured by God. A rabbinic tradition reads: "Greater is the miracle wrought for the sick than for Hananiah, Mishael and Azariah. [For] that of Hananiah, Mishael and Azariah [concerned] a fire kindled by man, which all can extinguish; whilst that of a sick person is [in connection with] a heavenly fire, and who can extinguish that?"[43] The answer is that none can extinguish it except God. It is therefore Christologically significant that Jesus can extinguish a heavenly fire—something only God or God's agent could do.

She began to wait on them (1:31). Being able to serve others was a sign of physical and mental wholeness; it was not demeaning. "To wait on them" is the same verb ("to serve") used to describe what the angels did for Jesus in 1:13. It is also a characteristic of discipleship as Jesus makes clear to his disciples (9:35; 10:41–45). The women who saw his death from afar are described as those who "in Galilee . . . followed him and cared for his needs" (15:41).

Prayer in a Lonely Place Before Going Out to the Whole of Galilee (1:35–39)

Jesus . . . went off to a solitary place, where he prayed (1:35). According to an ancient tradition, the "lonely place" was on the "ridge of hills" west of the village overlooking Tabgha and the Sea of Galilee.[44]

Healing a Leper (1:39–41)

A man with leprosy came to him (1:40). In the New Testament, leprosy does not refer to Hansen's disease but to various

REFLECTIONS

MANY TODAY ONLY RESORT TO prayer when they are in trouble. Jesus sets an example of a disciplined prayer life by regularly seeking solitude and receiving divine replenishment from prayer. Jesus would have been brought up to pray the Shema (Num. 15:37–41; Deut. 6:4–9; 11:13–21) and the Eighteen Benedictions at least twice a day, morning and evening. We get only a glimpse of Jesus' prayer life from Mark. Mark records three times of prayer: at the beginning, in the middle, and before the end of his ministry. He is always alone and prays at night or break of day and at times of tension (6:46; 14:32). His praying shows that he is not independent of God's help. His authority, strength, and power come from God.

kinds of skin diseases, such as dermatosis, psoriasis, burns, suspicious baldness, and white leprosy, where patches devoid of feeling develop on the skin. Four kinds of leprosy are distinguished in the Mishnah tractate on leprosy: bright white like snow, white like the lime of the temple, white as the skin of an egg, white like white wool.[45] Every suspected leprosy sign must be brought to the priest for examination because *only* a priest may declare lepers clean or unclean (Lev. 13:3).[46] The cases are described in detail in Leviticus 13–14 so that the priest can identify the presence or absence of particular physical signs, such as skin color change, hair color, infiltration, extension, or ulceration of the skin. There is no concern about a medical contagion; if it covers the whole body, he is considered clean of the disease (Lev.13:13)!

The law prescribed that lepers be excluded from the community.[47] As a result, lepers tended to be social derelicts. They were quarantined because they imparted ritual uncleanness to others, not because of any fear of physical contamination. Leprosy, like a corpse, imparts impurity to objects found within the same enclosure (known as the principle of a tent), so the leper is like a living corpse (see Num. 12:12).[48] Lepers could attend a synagogue if a screen was erected, but they had to enter first and leave last.[49] A different picture is presented in a later rabbinic text in which rabbis argue one should not pass within four cubits to the east of a leper or within one hundred cubits when a wind was blowing. Another tradition relates that when a certain rabbi saw a leper, he would throw stones at him and shout: "Go to your place and do not defile other people."[50]

Leprosy was regarded as a telltale sign that the victim had committed some hidden sin for which God was punishing him measure for measure. Most believed that God alone could heal leprosy (see 2 Kings 5:1–27). Only after being forgiven by God, as evidenced by the healing, could the purification process begin to reintegrate the leper into society.

Jesus shows compassion by stretching out his hand and touching the leper. The touch contrasts with Elisha's instructions to Naaman to go wash in the Jordan (2 Kings 5:10–11). The reader can only conclude that Jesus was so close to God that his touch could cleanse even the worst impurity.[51] "Jesus' power to cleanse is thus demonstrably greater than the power of the leprosy to contaminate."[52]

But go, show yourself to the priest and offer the sacrifices that Moses commanded for your cleansing (1:44). Though the man has been cleansed of his disease, he remains in social limbo until he has been examined and declared clean by a priest and has offered the appropriate sacrifices (see Lev. 14:1–32). The "testimony to them" may refer to the proof to the community into which the leper is being restored.

Healing of a Paralytic (2:1–12)

They made an opening in the roof above Jesus (2:4). Houses in Capernaum did not have large windows. Walls were built without true foundations and were made of rough basalt without mortar. The courses were leveled with small pebbles and soil. Such buildings could support little more than a thatch roof. The sloping flat roof consisted of wooden cross beams (usually made from trees, Isa. 9:10) overlaid with a matting of reeds, palm branches, and dried mud (see Ps. 129:6). The roof could be reached from open courtyards by a flight of stone steps or by a ladder. One could then dig into the earthen roof without causing irreparable damage. This explains why the men could dig through the roof without evoking howls of protest from the owner. The roof had to be replenished and rolled every fall before the onset of the winter rains.

right ▶

WATTLE AND MUD ROOF

Reconstruction of the roof of a typical rural home.

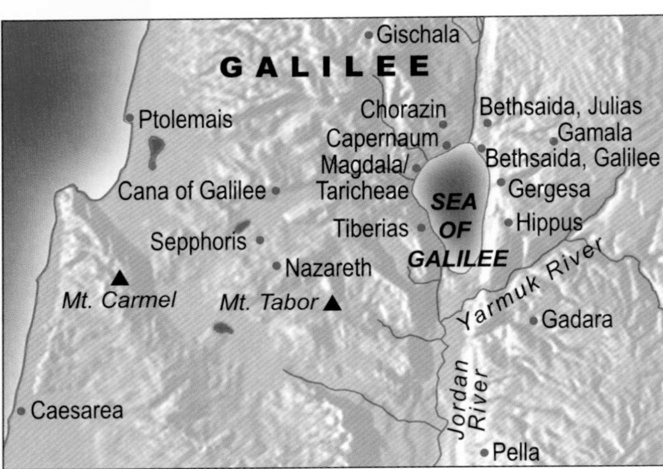

GALILEE

Capernaum was located on the north shore of the Sea of Galilee. ▼

The mat the paralyzed man was lying on (2:4). Mark uses a colloquial word for a poor man's mat (see John 5:8). The pallet was probably a "cheap mattress, like a bag filled with straw."[53] When the bystanders glorify God in response to this miracle, it confirms that Jesus is not guilty of blasphemy.

Son, your sins are forgiven (2:5). Readers might find it surprising that Jesus first announces that the man's sins are forgiven rather than healing him. The men bring him to Jesus for healing, not absolution. Moderns tend to dissociate sin and our relationship to God from our physical well-being. In Jesus' world, people took for granted a connection between sickness and sins (see John 5:14; 9:2). Healing appears in conjunction with forgiveness in 2 Chronicles 7:14 and Psalm 103:3. Most assumed that reconciliation with God must occur before healing could come. In the Prayer of Nabonidus, found at Qumran, the king of Babylon says, "I was smitten [by a malignant inflammation] for seven years, and banished far [from men, until I prayed to the God Most High] and an exorcist forgave my sins. He was a Je[w] from [the exiles]."[54] In the Talmud, we find a tradition that "a sick man does not recover from his sickness until all his sins are forgiven him, as it is written, 'Who forgiveth all thine iniquities, who healeth all thy diseases" (Ps. 103:3).'"[55] In another place, the rabbis appealed to Psalm 103:3–4 to explain why the prayer for forgiveness precedes the prayer for healing: "Redemption and healing come after forgiveness."[56]

A Jewish audience would surmise that the paralysis was a consequence of some sin.[57] To forgive the sin removes the consequences of the sin—the paralysis. The man's healing is therefore the result of the forgiveness of sins. The miracle shows that the coming of God's reign brings both forgiveness and healing.[58]

He's blaspheming! Who can forgive sins but God alone? (2:7). Jesus assumes the authority to remit sins as if he were God, even though he uses the divine passive, "Your sins are forgiven."[59] The teachers of the law conclude that Jesus blasphemously usurps God's prerogatives and affronts God's majesty, since only a priest could legitimately pronounce the forgiveness of sins on the basis of repentance, restitution, and sacrifice (Lev. 4; 5; 16; 17:11). Their hostile response unveils three things: (1) They admit that Jesus does something that they are unable to do—forgive sins. Their judgment confirms the crowd's earlier acclamation that Jesus teaches with new authority. (2) Blasphemy is a serious charge that emerges again during Jesus' trial (Mark 14:64). The text from Leviticus 24:16, that whoever "blasphemes the Name . . . must be put to death," cannot be far from their minds. The rejection of Jesus' authority to announce the forgiveness of sins will ultimately lead to his suffering and death for the forgiveness of sins. (3) Jesus knows hidden thoughts even as God does.[60] In *Joseph and Asenath* 23:8 and 26:6, prophets are said to perceive all things in their spirits (see Luke 7:39).

Which is easier: to say to the paralytic, "Your sins are forgiven," or to say, "Get up, and take your mat and walk?" (2:9). The alarm of these teachers of the law is

Scribes/Teachers of the Law

During the intertestamental period, the temple sacrificial cult was supplemented (not supplanted) by prayer and the study of the law in the synagogue. It was a lay institution that did not require the presence of a priest. As a result, the power of the priest became somewhat diluted by the learned scholar (teacher of the law or scribe). Unlike priests, scribes were not dependent on a special pedigree or institutional setting to function. Unlike prophets, they did not depend on direct contact with God or a charismatic personality. Judaism had become a book religion, and the scribe had authority on the basis of his erudition in sacred Scriptures and traditions. This does not exclude the possibility that scribes could be priests or Levites.

The hymn to the scribe in Sirach 38:24–39:11 presents the scribe as the ideal learned Jew. As interpreters of the law, they were regarded as custodians of the traditions on Jewish life and consulted by those in power (see Matt. 2:4). Some scribes were prominent advisors in the royal courts and leaders in the temple; others were lowly community officials or village copyists. Some were also visionaries.[A-8]

In Mark, the teachers of the law form a unified front in opposition to Jesus. His growing influence with the people imperils their importance. They appear alone (1:22; 2:6; 3:22; 9:11, 14; 12:28, 38), with the Pharisees (2:16; 7:5), and with the elders and chief priests (8:31; 11:27; 14:43, 53; 15:1).

legitimate, and Jesus takes it seriously. At this stage of his ministry, Jesus is willing to give doubting teachers proof. He parries their indictment with a riddle that confirms his claim to divine authority. Moses offered a criterion to verify whether someone is a true or a false prophet who presumes to utter in God's name what the Lord has not uttered: "If what a prophet proclaims in the name of the LORD does not take place or come true, that is a message the LORD has not spoken. That prophet has spoken presumptuously. Do not be afraid of him" (Deut. 18:22).

Jesus' statement does not mean that one thing is easier than the other but that the two are interconnected. If the paralytic leaves on his own power, it will reveal that his sins have been forgiven, resulting in his complete healing.

The Call of Levi the Tax Collector and Eating with Sinners (2:13–17)

He saw Levi son of Alphaeus sitting at the tax collector's booth (2:14). Since Levi is stationed in Galilee, he is most likely in the employ of Herod Antipas, a client king of Rome. The custom house is located near the border with Gaulanitus, under Herod Philip's rule, to collect tolls, tariffs, imposts, and customs on those goods entering and leaving the district or being transported through it. Levi also may have collected taxes from the fishing industry.

Toll collectors were renowned for dishonesty and extortion. Most pious Jews disdained them as desiring money more than honor or righteousness. They had sold out to a hostile culture. This would be particularly true for someone named Levi, assuming it was a typical name for Levites. In the *Testament of Levi* 13:1–2, Levi commands that his descendants learn to read and write so that they may read and understand the law. Levi's literacy may have opened up a quite different career path as an agent of an impious tetrarch.

Ironically, the rabbis sanctioned lying to a tax collector—except if one uses an oath, according to the School of Shammai, and even if one uses an oath, according to the School of Hillel.[61] Toll collectors were also detested throughout the Greco-Roman world. Plutarch wrote, "We are

▸ The Son of Man

No consensus exists about what this title (if it can be considered a title) was intended to conjure up in the minds of Jews in the first century. It appears thirteen times in Mark and only on the lips of Jesus. Was it supposed to evoke images of an apocalyptic heavenly figure, to punctuate his humanity (Ps. 8:4; 80:17; Ezek. 2:1), or simply to be understood as a circumlocution meaning "a man such as I"?[A-9]

When Jesus asked his disciples, "Who do people say I am?" "the Son of Man" was not one of the options cited (Mark 8:27–28). The obscurity of the term made it nearly free of any preconceived notions that Jesus' generation might entertain. It therefore was a mysterious and arresting title that Jesus could fill with his own meaning. In Mark, we do not get information about what the Son of Man is but what he does. He has authority to forgive sins (2:10) and is Lord of the Sabbath (2:28). He will be betrayed (14:21, 41), delivered up, suffer many things, die, and be raised (8:31, 38; 9:9, 12; 10:33). He came not to be served but to give his life as a ransom for many (10:45). He will come on the clouds (13:26) and will be seated at the right hand of power (14:62).

annoyed and displeased with customs-officials, not when they pick up those articles which we are importing openly, but when in the search for concealed goods they pry into baggage and merchandise which are another's property. And yet the law allows them to do this and they would lose by not doing so."[62] We should note, however, that Josephus cites John, the tax collector of Caesarea, as one of the leading Jews in the city, who took great risks in defending the sanctity of a synagogue.[63]

Many tax collectors and "sinners" were eating with him and his disciples (2:15). A celebratory meal was customary after conversion.[64]

One normally ate with one's relatives or with equals who would reciprocate. Jesus ate with toll collectors and sinners, that is, notorious sinners who had no intention of trying to conform to the demands of the law and became religious outcasts. By doing so, he made concrete God's offer of acceptance and forgiveness. Meals characterize

center

SILVER COIN

This coin depicts Tiberius, the Roman emperor during the ministry of Jesus (A.D. 14–37).

Pharisees

The Pharisees were collections of lay factions unified by their concern for rigorous obedience to the law. They believed that only the worship and obedience of a holy people could preserve the land of Israel from judgment. Most Pharisees were not priests, but they sought to extend the concerns of ritual purity usually associated with priests in the temple into the lives of ordinary Jews outside the temple. They were especially known for their attention to purity rules that organized and classified things, times, and persons. The name means the "separated ones," and it was essential to their sense of "separateness" (holiness) to know what was permissible or proscribed, clean or unclean.

Pharisaic purity rules specified not only what might be eaten but out of which vessel and with whom one might eat. The Pharisees were particularly anxious that foodstuffs be properly grown, tithed, and prepared. They shunned contact with people that they labeled "the people of the land," who were less conscientious about such things. The Pharisees regarded their table as an altar before God, and they sought to replicate the purity of the priests in the temple. Eating for them became a holy occasion.

In our culture, when we give a dinner party, we may worry about several things. Where will we eat—in the formal dining room or in the kitchen? Who sits where? Will the presence of a certain guest offend another guest? What should we serve? How do we prepare the food? What dinnerware do we use? What conversation is appropriate? What dress is appropriate? Guests at formal dinners may worry about which utensil to use with which course and may fear committing some gaffe. To the Pharisees, such questions had religious meaning. They gathered in hallowed groups to eat together in purity and reduce the risk of any pollution from the non-observant. The Pharisees believed that sinners should be kept at arm's length until decontaminated by proper repentance and the ceremonial rites.

Jesus' ministry and have a distinctive character. (1) They are spontaneous affairs not tied to the cycle of holy times (e.g., Passover), nor are they an expression of a strictly regimented communal pattern (e.g., Qumran). (2) They represent the joyous celebration of God's saving reign bursting into the lives of people. (3) By being open to all, Jesus shows no fear that he will be tainted by the impurity or iniquity of sinners. On the contrary, he will infect them with the grace of God.

Sharing a table with others was a sign of friendship and goodwill. In not being choosy about his eating companions, Jesus ignores purity boundaries and provokes the Pharisees' ire.[65] He torpedoes the whole system of ranking and classifying people where the devout are to be extolled and sinners shunned. Jesus accepts into his fellowship social outcasts and sinners forgiven by grace.

When the teachers of the law who were Pharisees saw him eating (2:16). "The teachers of the law who were Pharisees" reads literally "the scribes of the Pharisees." As laymen, most Pharisees were not learned scholars. The "scribes of the Pharisees" were those in the movement who had more formal study and had become expert guides in the law. These teachers laid out clear guidelines and boundaries for what was acceptable and unacceptable to God in all spheres of life.

Feasting was usually in the open, and people were attracted by the noise of conversation and the smell of food. The pious Pharisees, who so exalted the sacredness of meals, fume over Jesus' public behavior. He violates instructions laid down throughout Scripture not to associate with evildoers.[66] A later rabbinic tradition attributes to the wise this extreme saying, "Let not a man associate with sinners even to bring them near to the Torah."[67]

It is not the healthy who need a doctor, but the sick (2:17). The proverbial wisdom about physicians can be found in Hellenistic circles, where it notes the duty and habit of physicians to be with the diseased. Jesus uses the proverb to emphasize "the need of the sick to have a physician."[68] Jesus embodies God's mercy and purpose to take away the diseases, infirmities, and sins of the people.

The Question of Fasting (2:18–22)

How is it that John's disciples and the disciples of the Pharisees are fasting, but yours are not? (2:18). The Day of Atonement was the only time when God's law prescribed that the people were to deny themselves food.[69] The more ascetic disciples of John and the conscientious Pharisees fasted more often (see Luke 18:12). Observers, noting that Jesus' disciples do not fast, ask why.

Fasting was associated with three things: (1) sorrow for a deceased person; (2) penitential mourning to mollify the wrath of God and to avert calamity; and (3) petition to God.[70] According to the *Psalms of Solomon* 3:6–8, the righteous one avoids repeated sins, "searches his house to remove unintentional sins," and "atones for (sins of) ignorance by fasting and humbling his soul, and the Lord will cleanse every devout person and his house." Fasting could also be related to a fear of demons, who were thought to gain power over someone through eating.

How can the guests of the bridegroom fast while he is with them (2:19). Jesus explains his unwillingness to fast with a wedding analogy. Weddings were marked by music, laughter, feasting, and merrymaking. Anyone fasting at a wedding called attention to oneself and would be a grievous affront to the host. Jesus' rejection of fasting here is related to the joy, celebration, and hope that the presence of God's kingdom should excite. The Old Testament uses the image of the bridegroom for God, but clearly the image applies here to Jesus, who will be taken from them—the first allusion to his death in this Gospel.[71]

A patch . . . wineskins (2:21–22). The images of patching cloth and wineskins draw on everyday wisdom. The new stronger fabric of a patch will tear away from the old, weaker fabric when the garment is washed. Old wineskins already stretched to their limits will burst their seams when the new wine continues to ferment and emit gas. Combining new with old will result in torn garments, spilled wine, and ruined wineskins. The point is that the old—the old forms of Judaism—is incompatible with the new, not because the old is outmoded, but because the new packs such power that the old cannot contain it.

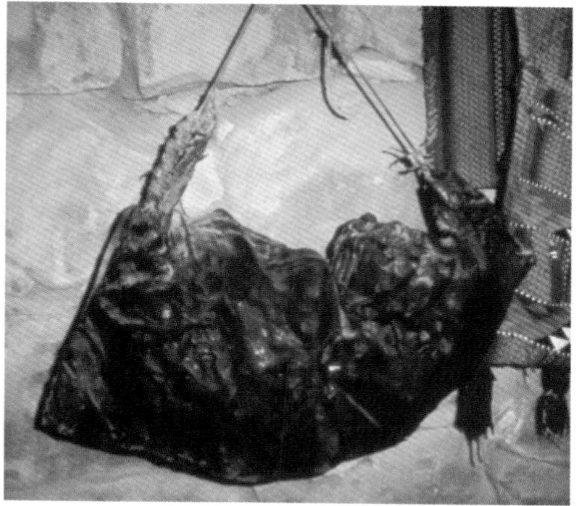

WINE SKIN

A goat skin on display at Qatrin in Golan.

Plucking Grain on the Sabbath (2:23–28)

They began to pick some heads of grain (2:23). Fields were not fenced but marked out by stones, so that taking shortcuts through planted fields was not unusual. The disciples may have followed a path

The Sabbath

The Sabbath was fundamental to Judaism as a sign of Israel's sanctification among all the nations. (1) It marked a joyful entry into sacred time (the time of the beginning before human work) and divine repose. Josephus claimed that "the word Sabbath in the Jew's language denotes cessation from all work."[A-10] (2) It allowed the people to honor God's holiness, who sanctified this day.[A-11] (3) It set Israel apart from the nations and served as a bulwark against assimilation to pagan culture. Keeping the Sabbath became a profession of faith. (4) Desecrating the Sabbath was akin to dishonoring the covenant (Isa. 56:4–6) and was worthy of death.[A-12] It was believed to unleash God's judgment on Israel (Neh. 13:18). This last concern may have motivated the Pharisees' consternation over perceived Sabbath violations.

Pietist groups in Israel multiplied the strict rules related to Sabbath observance. The earliest list of restrictions are found in *Jubilees* 2:17–33; 50:6–13 and CD 10:14–11:18. The Mishnah, the collection of the oral tradition compiled sometime before A.D. 220, contains three tractates specifically addressing Sabbath issues: *Šabbat* (prohibitions of work and what objects may or may not be carried), *ᶜErubin* (rules about extending the limits for movement on the Sabbath) and *Beṣah* (work permitted and prohibited on festivals). A rabbinic commentary on Exodus goes so far as to prohibit activities that merely detract from the restfulness of the day.[A-13] The rabbis recognized that the manifold Sabbath rules were only tenuously connected to scriptural law: "The rules about the sabbath, festal offerings and sacrilege are as mountains hanging by a hair, for Scripture is scanty and the rules many."[A-14] already struck by others and plucked grain as they went, rubbing it together before eating. Deuteronomy 23:25 permits gathering grain in another's field, but the Pharisees accuse the disciples of violating the Sabbath by harvesting, that is, extracting the edible content from something that had not previously been set aside for Sabbath consumption.[72] The disciples may also have violated the prohibition of moving beyond fixed boundaries on the Sabbath (see Ex. 16:29).

The Pharisees' accusation derives from their interpretation of the law. They would prefer that the disciples fast rather than eat, but one was also not supposed to fast on the Sabbath.[73]

In the days of Abiathar the high priest (2:26). Abiathar was Ahimilech's son, who had escaped the massacre by Doeg the Edomite. According to 1 Samuel 21:1–6, Ahimilech, not Abiathar, was the one who gave the bread of the Presence to David. Abiathar, however, was the high priest particularly associated with David, and this reference may be an example of eponymous dating for this period—during the Abiathar era (compare Luke 3:2).

The consecrated bread, which is lawful only for priests to eat (2:26). The loaves of presentation (Lev. 24:7–9) are set out before the Lord as an offering but belong to Aaron and his sons, who are to eat them in a holy place. The illustration from David is pertinent because he was not just any hungry man but God's anointed. His personal authority and the urgency of the situation made his violation of the law excusable. Jesus' argument assumes that if the regulations regarding the bread of the Presence could be set aside for David when he lied that the king had charged him with a mission (1 Sam. 21:2), how much more can holy regulations be set aside for one whom Mark has identified as the Messiah, the Son of God? His mission to proclaim the kingdom of God is not a falsehood and carries with it far greater urgency.

The Sabbath was made for man (2:27). Scholars have argued that rabbis would judge an appeal to 1 Samuel 21 to be invalid for establishing a legal precept regarding Sabbath observance. Historical passages could only be used to illustrate or corroborate a legal argument. This criticism, however, may help us see more clearly Jesus' purposes. He is not interested in convincing the hair-splitting legal experts but converting the more common-sense oriented masses. He also does

WHEAT

(left) A wheat field.

(right) A close-up of grains of wheat.

not want to set up more rules to decide what can or cannot be done on the Sabbath but wants to penetrate through the rules to unfold God's will for the Sabbath. God did not create the Sabbath for humans to obey but for human well-being. One can never interpret the law correctly unless one refers back to God's intention behind the law. God intended the Sabbath as a gracious gift to release human beings from the necessity of endless toil. Jesus emphasizes that David "had need" and "was hungry" and that human need has priority over regulations. The incident reveals that something new has broken in, and Jesus rules over the rules. Disciples need not concern themselves about appearing to be irreligious when they are carrying out the greater task of doing God's will. There will be plenty of other Sabbaths to keep holy.

Healing on the Sabbath (3:1–6)

Another time he went into the synagogue, and a man with a shriveled hand was there (3:1). The man with the shriveled hand would have stood out in the synagogue when the congregation rose and lifted their hands in prayer. A shriveled hand is frequently understood to be the punishment of God.[74] Jeroboam's hand "dried up" when he tried to take action against the rebellious prophets (1 Kings 13:4–6), and it was healed only after he pleaded that the prophet pray for his restoration.

They watched him closely to see if he would heal him on the Sabbath (3:2). Jesus makes the man the center of attention by calling him forward and healing him. This healing violates the Pharisees' interpretation that disallows minor cures on the Sabbath.[75] Rabbi Shammai was so strict that he is reported even to have opposed praying for the sick or visiting the sick on the Sabbath, since it conflicted with the day's character as one marked by joy.[76] All the later rabbis agreed that danger to life overrode the Sabbath; they only disagreed over the scriptural basis for this conclusion.[77] Since this man with a withered hand is not in a life or death situation, the opponents assume that he can and should wait for a cure.

But how does Jesus violate the Sabbath? He prepares no ointments and lifts nothing; he simply speaks. The text assumes that if this man's healing were not in accord with God's will, he would not have been healed. Jesus uses the healing to make the point that the Sabbath can become an occasion to do good rather than simply a time not to do work. Why should this man have to wait a day for help when the power to heal him is available now? The point: God did not send the Messiah to observe the Sabbath but to save life.

The Herodians (3:6). The precise identity of the Herodians (see also 12:13) is hazy. Most assume that they were supporters of the Herodian rule. In Galilee, they would be partisans of Herod Antipas and consequently influential. Economically and religiously they were comparable to the Sadducees, who had been pro-Hasmonean. Their agenda was less motivated by religious fervor than a concern to maintain the social and political status quo, which religion nicely abetted.

Others have guessed that "Herodians" was a tag that the common people gave to the Essenes. Josephus tells the story of an Essene teacher who won the favor of Herod the Great as a young boy by greeting him as king of the Jews and predicting a happy reign.[78] They became the favored religious party during his rule, inhabiting the Essene quarter in the southwest corner of Jerusalem.[79]

Summary of Jesus' Healing (3:7–12)

Many people came to him from Judea, Jerusalem, Idumea, and the regions across the Jordan and around Tyre and Sidon (3:8). The multitudes pressing on Jesus come from places that correspond to the land of biblical Israel. They swarm around the house he is in so that he is unable even to eat (3:20). This makes it necessary for him to prepare an escape route by boat (3:9).

Whenever the evil spirits saw him, they fell down before him and cried out, "You are the Son of God" (3:11). Only the demons know who Jesus really is, but they can never be agents of revelation. In the first-century setting, most would have considered it ominous for demons to shout out a name in recognition (see comments on 1:24). They would not assume that demons were paying Jesus homage but that they were attempting to control him by pronouncing his divine name. Jesus' rebuke shows his power over them.

PALESTINE

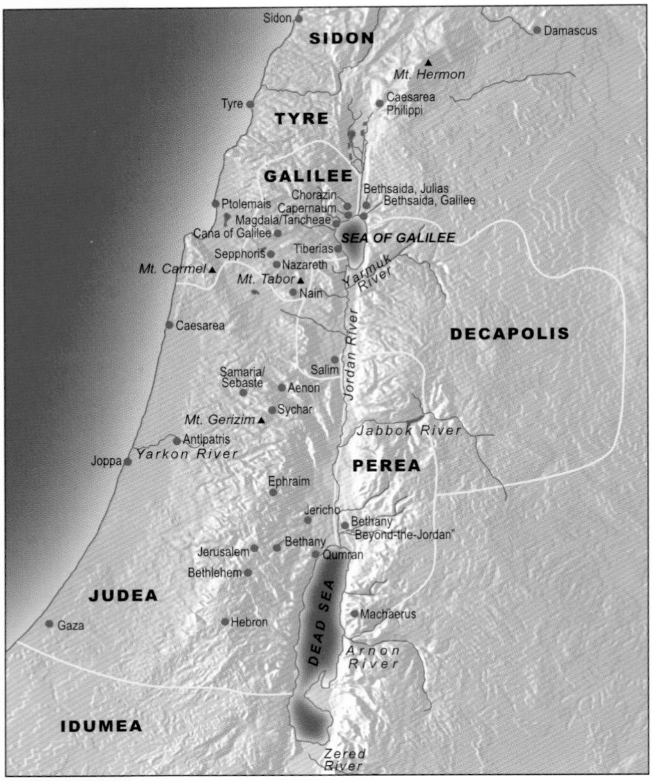

Calling of Disciples on the Mountain (3:13–19)

Jesus went up on a mountainside (3:13). Mark does not identify the mountain where Jesus calls the twelve disciples. Mountains serve in the Bible as places of revelation, but the mountain here is simply an isolated place that allows Jesus to be alone. Crowds do not follow him here; he calls those whom he wants.

He appointed twelve—designating them apostles (3:14). "Twelve" has symbolic significance, evoking God's promises of redeeming Israel. God commanded Moses to take men from each tribe to be "with him" as representatives of the "heads of the clans of Israel."[80] The twelve disciples represent the heads of the divisions of Israel, which are being restored; and Jesus stands over them as leader. His choice of twelve testifies to his self-understanding that he has been sent to gather Israel.

Simon (to whom he gave the name Peter) (3:16). Simon, James, and John head the list as the three most prominent disciples and appear at significant junctures in the story. Simon was a popular name and nearly all the Simons mentioned in the New Testament are given some distinguishing name: for example, Simon the Cananaean (3:18; NIV, the Zealot), Simon the Leper (14:3), Simon of Cyrene (15:21), Simon the Pharisee (Luke 7:40), Simon Iscariot (John 6:71), Simon the sorcerer (Acts 8:9), Simon the tanner (Acts 9:43), and Jesus' brother Simon (Mark 6:3). In the biblical tradition, however, God or a divine agent gives new names to persons who will have a significant role in the story of God's people.[81] When someone in the Bible is given a different name, it represents a promise to that person (see Gen. 17:15; 32:28).

Jesus calls Simon *petros*. The word *petros* in Greek usually means a free standing "stone" that can be picked up. The word *petra* usually means rock, cliff, or bedrock (see Matt. 7:24). Both terms could reverse their meanings, and no clear-cut distinction can be made between the two.[82] A rock could serve as a foundation or security, but it could also become a rock of stumbling and an obstacle to agriculture (Mark 4:16).

Boanerges, which means Sons of Thunder (3:17). James and John, previously introduced as the sons of Zebedee, are now presented as "Sons of Thunder." The word *Boanerges* means nothing in Greek and it is unclear what Aramaic phrase it might transliterate. It may imply excitability or anger (see Luke 9:54), but this is uncertain. God's voice is referred to as thunderous (Ps. 29:3), and in Revelation 16:18, the final judgment is ushered in with peals of thunder.

Simon the Zealot (3:18). The translation follows Luke 6:15 (Acts 1:13), but the text reads literally Simon the Cananaean. We are not to think that he was a revolutionary. The term *qannaîm* appears in rabbinic sources to refer to those who were especially zealous for the law and its observance. This notion may be connected to his label (see Gal. 1:14).

Judas Iscariot (3:19). The name may mean "man of Kerioth." Textual variants found in John 6:71; 12:4; 13:2; and 14:22 add *apo Karyomtou* (from Kariot), which represent an early explanation for the term's meaning. Kerioth could be a town in Moab (Jer. 48:24; Amos 2:2) or a town in southern Judea (Josh. 15:25). If this reading is correct, Judas would have been in the minority as a Judean among Jesus' Galilean disciples. Other less likely suggestions contend that the name refers to his membership in a group of assassins ("dagger man," *sicarius*) or a clan ("man of Issachar"), his deceit ("the false one"), his betrayal ("the one handing over"), his origin ("man from the city"), or his ruddy complexion.

Mention of betrayal hints of the death that awaits Jesus. Judas does not worm his way into the inner circle but is chosen by Jesus from the beginning. Jesus' culture cherished loyalty and trust and abhorred treachery that shreds the fabric of a close-knit community. Betrayal was regarded as inexcusable and unforgivable.

The Reaction of Family and Teachers of the Law (3:20–35)

Two groups try to quash Jesus' ministry for different reasons. His family seeks to protect him from danger and to protect the family honor, thinking that he is out of his mind. Teachers of the law from Jerusalem try to dishonor him with the people, claiming he works by Beelzebub.

He is possessed by Beelzebub! (3:22). The text reads literally, "He has Beelzebub," which parallels the charge that he has an unclean spirit (3:30). The origin of the term Beelzebub is vague, but it clearly is connected to "the prince of demons." The name may be a perversion of the name of a Philistine deity lampooned as "the lord of the flies." Beelzebul (which some MSS. read here) is identified as the prince of the demons in the *Testament of Solomon* 2:9–4:2. According to a rabbinic tradition, Jesus was condemned to death for practicing sorcery and misleading the people:

It has been taught: On the eve of Passover they hanged Yeshu. And an announcer went out, in front of him, for fourteen days [saying]: "He is going to be stoned because he practiced sorcery."[83]

This tradition independently confirms that Jesus was well known for doing miracles even though it attributes the source of his wonders to an evil power.

How can Satan drive out Satan? (3:23). Jesus' opponents concede that he is a successful exorcist, but they deliberately attempt to undermine him by labeling him as evil. Describing the enemy as subhuman or evil in some way makes it easier to justify doing away with him. They assume that someone who flouts his hallowed traditions can only be an undercover agent for Satan or for one who has made a compact with Satan.

Jesus exposes how absurd their accusation is. If they are correct, it must mean that civil war erupted in the ranks of Satan. Would Satan try to do himself in? Would he grant satanic power to someone to decimate his own minions? Satan extends his kingdom by sowing chaos and enslaving humans, not by setting them free. If it is unlikely that these exorcisms are worked by Satan's power, then how is it happening? Jesus answers only indirectly with an allegory about a stronger one who binds the previously reigning strong man and pillages his house. In Jesus' allegory, the strong one is Satan. His house is his domain, the present world he seeks to hold secure. His vessels are those hapless victims whom he has taken captive. The stronger one is Jesus, who has come from God (see 1:7; also Isa. 49:24–25), invaded Satan's stronghold, and bound him. Anyone with common sense would recognize that exorcisms bring healing, not harm. These opponents obdurately refuse to recognize that Jesus' ministry has to do with the collapse of Satan's kingdom, not its upsurge. Ironically, these experts from Jerusalem who seek to sabotage Jesus' ministry and blacken his reputation are the ones siding with the forces of Satan.

Whoever blasphemes against the Holy Spirit will never be forgiven (3:28). God is at work in Jesus. The sin referred to is willfully and spitefully denying the activity of God's Spirit in the ministry of Jesus and labeling it an unclean spirit. Jesus uses hyperbole to make his point and warn his listeners of its severity. In the Old Testament, defiant, high-handed sin is labeled unpardonable.[84] McNeile comments: "If the Lord spoke as a Jew to Jews and used the type of expression current in His day, and derived from the Old Testament, He meant, and would be understood to

REFLECTIONS

OBEYING JESUS' CALL CREATES family relationships within the community of God that transcend the boundaries of blood and marriage, the clan, and the nuclear family. Jesus does not mean that Christians do not need or should not have special people in their lives, but he does anticipate that his community will embrace and nurture all who belong to him, especially those who may have no other family.

mean, no more than that blasphemy against the Holy Spirit, by whose power He worked, was a terrible sin—more terrible than blasphemy against man."[85]

Who are my mother and my brothers? (3:33). In Jesus' world, people did not think of themselves as individuals but as members of a primary group, usually the family. Jesus' behavior brought unwanted attention to the family and dishonor since the accusations against him also reflect directly on them.

Parables Beside the Sea (4:1–34)

Again Jesus began to teach by the lake (4:1). Jesus' power exerts such a magnetic attraction that he speaks from a boat to crowds massed on the shore. A sloping amphitheater-like inlet lies halfway between Capernaum and Tabgha and has excellent natural acoustics, allowing someone to be heard easily on the shoreline. Jesus may have used this cove in teaching the crowds.

He taught them many things by parables (4:2). Parables are not simply illustrative yarns or earthly stories with heavenly meanings. The Hebrew *mashal* provides the backdrop for Jesus' parables. It "can mean a dark, perplexing saying that is meant to stimulate hard thinking."[86] The parables are "the opposite of prosaic, propositional teaching" and "attract attention by their pictorial or paradoxical language, and at the same time their indirect approach serves to tease and provoke the hearer."[87] They reveal the mystery while hiding it at the same time because a listener can only understand them by daring to become involved in their imaginative world. Even then, understanding the parables requires special help (4:33).

Listen! A farmer went out to sow his seed (4:3). In the Greco-Roman world, sower was a stock symbol for a teacher, sowing for teaching, seed for words, and soils for students.[88] These parallel ideas contrast with Jesus' parable. The Hellenistic writers compare farming to learning and refer to cultivation, toil, achievement, reward, and virtue. What stifles the seed from growing is a lack of intellect. The interpretation of Jesus' parable does not attribute the loss to some intellectual deficit. The failures are caused by cosmic forces—Satan snatching the seed; social forces—withering under persecution; and ethical breakdowns—temporal anxieties and the lure of riches. The reason for the failure of the seed is the lamentable spiritual state of the hearer's heart, not the lamentable state of the hearer's mind.[89]

A second difference is that sowing in Scripture is a metaphor for God's work. God promises to sow Israel to begin her renewal. In *4 Ezra* 8:6, the seed is understood as spiritual seed. God says, "For I sow my law in you, and it shall bring forth fruit in you, and you shall be glorified through it forever."[90] The reference to sowing, therefore, brings up three motifs. (1) It recalls God's promise of an end-time Israel planted by God. According to the vision in *1 Enoch* 62:8, "the congregation of the holy ones shall be planted [lit., sown], and all the elect ones shall stand before him." (2) Since sowing is a metaphor for God's work, this parable does not illustrate the effect that any teacher may have on pupils as in the Hellenistic parallels. It defines Jesus' ministry and implies that he comes as the end-time sower to renew Israel. How one responds to his teaching decides whether one will be included in God's kingdom. (3) The seeds sown are not just nuggets of wisdom. The seed is God's word, and

God says, "It will not return to me empty, but will accomplish what I desire and achieve the purpose for which I sent it" (Isa. 55:11).

Some fell along the path. . . . Some fell on rocky places. . . . Other seed fell among thorns (4:4–7). The parable pictures a farmer working marginal ground using a broadcast method of sowing where seeds fall everywhere—on the path, on rocky ground, and among thorns. What field in Palestine did not have its rocks and thorns and thistles? All seed sown does not prosper (*4 Ezra* 8:41), but against formidable odds, the miracle of a harvest will occur.

Some have tried to explain away the seeming carelessness of a farmer who casts good seed on the pathway, on a rocky substratum, and among thorn bushes to make the parable more realistic and less allegorical. They argue that plowing did not precede sowing, and the sower would later plow the seed into the ground. It would not help to plow thorns under, however, since they would only sprout up again. A pathway established by villagers would only be trampled down again.

Sowing did not always precede plowing.[91] One expert maintains that sowing may precede plowing only if the soil is silty or loamy and will form an even tilth when plowed. "Under any other soil conditions sowing in unploughed stubble would be condemned by any competent authority as a wasteful and slovenly proceeding."[92] This comports with the exhortation in Jeremiah: "This is what the LORD says to the men of Judah and to Jerusalem: 'Break up your unplowed ground and do not sow among thorns'" (Jer. 4:3).

It came up, grew and produced a crop, multiplying thirty, sixty, or even a hundred times (4:8). The harvest numbers do not refer to the bulk yield of the whole field. That was calculated from the proportion of the amount of seed sown to grain threshed. The varied yield refers instead to the numbers of grains produced by individual plants. Pliny mentioned that wheat with branching ears yielded a hundred grains.[93] Modern agronomists assert that wheat normally produces "two or three tillers under typical crowded field conditions, but individual plants on fertile soil with ample space may produce as many as 30 to 100 hundred tillers. The average spike (head) of common wheat contains 25 to 30 grains in 14 to 17 spikelets. Large spikes may contain 50 to 75 grains."[94] Wheat grown in ancient times approached these numbers. Strabo wrote that a deputy governor of a region in Africa reported to the emperor the incredible result of 400 shoots obtained from a single grain of seed and sent to Nero also 360 stalks obtained from one grain. He then reports that "at all events the plains of Lentini and other districts in Sicily, and the whole of Andalusia, and particularly Egypt reproduce at the rate of a hundredfold."[95]

REFLECTIONS

JESUS' DISCIPLES ARE TO CONTINUE THE TASK OF sowing, and this parable provides a note of encouragement for the sower and warning to the soil. The sower in this parable is not responsible for success but only for sowing. We should mark that the sower does not prejudge the soil's potential before casting the seed but sows with abandon. Sowing will not meet with universal success, but no farmer refrains from scattering the seed out of fear that some might be wasted. Success comes from God (1 Cor. 3:5–9), and contemporary sowers are called only to be faithful in the task and to allow the seed to do its work. The parable also identifies, and therefore warns about, conditions that make bad soil barren. It does not say what makes productive soil good except to caution listeners to be careful how they hear.

The secret of the kingdom of God (4:11). Because the parables are characterized as secret, everyone needs Jesus' interpretation to unlock the mystery. The word translated "secret" is "mystery." It does not refer to something baffling or unintelligible but to something that could not be known except by divine revelation. Behind this concept is the Old Testament idea of God's secret that cannot be discovered by human wisdom but can only be revealed by God. What was once hidden—how God is establishing his sovereignty over the world—is now being revealed.[96]

The idea that many remain in the dark is familiar in Jewish apocalyptic ("You do not reveal your mysteries to many," *2 Bar.* 48:2–3). We find a similar idea expressed in the Dead Sea Scrolls. The wicked are those who have not inquired nor sought God "to know the hidden matters in which they err."[97] The outsiders' unbelief is therefore not caused by the parables' obscurity but by their unwillingness to try to stretch their minds around Jesus' unconventional visions of God's kingdom. Insiders want to know more and come to him to ask for clarification.

Satan comes and takes away the word that was sown in them (4:15). Ancient Jewish texts also liken Satan to a bird or birds.[98] *Second Enoch* 29:5 pictures Satan's expulsion from heaven as resulting in his flight: "And I threw him out from the height with his angels, and he was flying in the air continuously above the bottomless."

Do you bring in a lamp to put it under a bowl or a bed? (4:21). Lamps were associated with gladness and marriage and were also important in the religious life of the Jewish household.[99] The Sabbath lamp was lit at dusk since fire could not be kindled on the Sabbath (Ex. 35:3), the Day of Atonement, or the Passover. The words of the prophets are likened to a light shining in a dark place (2 Peter 1:19). In *4 Ezra* 12:42, Ezra is compared to a lamp in a dark place (and a haven for a ship saved from a storm).

REFLECTIONS

THE PARABLE REMINDS US THAT we live in the in-between-time, when humans tend to overlook God's reign or dismiss it as inconsequential or lacking certifiable proof. Before one can see how God's purposes are being accomplished in the world through the cross of Christ, one needs spiritual discernment, given only by God.

ANCIENT OIL LAMPS

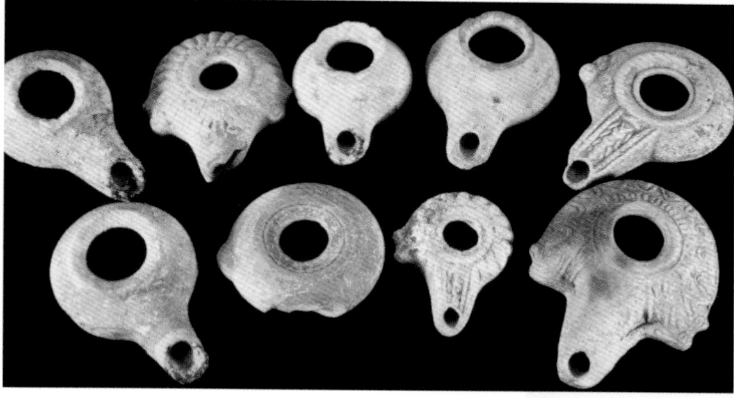

With the measure you use, it will be measured to you—and even more (4:24). This parable affirms that those who do not hear rightly will become have-nots who lose everything. Those who hear well will receive more explanation and understanding. A rabbinic tradition professes:

> Observe how the character of the Holy One, blessed be He, differs from that of flesh and blood. A mortal can put

something into an empty vessel, but not into a full one. But the Holy One, blessed be He, is not so; He puts more into a full vessel, but not an empty one; for it says, "If hearkening you will hearken" (Ex. 15:26), implying, if you hearken you will go on hearkening, and if not you will not hearken.[100]

A man scatters seed on the ground (4:26). Jesus again compares the things of God to the everyday world of a farmer in the only parable peculiar to Mark. It reflects a Palestinian perspective. The farmer first sleeps and then rises because the day begins in the evening, not in the morning.

All by itself the soil produces grain (4:28). The seed holds within itself the secret of its growth that follows an appointed order of development that cannot be hurried or skipped. This parable expresses the belief that the growth of plants is the wondrous work of God. His purposes will be fulfilled in his way and his time.

It is like a mustard seed, which is the smallest seed you plant in the ground (4:31). The mustard seed was proverbially small (see Matt. 17:20, "if you have faith as small as a mustard seed"). The Mishnah uses the phrase "even as little as a grain of mustard" to describe the smallest possible quantity.[101] It requires 725–760 seeds from the black mustard to make a gram.[102] The parable contrasts the mustard bush's microscopic beginning with its lush outcome. The kingdom of God is something present and yet something that will be transformed and is therefore yet to come. The present activity of God, "not the plausibility of the evidence, guarantees that great ending."[103]

Yet when planted, it grows and becomes the largest of all garden plants, with such big branches that the birds of the air can perch in its shade (4:32). The mustard bush was cultivated in the field (Matt. 13:31) and grown for its leaves as well as its grains. Wild mustard (charlock) was unwelcome since it was almost impossible to get rid of it. Pliny claims that "mustard . . . with its pungent taste and fiery effect is extremely beneficial for the health. It grows entirely wild, though it is improved by being transplanted: but on the other hand when it has once been sown it is scarcely possible to get the

MUSTARD PLANTS AND SEEDS

place free of it, as the seed when it falls germinates at once."[104]

The NIV translation of the verb *kataskēnoō* as "perch" is based on the assumption that the mustard bush was hardly a suitable place for the birds of the air to nest. It is a fast-growing annual plant that grows to a height of eight to ten feet. Spring is the time when birds build their nests, but the mustard has not yet grown large enough for the birds to build nests in its branches.[105] It is assumed that the birds are attracted to the bush by the seeds. But the verb means to dwell, lodge, or nest. The noun form *kataskēnōsis* is used for bird nests in Matthew 8:20 and Luke 9:58. The image recalls Old Testament texts. Daniel 4:12, 21 refers to a tree in which "the birds of the air" have nesting places. In Ezekiel 17:23 and 31:6, God promises to plant a noble cedar on the mountain height of Israel that towers over all the trees of the field, and in its boughs "birds of every kind will nest."[106]

The "birds of the air" was a transparent symbol for the nations of Gentiles.[107] The image of lodging or shelter appears in *Joseph and Asenath* 15:6 for the incorporation of the Gentiles in the people of God. After Asenath is converted, an angel appears to her and tells her that she will be given the name "City of Refuge, because in you many nations will take refuge with the Lord God, the Most High, and under your wings many peoples trusting in the Lord God will be sheltered [*kataskēnousi*]."

This background may point to more subtle meanings hidden in the parable of the mustard bush. The tree mentioned in the Old Testament is planted on a high and lofty mountain (Ezek. 17:22), and its top reaches to heaven so that it is visible to the ends of the earth (Dan. 4:11, 20). When one is talking about the kingdom of God and birds of heaven lodging under the protection of trees with great branches, the Jewish listener was conditioned by Scripture and tradition to think in terms of the salvation of pagans through Israel's triumph.[108] Does this parable cleverly undermine notions of grandeur with its jarring image of a mustard bush?

The Stilling of the Storm (4:35–41)

Let us go over to the other side (4:35). The inclusion of "other boats" means that the group of insiders surrounding Jesus was not limited only to the twelve. The Sea of Galilee was also known as the Sea of Tiberias (John 21:1) and the Lake of Gennesaret.[109] It is thirteen miles long and seven miles wide. Going across to the other side of the lake is mentioned in Mark 4:35; 5:1, 21; 6:45; 8:13. Josephus describes the Jordan River as "cutting across the Lake" so that the river's entry and exit points "formed an imaginary line which determined whether a location was 'on the side' or 'on the other side' of the lake."[110]

They took him along, just as he was, in the boat (4:36). An ancient boat was discovered buried in the silt of this lake

THE SEA OF GALILEE

Choppy waves on the sea.

during a prolonged dry season. It has allowed us the opportunity to picture exactly the kind of boat Jesus and his disciples would have sailed. Carbon 14 testing dates the boat from this time period, 120 B.C. to A.D. 40. An oil lamp inside the boat was dated to the mid-first century B.C., and coins from A.D. 29–30 were also found. The boat measured 25.5 feet long, 7.5 feet wide, and 4.5 feet in depth. It had a deck in the bow and the stern and could be powered by sails or by four oars. It normally would have a crew of five with a capacity for ten passengers or in excess of a ton of cargo.[111]

A furious squall came up (4:37). Two extensive valleys on the western side of the lake funnel wind onto the lake. Westerly gusts can arise in the afternoon, turning the placid lake into a high sea with waves soaring up over seven feet.[112] The lake also is 682 feet below sea level, which makes it susceptible to downdrafts when "cool air from the Golan Heights meets the warm air coming off the lake, and these contribute to sudden and unpredictable storms."[113] Sudden storms are therefore familiar sailing hazards.

Jesus was in the stern, sleeping on a cushion (4:38). Jesus has probably fallen asleep under the stern deck, which affords the most protection from the elements and keeps him out of the way of those sailing the vessel. The "cushion" is probably a sandbag used for ballast. Two types were used: a sack of a hundred to a hundred and twenty pounds; and a pillow of around fifty pounds.

The storm at sea should be read against an Old Testament backdrop. Jonah was in a deep sleep in the midst of a storm that terrified the sailors. In Psalm 107:23–32, imperiled sailors cry out to the Lord in their trouble, and he "stilled the storm to a whisper; the waves of the sea were hushed."[114] The incident reveals that Jesus has mastery over the sea, the place of chaos and evil, as does God. Jesus awakes to muzzle the sea in the same way he rebuked demons (1:25; 3:12; 9:25).[115] His sleep during the storm contrasts with the disciples' terror. God "grants sleep to those he loves" (Ps. 127:2), and Jesus' sleep reflects his serene trust in God, who watches over him.[116]

GALILEE

Gergesa and Gadara were located east of the Sea of Galilee. Jerash was about 40 miles southeast of the sea (off this map).

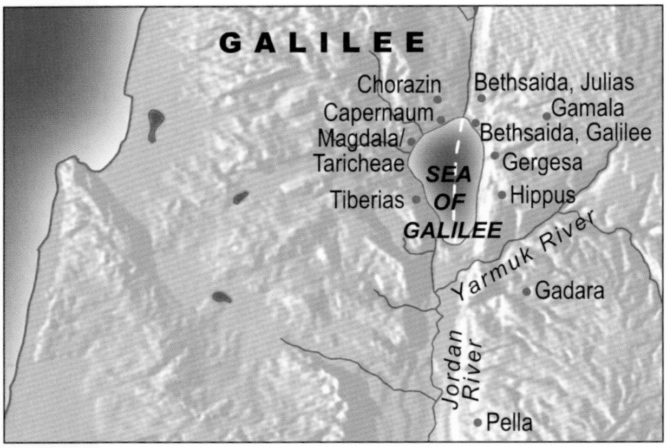

The Gerasene Demoniac (5:1–20)

They went across the lake to the region of the Gerasenes (5:1). Gerasa, modern Jerash, was thirty miles from the lake. That distance from the sea probably prompted the textual variants locating the incident at Gadara or Gergesa. Some have suggested that the original reference was to a town that is now called Kersa or Koursi, which was later mistaken for the better-known Gerasa, a member of the Decapolis. Most likely, however, this is territory controlled by Gerasa, which extends to the Sea of Galilee.

This man lived in the tombs, and no one could bind him any more, not even with a chain (5:3). Mark emphasizes both the fierce strength of the man, who could not e subdued even with chains, and the rastic nature of his possession, which rove him to lacerate himself. In the New estament, demoniacs are never aggres-ve, unless one interferes with them. ather, they are victims who need an xternal power to liberate them from ıeir thralldom.

This demonized soul, screaming in his ortured isolation, lives in the unclean lace of the dead and has become himself dwelling place for unclean spirits. Tombs vere frequently located in caves and were nown as haunts for demons.[117] The man ts the four characteristics of madness ound in rabbinic literature: running bout at night, staying overnight in burial laces, tearing apart one's clothes, and estroying what one has been given.[118]

Vhat do you want with me, Jesus, Son of he Most High God? Swear to God that ou won't torture me! (5:7). Unlike umans, who never quite fathom the eality of the divine breaking into human istory (4:41), the unclean spirits always ecognize Jesus' divine origin and his hreat to them (1:24; 3:11; see James :19). Ancient listeners to this account vould have recognized the irony that hese demons attempt to resist exorcism vith gimmicks from an exorcist's bag of ricks. They attempt to control Jesus by pronouncing aloud his holy name. Knowing the names of demons was believed to give one control over them.[119] Ironically, they try to invoke the name of God to protect themselves.

"What is your name?" . . . "My name is Legion" (5:9). Jesus counters these diversionary tactics by asking for the demon's name. The unclean spirits evade the question by giving a number instead of a name. "Legion" was the term for a Roman regiment commanded by a senator of praetorian rank and generally consisting of 5,400 foot soldiers and 120 horsemen. The man was possessed by an army of demons.

The demons begged Jesus, "Send us among the pigs; allow us to go into them" (5:12). Ancients understood that demons always want to inhabit something rather than wander about aimlessly.[120] Some were thought to be land demons, who would be destroyed in water. In the *Testament of Solomon* 5:11 (see 11:6), a demon about to be exorcised pleads: "Do not condemn me to water."

The enormously large herd of 2,000 pigs grubbing on the hillside must have belonged to a swine cooperative and marks this as a pagan area. Isaiah lumps

A Spell for Driving out Daimons from the Greek Magical Papyri

Place an olive branch before him and stand behind him and say:

> Hail, God of Abraham; hail, God of Isaac, God of Jacob; Jesus Chrestos [excellent one], the Holy Spirit, the Son of the Father, who is above the Seven, who is within the Seven. Bring Iao Sabaoth; may your power issue forth from him, [name to be inserted], until you drive away this unclean daimon Satan who is in him. I conjure you, daimon, whoever you are, by this God, SABARBARBATHIOMTH SABARBARBATHIOUTH SABARBARBATHIOMNEMTH SABARBARBAPHAI. Come out, daimon, whoever you are, and stay away from him, [name to be inserted] now, now; immediately, immediately. Come out, daimon, since I bind you with unbreakable adamantine fetters, and I deliver you into the black chaos in perdition.[A-15]

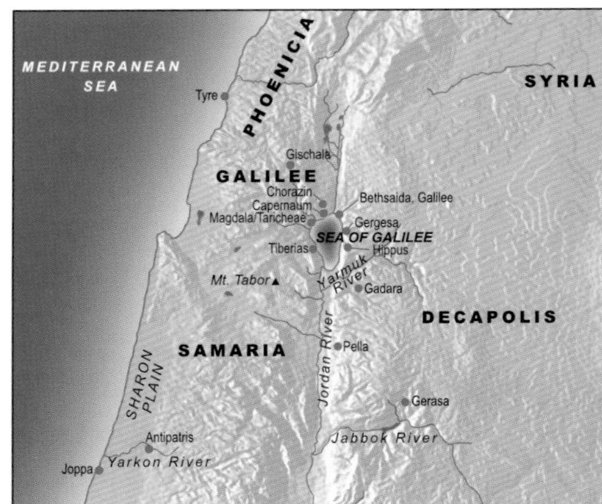

THE REGION OF THE DECAPOLIS

pork eaters, tomb dwellers, and demon worshipers together (Isa. 65:3–4). Demons try to destroy whatever they inhabit and never leave their victims quietly (Mark 1:26; 9:26). When Jesus grants the demons' request to enter into the pigs, these very un-herdlike animals stampede down the bank and into the waters, where Jesus has just demonstrated his dominion (4:39, 41). The text assumes that both animals and demons are destroyed in the sea.

This story would have evoked glee in a Jewish audience. Pigs were unclean animals to them (Lev. 11:7; Deut. 14:8) and were sacrificed in some pagan cults. More significantly, swine called up memories of the torture of martyrs in the days of Antiochus Epiphanes. He had polluted the temple by sacrificing swine on the altar and attempted to eradicate Jewish distinctives with a savage campaign of persecution (1 Macc. 1:41–61). During this time, abstaining from eating pork became compelling proof of loyalty to God.[121] Swine were thus associated with pagan attempts to abolish Judaism.

Those reading this story after the destruction of Jerusalem may have made another connection. The Tenth Roman Legion (Fretensis) took part in the sieges of Jerusalem and Masada and was stationed in Jerusalem after its fall. Its standards bore the image of a wild boar. According to Josephus, it had a complement of a thousand horses and two thousand foot soldiers.[122] Many Jews would have liked nothing better than to see this Roman legion—guilty of defiling the land, destroying the holy city, and killing and enslaving thousands—driven into the sea.

KURSI (OR, GERGESA)

The possible site of the demoniac episode.

So the man went away and began to tell in the Decapolis how much Jesus had done for him (5:20). The Decapolis was a league of free Greek cities under the protection of the Roman governor of Syria: Damascus, Raphana, Dion, Canantha, Scythopolis, Gadar, Hippos, Pella, Gerasa, and Philadelphia. The great calm that came over the sea matches the great calm that now governs the man, sitting quietly and fully clothed at Jesus' feet. The man's deliverance will spread the word into the heavily pagan Decapolis.

Jairus' Daughter and the Woman with the Flow of Blood (5:21–43)

Then one of the synagogue rulers, named Jairus, came there (5:22). Jairus is a male leader of the synagogue and

Mark identifies him by name. The woman with the flow of blood is nameless, and her complaint renders her ritually unclean, making her unfit to enter into a synagogue or the temple. The two individuals come from opposite ends of the social and purity spectrum.

And a woman was there who had been subject to bleeding for twelve years (5:25). The text does not specify the nature of the woman's loss of blood, but we can presume that it was related to uterine bleeding. Menstruation was a normal part of life that, nevertheless, made a woman unclean and confined her to home (see Ezek. 36:17). Leviticus 15:19–24 deals with normal female discharges. Her family was to refrain from lying in her bed, sitting on her seat, or touching her. Those contaminated by her had to purify themselves by bathing and laundering their clothes and remained unclean until the evening.

Outside of Judaism, Pliny reported that the touch of a menstruating woman was considered harmful.[123] An extreme view is found in the sectarian Ramban, who said that such women were not to approach people or speak with them because their breath is harmful and their gaze detrimental. Learned men were forbidden to greet a menstruant, or to walk after her and tread in her footsteps.[124]

This woman's condition was abnormal, making her unclean all the time. It would not have been kept secret in a small village society. She was subject to regulations listed in Leviticus 15:25–31, which sought to prevent impurity from infringing on the realm of God's holiness. As a bearer of such impurity, she was not permitted to participate in the religious feasts or enter the temple precincts,[125] and she was excluded from normal social intercourse for twelve years. Such an affliction must have caused her physical, psychological, social, and economic suffering. Jesus' healing demonstrates that God's holiness cleanses human impurity and restores individuals to wholeness.

She had suffered a great deal under the care of many doctors and had spent all she had (5:26). Only the wealthy could afford the care of physicians, and now this woman has become impoverished (cf. Tobit 2:10). Doctors were not always revered.[126] We find complaints about their fees,[127] statements that even the best of doctors are destined for hell,[128] and advice not to stay in a town where the leading citizen is a physician.[129] A list of procedures for curing a woman who suffers from a flow of blood appears in the Babylonian Talmud. Possibly this poor woman endured some of them:

> Let them procure three kapiza of Persian onions, boil them in wine, make her drink it, and say to her, "Cease your discharge." But if not, she should be made to sit at cross-roads, hold a cup of wine in her hand, and a man comes up from behind, frightens her and exclaims, "Cease your discharge!" But if not, a handful of cummin, a handful of saffron, and a handful of fenugreek are brought and boiled in wine, she is made to drink it, and they say to her, "Cease your discharge." But if not, let sixty pieces of sealing clay of a [wine] vessel be brought, and let them smear her and say to her, "Cease your discharge."

It offers five more remedies; the last suggests fetching a barley grain from the dung of a white mule. When she eats it and holds it in one day, her discharge will cease for one day, if for two days, her discharge will cease for two days, if for three days, it will cease forever.[130]

When she heard about Jesus, she came up behind him in the crowd and touched his cloak (5:27). In popular belief, the clothes of holy men, and especially the fringes, were thought to possess miraculous power. Touching Jesus' garment is mentioned four times here (5:27, 28, 30, 31). Already in 3:10, many who suffered diseases pushed forward to touch him. In 6:56, they beg him to let them touch the hem of his cloak, and all who touch him are healed. The belief that the power of a person is transferred to what he wears or touches is also found in Acts 5:15 and 19:12. To touch a man in public would have been highly irregular, and this woman tries to do it on the sly.

Daughter, your faith has healed you (5:34). God controls the power residing in Jesus, for the emphasis in this story is placed on the woman's faith, not on Jesus' power. Faith transfers divine power to those who are utterly powerless. When a woman was healed from this type of affliction, she was supposed to bring a sacrifice (Lev. 15:29–30), but Jesus makes no mention of this as he did for the leper (Mark 1:44). The miracle nicely dovetails with the next miracle. The woman's faith in Jesus reverses the loss of blood that betokened the ebbing away of life. Resurrection awaits all those who trust in Jesus, but even now they can see the forces of death being held at bay through their faith.

Your daughter is dead (5:35). Child mortality rate was high in this era. Sixty percent of children who survived childbirth died by their mid-teens.

Jesus saw a commotion, with people crying and wailing loudly (5:38). Burial was swift, usually on the same day of death, and relatives, neighbors, and mourners were employed for the occasion and gathered quickly to make loud, theatrical demonstrations of sorrow (see Jer. 9:17–19).

He took her by the hand and said to her, "Talitha koum!" (5:41). *Talitha koum* is an ordinary Aramaic phrase made memorable by the extraordinary miracle.[131] By providing the translation, "Little girl, rise," Mark makes it clear that it was not some arcane, magical formula. Eating food proves that the child is really alive and not some disembodied spirit (cf. Luke 24:39–43).

Jesus Dismissed by His Own (6:1–6)

Jesus left there and went to his hometown (6:1). Nazareth was located in the hills of Galilee and had a population of approximately 150–200 people. It was within an hour's walking distance of the large city of Sepphoris. It receives notice only in the New Testament and is not mentioned in the Old Testament, Apocrypha, or rabbinic literature.

Jesus alludes to his kinsmen and his house in 6:4. The clan members were descendants of King David, who possibly settled here after returning from the Babylonian exile. They may have given

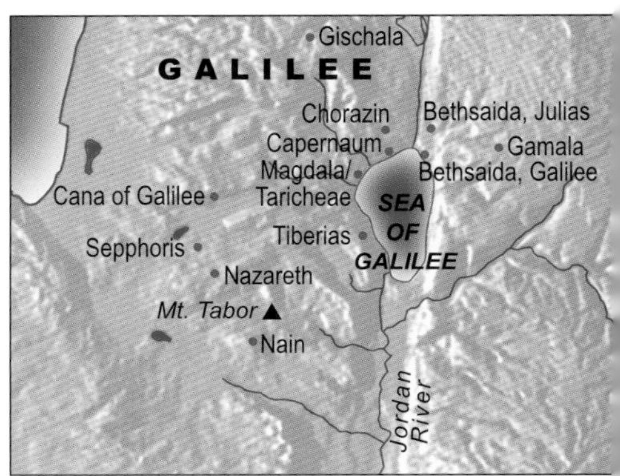

right ▶
GALILEE

the place an intentionally messianic name, Little-Netzer (offshoot [of David]), under the influence of Isaiah 11:1–2.[132]

Isn't this the carpenter? (6:3). When Jesus teaches in the synagogue, the astonishment of the "many," a Semitism for "all" (10:45), quickly turns into suspicion. Where did he come by all this? A lowborn village artisan had no business becoming a public figure. Jesus has stepped outside the bounds of his honor rating. "Isn't this the carpenter?" is therefore a sneer. In a later tale, Asenath angrily scorns Joseph as a potential husband by saying, "Is he not the shepherd's son from the land of Canaan?"[133]

The noun translated "carpenter" (*tektōn*) refers to someone who works with hard materials: wood, metal, stone. If Jesus were a carpenter, as tradition assumes, he would have been engaged in making farm tools such as plows, yokes, carts, wheels, winnowing forks, and threshing boards, as well as house parts, doors, frames, locks, window lattices, beds, tables, lampstands, boxes, cabinets, and chests. He also may have built and repaired boats. The excavated Galilean boat had been repaired often. Meier asserts: "The airy weakling often presented to us in pious paintings and Hollywood movies would hardly have survived the rigors of being Nazareth's *tektōn* from his youth to his early thirties."[134]

In the Greco-Roman world, most would have regarded a person in such a craft as uneducated and uncouth. Secundus (an Athenian orator) was mocked as a "wooden nail" because he was the son of a carpenter. Celsus derides Jesus for having been simply a carpenter, connecting his work to his crucifixion; Origen weakly counters that the Gospels never describe Jesus as working with his hands.[135] In Sirach 38:24–32, the skillful artisan who works with his hands is commended, but it is assumed that his business keeps him from ever becoming wise like the scribe. The scribe has greater leisure and can devote himself to the study of the law to gain greater wisdom (Sir. 39:1–11).

Isn't this Mary's son? (6:3). A man was normally identified as the son of his father. To be identified only as the son of the mother could be an insult (see Judg. 11:1–2), but there is no grounds to claim that it intimates some confusion about Jesus' father's identity. Possibly, the brothers and sisters listed were the children of Joseph's hypothetical first wife. Note that Mark uses the word "brother" in Mark 6:17 to identify the half brothers Herod Antipas and Herod Philip. Outside of Nazareth, where the family was unknown, Jesus would have been identified simply as the son of Joseph.[136] It seems more likely, however, that Jesus' father is no longer living. The townsfolk simply identify him as a "local boy" whose mother (and brothers and sisters) is well known.

The brother of James, Joseph, Judas and Simon (6:3). James (Jacob) and Joseph are the names of two of the patriarchs, and Judah and Simon are names of two of the famous Maccabee brothers. These names suggest a family that hoped for the redemption of Israel.

The argument that these are Jesus' cousins has been concocted to support the idea of Mary's perpetual virginity and has no basis in the Greek. Paul refers to James, whom he met, as "the Lord's brother" (Gal. 1:19), and to "the Lord's brothers" (1 Cor. 9:5); he does not use the Greek word for "cousins" (*anepsioi*), which he knows and uses elsewhere (Col. 4:10).[137]

Aren't his sisters here with us? (6:3). His sisters are unnamed and unnumbered, reflecting the ancient bias that females' identities are embedded in males and do not merit special attention.

The Sending Out of the Disciples (6:7–13, 30)

He sent them out two by two (6:7). Sending the disciples two by two satisfies the requirement of two or three witnesses and provides them a measure of protection. Jesus' authority over unclean spirits is invested in the disciples (see 3:15).[138] In Numbers 27:20, some of Moses' dignity is invested in Joshua so that the Israelite community might obey him.

Take nothing (6:8). Jesus directs his disciples to take nothing normally required for trips: no bread, no satchel for provisions, no money (copper) in the belt, and no change of clothing. The disciples go unencumbered, entirely dependent on the hospitality of hosts, a virtue particularly cherished by Jews. They may take a staff, which may refer to the traveler's stick that Parrot describes as "a supple and flexible cane. When slipped behind the back under the arms, it works as a brace and makes one's gait more rapid and supple."[139] But the staff also has a rich imagery in the history of God's dealings with Israel, beginning with Moses' staff (Ex. 4:2–5, 20). The reference here may be connected to the staff of the twelve tribes (Num. 17), a symbol of a tribal leader's authority. It therefore may have some symbolic connection to the covenant renewal of Israel.[140]

Shake the dust off your feet when you leave (6:11). Jews shook the dust from their feet when they returned to Israel from Gentile territory.[141] The gesture may serve as a prophetic warning that the defiant will be cut off from Israel for failing to respond to the reign of God or as a sign that they were washing their hands of them (Acts 18:6), as if to say, "We do not even want your dust."

Anointed many sick people with oil and healed them (6:13). The *Testament of Solomon* is a collection of legends and beliefs that offers magical wisdom on how to exorcise demons. In 18:34, a demon that purportedly brings on long-term illnesses says, "If anyone puts salt into (olive) oil and massages his sickly (body with it) saying, 'Cherubim, seraphim, help (me),' I retreat immediately." The oil used by the disciples is probably olive oil, but they do not resort to magical healing arts. Jesus does not instruct them in any hocus-pocus. The oil may have been warmed and rubbed into the skin, and the human touch, not to mention prayer accompanying it, may have been part of the healing. Philo claims that olive oil was an excellent ointment that "produces smoothness, and counteracts physical exhaustion, and brings about good condition. If a muscle be relaxed it braces it and renders it firm,

TYPICAL VILLAGE

The village of Yata, near Hebron, that preserves the appearance of a typical ancient village in Judea.

nor is there anything surpassing it for infusing tone and vigour."[142]

The Death of John the Baptizer (6:14–29)

King Herod heard about this, for Jesus' name had become well known (6:14). The growing reputation of Jesus from his miracles causes jitters in Herod's court. A flashback relating the slaying of John the Baptizer explains the dread that Jesus may be the sequel: John the Baptist II.

He had him bound and put in prison (6:17). John's bold censure of the powerful Antipas earned him imprisonment. Josephus identifies the prison as Machaerus.[143] This fortress-palace (like Masada and Herodium) was situated atop a mountain in southeastern Perea, five miles east of the Dead Sea and thirteen miles southeast of Herodium. Josephus described the citadel as luxurious.[144] Archaeologists have uncovered two large *triclinia* (dining rooms) that would have been suitable for a banquet and a small one where the women would have eaten during the banquet.

He did this because of Herodias, his brother Philip's wife, whom he had married (6:17). Herodias, the daughter of Aristobulus (son of Herod the Great) and Bernice (daughter of Herod the Great's sister, Salome), was married to Herod Philip, another son of Herod the Great. She was therefore the half niece of both Herods and the sister-in-law of Antipas. This Philip is not the better

COINS OF HEROD PHILIP

Herod Antipas

Herod the Great had ten wives, and every son had the name Herod as the family designation. Herod Antipas, whom Mark identifies only as Herod, was the son of Herod the Great and Malthace, a Samaritan. He was raised in Rome and served as "tetrarch" (ruler of a fourth part) of Galilee and Perea from 4 B.C. to A.D. 39.[A-16] Mark's mention of him as king may reflect popular usage or may be intentionally ironic. Augustus had specifically denied him that royal title when his father Herod died and his kingdom was carved up among his heirs.[A-17]

Herod Antipas's wife, Herodias, was exceedingly jealous when Herod Agrippa later received the title king from the emperor Gaius (Caligula). She egged on Antipas to request that the emperor also give him the title king. His ill-advised petition led to his dismissal and exile when opponents accused him of treachery against Rome in amassing a stockpile of weapons.[A-18]

Mark may be scornfully mocking Herod's royal pretensions by giving him the title he so coveted and that led to his ruin. Chapman aptly describes the Galilean dislike of Antipas:

> The Jews hated his father. Antipas had close ties with Rome, and the Jews hated Rome. His mother was a Samaritan, and the Jews hated Samaritans. He built or rebuilt towns or cities naming them after *Roman* royalty. To populate Tiberias, he forcibly relocated his subjects (today's Palestinian controversy should cast light on how popular that move must have been). In Tiberias, he built a royal palace and adorned it with a frieze of animal figures, in violation of the Second Commandment.[A-19]

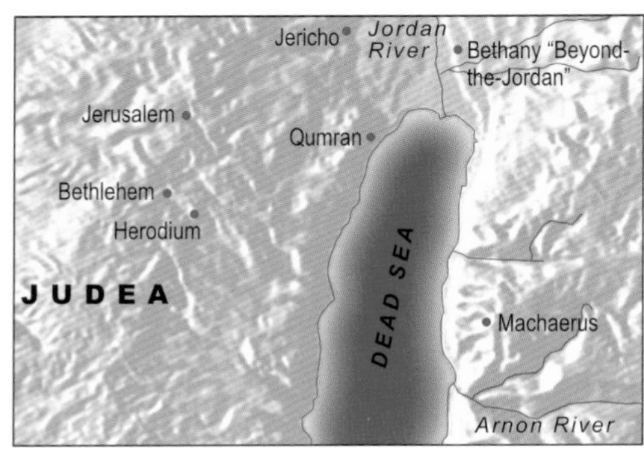

JUDEA

Machaerus was located east of the Dead Sea.

known son of Herod and Cleopatra, who was the tetrarch. He is the son of Mariamne II and lived privately in Rome. When Herod Antipas was staying with them on a visit to Rome, he fell in love with Herodias and brazenly proposed marriage. She agreed upon the condition that he divorce his current wife, the daughter of Aretas IV, king of Nabatea. The outraged Aretas began a border war that led to serious military losses for Herod Antipas.[145] The divorce also touched off religious protests at home because marrying the wife of his half brother was forbidden and regarded as incest (Lev. 18:16; 20:21). Antipas would have deemed John's attack on his remarriage as a political threat.

Josephus and Mark recount John's death from different perspectives. Josephus claims that John was imprisoned and executed because Herod Antipas feared the political unrest he aroused.[146] Mark reports that Herod executed John because of a public oath that leads him to bow to the will of Herodias.[147] Josephus has a marked interest in the suppression of potential uprisings, a critical Roman concern. Mark is primarily interested in the moral issues and the conniving of Herodias, which has biblical overtones. The Herodian family was infamous for its intrigues and grudges, and it is no surprise that Herodias conspired to destroy one who called for her removal from the halls of power. Josephus and Mark do not contradict each other; "political ends and the anger of an insulted woman cannot be regarded as mutually exclusive."[148]

HEROD'S FORTRESS AT MACHAERUS

On his birthday Herod gave a banquet for his high officials and military commanders and the leading men of Galilee (6:21). The account reeks of gross impiety. Birthdays were pagan celebrations.[149] Drunken revelry, a princess dancing at a stag party (she must leave to consult her mother), and execution without a trial all smack of rank paganism.[150] The grisly detail of John's head brought to them on a platter caps off a banquet already polluted by excess.

Whatever you ask I will give you, up to half my kingdom (6:23). As a puppet of Rome, Herod did not have the right to give half of his kingdom away. To preserve his honor by keeping his oath, Herod brings greater dishonor to his name.

Feeding the Five Thousand (6:32–44)

But many who saw them leaving recognized them and ran on foot from all the towns and got there ahead of them (6:33). The crowd races around the lake in its relentless pursuit of Jesus and beats the boat to its destination, further proof of Jesus' immense popularity. A tradition that the pilgrim Egeria (ca. 383–95) supports claims that the feeding took place at the Seven Springs, present-day Tabgha. Grass grows abundantly in this area. The crowd could hardly outrun the boat to the other side of the lake, a distance of fifteen to twenty miles. In springtime, the Jordan is high, and the crowds could not have easily crossed it.

You give them something to eat (6:37). The disciples want the crowds to go off to buy their own food and ask Jesus to send them away. Earlier they lived off the hospitality of others (6:8); now Jesus insists that they are to return the favor.

Eight months of a man's wages (6:37). Two hundred denarii is what this translates, which, according to Matthew 20:2, was a day's pay for a day laborer and would buy approximately 2400 loaves of bread, one-half inch thick and seven to eight inches in diameter.[151]

They were like sheep without a shepherd (6:34). The image of sheep without a shepherd echoes Moses' request for his successor when he is informed that he cannot lead them into the promised land (Num. 27:15–17). The shepherdless throng is soon organized by Jesus (see Ps. 23; Ezek. 34:23).

So they sat down in groups of hundreds and fifties (6:40). The assembly into orderly rows suggests the grouping of an army and recalls Israel's encampment.[152] Five thousand was also the typical number in a Roman legion and the number of Galilean troops Josephus said that he assembled for battle against the Romans in A.D. 67.[153] Rebel movements were known for gathering in the desert during this era, but Jesus is feeding a spiritual army, not a military company.

The feeding of bread and fish recalls several Old Testament themes. During Israel's sojourn in the desert God miraculously provided manna and quail. The disciple's astonished question when asked to feed the crowd parallels Moses' dismay at being asked to feed the people (Num. 11:22). The few small fish may connect to the complaints of Israel in the desert (11:4–6), and the collection of an abundance of leftovers shows that Jesus provides what Moses could not, bread that did not decay overnight. Unlike the disgruntled gathering around Moses, everyone is satisfied.

The feeding also challenges Roman propaganda. The Julia coins depict Livia, the wife of Augustus, as the goddess Demeter providing abundance. This miracle shows Jesus to be the true giver of bread.

Walking on Water and Summary of Healings (6:45–56)

Jesus made his disciples get into the boat and go on ahead of him to Bethsaida (6:45). Bethsaida means "house of the fisher." It was located just east of the Jordan, so it qualified as being on "the other side" of the lake (see comments on 4:35). This is the first mention of Bethsaida (see 8:22), though the Gospel of John tells us that Jesus' disciples Philip, Andrew, and Peter hailed from there (John 1:44; 12:21). Jesus pronounces woes on the city and on Korazin (Matt. 11:20–22; Luke 10:13–14), condemning their failure to repent after the mighty works he had done there (see Mark 8:22–26).

Josephus credits Philip, the son of Herod the Great who was appointed Tetrarch of Batanea, Trachonitus, Auranitus, Gaulonitus (from 4 B.C. to A.D.

GALILEE

Bethsaida was located on the north shore of the Sea of Galilee. Gennesaret was a plain on the northwest side of the Sea between Tiberias and Capernaum.

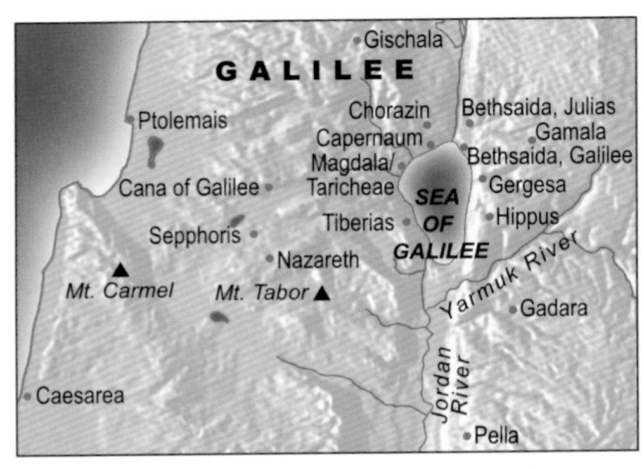

33/34) by the emperor Augustus, for raising the village of Bethsaida to the status of a city and renaming it Julias to honor the emperor's daughter.[154] From the coin evidence, the dedication of the city does not appear to have occurred until A.D. 30. Presumably, the refounding of the city with extensive building projects and an influx of new settlers took place during Jesus' ministry.

Three sites have been connected with Bethsaida: et-Tell, now almost two miles from the lake, and el-Araj and el-Mess'adiyye on the lake's current shoreline. Geological evidence, however, indicates that in the past the sea or its estuaries extended closer to the base of the hill at et-Tell and that the shoreline, after two thousand years, has been altered by the passing of continental plates, earthquakes, floods, and silting.[155]

After leaving them, he went up on a mountainside to pray (6:46). Jesus disperses the crowds after they have eaten. Mark gives no explanation as to why he forces them into the boat (contrast John 6:15). If the tradition that places the feeding at Tabgha is correct, Jesus could go up the Eremos ridge and see the disciples struggling on the lake.

About the fourth watch of the night he went out to them, walking on the lake (6:48). Mark depicts Jesus as walking on the sea (not on the shore!). This account is not simply about rescuing the disciples in distress but describes the unveiling of Jesus as a heavenly figure. The scene is intended to hark back to Old Testament images of God as one who tramples the waves.[156] Jesus is more than a successor to Moses who fills up bread baskets in the desert; he is God with us.

He was about to pass by them (6:48). "He wanted to pass by them" accords with an Old Testament theophany scene where God parades by someone.[157] In Genesis 32:31–33 (LXX), the face of God "passed by" Jacob wrestling with the angel. By passing by, Jesus intends to reveal to them his transcendent majesty.

When they saw him walking on the lake, they thought he was a ghost (6:49). The sight of Jesus throws the disciples into a panic. According to Wisdom 17:3, 15, fearsome apparitions smite the wicked.

"It is I" (6:50). Jesus responds to their fear with the divine formula of self-revelation, "I am."[158] This self-revelation answers the disciples' question in 4:41, "Who is this? Even the wind and the waves obey him!" A rabbinic tradition has it that when waves that would sink a ship are struck with clubs on which is engraven "'*I am that I am,*' Yah, the Lord of Hosts, Amen, Amen, Selah," they subside.[159]

When they had crossed over, they landed at Gennesaret and anchored there (6:53). Jesus dispatched the disciples to Bethsaida (6:45), but they land in Gennesaret. Bethsaida was a town on the northeast side of the Sea of Galilee; Gennesaret probably refers to a district between Tiberias and Capernaum three and a half miles long and a mile wide on he northwest side of the sea. The district was a densely populated, fertile plain and ncluded the city of Taricheae or Magdala. The region also lent its name to the Sea of Galilee (see Luke 5:1, "Lake of Gennesaret"). Josephus describes it as being remarkably beautiful, producing abundant varieties of fruits and trees.[160]

Perhaps the disciples were blown off course by the wind, making landing in Bethsaida difficult or undesirable. Perhaps Mark wants the reader to see some significance in this detour. The disciples are unable to go to Bethsaida since they are unable to understand about the loaves (6:52) and do not reach this destination until later (8:22).

They begged him to let them touch even the edge of his cloak (6:56). The edge of Jesus' cloak refers to the tassels with a blue cord that the law obliged Jewish males to wear and that was to remind them of the commandments of the Lord (Num. 15:37–41; Deut. 22:12). A bundle of dyed unspun wool to make these fringes was found in the caves of Bar Cochba. Some unfinished fringes revealed how they were made.[161]

Dispute Over Purity Issues (7:1–23)

The Pharisees and all the Jews do not eat unless they give their hands a ceremonial washing (7:3). The Pharisees protest

▸ Purity

The Pharisees' attention to purity derived from God's command for Israel to be a holy people and from the many biblical directives about holiness.[A-20] Purity is important because impurity drives God's presence from the midst of the people and will result in their expulsion from the land (18:24–30). Impurity belongs to the realm of death and demons and cuts a person off from God. It clings to a person and can be transferred to other persons, vessels, clothes, and houses by touching, lying, or sitting.[A-21] Serious impurity occurring anywhere among the people pollutes the sanctuary where God dwells (15:31). Impurity is not a sin; it comes naturally in the course of life, but it prevents one from approaching what is holy. What the Pharisees considered sinful was choosing not to avail oneself of the opportunity to be cleansed of the impurity.

The Pharisees clarified purity rules that label persons, objects, and places as pure or polluted and susceptible to impurity. Something becomes "impure" or "dirty" when "it is the wrong *thing* appearing in the wrong *place* at the wrong *time*."[A-22] Interest in purity, therefore, stems from a universal human aversion to dirt, disease, and death and to the desire to keep everything in its proper place. Washing was the normal means of removing most impurity.

The Pharisees sought to promote obedience to God's law among the people and took for granted that true obedience would conform to their particular interpretation of the law. With their purity maps charting what was clean or unclean, permissible or forbidden, the Pharisees strove to impose their vision of what God required on all Israel. Maintaining purity was a key item in their agenda, and they applied to everyone many purity laws meant only for priests serving in the temple. The legislation in Exodus 30:18–21 (see 40:12, 31), for example, required priests engaged in the tabernacle service to wash their hands. Nowhere does the Bible stipulate that others must wash their hands for ritual purity.

To understand the Pharisees' concerns, we might apply a variation of the aphorism that a man's home is his castle. The Pharisees believed that a man's home is his temple, and he must apply the purity concerns that in the Scripture only pertained to priests.[A-23] Holiness is not given to priests alone but to priests, Levites, and all Israel.[A-24] Every Israelite must be prepared to come into God's presence.

publicly that Jesus' disciples eat with defiled (lit., "common") hands. "Common" is the opposite of "holy, devoted to God." Mark explains further that "unclean hands" refer to "unwashed" hands (7:2) and inserts an explanation about Jewish ritual washings for Gentile readers unfamiliar with these customs (7:3–4). The disagreement over washing hands has nothing to do with hygiene but is a matter of purity, the fitness to offer sacrifice or to take part in a meal.

The Old Testament law does not require ordinary meals to be eaten in a state of purity.[162] Only priests eating sacrificial offerings (Lev. 22:3–9) and laypersons eating their portion of their fellowship offerings (7:20–21) must eat in a state of purity. The Pharisees have broadened the law to include all Jews eating anything at any time.

The Bible also prescribes immersion to cleanse impurity, but the Pharisees innovated with their tradition to meet the needs of the urban Jew in a Hellenistic age. They reduced the biblical requirement of bathing the whole body and laundering clothes to the simple act of washing hands.[163] By contrast, Josephus describes the Essenes as so scrupulous that they would not eat without first immersing their entire bodies in cold water.[164]

ANCIENT LATRINE

A Roman-era public facility at Beth Shean.

Holding to the tradition of the elders (7:3). "The tradition of the elders" was unscriptural law based on interpretations that tried to fill the gaps and silences in the regulations found in Scripture. Because they based their decisions on the logical analysis of the explicit and implicit data in Scripture, the Pharisees regarded them as rooted in Scripture and equal in authority.

In the first century, washing hands had become a widespread custom and a sign of piety and fidelity to God. The *Letter of Aristeas*, describing the translation of the Pentateuch into Greek and written no later than the first century B.C., cites the practice: "Following the customs of all the Jews, they washed their hands in the sea in the course of their prayers to God, and then proceeded to the reading and explication of each point."[165] Later rabbinic tradition, which contains the legacy of Pharisaism, insisted that washing hands did have an explicit biblical basis. "When he washes his hands, he should say, 'Blessed is He who has sanctified us with his commandments and commanded us concerning the washing of hands.'"[166] The Pharisees and their spiritual heirs also asserted that God had delivered their tradition to Moses.[167]

When they come from the marketplace they do not eat unless they wash (7:4). Presumably, the elders fear some contamination from contact even with fellow Jews who are nonobservant. According to Josephus, the sectarians at Qumran were far more extreme and regarded it necessary to bathe even after touching a junior member as if he were an alien.[168]

They observe many other traditions, such as the washing of cups, pitchers and kettles (7:4). The concern for the purity

The Purposes of the Tradition of the Elders

The development of "the tradition of the elders" (Mark 7:3) sought to achieve three goals. First, it made the basic requirement that Israel be holy to the Lord something attainable for every Jew in everyday life. The Pharisees never thought that they were voiding the commands of God—only making them applicable. Their tradition sought to provide clear-cut instructions on every aspect of daily life so that Jews could live in accord with God's law.

Second, the tradition of the elders sought to forestall the dominant pagan culture from making inroads into Jewish life (see Lev. 20:1–7). The *Letter of Aristeas* exults in the law that "surrounds us with unbroken palisades and iron walls, to prevent our mixing with any of the other peoples in any matter being thus kept pure in body and soul, preserved from false beliefs, and worshiping the only God omnipotent over all creation" (139). The tradition of the elders helped raise the wall even higher. It encouraged the devout to make conscious efforts to set themselves apart from the unwashed hordes destined for destruction. Actions such as immersion and washing hands were tangible, positive gestures that displayed who God's elect were and who would be vindicated at the end of the age. Purity laws were elevated "because they plainly distinguished Israel from non-Israel and defined Israel as physical and dependent on history and genealogy not on a universal, spiritual idea."[A-25]

The outward signs of obedience in Jesus' day, circumcision, keeping the Sabbath, observing food laws and washing hands, became the badges that marked out the elect as those who were "in." The feelings about this issue could be strong. As one rabbi from a later period expressed it, "Whoever eats bread without previously washing the hands is as though he had intercourse with a harlot."[A-26] Another rabbi was placed under the ban for casting doubt on the tradition of the elders concerning the cleansing of hands.[A-27]

Third, the tradition of the elders assumes that God created order and that human affairs prosper only when things are divinely ordered—even when they may seem only to be minor issues. Eleazar's speech to Antiochus Epiphanes explaining his refusal to eat anything unclean, even when he has been brutally tortured and threatened with death, movingly captures this conviction (*4 Macc.* 5:16–21):

> We, O Antiochus, who have been persuaded to govern our lives by the divine law, think that there is no compulsion more powerful than our obedience to the law. Therefore we consider that we should not transgress it in any respect. Even if, as you suppose, our law were not truly divine and we had wrongly held it to be divine, not even so would it be right for us to invalidate our reputation for piety. Therefore do not suppose that it would be a petty sin if we were to eat defiling food; to transgress the law in matters either small or great is of equal seriousness, for in either case the law is equally despised.

The tradition tried to be as precise as possible—hence its reputation for hairsplitting. The rules preserved in the Mishnah about washing hands, for example, specified the quantity of water required, the position of the hands, and the type of vessel to be used. Hands were suspected of being generally unclean because they were fidgety and likely to touch something unclean,[A-28] and the rabbis vigorously debated the degree of uncleanness that hands incurred.[A-29] Such regulations may seem inconsequential to us, but they gave a mundane act holy significance and allowed individuals to show devotion to God in deliberate, tangible ways. They also led some to become so painstaking in their obedience to these rules that they neglected the weightier matters of the law (see Matt. 23:23–25). In the case Jesus presents, such fastidiousness overrides obedience to God's law.

of cooking pots and bowls is found in Zechariah 14:20–21:

> On that day HOLY TO THE LORD will be inscribed on the bells of the horses, and the cooking pots in the LORD's house will be like the sacred bowls in front of the altar. Every pot in Jerusalem and Judah will be holy to the LORD Almighty, and all who come to sacrifice will take some of the pots and cook in them.

This text has to do with the temple's becoming a fit place to worship God in the coming new age. The Pharisees extended the concern to all vessels everywhere. One of the largest tractates in the Mishnah, *Kelim* ("Vessels"), has to do with vessels of all kinds and with their susceptibility to uncleanness.

"Why don't your disciples live according to the tradition of the elders?" (7:5). In Jesus' day, people viewed a teacher as entirely responsible for the conduct of his disciples.[169] By publicly belittling Jesus' disciples for blatantly failing to observe basic Jewish tradition, his challengers seek to make him lose face. Someone so popular threatens to reduce their sphere of influence when he disregards sacred boundaries carefully erected by their rules and calls into question their role as interpreters. Consequently, they seek ways to smudge his reputation before the crowds. Jesus will not answer insincere questions but instead regains command of the situation with a blistering counterattack.

Isaiah was right when he prophesied about you hypocrites (7:6). Hypocrisy is a perceived discrepancy between one's alleged principles and one's behavior. Because the Pharisees so insistently championed strict obedience to the law, they left themselves open to the charge. Hypocrisy can take two forms. A hypocrite may be a play actor who deliberately feigns piety to cloak an inner godlessness; this kind of hypocrite seeks to deceive others. A hypocrite may also be self-deceived; this form of hypocrisy is the more insidious because nothing is easier to prove to oneself than one's own sincerity. Jesus' response shows how those who accuse his disciples of transgressing the tradition of the elders sanction far worse transgressions of the law by means of their traditions.

Whatever help you might otherwise have received from me is "Corban" (that is, a gift devoted to God) (7:11). God commands children to honor their parents, and in Jewish tradition that entailed giving them physical necessities.[170]

> Our rabbis taught: What is 'reverence' [for parents] and what is honor? Reverence [refers to one who] does not sit in his parent's place and does not stand in his [parent's] place, he does not contradict his [parent's] opinions, and does not judge [his parent's disputes]. 'Honor' [refers to one who] feeds [his father or mother] and gives him (or her) drink; he clothes him (or her) and covers him (or her), and helps him (or her) to enter and exit.[171]

Jesus gives an extreme example of a son who spitefully or selfishly vows that his property is an offering dedicated to the temple. "Corban" refers to something that is taboo as an offering to God. The property becomes "most sacred" even before it is brought to the temple and bars the one who makes the vow or others who are specified in the vow from gaining profit from it (based on the exegesis of Lev. 6:18; Deut. 26:14). In this case, the son prevents his parents from having any benefit from the property. The term "Corban" also applies to the dedicatory formula used in a vow to set aside property for God.[172] As a legal device, it only expresses an intention to give property to God and is not the actual disposal of it. The person could keep the property in his possession but say to his parents that he cannot offer them any help because he has dedicated it to God.

The Pharisees regarded breaking this vow to use the property in any way to help the parents as a grave sin. One example from the Mishnah shows how intricate legal fictions developed around such vows:

> If a man was forbidden by a vow to have any benefit from his fellow, and he had naught to eat, his fellow may give [the food] to another as a gift, and the first is permitted to use it. It once happened that a man at Beth Horon, whose father was forbidden by a vow to have any benefit from him, was giving his son in marriage, and he said to his fellow, "The courtyard and the banquet are given to thee as a gift, but they are thine only that my father may come and eat with us at the banquet." His fellow said, "If they are mine, they are dedicated to Heaven." The other answered, "I did not give thee what is mine that thou shouldst dedicate it to Heaven." His fellow said, "Thou didst give me what is thine only that thou and thy father might eat and drink and be reconciled one with the other, and that the sin should rest on his head!" When the case came before the Sages, they said: Any gift which, if a man would dedicate it, is not accounted dedicated, is not a [valid] gift.[173]

In Jesus' example, the command to honor parents (Ex. 20:12; Deut. 5:16) and the command to honor vows (Deut. 23:21–23) clash head-on. From his point of view, the command from the Decalogue to honor parents soars above the command to honor vows. The Pharisees' tradition, however, turns the law on its head by insisting that the sanctity of the vow supersedes the parents' right to support. Jesus assumes that such a vow is automatically invalid because it violates God's command to honor parents.

Nothing outside a man can make him "unclean" by going into him. Rather, it is what comes out of a man that makes him "unclean" (7:15). Jesus not only disputes the legitimacy of the Pharisees' tradition, he rejects the entire basis of Jewish food

REFLECTIONS

CHRISTIANS SHOULD BE MINDFUL that they also have oral traditions that direct their behavior and dictate their beliefs. These are necessary for preserving the Christian heritage, drawing boundaries to set them apart from an unbelieving world, and mapping out how they can be expected to live. But these traditions can become snares that will trip up believers if they regard them as sacred and inviolable or apply them to repulse those whom God wishes to embrace. Christians, too, must guard against accentuating minutiae and making such things paramount while ignoring the weightier commands of God's law.

laws by proclaiming that contact with supposedly impure things or persons does not defile a person. He illustrates his point with an indelicate reminder of what happens to food when it is consumed. It passes through the digestive tract and winds up in the latrine. He concludes from that process that God only cares about defilement that touches the heart (7:21, 23). The heart is the core of motivation, deliberation, and intention. Food does not enter the heart, and what does not enter the heart cannot make a person unclean. How one handles food is therefore morally irrelevant. Nothing from outside pollutes a person.

Jesus reiterates for emphasis that what comes out of a man is what makes him "unclean" (7:20) and then lists vices that flow from the heart. These cannot be cleansed by a fistful of water in cupped hands. God requires that we scour our hearts. If the only thing that matters to God is what comes from a person's heart, then this opens the door for the recognition that God will accept all persons who cleanse their hearts and exhibit faith. Clean/unclean laws establish boundaries, and the Pharisees set themselves up as the border guards. Jesus breaks down the boundaries and claims that true uncleanness has to do with moral impurity, not ritual impurity.

(In saying this, Jesus declared all foods "clean") (7:19). The parenthesis in the NIV text interprets this statement as a narrator's aside drawing the conclusion that Jesus declares all foods clean. The phrase, "In saying this, Jesus declared," is not in the Greek text. Literally, it reads, "cleansing all foods." The nominative participle, "cleansing" would modify the verb "he says" in 7:18.

A variant reading, however, has an accusative singular participle that would modify the noun "latrine" immediately preceding it. If this is the original reading, the statement affirms that the food has become clean in the process of elimination. This reading surprisingly fits the rabbinic laws of clean and unclean. According to the Mishnah, excrement is not ritually impure.[174] Rabbi Jose is said to ask: "Is excrement impure? Is it not for purposes of cleanliness?"[175] Even the excrement of a person suffering an unclean emission is not impure.[176] By contrast, the much stricter Qumran sectarians, under the influence of Deuteronomy 23:12–14 and Ezekiel 4:12–15, considered it to be impure.[177] This startling judgment may be the key to Jesus' argument. Jesus may not declare all foods clean—although that is a legitimate inference—but with droll humor may be exposing the illogic of the Pharisee's arguments. If food defiles a person, as the Pharisees claim, why do they not regard it as unclean when it winds up in the latrine? Defilement must come from some other source than food. The logic derives from the Pharisees' own rules regarding clean and unclean and sets up his concluding words on the real source of defilement: what comes from the heart.

The Syrophoenican Woman (7:24–30)

Jesus left that place and went to the vicinity of Tyre (7:24). After the controversy of 7:1–23, Jesus withdraws and seeks to remain incognito. In the Old Testament, Tyre was a godless city, and Josephus identifies the people from Tyre "as our bitterest enemies."[178] People from Tyre and Sidon, however, have already flocked to Jesus, which explains how his fame has preceded him (3:8).

The woman was a Greek, born in Syrian Phoenicia (7:26). The Romans distin-

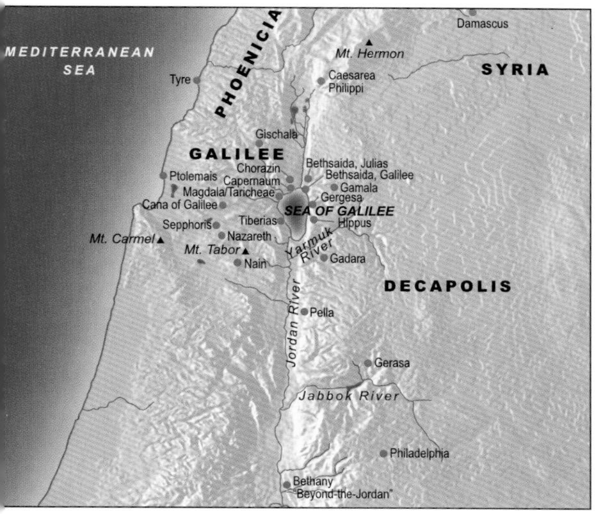

guished between Lybiophoenicians and Syrophoenicians; this note would seem to reflect a Roman orientation.[179] She is a pagan who comes from a Greek-speaking, more affluent class.

First let the children eat all they want (7:27). Israel identified itself as the children of God.[180] A rabbinic tradition expands on Deuteronomy 14:1: "Beloved are Israel, for they were called children of God; still greater was the love in that it was made known to them that they were called children of God, as it is written: Ye are the children of the Lord your God."[181] Jesus' response assumes that Israel has priority in the blessings of the gospel.

For it is not right to take the children's bread and toss it to their dogs (7:27). For Israel, "dogs" evoked an image of repulsive scavengers; they will eat anything and never seem satisfied. The word became a term of ultimate scorn and was applied to Gentiles, all of whom were considered to be inherently unclean: "He that separates from the foreskin [Gentile] is as one who separates himself from a grave."[182] Another rabbinic tradition explains that "as the sacred food was intended for men, but not for the dogs, the Torah was intended to be given to the Chosen People, but not to the Gentiles."[183] Asenath, after her conversion, took her royal dinner of food that had been sacrificed to idols and threw it out the window, saying, "By no means must my dogs eat from my dinner and from the sacrifice of the idols, but let the strange dogs eat those."[184]

Does Jesus share this Jewish prejudice against Gentiles? There is no indication in the text that Jesus is struggling with the scope of his mission, and this woman helps him to clarify it by opening his eyes to a wider mandate. He has already received people from Tyre and Sidon (3:8).

Jesus may be reacting to a member of the oppressive upper class.[185] Economically, Tyre took bread away from Galilee. This region was well stocked with food

left

GALILEE AND PHOENICIA

Tyre was located on the coast northwest of Galilee.

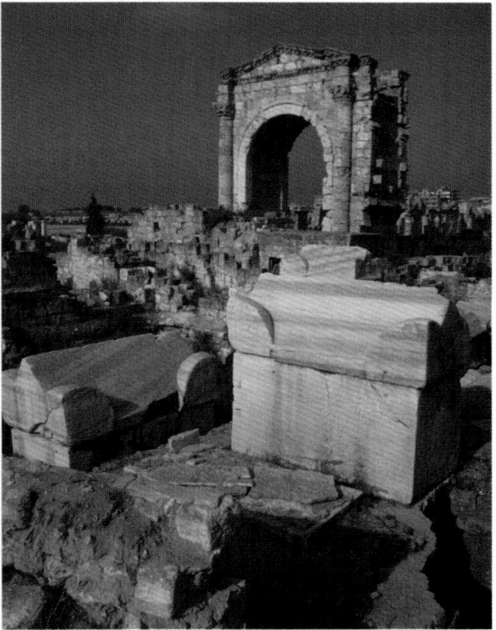

TYRE

Roman remains in the ancient city of Tyre.

produced in the Galilean hinterland while Galileans went hungry (see Acts 12:20).[186] Galileans perceived Tyre as a bloated bully and had long despised it for amassing wealth at the expense of the poor.[187] The probing of this woman's faith occurs in the historical context of the animosity between Jews and heathens and Galilean resentment over Tyre's socioeconomic domination.

But even the dogs under the table eat the children's crumbs (7:28). This clever woman understands that he is talking about the priority of Israel over Gentiles and that the time for Gentiles has not yet come. But her desperation and faith keep her from taking no for an answer. She comes like a dog begging for a scrap and displays extraordinary faith. She will not be put off by his initial rejection and pleads for help, knowing that she has no merit and nothing to commend her.

A Deaf Tongue-tied Man Regains His Hearing (7:31–37)

Then Jesus left the vicinity of Tyre and went through Sidon, down to the Sea of Galilee and into the region of the Decapolis (7:31). Returning from the district of Tyre by way of Sidon to the Sea of Galilee through the district of the Decapolis is a circuitous route. Sidon is twenty-five miles north of Tyre. This indirect route may hint that Jesus was evading the long arm of Herod Antipas. Mark places Jesus in a culturally pagan region.

After he took him aside, away from the crowd, Jesus put his fingers into the man's ears. Then he spit and touched the man's tongue (7:33). Healing in the ancient world was a hands-on activity. Healers were expected to do some purposeful action to restore health. Such physical gestures would be particularly important for one who could not hear the spoken words of healing. Putting his fingers in the man's ears was symbolic of opening them and spitting and touching his tongue was symbolic of loosening his tongue. Saliva was also believed to have healing properties.

He looked up to heaven and with a deep sigh said to him, "Ephphatha!" (which means, "Be opened!") (7:34). Jesus' healing words in Aramaic are translated to make clear that he is not using some magical incantation. A parallel story about the newly enthroned emperor Vespasian is instructive:

> Vespasian as yet lacked prestige and a certain divinity, so to speak, since he was an unexpected and still new-made emperor; but these were also given to him. A man of the people who was blind, and another who was lame, came to him together as he sat on his tribunal, begging for the help for their disorders which Serapis had promised in a dream; for the god declared that Vespasian would restore the eyes, if he would spit upon them, and give strength to the leg, if he would deign to touch it with his heel.
>
> Though he had hardly any faith that this could possibly succeed, and therefore shrank even from making the attempt, he was at last prevailed upon by his friends and tried both things in public before a large crowd, and with success.[188]

The story reflects the belief that the saliva of a revered person has healing power. In contrast with Vespasian, Jesus does not perform miracles with any hesitancy about his ability or to win prestige

The Feeding of Four Thousand (8:1–12)

Jesus' compassion prompts him again to feed a large crowd that had been with him for three days without anything to eat (8:2; see 6:34). In this second feeding, the number fed drops from five thousand to four thousand. The loaves and fishes increase from five loaves and two fishes (6:41) to seven loaves and a few small fish (8:5, 7).

Seven basketfuls (8:8). The number of baskets of fragments left over diminishes from twelve (6:43) to seven (8:8). The word *kophinoi* (6:43; 8:19) is associated with Jews by Juvenal, but that does not make the common word *spyrides* (8:8; 8:20) into a Gentile basket.[189]

He got into the boat with his disciples and went to the region of Dalmanutha (8:10). Jesus sets sail with his disciples to Dalmanutha, a place that is never mentioned elsewhere in ancient literature. The best guess is that it refers to the anchorage of the district of Magdala.

He sighed deeply and said, "Why does this generation ask for a miraculous sign? I tell you the truth, no sign will be given to it" (8:12). This generation, represented by the Pharisees, asks Jesus for some apocalyptic sign to signal Israel's final deliverance from her enemies. A sign from heaven is something that "is apocalyptic in tone, triumphalistic in character, and the embodiment of one of the 'mighty deeds of deliverance' that God had worked on Israel's behalf in rescuing it from slavery."[190]

The English translation misses how sharply Jesus refuses. The text reads literally, "If a sign shall be given to this generation." It comprises part of a vehement oath formula that would begin or conclude: "May God strike me down" or "May I be accursed of God" if a sign is given to this generation. Only false prophets will give signs to this generation (13:22, 30).

The Disciples' Incomprehension (8:13–21)

Watch out for the yeast of the Pharisees and that of Herod (8:15). "Yeast" connotes to moderns something fresh and wholesome that makes dough rise and gives bread a pleasing light texture. "Leaven," the word used, was far more dangerous. It was produced by keeping back a piece of the previous week's dough, storing it in suitable conditions, and adding juices to promote the process of fermentation, much like sourdough. This homemade rising agent was fraught with health hazards because it could easily become tainted and infect the next batch. In the Old Testament, leaven symbolizes corruption and the infectious power of evil. This image was widely understood. Plutarch wrote that leaven "is itself also the product of corruption, and produces corruption in the dough with which it is mixed . . . and altogether

MAGDALA

Magdala was located on the northwest coast of the Sea of Galilee.

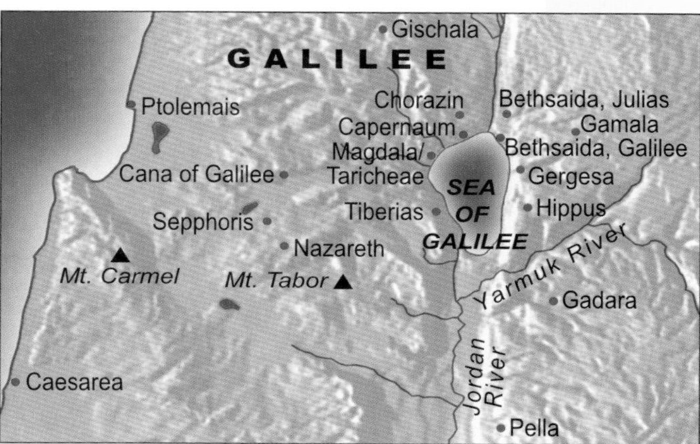

the process of leavening seems to be one of putrefaction; at any rate if it goes too far, it completely sours and spoils the dough."[191]

Healing a Blind Man (8:22–26)

They came to Bethsaida, and some people brought a blind man and begged Jesus to touch him (8:22). Bethsaida was reached by sea, not by land, from Capernaum. After refusing to give the Pharisees a sign (8:11–13), this healing reveals that Jesus does miracles to meet genuine needs. Dust, poor hygiene, and the bright sun made eye diseases common in the ancient world. Mark describes Jesus taking the blind man away from the village, where he probably had come to beg.

When he had spit on the man's eyes and put his hands on him (8:23). Pliny recommends the use of saliva for eye diseases.[192] Jesus' first attempt to heal the man meets with only partial success. This detail communicates two things. First, his blindness is stubborn and hard to cure but Jesus has power to heal even the most difficult cases. Second, on a literary level, curing the stubborn spiritual blindness of the disciples will also take a second touch.

REFLECTIONS

THE PHARISEES AND HEROD HAVE NOTHING IN COMmon except their refusal to believe in spite of the evidence. They deny the truth evident in Jesus' ministry. The disciples, too, are in danger of succumbing to the spiritual virus of hardened hearts that causes them to fail to recognize the miraculous truth about Jesus even though they have witnessed his deeds firsthand.

Their failure, before the resurrection, to grasp everything reflects the condition of those governed by the spirit of human wisdom who have not received God's Spirit to reveal God's ways. The disciples are mirror images of modern-day disciples. "The disciples' major problem is not simply their blindness, but the failure to recognize that they are blind."[A-30] We are no less slow-witted or subject to confusion.

The text does its work when readers can see their own blindness in the disciples' blindness. If we ask, "How could the disciples be so dense?" we need immediately to ask the same question of ourselves. The disciples saw dimly in a glass coated with the dust of traditional ways of viewing things and warped by the curvature of their own dreams and ambitions. The glass we look through is no different. We are no less in need of healing before we can see what God is doing, and it may not take on the first try.[A-31]

Announcement of Jesus' Death and Resurrection (8:27–9:1)

This passage is the axis on which the two halves of the Gospel turn. The first half reveals Jesus performing mighty works; the second half shows him bound for the cross and crucified in weakness.[193]

Jesus and his disciples went on to the villages around Caesarea Philippi (8:27). Caesarea Philippi lay twenty-four miles north of the Sea of Galilee at the southwestern base of Mount Hermon range. It was the capital of Herod Philip's tetrarchy. Jesus may have retreated to the territory of Herod Philip to escape danger from the more threatening Herod Antipas. Originally, the city was called Panion, which refers to a cave sanctuary dedicated to the Greek God Pan, and the cult was still thriving in the first century. Josephus describes the cave as near the source of the river Jordan.[194] Ironically, Peter's confession occurs in the area where Herod the Great built a grand marble temple to honor the emperor[195] and where his heir enlarged the city and renamed it to honor Caesar.[196] It is "theologically significant that Jesus' dignity was recognized in a region devoted to the affirmation that Caesar is lord."[197]

They replied, "Some say John the Baptist; others say Elijah; and still others, one of the prophets" (8:28). Popular opinion regards Jesus as some kind of prophet figure (see also 6:14–15). Identifying Jesus as a prophet attributes significant status to him and should not be missed. Many Jews in this time believed that the prophetic Spirit had been withdrawn from Israel. In 1 Maccabees 4:41–46, Judas Maccabeus has cleansed the sanctuary and torn down the altar defiled by the pagan sacrifices of Antiochus Epiphanes. He stored "the stones in a convenient place on the temple hill until a prophet should come to tell what to do with them" (4:46). The end of 1 Maccabees records the decision that Simon (and the Hasmonean line) should be "their leader and high priest forever, until a trustworthy prophet should arise" (14:41). This view presumes that trustworthy prophets have left the scene, and this prophet is yet to come (Deut. 18:15; Mal. 4:5). Some expected the great prophets such as Isaiah and Jeremiah to return at the end (*5 Ezra* 2:18).

You are the Christ (8:29). Under Jesus' interrogation, Peter makes the right confession. By the time of the first century the word Christ (i.e., Messiah) was understood by most Jews to refer to a king-like figure who would triumphantly appear in the final days to deliver Israel from her enemies. The dream did not die even after the debacle with Rome.

Peter's answer is correct since it corresponds to the title of the Gospel (1:1), but Jesus modifies standard expectations by announcing his impending suffering (8:31). Jesus will not take up the crown but the cross. Suffering, rejection, and death will be God's means of deliverance. Only then will resurrection follow.

He then began to teach them that the Son of Man must suffer many things . . . , and that he must be killed (8:31). Mark records three instances when Jesus informs his disciples that the Son of Man must suffer, die, and then be raised (8:31; 9:30–31; 10:32–34). Significantly, he speaks about this suffering *plainly* (8:32), not in parables (cf. 4:33). Each time, however, the disciples demonstrate in some way that they fail to grasp his meaning. They may have shared the expectations of most Jews, who hoped for a Messiah. He would be a kingly figure who would reign triumphantly as David had (see "Messianic Expectation in Judaism"). No wonder the disciples have trouble assimilating Jesus' announcements about his suffering if they believe he is the Messiah. It runs counter to their every expectation about the Messiah.

And after three days (8:31). "After three days" can mean "a short time later." The third day is the time when God has been known to intervene.[198] The intention of

THE JORDAN RIVER AT CAESAREA PHILIPPI

The waterfall at Banias, near the source of the river.

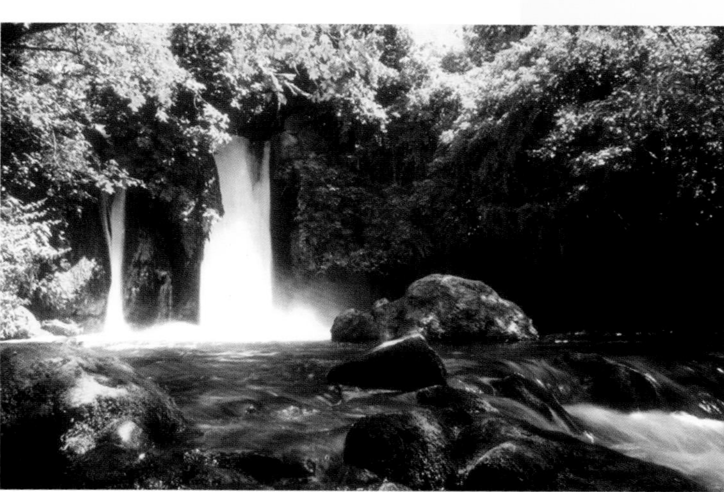

this prophetic utterance was not to pinpoint in advance the timing of his resurrection but to certify that it will happen in fulfillment of God's plan. "The full import of the prophecy cannot be grasped until after the event."[199]

Get behind me, Satan! (8:33). The archenemy appears in Jesus' most prominent disciple. It is satanic to plot Jesus' death for selfish reasons (3:6, 23–26); it is equally satanic to try and block it for selfish reasons (8:33). Ironically, Satan uses one disciple, Peter, to try to turn Jesus away from death, and another disciple, Judas, to lead him to death.

Jesus' stern rebuke is a teaching tool, not a rejection of Peter. In the Qumran literature, chastisement by God was considered to be a requisite for spiritual growth and something for which to be grateful to God.[200] Harsh censure was considered appropriate in the case of recalcitrant students. Philodemus, for example, believed that teachers should use harsh remedies as wise doctors do and show benevolent care by using blame.[201]

If anyone would come after me, he must deny himself and take up his cross and follow me (8:34). Jesus does not speak only to the twelve disciples but also to the crowds. He does not want them simply to marvel but to follow him. The cross is a startling image because only criminals and slaves were crucified and carried crosses to the place of execution. Plutarch reports, "Every criminal condemned to death bears his own cross on his back."[202] Dionysius of Halicarnassus gives this account:

> A Roman of some note had handed over a slave to his fellow slaves for them to execute. In order to make the punishment generally known, their master ordered them to drag the condemned man first through the forum and other public places and to scourge him while doing so. . . . The slaves who

▸ Messianic Expectation in Judaism

Three important texts illustrate the kind of Messiah Jews living at the time of Jesus were looking for. *Psalms of Solomon* 17:21–25 expresses the earnest longing for a mighty king to come and reign:

> See, Lord, and raise up for them their king, the son of David, to rule over your servant Israel in the time known to you, O God. Undergird him with the strength to destroy the unrighteous rulers, to purge Jerusalem from gentiles who trample her to destruction; in wisdom and in righteousness to drive out the sinners from the inheritance; to smash the arrogance of sinners like a potter's jar; to shatter all their substance with an iron rod; to destroy the unlawful nations with the word of his mouth; at his warning the nations will flee from his presence; and he will condemn sinners by the thoughts of their hearts.

The author of *4 Ezra* pictures the Messiah as a lion from the *posterity* of David, who will triumph over the eagle (the Romans). He will judge the world and deliver the faithful remnant of Israel (12:31–34).

The *Targum Yerušalmi* to Genesis 49:11 exults:

> "How fine is the King, the Messiah, who will arise from those of the house of Judah! He girds his loins and goes forth and sets up the ranks of battle against his enemies and kills the kings together with their commanders and no king and commander can stand before him. He reddens the mountains with the blood of their slain and his garments are dipped in blood. . . ."[A-32]

had been thus commanded stretched out both the man's arms and tied them down to a piece of wood which reached across breast and shoulders to his wrists. They chased him and lacerated his naked body with their lashes. Overcome by this cruel treatment, the convict not only uttered the most heartrending cries, but under the painful impact of the lashes he also made indecent movements.[203]

Besides the cruel horror of crucifixion, the Jews also believed that anyone who was hanged on a tree was accursed of God (Deut. 21:22–23). By inviting followers to take up a cross, Jesus offers them a shameful stigma to go with agonizing suffering.

The Transfiguration (9:2–13)

After six days Jesus took Peter, James and John with him and led them up a high mountain, where they were all alone (9:2). "After six days" means that Jesus' transfiguration occurs on the seventh day after Peter's confession. Tradition associates the high mountain with Mount Tabor (1,843 feet), but since a Roman camp was located there[204] and Jesus is still in the region of Caesarea Philippi, it is more likely to be the much higher Mount Hermon (9,166 feet).

There he was transfigured before them (9:2). Jewish readers would associate "dazzling white garments" with traditions about the radiant clothing of divine figures (Dan. 7:9) and of the righteous in the resurrection.[205] This event may foreshadow Jesus' resurrection, but Otto concludes: "It is not a vision of *what is to be*, but a revelation of *what already is*, a revelation of the unchanging divine glory which has been concealed beneath the lowliness of a human body."[206] The transfiguration is like a hologram that allows disciples to glimpse Jesus' divine glory.

And there appeared before them Elijah and Moses, who were talking with Jesus (9:4). Elijah ascended in a whirlwind into heaven (2 Kings 2:11). Later rabbinic interpretations combined the reference to Moses' death, "no one knows . . . his grave" (Deut. 34:6), with the passage "and [he] was there with the LORD" (Ex. 34:28) to conclude that Moses was taken to heaven without death, like Enoch and Elijah. This may have been a popular belief in Jesus' time.[207] Their translation to heaven meant that they were believed able to return to earth. What does their presence signify?

(1) Both were faithful servants who suffered because of their obedience, were rejected by the people of God, and were vindicated by God. The same thing will happen to Jesus.

(2) The people expected a prophet like Moses (Deut. 18:15), Israel's first deliverer, to liberate them once and for all. Elijah was supposed to appear at the dawning of the end time and God's ultimate redemption of Israel. According to *4 Ezra* 6:25–26, one of the signs of the end of the age is that those who are left will "see those who were taken up, who

MOUNT TABOR

Tradition associates the transfiguration of Jesus with this mountain, located in lower Galilee.

from their birth have not tasted death; and the heart of the earth's inhabitants shall be changed and converted to a different spirit." According to a later rabbinic midrash, God swore to Moses, "in the time to come when I send Elijah, the prophet, unto them [Israel], the two of you shall come together."[208] Their return here denotes the debut of the final age (Deut. 18:15; Mal. 4:5–6).

(3) Their presence with Jesus accredits him for his role as the deliverer sent by God. The voice from heaven (9:7) clinches it.

Peter said to Jesus, "Rabbi, it is good for us to be here. Let us put up three shelters—one for you, one for Moses and one for Elijah" (9:5). The word translated "shelters" is the word for "tabernacles" or "booths." Otto asks whether this should not be punctuated as a question: "Is it good for us to be here?"[209] This punctuation suggests a measure of fear appropriate to the Sinaitic background of the event and would harmonize with the statement that they were so frightened (9:6).

The *Targum Pseudo-Jonathan* to Exodus 24:10–11 develops the account of those who went up the mountain with Moses and saw God. It reads it in light of the declaration that no one will see God and live (Ex. 33:20) and adds that Nadab and Abihu were struck down on the eighth day because they had seen the divine glory. Witnessing Jesus' divine glory would have been terrifying (compare Ex. 19:21) since it could kill those who were unworthy. Peter is a sinner, not a priest, nor is he ritually purified. He does not think it is good to be there in the presence of divine glory; thus he wants to build tabernacles to protect him and the others, physically and psychologically. The tabernacles would veil them from this divine glory radiating from these glorified saints and Jesus.

Otto comments, "The only means by which the people may approach God was through their elect mediator in the *skēnē*, the tabernacle and the tent of meeting, where the power of God's glory was veiled by the cloud."[210] The overshadowing cloud that descends on them signifies the divine glory but also provides them protection. Exodus 19:9 provides the backdrop: "The LORD says to Moses [on Sinai], 'I am going to come to you in a dense cloud, so that the people will hear me speaking with you and will always put their trust in you.'" The command to listen to Jesus means that God is now speaking directly through him.

GALILEE AND THE NORTH

Mount Hermon is the likely place of Jesus' transfiguration.

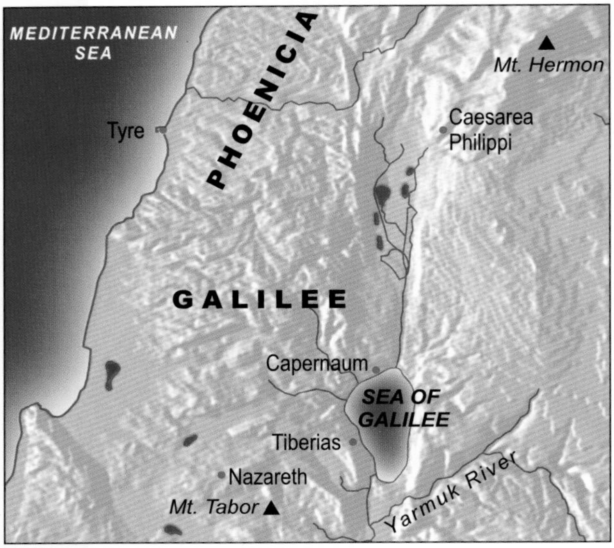

Descent From the Mountain (9:9–13)

Jesus gave them orders not to tell anyone what they had seen until the Son of Man had risen from the dead (9:9). The transfiguration is sandwiched between announcements of Jesus' death. The truth about Jesus' glory can only be fully understood when coupled with his suffering, death, and resurrection. Until that takes place, the secret is not yet ready for public proclamation.

They asked him, "Why do the teachers of the law say that Elijah must come first?" (9:11). The teachers of the law based their opinion on Malachi 4:5–6 (see Sir. 48:10). Jesus confirms the scribal opinion, but surprisingly asserts that Elijah has already come.

Speculation about Elijah's return and his task of restoration appears to have been diffuse in Judaism. The later rabbis mostly assume that Elijah will solve legal disputes.[211] Others imagine that he will revive the dead, bring back Moses and the desert generation, recover the lost sacred temple vessels, crush mountains like straw, and reveal the great mystery. The disciples' question assumes that some connection between Elijah and the coming of the Messiah existed in Jesus' day, which seems to have faded in later rabbinic literature. Christian literature preserves the conviction that Elijah will identify and anoint the Messiah.[212] Contrary to any current expectation, Jesus announces that Elijah has come and was mistreated.

Jesus rejects any personal identification with Elijah (8:28) and can only have in mind John the Baptizer, who came in the garb of Elijah. Clearly his coming does not herald imminent messianic splendor for Israel. "Restor[ing] all things" has to do with repentance, which was fulfilled when all Judea and Jerusalem came to John to be baptized, confessing their sins (1:5).

A Father's Plea for His Possessed Son (9:14–29)

Jesus returns from the mountain to the everyday world of human and demonic mayhem. The disciples have proven incapable of exorcising a demon, threatening the life of a little boy.

Teacher, I brought you my son, who is possessed by a spirit that has robbed him of speech. Whenever it seizes him, it throws him to the ground. He foams at the mouth, gnashes his teeth and becomes rigid (9:17–18). Many have pointed out that the boy's symptoms fit descriptions of epileptic seizures (see Matt. 17:15), but Mark intends to describe the severity of the boy's suffering under the power of an unclean spirit rather than to give evidence for some medical diagnosis. Pilch argues, "The Western tendency to rationalize the ancient understanding of spirits is rooted in the fact that the Westerners have much more power over their lives and circumstances than the ancients believed they had."[213] Attempts to give the boy's self-destructive affliction (Mark 9:22) a modern medical name do not alleviate the evil behind it. Demonic powers always seek to destroy. Josephus comments in an aside that what are called demons "enter the living and kill them unless aid is forthcoming."[214]

The exorcisms in Mark are not simply deeds of kindness and compassion but demonstrations of the divine power and wrath against Satan. In contrast to 5:1–13, this exorcism is not a struggle with a demon but a struggle for faith (9:21–24). It serves as a concrete example of the truth of Paul's statement that the gospel "is the power of God for the salvation of everyone who believes" (Rom. 1:16).

The spirit shrieked, convulsed him violently and came out. The boy looked so much like a corpse that many said, "He's dead" (9:26). Demons always cause some kind of harm or noise when they exit. The final attack elicits the crowd's skeptical deduction. In 9:27, Jesus takes the boy by the hand (see 1:31; 5:41) and by his power "raises him" (the literal Greek rendering), as it were, from the dead.

His disciples asked him privately, "Why couldn't we drive it out?" (9:28). The scene reveals how feeble the disciples are when left to their own devices. In the ancient world, magicians sought to hit the right combination to invoke the power to achieve the desired goals. They weaved esoteric spells using special words, performed unusual actions, and utilized special instruments. Success was all a matter of technique that would force the power to do the bidding of the sorcerer. The disciples' question about what they did wrong verges on this attitude.

[And fasting] (9:29). This phrase appears in most of the later New Testament manuscripts but is unlikely to be original. Fasting was an interest of the early church, and the phrase was frequently combined to references to prayer (see its addition to the text in Acts 10:30; 1 Cor. 7:5).[215] Fasting does not fit the context because Jesus has already discouraged fasting as inappropriate until the bridegroom is taken away (Mark 2:18–20). He can hardly fault the disciples for failing to do what he has discouraged. He also stresses that the power for exorcism emanates from humble dependence on God, not from some work they perform.

REFLECTIONS

JESUS' ANSWER REVEALS THAT prayer is not a magical incantation but a total openness to God's action in and through us. Prayer stops looking to us asking, Why couldn't *we* drive it out? Disciples do not need to learn better techniques but must make themselves more receptive to the action of God. Since Jesus does not pray before performing the exorcism, prayer is not a one-time invocation of God's power. While special prayers for healing are uttered by Christians (Acts 9:40; 28:8; James 5:15), effective prayer is a continuous posture, not simply an emergency procedure.

The Second Announcement of Jesus' Death and Resurrection (9:30–37)

Jesus did not want anyone to know where they were, because he was teaching his disciples (9:30–31). Jesus' public ministry in Galilee is coming to an end, and he desires to spend time teaching his disciples privately, particularly about his suffering and death.

He took a little child and had him stand among them (9:36). To squelch the disciples' hankering for worldly greatness, Jesus uses a child as an illustration of kingdom greatness. No romanticized notion of children existed in the first century. Children had no power, status, or rights. They were not considered full persons and were regarded as somewhat akin to property. They were dependent, vulnerable, unlearned, and entirely subject to the authority of the father. The rabbis classified children with the deaf, the dumb, the weak-minded, and slaves. Nowhere else in this period do we find children appealed to as examples to be imitated. To become as a child basically means to recognize one's insignificance. What evokes repentance is the realization that one is as small and slight as a child before God.

The Strange Exorcist (9:38–41)

Do not stop him (9:39). Jesus' response to the exorcist who "was not one of us" is similar to Moses' answer when Joshua pled with him to stop unauthorized prophets (Num. 11:26–30). Moses responded, "Are you jealous. . . ? Would that all the LORD's people were prophets" (11:29). Disciples are up against hostile forces and will need all the friends they can get. Jesus therefore blesses the humblest act of compassion shown to those who bear his name.

Temptations to Sin (9:42–50)

It would be better for him to be thrown into the sea with a large millstone tied around his neck (9:42). A "large millstone" reads literally "a millstone of a donkey," that is, a donkey-powered millstone. This millstone was pierced in the middle to fit a beam attached to a blindfolded donkey, who circled round and round to grind grain or olives.

If your hand . . . foot . . . eye causes you to sin (9:43, 45, 47). The eye is the cause of covetousness, stinginess, and jealousy. A rabbinic tradition speaks of adultery with the hand (masturbation) and with the foot (a euphemism for the male member), but we cannot limit this passage only to sexual sins.[216] Self-mutilation was prohibited in Judaism, so Jesus does not intend for one to carry this out literally.[217] He means it is better to accept rigorous discipline now than be punished later.

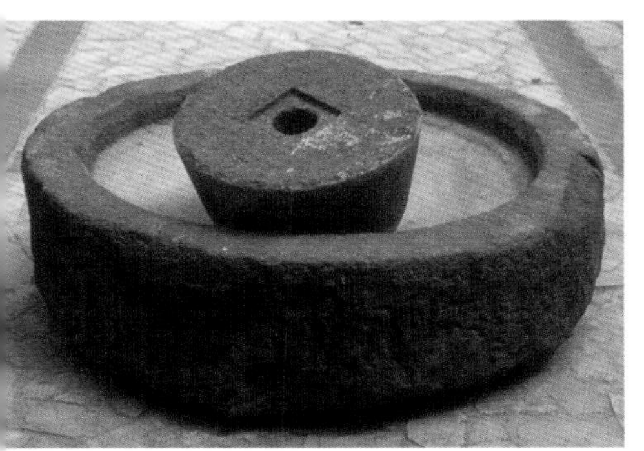

◀ *left*

MILLSTONE

A large olive press made from basalt found in Galilee at Tabgha.

Thrown into hell (9:47). *Gehenna* (translated "hell") derives from the valley of Ben Hinnom outside Jerusalem, where idolaters had once offered child sacrifices.[218] It was later used as a garbage dump, and the burning waste became a vivid image for the place of final punishment.

Where "'their worm does not die, and the fire is not quenched'" (9:48). Jesus quotes the last line of Isaiah (66:24). Worms and fire are images of putrid decay (see Acts 12:23) and flaming destruction (see Rev. 14:11; Judith 16:17), but eternal worms and unquenchable fire (see also Mark 9:43), emitting a noxious stench and an impenetrable column of smoke, refer to everlasting torment. It also means that these sinners will serve as an enduring warning to others of the dangers of sin.

Everyone will be salted with fire (9:49). Salt had many functions. It could be used to preserve and purify or to destroy (Judg. 9:45).[219] An early interpretation of this saying appears in a textual variant: "for every sacrifice will be salted with salt" (from Lev. 2:13). The thought may be that disciples are to become sacrifices to God offered up in fiery persecutions. An apocalyptic text reads: "And then all will pass through the blazing river and the unquenchable flame. All the righteous will be saved. But the impious will then be destroyed for all ages. . . ."[220]

Have salt in yourselves, and be at peace with each other (9:50). These sayings are parallel. Having salt "among yourselves" means to share salt or eat together (Ezra

4:14 [lit. trans.]; Acts 1:4), which is to be done in a spirit of peace.

Question about Divorce (10:1–12)

Jesus then left that place and went into the region of Judea and across the Jordan (10:1). "Judea and across the Jordan" reverses the natural geographical order but indicates that Judea is the goal of the journey (see 11:1, where Jerusalem is mentioned before Bethphage and Bethany).

"JUDEA" COINS

First Jewish coins struck in the land of Israel. These date from 333 B.C. and bear the Hebrew inscription, "Yehud," the Aramaic name for the Persian satrapy of Judea.

They said, "Moses permitted a man to write a certificate of divorce and send her away" (10:4). In biblical times, divorce was not a judgment decided by some court of law. It was an independent action taken by a husband against his wife. The husband's absolute right to divorce his wife was taken for granted by nearly all Jews. According to the rabbis, "The man that divorces is not like the woman that is divorced; for a woman is put away with her consent or without it, but a husband can put away his wife only with his consent."[221] Josephus shares that he divorced his second wife because he was "displeased with her behavior."[222] The husband was only restrained from divorcing his wife if she were insane and unable to care for herself, in captivity,[223] or too young to understand,[224] if he had brought false charges of premarital fornication (Deut. 22:13–19) against her, or if he had seduced her and thus had to marry her (22:28–29).

Malachi 2:13–16 contains the only protest against putting away a wife in the Old Testament, but the Targum to Malachi 2:16 refashions the text to match common practice, rendering it, "If you hate her, divorce her." One rabbi even claimed it was meritorious to divorce a bad wife (citing Prov. 18:22). If her *ketuba*, the sum the husband agreed to pay the wife if he divorced her, was large, he advised marrying another to subject her to the anguish of having a rival.[225]

The instruction given in Deuteronomy 24:1–4 was intended to regulate the practice of putting away a wife, not to give the legitimate grounds for divorce. When a husband decided to divorce his wife, the law of Moses required him to give her a bill of divorce and forbad him from ever remarrying her after she became the wife of another man who later divorced her or died. The abomination is not divorce but remarrying the first wife. The law was primarily aimed at preventing this abomination from occurring in Israel.

The Temple Scroll from Qumran envisaged a time when God would renew the people of Israel and the laws concerning divorce, among others, would become passé since there would be no divorce.[226] Jesus' teaching on divorce assumes that this renewal has already dawned.

But at the beginning of creation God "made them male and female" (10:6). Jesus asks what Moses *commanded* (10:3) and his opponents respond with what Moses *permitted* (10:4). This response opens the door for Jesus to make his point: Divorce is not a command but a concession because of hardness of heart. The legal stipulations regarding divorce do not mean that God approves of divorce. God's will is to be found in the beginning, in creation. Citing texts combined from the first book of Moses (Gen. 1:27; 2:24), Jesus implies that they contain God's intention for marriage and Moses' real command.

Anyone who divorces his wife and marries another woman commits adultery against her (10:11). Jesus contends that marriage is not simply a legal bond but becomes a blood relationship of two persons joined together by God. In Sirach 25:26, we find the advice that if your wife does not go as you would have her go, you should cut her off from your flesh. Jesus rejects any view that regards the spouse as a superfluous limb that can be easily severed. The one flesh relationship is dissolved only by death.

By definition, adultery was the violation of the marriage of your fellow of the covenant, adulterating his property. A man does not violate his own marriage or commit adultery against his wife but only violates the marriage of another married man. Jesus' radical pronouncement holds the husband guilty of adultery against his wife for remarrying.

If she divorces her husband and marries another man, she commits adultery (10:12). Only Mark's account of Jesus' teaching on divorce reckons with the possibility of a woman initiating divorce. In the Greco-Roman world, wives were allowed to divorce their husbands, but this action was disallowed in Judaism. A wife could only take steps that would induce her husband to divorce her. We find accounts, however, of women from the Jewish upperclass divorcing their husbands. Josephus reports that Salome, the sister of Herod the Great, sent her husband a bill of divorce and self-righteously declares that it "was not in accordance with Jewish law." He goes on to comment, "For it is (only) the man who is permitted by us to do this, and not even a divorced woman may marry again on her own initiative unless her former husband consents."[227] Josephus also reports that Drusilla, the sister of Herod Agrippa (Acts 25:13), "was persuaded to

Certificates of Divorce in Judaism

Gittin, a tractate in the Mishnah, is devoted to the legal ins and outs of divorce bills. It outlines the procedures to be followed in securing witnesses, the contents of the bill, how it is to be delivered (e.g., the husband is not to slip it in her hands at night while she is asleep), and what to do if he should want to withdraw it. The certificate of divorce meant that the husband gave up his right to his wife. It basically said: "Lo, thou art free to marry any man."[A-33] This certificate allowed her to remarry without fear of being accused of adultery or of being reclaimed by her former husband.

The marriage contract was vital because it specified the amount of money she was to receive if she were divorced or if her husband died. A copy of one belonging to a woman named Babata was uncovered in the Bar Cochba caves. The document was specially wrapped among bundles of others that she kept in a leather purse. It reads, "If I go to my resting place before you, you shall dwell in my house and receive maintenance from it and from my possessions, until such time as my heirs choose to pay you your *Kethuba* money."[A-34] Yadin speculates that she "spent most of her life in litigation, either suing the guardians of her fatherless son or being sued by the various members of her deceased husbands' families."[A-35] transgress the ancestral laws" by leaving her husband to marry the Roman governor, Felix.[228] Josephus describes Herodias, who left her husband to marry Herod Antipas, as "taking into her head to flout the ways of our fathers."[229] Jesus may be alluding to this case here.

Bringing Children to Jesus (10:13–16)

People were bringing little children to Jesus to have him touch them (10:13). Infant mortality was high in this time. Six of every ten children died before the age of sixteen. "The picture is one of peasant women, many of whose babies would be dead within their first year, fearfully holding them out for Jesus to touch."[230] These parents come from outside the circles of the disciples, and they hope his touch will protect their children from evil. Jesus' loving response reveals that the new community he founds embraces little ones.

The Rich Man (10:17–31)

"Why do you call me good?" Jesus answered. "No one is good—except God alone (10:18). Jesus responds sharply to the man's deference. Malina and Rohrbaugh contend concerning this culture:

> Compliments conceal envy, not unlike the evil eye. Jesus must fend off the aggressive accusation by denying any special quality of the sort that might give offense to others. Such a procedure is fully in line with the canons of honor. The honorable person, when challenged, pushes away the challenge and diffuses any accusations that might fuel the position of his opponents.[231]

The man may be implying that while Jesus is a good teacher, he is a good man and should have as great a reputation as he has.

Go, sell everything you have and give to the poor, and you will have treasure in heaven. Then come, follow me (10:21). At Qumran, members were required to contribute all their wealth to the common treasury (see also Acts 4:32–37; 5:1–11). The rabbis, however, forbad giving away one's property. They limited giving to no more than 20 percent to prevent one from being reduced to poverty by excessive generosity.[232]

But this man is identified as a rich man (10:22–23). The average peasant assumed that the rich had defrauded others by taking more than their fair share of a limited pie.[233] In the New Testament, the rich are condemned as those who oppress the poor (James 2:6), plunder the property of helpless widows (Mark 12:40; Luke 20:47), and defraud their laborers (James 5:1–6). They live in incredible luxury and fare sumptuously (Mark 6:17–23; Luke 16:19–21) while ignoring the abject poverty of those at their doorstep. They built up surpluses only for themselves, disregarding the disastrous consequences for the rest of society (Luke 12:13–21).

When we read "rich" in the New Testament, we should understand it to mean the greedy, dishonorable rich, unless they act in notably charitable ways (see Matt. 27:57–60). Therefore, when Jesus asks this man to sell all that he has and give to the destitute, he is simply asking him to redistribute his wealth among those who lack the necessities of life because their portion has been snatched from them. He will simply be returning to them their share. Almsgiving was also associated with true conversion (see Luke 19:8).[234]

It is easier for a camel to go through the eye of a needle than for a rich man to enter the kingdom of God (10:25). Jesus uses a deliberately absurd image. The opening of a needle was the smallest thing imaginable, and the camel was the largest animal in Palestine (cf. Matt. 23:24, where camels are contrasted with gnats). A rabbinic tradition from the Babylonian Talmud remarks that dreams are a reflection of man's thought: "This is proven by the fact that a man is never shown in a dream a date palm of gold or an elephant going through the eye of a needle."[235] The elephant was the largest animal in Mesopotamia, where this tradition was compiled.

Interpretations that try to reduce the size of the camel or enlarge the needle's eye are suspect. There is no basis for the widely circulated tradition that the eye of the needle was the name of a gate in Jerusalem. Walled cities had smaller gates beside or built into a larger gate so that people could enter when the larger gate was closed. Large animals might be able to squeeze through such a gate. Theophylact (eleventh century) seems to have been the first to make this suggestion.[236] Luke uses a different word in Greek for "needle" (*belonē*, Luke 18:25) than Mark (*raphis*). If a gate had been known as "The Needle's Eye," it seems likely that only one Greek term would have been used. Also to be rejected is the textual variant in a couple ancient versions that have the similar sounding *kamilos*, meaning a rope or ship's cable, instead of camel (*kamēlos*). The disciples' shocked response (Mark 10:24a, 26a) reveals that they understand Jesus' statement to be extreme.

Jesus clearly rejects the presumption that prosperity equals divine blessing.[237] His pronouncement recalls the danger of the deceit of riches choking the seed (4:19) and makes clear that salvation is only a divine possibility. It does not mean, however, that wealth is the only obstacle to salvation.

Jesus' Third Announcement of His Death and Resurrection (10:32–45)

They were on their way up to Jerusalem (10:32). Regardless of the direction from which one came, one always "went up" to the holy city. Jesus leads the way to his Passion, as he will later lead the way to Galilee after the resurrection (14:28; 16:7).

Let one of us sit at your right and the other at your left in your glory (10:37). The disciples recognize that Jesus is destined for great power and ask for special distinction in his messianic kingdom. When Vitellius accepted the title of emperor in A.D. 68, he praised his generals and "placed them on either side of his curule chair."[238] According to the *Psalms of Solomon* 17:26, the Messiah will judge the tribes of Israel, and the disciples may be bidding to share in this messianic authority. Jesus censures the sinful human craving for positions of honor above others.

Can you drink the cup I drink or be baptized with the baptism I am baptized with? (10:38). The cup is the cup of suffering from divine judgment.[239] Baptism paints an image of being submerged in suffering (Ps. 42:7; 69:1). The disciples, however, will sleep as Jesus confronts alone in prayer the cup of his bitter destiny (Mark 14:36–41).

Whoever wants to be first must be slave of all (10:44). The years have dulled the shocking nature of this statement. Plato has Callicles ask: "How can anyone be happy when he is the slave of anyone else at all?"[240] The slave experienced "civil death" with no legal or human rights. Seneca characterizes a slave as one who "does not have the right to refuse."[241] The slave's entire life was at the disposal of the master.

For even the Son of Man did not come to be served, but to serve, and to give his life as a ransom for many (10:45). To ransom someone or something means to pay a price to secure its freedom, but it is also a biblical image for the redemption of God's people.[242] Isaiah speaks of making the life of the Suffering Servant "a guilt offering," which brings forgiveness for the lives of the many.[243] In *4 Maccabees* 6:28–29 and 17:20–22, the death of martyrs is understood to afford vicarious atonement for the people. The difference from Jesus' statement here is that it understands the martyr's death as providing victory over an evil tyrant, whereas Jesus' death offers final deliverance from all evil.

Malina and Rohrbaugh point out that only one of supreme honor could ransom a great number of others who collectively have less honor. Though the king might be just one person, he is worth a whole kingdom of other individuals.[244]

JUDEA

The route from Jericho to Jerusalem.

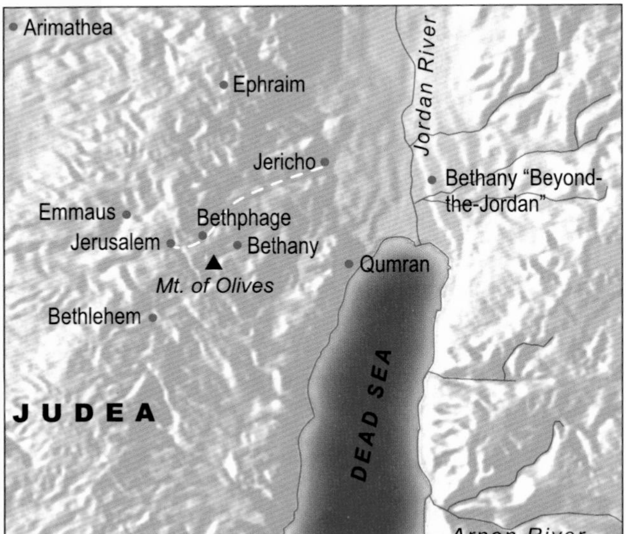

The word "many" may suggest an elite number—many but not all. The "many," however, is a Semitism for "all" (see Mark 1:34; Rom. 5:15, 19). They stand over against the one Son of Man, who acts on their behalf.

Blind Bartimaeus (10:46–52)

Then they came to Jericho (10:46). Galilean Jews on pilgrimage to Jerusalem took a detour around Samaria by passing through Perea on the east side of the Jordan. Coming to Jericho, they would make the journey's final leg up the steep road to Jerusalem.

A blind man, Bartimaeus (that is, the Son of Timaeus), was sitting by the roadside begging (10:46). Bartimaeus camps along this road to beg alms of the pilgrims. As a blind man, he is not only impoverished but also excluded from participation in the temple worship.[245] A text from Qumran even excludes the blind from the messianic banquet.[246] Since there were so many blind persons in this world, the crowds have become inured to their plight.

Jesus, Son of David, have mercy on me! (10:47). The title "Son of David" appears only here in Mark. In this context, it does not have the nationalistic and militaristic connotation normally associated with the term (see *Pss. Sol.* 17). It affirms Jesus' royal authority "expressed in therapeutic works of mercy and deliverance."[247] The healing is linked to another Isaian theme (Isa. 35:1–7; 42:16).

Throwing his cloak aside, he jumped to his feet and came to Jesus (10:50). The cloak was placed before him to collect alms. It may be his sole worldly possession.[248] He abandons it to come to Jesus

Rabbi, I want to see (10:51). He addresses Jesus as *Rabbouni* in the Greek (see John 20:16). This means "My dear Rabbi" and expresses more reverent homage than simply "Rabbi" (see Mark 9:5).

Entry into Jerusalem (11:1–11)

As they approached Jerusalem and came to Bethphage and Bethany at the Mount of Olives (11:1). Bethphage (meaning "house of early figs") is located closer to Jerusalem than Bethany and is near the summit of the Mount of Olives. Bethany is on the southeastern slopes of the Mount of Olives.

You will find a colt tied there, which no one has ever ridden. Untie it and bring it here (11:2). Jesus has walked everywhere else in his ministry except when he crossed the lake in a boat. Riding a colt on this last stage of his journey becomes an enacted symbol that communicates forcefully and dramatically that Jesus is the king of Israel. (1) He impresses the animal as a king would. "The Lord needs it" is the same phrase used to justify David's eating of the bread of the Presence (cf. 2:25). (2) He impresses the use of a young donkey that has never been ridden. This fits a royal motif. It is an animal suitable for a sacred purpose and worthy of a king.[249] According to the Mishnah, no one else may ride a king's horse.[250] (3) The disciples saddle it with their own garments. When Jehu is anointed king, every man took his garment, put it under him on the steps, and proclaimed, "Jehu is king" (2 Kings 9:12–13). This entry into the city may have fueled the charge brought against Jesus to Pilate that he was king of the Jews (Mark 15:2).

A donkey would be apt for a king, but Mark does not identify the animal. Riding "a colt" may express humility. This idea is drawn from Zechariah 9:9, though Mark makes no explicit reference to this verse. He does use the word for the donkey's foal that appears in the LXX version

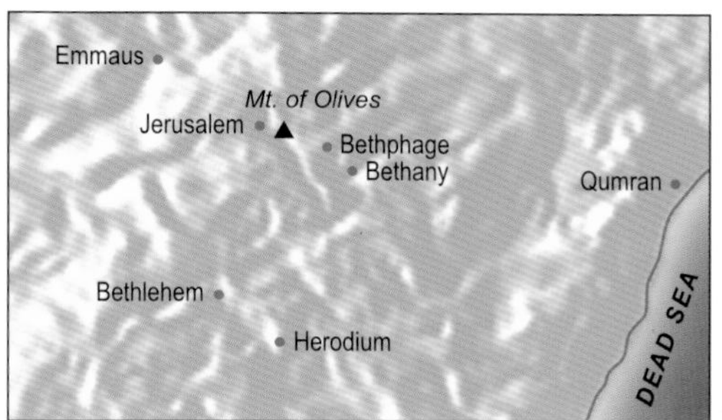

BETHPHAGE, BETHANY, AND JERUSALEM

BETHANY

(left) The location of the ancient road from Bethany to Bethphage. *(right)* The countryside near Jerusalem.

of Zechariah 9:9. A later rabbinic tradition interprets Daniel 7:13 and Zechariah 9:9 to mean that if Israel is worthy, the Messiah will come upon the clouds; and if not, he will come on a donkey.[251] We cannot know if this tradition was current in the first century.

As they untied it (11:4). Twice Mark mentions that the colt is bound and must be untied. This factor may purposely link to Genesis 49:10–12, where the one to whom the scepter of Judah belongs binds his colt to the choicest branch and washes his garments in wine.

Others spread branches they had cut in the fields (11:8). The practice of spreading branches occurred at various festivals—at the Feast of Dedication and the Feast of Tabernacles.[252] It fits the joyous nature of the Passover celebration.

Hosanna! Blessed is he who comes in the name of the Lord! (11:9). "Hosanna" is a Greek transliteration of the Hebrew *Hôšî'âh nā'*, which means "save" or "help, please." Jesus' eye-catching entry into Jerusalem parallels other triumphant entries into the city. After Simon destroyed the last shred of opposition to Maccabean rule by capturing the citadel in the city, "the Jews entered it with praise and palm branches, and with harps and cymbals and stringed instruments, and with hymns and songs, because a great enemy had been crushed and removed from Israel" (1 Macc. 13:51). Josephus reports that in the rebellion against the census of Quirinius, Menahem broke into King Herod's armory on Masada and "returned like a veritable king to Jerusalem" and became a leader of the revolution laying siege to the palace.[253] Jesus' entry may have set up expectations of a kingly rule, but his purpose and actions starkly contrast with those of military ambitions.

Jesus entered Jerusalem and went to the temple. He looked around at everything (11:11). Jesus' surveying the area and then leaving recalls Malachi's prophecy of the Lord visiting his temple.[254]

Worshipers entered and exited the temple grounds through the Double Gate in the south wall.[255] From a broad plaza one climbed thirty steps that alternated

▸ Josephus Offers a Firsthand Description of the Temple

All who ever saw our Temple are aware of the general design of the building, and the inviolable barriers which preserved its sanctity. It had four surrounding courts, each with its special statutory restrictions. The outer court was open to all, foreigners included; women during their time of impurity were alone refused admission. To the second court all Jews were admitted, and, when uncontaminated by any defilement, their wives; to the third male Jews, if clean and purified; to the fourth the priests robed in their priestly vestments.

The sanctuary was entered only by the high priests, clad in the raiment peculiar to themselves. So careful is the provision for all the details of the service that the priests' entry is timed to certain hours. Their duty was to enter in the morning, when the Temple was opened, and to offer the customary sacrifices, and again at mid-day, until the Temple was closed.

One further point: no vessel whatever might be carried into the Temple, the only objects in which were an altar, a table, a censer, and a lampstand, all mentioned in the Law. There was nothing more; no unmentionable mysteries took place, no repast was served within the building.[A-36]

between steps and landings to force an unhurried, reverent ascent. The steps are estimated to have been 210 feet wide. The arch and the original lintel of the Double Gate are still intact, though partially concealed by the remains of a tower built by the Crusaders. Inside the vestibule were domes, sixteen feet in diameter, chiseled with beautifully painted floral and geometric designs. One climbed the tunnel passageway and exited in the temple esplanade. The Royal Stoa lay behind.

The Triple Gate was used by priests and to reach the storerooms for the wine, oil, and flour. In between these gates stood a bathhouse for ritual purification and a council house. Three such courts are mentioned in the Mishnah: a court at the gate of the temple mount, at the entrance to the temple court, and in the Chamber of Hewn Stone (*m. Sanh.* 11:2).

The Temple Incident and the Cursing of the Fig Tree (11:12–25)

Then he said to the tree, "May no one ever eat fruit from you again" (11:14). Pliny, the Elder, observed, "The fig tree is also the only tree whose leaf forms later than its fruit."[256] Since it sets its fruit before producing leaves, once it has broken into leaf, it should have produced fruit.

Jesus' odd cursing of a fig tree—the only miracle that brings death and not life—becomes an enacted parable. Jeremiah's outburst against the temple provides the backdrop for understanding it. God forbids the prophet to make any intercession for the people (Jer. 7:16) and then says that his "wrath will be poured out on this place, on man and beast, on the trees of the field and on the fruit of the ground, and it will burn and not be quenched" (7:20). The parable of the tenants of the vineyard makes the same point: The tenants [of the temple] have borne no fruit to give to the owner and are subsequently destroyed.

Fruitfulness was a symbol of Israel's covenant relation to God. At one point, God delighted in Israel because it was like seeing the early fruit on the fig tree (Hos. 9:10). The blighted tree in a land where trees are scarce becomes a symbol of God's judgment.[257] Withered to the roots, there is no hope for this fig tree's renewal.

FIG BRANCH

REFLECTIONS

THE TEMPLE HAD BECOME A SACRED COW, PARTICULARLY for those whose livelihood and dominance depended on the sacrificial system. Jesus recognizes that this institution is barren despite the veneer of piety and holiness. In challenging it, he takes on a massive mountain of tradition and entrenched power. Boldly condemning religious or political corruption has its costs. Holders of power usually do not placidly tolerate denunciation but will strike out to crush their nemeses. Many Christians, therefore, remain shamefully silent before wickedness, particularly when it is manifested within their own group. Jesus' prophetic defiance cost him his life. The result is an atoning sacrifice that replaces once and for all the system of animal sacrifices.

Jesus . . . began driving out those who were buying and selling there (11:15). Those buying and selling are trafficking in animals for the sacrifices. The priestly aristocracy's wealth and influence are directly attributable to their control of the fiscal affairs of the temple. Since Jesus throws out *both* buyers and sellers, something more than dishonest profiteering provokes him.

Archaeological discoveries suggest that the temple market was inside the Royal Stoa and not spread out all over the so-called court of the Gentiles.[258] The Royal Stoa was at the intersection of the paved streets of Jerusalem. The main street that ran the length of the Tyropoeon Valley headed north along the western wall of the temple was directly accessible via the steps leading down from Robinson's Arch to the markets on the streets below. The main part of the Stoa was a long rectangular Hall of Columns built in the design of a basilica, with 162 columns in four rows stretching the length of the hall. Josephus describes it as "a structure more worthy to be spoken of than any other under the sun."[259] Mazar concludes that the Royal Stoa contained a smaller market that "served primarily for commerce in the cultic provisions for the Temple."[260]

We should not suppose that the changing of money and the selling of sacrificial objects compromised the holiness of the temple. Some kind of market was

TYRIAN SHEKELS

necessary for the daily operation of the temple. The biblical requirement of offering unblemished sacrifices to God necessitated having a supply of sacrificial animals on hand, a means of inspecting the animals for disqualifying blemishes, and a monetary exchange for pilgrims. This activity does not take place within the sacred space of the sanctuary.

He overturned the tables of the money changers (11:15). Tables were set up in the outer courts three weeks before Passover to receive the annual half-shekel tax required of every Jewish male (Ex. 30:11–16).[261] This tax funded the daily sacrifices for the atonement of sin.[262] For a modest commission, money changers exchanged inadmissible local currencies for the sanctioned Tyrian shekel used to pay the tax. Jewish authorities were forbidden to mint silver coins, and they adopted the Tyrian shekel because of its high quality and because it did not flaunt Rome's dominion over Israel. These coins, however, had an image of the god Melkart (Herakles) on the obverse and an eagle with the inscription, "Tyre the holy and inviolable," on the reverse.

The benches of those selling doves (11:15). Doves were the staple sacrifice of the poor who could not afford animals for sin offerings (Lev. 5:7). They were also used for the purification of poor women after child birth (12:6, 8; Luke 2:22–24), for men and women who had a bodily discharge (Lev. 15:14, 29), and for poor ex-lepers (14:21–22). An incident recorded in the Mishnah describes a time when the cost of doves was exorbitant (two golden dinars for a pair of doves). Fearing that the poor would not bring their offerings at these prices, Rabbi Simeon, the son of Gamaliel, gave a ruling that only one offering would suffice for the five that were required. The bottom fell out of the price in one day to half a silver dinar (1 percent of the original cost).[263]

He . . . would not allow anyone to carry merchandise through the temple courts (11:16). This translation is misleading. It is perhaps based on Josephus's report that no one was allowed to carry vessels into the sanctuary[264] and a passage from the Mishnah that forbids using the temple as a shortcut.[265] The text, however, says that Jesus prevents them from carrying a "*vessel* through the temple." "Vessel" is used in the LXX for the sacred temple vessels for the bread of the Presence, lamp oil, and incense censers (see Isa. 52:11: "the vessels of the LORD").

The people involved are probably stunned by the power of Jesus' moral indignation. It is a modest clash since it does not spark the intervention of the Roman soldiers, who monitor the crowd from their post above the temple court in the Antonia Fortress (contrast Acts 21:34). Jesus' actions in the temple market, therefore, do not seem to be some attempt to reform the temple practice. Overturning and driving out evoke images of judgment rather than reform. Those involved will soon set right their tables and pick up the scattered money. There is little comparison to what Jesus did and the purification of the temple by Josiah (2 Kings 23) or Judas Maccabeus (1 Macc. 4:36–59).

He is not clearing commercial space for prayer. There is no evidence that the outer court was thought of positively as the place where Gentiles could worship. On the contrary, it was thought of as an area beyond which Gentiles could not go. The balustrade surrounding the sanctuary had warning signs cautioning any Gentile against proceeding any further, threatening death to violators (see Acts

REFLECTIONS

JESUS' ACTIONS ARE INTENTIONALLY symbolic. Like prophets of old, he makes a dramatic gesture acting out God's rejection of the temple cult and its coming destruction. He assaults the foundation of the temple's operation: the contributions and sacrifices. If money cannot be exchanged into the holy currency, then monetary support for the temple sacrifices and the priesthood must end. If sacrificial animals cannot be purchased, then sacrifice must end. If no vessel can be carried through the temple, then all cultic activity must cease. He makes his point. The chief priests will take up his challenge and ask him by what authority he does these things (11:28).

Jesus also attacks the temple operations that tended to encourage the merchandising of religion. Any church or ministry that tries to take advantage of the presence of God to make a profit, to hawk religious benefits like the peddlers in the bazaar, or to build a financial empire stands under his judgment.

THE ANTONIA FORTRESS

A model of the Roman fortress showing the temple precincts in the foreground.

21:27–30). There was plenty of room for Gentiles to pray in the outer court, and clearing a place for them to pray does not remove the barrier that kept them from the sacred place.

But you have made it "a den of robbers" (11:17). This citation from Jeremiah condemns the Jewish leaders for turning God's sanctuary into a sanctuary for bandits. The den was the hideout where robbers retreated after committing their crimes—their place of security and refuge.

Therefore I tell you, whatever you ask for in prayer (11:24). The temple was regarded as the place where prayer was particularly effective; thus, when one was not in the temple, one should orient oneself toward it in prayer.[266] This belief is reflected in the high priest's prayer in *3 Maccabees* 2:10: "And because you love the house of Israel, you promised that if we should have reverses and tribulation should overtake us, you would listen to our petition when we come to this place and pray." Lament over the effect of the temple's destruction on Israel's prayer is recorded in the Talmud:

> R. Eleazar said: From the day on which the Temple was destroyed, the gates of prayer have closed, as it says, "Yea, when I cry for help, He shutteth out my prayer" (Lam. 3:8).... R. Eleazar also said: Since the day that the Temple was destroyed, a wall of iron divides between Israel and their Father in Heaven; as it says, "And take thou unto thee an iron griddle and set it for a wall of iron between thee and the city" (Ezek. 4:3).[267]

Jesus' statement implies that the effectiveness of prayer has nothing to do with the temple or its sacrifices. He will later affirm the judgment of a teacher of the law who says that loving your neighbor as yourself "is more important than all burnt offerings and sacrifices" (12:33).

By what authority are you doing these things? (11:28). The priestly hierarchy take seriously any threats against the temple. Not only is it the holy place where God dwells, it provides the priestly caste its livelihood and status and has an enormous impact on the whole Jerusalem economy. Josephus reports that prior to the war against Rome, the leading citizens of Jerusalem arrested a coarse peasant named Jesus, son of Ananias. He had pronounced woes day and night against the city, the people, and the sanctuary. After arresting him, the magistrates were still unable to silence him. In hopes of doing away with him once and for all, they brought him before the Roman governor, who judged him to be a maniac and had him flayed to the bone.[268]

John's baptism—was it from heaven, or from men? Tell me! (11:30). Answering a question with a counterquestion was a normal debate tactic that changed the power equation. Jesus will answer their question only on his terms—after they answer him. It puts him "in the driver seat."[269] The priests cannot afford to declare John a charlatan and alienate his pious supporters, nor can they openly endorse him and risk accrediting other charismatic prophets who followed after him—like Jesus. The implication is that John was an eschatological prophet whose divine authority had bypassed institutional lines of command, such as the temple hierarchy. The same holds true for Jesus. His action in the temple is that of a prophet directed by God and not a conventicle of priests and teachers of the law.

The Parable of the Tenants (12:1–12)

He put a wall around it, dug a pit for the winepress and built a watchtower (12:1). Stone walls were erected around vineyards to keep out animals and foragers. The towers provided some shelter and a lookout during the grape harvest. The description of the vineyard has striking parallels to Isaiah 5:2 (LXX). Since the hedge, winepress, and tower have no significance in the later development of the story, these details are only included to recall the context in Isaiah that pictures God's lavishing care on the vineyard, his people, but meeting only with ingratitude and unfruitfulness (5:1–7). Jesus' parable is thus an allegory of God's troubled relationship with Israel. A fragment from Qumran has been interpreted as applying Isaiah 5 to the temple.[270] The problem is not a vineyard that yields bad fruit, but tenants who yield no fruit.

Then he rented the vineyard to some farmers and went away on a journey (12:1). The parable reflects the real world of absentee landlords. Resentment against them was typical, but few would ever dare to behave as the parable's tenants did.[271] In Longus's novel, *Daphnis and Chloe* (4.1–14), the master plans to visit the estate where the hero and heroine keep sheep. They work hard to make things as presentable as possible. Daphnis is uneasy about seeing the master who heretofore has been only a name and referred to as the dreaded master. They panic when an enemy vandalizes their garden, assume the master will have them hanged, and pray that he will never come. Then news comes by messenger that their master will arrive in three days but that his son is coming first and will be there the next day. All goes well as Daphnis is commended to the master for doubling his flock.

Then he sent another servant to them (12:4). The word "servant" is a transparent metaphor for the prophets since the Old Testament uses it frequently to describe them.[272] God continually sent prophets to Israel (Jer. 7:25–26). Persistent mistreatment of them was proverbial.[273]

They will respect my son (12:6). Some interpreters debate whether the word

VINEYARD AND WATCHTOWER

(left) A vineyard near the tel of Lachish.

(right) A watchtower in the hills of Samaria.

"son" would have been interpreted messianically in the first century. Evidence from the Dead Sea Scrolls referring to the Son of God and Son of the Most High lends credence to the probability that "son" would have been understood in a messianic sense by the audience.[274]

This is the heir. Come, let's kill him, and the inheritance will be ours (12:7). The son is on a different level than the servants and crucial for a case involving the disputed ownership of a vineyard. The phrase "Come let us kill him" is the same phrase used by Joseph's brothers in Genesis 37:20a (LXX). It serves to heighten the tenants' guilt, which is compounded by their failure to give the body a burial. To be refused honorable burial is a powerful image of humiliating punishment in Scripture.[275]

The stone the builders rejected has become the capstone (12:10). A portion of Psalm 118 was chanted to greet Jesus as he entered Jerusalem (Mark 11:9–10/Ps. 118:25). It is now invoked to explain that the one who is rejected will be vindicated (Ps. 118:22–23). The block of stone that the builders rejected becomes the keystone—the wedge-shaped stone placed in the top of an arch that locks the others into position. It is the head of the new structure. An Aramaic play on words between "son" (*ben*) and "stone" (*'eben*) may lie behind this saying.

Taxes to Caesar (12:13–18)

Pharisees and Herodians (12:13). See comments on 3:6.

Is it right to pay taxes to Caesar or not? (12:14). Judea became a Roman province in A.D. 6 and was subject to the poll tax (or head tax, distinct from the tax on property and customs on articles). The census provided the data (computed in acres and human heads) from which the Romans levied this tax. Its establishment provoked the revolt of Judas of Galilee because it placed God's own land at the service of foreigners.[276] A "yes" answer to Jesus' question invites the charge of turning traitor to God by endorsing Caesar's hegemony over the land. It was also an emotionally charged issue since most residents of Palestine knew someone the Romans sold into slavery, executed, or forced off their land by the whirlpool of debt from the spiraling tax burden. A "no" answer, by contrast, invites the charge of sedition.

Bring me a denarius and let me look at it (12:15). By asking for a denarius that he does not possess, Jesus throws them off their guard. In this era, coins served propaganda purposes. Assuming that they show him a Tiberian denarius, the obverse side bore the image of the emperor with the superscription: "TI[berius] CAESAR DIVI AVG[usti] AVGVSTUS." The reverse had a female

right ▶

COINS

(top) Silver denarius with a portrait of the Roman emperor Tiberius (A.D. 14–37).

(bottom) A coin depicting the emperor Nero (A.D. 54–68).

figure facing right, seated on a throne, with a crown and holding a scepter in the right hand and a palm or olive branch in the left. The superscription reads: "Pontif[ex] Maxim[us]." The Pharisees and Herodians possess a coin oozing idolatry and blasphemy. It touts Tiberius as a divine or semidivine being as the son of the divine Augustus. The woman is a priestess or the wife of Augustus, Livia, proclaiming the *Pax Romana* that places all peoples in subjection.[277]

Give to Caesar what is Caesar's and to God what is God's (12:17). This statement places a limit on Caesar's authority. Those things stamped with Caesar's image, such as mere coins, belong to him. Those things stamped with God's image, such as human beings, belong to God. The image that humans are a coin stamped by God's seal is found in a discussion about idolatry and immorality in the Talmud. Sinful humans misuse the sexual instinct God gives them, resulting in the conception of illegitimate children. God complains about this, "Not enough that the wicked put My coinage to vulgar use, but they trouble Me to set My seal thereon!"[278]

The Question about the Resurrection (12:18–27)

Then the Sadducees, who say there is no resurrection (12:18). The Sadducees considered the Mosaic directives alone as binding and rejected what they perceived to be theological innovations. Consequently, they did not believe in a resurrection since it does not appear in the Pentateuch.[279] Their attitude may be captured in the hymn to honor ancestors in Sirach 44:1–23: The only immortality one can hope for is having posterity and being remembered.[280]

When the dead rise, they will neither marry nor be given in marriage; they will be like the angels in heaven (12:25). The Sadducees understand resurrection to be only reanimation. Jesus declares that life in heaven should not be confused with life on earth. He compares it to the life of angels, who are immortal, making procreation and therefore marriage unnecessary.

Have you not read in the book of Moses, in the account of the bush (12:26). The reference to the "bush" passage reflects how Scripture was cited before chapter and verse divisions. The point is that the living God will not tie his name to three corpses.

The Question about the Great Commandment (12:28–34)

Of all the commandments, which is the most important? (12:28). One rabbi declared that of the 613 commandments given to Moses, 365 were negative precepts, "corresponding to the number of solar days," and 248 were positive commandments, "corresponding to the number of members of a man's body."[281] The Talmud passage goes on to claim that David reduced them to eleven essential principles, Isaiah to six, Micah to three, and Isaiah, again, to two, and Amos to one.[282] This discussion reflects the debate over the relative weight of the various commandments. The rabbis divided them up into light and heavy commandments according to three varying criteria: how severe the penalty was for failing to obey them, how great or little the reward for obeying them, or how easy or difficult they were to fulfill.[283]

Hear, O Israel . . . (12:29). Jesus identifies as absolute the first line in the Shema (Deut. 6:4), recited morning and evening by devout Jews, which commands exclusive love for God. He adds a second that is on the same order, love of one's neighbor. Since love is something that is commanded, it has to do with actions rather than feelings.

Well said, teacher (12:32). The teacher of the law assumes he is in a superior position and able to pass judgments on Jesus' teaching. Jesus, however, is the final arbiter of the law and of who is near or far from the kingdom of God, and he regains mastery by commending his response.

Jesus' Question about David's Son (12:35–37)

Psalm 110 was assumed to refer to a Davidic figure who would reign with God's authority and crush Israel's enemies. Jesus challenges the views about this abstract figure. Sons may address their fathers as "Lord," but never vice versa. Therefore, Jesus uses the psalmist's words to pose a conundrum about himself as the Son of David (Mark 10:47, 48; 11:10).

The Denunciation of the Scribes (12:38–40)

Teachers of the law (12:38). See "Scribes / Teachers of the Law" at 2:7.

They like to walk around in flowing robes (12:38). Jesus attacks the human fondness to seek honor, to parade one's caste, and to call attention to one's piety. The long robes refer to the distinctive white linen robes that set them apart from others. They also expect others to show them the greatest respect and greet them as "Rabbi," "Father," "Master" (Matt. 23:7–9), or "Good teacher" (Mark 10:17) and to offer them the seats of honor.

They devour widows' houses (12:40). Widows are a traditional symbol of the helpless in the Old Testament. Widows without male offspring to protect them were particularly vulnerable, and abusing them is sternly denounced in the Old Testament.[284]

The Widow's Offering (12:41–44)

Jesus sat down opposite the place where the offerings were put and watched the crowd putting their money into the temple treasury (12:41). Jesus' presence in the temple began with his condemnation of the buyers and sellers for the animal sacrifices and ends with his commendation of one who sacrifices her all for God. "Opposite the place where the offerings were put" may refer to a special room in the temple or to one of thirteen chests, shaped like a trumpet, that stood around the Court of Women. The verb translated "putting" is the verb "to throw" and suggests throwing something into a chest. The Mishnah mentions shofar-chests labeled for different types of offerings: "new shekel dues," "old shekel dues" (paid only by males), "bird offerings" (for the purchase of turtle doves), "young birds for whole offerings" (for the purchase of

right ▶

BRONZE LEPTA

A horde of lepta and a terra cotta jar in which they were found.

pigeons), "wood" (for burning on the altar), "frankincense," and "gold for the mercy seat"; six were designated "freewill offerings."[285] The small amount of the widow's contribution means that her gift can only go to the freewill offering, which goes to the building of the temple (see Ex. 35–36; 1 Chron. 29), or burnt offerings, from which the priests receive the hides.[286]

But a poor widow came and put in two very small copper coins, worth only a fraction of a penny (12:42). A widow is indeed poor if she has only two *lepta*. The *lepton* was a tiny copper coin with the least value of any in circulation in the time of Jesus, about one-eighth of a Roman *assarion*. The two *lepta* are said to be worth a *quadrans*, the smallest Roman coin. Four *quadrans* equal an *assarion* which was worth one-sixteenth of a *denarius*. If a day laborer earned a *denarius* for a day's wage (Matt. 20:2), this woman has one-sixty-fourth of that wage. If this is all she has to live on, she is indeed destitute.

A similar story occurs in later rabbinic literature:

> Once a woman brought a handful of fine flour [for a meal offering, Lev. 11:2], and the priest despised her, saying: "See what she offers! What is there to eat? What is there to offer up?" It was shown to him in a dream: "Do not despise her! It is regarded as if she had sacrificed her own life."[287]

Jesus does not need a dream vision to recognize the worth of her extraordinary sacrificial giving.

The Olivet Discourse (13:1–37)

As he was leaving the temple, one of his disciples said to him, "Look, Teacher! What massive stones! What magnificent buildings!" (13:1). The highest walls of the temple mount reached 165 feet. Philo reports that Marcus Agrippa, the grandfather of the emperor Gaius (Caligula), visited Jerusalem and could talk of nothing else "but praise for the sanctuary and all that pertained to it."[288] The wonderful buildings elicited pride and a sense of security because of the conviction that the temple was the place where God dwelt: "This is my resting place for ever" (Ps. 132:14). What the disciples did not see was that this temple was like a barren fig tree.

Not one stone here will be left on another; every one will be thrown down (13:2). We get a glimpse of the devastation wrought by the Roman army's destruction of the temple in A.D. 70 from the imprint of arches burnt into the bedrock foundations of chambers adjoining the southern retaining wall, east of the Triple Gate. The Ritmeyers explain:

> The limestone ashlars used in the Herodian construction can be reduced to powder when exposed to very high temperatures. The Roman soldiers must have put brushwood inside the chambers and the blaze

MODEL OF THE JERUSALEM TEMPLE

HEROD'S TEMPLE

20 B.C. – A.D. 70
Aerial view showing
outer courts

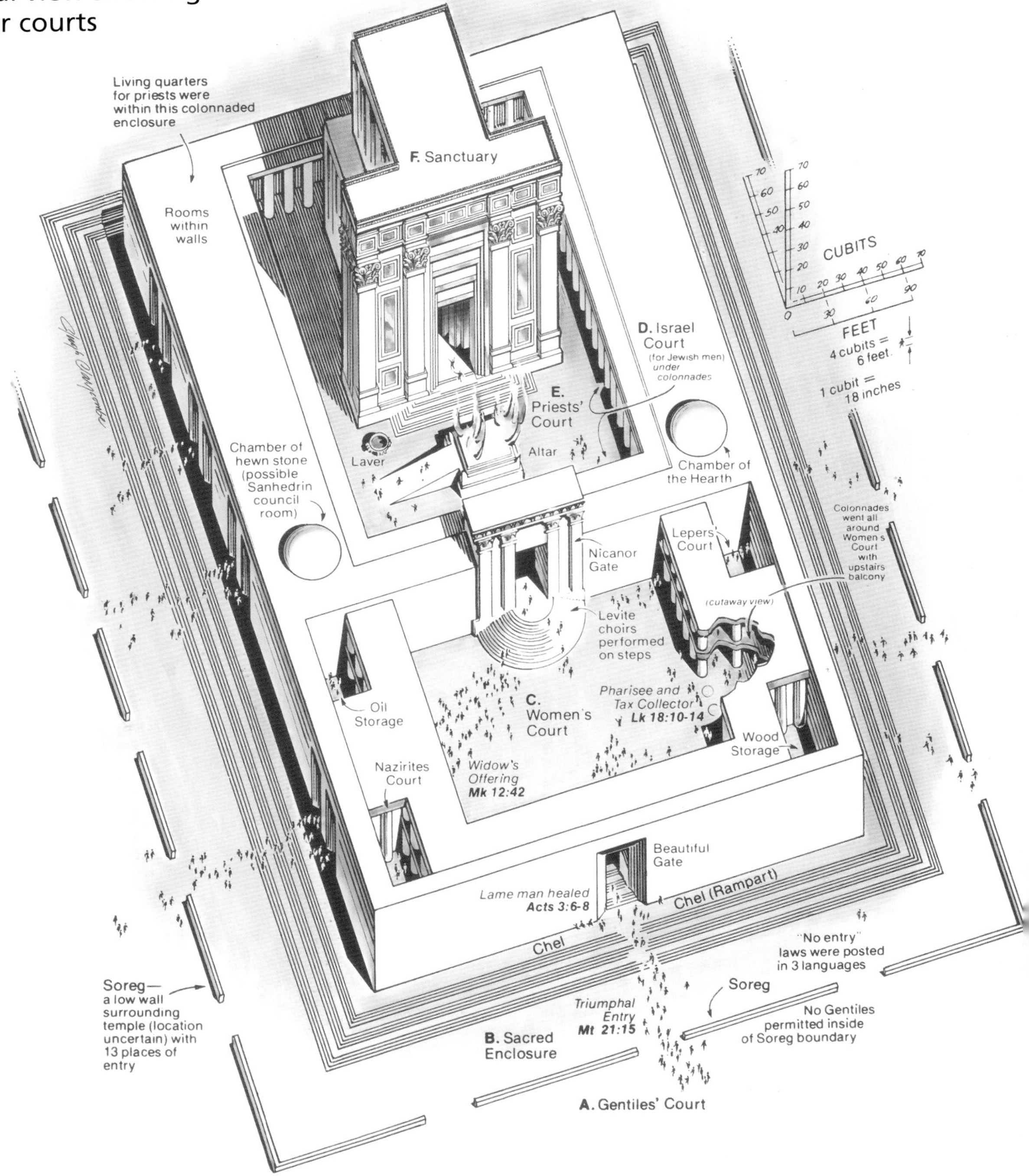

Living quarters for priests were within this colonnaded enclosure

F. Sanctuary

Rooms within walls

CUBITS

FEET

4 cubits = 6 feet

1 cubit = 18 inches

D. Israel Court (for Jewish men) under colonnades

E. Priests' Court

Altar

Laver

Chamber of hewn stone (possible Sanhedrin council room)

Chamber of the Hearth

Colonnades went all around Women's Court with upstairs balcony

Lepers' Court

Nicanor Gate

(cutaway view)

Levite choirs performed on steps

Oil Storage

C. Women's Court

Pharisee and Tax Collector *Lk 18:10-14*

Wood Storage

Nazirites Court

Widow's Offering ***Mk 12:42***

Beautiful Gate

Lame man healed ***Acts 3:6-8***

Chel (Rampart)

Chel

"No entry" laws were posted in 3 languages

Soreg

No Gentiles permitted inside of Soreg boundary

Soreg—a low wall surrounding temple (location uncertain) with 13 places of entry

Triumphal Entry ***Mt 21:15***

B. Sacred Enclosure

A. Gentiles' Court

Dimensions are stated in history (Josephus and the Mishnah) but are subject to interpretation, and all drawings vary.

created when this was set alight would have caused the arches to collapse. The street that was carried by these arches also collapsed. Before the arches collapsed, the fire burnt into the back wall of the chambers, leaving the imprint of the arches as evocative testimony to the dreadful inferno.[289]

As Jesus was sitting on the Mount of Olives opposite the temple (13:3). According to Ezekiel 11:23, the glory of the Lord retreats from a corrupt Jerusalem to the Mount of Olives (see Zech. 14:4). The Mount of Olives was severely deforested by the Romans during their siege of Jerusalem.[290] In Jesus' day, its groves of pines and olives offered pleasant seclusion.

Many will come in my name, claiming, "I am he," and will deceive many (13:6). Jesus warns of a procession of impostors to come (see also 13:21–22). Josephus claimed that what incited the nation to war against Rome more than anything else was "an ambiguous oracle" found "in their sacred scriptures, to the effect that one from their country would become ruler of the world."[291] He himself concluded that

"MASSIVE STONES" OF THE TEMPLE

The western wall ("the wailing wall") of the temple with massive stones from the platform of the Herodian temple.

Josephus on the Magnificence of the Temple

With pride Josephus describes the former glory of the temple:

> Now the exterior of the building wanted nothing that could astound either mind or eye. For, being covered on all sides with massive plates of gold, the sun was no sooner up than it radiated so fiery a flash that persons straining to look at it were compelled to avert their eyes as from solar rays. To approaching strangers it appeared from a distance like a snow-clad mountain; for all that was not overlaid with gold was of purest white.... Some of the stones in the building were forty-five cubits in length, five in height and six in breadth.[A-37]

REFLECTIONS

JESUS DOES NOT ANSWER THE disciples' questions about the signs and timing of the consummation of the age, but gives instructions on how to discern false signs, punctuated by warnings not to be fooled. The emphasis does not fall on *what* to know but on *how* to know. Geddert concludes, "The disciple is not called to *eliminate* his ignorance of the timing of the End, he is called to *cope* with it, and respond to it appropriately."[A-38]

Jesus warns that God's cause will meet with greater and greater resistance from the powers of evil until the end. "The eschatological drama will run its course, scene by scene. But the actors on the stage have only vague clues about where they are precisely in the play. Only the stage director knows. He has given the actors instructions about what to do and what to say when they see certain things happen. But that is it. They know how the play ends, but they do not know when the curtain will fall."[A-39]

MASADA

Roman ramp built up for the assault on Masada in A.D. 70.

it referred not to some Jewish leader but to the Roman general Vespasian and castigates those whom he claimed were worse than the violent revolutionaries:

> Another group of scoundrels, in act less criminal but in intention more evil. . . . Cheats and deceivers, claiming inspiration, they schemed to bring about revolutionary changes by inducing the mob to act as if possessed and by leading them out into the wild country on the pretence that there God would give them signs of approaching freedom.[292]

In the second century, Simon was designated the Messiah by R. Akiba, who dubbed him Bar Cochba, "son of the star." After his defeat, later rabbis called him Bar Cosiba, "son of the lie."

When you hear of wars and rumors of wars, do not be alarmed. Such things must happen, but the end is still to come (13:7). Jesus' warning is exactly the opposite of what is found in *4 Ezra* 9:1–6. In that text, "earthquakes, tumult of peoples, intrigues of nations, wavering of leaders, confusion of princes" are signs of the end. Jesus says that such things are *not* true signs of the end, and they should not cause panic when they occur. They are to be expected along with the persecution that will inevitably befall his followers (13:9–11).

When you see "the abomination that causes desolation" standing where it does not belong (13:14). "Abomination" refers to what is detestable and rejected by God. It is either an abomination (filth) that causes horror (such as pagan idols, Deut. 29:17) or an appalling sacrilege that makes desolate.[293] The warning relates to events surrounding the destruction of Jerusalem. It will be useless to flee to some mountain refuge at the end of the ages. Those who do will have no time to retrieve precious possessions, even essentials, such as cloaks.

If the abomination refers to something before the Jewish revolt, Gaius Caligula commanded that his statue be erected in the temple. Petronius, the legate of Syria, however, stalled in carrying out the order, and Gaius's assassination prevented a confrontation.[294] If it refers to something during the revolt, the Zealots who occupied the temple precincts committed multiple sacrileges.[295] If it refers to something after the revolt, Josephus reports that after the Romans captured Jerusalem, the soldiers set up their standards in the temple and sacrificed to them, and the general Titus stood in the Most Holy Place.[296] But what good will flight do at this point? If it refers to none of these things, it applies to anything or anyone who seeks to usurp God's place, and the flight should be understood metaphorically.[297]

Let the reader understand (13:14). This direction may be some kind of interpretive hint for an esoteric reading of Daniel, or it may be an aside for the one who publicly reads Mark's Gospel to the assembly.[298] Today, personal copies of the Bible are widely available, and many read their Bibles privately. This was not the case in Mark's day, an age of limited literacy. His Gospel would have been read publicly.

Note that the "abomination that causes desolation" is a neuter noun. Good grammar requires the participle "standing" also be neuter, but it is masculine. The aside instructs the one reading the Greek text not to correct the masculine participle with a neuter noun out of some mistaken grammatical sensitivity. What Mark has written, he has written deliberately. The masculine participle makes the abomination refer to a person. Best likens it to our modern *sic*, which is placed after a word that seems odd or misspelled: "But when you see that thing, the abomination of desolation, standing where he [*sic*] should not be. . . ."[299]

Let those who are in Judea flee to the mountains (13:14). Eusebius reports:

> But before the war, the people of the Church of Jerusalem were bidden in an oracle given by revelation to men worthy of it to depart from the city and to dwell in a city of Perea called Pella. To it those who believed in Christ migrated from Jerusalem. Once the holy men had completely left the Jews and all Judea, the justice of God at last overtook them, since they had committed such transgressions against Christ and all his apostles. Divine justice completely blotted out that impious generation among men.[300]

By contrast, Josephus tells of numerous prophets who deluded the people by encouraging them to wait for God's help and to seek refuge in the supposedly inviolate temple court.[301]

Dio Chrysostom expresses amazement at the Jewish resistance to the very end during the revolt:

> The Jews resisted [Titus] with more ardor than ever, as if it were a kind of windfall [an unexpected piece of luck] to fall fighting against a foe far outnumbering them; they were not overcome until a part of the Temple had caught fire. Then some impaled themselves voluntarily on

the swords of the Romans, others slew each other, others did away with themselves or leaped into the flames. They all believed, especially the last, that it was not a disaster but victory, salvation, and happiness to perish together with the Temple.[302]

Let no one on the roof of his house go down or enter the house to take anything out (13:15). Since Palestinian roofs were flat, they served as an extra room of the house. People used them to dry produce (Josh. 2:6), to sleep on during the hot summer months (1 Sam. 9:25), to wile away the hours in talk, and to pray in private (Acts 10:9).

Pray that this will not take place in winter (13:18). Winter is the time of heavy rains in Palestine, flooding roads and wadis.[303] Gadarene refugees during the first revolt sought shelter in Jericho but could not cross the swollen Jordan and were slain by the Romans.[304] Winter travel is also hazardous if people are to traverse mountain passes.

Because those will be days of distress unequaled from the beginning (13:19). All wars bring in their wake horrible suffering. Josephus narrates a lurid tale of terrible famine and a prominent woman cannibalizing her son during the last stages of the siege of Jerusalem as an "act unparalleled in the history whether of Greeks or barbarians and as horrible to relate as it is incredible to hear."[305] Sensationalized stories of cannibalism are not an uncommon feature of siege stories, and this account probably has no factual basis. Josephus simply wanted to convey the horrifying distress that was real.

His description of the terrible inferno that engulfed the city can be verified archaeologically. The Roman soldiers set fire to the temple and the city and plundered and slaughtered the remaining

MEMORIAL OF THE 10TH ROMAN LEGION

The pillar commemorates *Legio X Fretensis,* a key army involved in the attack on Jerusalem and the destruction of the temple.

REFLECTIONS

JESUS CALLS HIS DISCIPLES TO place their trust only in him and his words and to abandon their cherished heritage and false trust in the protection of what is now a spiritually bankrupt temple. God will not save it from destruction. Flight is better than fighting for a lost and unworthy cause. Sadly, Israel fought three wars in A.D. 66–70 (74), 115–17, and 132–35, spurred by nationalistic hopes centered on the temple, until the Romans finally expelled them from Jerusalem and made it an entirely forbidden city to Jews. Christians today should be wary of tethering their hopes to nationalistic aspirations or crusades.

◀ *left*

REMAINS OF THE ROMAN DESTRUCTION OF JERUSALEM

The skeletal remains of a woman's severed arm found in the charred ruins of a first-century Jewish home in Jerusalem.

inhabitants so that "the ground was nowhere visible through the corpses; but the soldiers had to clamber over heaps of bodies in pursuit of the fugitives."[306] The basement of a house in the upper city of Jerusalem was excavated in 1970 and designated the "burnt house" because of the massive amount of ash and soot. Since the coins discovered in the ruins included those minted by the rebels in A.D. 67, 68, and 69 and none is after 70, the conflagration that destroyed this house was caused when the Romans burned the Upper City.[307] Josephus vividly recounts the events (see comments on 13:2).[308]

Now learn this lesson from the fig tree: As soon as its twigs get tender and its leaves come out, you know that summer is near (13:28). The fig tree was one of the few deciduous trees in Palestine. Its leafing out is a harbinger of summer. In Isaiah 28:4, the first ripe fig of summer is an image for Israel's defenselessness, and the basket of summer fruit in Amos 8:1–2 is an image of judgment.

I tell you the truth, this generation will certainly not pass away until all these things have happened (13:30). Josephus laments the fate of Jerusalem at the end of the war. He writes that it was "a city undeserving of these great misfortunes" except that "she produced a generation such as that which caused her overthrow."[309]

Heaven and earth will pass away, but my words will never pass away (13:31). This saying affirms the validity of Jesus' prophecy, but the passing away of heaven and earth may not refer to the crumbling of the material universe. It may refer allusively to the temple, which was understood not only as the meeting point of heaven and earth but a miniature replica of heaven and earth.[310] This idea is found in Psalm 78:69, which pictures God as building the sanctuary like the high heavens and the earth. If this reading is correct, it reinforces Jesus' prediction of the temple's destruction (13:2).

It's like a man going away: He leaves his house and puts his servants in charge, each with his assigned task, and tells the one at the door to keep watch (13:34). This last parable in Mark picks up on the phrase "right at the door" (13:29). Literally, it reads that the master "gives authority to his slaves, to each one his work." This phrasing matches a papyrus

REFLECTIONS

THE KEY ELEMENT IN THE PARABLE IS THAT THE SERVANTS have no prior warning when the master of the house will return. They must be vigilant, which means "patient waiting at one's post, not speculation about how much longer the delay will be."[A-40] Unceasing vigilance means that Christians will not fall apart when earthly disasters strike, nor will they become spiritually lethargic when others are heralding "peace and safety" (1 Thess. 5:3).

fragment in which a master writes to a slave: "Since for some time you have been my slave-girl, I give you authority henceforth to go wherever you wish without being accused by me."[311]

The Anointing and Plans for Betrayal (14:1–11)

Now the Passover and the Feast of Unleavened Bread were only two days away (14:1). In the time of Jesus, the Festival of the Passover Offering, commemorating God's redemption of Israel, had become a national holy day celebrated in Jerusalem. The Passover lambs (one-year-old sheep) were slaughtered on the afternoon of Nisan 14 and eaten in a family or fraternal gathering between sunset and midnight, technically the next day, Nisan 15, since the Jewish day was reckoned from sunset to sunset (cf. Gen. 1:5). The Feast of Unleavened Bread is the seven-day feast following Passover, beginning on Nisan 15.[312] By avoiding bread with yeast and rejoicing in a feast, those unable to journey to Jerusalem or too poor to purchase a sacrificial lamb for Passover could celebrate the festival of Unleavened Bread. The two festivals had essentially become one in the minds of many.[313] Leaven was removed in a ceremonial search of the dwelling on the morning the Passover lambs were sacrificed, and some thought of it as the first day of Unleavened Bread, although technically it began the next day.

The chief priests and the teachers of the law (14:1). The "chief priests" in view here were those permanently employed at the temple as an executive committee, overseeing its daily operations. They include the high priest, the captain of the temple (responsible for the worship), and the temple treasurers. Their wealth and power alienated them from the ordinary priests. "The teachers of the law" (scribes) are those scholars allied with the priestly hierarchy.

"But not during the Feast," they said, "or the people may riot"(14:2). The fears of the Jewish leaders about a tumult of the people were realistic since Passover was the celebration of the liberation from Egypt, and many viewed it as the prototype of God's final liberation of Israel. It is estimated that anywhere from 85,000 to 300,000 pilgrims converged on Jerusalem, that normally had a population of 25,000 to 30,000, filling it with the sounds and smells of hordes of people and animals. Most pilgrims slept in tents or boarded in the towns of the surrounding countryside.

The chief priests' guards had the main responsibility for policing the city, and the Romans had only a small garrison in Jerusalem. Since the atmosphere in Jerusalem was so explosive at this time of year, the Roman governor moved with more troops from his headquarters in Caesarea to Jerusalem to thwart any violent uprisings. In spite of these precautions, Josephus records numerous protests and riots during the Passover season.

The Anointing (14:3–9)

A woman came with an alabaster jar of very expensive perfume, made of pure nard. She broke the jar and poured the perfume on his head (14:3). Jerusalem was filled with a strong smell from the temple sacrifices. If the wind blew from the east, the smoke from the altar turned back not only into the temple courts but over the whole city, bringing a mixture of the horrible reek of burning flesh and the heady smell of incense. Women who could afford it tended to use a great deal

◀ *left*

PERFUME JARS

Ointment jars and surgical instruments dating to the Hellenistic era.

of scent, though the rabbis argued in vain that the incense of the temple ought to be enough for a person.[314]

Anointing was common at feasts (see Luke 7:46: "You did not put oil on my head").[315] Alabaster jars were made from translucent calcite stone and stood five to nine inches high. A narrow neck restricted the flow of oil or perfume. Breaking the whole jar indicates that its entire contents were used. Nard was a highly valued plant from India. Its value is pegged here at three hundred denarii, which represented almost a year's wage for a day laborer. According to Mark 6:37, two hundred denarii was sufficient to provide a meal for five thousand people.

A social divide existed between male space and female space in the ancient world. Men and women did not intermingle even in the home. Women only crossed into the public male world to wait on men and then retreated.

The Last Supper (14:12–31)

Judas Iscariot (14:10). See comments on 3:19.

On the first day of the Feast of Unleavened Bread, when it was customary to sacrifice the Passover lamb (14:12). On the eve of Passover, work normally ceased at noon. The ritual slaughter of the Passover lambs began around 3:00 P.M. as the heads of the household brought their animals to the temple.[316] The priests sprinkled the blood of the lamb against the base of the altar and offered the fat on the altar. With the legs unbroken and the head still attached to the carcass, it was wrapped in its skin and returned to the worshipers. The forecourt of the temple had been the place to eat the meal, but the large number of people made that now impossible. It was only stipulated that the meal had to be eaten in Jerusalem with a minimum of ten persons. This took place in the evening on Nisan 15—strictly speaking, the first day of Unleavened Bread.

A man carrying a jar of water will meet you (14:13). Since Jesus probably stays with Simon the Leper in Bethany, his company probably enters Jerusalem either through the Fountain Gate by the

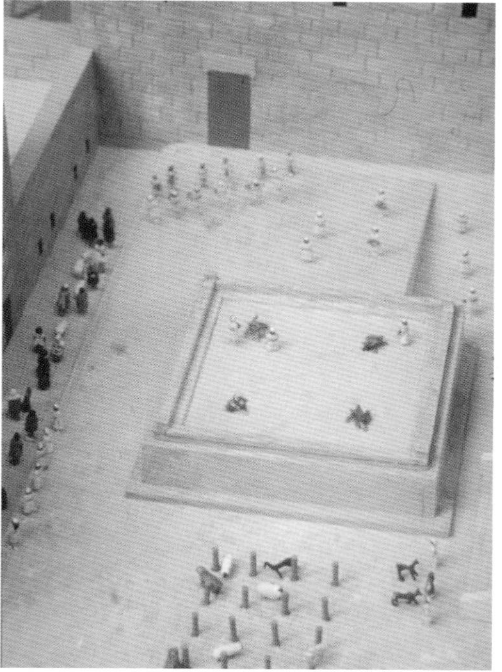

◀

PASSOVER TEMPLE SCENE

A model of the sacrificial altar in the court of priests of the Jerusalem temple.

Gihon Spring, the Casemate Gate or Water Gate by the King's Garden, or the Potsherd Gate near the pool of Siloam. It would be usual to spot someone carrying a water jar at any of these gates,[317] but it would be unusual to find a man doing so, since women normally fetched water.

He will show you a large upper room, furnished and ready (14:15). The upper room was "a smaller box on top of a bigger box."[318] It was used as a guest room, storeroom, and a place of retreat; such a room was usually reached by an outside stairway that allowed one to enter it without going through the main room of the house. The sages met their students in upper rooms to teach, according to later rabbinic traditions. This room apparently was furnished with a table that would have been a low U-shaped one. Couches or cushions would have been used for reclining at the meal.

right ▶

BETHANY

The site of the ancient village of Bethany.

One who dips bread into the bowl with me (14:20). Diners shared from the same dish and used the bread as their utensil. In this culture, eating bread with someone barred one from hostile acts against a fellow eater (see Ps. 41:9). In *The Sentences of the Syriac Menander* 2.215–16 we find this admonition: "And he with whom you had a meal, do not walk with him in a treacherous way."

THE UPPER ROOM

A historical tradition locates the last supper in the Cenacle on Mount Zion. This present structure was reconstructed by Franciscans in 1335.

▼

While they were eating, Jesus took bread, gave thanks and broke it, and gave it to his disciples, saying, "Take it; this is my body" (14:22). The visible union between Jesus and his disciples will dissolve at his death, but he provides a symbol by which it is to be replaced by an invisible one. He gives a special interpretation of the shared loaf and the shared wine, linked to the familiar rite of pronouncing a blessing before a meal. At every meal, the head of the family took the bread, lifted it up, and said, "Praise be Thou, O Lord our God, King of the Universe, who causes bread to come forth from the earth." After the "Amen" response, the bread was broken and distributed, mediating the blessing to each one who ate. Jesus gives the traditional blessing of the bread a new twist by saying that it is his body.

Then he took the cup (14:23). The *Book of Jubilees* provides evidence for the association of wine with the Passover festival (*Jub.* 49:6). Wine was always diluted with at least three parts water to one part wine (2 Macc. 15:39).

They all drank from it (14:23). Jesus uses the suggestive symbolism of the wine as the blood of the grape, plucked from the vine and crushed. Drinking the cup of someone was understood as a means of entering into a communion relationship with that person to the point that one shared that person's destiny, for good or ill (see Ps. 16:4–5).

I tell you the truth, I will not drink again of the fruit of the vine until that day when I drink it anew in the kingdom of God (14:25). "Not drinking again" becomes a metaphor for death.[319] With this statement, Jesus again prophesies his death. He will die before he will join in another festive banquet.[320] "Drinking again" is a metaphor for God's saving action when his kingdom comes.

When they had sung a hymn, they went out to the Mount of Olives (14:26). We should not immediately associate this hymn with the Hallel Psalms sung at Passover. The Passover rituals known to us from the Mishnah developed after the destruction of the temple when it no longer was a pilgrimage feast. Before then, the Passover practices were not uniform; and these later traditions may not have been the custom in Jesus' day. The hymn may simply convey the "prayerful context as the meal closed."[321]

Tonight—before the rooster crows twice (14:30). The cock's crow may refer to a real rooster crowing or to the bugle call of the *gallicinium* (cockcrow) that signaled the third watch of the night in Roman military reckoning (from 12:00 to 3:00 A.M.). The two cockcrows may refer to the signals at the beginning and the end of that watch. The text, however, lacks the definite article before the word for rooster, and this absence suggests that Mark understands it to refer to a fowl rather than a night watch.

Rabbinic evidence conflicts on whether one was allowed to raise poultry in the city of Jerusalem. A tradition from the Mishnah forbids it;[322] a tradition from the Jerusalem Talmud assumes their presence in the city.[323] Whether or not this conflicting testimony is relevant for the first century, a rooster would not need to have been within the walls of Jerusalem to have been heard.

The second cockcrow was connected to the dawn or rising sun.[324] Jesus' statement essentially means "before the next dawn."[325]

Prayer in Gethsemane (14:32–52)

They went to a place called Gethsemane (14:32). The word Gethsemane comes from a Hebrew/Aramaic word (*Gatz šᵉmānî*), meaning "oil press." Mark does not identify it as a garden (John

Contrasts Between Passover and the Lord's Supper	
Passover	**Lord's Supper**
In the old age of law	In the new age of the kingdom
The great festival meal celebrating the birth of God's people	The new celebratory meal of the birth of God's people
Participants associate themselves with deliverance and the old covenant	Participants associate themselves with redemption and the new covenant
Looks back to the Exodus and forward to God's salvation	Looks back to the cross and forward to the consummation

18:1) but simply as a "place"; four different locations on the Mount of Olives claim the honor of being the authentic site. Taylor contends that Gethsemane does not refer to an olive grove but to a spacious cave (about 55 feet long and 29-1/2 feet wide) within a cultivated enclosure, adjacent to the Church of All Nations, where olives were pressed for oil.[326] The press would have been in operation in the fall and winter after the olive harvest but would have been idle and used only for storage in the spring. Such a locale, close to the city, would have made an excellent place to spend a chilly night that had others kindling fires for warmth (14:54). It would have been "warm, dry, and roomy, with a cistern inside for water."[327] This location may explain why the young man there is attired only in a linen garment (14:51–52) as he presumably sleeps on his cloak. In the shelter of the cave, such a decision is understandable; out in the open, exposed to frigid air, it is not. Jesus may have left the cave to go further away in the enclosure to pray by himself.

Taylor cites as the earliest evidence for its location Egeria's account of her pilgrimage to the Holy Land. She said that pilgrims go "into Gethsemane" and are given candles "so that all can see." Theodosius, in the sixth century, explicitly identifies it as a cave.[328]

ALTAR IN CAVE IN GETHSEMANE

He fell to the ground and prayed that if possible the hour might pass from him (14:35). The normal Jewish attitude of prayer was to lift one's hands toward heaven and to pray aloud while standing. When one was in particular distress, one prayed lying prostrate. Jesus prostrates himself before his Father to pray in the same way that others in Mark's story fell before him to make their requests (5:22; 7:25).

Jewish prayers are sometimes remarkable for their loud complaint and directness. They approach God as a trusting child does, willing to complain bitterly and ask for anything. These prayers may seem insolent to us, but they reveal an intimacy with God, who is believed to listen sympathetically and grant requests.[329] Jesus' prayer conforms to this tradition. He trusts completely in God as his Father and is obedient.

Abba, Father (14:36). "Abba" is the Aramaic word term for father, and there is "no evidence in the literature of pre-Christian or first-century Palestinian Judaism that '*abbā*' was used in any sense as a personal address for God by an individual."[330] This unusual way of addressing God was remembered by Jesus' followers because his disciples also experienced such closeness to God in prayer through the Spirit (Rom. 8:15; Gal. 4:6). The term does not mean, "Daddy," however.[331] In translating it for Greek readers, Mark uses the regular word for "father" (*patēr*), not a diminutive form. The word was used both by children for their father and by disciples for an esteemed teacher. While the address

REFLECTIONS

JESUS LEARNS GOD'S WILL IN THE face of evil in exactly the same way we do—through prayer. Jesus overcomes intense distress with intense prayer. Mark teaches us how to pray from Jesus' example. He describes his bearing, his intimate address, his confession of God's omnipotence, his plea to be spared suffering, and his obedient submission to God's will. His posture conveys his helplessness apart from God's enablement and his submission to God's will. He prays desiring God's deliverance but accepting the cup of suffering. Having prostrated himself before God, Jesus can now stand before men.

may exhibit intimacy, it is not flippant. As Father, God requires obedience.

Now the betrayer had arranged a signal with them: "The one I kiss is the man" (14:44). One normally greeted a teacher or rabbi with a kiss on the hand or cheek if one considered oneself to be an equal (see Luke 7:45, "You did not give me a kiss"). See the parting kiss given to Paul by the Ephesian elders (Acts 20:37). Judas addresses him as rabbi and kisses him (Mark 14:45). He may have kissed him affectionately (the same word appears in Luke 15:20) or on the hand or even the foot (Luke 7:38, 45). The customary greeting of respect is turned into a sign of infamy and death.

Am I leading a rebellion . . . that you have come out with swords and clubs to capture me? (14:48). The high priests paid Judas to lead them to Jesus where they can quietly arrest him without a skirmish, yet they come ready for combat. The question, "Am I leading a rebellion?" interprets the Greek phrase, "Have you come out against a robber?" Josephus uses the term "robber" for the social bandits that badgered the aristocracy. He "never uses the term *lēstēs* to describe a revolutionary against Rome."[332] These bandits were usually peasants driven from their land. In response to injustice, they chose outlawry rather than meek submission and preyed on the rich in the countryside. Galilee was famous as a haven for bandits; Josephus notes their "habitual malpractices, theft, robbery, and rapine."[333]

Yet Mark is writing in a time during or shortly after the Jewish revolt against Rome. He may intend for readers to see the clear contrast between Jesus and contemporary assassins and revolutionaries.

A young man, wearing nothing but a linen garment, was following Jesus (14:51). This man apparently was sleeping in his undergarment, a linen cloth, and attempts to follow along with Jesus. When the arresting posse tries to seize him, he wriggles free from their grasp, fleeing into the darkness naked (presumably with only his loin cloth).

The young man is unidentified. Some, appealing to John 18:15, identify him as "[the other] disciple" known to the high priest, perhaps John, son of Zebedee. Others have guessed it is Mark himself, whose mother Mary has a house in Jerusalem (Acts 12:12). Remembering his disgrace, Mark gives himself a cameo role in his Gospel. It is more likely, however, that this anonymous figure epitomizes the "save yourself if you can" mentality that causes all the disciples to desert Jesus in a panic. Unprepared for testing, they break down completely, just as Jesus prophesied they would (Mark 14:27). The last remnant of their respectability is stripped away.

The Sanhedrin Hearing (14:53–65)

They took Jesus to the high priest (14:53). We learn from Acts 4:6 that the high priest was Joseph Caiaphas, the son-in-law of Annas (who held the office from A.D. 6 until he was deposed in A.D.15). Annas remained a kind of godfather controlling the reins of power with five sons holding the office of high priest.[334] The clan of Annas is remembered in the Babylonian Talmud for its knavery: "Woe unto me because of the house of Hanin [Annas], woe unto me because of their whisperings."[335] Josephus refers to the son of Annas, Ananas II (high priest in A.D. 62), as following the school of the Sadducees, who were "more heartless than any of the other Jews . . . when they sit in judgment."[336]

Pilate's predecessor, Valerius Gratus, removed four high priests during his eleven-year tenure as governor. Caiaphas had to be an artful politician to have held office as high priest for eighteen years from A.D. 18 to 36, serving throughout Pilate's tenure.[337] The family tomb of Caiaphas has been discovered. The name of Joseph bar Caiaphas is inscribed in Aramaic (*Yhwsp br Qp'*) on an elaborately decorated bone box containing the bones of a sixty-year-old man.[338]

We do not know where the high priest's home was. Some suggest it was located on the old Hasmonean palace on the West Hill of Jerusalem that "stood above the Xystus on the opposite side of the upper town."[339] Others claim it was near the Zion Gate in the southern section of the Western Hill.

The chief priests, elders and teachers of the law came together (14:53). In addition to the chief priests (see comments on 14:1), this group may also include the leader of the weekly course of priests and the leaders of the daily courses of priests. The elders are likely the heads of the distinguished families who are not priests but are aligned with the governing priestly faction. They are distinct from the elders who were the scholars behind "the tradition of the elders" (7:5).

The chief priests and the whole Sanhedrin (14:55). The Mishnah identifies the Great Sanhedrin as consisting of seventy-one members (see Num. 11:16).[340] The Mishnah, however, is not a reliable source for understanding how this body functioned in the first century or the juridical procedure against Jesus. The term *sanhedrin* can denote any council (see Mark 13:9, "councils," lit., "sanhedrins"). Rather than referring to a fixed body of members suddenly called into session in the middle of the night, it is more likely an ad hoc group of powerful noblemen, a sanhedrin of judges, whom the high priest assembles for an inquest to prepare charges before Pilate.

The Jewish people did not have the right to administer capital punishment at this time (John 18:31). The Jerusalem Talmud states: "Forty years before the destruction of the Temple, the right to judge capital cases was withdrawn."[341] It was the most jealously guarded of all the attributes of government. According to Josephus, the high priest Ananus was deposed for convening a Sanhedrin that condemned James, the brother of Jesus, to death during a transition from one governor to the next; he was accused of acting without the governor's permission.[342] The Sanhedrin gathered to judge Jesus, therefore, cannot pronounce a real death sentence because only Pilate, the governor, can carry out the death penalty after reaching his own verdict. He is not

The So-Called Illegalities of Jesus' Trial

The trial described by Mark is highly irregular according to rules listed in the Mishnah tractate *Sanhedrin* concerning the procedure for courts conducting capital trials.

(1) Capital cases were to be tried during the daytime, and the verdict must be reached during the daytime (*m. Sanh.* 4:1).

(2) Trials were not to be conducted on a Sabbath eve or on the eve of a festival day (*m. Sanh.* 4:1; see Acts 12:4, which reports that Herod intended to bring Peter to the people *after the Passover*).

(3) Capital cases were supposed to begin with reasons for acquittal and not with reasons for conviction (*m. Sanh.* 4:1). Attempts were to be made to find witnesses and arguments for the defense. If on the way to stoning someone should say, "I have somewhat to argue in favor of his acquittal," or even if the accused does so, they bring him back four or five times. The herald was to cry: "Such a one, the son of such a one is going to be stoned for he committed such or such an offense. Such and such are witnesses against him. If any man knoweth aught in favor of his acquittal let him come and plead it" (*m. Sanh.* 5:4). A later rabbinic tradition imagines that this was indeed done in Jesus' case:

On the Eve of Passover Yeshu [one text adds the Nazarean] was hanged. Forty days before his execution took place, a herald went forth and cried, "He is going forth to be stoned because he practised sorcery and enticed Israel to apostasy. Any one who can say anything in his favour, let him come forward and plead on his behalf." But since nothing was brought forward in his favour he was hanged on the eve of Passover![A-41]

(4) Verdicts of acquittal could be reached on the same day, but verdicts of conviction must be confirmed on the following day after a night's sleep (*m. Sanh.* 4:1).

(5) Condemnation required the evidence of two witnesses.[A-42] When witnesses disagreed, their evidence was null and void (*m. Sanh.* 5:2). If they were found to be false witnesses, they were required to suffer the "same death-penalty to which the accused had been made liable."[A-43]

(6) The Mishnah assumes that the Sanhedrin met in the inner courts of temple, the Chamber of Hewn Stone, not in the high priest's home.[A-44]

Mark's report of Jesus' trial depicts the nation's religious leaders gathering furtively in the middle of the night and conducting a hasty and blatantly prejudicial proceeding against Jesus. Some scholars have concluded that Mark has invented the Jewish hearing to transfer Roman guilt for Jesus' arrest and crucifixion to the Jews. But this Mishnaic tractate, compiled around A.D. 220, reflects the circumstances and scruples of a later era. The laws regarding capital cases in Mishnah *Sanhedrin* may not be representative of the historical procedure for the Sanhedrin in the first century or, for that matter, any period. They are idealized and theoretical, assuming, for example, that the king rules, not a high priest under the thumb of a Roman governor. The laws for the Sanhedrin are perceived through the lens of the wishful thinking of the post-war rabbis who compiled the oral law—this is the way it should be when the temple is restored, and it is assumed that this is the way it must have always been.

A Sanhedrin controlled by the high priest was also unlikely to follow Pharisaic procedures. If it were an informal hearing gathering evidence to bring to the governor, it would not need to observe legal formalities. According to Deuteronomy 18:20, a false prophet is to be killed immediately—even on a feast day. The chief priests considered Jesus such a serious threat that they made every effort to eliminate him by getting the Roman governor to put him to death and discredit him forever with death by crucifixion.

a rubber stamp and can overrule whatever they decide.

I will destroy this man-made temple and in three days will build another, not made by man. (14:58). Mark describes this as false testimony, and it is difficult to identify precisely how it is false. Possibly, the Jewish leaders wish to paint Jesus as a dangerous crank. Josephus describes the false Egyptian prophet gathering followers on the Mount of Olives and promising that at his command the walls of Jerusalem will fall down.[343] They may want to associate this boast with Jesus' claim to be the Messiah. Since 2 Samuel 7:13 mentions that David's offspring will build a house for God's name, some may have assumed that one of the tasks of the coming Messiah was to rebuild the temple (see Zech. 6:12–13). The Targum to Isaiah 53:5 reads: "But he shall build the sanctuary that was polluted because of our transgressions and given up because of our iniquities. . . ."[344]

HIGH PRIEST

Artistic interpretation of the Jewish high priest.

"Without human hands" (NIV "not made by man"; cf. Dan. 2:34, 45) means not of human origin. It will be a spiritual sanctuary.[345]

The high priest tore his clothes (14:63). Tearing one's garments was an ancient way of expressing distress and mourning.[346] The gesture is a fitting response to blasphemy and a dramatic way of getting the others to agree with him.

You have heard the blasphemy (14:64). According to Mishnah *Sanhedrin* 7:5, "'The blasphemer' is not culpable unless he pronounces the Name itself" (see Lev. 24:16). Measured by this rule, Jesus is not technically guilty. This ruling may not have been operative in Jesus' time, and what people regard as sacrilege need not fit any technical definition. Jesus' admission that he is the Messiah supposedly infringes on God's prerogative to declare who the Messiah is and to enthrone him.

Jesus' answer that the Son of Man will be sitting at the right hand of God in power also implies that he is on the same level with God. The Talmud records a dispute in which Rabbi Akiba interprets the phrase in Daniel 7:9, "till thrones were placed," as referring to two thrones, one for God and one for David (the Messiah), so that "one like a son of man is identified as the royal Messiah." His colleagues vigorously reject this interpretation as profaning the Divine Presence.[347]

A text from Qumran refers to the last enemy of God calling himself the son of the Most High and demanding adoration and obedience.[348] Flusser calls it "important evidence for a Jewish tradition about the superhuman hubris of the Antichrist."[349] Jesus' assertion perhaps

:onfirms the high priest's suspicions that esus is a figure like this who tries to educe the world.

In his summary of the Jewish law, osephus freely renders Leviticus 24:16: Let him that blasphemeth God be toned, then hung for a day, and buried gnominiously and in obscurity."[350] The ıigh priest may not be able to stone esus, but he has every intention that esus be put to death and suffer the ıumiliation of being hanged and given a lishonorable burial.

Then some began to spit at him; they blindfolded him, struck him with their ists, and said, "Prophesy!" (14:65). The aunt to prophesy derives from Jesus' mplicit claim to be the Messiah, who vas supposed to have a prophetic gift. According to an anecdote in the Babylonian Talmud, the Messiah is able to udge by smell:

> Bar Koziba ["son of lies," see comments on 13:6] reigned two and a half years, then said to the rabbis, "I am the messiah." They answered, "Of the messiah it is written that he smells and udges; let us see whether he can do so." When they saw that he was unable to udge by scent, they slew him.[351]

REFLECTIONS

THESE EVENTS REVEAL THAT GOD'S power is revealed in weakness, and they confirm that Jesus indeed is the Messiah and the Son of God. Humans have always stumbled over how one whom they assume should be associated with power and glory could possibly be linked to suffering and death. The mystery of God's love and power expressed in the cross consequently remains a riddle to many.

The torturers may also be playing a cruel version of the game of blindman's bluff, known from this era, where the person must guess who is hitting him.[352]

Peter's Denial (14:66–72)

While Peter was below in the courtyard (14:66). Peter's denial of Jesus wraps around the trial of Jesus, indicating that they both take place at the same time. While Jesus is interrogated by the high priest, Peter waits in the courtyard (though the word *aulē* may refer to a court in the house). The courtyard was the open space around which rooms were arranged; the "entryway" (14:68) was the vestibule leading to the courtyard.

Surely you are one of them, for you are a Galilean (14:70). In rabbinic literature, Galileans are portrayed as simpletons and riffraff (see the prejudice reflected in John 7:45–52). They can be identified by their Aramaic accents (Matt. 26:73). Jerusalem merchants taunt a Galilean wanting to purchase an *amar*:

> "Foolish Galilean," they said to him, "do you mean an 'ass' for riding [*hamār*], 'wine' to drink [*hamar*], 'wool' for clothing [*ʿamar*] or a 'lamb' for killing [*immar*]?"[353]

Vermes explains with an example from modern British English: "In careless everyday conversation the Galileans dropped their aitches."[354]

He began to call down curses on himself (14:71). The text does not say that Peter called down curses on himself. The verb has no object in the Greek text, and it is possible to construe it that he goes so far as to curse Jesus. Pliny the Younger was appointed by the emperor Trajan to govern Bithynia-Pontus and reported that he asked suspected Christians three times with threats of punishment, "Are you a Christian?"[355] The accused proved their innocence by cursing Jesus, which, he says, "those who are really Christians cannot be made to do."[356] In the *Martyrdom of Polycarp* 9:3, the proconsul adjures Polycarp, "Swear and I will release you." Polycarp replies, "How can I blaspheme the King who saved me?"

The Trial Before Pilate (15:1–20)

Very early in the morning (15:1). The working day of a Roman official began at the earliest hour of daylight. Seneca attests that Roman trials could begin at daybreak.[357] Pliny completed his work by 10:00 A.M.; Vespasian finished before dawn.[358] If the council spent the early hours of daylight examining Jesus, they may have been too late for Pilate's tribunal.

They bound Jesus, led him away and handed him over to Pilate (15:1). Pilate's official title was prefect (see inscription found in Caesarea identifying him as *Praefectus Iudaeae*). The governors were called procurators only after A.D. 44. As governor, Pilate had the power of life and death over all the inhabitants of his province.[359] He was of equestrian rank (knight, wealthy enough to own a horse). In this rank, he would have had no assistants of a similar status and no team of Roman officials to handle all of the administrative matters. A large part of the everyday chores of government and administration was thus carried out by the local councils and magistrates. They had the power to arrest, take evidence, and make a preliminary examination in order to present a case before a governor for a formal trial. The Roman authorities held them accountable for outbreaks of violence and would replace them. The governor, however, was ultimately responsible for ensuring that order was maintained and for deciding the death penalty.

COINS MINTED UNDER PONTIUS PILATE

The chief priests accused him of many things (15:3). No criminal code existed for the non-Roman citizen tried in the provinces. It was technically known as a "trial outside the system." The governor was free to make his own rules and judgments as he saw fit, to accept or reject charges, and within reason to fashion whatever penalties he chose. Governors,

Pilate

Pilate was nominated to his post in A.D. 26 by Lucius Aelius Sejanus as the fifth Roman prefect of Judea. Sejanus rose to become the prefect of the Praetorian Guard under Tiberius and became his trusted advisor. He gained greater influence in the affairs of government when the moody Tiberius retired to Campania and Capri in 27 and handled most of the government affairs and complaints.[A-45] In 31, he was named consul with Tiberius, which made him de facto joint emperor and the heir apparent. According to Philo, Sejanus manifested anti-Semitic attitudes and attacked the Jewish inhabitants of Rome with slander because he wished to do away with the nation.[A-46] Under the sponsorship of the powerful Sejanus in Rome, Pilate did not fear repercussions from his various run-ins with the Jewish sensibilities in Palestine.

continued next page

We get the impression from Josephus that Pilate believed staunchly in Roman sovereignty and wished to ram it down the Judeans' throat. When he first arrived, he brought in army standards with Roman religious symbols into Jerusalem under the cover of night and precipitated a riotous reaction. Crowds thronged to Caesarea, where they bared their necks to the Roman swords, forcing him to back down.[A-47] Later, he confiscated funds from the treasury to finance an aqueduct from Bethlehem to Jerusalem. Another disturbance followed with many killed.[A-48] At some point, he was responsible for the deaths of Galileans whose blood was mingled with their sacrifices (Luke 13:1–2). His last outrage occurred when he heard that a prophet in Samaria had gathered with a crowd to uncover sacred vessels buried by Moses. Pilate overreacted with a preemptive strike and wiped them out. The Samaritans protested, and Pilate was recalled to Rome in 36.[A-49]

On October 18, 31, Sejanus conspired to grab power completely for himself. The plot was uncovered, and Tiberius had him executed hours later. What was known as the Tiberian terror followed, uprooting all of Sejanus's supporters. No one who had been associated with Sejanus and his policies could feel secure. Philo contended that a dramatic change in policy toward the Jews also occurred:

> Tiberius... knew at once after Sejanus's death that the accusations made against the inhabitants of Rome were false slanders.... And he charged his procurators on every place to which they were appointed to speak comfortably to the members of our nation in the different cities assuring them that the penal measures did not extend to all but only to the guilty, who were few, and to disturb none of the established customs but even to regard them as a trust committed to their care, the people as naturally peaceable, and the institutions as an influence promoting orderly conduct.[A-50]

Philo regarded Pilate as an agent of Sejanus's policy, and this information may help make sense of Pilate's behavior as it is reported in the Gospels. He describes Pilate as "naturally inflexible, a blend of self-will and relentlessness," stubborn, vindictive, hot tempered, but afraid that the Jews would report to the emperor "his briberies, insults, robberies, outrages and wanton injuries."[A-51] After the Sejanian conspiracy was exposed, Pilate was vulnerable. He could not chance a Jewish appeal to Rome and had to demonstrate unwavering loyalty to Tiberius.

Pilate served a long time in his office, and Josephus gives an anecdote explaining Tiberius's policy of appointing governors:

> Once a man lay wounded, and a swarm of flies hovered about his wounds. A passer-by took pity on his evil plight and, in the belief that he did not raise a hand because he could not, was about to step up and shoo them off. The wounded man, however, begged him to think no more of doing anything about it. At this the man spoke up and asked him why he was not interested in escaping from his wretched condition, "Why," said he, "you would put me in a worse condition if you drove them off? For since these flies have already had their fill of blood, they no longer feel such pressing need to annoy me but are in some measure slack. But if others were to come with fresh appetite, they would take over my now weakened body and that would indeed be the death of me." He too, he said, for the same reason took the precaution of not dispatching governors continually to the subject peoples who had been brought to ruin by so many thieves; for the governors would harry them utterly like flies. Their natural appetite for plunder would be reinforced by their expectation of being speedily deprived of that pleasure. The record of Tiberius's acts will bear out my account of his humor in such matters. For during the twenty-two years that he was emperor he sent altogether two men, Gratus and Pilate, his successor, to govern the Jewish nation.[A-52]

however, tended to follow the legal custom with which they were familiar.

Trials normally took place in a public setting before the governor, who sat on his tribunal. Since there were no public prosecutors, a prosecution's case was brought by private third parties, who presented formal charges (cf. the trials of Paul, Acts 24:1–9; 25:1–27).

The Roman governor would not have put anyone on trial for his life simply for transgressing Jewish religious regulations. When Paul was arrested, the Roman garrison commander wrote to the governor Felix in Caesarea, "I found that the accusation had to do with questions about their law, but there was no charge against him that deserved death or imprisonment" (Acts 23:29; see the reaction of Gallio in 18:14–17). The Sanhedrin may have found Jesus guilty of blasphemy and deserving of death, but a religious charge would not suffice for Pilate to take action. The governor only cared that matters religious did not become matters political. The chief priests must thus formulate a charge that will capture his attention and carry a death sentence. The charges need to be political, which explains why Pilate asks Jesus, "Are you the king of the Jews?" (Mark 15:2). Charges of *maiestas*, "the diminution of the majesty of the Roman people," were increasingly frequent under Tiberius.[360]

Josephus bemoaned the various would-be kings who rose up and caused disturbances:

> And so Judaea was filled with brigandage. Anyone might make himself king as the head of a band of rebels whom he fell in with, and then would press on to the destruction of the community, causing trouble to few Romans and then only to a small degree but bringing the greatest slaughter upon their own people.[361]

Now it was the custom at the Feast to release a prisoner whom the people requested (15:6). This tradition may derive from the days of the Hasmonean kings, and the Romans may have continued it when it suited their purposes. A papyrus from A.D. 85 contains a report of judicial proceedings before the prefect of Egypt and quotes the words from the governor to the prisoner: "You were worthy of scourging . . . but I will give you to the people."[362] A text from the Mishnah rules, "They may slaughter (the Passover lamb) . . . for one whom they (the authorities) have promised to release from prison."[363]

A man called Barabbas (15:7). The name Barabbas means "son of Abba." This name distinguishes him from others with the same personal name.

The crowd came up and asked Pilate to do for them what he usually did (15:8). Governors were known to enter into conversation with the crowd, although a first-century papyrus warns against this since it may lead to injustice. The crowd is probably composed of partisans supporting the priestly hierarchy. It would be easy to stir them up if they were led to believe that Jesus has somehow threatened the temple. The temple was not only a potent religious symbol, it provided employment to a large segment of the population of Jerusalem.

The Mocking and Crucifixion of Jesus (15:15–41)

He had Jesus flogged, and handed him over to be crucified (15:15). Scourging was a customary preliminary to crucifixion. The prisoner was bound to a pillar or post and beaten with a *flagellum*. This whip consisted of leather thongs plaited with pieces of bone, lead, or bronze or with hooks and was appropriately called a scorpion. Gladiators sometimes fought with them. There was no prescribed number of lashes so that in some cases the scourging itself was fatal. The balls would cause deep contusions as the flesh was literally ripped into bloody ribbons. It was so horrible that Suetonius claimed even Domitian was horrified by it.[364] Significant blood loss could also occur, critically weakening the victim.

The soldiers led Jesus away into the palace (that is, the Praetorium) (15:16). During his sojourns to Jerusalem, Pilate probably stayed in the luxurious palace of Herod the Great (near the Tower of David and the Jaffa Gate), the highest point in the city. Philo recalls that when Pilate was first appointed governor he stayed in Herod's palace.[365] Others argue that he resided in the Antonia Fortress (named after Mark Anthony) adjacent to the northwest corner of the temple; it served as the barracks for the Roman cohort. It seems more likely that the governor would choose to lodge in Herod's more opulent palace.

They put a purple robe on him (15:17). The mocking of Jesus by the soldiers is intended to parody the charge that he is king of the Jews. The purple cloak probably refers to the oblong-shaped garment fastened around the neck by a brooch that was a foot soldier's equipment (*chlamys*), or perhaps the cloak of the lictor. According to Suetonius, Caligula wore one.[366] It is intended to be a mock royal robe.[367]

They twisted together a crown of thorns and set it on him (15:17). This crown may or may not be an instrument of torture. The soldiers are improvising and grab whatever is at hand. Thus the thorns may come from a type of palm tree common to Jerusalem, a dwarf date palm or thorn palm, which grew as an ornamental and had formidable spikes. The leaves could be easily woven and the long spikes from the date palm inserted to resemble a radiate crown.[368] Evidence for this type of crown is found in seals excavated from

TREE USED FOR MAKING CROWN OF THORNS

left

SOLDIER GAMES

A Roman era pavement inscribed with lines related to "the king's game."

the Roman camp in Jerusalem. Or, the soldiers may have simply grabbed a clump of thorns and put them on his head like a cap.

Hail, king of the Jews! (15:18). The homage of the soldiers parodies that given to the emperor, "Ave Caesar, victor, imperator." Philo records similar mockery of an imbecile named Carabas in Alexandria. He was used as a stand-in to lampoon Herod Agrippa I when he was proclaimed king of Judea.[369]

A certain man from Cyrene, Simon, the father of Alexander and Rufus (15:21). The names are Greek and Latin, although Simon may reflect the Hebrew Simeon. If Simon is a Jew, which seems likely, he may have been a member of the synagogue of Cyrenians that later opposed Stephen (Acts 6:9). Apparently, Rufus and Alexander are known to the first readers of this Gospel. A Rufus is mentioned in Romans 16:13 and in Polycarp's letter to the Philippians 9:1. An ossuary with the name "Alexander, son of Simon" has been discovered in Jerusalem.[370]

They forced him to carry the cross (15:21). Normally, a condemned person carried the crossbeam (*patibulum*) to the crucifixion site, where a vertical post (*stipes, staticulum*) had already been fixed in the ground. Wood was scarce, and crosses were probably used more than once. Plutarch says that "every criminal who goest to execution must carry his own cross on his back."[371]

Mark does not tell us why Jesus is unable to carry his own cross. We can surmise that he was too weak or too slow after the ordeal of his scourging, which also may explain his quick death (15:44). Cicero mentions an executioner's hook used to drag the condemned to the place of execution.[372] "Compel" is a technical term for commandeering a person or his property (see Matt. 5:41). Simon is grabbed from the crowd and forced to carry the crossbeam to the place where Jesus will be crucified.

They brought Jesus to the place called Golgotha (which means The Place of the Skull) (15:22). According to Roman law (and Jewish, Lev. 24:14), crucifixion was to take place outside the city. Quintilian commended crucifixion as a deterrent and noted that the executioners chose "the most crowded roads where the most people can see and be moved by this fear."[373] Josephus reports that during the siege of Jerusalem, the Romans crucified five hundred or more victims every day opposite the wall, nailing their victims in different postures as a spectacle for those in the city.[374] The crucifixion site would be near roads leading into the city where

REFLECTIONS

THE IRONIC RECOGNITION OF JESUS is now complete. He was "anointed" by a woman in the home of a leper but it was for his burial (14:3–9). He was identified as the Christ (the Anointed One), the son of the Blessed One, by the high priest, who declares it blasphemy. He was announced as king by Pilate (15:17–19) and saluted by the soldiers (15:16–19). These anoint him with spit, crown him with thorns, and will soon enthrone him on a cross.[A-53] One scholar writes: "So powerful is the kingdom that it reaches down even into the hate-filled minds and venomous lips of its foes, drawing unwitting testimony from those who look without seeing."[A-54] eople could learn what happens to nalefactors and would-be kings.

Jesus is taken to a place called Gol-gotha, which Mark interprets for his Greek-speaking readers as "skull place." The more familiar term Calvary derives rom the Latin translation *calvaria*, vhich means "skull". The name Golgotha loes not appear in any other extant ource from antiquity other than the Gospels. The name may refer to (1) the hape of the outcropping of rock that esembled a skull, (2) the place where executions were carried out, or (3) a egion that included the place of execu-ion and a cultivated tract of land where here were tombs.[375] This last option eems best. Taylor concludes:

> Golgotha was probably an oval-shaped abandoned quarry located west of the sec-ond wall, north of the first wall. Jesus may have been crucified in the southern part of this area, just outside the Gennath Gate, and near the road going west, but at a site visible also from the road north and buried some 200 m. away to the north, in a quieter part of Golgotha where there were tombs and gardens.[376]

This site is not far from the Gennath Gardens) Gate mentioned by Josephus; t was located in the first wall and fits ohn's mention of a garden in the place John 19:41).[377] Exposed rock in this area hows evidence of ancient quarrying, and t may have been a rejected portion of an ancient preexilic white stone quarry. One cholar suggests that the early Christians knew that Golgotha was a rejected quarry tone, which brings to mind Psalm 118:22, nentioned in Mark 12:10 (see also Acts 4:11 and 1 Peter 2:7).[378]

Constantine drew on local tradition o build "a great sacred enclave" in this area in 325–35.[379] The Church of the Holy Sepulchre is currently located on his site. Despite this ancient tradition, several questions remain. Was it outside the city wall in the first century? Was it not too close to the temple (and the palace of Herod)? Since the prevailing winds came from the west, nearly all extant tombs are found to the north, east, and south of Jerusalem. Did the Gennath Gate open onto a roadway?

Then they offered him wine mixed with myrrh (15:23). According to a Talmudic tradition, the women of Jerusalem offered a narcotic drink to people con-demned to death in order to alleviate the pain of execution, but it refers to wine and frankincense (see Prov. 31:6–7).[380] The text, however, implies that the exe-cutioners, not pious women, offer the drink. Pliny regarded the finest wine as that "spiced with the scent of myrrh."[381] The Romans did not consider it to be intoxicating but more of a woman's drink.[382] The executioners may have given this drink to exhausted prisoners on the way to the place of execution to give them more strength so that they would last longer and suffer longer.

Another possibility is that this gesture continues the mocking of Jesus as a tri-umphant king. At the end of a Roman tri-umphant procession, the triumphator is offered a cup of ceremonial wine that he refuses to drink but pours out on the altar at the moment of sacrifice.[383]

Jesus rejects the offer of wine because he has made a vow of abstinence at the Last Supper (14:25) and wishes to re-main fully conscious to the bitter end. He will drink the Father's cup instead (14:36).

They crucified him (15:24). Mark does not need to describe crucifixion to his readers since they would be familiar with it. The victim is stripped to increase the humiliation and fastened to the crossbeam with nails and/or ropes. The executioners lift up the crossbeam with forked poles until the victim's feet clear the ground and then attach it to the stake. Most guess that "Jesus' cross stood some 7 ft. high."[384] Since the nails do not support the whole body, a plank (*sedile, sedecula*) is fastened to the *stipes* to support the buttocks, which explains Seneca's mention of "sitting on a cross."[385]

The only extant bones of a crucified man were discovered in Jerusalem in 1968 at Giv'at ha-Mivtar in a group of cave tombs dating from the second century B.C. to A.D. 70. A man named Jehohanan had been crucified sometime between A.D. 7 and 66.[386] Initial analysis suggested several possibilities that have later been refuted. (1) A scratch on the forearm near the wrist was interpreted to mean that he was nailed to the cross beam through the forearms. Thus it is possible that Jesus was not nailed to the cross through his palms, as Christian art has normally depicted it, but through the wrists or arms. The word translated "hands" in Luke 24:39–40 and John 20:20, 25, 27 may refer to wrist or arm.[387] Later analysis, however, has revealed that Jehohanan's arms and hands had not undergone violent injury, and it is more likely that he had been tied to the crossbeam with ropes.

CRUCIFIED BONE

The heel bone of a man crucified with an iron nail that pierced the bone and fastened him to the wood. The bone was found in an ossuary (burial box) in a Jerusalem tomb.

Zugibe has determined that the upper part of the palm of the hand can support the weight of the body nailed to a cross.[388] It is therefore possible that tradition is correct, and Jesus was nailed to the cross through the palms of his hands.

(2) The iron nail piercing the man's heel bone had apparently hit a knot when it was driven into the cross and was bent, making it difficult to extract from the bone. The initial report suggested that this nail had been driven through both heels and that the man's legs were either pressed together and twisted so that the calves were parallel to the crossbeam or possibly were spread apart. Later analysis showed that the nail was shorter than first described and was driven through the right heel, suggesting that the man had straddled the upright beam with each foot nailed laterally to the beam. Executioners employed a variety of ways of crucifying victims, and we cannot know precisely how Jesus was affixed to the cross.

(3) It was initially reported that the man's legs were fractured from a blow from a massive weapon shattering the right shin into slivers and fracturing the left one. This procedure was known as *crurifragium* and hastened death. According to the fictional *Gospel of Peter* 4:14, the people were angry with the penitent thief and did not allow his legs to be broken so that he would suffer longer. Later analysis of the bones, however, has questioned whether the man's legs had been broken.

Death by crucifixion normally came slowly and tortuously. Horace records a jeer that reflects this protracted suffering: "You'll hang on no cross to feed crows."[389] Seneca's letters offer gruesome images of crucifixion:

> Can anyone be found who would prefer wasting away in pain dying

> limb by limb, or letting out his life drop by drop, rather than expiring once for all? Can any man be found willing to be fastened to the accursed tree, long sickly, already deformed, swelling with ugly weals on shoulders and chest, and drawing the breath of life amid long drawn-out agony? He would have many excuses for dying even before mounting the cross.[390]

n another letter he writes:

> Yonder I see instruments of torture, not indeed of a single kind, but differently contrived by different peoples; some hang their victims with head toward the ground, some impale their private parts, others stretch out their arms on fork-shaped gibbet; I see cords, I see scourges, and for each separate limb and each joint there is a separate engine of torture.[391]

Reading this, one better understands the meaning of the word "excruciating," which derives from the Latin *excruciatus*, out of the cross.

Dividing up his clothes, they cast lots to see what each would get (15:24). Executioners customarily shared out the minor personal belongings of the condemned.[392] Not only does the victim suffer from the excruciating pain and thirst as well as the torture of insects burrowing into open wounds, he must also endure the humiliation of exposure. It is likely that Jesus was left with a loin cloth out of deference to Jewish scruples about nakedness.

The written notice of the charge against him read: THE KING OF THE JEWS (15:26). Jesus, who resisted any political overtones to his messiahship, is executed as a political Messiah. A placard citing the basic charge against him is probably hung around his neck as he departs for the execution site. To the Romans, any claim to kingship was treasonous.

They crucified two robbers with him, one on his right and one on his left (15:27). The robbers may have been involved in the insurrection with Barabbas (15:7), or they may be common thieves or bandits (11:17; see 2 Cor. 11:26).

Those who passed by hurled insults at him (15:29). Mocking a victim was customary and stemmed from the mob mentality of kicking a man when he is down. A rabbinic story tells of the crucifixion of Jose ben Joezer and the scorn hurled at him by his wicked nephew Jakum. He came up riding a horse on the Sabbath and mocked him: "Behold my horse which my master lets me ride and thy horse which thy Master (God) makes thee sit."[393] The "Aha" appears as a derisive cry in the Psalms, and the wagging of heads is a gesture of contempt.[394]

At the sixth hour darkness came over the whole land until the ninth hour (15:33). The darkness would have evoked several different images for ancient readers. (1) It was a sign of mourning (Jer. 4:27–28). According to a Talmudic tradition, when the president of the council dies, the sun is darkened; the rabbis comment that the sun mourns for the man even if humans do not.[395] (2) Darkness was associated in the ancient world with the death of great men. Philo saw the sun and moon as natural divinities and wrote that eclipses announce the death of kings and the destruction of cities.[396] Vergil wrote: "The Sun will give you signs. Who dare say the Sun is false? Nay, he oft warns us that dark uprisings threaten, that treachery and hidden wars are upswelling. Nay, he had pity for Rome when, after Caesar sank from sight, he veiled his shining face in dusky gloom, and a godless age feared everlasting night."[397] (3) In the Scriptures, darkness is an apocalyptic sign of judgment and could be construed as signaling the advent of divine judgment.[398] The darkness that descended during Jesus' crucifixion turns upside down the expectation derived from Isaiah 60:2 that though darkness covers the earth and dark night the nations, God's light will shine on Jerusalem. (4) The darkness also announces the great Day of the Lord in prophets such as Amos, and the darkness that settles on the land signifies that the day has dawned with a new beginning. (5) The darkness may veil the shame of the crucifixion: "God hides the Son from the blasphemer's leering."[399]

"Eloi, Eloi, lama sabachthani?"—which means, "My God, my God, why have you forsaken me?" (15:34). Jesus does not form the words of the prayer himself as he did in Gethsemane ("*Abba*"); rather, he cites a proverbial expression of distress from Psalm 22:1. One could not expect a crucifixion victim to recite an entire psalm, but it is possible that citing the first verse of the psalm refers to the entire psalm. Without chapters and verses to identify specific passages, initial words or key phrases were cited (see Mark 12:26). If this is the case here, Jesus prays the opening words of this lament psalm that, when read through to the end, expresses not only bitter despair but also supreme confidence. This interpretation does not deny the real anguish that Jesus experiences but understands his cry as an expression of trust that God will intervene and ultimately vindicate him.

Listen, he's calling Elijah (15:35). The final taunt arises from the popular belief that Elijah comes to aid those in mortal danger. According to a story in the Talmud, Elijah was said to have rescued one Eleazar ben Perata from the Romans and removed him four hundred miles away.[400]

One man ran, filled a sponge with wine vinegar (15:36). The name of this sour wine derives from the Greek word for sharp (*oxys*) and was made from water, egg, and vinegar. It was a soldier's drink. Marcus Cato was said to have called for it when he was in a raging thirst or when his strength was failing.[401] The one who went to get the wine may have hoped to give Jesus a spurt of energy to enable him to hold out until Elijah arrived.

With a loud cry, Jesus breathed his last (15:37). "Breathed out" (*ekpneueo*) is a rare word for death. Scholars have argued that death was caused by (1) a rupture of the heart; (2) asphyxiation as breathing became more difficult; or (3) shock from extreme physical punishment. From carefully conducted experiments, Zugibe refutes the asphyxiation theory and argues that Jesus' death was caused by traumatic shock from the effects of dehydration and loss of blood.[402]

The curtain of the temple was torn in two from top to bottom (15:38). Mark may refer to the outer curtain that separated the sanctuary from the outer porch[403] or to the inner veil between the Holy Place and the Most Holy Place.[404] The high priest on the Day of Atonement could go behind this veil into the Most Holy Place for only a brief moment. The veil was made of the finest wool—blue, purple and scarlet; and, according to the Mishnah, was one handbreadth thick, forty ubits long, and twenty cubits broad and ook three hundred priests to immerse t.[405] Josephus, a priest who would have irsthand knowledge of the veil, describes t as

> of Babylonian tapestry, with embroidery of blue and fine linen, of scarlet and also purple, wrought with marvelous skill. Nor was this mixture of materials without its mystic meaning: it typified the universe. For the scarlet seemed emblematical of fire, the fine linen of the earth, the blue of the air, and the purple of the sea; the comparison of the two cases being suggested by their colour, and in that of the fine linen and purple by their origin, as the one produced by the earth and the other by the sea. On this tapestry was portrayed a panorama of the heavens, the signs of the Zodiac excepted.[406]

The veil's rending may have both a egative and positive significance. Being orn from top to bottom points to its irreediable destruction and to God as the gent. It may signify the end of the Jewsh cult and the destruction of the temple. osephus records strange portents that he laimed gave early warning of the destrucion that would later befall the temple. The massive, brass eastern gate of the temle's inner court took twenty men to close t every evening and fasten it shut with ron bars anchored to solid blocks of stone. Some years before the temple's destrucion, it supposedly opened of its own ccord.[407] The *Lives of the Prophets*, comiled by a Jew in the first century A.D. but reserved and edited by Christians, conains the following prophecy attributed to Habakkuk:

> And concerning the end of the Temple he predicted, "By a western nation it will happen." "At that time," he said, "the curtain of the *Dabeir* [transliteration of the Hebrew for the inner sanctuary, the Most Holy Place] will be torn into small pieces, and the capitals of the pillars will be removed and no one will know where they are" (12:12).

A Talmudic tradition also connects the rending of the veil with the temple's destruction. It records the Roman general Titus entering into the Most Holy Place and rending the veil with his sword, and blood poured out.[408]

The rending of the veil may also be interpreted as a decisive opening. All barriers between God and the people have now been removed (Heb. 10:19–20).

And when the centurion, who stood there in front of Jesus, heard his cry and saw how he died, he said, "Surely this man was the Son of God!" (15:39). Petronius, a courtier of Nero, recounts in his satiric novel, *Satyricon*, a soldier guarding the crosses of crucified thieves at night to prevent anyone from removing the bodies for burial.[409] It is probable that this was not the first crucifixion detail that the centurion had commanded. According to Mark, the centurion witnesses Jesus' death, not the rending of the veil. Consequently, we should not attempt to place the scene of the crucifixion at a spot where one might be able to see the veil being torn.

After Julius Caesar was deified, his adopted son, Augustus, became widely known as "son of god" (*divi filius*). It was not a title applied to emperors in general. This soldier transfers the title from the most revered figure in the Roman imperial cult to a Jew who has just been executed. The opening words of the Gospel (1:1) and this confession directly challenge the claims of the imperial cult.

Jesus, not Augustus nor any other emperor, is Savior and Lord.[410]

Some women were watching from a distance. Among them were Mary Magdalene, Mary the mother of James the younger and of Joses, and Salome (15:40). Women customarily gathered in groups segregated from men. Magdalene suggests that Mary came from Magdala, three miles northeast of Tiberias and known as Taricheia in Greek. Church tradition says that she had been a prostitute, but there is no evidence in the New Testament for this.

It was Preparation Day (15:42). Mark explains that Preparation Day is the day preceding the Sabbath. Quitting all work on the Sabbath required much forethought and preparation. Before sunset, all business must be discharged, journeys ended, food prepared, and lamps fixed to burn longer since no light could be kindled on the Sabbath.

Joseph of Arimathea, a prominent member of the Council, who was himself waiting for the kingdom of God, went boldly to Pilate and asked for Jesus' body (15:43). The Romans frequently did not allow the bodies of executed persons to be taken down and buried.[411] Philo protested against the prefect Flaccus:

> On the eve of a holiday of this kind, people who have been crucified have been taken down and their bodies delivered to their kinsfolk, because it was thought well to give them burial and allow ordinary rites. For it was meet that the dead also should have the advantage of some kind treatment upon the birthday of an emperor and also that the sanctity of the festival should be maintained.

Flaccus gave no orders to take down the bodies of the executed Jews but crucified more instead.[412]

Deuteronomy 21:22–23 became the basis for the Jewish belief that one was obligated to bury the body of criminals and even enemies on the day of their death. Philo paraphrases the text, "Let not the sun go down upon the crucified but let them be buried in the earth before sundown."[413] Josephus writes about the treacherous attack of the Idumeans in the first revolt when they killed the chief priests and refused to allow them to be buried: "They actually went so far as to cast out the corpses without burial, although the Jews are so careful about funeral rites that even the malefactors who have been sentenced to crucifixion are taken down and buried before sunset."[414]

Arimathea may designate that Joseph comes from Ramathaim (1 Sam. 1:1), east of Joppa, or Rathamin to the northwest (1 Macc. 11:34). He is described as someone of high standing and noble repute. He may have been a member of his local ruling body or a member of the council that decided Jesus deserved death. Why would he then wish to claim the body? Joseph is described with emphasis as looking for the kingdom of God, which identifies him as a pious man (see the description of Simeon and Anna, Luke 2:25, 38). The statement that it is already the evening of the Preparation Day, the day before Sabbath (Mark 15:42), provides the motivation for why he wishes to act and act quickly. A body must not be allowed to hang beyond sundown into the Sabbath. Joseph fulfills the pious obligation to bury the dead and thus prevents a body left on the cross from affronting God and defiling the land and the Sabbath (Deut. 21:23).

If Joseph is not a follower of Jesus at his point, it may explain why the vomen do not come near and assist in he burial but watch from a distance. In Acts 8:2, when Stephen was stoned, ious men, *not* Christians, buried him nd made great lamentation over him. Regarding Jesus' burial, Acts 13:29 sserts that when "they had carried out ll that was written of him, they took him own from the tree and laid him in a omb." The context implies that enemies f Jesus buried him.

Ordinarily, family or friends requested he body of one who was executed (see he disciples of John the Baptist, 6:29). Yet esus' disciples do not do this. That Joseph went boldly" to ask Pilate for the body uggests that the request involved some isk. Jesus has been executed for treason s the king of the Jews. To ask for the body f one guilty of *maiestas* could be looked ıpon as sympathizing.

In Matthew 27:57, Joseph is identiied as a disciple and rich. The aorist verb, however, may be translated that he became a disciple at a later time and need not mean that he was counted among the disciples when he buried Jesus. In Luke 23:50–51, he is identified as a good and righteous man, who did not consent to their plan and action and who was waiting for the kingdom of God. In John 19:38, he is identified as a secret disciple. Possibly, Joseph became a follower of Jesus after the resurrection, which explains why his name was remembered in the tradition.

So Joseph bought some linen cloth, took down the body, wrapped it in the linen, and placed it in a tomb cut out of rock (15:46). "Some linen cloth" translates the word *sindon* (see 14:51–52). It may refer to pieces of cloth to wrap the body but more likely refers to a single piece of linen cloth not unlike the spurious Shroud of Turin.

The surviving tombs from this period appear to belong to wealthier families. Most of the population apparently were buried in "simple shallow pits" that have not survived.[415] Wealthier Jews practiced secondary burial. When the flesh had decomposed, the bones were carefully gathered up and placed in an ossuary

ROCK-HEWN TOMBS

Examples of Roman-era rolling stone tombs in Israel.

TOMB OF JOSEPH AND THE EDICULE

Looking at the present edicule, it is impossible to know what the original tomb of Jesus looked like. We can now reconstruct that original by comparison with 63 other round-stone tombs from the time of Christ. Probably the closest of these 63 would be Heshbon Tomb F.1 which of all 63 most closely follows the plan found in the Mishnah Baba Bathiza 6:8. This form temporarily died out at A.D. 70 with the Roman destruction, but was brought back in the 4th century A.D.

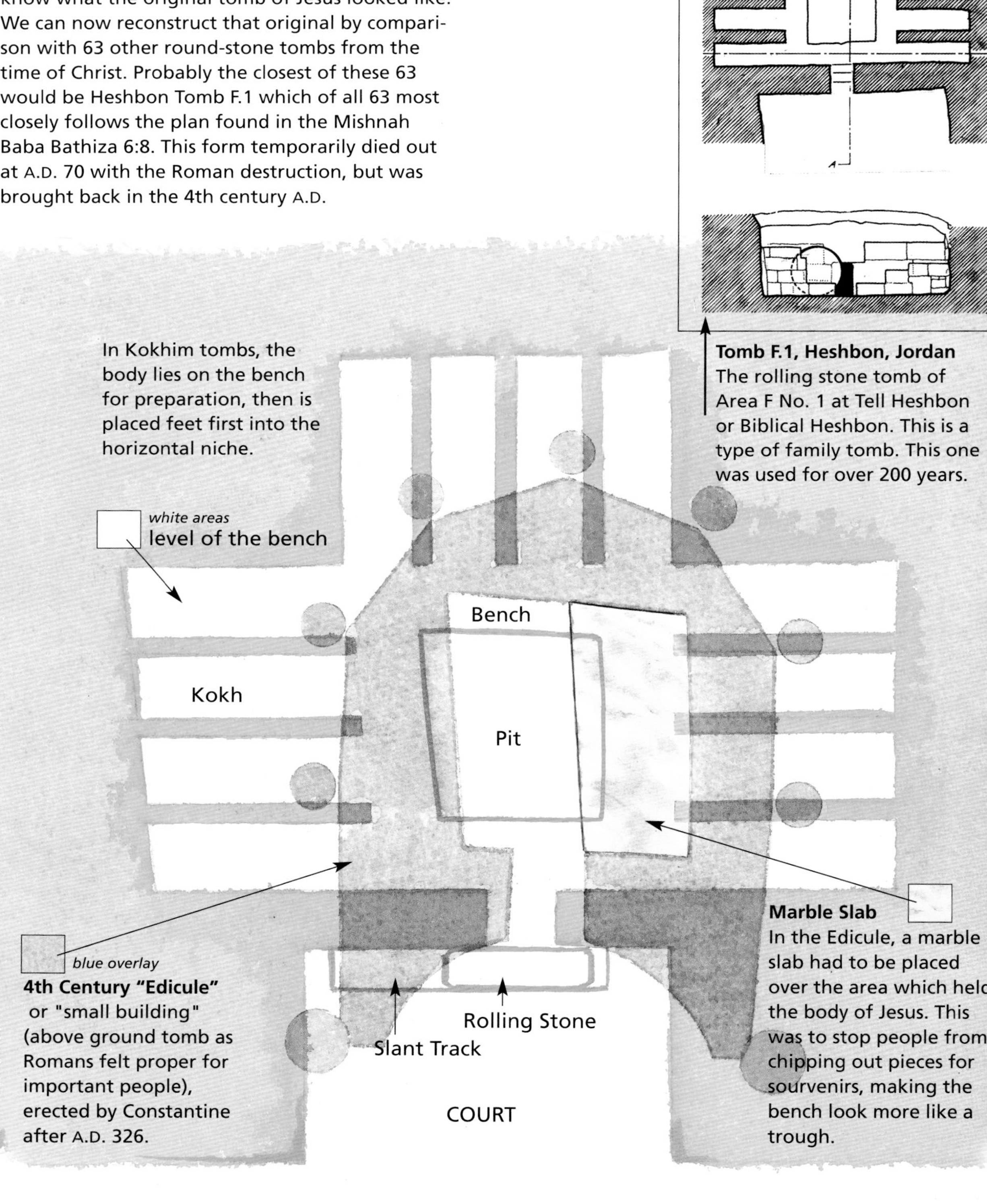

Tomb F.1, Heshbon, Jordan
The rolling stone tomb of Area F No. 1 at Tell Heshbon or Biblical Heshbon. This is a type of family tomb. This one was used for over 200 years.

4th Century "Edicule" or "small building" (above ground tomb as Romans felt proper for important people), erected by Constantine after A.D. 326.

box, the larger bones on the bottom and smaller bones on top. This practice allowed tombs to be reused. The coffinless body would be placed in a niche (*kokh*, up to 2 ft wide and 7 ft deep) cut horizontally into the wall of the tomb chamber. Another type of tomb had trough-like shelves hewn along the sides of the chamber with an arched ceiling (*acrosolinium*). A third type of tomb had a low bench cut around three sides of the chamber. Mark's account of the angel sitting inside on the right (16:5) seems to describe a tomb with a bench, and John 20:6, 8 suggests it has an anteroom.

Then he rolled a stone against the entrance of the tomb (15:46). The tombs in this period had small, low openings into cave-like chambers that were closed with stone blocks (see John 11:38–39) or with rolling stones (like a mill stone) in slanted tracks. Sealing the tomb prevented the body from being disturbed and shut out dirt. But it also shut down its potential defiling effects. A tomb with a door was ruled as not spreading defilement on all sides, and one could safely walk above it without being defiled.

A discussion in the *Tosepta* describes the case of a man who died on the eve of Passover. To bury him, the women tied a rope to the rolling stone and the men pulled on the rope from outside to move it. The women then entered the tomb and buried the man. By not touching directly the body or the rolling stone, the men remained in a state of purity and were able to eat the Passover.[416]

The tomb in which Jesus was laid had to be nearby since the body had to be buried quickly before the Sabbath. Visitors to Jerusalem are frequently shown the garden tomb, discovered in 1867, as the site of Jesus' burial. It is a more peaceful and picturesque locale than the Holy Sepulchre church and definitely outside the city wall. The archaeological evidence, however, rules it out, since it was hewn in Iron Age II (eighth to seventh century B.C.). No other tombs that can be dated to the time of Jesus have been uncovered in this area, and it differs from other excavated burial caves that date from the first century.[417]

The Report of the Resurrection (16:1–8)

When the Sabbath was over, Mary Magdalene, Mary the mother of James, and Salome bought spices so that they might go to anoint Jesus' body (16:1). It was customary to check a tomb before three days to make sure that the person was dead. "After the Sabbath" explains why the women do not come to the tomb sooner; they do not want to violate the Sabbath.

Anointing a body with aromatic oils neutralized the smell from its decomposition, and sometimes anointing the body was repeated. Gundry contends that Jews customarily used oil, not aromatics, and argues that the burial of a king was the exception (see 2 Chron. 16:14; Song 4:10).[418] The dignity of anointing Jesus' body with spices is an attempt to remove the disgrace of the crucifixion for the Son of God, who deserves no less than a king. The women may have judged that what Joseph did was insufficient.

Who will roll the stone away from the entrance of the tomb? (16:3). Stones required some force to move them back along the sloped groove. The entrance would have been small and one needed to stoop to enter, but the inner court would have been high enough for one to stand.

As they entered the tomb, they saw a young man dressed in a white robe sitting on the right side (16:5). The white robe is the characteristic dress of heavenly beings.[419] Angels were not pictured with wings. Only the seraphim had wings, and they numbered six (Isa. 6:2). Cherubim had animal and human features, but the Bible describes angels as quite human-like.[420] In 2 Maccabees 3:26, angels are described as "two young men . . . remarkably strong, gloriously beautiful and splendidly dressed." Josephus describes the angel who appears to Manoah's wife (Judg. 13:13) "as being in the likeness of a beautiful youth."[421]

Don't be alarmed (16:6). Angels typically urge those to whom they appear not to be afraid or amazed.[422]

They said nothing to anyone, because they were afraid (16:8). The earliest and most reliable texts conclude Mark's gospel at 16:8. This abrupt ending has caused consternation for many, however. How could a Gospel end on a note of apparent failure and with no resurrection appearances? Two other existing endings to Mark's Gospel testify to early dissatisfaction or an uneasiness with this finale. (1) A shorter ending, extant in only a handful of later manuscripts, is clearly a subsequent attempt to tie up the loose ends. The phrase "the sacred and imperishable proclamation of eternal salvation" plainly derives from the church's language of a later era.

(2) A better-attested longer ending (16:9–20), recording three appearances of Jesus and his ascension, contains vocabulary and style that differ noticeably from that found in the rest of Mark. The transition from verse 8 to verse 9 is rough, suddenly switching to Jesus' appearing to Mary Magdalene and completely ignoring the other two women. Mary Magdalene was introduced in 15:40, 47 and 16:1 without any further description, but she now is identified as the one out of whom Jesus cast out seven demons (see Luke 8:2). Careful analysis points to a later scribe in the second century reworking accounts from the other Gospels or oral traditions to compose a more reassuring ending for Mark.

Speculations about a lost ending or suggestions that Mark somehow may have failed to complete his Gospel are not helpful. Mark may have felt no need to relate resurrection appearances already familiar to his readers. The Gospel begins as abruptly as it ends, and it is more likely that Mark intends this suspenseful ending to provoke a reaction in the reader. The reader knows the disciples eventually reunite with Jesus in story time if not in

REFLECTIONS

THE TITLE OF THIS NARRATIVE IS "The beginning of the gospel about Jesus Christ, the Son of God" (1:1). Mark understands that the story cannot end with the report of the resurrection of Jesus. The readers also must go to Jesus, who goes on ahead of them. They must not only tell about his resurrection but must tell the entire story from the beginning. Will they take the baton that is being passed to them, run faithfully their part of the race, and pass the baton to others? Or will they retreat in fear and silence? Hearing the announcement of Jesus' resurrection is not enough. All who would be Jesus' disciples must take up their cross and follow him where he goes and where he bids.

the plotted time of the Gospel; otherwise, this Gospel would never have been written. Paul says he reminded the Corinthians that he related these events to them as of first importance (1 Cor. 15:3–5). The word of Jesus' resurrection has clearly been made public. The repetition of Jesus' prediction that they will meet him in Galilee (Mark 16:7; cf. 14:28) also guarantees that these things do come to pass, because the other predictions he made in the Passion Narrative were fulfilled to the letter.

Since Mark does not narrate how this reunion occurs, the reader can only conclude that God overrode human fear, failure, and disobedience to accomplish it—as God always does. One must infer that success does not depend on the heroism of individual believers, whose flesh is weak and whose spirit is not always willing, but on the power of God.

ANNOTATED BIBLIOGRAPHY

France, R. T. *Divine Government: God's Kingship in the Gospel of Mark*. London: SPCK, 1990.

A compelling overview of a key theme in Mark.

Garland, David E. *Mark*. NIVAC. Grand Rapids: Zondervan, 1996.

A commentary that combines analysis of the original meaning of the text with discussion of how to bridge the contexts to our world and make contemporary application.

Geddert, Timothy J. *Watchwords: Mark 13 in Markan Eschatology*. JSNTSup 26. Sheffield: JSOT, 1989.

A brilliantly conceived dissertation that is not only readable but offers keen insights into the text of Mark.

Gundry, Robert H. *Mark: A Commentary on His Apology for the Cross*. Grand Rapids: Eerdmans, 1993.

A carefully argued commentary with extensive interaction with the technical scholarship on Mark.

Hooker, Morna D. *The Gospel According to Saint Mark*. BNTC. Peabody, Mass.: Hendrickson, 1991.

A more popular commentary by an astute interpreter of Mark.

Juel, Donald. *A Master of Surprise*. Philadelphia: Fortress, 1994.

An excellent overview of the Gospel.

Lane, William L. *Commentary on the Gospel of Mark*. NICNT. Grand Rapids: Eerdmans, 1974.

One of the classic commentaries on Mark that has stood well the test of time.

Schweizer, Eduard. *The Good News According to Mark*. Richmond, Va.: John Knox, 1970.

A scintillating treatment of Mark by a renown biblical scholar.

Main Text Notes

1. See also Col. 4:10; Philem. 24; 1 Peter 5:13.
2. Tacitus, *Hist.*1.2–3.
3. Joel Marcus, *The Way of the Lord: Christological Exegesis of the Old Testament in the Gospel of Mark* (Louisville: Westminster/John Knox, 1992), 76.
4. See Gen. 6:2; Job 1:6; 2:1; 38:7; Ps. 82:6; Dan. 3:25.
5. See Ex. 4:22–23; Deut. 1:31; 14:1; 32:5–6; Jer. 31:9, 20; Hos. 11:1; see also Wisd. Sol. 18:13; *Jub. 1:24–25; T. Mos.* 10:3; *Pss. Sol.* 17:27; 18:4; *Sib. Or.* 3:702.
6. See Wisd. Sol. 2:18; Sir. 4:10; compare Matt. 5:9.
7. *Jos. Asen.* 6:3, 5; 13:10; 21:3; 23:10.
8. 2 Sam. 7:14; Ps. 2:7; cf. 89:26–27.
9. See *4 Ezra* 7:28–29; 13:32, 37, 52; 14:9; 4QFlor 1:11–13; 1Qsa 2:11–12; *1 En.* 105:2; see also *b. Sukkah* 52a. Later Judaism would have expunged such usage because of Christian use of the title for Jesus.
10. Adolf Deissmann, *Light from the Ancient East* (1922; reprint, Grand Rapids: Baker, 1978), 295.
11. Robert H. Gundry, *Mark: A Commentary on His Apology for the Cross* (Grand Rapids: Eerdmans, 1993), 34.
12. Mark characteristically fuses Scripture, see 1:11 (Isa. 42:1/Ps. 2:7); 11:1–11 (Zech. 9:9/Ps. 118:25–26); 11:17 (Isa. 56:7/Jer. 7:11); 12:1–12 (Isa. 5:1–2/Ps. 118:22–23); 13:24–26 (Isa. 13:10/34:4/Ezek. 32:7–8/Joel 2:10); 14:62 (Dan. 7:13/Ps. 110:1).
13. Marcus, *The Way of the Lord*, 20.
14. Ex. 2:15; 1 Sam. 23:14; 1 Kings 19:3–4.
15. See 2 Macc. 5:27; Philo, *Decalogue* 1.2.
16. 1QS 8:13–14.
17. *b. Ker.* 9a; 81a; *b. Yebam.* 46a; see 1 Cor. 10:2.
18. Ezek. 36:25–27; see also Isa. 4:3–4; Zech. 13:1; 1QS 4:20–21.
19. *m. Miqw.* 8:5; 9:1.
20. Josephus, *Ant.* 18.5.2 § 117.
21. 2 Kings 1:8; see Zech. 13:4.
22. Gustav Dalman, *Sacred Sites and Ways*, trans. Paul P. Levortoff (New York: Macmillan, 1935), 84.
23. Josephus, *J.W.* 4.8.3 § 469.
24. *Mekilta Nezikin* 1 to Ex. 21:2; *Mekilta de-Rabbi Ishmael* trans. Jacob Z. Lauterbach (Philadelphia: Jewish Publications Society of America, 1935), 3:5–6.
25. See Ezek. 1:1; 3; John 1:51; Acts 7:56; Rev. 4:1; 11:19; 19:11.
26. Josephus, *Ant.* 20.5.1 §97.
27. *b. Ḥag.* 15a.
28. F. E. Greenspahn, "Why Prophesy Ceased," *JBL* 108 (1989): 37–49.
29. *y. Soṭah* 13:2.
30. The same verb occurs in Mark 3:19; 9:31; 10:33; 14:10, 11, 18, 21, 41, 42, 44; 15:1, 10, 15.
31. See *4 Ezra* 4:36–37; 9:5; 11:44; *2 Bar.* 40:3.
32. Charles R. Page II, *Jesus and the Land* (Nashville: Abingdon, 1995), 73.
33. Mendel Nun, *The Sea of Galilee and Its Fishermen in the New Testament* (Tiberias: En Gev, 1989); John J. Rousseau and Rami Arav, *Jesus and His World: An Archaeological and Cultural Dictionary* (Minneapolis: Fortress, 1995), 94; K. C. Hanson, "The Galilean Fishing Economy and the Jesus Tradition," *BTB* 27 (1997): 105.
34. Jer. 16:14–16; Ezek. 29:4; 32:3; Amos 4:2; Hab. 1:14–17.
35. *Jos. Asen.* 21:21.
36. James F. Strange and Hershel Shanks, "Synagogue Where Jesus Preached Found at Capernaum," *BAR* 9 (1983): 24–31.
37. Daniel K. Falk, "Jewish Prayer Literature and the Jerusalem Church in Acts," in *The Book of Acts in Its First Century Setting;* vol. 4 of *Palestinian Setting*, ed. Richard Bauckham (Grand Rapids: Eerdmans, 1995), 282.
38. Sherman E. Johnson, *Jesus and His Towns* (GNS 29; Wilmington Del.: Michael Glazier, 1989), 69.
39. G. B. Caird, *New Testament Theology*, ed. L. D. Hurst (Oxford: Clarendon, 1994), 109.
40. William L. Lane, *Commentary on the Gospel of Mark* (NICNT; Grand Rapids: Eerdmans, 1974), 74, citing O. Bauernfeind, *Die Worte der Dämonen in Markusevangelium* (Stuttgart, 1927).
41. *m. Demai* 3:6.
42. See John Granger Cook, "In Defense of Ambiguity: Is There a Hidden Demon in Mark 1.29–31?" *NTS* 43 (1997): 184–208.
43. *b. Ned.* 41a.
44. Bargil Pixner, *With Jesus through Galilee According to the Fifth Gospel* (Collegeville: Liturgical, 1992), 34.
45. *m. Neg.* 1:1.
46. *m. Neg.* 3:1; 4:7–10; *t. Meg.* 1:1.
47. Lev. 13:45–52; Num. 5:2–4.
48. The interpretations of the rabbis argued that one became defiled by a leper by passing under a tree where a leper was standing (*m. Neg.* 13:7; *b. Ber.* 25a), entering a leprous house (*b. Ber.* 41a), or being in a house which a leper entered (*m. Neg.* 13:11; *m. Kel.* 1:4).
49. *m. Neg.* 13:12; *t. Neg.* 7:11.

50. *Lev. Rab.* 16:3.
51. M. Wojciechowski, "The Touching of the Leper (Mark 1,40–45) as a Historical and Symbolic Act of Jesus," *BZ* 33 (1989): 114–119.
52. Morna D. Hooker, *The Gospel According to Saint Mark* (BNTC; Peabody, Mass.: Hendrickson, 1991), 79.
53. Rousseau and Arav, *Jesus and His World*, 340.
54. 4Q242.
55. *b. Ned.* 41a.
56. *b. Meg.* 17b.
57. See the paralysis of Alcimus in 1 Macc. 9:55, and of Ptolemy IV Philopator in *3 Macc.* 2:21–23.
58. See Isa. 33:24; Jer. 31:34; and Mic. 7:18.
59. 2 Sam. 12:13; Isa. 6:7; 43:25; 44:22.
60. 1 Sam. 16:7; 1 Chron. 28:9; Ps. 139:1–2, 6, 23; Jer. 11:20; 17:9–10; Acts 1:24.
61. *m. Ned.* 3:4.
62. Plutarch, *On Curiosity* 518E.
63. Josephus, *J.W.* 2.14.4 § 287; 2.14.5 § 292.
64. See Acts 16:34; *Jos. Asen.* 20:8.
65. John Riches, *Jesus and the Transformation of Judaism* (New York: Seabury, 1982), 105.
66. See, e.g., Ps. 1:1, "Blessed is the man who does not walk in the counsel of the wicked or stand in the way of sinners or sit in the seat of mockers."
67. *Mekilta Amalek* 3 to Ex. 18:1.
68. Gundry, *Mark*, 129.
69. Lev. 16:29, 31; 23:27, 32; Num. 29:7.
70. 1 Sam. 31:13; 2 Sam. 1:12; 3:35; 12:21; 1 Kings 21:27; Est. 4:3; Ps. 35:13–14; 69:10; Isa. 58:5; Jonah 3:5.
71. Isa. 62:5; Ezek. 16:7–14; see Isa. 54:4–8.
72. *m. Šabb.* 7:2.
73. See Judith 8:6; *Jub.* 50:2; *m. Taʿan.* 1:6.
74. Ps. 137:5; Zech. 11:17.
75. CD 11:10; *m. Šabb.* 14:3–4; *t. Šabb.* 12:8–14.
76. *t. Šabb.* 16:22; *b. Šabb.* 12a.
77. *m. Yoma* 8:6; *Mekilta Shabbata* 1 to Ex. 31:12.
78. Josephus, *Ant.* 15.10.4–5 §§ 371–79.
79. Otto Betz, "Jesus and the Temple Scroll," *Jesus and the Dead Sea Scrolls*, ed. J. H. Charlesworth (New York: Doubleday, 1992), 76–78.
80. Num. 1:1–19, 44; see also Gen. 49:28.
81. See Gen. 17:5, 15; 32:28.
82. Chrys C. Caragounis, *Peter and the Rock* (BZNW 58; Berlin/New York: Walter de Gruyter, 1990), 12, 15.
83. *b. Sanh.* 43a. See also *b. Soṭa* 47a; 107b; *t. Šabb.* 11:15; John 7:20; 8:48, 52; 10:20.
84. Num. 15:30–31; 1 Sam. 3:14; Isa. 22:14.
85. Alan Hugh McNeile, *The Gospel According to St. Matthew* (London: Macmillan, 1915), 179.
86. C. E. B. Cranfield, *The Gospel According to St. Mark* (CGTC; Cambridge: Cambridge Univ. Press, 1966), 159.
87. R. T. France, *Divine Government: God's Kingship in the Gospel of Mark* (London: SPCK, 1990), 30.
88. Seneca, *Mor. Ep.* 38.2; 73.16; Quintilian, 5.11.24; Burton L. Mack and Vernon K. Robbins, *Patterns of Persuasion in the Gospels* (Sonoma: Polebridge, 1989), 156.
89. Mack and Robbins, *Patterns of Persuasion in the Gospels*, 156.
90. Jer. 31:27–28; Ezek. 36:9; Hos. 2:21–23; *4 Ezra* 9:31; see Mark 3:20.
91. See Ezek. 36:9; Hos. 10:11–12; *Jub.* 11:11.
92. K. D. White, "The Parable of the Sower," *JTS* 15 (1964): 304.
93. Pliny, *Nat. Hist.* 18.21.94–95. Varro said seed in Syria could yield a hundred fold (*On Agriculture* 2.9.5–6).
94. John H. Martin, Warren H. Leonard, and David L. Stamp, *Principles of Field Crop Production* (New York: Macmillan, 1976), 436.
95. Strabo, *Geogr.* (SBL 261) 15.3.11.
96. Job 15:8; Ps. 25:14; Prov. 3:32; Amos 3:7.
97. 1QS 5:11.
98. See *Jub.* 11:5–24; *b. Sanh.* 107a.
99. Jer. 25:10; Matt. 25:1–13; Rev. 18:22–23.
100. *b. Ber.* 40a.
101. *m. Nidda* 5:2; *m. Nazir* 1:5; *m. Tohar.* 8:8.
102. Claus-Hunno Hunzinger, "σίναπι," TDNT, 7.289.
103. Charles E. Carlston, *The Parables of the Triple Tradition* (Philadelphia: Fortress, 1975), 162.
104. Pliny, *Nat. Hist.* 19:170–71.
105. Gundry, *Mark*, 267.
106. See Ps. 104:12, 16–17.
107. *1 En.* 90:30, 33, 37; *Midr. Ps.* 104:10.
108. 1QH 6:14–17; 8:4–8.
109. Luke 5:1; "Sea of Kinnereth," Num. 34:11; Josh. 12:3; 13:27.
110. Pixner, *Galilee*, 89. See Josephus, *J.W.* 3.10.7 § 515.
111. Shelley Wachsmann, *The Sea of Galilee Boat: An Extraordinary 200 Year Old Discovery* (New York: Plenum, 1995), 349; Hanson, "The Galilean Fishing Economy," 106.
112. Rousseau and Arav, *Jesus and His World*, 246.
113. Page, *Jesus and the Land*, 183, n. 30.
114. See also Ps. 69:1–2; 89:9–10; 104:7.
115. See also Ps. 104:7; 106:9; Isa. 50:2; Nah. 1:4.
116. Ps. 3:5; 4:8; 46:1–3; Prov. 3:23–26.
117. See Job 30:6; Heb. 11:38; *b. Ber.* 3b; *b. Šabb.* 67a; *b. Giṭ.* 70a; *b. Sanh.* 65b.
118. Cf. Str-B 1.491–92.
119. *T. Sol.* 5:1–13; 13:1–17. See *PGM* 1.160–61 for asking a demon to divulge its name: "What is your divine name? Reveal it to me ungrudgingly, so that I may call upon it."

120. Matt. 12:43; Luke 11:24; see also Tobit 8:3.
121. 1 Macc. 1:62–64; 2 Macc 6:18–7:42.
122. Josephus, *J.W.* 3.7.31 § 289.
123. Pliny, *Nat. Hist.* 7.64.
124. Noted by Jacob Milgrom, *Leviticus 1–16* (AB; New York: Doubleday, 1991), 948.
125. Josephus reports that the temple was closed to women during their menstruation (*J.W.* 5.5.6 § 227; *Ag. Ap.* 2.8 §§103–4).
126. See 2 Chron. 16:12; Job 13:4; Jer. 46:11; 51:8; and Philo, *Sacrifices* 70–71.
127. *t. B. Bat.* 10:6.
128. *m. Qidd.* 4:14.
129. *b. Pesaḥ.* 113a.
130. *b. Šabb.* 110a.
131. John P. Meier, *A Marginal Jew: Rethinking the Historical Jesus* (New York: Doubleday, 1991), 1.785.
132. An inscription shows that Nazareth was spelled with the Hebrew letter tzade (Pixner, *Galilee,* 15).
133. *Jos. Asen.* 6:10.
134. Meier, *A Marginal Jew,* 1.281.
135. Origen, *Contra Celsum* 6.36.
136. Richard Bauckham, "The Brothers and Sisters of Jesus: An Epiphanian Response to John P. Meier," *CBQ* 56 (1994): 698–700.
137. Josephus also refers to James as "the brother of Jesus" (*Ant.* 20.9.1 § 200).
138. Num. 35:30; Deut. 17:6; 19:15; 2 Cor. 13:1; 1 Tim. 5:19.
139. André Parrott, *Land of Christ: Archaeology, History, Geography* (Philadelphia: Fortress, 1968), 48–49.
140. See also Ex. 12:11; Ezek. 20:37; 37:15–28.
141. *m. ʾOhal.* 2:3; *m. Ṭehar.* 4:5.
142. Philo, *Dreams* 2.58.
143. Josephus, *Ant.* 18.5.2 § 119.
144. Josephus, *J.W.* 7.6.2 §§ 171–77.
145. Josephus, *Ant.* 18.5.1 §§ 109–15.
146. Ibid., 18.5.2 §118.
147. Compare the story of the pledge of the emperor Gaius to Agrippa (Josephus *Ant.* 18.8.7 §§ 289–304).
148. Vincent Taylor, *The Gospel According to St Mark* (London: Macmillan, 1966), 311.
149. *m. ʿAbod. Zar.* 1:3.
150. The story of another dancing girl appears in Josephus, *Ant.* 12.5.6 §§186–89.
151. The dimensions of a loaf according to *m. Peʾah* 8:7. It probably looked somewhat like modern pita bread.
152. See Ex. 18:21, 25 (officers over thousands, hundreds, fifties, and tens); 1QS 2:21–22; 1QSa 1:14–15, 27–2:1; 2:11–22; 1QM 4:1–5:16; CD 13:1.
153. Josephus, *Life* §§ 398–406.
154. Josephus, *Ant.* 18.2.1 § 28; but see idem *J.W.* 2.9.1 § 168, which seems to connect it to the wife of Augustus, Livia (given the name Julia after her death in 29 B.C.), instead of his daughter, who had been discredited. Her third marriage in 11 B.C. to Tiberius, the stepson of Augustus, ended in estrangement; and her father exiled her for her adulteries in 2 B.C. On this issue, see Fred Strickert, *Bethsaida: Home of the Apostles* (Collegeville, Minn.: Liturgical, 1998), 91–107.
155. Ibid., 41–45.
156. Job 9:8; 38:8–11; Prov. 8:29; Isa. 43:16; 51:10; Hab. 3:15; Sir. 24:5–6.
157. See Ex. 33:19–23; 34:5–6; 1 Kings 19:11; Job 9:8, 11 (see LXX; "He walks upon the waves of the sea. . . If he goes by me, I will not see him, and if he passes by me, I will not recognize him"); Dan 12:1 (LXX) describing the glory of the Lord passing by; Amos 7:8; 8:22.
158. Ex. 3:14; Deut. 32:39; Isa. 41:2–14; 43:1–13 (cf. v. 2, "When you pass through the waters I will be with you"); 44:1–5; 46:4; 48:12; 51:9–16; 52:6.
159. *b. B. Bat.* 73a; cited by Lane, *Mark,* 237.
160. Josephus, *J.W.* 3.10.7–8 §§506, 516–21.
161. Yigael Yadin, *Bar-Kokhba* (London: Weidenfeld and Nicolson, 1978), 81–85.
162. Deut. 12:15, 22; 15:22.
163. Lev. 15:7; 16:26, 28; 17:15–16; 22:1–7.
164. Josephus, *J.W.* 2.8.5 § 129.
165. *Let. of Aris.* 305–6.
166. *b. Ber.* 60b.
167. *m. ʾAbot* 1:1–2.
168. Josephus, *J.W.* 2.8.10 § 150.
169. See *b. Ber.* 47b.
170. See Prov. 28:24; 1 Tim. 5:4.
171. *b. Qidd.* 31b.
172. Josephus considers it to be a distinctive Jewish oath, see *Ant.* 4.4.4 § 73; *Ag. Ap.* 1.166–67.
173. *m. Ned.* 5:6.
174. *m. Makš.* 6:7; *t. Miqw.* 7:8.
175. *y. Pesaḥ.* 7:11.
176. According to *Sifra Mes. Zab.* 1:12–13.
177. See Josephus *J.W.* 2.8.9 §§ 148–49; 1QM 7:3–7; 11QT 46:15–16. See further the discussion in Harrington, *Impurity Systems of Qumran,* 100–103.
178. Josephus, *Ag. Ap.* 1.70. See also Isa. 23; Jer. 25:22; 27:3; 47:4; Ezek. 26–28; Joel 3:4; Amos 1:9; Zech. 9:2. In Matt. 11:21–24, Tyre and Sidon are equivalent to Sodom and Gomorrah.
179. Martin Hengel, *Studies in the Gospel of Mark* (London: SCM, 1985), 29.
180. Deut. 32:6; Isa. 1:2; Jer. 31:9; Hos. 11:1; Rom. 9:4.
181. *m. ʾAbot.* 3:15.

182. See 1 Sam. 17:43; 24:14; 2 Sam. 3:8; 9:8; 16:9; 2 Kings 8:13; Prov. 26:11; Eccl. 9:4; Isa. 56:10–11; *m. Pesaḥ.* 8:8.
183. *b. Ḥag.* 13a.
184. *Jos. Asen.* 10:13.
185. Gerd Theissen, *The Gospels in Context: Social and Political History in the Synoptic Tradition* (Minneapolis: Fortress, 1991), 61–80.
186. See Sean Freyne, *Galilee: From Alexander the Great to Hadrian 323* BCE *to 135* CE (Edinburgh: T. & T. Clark, 1980), 8, 117–21.
187. See Ezek. 26:1–27:36; Joel 3:4–21; Amos 1:9–10; Zech. 9:1–4.
188. Suetonius, *Vespasian* 8:7.
189. Juvenal, *Sat.* 3.14; 6.542.
190. Jeffrey B. Gibson, "Jesus' Refusal to Produce a 'Sign' (Mark 8.11–13)," *JSNT* 38 (1990): 53.
191. Plutarch, *Roman Questions* 289F; see also Pliny, *Nat. Hist.* 18.26.
192. Pliny, *Nat. Hist.* 28.37.
193. Francis Watson, "Ambiguity in the Marcan Narrative," *KTR* 10 (1987): 12.
194. Josephus, *Ant.* 15.10.3 § 364.
195. Ibid., 15.10.3 § 364; idem, *J.W.* 1.21.3 §§ 404–5.
196. Josephus, *Ant.* 18.2.1 § 28; *J.W.* 2.9.1 § 168.
197. Lane, *Mark*, 288.
198. Gen. 22:4; Hos. 6:2; cf. Jonah 2:1.
199. Lane, *Mark*, 296.
200. 1QS 2:13–14; 6:14–15; 10:12–13; 1QH 9:23.
201. Clarence E. Glad, "Frank Speech, Flattery, and Friendship in Philodemus," in *Friendship, Flattery and Frankness of Speech: Studies on Friendship in the New Testament World*, ed. John T. Fitzgerald, (NovTSup 82; Leiden: Brill, 1996), 42.
202. Plutarch, *Moralia* 554A/B.
203. Dionysius of Halicarnassus, *Roman Antiquities* 7.69.1–2.
204. Josephus *J.W.* 4.1.8. §§ 54–61.
205. See Dan. 12:3; Matt. 13:43; Rev. 7:13–14; *1 En.* 38:4; 58:3; 62:15–16; 104:2; *2 En.* 22:8; 66:7; *2 Apoc. Bar.* 51:1–3, 10, 12.
206. Randall E. Otto, "The Fear Motivation in Peter's Offer to Build τρεῖς σκηνάς," *WTJ* 59 (1997): 105.
207. Wayne A. Meeks, *The Prophet-King: Moses Traditions and the Johannine Christology* (Leiden: Brill, 1967), 124; Marcus, *The Way of the Lord*, 89.
208. *Deut. Rab.* 3:17.
209. Otto, "The Fear Motivation in Peter's Offer," 106.
210. Ibid., 104.
211. *m. ʿEd.* 8:7; *m. Šeqal.* 2:5; *m. B. Meṣiʿa* 1:8.
212. Justin Martyr, *Dialogue With Rabbi Trypho* 8.4; 49.1.
213. John J. Pilch, *The Cultural World of Jesus* (Collegeville: Liturgical, 1996), 30.
214. Josephus, *J.W.* 7.6.3 § 185.
215. Acts 13:2; 14:23; *Did.* 7; 8; Justin, *Apology* 61.
216. *b. Nid.* 13b.
217. Deut. 14:1; 1 Kings 18:28; Zech. 13:6.
218. 2 Chron. 28:3; 33:6; Jer. 7:31–32.
219. 2 Kings 2:21–22; Ezek. 16:4; 43:24.
220. *Sib. Or.* 2:252–55.
221. *m. ʿArak.* 5:6; see also *m. Yebam.* 14:1.
222. Josephus, *Life* § 427.
223. *m. Ketub.* 4:9.
224. *m. Giṭ.* 6:2.
225. *b. Yebam.* 63b.
226. Michael O. Wise, *A Critical Study of the Temple Scroll from Cave 11* (Chicago: Oriental Institute of the Univ. of Chicago, 1990), 161–75. See 11Q Temple 57:11–19; CD 4:18–21.
227. Josephus, *Ant.* 15.7.10 § 259.
228. Ibid., 20.7.2 §§ 141–43.
229. Ibid., 18.5.4. § 136.
230. Malina and Rohrbaugh, *Social-Science Commentary on the Synoptic Gospels*, 243.
231. Ibid., 244.
232. Martin Hengel, *Poverty and Riches in the Early Church* (Philadelphia: Fortress, 1974), 8. See *m. ʿArak.* 8:4; *b. Ketub.* 50a; *b. Taʿan.* 24a.
233. G. W. E. Nickelsburg, "Riches in 1 Enoch 92–95," *NTS* 25 (1979): 327. See also Bruce J. Malina, "Wealth and Poverty in the New Testament," *Int* 41 (1987): 361; *The New Testament World: Insights from Cultural Anthropology* (Atlanta: John Knox, 1981), 75–85. See also Sir. 13:3–4; 34:20–22.
234. See *Jos. Asen.* 10:11–13. On Asenath's conversion, she threw all her goods out her palace window for the poor and the beggars.
235. *b. Ber.* 55b; *b. B. Meṣiʿa* 38b.
236. See P. S. Minear, "The Needle's Eye: A Study in Form Criticism," *JBL* 61 (1942): 157–69.
237. See Job 1:10; 42:10; Ps. 128:1–2; Isa. 3:10.
238. Tacitus, *Hist.* 2.59.
239. Ps. 75:8; Isa. 51:17, 22; Jer. 25:15, 28; 49:12.
240. Plato, *Gorgias* 491E.
241. Seneca, *On Benefits* 3.19.1.
242. Ex. 21:30; Lev. 25:51–52; Num. 18:15; 35:31–32; Isa. 35:10; 51:11.
243. Isa. 52:13–53:12 [esp. 53:10]; cf. 1 Tim. 2:5–6.
244. Malina and Rohrbaugh, *Social-Science Commentary on the Synoptic Gospels*, 246.
245. Lev. 21:18; 2 Sam. 5:8.
246. 1QSa 2:8–9.
247. Christopher D. Marshall, *Faith as a Theme in Mark's Narrative* (SNTSMS 64; Cambridge: Cambridge Univ. Press, 1989), 128.

248. See Ex. 22:26–27; Deut. 24:12–13.
249. See Num. 19:2; Deut. 21:3; 1 Sam. 6:7.
250. *m. Sanh.* 2:5.
251. *b. Sanh.* 98a.
252. Hanukkah; 1 Macc. 13:51; 2 Macc. 10:7; *m. Sukkah* 3:9.
253. Josephus, *J.W.* 2.17.8 § 434.
254. Mal. 3:1–2, cited in Mark 1:2.
255. Kathleen and Leon Ritmeyer, "Reconstructing Herod's Temple Mount in Jerusalem," *Archaeology in the World of Herod, Jesus, and Paul* (Washington: Biblical Archaeology Society, 1990), 2:43–45.
256. Pliny, *Nat. Hist.* 16.49.
257. Isa. 28:3–4; Jer. 8:13; Hos. 9:16; Joel 1:7, 12; Mic. 7:1; Hab. 3:17–18.
258. Jostein Ådna, "The Attitude of Jesus to the Temple," *Mishkan* 17–18 (1992–93): 68.
259. Josephus, *Ant.* 15.11.5 § 412.
260. Benjamin Mazar, "The Royal *Stoa* in the Southern Part of the Temple Mount," in *Recent Archaeology in the Land of Israel*, ed. H. Shanks (Washington/Jerusalem: Biblical Archaeology Society, 1984), 141–47.
261. *m. Šeqal.* 1:3; 4:7–8.
262. *t. Šeqal.* 1:6.
263. *m. Ker.* 1:7.
264. Josephus, *Ag. Ap.* 2.8 §106.
265. *m. Ber.* 9:5.
266. 1 Sam. 1:1–28; 1 Kings 8:27–51; Dan. 6:10.
267. *b. Ber.* 32b.
268. Josephus, *J.W.* 6.5.3 §§ 300–309.
269. Meier, *A Marginal Jew,* 164.
270. 4Q500 (4QBenediction); J. M. Baumgarten, "4Q 500 and the Ancient Conception of the Lord's Vineyard," *JJS* 40 (1989): 1–6.
271. See S. R. Llewellyn, "The Lease Agreement and the Parable of the Wicked Tenants," *New Documents Illustrating Early Christianity* (Sydney: Macquarie University, 1992): 88–107.
272. See 1 Kings 14:18; 15:29; 18:36; 2 Kings 9:36; 10:10; 14:25; Jer. 7:25; Dan. 9:6; Amos 3:7.
273. 2 Chron. 24:18–19; 36:15–16; Neh. 9:26.
274. 4Q Florilegium 1:11 on 2 Sam. 7:11; 1QSa 2:11–12 on Ps. 2:7.
275. Deut. 28:26; Jer. 7:33; 8:1; Ezek. 6:5; 29:5; 39:17; see Jer. 22:19, "He will have the burial of a donkey—dragged away and thrown outside the gates of Jerusalem."
276. Josephus *J.W.* 2.8.1 § 118; idem *Ant.* 18.1.1 §§ 1–10.
277. P. C. Finney, "The Rabbi and the Coin Portrait (Mark 12:15b, 16): Rigorism Manqué," *JBL* 112 (1993): 629–44.
278. *b. ʿAbod. Zar.* 54b.
279. See Acts 23:8; Josephus, *Ant.* 18.1.4 §§ 16–17; idem *J.W.* 2.8.14 §§ 164–65; *b. Nid.* 70b. A similar story in *Qoh. Rab.* 5.10 § 1 has a Samaritan (who also relied only on the Pentateuch) asking questions to ridicule belief in the resurrection.
280. See also Wisd. Sol. 2:1–5.
281. *b. Mak.* 23b.
282. *b. Mak.* 24a.
283. Ephraim E. Urbach, *The Sages: Their Concepts and Beliefs* (Jerusalem: Magnes, 1975), 1:343–65.
284. See Ex. 22:21–23; Deut. 10:17; 24:17; Isa. 1:17, 23; 10:1–4; Ezek. 22:7.
285. *m. Šeqal.* 6:5–6.
286. *m. Šeqal.* 6:6; *t. Šeqal.* 3:8.
287. *Lev. Rab.* 3.5.
288. Philo, *Embassy* 294–97.
289. Kathleen and Leon Ritmeyer, "Reconstructing Herod's Temple," 45, 48.
290. Josephus, *J.W.* 6.1.1 §§ 5–7.
291. Josephus, *J.W.* 6.5.4. § 312.
292. Ibid., 2.13.4 §§ 258–60.
293. See Dan. 9:27; 11:31; 12:11; see also 1 Macc. 1:54.
294. See Josephus; *Ant.* 18.8.2–9 §§ 257–309; Philo, *Embassy*; Tacitus *History* 5.9.
295. Josephus, *J.W.* 4.3.7 §§ 151–54; 4.3.10 § 162; 4.5.4 §§ 341–43.
296. Ibid., 6.6.1 § 316.
297. "Blessed is the one who reads . . . this" in Rev. 1:3 refers to the public reader.
298. Dan. 8:15–17; 9:22; see also Mark 11:23; 12:10; see Rev. 1:3.
299. Ernest Best, "The Gospel of Mark: Who is the Reader?" *IBS* 11 (1989): 129.
300. Eusebius, *Eccl. Hist.* 3.5.11, 32.
301. Josephus, *J.W.* 6.5.2 §§ 285–87.
302. Dio Chrysostom, *Orations* 66.6–2–3.
303. Josephus, *J.W.* 4.7.5 §§ 433–36.
304. Ibid., 4.4.5 §§ 286–87.
305. Ibid., 6.3.5 §§ 214–19.
306. Ibid., 6.5.1 § 276; 6.6.3 §§ 354–55.
307. Nahman Avigad, "The Burnt House Captures a Moment in Time," in *Archaeology in the World of Herod, Jesus, and Paul;* vol. 2, ed. Hershel Shanks and Dan P. Cole (Washington: BAS, 1990), 96–104.
308. Josephus, *J.W.* 6.8–10 §§ 374–442.
309. Ibid., 6.8.5 § 408.
310. Crispin H. T. Fletcher-Louis, "The Destruction of the Temple and the Relativization of the Old Covenant: Mark 13:31 and Matthew 5:18," in *"The Reader Must Understand": Eschatology in Bible and Theology*, ed. K. E. Brower and M. W. Elliott (Leicester: Apollos, 1997), 145–69.
311. S. R. Llewelyn and R. A. Kearsley eds., *New Documents Illustrating Early Christianity*, ed. (Sydney: Macquarie University, 1992), 60.
312. Ex. 12:1–20; 23:15; 34:18.

313. See 2 Chron. 35:17; Josephus, *Ant.* 14.2.1 §21; 17.9.3 § 213.
314. Henri Daniel-Rops, *Daily Life in the Time of Jesus* (Ann Arbor: Servant, 1980), 96.
315. See Deut. 28:40; Ruth 3:3; Ps. 23:5; Eccl. 9:7–8; Ezek. 16:9; Dan. 6:15; Micah 6:15; Judith 16:7–8; *b. Šabb.* 41a, 61a; *b. Soṭah* 11b; *b. Ketub.* 66b.
316. See *Jub.* 49:10–12.
317. Rousseau and Arav, *Jesus and His World*, 341.
318. William Barclay, *The Gospel of Mark* (Philadelphia: Westminster, 1956), 347–48.
319. Cf. 9:1; Luke 2:26; John 21:23.
320. Meier, *A Marginal Jew*, 2.307.
321. Raymond E. Brown, *The Death of the Messiah* (New York: Doubleday, 1994), 1:123.
322. *m. B. Qam.* 7:7.
323. *y. ʿErub.* 10:1, 26a.
324. Juvenal, *Satire* 9.170–178.
325. Brown, *The Death of the Messiah*, 1:137.
326. Joan F. Taylor, "The Garden of Gethsemane Not the Place of Jesus' Arrest," *BAR* 21 (1995): 26–35, 62.
327. Ibid., 34.
328. Ibid., 35, citing Egeria, *Itinerarium* 36.2; and Theodosius, *De Sittu Sanctae* 10.
329. Brown, *The Death of the Messiah*, 1:167.
330. Joseph A. Fitzmyer, "Abba and Jesus' Relation to God," *À cause de l'évangile* (Paris: Cerf, 1985), 29–30.
331. James Barr, "'*Abba*' Isn't Daddy," *JTS* 39 (1988): 28–47.
332. Brown, *The Death of the Messiah*, 1:688.
333. Josephus, *J.W.* 2.20.7 § 581.
334. Josephus, *Ant.* 20.9.1 § 198.
335. *b. Pesaḥ.* 57a; *t. Menaḥ.* 13:21.
336. Josephus, *Ant.* 20.9.1 § 199.
337. Ibid., 18.2.2 §§ 34–35.
338. Zvi Greenhut, "Burial Cave of the Caiaphas Family," *BAR* 18/5 (1992): 28–36, 76; Ronnie Reich, "Caiaphas' Name Inscribed on Bone Boxes," *BAR* 18/5 (1992): 38–44, 76.
339. Josephus, *J.W.* 2.16.3 § 344.
340. *m. Sanh.* 1:6.
341. *y. Sanh.* 1.1, 18a. On the issue of Jewish power to carry out the death penalty, see Brown, *The Death of the Messiah*, 363–72.
342. Josephus, *Ant.* 20.9.1 §§ 200–203.
343. Josephus, *Ant.* 20.8.6 §§ 169–70.
344. See also *1 En.* 90:28–29.
345. See *2 Bar.* 4:2–6.
346. See Gen. 37:29; 2 Sam. 1:11; 2 Kings 18:37; 22:11–13; Isa. 37:1; Acts 14:14.
347. *b. Sanh.* 38b; *b. Ḥag.* 14a.
348. 4Q246.
349. David Flusser, "The Hubris of the Antichrist in a Qumran Fragment," *Judaism and the Origins of Christianity* (Jerusalem: Magnes, 1988), 210.
350. Josephus, *Ant.* 4.8.6 § 202.
351. *b. Sanh.* 93b citing Isa. 11:2–4.
352. David Flusser, "Who Is It That Struck You?" *Imm.* 20 (1986): 27–32.
353. *b. ʿErub.* 53b.
354. Geza Vermes, *Jesus the Jew* (Philadelphia: Fortress, 1973), 53.
355. Pliny, *Ep.* 10.96.3.
356. Ibid., 10.96.5.
357. Seneca, *On Anger* 2.7.3.
358. Brown, *The Death of the Messiah*, 1:629.
359. Peter Garnsey, "The Criminal Jurisdiction of Governors," *JRS* 58 (1968): 51–59.
360. Tacitus, *Ann.* 2.50; 3.38; Suetonius, *Tiberias* 58.
361. Josephus, *Ant. 17.10.8 §285.*
362. PFlor 1.61.59; cited by Deissmann, *Light*, 268–69.
363. *m. Pesaḥ.* 8:6.
364. Suetonius, *Dom.* 11.
365. Philo, *Embassy* 299.
366. Suetonius, *Cal.* 19.
367. Josephus reports an incident when Herod came to the Sanhedrin "clothed in purple" (*Ant.* 14.9.4 § 173).
368. H. St. J. Hart, "The Crown of Thorns in John 19.2–5," *JTS* 3 (1952): 66–75.
369. Philo, *Flaccus* 6.36–41.
370. Nahman Avigad, "A Depository of Inscribed Ossuaries in the Kidron Valley, *IEJ* 12 (1962): 9–11.
371. Plutarch, *On the Delays of the Divine Vengeance* 554B.
372. Cicero *Rab. Post.* 5.16.
373. Quintilian, *Training in Oratory* 274.
374. Josephus, *J.W.* 5.11.1 §§ 449–451.
375. Joan E. Taylor, "Golgotha: A Reconsideration of the Evidence for the Sites of Jesus' Crucifixion and Burial," *NTS* 44 (1998): 180–203. See also Shimon Gibson and Joan E. Taylor, *Beneath the Church of the Holy Sepulchre: The Archaeology and Early History of Traditional Golgotha* (London: Palestine Exploration Fund, 1994).
376. Taylor, "Golgotha," 201.
377. Josephus, *J. W.* 5.4.1 § 146.
378. James H. Charlesworth, *Jesus Within Judaism: New Light from Exciting Archaeological Discoveries* (New York: Doubleday, 1988), 124.
379. Brown, *The Death of the Messiah*, 2:937–38, 1281–83. See Eusebius's account of the discovery of the tomb in *The Life of Constantine* 3.25–32.
380. *b. Sanh.* 43a.
381. Pliny, *Nat. Hist.* 14.15.
382. Wilhelm Michaelis, "σμυρνίζω," *TDNT*, 7:458–59.

383. T. E. Schmidt, "Mark 15.16–32: The Crucifixion Narrative and the Roman Triumphal Procession," *NTS* 41 (1995): 11–12.
384. Brown, *The Death of the Messiah*, 2:949.
385. Seneca, *Mor. Ep.* 101.12.
386. N. Haas, "Anthropological Observations on the Skeletal Remains from Giv'at ha-Mivtar," *IEJ* 20 (1970): 38–59; V. Tzaferis, "Jewish Tombs at and near Giv'at ha-Mivtar, Jerusalem," *IEJ* 20 (1970): 18–32; "Crucifixion—the Archeological Evidence," *BAR* 11/1 (1985): 44–53; J. Zias and E. Sekeles, "The Crucified Man from Giv'at ha-Mivtar—A Reappraisal," *IEJ* 35 (1985): 22–27; and Joe Zias and James H. Charlesworth, "Crucifixion: Archaeology, Jesus, and the Dead Sea Scrolls," *Jesus and the Dead Sea Scrolls*, ed. J. H. Charlesworth (New York: Doubleday, 1992), 273–89.
387. *LSJ*, 1983.
388. Frederick T. Zugibe, "Two Question About Crucifixion: Does the Victim Die of Asphyxiation? Would Nails in the Hands Hold the Weight of the Body?" *B Rev* 5/2 (1989): 34–43.
389. Horace, *Ep.* 1.16.48.
390. Seneca, *Ep.* 101.14.
391. Seneca, *To Marcia On Consolation* 20.3.
392. A. N. Sherwin-White, *Roman Society and Roman Law in the New Testament*, (Oxford: Clarendon, 1963), 46; Justinian, *Digest* 48.20.6.
393. *Gen. Rab.* 65:22; *Midr. Ps.* 11:7.
394. Ps. 35:21; 40:15; 70:3; 2 Kings 19:21; Job 16:4; Ps. 22:7; 109:25; Isa. 37:22; Jer. 18:16; Lam. 2:15; Sir. 12:18.
395. *b. Sukkah* 29a.
396. Philo, *Providence* 2:50.
397. Vergil, *Georgics* 1.463.
398. Joel 2:10; 3:14–15; Amos 5:18, 20; 8:9; see also Isa. 13:9–13; Jer. 15:9.
399. Gundry, *Mark*, 947.
400. *b. Ned.* 50a.
401. Plutarch, *Lives* 336, 1.7.
402. Zugibe, "Two Questions About Crucifixion: Does the Victim Die of Asphyxiation?" 34–43.
403. Ex. 26:37; 38:18; Num. 3:26.
404. Ex. 26:31–35; 27:16, 21; 30:6; 40:21; Lev. 16:2, 12–15; 21:23; 24:3.
405. *m. Šeqal.* 8:5.
406. Josephus, *J.W.* 5.5.4 §212–13.
407. Josephus, *J.W.* 6.5.3 §§ 293–95; see also *b. Yoma* 39b.
408. *b. Giṭ.* 56b.
409. Petronius, *Satyricon* 111.
410. Tae Hun Kim, "The Anarthrous υἱὸς θεοῦ in Mark 15, 39 and the Roman Imperial Cult," *Bib* 79 (1982): 238.
411. Raymond E. Brown, "The Burial of Jesus (Mark 15:42–47)," *CBQ* 50 (1988): 233–45.
412. Philo, *Flaccus* 83–84.
413. Philo, *Spec. Laws* 3.151–52.
414. Josephus, *J.W.* 4.5.2 § 317.
415. Rousseau and Arav, *Jesus and His World*, 167.
416. *t. ᵓOhal.* 3:9.
417. Gabriel Barkay, "The Garden Tomb: Was Jesus Buried Here?" *BAR* 12/2 (1986): 40–57.
418. Gundry, *Mark*, 989.
419. See Dan. 7:9; Acts 1:10; 10:30; 2 Macc. 11:8–10.
420. Gen. 18:2; 19:1–3; Dan. 8:15–16; 9:21.
421. Josephus, *Ant.* 5.8.2 § 277.
422. Dan. 8:17–18; 10:8–12; Luke 2:10.

Sidebar and Chart Notes

A-1. Ps. 103:19; Zech. 14:9.
A-2. *m. ᵓAbot* 1:1.
A-3. Josephus, *J.W.* 3.10.8 §§ 516–21; see *Life* § 403.
A-4. L. I. Levine, "The Second Temple Synagogue: The Formative Years," in *The Synagogue in Late Antiquity*, ed. L. I . Levine (Philadelphia: Fortress,1987), 7.
A-5. Josephus, *Ag. Ap.* 2.17 § 175.
A-6. On the debate over the date of this inscription, see Rainer Riesner "Synagogues in Jerusalem," in *The Book of Acts*, ed. Bauckham, 192–99.
A-7. Philo, *Dreams* 2.127.
A-8. See *1 En.* 12:3–4; 15:1; *2 Bar.* 2:1; 9:1–10:4.
A-9. See Dan. 7:13; *1 En.* 46–53.
A-10. Josephus, *Ag. Ap.* 2:27 §3.
A-11. Gen. 2:3; Ex. 20:8–11; 31:14; Deut. 5:12–15.
A-12. Ex. 31:14–15; 35:2; Num. 15:32–36.
A-13. *Mekilta Kaspa* 4 to Ex. 23:13.
A-14. *m. Ḥag.* 1:8.
A-15. *PGM* 4.1227–64, found in H. D. Betz, ed., *The Greek Magical Papyri in Translation*, 2d ed. (Chicago/London: Univ. of Chicago Press, 1992), 62.
A-16. See Matt. 14:1; Luke 3:19; 9:7.
A-17. Josephus, *Ant.* 17.18.1 § 188; 17.9.4 §§ 224–7l; 17.11.4 § 318; idem, *J. W.* 2.2.3 §§ 20–22; 2.6.3. §§ 93–95.
A-18. Ibid., *Ant.*, 18.7.1–2 §§ 240–56; idem, *J. W.* 2.9.6 §§ 181–83.
A-19. D. W. Chapman, *The Orphan Gospel: Mark's Perspective on Jesus* (The Biblical Seminar 16; Sheffield: JSOT, 1993), 186.
A-20. Lev. 11:44; 19:2.
A-21. Herbert Danby includes a synopsis of the rules of uncleanness from *Eliyahu Rabbah*, a commentary on the sixth division of the Mishnah '*Tohorot*' by Elijah,

the Gaon of Wilna (*The Mishnah* [Oxford: Oxford Univ. Press, 1933], 800–804).

A-22. Jerome H. Neyrey, "The Idea of Purity in Mark's Gospel," *Semeia* 35 (1986): 92.

A-23. David H. Stern, *Jewish New Testament Commentary* (Clarksville, Md.: Jewish New Testament Publications, 1992), 92.

A-24. Daniel R. Schwartz, *Studies in the Jewish Background of Christianity* (WUNT 60; Tübingen: J. C. B. Mohr [Paul Siebeck], 1992), 64, citing a late midrash *Tanna Debe Eliyahu* 16.

A-25. H. Harrington, *The Impurity Systems of Qumran and the Rabbis: Biblical Foundations* (SBLDS 143; Atlanta: Scholars, 1993), 164. See *Jub.* 22:16; Acts 10:28.

A-26. *b. Soṭah* 4b.

A-27. *m. ʿEd.* 5:6.

A-28. *m. Ṭehar* 7:8; *b. Šabb.* 14a; *b. Sukkah* 26b; see Ex. 30:19, 21; 40:31.

A-29. *m. Yad.* 3:1; *m. Zabim* 5:12; *m. Parah* 11:5; *m. Soṭah* 5:2; *m. Ṭehar* 2:2.

A-30. David E. Garland, *Mark* (NIVAC; Grand Rapids: Zondervan, 1996), 316.

A-31. Ibid.

A-32. Cited by Martin Hengel, *The Zealots* (Edinburgh: T. & T. Clark, 1989), 277.

A-33. *m. Giṭ.* 9:3.

A-34. Yigael Yadin, *Bar-Kokhba* (London: Weidenfeld and Nicolson, 1978), 239.

A-35. Ibid., 222.

A-36. Josephus, *Ag. Ap.* 2.8 §§ 102–7.

A-37. Josephus, *J.W.* 5.5.6 §§ 222–24. On the whole description of the temple, see *J.W.* 5.5.1–6 §§ 184–226; and *Ant.* 15.11.3 §§ 391–402.

A-38. Timothy J. Geddert, *Watchwords: Mark 13 in Markan Eschatology* (JSNTSup 26; Sheffield: JSOT, 1989), 283, n. 53.

A-39. Garland, *Mark*, 505.

A-40. Morna D. Hooker, *The Gospel According to Saint Mark* (BNTC; Peabody, Mass.: Hendrickson, 1991), 302.

A-41. *b. Sanh.* 43a.; see also *t. Sanh.* 10:11; *y. Sanh.* 7:12.

A-42. Num. 35:30; Deut. 17:6; 19:15; *m. Sanh.* 4:1.

A-43. *m. Sanh.* 11:6; Deut. 19:16–21.

A-44. *m. Mid.* 5:4; *m. Sanh.* 11:2.

A-45. Tacitus, *An.* 3.38; 4.41, 57; Suetonius, *Tiberias* 41, 58; Cassius Dio, *Roman History* 58.2, 7; 3.8.

A-46. Philo, *Embassy* 24, 159–61.

A-47. Josephus, *J.W.* 2.9.3–4 § 175–77; *Ant.* 18.3.2 §§ 60–62.

A-48. Josephus, *Ant.* 18.4.1 §§ 85–87.

A-49. Ibid., 18.4.2 §§ 88–89.

A-50. Philo, *Embassy* 24, 159–61.

A-51. Ibid., 299–305.

A-52. Josephus, *Ant.* 18.6.5 §§ 174–78.

A-53. Jerry Camery-Hoggatt, *Irony in Mark's Gospel: Text and Subtext* (SNTSMS 72; Cambridge: Cambridge Univ. Press, 1991), 170–71.

A-54. Joel Marcus, *The Mystery of the Kingdom of God* (SBLDS 90; Atlanta: Scholars, 1986), 117.

LUKE

by Mark Strauss

Unity and Main Themes of Luke and Acts (Luke-Acts)

It is widely recognized today that Luke and Acts are two parts of a single two-volume work (Luke-Acts). Acts picks up where the Gospel ends and claims to be a continuation of the story that began with Jesus' life, death, and resurrection (Acts 1:1–2). The two works share not only a common style and vocabulary, but also a common purpose, themes, and theology.

1. Promise-fulfillment. The central theme running throughout Luke-Acts is that the coming of Jesus the Messiah heralds the dawn of the new age—the age of salvation. What was promised by the Old Testament prophets is now being fulfilled. Through Jesus' life, death, and resurrection forgiveness of sins is now offered to all people.

2. The age of the Spirit. The new age of salvation is the age of the Spirit. In Luke's birth narrative (Luke 1–2),

EAST OF JERUSALEM TOWARD JERICHO

Luke IMPORTANT FACTS:

- **AUTHOR:** Luke: physician, coworker, and traveling companion with the apostle Paul. Probably the only New Testament work written by a Gentile.
- **PORTRAIT OF CHRIST:** Jesus, the Savior for all people.
  Part One of a Two-Volume Work: Luke's Gospel is the first half of a single two-volume work ("Luke-Acts"), sharing purpose, themes, and theology with the book of Acts.
- **CENTRAL THEME OF LUKE-ACTS:** Luke seeks to show that *God's great plan of salvation has come to fulfillment in the life, death, resurrection, and ascension of Jesus the Messiah, and continues to unfold as the Spirit-filled church takes the message of salvation from Jerusalem to the ends of the earth.*
- **OTHER KEY THEMES:**
  1. Promise-fulfillment: The age of salvation has arrived in Jesus the Messiah.
  2. The age of the Spirit: The sign of the new age is the coming of the Spirit in the ministry of Jesus and the early church.
  3. The gospel is "good news" for all people, regardless of race, gender, or social status.
- **PURPOSE IN WRITING:** To defend and legitimize the claims of the church as the authentic people of God in the present age.
- **RECIPIENT:** Theophilus, but intended for a larger Christian audience.

the long-silent Spirit of prophecy suddenly breaks forth in praise and prophetic declaration through Zechariah, Mary, Elizabeth, and Simeon—representatives of Israel's righteous remnant. At Jesus' baptism the Spirit anoints and empowers him to accomplish the messianic task (3:22; 4:1, 14, 18). Finally, in Acts Jesus pours out his Spirit on the church, empowering its members to take the gospel to the ends of the earth. As promised by the Old Testament prophets, the coming of the Spirit means that the last days have arrived, so that "everyone who calls on the name of the Lord will be saved" (Acts 2:21, citing Joel 2:28–32).

3. A gospel for all nations. Closely related to the theme of promise-fulfillment is the universal application of the message of salvation. While the gospel message arises from within Israel and fulfills the promises made to her, it is a message for all people. Just as the prophets predicted, the coming of the Messiah inaugurates a new era, when all nations will be called to participate in the salvation available through Jesus the Messiah. The key for Luke is the *continuity* between the history of Israel, the person and work of Jesus, and the expansion of his church from Jerusalem to the ends of the earth. This theme is introduced in the Gospel and comes to fruition in the worldwide mission of the church in Acts.[1]

4. A gospel for the outcasts. The theme of God's love for all people is most evident in this Gospel with Jesus' concern for social outcasts, sinners, and the poor. The message of salvation crosses all racial and social barriers. At the inauguration of his ministry, Jesus enters the Nazareth synagogue and epitomizes his message as good news to the poor (4:16–22). He

JERUSALEM

An artistic reconstruction of Jerusalem at the time of Christ.

associates with sinners and tax collectors, and tells parables where a hated Samaritan is the hero (10:25–37) and where a wayward son is graciously received back by his father (15:11–32). The message throughout is that God loves the lost, those who with a contrite and humble heart will return to him. Repeatedly Jesus' parables reveal the great reversal of fortunes that the kingdom of God will bring: The rich, proud, and mighty will be humbled, while the poor, humble, and oppressed will be exalted (12:13–21; 14:15–24; 16:19–31).

5. A gospel for women. This Gospel also crosses gender barriers, for women play a more prominent role in Luke than in the other Gospels. The birth narrative is told from the perspective of women (Mary, Elizabeth, and Anna). Women support Jesus' ministry financially (8:1–3). Mary sits at Jesus' feet, learning from him as a disciple (10:38–42). In contrast to the low status of women in Palestinian society, Jesus lifts them up to full participation in the kingdom of God. The gospel of Jesus is for all people.

Purpose in Writing

Why then did Luke write? Luke's prologue identifies his general purpose as the confirmation of the gospel, seeking to confirm for Theophilus "the certainty of the things you have been taught" (1:1–4). More specifically, Luke appears to be writing for a Christian community—probably predominantly Gentile, but with Jewish representation—struggling to legitimize its claim as the authentic people of God, the heirs of the promises made to Israel. In defending the identity of Christ, Luke seeks to show that Jesus is the Messiah promised in the Old Testament and that his death and resurrection were part of God's purpose and plan. In defense of the increasingly Gentile church, he confirms that all along it was God's plan to bring salvation to the Gentiles, and that Israel's rejection of the gospel was predicted in Scripture and was part of her history as a stubborn and resistant people. The theme that holds these threads together is promise and fulfillment. The church made up of Jews and Gentiles is the true people of God because it is for her and through her God's promises are being fulfilled.

The Author

The third Gospel has been traditionally ascribed to Luke, a physician, friend, and missionary companion of the apostle Paul.[2] In addition to the unanimous testimony of early church writers, there is also internal evidence consisting of several "we" sections (first-person accounts) in Acts. These reveal that the author was with Paul briefly on his second missionary journey (Acts 16:10–17), and then rejoined him at Philippi on Paul's return from his third journey (20:5–21:18). He stayed with Paul at Caesarea after Paul's arrest and accompanied him to Rome (27:1–28:16).

We know a little about Luke from Paul's letters. In two letters from prison in Rome, Paul identifies him as a physician (Col. 4:14) and fellow worker (Philem. 24). Luke also appears as Paul's faithful companion during his second Roman imprisonment (2 Tim. 4:10–11). In Colossians 4:11, 13–14, Paul associates Luke with his Gentile rather than Jewish companions. This Gentile identity helps to explain Luke's keen interest in the universal application of the gospel message. The gospel is for all peoples, Jew and Gentile alike.

Luke writes as a second-generation Christian, claiming not to have been an eyewitness of the events of Jesus' ministry, but to have thoroughly investigated the events before composing his Gospel (Luke 1:1–4). He writes as both historian and theologian, seeking to provide an accurate and trustworthy account of the events, while confirming the profound spiritual significance of these events.

Date, Recipients, Destination

The date of the Gospel of Luke is uncertain, but it is closely tied to its companion volume Acts. Since Acts ends with Paul in prison in Rome (about A.D. 60), the book was probably written before his release, rearrest, and subsequent martyrdom. This would place its date around A.D. 60–63. The Gospel must have been completed sometime before this, perhaps in the late 50s or early 60s. It is possible, of course, that Luke wrote after Paul's death, but had a different reason for ending his two-volume work with Paul in Rome. This could be to show that the gospel had reached "the ends of the earth" (cf. Acts 1:8)—the furthest reaches of the empire. In this case, a much later date is possible, anytime from the 60s to the 80s.

Both Luke and Acts are addressed to Theophilus, who may have been: (1) the patron who sponsored the publication of Luke's work, (2) an influential unbeliever with an interest in Christianity, (3) a new Christian in need of further instruction, or even (4) the Roman official overseeing Paul's trial. This last possibility arises from the fact that Acts ends with Paul awaiting trial in Rome (Acts 28:30–31). The first of these is the most likely, perhaps in combination with the third. The writing of a book of this length was an expensive endeavor in the ancient world, both in terms of time and resources, and it was common to dedicate such a work to an influential patron. See further comments on Luke 1:3 and "The Prologues of Luke and Josephus."

Though Luke dedicates the work to Theophilus, it seems certain that he, like the other Gospel writers, writes for a wider audience. That this audience is predominantly Gentile is suggested by Luke's profound interest in the universality of the gospel message. It is good news for all peoples and for all nations.

There are few clues as to specific destination of the letter. Rome, Greece, Caesarea, and Alexandria have all been suggested.

Historians of Luke's Time

Critics of Luke's claim to be an accurate historian have sometimes said that historical writing in the modern sense was unknown in the ancient world. Ancient "historians" played fast and loose with the facts, freely creating stories to suit their own purposes.

While it is true that some historians of antiquity were not as careful as others, it is overstating the case to deny that good history existed. The Hellenistic historian Polybius criticizes other writers for making up dramatic scenes and calls on them to "simply record what really happened and what really was said . . ." (2.56.10).[A-1] Other ancient historians make similar comments. This confirms that intelligent writers and readers of the first century were concerned with distinguishing fact from fiction.

This is not so different from today, where the careful reader must discern between accurate news accounts and supermarket tabloid journalism. Luke's reliability as a historian must be judged from a careful examination of the events he records, not with sweeping generalizations about ancient history.[A-2]

The Prologue (1:1–4)

Luke introduces his two-volume work with a formal literary prologue similar in style to the Hellenistic writers of his day (see "The Prologues of Luke and Josephus"). These four verses represent some of the finest Greek in the New Testament. The author is obviously an educated and skilled writer, a worthy candidate to compose the longest and most comprehensive account of the words and deeds of the central figure in human history.

Luke begins by setting forth the purpose of his work. What strikes the reader first is the piling up of terms of historical reliability. Not only has Luke received his information from first–generation Christians—eyewitnesses and the original ministers of God's message of salvation—but he has also gone back and carefully investigated these accounts to ensure that they are true. Yet Luke does not write from historical motivations alone. His goal is also theological. He is seeking to assure Theophilus of the truth of the gospel message.

This brings up an important point about the nature of the New Testament Gospels. None of the writers wrote from purely biographical or historical interest. All were convinced that God had acted in history to bring salvation to the world through his Son Jesus Christ. All had a burning desire to convince others of the truth of this message. The Gospel writers are called "Evangelists" (from *euangelion*, the Greek word for "Gospel") because their works are *written* versions of the *oral* proclamation of the good news about the salvation that has been achieved in Jesus Christ. The Gospels were written to be preached, and they were written to be believed.

Many have undertaken to draw up an account (1:1). Authors of Luke's day often cited similar works when describing their reason for writing. In some cases this was to show the inadequacy of previous writings; in others it was to justify their reason for writing or to lend credibility to their own works. In his history of the *Jewish War*, the Jewish historian Josephus claims he is writing to correct others who "misrepresented the facts" of the war to flatter the Romans or because of their hatred for the Jews.[3] The closest ancient parallel to Luke's prologue appears in the introduction to Josephus's *Against Apion* (see "The Prologues of Luke and Josephus" at 1:3).

While Luke does not say that these "many" other writings were inaccurate or inferior, he must have seen something inadequate in them for the situation he was addressing, since he felt the need to write his own. If Luke is using Mark as one of his sources, as most scholars believe, he may have wanted a more comprehensive account than Mark provided and one that addressed the universality of the gospel message more clearly.

An account (1:1). The term *diēgēsis* is used frequently in Greek literature of a historical narrative, especially one that set out a comprehensive and orderly account of events.[4]

Handed down to us by . . . eyewitnesses and servants of the word (1:2). The term "handed down" (*paradidōmi*, 1:2) often occurs as a technical term for the passing down of authoritative tradition. The rabbis of Jesus' day had a large body of oral traditions that they carefully memorized and passed on to their disciples (cf. Mark 7:13). Paul uses the same term regarding the handing down of the authoritative accounts of the Lord's Supper (1 Cor. 11:2, 23) and of the resurrection appearances (1 Cor. 15:3–8). The use of such terms indicates that the apostles, like the rabbis of their time, carefully preserved and passed on the words and deeds of their teacher. This contradicts the claim of some critics that the early church cared little about preserving accurate historical material about Jesus (see "Historians of Luke's Time").

The phrase "eyewitnesses and servants of the word" probably refers to one rather than two groups and means "the eyewitnesses who became the ministers of the message." This would refer primarily to the twelve apostles, but would also include the larger body of Jesus' disciples (see the reference to 120 believers in Acts 1:15).

An orderly account (1:3). Literally, "accurately in order." The phrase does not necessarily denote a strict chronological order (some events in Luke's Gospel are *not* chronological), but rather a systematic or logical account of the events.

Most excellent Theophilus (1:3). The word "Theophilus" means "beloved of God" or "one who loves God"; some have therefore suggested that Luke is writing generally to all believers who love God. Theophilus, however, was a common personal name in Luke's day, and it is much more likely that he refers here to an actual individual. The designation "most excellent" was used of anyone of high social status and was especially common for those of the equestrian order (the "knights") of Roman society. The term is used in Acts of the Roman governors Felix (Acts 24:3) and Festus (Acts 26:25). For more on the identity of Theophilus see the Introduction above.

The Birth of John the Baptist Foretold (1:5–25)

Only Luke and Matthew include accounts of Jesus' miraculous conception

The Prologues of Luke and Josephus

While there are many Greek and Roman works that have introductions similar to Luke's, the Jewish historian Josephus's two-volume work *Against Apion* is perhaps the closest. Josephus, like Luke, dedicates his work to a patron, "most excellent Epaphroditus," refers to previous works on the subject (his own in this case), and describes his purpose for writing:

> In my history of our Antiquities, most excellent Epaphroditus, I have, I think, made sufficiently clear to any who may peruse that work the extreme antiquity of our Jewish race.... Since, however, I observe that a considerable number of persons, influenced by the malicious calumnies of certain individuals, discredit the statements in my history concerning our antiquity ... I consider it my duty to devote a brief treatise to all these points; in order at once to convict our detractors of malignity and deliberate falsehood, to correct the ignorance of others, and to instruct all who desire to know the truth concerning the antiquity of our race.[A-3]

Josephus's second volume, like Acts, refers back to the first:

> In the first volume of this work, my most esteemed Epaphroditus, I demonstrated the antiquity of our race, corroborating my statements by ... citing as witnesses numerous Greek historians.... I shall now proceed to refute the rest of the authors who have attacked us.[A-4]

and birth. (Mark begins with the ministry of John the Baptist, John with a statement of Jesus' preexistence.) While the birth narratives of Matthew and Luke differ significantly from each other in terms of content, both draw strongly on the themes of messiahship and promise-fulfillment. Jesus is the promised Messiah, the descendant of David born to be king. His coming represents the fulfillment of the hopes and expectations of faithful Jews throughout the ages. Matthew's story centers on Joseph, whose dreams and actions link the narrative together. Luke's centers on Mary.

Luke's birth narrative (1:5–2:52) is not intended merely to fill in the details about Jesus' early years for the curious reader. It serves rather as an overture, setting the stage and preparing the reader for the rest of the Gospel and Acts. Many of Luke's important themes are introduced in these two chapters, including (1) the arrival of God's promised salvation and the fulfillment of his promises to Israel, (2) the place of John the Baptist as the forerunner of the Messiah, (3) the central role of the Holy Spirit in the age of salvation, (4) the gospel as good news for the poor and oppressed, (5) Jesus as the Messiah from David's line, and (6) the gospel as salvation for the Gentiles as well as the Jews.

As the reader moves from Luke's formal introduction in 1:1–4 to the story of John the Baptist, the writing style changes dramatically. From the very fine Greek literary style of the prologue, the language suddenly takes on an "Old Testament" flavor, reminiscent of the Septuagint (LXX), the Greek translation of the Old Testament. This stylistic change is used by Luke to bring the reader into another world—the world of the Old Testament and of Judaism. The characters we meet represent the righteous "remnant" of faithful Israel, Jews anxiously awaiting the coming of their Messiah. Zechariah is a priest, one of Israel's spiritual elite, and his wife Elizabeth is of priestly ancestry. Both are upright before God and faithful to his law. Zechariah is in the temple in Jerusalem, the center of Israel's religious life, offering incense before the Lord. Luke's goal here is to introduce his readers to the Old Testament people of God and to the promises that he has made to them, setting the stage for the fulfillment of those promises. The fulfillment begins with the announcement of the birth of John the Baptist, who will be "a voice of one calling in the desert" (3:4), preparing the way for the Messiah.

THE KINGDOM OF HEROD THE GREAT

In the time of Herod king of Judea (1:5). In line with his historical purpose, Luke connects the birth of John the Baptist with Herod the Great, who reigned from 37–4 B.C. over a kingdom that included Judea, Galilee, Samaria, and much of Perea and Coele-Syria (see map and "Herod the Great"). When Luke calls him "king of Judea" he is probably using the term "Judea" in the broader sense of "greater Palestine," encompassing all of these regions.

A priest named Zechariah, who belonged to the priestly division of Abijah (1:5). The priesthood in Israel was divided into twenty-four courses, each providing temple service for one week twice a year (1 Chron. 24:1–19). Abijah is identified as the eighth division of the priesthood in 1 Chronicles 24:10.

His wife Elizabeth was also a descendant of Aaron (1:5). Literally, a "daughter of Aaron." Though priests could marry any godly Israelite woman, it was a sign of special piety to marry a woman of priestly ancestry.

But they had no children, because Elizabeth was barren (1:7). In a culture where the primary social unit was the family and where one's ancestry was of critical importance, childlessness was a cause of great concern and shame. Such shame is a common theme in the Old Testament, appearing in the stories of Sarah, the mother of Isaac (Gen. 18); Rebekah, the mother of Jacob and Esau (25:21); Rachel, the mother of Joseph (30:22–23); the unnamed mother of Samson (Judg. 13); and Hannah, the mother of Samuel (1 Sam. 1). Sarah provides the closest analogy to Elizabeth, since she was not only barren but also past child-bearing years. In all of these cases, the tragedy of childlessness provides an opportunity for God to show his grace and power. When God miraculously opens the womb, the child who is born is a special and unique gift from God and fulfills a special destiny in his plan.

When Zechariah's division was on duty . . . chosen by lot (1:8–9). During one of the two weeks of service for Zechariah's priestly division, he is chosen by lot to offer incense in the Holy Place. The casting of lots (something like throwing dice) was a common method of discerning God's will in the Old Testament. Proverbs 16:33 says, "The lot is cast into the lap, but its every decision is from the LORD."[5] Lots were cast by the disciples for the replacement of Judas in Acts 1:26. Regulations for the lot are given in the Mishnah.[6] In the New Testament era such a procedure is unnecessary since believers possess the permanent indwelling of the Holy Spirit for guidance (Rom. 8:14).

To go into the temple of the Lord and burn incense (1:9). The word "temple" here is *naos,* which Luke uses to designate the Holy Place and/or the Most Holy Place (see diagram of temple). Luke uses a different word, *hieron,* to identify the temple in general or the larger temple precincts (see comments on 2:27). The Most Holy Place, which held the ark of the covenant, was entered only once a year by the high priest on Israel's Day of Atonement, when sacrifices were offered for the whole nation (see Lev. 16:1–34; Heb. 9:6–7). Incense was offered in the Holy Place twice daily, before the morning sacrifice and after the evening sacrifice. The Holy Place held the altar of incense, the golden lampstand,

and the table of consecrated bread. The chosen priest would enter, clean the altar, and offer fresh incense. The incense was to be kept burning continually before the Lord (Ex. 30:7–8). Because of the large number of priests, this privilege may have come only once in a lifetime for a particular priest. This was a special occasion in Zechariah's life.

An angel of the Lord appeared (1:11). Visions or messages from God occasionally occur in the temple in the Old Testament (1 Sam. 3; Isa. 6; Zech. 3:1) and in later Judaism. Josephus describes how the Maccabean king and high priest John Hyrcanus, while offering incense in the temple, heard a heavenly voice telling him his sons had just won victory in battle.[7] Such precedents explain why in Luke 1:22 the people conclude that Zechariah has seen a vision.

In the Old Testament "the angel of the LORD" is an exalted figure who appears as God's messenger and is at times identified with the Lord himself (see Gen. 16:7, cf. v. 13). Some identify him as the preincarnate Christ. Here, however, he is identified as Gabriel (see Luke 1:19).

Zechariah . . . was gripped with fear (1:12). Fear is a common Old Testament response to the appearance of God or an angel. See the reactions of Gideon (Judg. 6:22–23), Manoah (13:22), and Daniel (Dan. 8:16–17; 10:10–11), and especially Isaiah's terror at his awesome vision of God (Isa. 6:5). Such fear is usually followed by a reassuring word of comfort, "Do not be afraid" (Luke 1:13; cf. 1:29–30).

Your wife Elizabeth will bear you a son (1:13). Predictions of the birth of a special child are common in the Old Testament and frequently follow the pattern of announcement and naming found here. See the accounts of Ishmael (Gen. 16:11), Isaac (17:16, 19; 18:1–15), Samson (Judg. 13:2–23), and "Immanuel" (Isa. 7:14). The announcement to Mary in Luke 1:30–33 will follow a similar pattern.

You are to give him the name John (1:13). The meaning of names, especially those bestowed by God, had greater significance in biblical times than today. They could relate to the circumstances of the child's birth or might predict his future role. "John" means "the Lord has shown favor." God is showing favor to Elizabeth by giving her a child in her old age and also to the nation Israel by providing the forerunner of the Messiah.

He is never to take wine or other fermented drink (1:15). The Greek word for "fermented drink" (*sikera*) can mean any alcoholic beverage not made from grapes, but usually referred to grain-based alcohol ("beer"). This abstinence from alcohol is probably to be identified with a Nazirite vow, which was for an

THE JERUSALEM TEMPLE

A model of the temple looking at the entrance to the holy place. This portion of the temple would have been 172′ high.

Israelite a period of special consecration to God. During the vow no alcohol was to be drunk, the hair was to remain uncut, and no dead body was to be touched (touching a body rendered an individual ceremonially unclean) (Num. 6:1–21). Though normally temporary, in the case of John the Baptist, as with Samson (Judg. 13:4–7) and Samuel (1 Sam. 1:11, 15), this vow was lifelong.

He will be filled with the Holy Spirit even from birth (1:15). "Even from birth" is better translated "even while still in the womb," as 1:41 makes clear. The filling of the Spirit provided an individual with God's presence and power to accomplish his sovereign purpose. While in the Old Testament period, the Spirit came upon individuals intermittently to accomplish particular tasks, John will have a permanent possession of the Spirit (cf. 1 Sam. 16:13). This previews the role of the Spirit in the church from the day of Pentecost onward.

In the spirit and power of Elijah (1:17). This verse alludes to Malachi, where the prophet predicts that Elijah will return before the great Day of the Lord to bring about reconciliation within families (Mal. 4:5–6) and to prepare the way for the coming of the Lord (Mal. 3:1; see Luke 1:76). The reference to Elijah's "spirit" recalls 2 Kings 2:9–10, where Elijah's successor Elisha asks for and receives a "double portion" of his spirit. The "power" of Elijah probably refers to his prophetic authority rather than to his miracles (cf. 1 Kings 17–18) since Luke does not record miracles by John. His role, rather, is to "make ready a people prepared for the Lord."

There was speculation in Judaism concerning the return of Elijah, much of it related to Elijah's role as interpreter of the law.[8] Even today Jews leave an empty chair at Passover in the hopes that the prophet Elijah will come.

How can I be sure . . . ? (1:18). Requests for a sign are common in the Old Testament. Abraham (Gen. 15:8), Gideon (Judg. 6:17), and Hezekiah (2 Kings 20:8) all asked for signs. Paul says in 1 Corinthians 1:22, "Jews demand miraculous signs and Greeks look for wisdom."

I am Gabriel (1:19). Gabriel is one of only two angels specifically named in the Old Testament, though others are named in intertestamental Jewish literature. Both Gabriel and Michael appear in the New Testament (Gabriel in Luke 1:19 and 1:26, Michael in Jude 9 and Rev. 12:7). In Daniel Gabriel explains the vision of seventy weeks, a prophecy concerning the coming Messiah (Dan. 9:24–27). He will now announce the birth of that Messiah.

The people were waiting . . . and wondering why he stayed so long in the temple (1:21). Replacing the incense took only a short time, so the people may have been concerned that Zechariah had incurred God's judgment for some act of disrespect. A passage from the Mishnah (*c.* A.D. 200) concerning the entrance of the high priest into the Most Holy Place on the Day of Atonement provides insight into Luke's text:

> When he [the high priest] reached the Ark he put the fire pan between the two bars. He heaped up the incense on the coals and the whole place became filled with smoke. He came out by the way he went in, and in the outer space he prayed a short

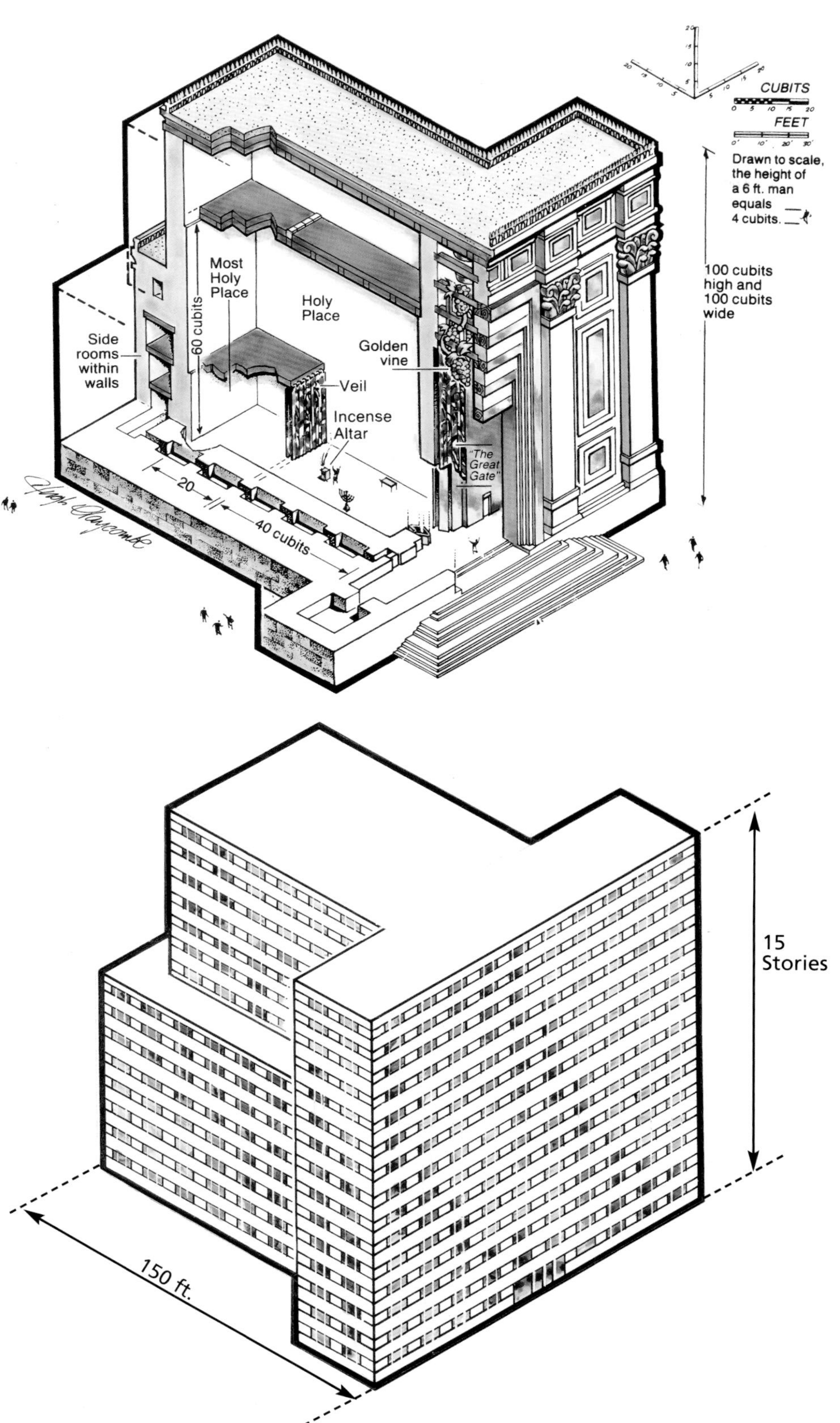

HEROD'S TEMPLE COMPARED TO A MODERN BUILDING

prayer. But he did not prolong his prayer lest he put Israel in terror.[10]

Though Zechariah did not enter the Most Holy Place, the altar of incense just outside in the Holy Place stood very close to the ark and hence to the awesome power and presence of God (see 2 Sam. 6:1–15 for the danger of casually touching the ark).

He returned home (1:23). Zechariah and Elizabeth lived outside of Jerusalem "in the hill country of Judea" (1:39). When not fulfilling his role as a priest, Zechariah probably practiced a secular trade as a small farmer or craftsman. Though the priests were supposed to receive portions of sacrifices (1 Cor. 9:13) and temple tithes (Heb. 7:5), these tithes were not always paid because of poverty or corruption, and many priests remained poor. Since they served in the temple only a few weeks a year, most practiced a secular trade.[11]

Elizabeth . . . for five months remained in seclusion (1:24). There is no known Israelite custom that required such seclusion. This may have been a spiritual retreat for grateful prayer, or perhaps it was Elizabeth's way of respecting God's silence imposed on Zechariah.

Herod the Great

Herod "the Great" ruled Palestine under the Romans from 37–4 B.C. He was the son of Antipater, an advisor to the Hasmonean kings who had ruled Israel during the period of independence won by the Maccabees (see "The Maccabees"). When the Hasmonean dynasty collapsed, the Romans appointed Herod to rule as king of the Jews. A cunning politician, he had at first supported Mark Antony and Cleopatra in their struggle against Octavian (Caesar Augustus). When Octavian proved superior, Herod quickly switched sides and convinced the emperor of his loyalty.

Herod was a strange mix of an efficient ruler and a cruel tyrant. On the one hand, he appeared as the protector of Judaism and sought to gain the favor of the Jews. He encouraged the development of the synagogue communities and in time of calamity remitted taxes and supplied the people with free grain. He was also a great builder, a role that earned him the title "the Great." His greatest project was the rebuilding and beautification of the temple in Jerusalem, restoring it to the splendor of the time of Solomon (see Mark 13:2).

At the same time, Herod was distrustful, jealous, and cruel, ruthlessly crushing any potential opposition. Because he was an Edomite and not Jewish, the Jews never accepted him as their legitimate king—a rejection that infuriated him. To legitimize his claim to the throne, he divorced his first wife and married the Hasmonean princess Miriamne—later executing her when he suspected she was plotting against him. Three of his sons and another wife met the same fate when they, too, were suspected of conspiracy. The emperor Augustus once said he would rather be Herod's *hys* ("pig") than his *huios* ("son"). Herod, trying to be a legitimate Jew, would not eat pork, but he freely murdered his sons!

Herod died in 4 B.C. (cf. Matt. 2:19), probably from intestinal cancer. As an act of final vengeance against his rebellious subjects, he rounded up leading Jews and commanded that at his death they should be executed. His reasoning was that if there was no mourning *for* his death, at least there would be mourning *at* his death. (The order was never carried out.) Matthew's story of the slaughter of the infants in Bethlehem comes to life when seen in the context of Herod's extraordinary paranoia and quest for power (Matt. 2:1–18).[A-5]

The Lord has . . . taken away my disgrace among the people (1:25). Similar praise is expressed in the Old Testament by the barren women whom God blesses with children (Gen. 21:6–7; 1 Sam. 2:1–11). Rachel, like Elizabeth, rejoices that "God has taken away my disgrace" (Gen. 30:23).

The Birth of Jesus Foretold (1:26–38)

Having announced the birth of John, the forerunner of the Messiah, Luke's story now turns to the Messiah himself. While Jesus and John are viewed together as co-agents in God's great plan of salvation, Jesus is superior, for he is the Messiah.

In the sixth month (1:26). This is the sixth month of Elizabeth's pregnancy (1:36). The reference links this story with the previous one.

Nazareth, a town in Galilee (1:26). Nazareth was a small and insignificant village in Galilee (see Nathanael's comment in John 1:46: "Can anything good come from [Nazareth]?"). The town is never mentioned in the Old Testament or in Jewish writings of the day. Its existence was confirmed by an inscription discovered in 1962 at Caesarea Maritima (see "Inscription Bearing the Name of Nazareth'").

To a virgin pledged to be married (1:27). The word translated "virgin" (*parthenos*) means a young, unmarried girl and normally indicates virginity. A young Jewish girl would normally be engaged between twelve and fourteen years old. This engagement was far more formal than today. A legal marriage contract would be drawn up (which could only be broken by "divorce"), the girl would be called her fiancé's "wife," and infidelity would be treated as adultery. Yet she would continue to live with her parents until the marriage ceremony a year or so later.[12]

Joseph, a descendant of David (1:27). Literally "of the house of David," meaning the family (= ancestry) with implications of "dynasty." Jesus is a legitimate heir to the throne of David (see 1:32–33).

You will be with child and give birth to a son (1:31). This verse follows a common pattern of birth announcements and especially echoes Isaiah 7:14: "The virgin will be with child and will give birth to a son, and will call him Immanuel."

You are to give him the name Jesus (1:31). "Jesus" is the Greek equivalent of the Hebrew *Yeshua*, or Joshua, and means "Yahweh saves." Unlike Matthew (Matt. 1:21), Luke does not specifically refer to the meaning of the name.

Most High . . . .The Lord God (1:32). Both of these are Greek translations of

GALILEE

Nazareth was located west of the Sea of Galilee near the Roman city of Sepphoris.

Inscription Bearing the Name of "Nazareth"

Though the site has long been known to Christian pilgrims, until 1962 there was no literary or epigraphic evidence for ancient Nazareth. This fragmentary inscription discovered at Caesarea Maritima lists the twenty-four priestly courses (see comments on Luke 1:5), and tells in which towns they reside. The eighteenth course, Happizzez (1 Chron. 24:15), is identified with Nazareth.

Old Testament names for God. The first is from *El Elyon*, "God Most High," and the second from *Yahweh Elohim*, "Yahweh God."

The throne of his father David . . . he will reign . . . forever (1:32–33). The verse epitomizes the covenant made to David (2 Sam. 7; Ps. 89), where David was promised that God would raise up his "seed" after him, who would have a "father-son" relationship with God (see Luke 1:35) and who would reign forever on his throne. This promise to David was taken up by the prophets and became the foundation for Israel's hope for a coming Messiah (see "Messianic Expectation in Jesus' Day").[13] Luke repeatedly refers to this promise.[14]

His kingdom will never end (1:33). Though an eternal kingdom was part of the covenant made to David (2 Sam. 7:16; Isa. 9:6), the verse also recalls the eternal kingdom of Daniel 7:14.

The Holy Spirit will come upon you . . . will overshadow you . . . (1:35). The verb "come upon" is used similarly in Isaiah 32:15 LXX, where it refers to the Spirit's coming upon the land to make it fertile. Luke uses the same verb in Acts 1:8 of the Spirit's coming upon the believers at Pentecost. The verb "overshadow" appears in Exodus 40:35 (LXX) with reference to God's presence or Shekinah "overshadowing" the tabernacle in a cloud (cf. Num. 10:34), and a similar reference to God's overshadowing presence appears in the transfiguration account (Luke 9:34).

In the past, attempts have been made to draw parallels between this passage and pagan texts related to a god's impregnating a human woman. But there is no hint here of sexual union, and these parallels have now generally been rejected by scholars.

The Son of God (1:35). While the title always points to Jesus' unique relationship with the Father, it carries various nuances in the New Testament. In 1:32 the emphasis is on Jesus' messiahship, since the Old Testament promised that the Messiah would have a special father-son relationship with God.[15] This use of the title is common in the New Testa-

REFLECTIONS

WHEN GABRIEL ANNOUNCED TO Mary that she would give birth to Jesus, he was proclaiming the fulfillment of a promise made nine hundred years earlier to King David. Jesus would be the promised Messiah, the king who would reign forever on David's throne. The Annunciation reminds us that God is a God who always keeps his promises. We can trust him for that today.

ment.[16] Elsewhere, as here in 1:35, the title emphasizes Jesus' essential deity.[17]

Elizabeth your relative (1:36). The term "relative" (*syngenis*) is not specific and could refer to a cousin, aunt, or other relation.

Nothing is impossible with God (1:37). The verse echoes Genesis 18:14 (LXX), "Nothing is impossible with God," a reference to God's miraculous intervention for the barren and aged Sarah. God's intervention in the case of Elizabeth (and Sarah) is proof that he can accomplish anything, even the virginal conception promised to Mary.

I am the Lord's servant (1:38). The term "servant" (*doulē*) is also used by Hannah (1 Sam. 1:11 LXX), whose hymn of joy has parallels to Mary's *Magnificat* in the following passage (1 Sam. 2:1–10; Luke 1:46–55).

Mary Visits Elizabeth (1:39–45)

The stories of the births of Jesus and John now come together as Mary sets off to visit her relative Elizabeth. John's role as forerunner and witness to Christ begins already as the child leaps for joy in Elizabeth's womb at Mary's arrival. Filled with the Spirit (see comments on 1:41), Elizabeth proclaims a blessing on Mary and on her child, and Mary responds with a song of praise to God. This theme of joy and rejoicing at the arrival of God's salvation is an important one for Luke and will recur throughout his Gospel.

▸ Messianic Expectation in Jesus' Day

In the century leading up to Jesus' birth, when the powerful Roman empire dominated Palestine, hope for the coming Messiah to free God's people from their oppressors became particularly intense. Though these expectations were diverse in the various strands of first-century Judaism,[A-6] the dominant hope was for a messianic deliverer from King David's line. In the *Psalms of Solomon,* a pseudepigraphic work (written under an assumed name) from the first century B.C., the following hope is expressed:

> See, Lord, and raise up for them their king, the son of David,
> to rule over your servant Israel....
> Undergird him with the strength to destroy the unrighteous rulers,
> to purge Jerusalem from gentiles who trample her to destruction;
> in wisdom and in righteousness to drive out the sinners from the inheritance;
> to smash the arrogance of sinners like a potter's jar;
> To shatter all their substance with an iron rod [cf. Ps. 2:9]
> to destroy unlawful nations with the word of his mouth; [cf. Isa. 11:4]
> At his warning the nations will flee from his presence;
> and he will condemn sinners by the thoughts of their hearts.
>
> (*Pss. Sol.* 17:21–25)

The Gentiles who "trample [Jerusalem] to destruction" are the Romans. It is not difficult to see why such excitement surrounded Jesus and even John the Baptist (Luke 3:15), when people suspected either might be the Messiah, the Son of David.

Similar expectations for a Davidic Messiah appear in apocalyptic Judaism[A-7] and in the Qumran (Dead Sea) scrolls.[A-8] The community at Qumran awaited two messiahs: a royal Davidic one and a priestly one from the line of Aaron.[A-9]

A town in the hill country of Judea (1:39). Lit. "into the hill country, to a city of Judah" (see 2 Sam. 2:1). Judah, one of the twelve tribes of Israel, occupied much of southern Canaan after the Israelites conquered the Promised Land (Josh. 15). David, a Judahite, was first made king over Judah (2 Sam. 2) and then later of all of Israel (2 Sam. 5). When the kingdom divided in civil war after the death of David's son Solomon, the southern kingdom was known as "Judah" and the northern kingdom "Israel." Luke probably uses the term to describe the whole southern region of Israel—what became the Roman province of "Judea." Luke's description of the location is imprecise, but in light of Zechariah's temple service one would expect a village in the hills near Jerusalem. Depending on the location, Mary' journey may have taken her between three and five days. If taken alone, such a journey would have been unusual and potentially dangerous for a woman of Mary's age.

HILL COUNTRY OF JUDEA

The baby leaped in her womb (1:41). Leaping is an expression of joy (Mal. 4:2). David "leaped" and danced before the Lord (2 Sam. 6:16). The recognition of prenatal actions as significant appears elsewhere in Jewish literature. The struggle between Esau and Jacob in the womb (Gen. 25:22) is interpreted in Jewish tradition as a conscious struggle. In another tradition, the unborn children sang a song at the Exodus.[18]

Elizabeth was filled with the Holy Spirit (1:41). In the Old Testament, as here, the filling of the Spirit is often associated with the prophetic gift. After four hundred years of silence, the Spirit of prophecy is appearing again in Israel (cf. 1:67; 2:25, 27).

Mother of my Lord (1:43). "My Lord" here is a court expression, roughly equivalent to "my king." Elizabeth recognizes

HILL COUNTRY OF JUDEA

The area just north of Hebron.

that Mary is bearing the Messiah, the future king of Israel (see 2 Sam. 24:20–21, where Araunah expresses similar unworthiness that he should be visited by King David).

Mary's Song (1:46–56)

Mary's joyful song of praise (called the *Magnificat*, "he/she magnifies," from the first word in the Latin translation) has a strong Old Testament flavor and is the first of four similar "hymns" of praise in the birth narrative (see also 1:68–79; 2:29–32; 2:14). It has many parallels with Hannah's prayer in 1 Samuel 2:1–10, which celebrates God's blessing in overcoming her barrenness and providing her with a child. Hannah, like Mary, praised God for lifting up the poor and the humble and bringing down the mighty and the proud. This theme of the reversal of fortunes, which will accompany God's salvation (see comments on 1:52), is an important one for Luke and will appear again in his rendition of the Beatitudes (6:20–21, 24–25) and in the parable of the rich man and Lazarus (16:19–31; cf. 12:13–21; 21:1–4).

My soul . . . my spirit (1:46–47). Synonymous parallelism, where a second line restates the first line in some way, is characteristic of Hebrew poetry and appears throughout the Psalms. See Psalm 16:9: "Therefore my heart is glad, and my soul rejoices; my body also dwells secure" (RSV). "My soul" is a Hebrew way of saying "I" (Ps. 34:2).

God my Savior (1:47). God is often called "Savior" in the Old Testament, especially in the Psalms and Isaiah. Physical salvation (but always with spiritual dimensions) is usually intended.

All generations will call me blessed (1:48). The honor given to one's name by future generations was of great importance in the ancient Near East.

Those who fear him (1:50). Fear here means reverence, humility, and obedience before God's awesome person and presence. It is the appropriate attitude of all God's people.

He has performed mighty deeds with his arm (1:51). God's "arm" is an Old Testament anthropomorphism for God's mighty power (cf. Ps. 98:1; Isa. 40:10). It is especially used of God's strength in bringing the Israelites out of Egypt.[19]

He has brought down rulers . . . lifted up the humble . . . filled the hungry . . . sent the rich away empty (1:52–53). God's justice in reversing social and political fortunes is a common theme in the Old Testament. Hannah's song says, " . . . those who were hungry hunger no more. . . . The LORD sends poverty and wealth; he humbles and he exalts."[20] The theme also appears in the wisdom literature of intertestamental Judaism. Sirach 10:14 reads, "The Lord overthrows the thrones of rulers, and enthrones the lowly in their place." For the "poor" as God's righteous people, see comments on Luke 6:20.

His servant Israel (1:54). Israel is frequently called God's "servant" in Isaiah 41–49 (see comments on Matt. 3:22; 12:15–18).

To Abraham and his descendants forever (1:55). Just as Gabriel's words in 1:33–34 recalled God's covenant with David, so now Mary alludes to the Abrahamic covenant. God made an "everlasting covenant" with Abraham and with his descendants to be his God, to make his name great, to bless him, to make him the father of a great nation (Israel) and of many nations, and to give him the land of Canaan as an eternal inheritance (Gen. 12:1–3; 17:3–8). Abraham became the father of the nation Israel as well as the father of all who share his faith in God's promises (Rom. 4:16–17). Luke often refers to Abraham and his covenant.[21]

The Birth of John the Baptist (1:57–66)

The account of John's birth centers around his circumcision and naming. Elizabeth and Zechariah demonstrate their faithfulness and obedience to God by naming the child "John" (see 1:6, 13). Their friends and neighbors are amazed at their unwillingness to name the child after Zechariah or another relative, and are astonished at the miracle that Zechariah can speak again. Word of these extraordinary events spreads throughout the countryside and all wonder what special role this child will play in God's plan. God is once again at work among his people!

Her neighbors and relatives . . . shared her joy (1:58). A birth, especially the birth of a son (because it meant the family name would be carried on), was a time of great celebration (as today!). For Elizabeth's family and friends, the joy was even greater since God had mercifully removed the shame of her barrenness (see comments on 1:7).

On the eighth day they came to circumcise the child (1:59). God commanded first Abraham and then the nation Israel to circumcise every male child on the eighth day (Gen. 17:9–14; Lev. 12:3). The procedure represented the child's incorporation into God's covenant community. Circumcision was generally viewed as essential for recognition as an authentic Jew (Phil. 3:5). At this time it was normally performed by the head of the household.

To name him after his father (1:59). It was common to name a son after a relative, usually either his father or (more often) his grandfather. In the Old Testament the naming normally occurred at birth (see Gen. 4:1; 25:25–26), so waiting eight days is unusual. The Greeks and Romans often named their children around the seventh or tenth day, so perhaps this practice had been adopted by some in Palestine.[22]

He asked for a writing tablet (1:63). This would normally be a wood board with a wax surface that could be inscribed with a sharp object.

For the Lord's hand was with him (1:66). Another Old Testament anthropomorphism (see 1:51). It can indicate either God's guidance and protective power, as here, or his hand of judgment, as in Acts 13:11.[23]

Zechariah's Song (1:67–80)

Zechariah's song of praise, known as the *Benedictus* ("blessed" or "praised," after the first word of the hymn in the Latin Vulgate), is the second of four songs of praise in Luke's birth narrative.[24] Like Mary's, Zechariah's hymn has a strong nationalistic tone, focusing on Israel's physical salvation. It recalls similar psalms in the Old Testament and Judaism. Yet while Mary's was primarily a psalm of praise, Zechariah's is also prophetic, predicting the roles of Jesus and John. It is thus similar to the messianic or "royal" psalms of the Old Testament.[25] While praising God for the part his son John will play in God's plan (1:76–77), the hymn focuses especially on God's salvation through his Messiah. It is with this latter theme that the hymn begins and ends (1:68–75, 78–79).

His father Zechariah was filled with the Holy Spirit (1:67). See comments on 1:41.

Praise be to the Lord, the God of Israel (1:68). A common Old Testament phrase in hymns of praise.[26]

Because he has come and has redeemed his people (1:68). The idea of "visiting to redeem" recalls especially God's great act of salvation in the Exodus from Egypt (see Ex. 3:7–10, 17–20) and the "new exodus" promised by the prophets (see Isa. 40). Luke will return to this theme in 1:78 and 7:16.

He has raised up a horn of salvation (1:69). "Horn" indicates the horn of a powerful animal, a symbol of strength (Deut. 33:17). The lifting or exalting of a horn denotes an increase in power. The horn of David is exalted by the Lord in Psalm 89:24, a messianic context (cf. 1 Sam. 2:10). The image of "raising up" a horn is close to Psalm 132:17, another messianic passage, where it is said that a horn will "sprout" or "grow up" for David.

In the house of his servant David (1:69). See comments on 1:27.

Salvation from our enemies . . . to rescue us (1:71–74). While the language here is strongly nationalistic and political, in the Old Testament such salvation is always accompanied by spiritual and moral renewal. Notice the goal here is "to enable us to serve him . . . in holiness and righteousness" (1:74–75).

Covenant . . . to our father Abraham (1:72–73). See comments on 1:55.

You will go on before the Lord to prepare the way for him (1:76). The verse recalls God's messenger of salvation in Malachi 3:1 and the voice announcing a new exodus deliverance in Isaiah 40:3 (see comments on Luke 1:17; 3:4; 7:27).

The knowledge of salvation through the forgiveness of their sins (1:77). Forgiveness of sins, an important theme for Luke, was an integral part of the new covenant promised through Jeremiah.[27]

The rising sun will come to us . . . to shine on those living in darkness (1:78–79). The Greek word translated "rising sun" (*anatolē*; "Sunrise," NASB; "dawn," NRSV) denotes a "rising" and can refer to a rising heavenly body ("sunrise" or "east" [= where the sun rises]) or to a growing plant ("shoot" or "branch"). Both images have messianic connotations. The Messiah is called the "shoot" from David's line[28] but is also identified as a light shining on those in darkness.[29] The reference to shining here confirms that the latter sense is primary. In Isaiah 9:1–7 the light that shines on those in darkness heralds the birth of the child who will reign forever on the throne of David. Similarly, Numbers 24:17, which speaks of a star coming forth from Jacob, was widely interpreted in Judaism with reference to the Messiah.[30] Rising light imagery also appears in the Old Testament with reference to God's end-time salvation.[31]

The child grew and became strong in spirit (1:80). This phrase echoes the

QUMRAN

(top) The cliffs where the principal cave (cave 4) of the Dead Sea Scroll discoveries is located.

(bottom left) The remains of the scriptorium.

(bottom right) The entrance to cave 4.

John the Baptist and the Community at Qumran

There has been much speculation among scholars as to whether John the Baptist may have had contact with the desert community of Essenes at Qumran, which produced the Dead Sea Scrolls. John's early years in the Judean Desert (Luke 1:80) may well have been in the vicinity of the Qumran community near the Dead Sea. If John's aged parents died before he reached adulthood, it is not impossible that he was raised by such a community. In an intriguing comment, the Jewish historian Josephus writes of the Essenes that "marriage they disdain, but they adopt other men's children, while yet pliable and docile, and regard them as their kin and mould them in accordance with their own principles."[A-10]

John's message and ministry also has some interesting points in common with the Essenes. Both share a strong expectation for the soon arrival of God's final salvation, both identify with the prophecy of Isaiah 40:3, both associate themselves with the righteous remnant called out from apostate Israel, and both practice ritual washings of some sort (baptism in John's case).

Unfortunately, there is not enough evidence either to confirm or disprove this fascinating hypothesis.

descriptions of Samson and especially Samuel.[32]

He lived in the desert (1:80). The reference is probably to the Jordan River Valley west of the Dead Sea. The desert in the Bible is a place of solitude and spiritual reflection, but also one of testing and preparation (see comments on 4:2 and "John the Baptist and the Community at Qumran").

The Birth of Jesus (2:1–7)

The account of Jesus' birth in Bethlehem brings together various themes of significance for Luke. By linking Jesus' birth to the census decree of Caesar Augustus, Luke provides his narrative with a firm historical framework (cf. 1:1–4; 3:1–2) and hints at the worldwide significance of seemingly trivial events in Judea. God's sovereign control over history is evident as Caesar Augustus, emperor of the world, issues a decree that inadvertently moves God's plan forward. Joseph and Mary are required to take the arduous trip to Bethlehem and so fulfill the prophecy of the Messiah's birth (Mic. 5:2). The commonness of the birth and the lowly shepherd visitors further confirm that this child, though destined to reign in power and glory (Luke 1:32–33), will first bring good news and salvation to the humble, the poor, and the outcasts.

Caesar Augustus (2:1). See "Caesar Augustus, the First Roman Emperor."

A census should be taken of the entire Roman world (2:1). Censuses were common in the Roman empire and were used as registration for tax purposes. Although we have no written evidence of such a single worldwide census during this time, Augustus reorganized the administration of the empire and conducted numerous local censuses. Luke may be referring to an otherwise unknown census, or he may be treating a local Palestinian census as part of the emperor's administrative policy.

The Greek word *oikoumenē* (NIV: "the Roman world") literally means "the inhabited world" and is used here of the Roman empire—civilization as perceived through Roman eyes.

The first census . . . while Quirinius was governor of Syria (2:2). Like the census itself, the reference to Quirinius represents a historical difficulty. According to Josephus, the governorship of Quirinius over Syria began in A.D. 6–7, and a census he conducted is described for Judea around A.D. 6.[33] This particular census and the revolt that followed are also mentioned by Luke in Acts 5:37. The problem is this would be ten years too late for the present account, since the birth of Jesus occurred prior to Herod's death in 4 B.C. (Matt. 2:1–19; Luke 1:5).

Various solutions to this problem have been proposed. (1) There is some inscriptional evidence that Quirinius may have been governor of Syria twice, first in 10–7 B.C. and then again in A.D. 6–9.[34] Luke's reference would be to his first governorship and a prior census. (2) Others suggest that prior to his governorship, Quirinius held a broad administrative post over the eastern empire, and it was at this time that this first census was taken. The Greek actually says, "while Quirinius was governing [or had charge over] Syria." (3) A third possibility is that Quirinius was completing a census that a previous governor had begun. In these first three proposals Quirinius would have been overseeing a census imposed by Caesar upon Herod the Great's territory. (4) Another novel solution separates Quirinius from Luke's census by translating the Greek word *prōtē* as "before" rather than "first." Luke might be saying this census took place *prior* to Quirinius's governorship of Syria. In any case, there is not enough evidence available to draw a decisive conclusion either for or against Luke's account.

Everyone went to his own town (2:3). Though the Romans did not generally require citizens to return to their ancestral homes during a census, there is some Egyptian evidence that property owners had to return to the district where they owned land.[35] Perhaps Joseph owned property in Bethlehem. Another possibility is that the Romans here, as on other occasions, allowed their client states to conduct affairs according to local customs, which in the case of Judea would involve ancestral tribal divisions.

BUST OF CAESAR AUGUSTUS

COIN INSCRIBED WITH "CAESAR"

This coin depicts captives of Julius Caesar.

So Joseph also went up ... to Judea (2:4). In the Old Testament one always went "up" to Judea and to Jerusalem. This is not just because of their elevation (Bethlehem is in "the hill country of Judea"; cf. 1:39), but especially because Jerusalem was the city of God.

Bethlehem the town of David (2:4). "Bethlehem" is from a Hebrew word meaning "house of bread." The Greek term *polis* can refer to a village, town, or city. Since Bethlehem was a small village, the NIV's "town" is accurate. Located about five miles south of Jerusalem, Bethlehem was closely associated with David in the Old Testament, being his birthplace and original home.[36] This David connection is the key to the prophecy of Micah 5:2, which predicts the Messiah's birth in Bethlehem (cf. Matt. 2:6). The Messiah was to be a new and greater "David."

Joseph ... line of David (2:4). See comments on 1:27.

Mary, who was pledged to be married to him (2:5). See comments on 1:27.

Her firstborn, a son (2:7). "Firstborn" is not meant to indicate that other children would be born, but to demonstrate Jesus' consecration to God and his rights to the privileges of a firstborn son.[37]

She wrapped him in cloths (2:7). The traditional "swaddling clothes" were strips of cloth intended to keep the limbs straight—a sign of motherly care and affection. In Ezekiel 16:4 Jerusalem is metaphorically described as a infant for whom no one cared: "On the day you were born your cord was not cut, nor were you washed with water to make you clean, nor were you rubbed with salt or wrapped in cloths."[38]

A manger (2:7). A manger (*phatnē*) was a feeding trough for animals. The word could also be used of a stall or enclosure where animals would be fed, but the reference to being "placed" there suggests the former.

Because there was no room for them in the inn (2:7). Contrary to the traditional Christmas story, the "inn" (*katalyma*) was probably not an ancient hotel with rooms to rent and an innkeeper, but either a guest room in a private residence (see 22:11) or an informal public shelter (a "caravansary") where travelers would gather for the night.[39] In the parable of the Good Samaritan, Luke uses a different term for a public inn (*pandocheion,* 10:34). In any case, crowded conditions force Joseph and Mary from normal lodging to a place reserved for animals. This could have been (1) a lower-level room or stall for animals attached to the living quarters of a private residence, (2) a cave used as a shelter for animals (as some

Caesar Augustus, the First Roman Emperor

Born Gaius Octavius in 63 B.C. (known to historians as "Octavian"), Caesar Augustus was emperor of the Roman world at the time of Jesus' birth. The grand-nephew of Julius Caesar, Octavian's rise to power began when Caesar was assassinated in 44 B.C. In his will, Caesar had adopted Octavian as his son. Now known as Gaius Julius Caesar Octavianus, Octavian at first shared power with a three man "triumvirate," or board of three, including himself and two of Julius Caesar's aids, Marcus Lepidus and Mark Antony. After Lepidus fell from power in 36 B.C., civil war broke out between Antony and Octavian. Antony allied himself with Cleopatra, queen of Egypt, but their combined forces were defeated by Octavian at Actium in 31 B.C. Octavian conquered Egypt in the following year and Antony and Cleopatra committed suicide. The Roman Senate recognized Octavian as supreme leader of Rome, and in 27 B.C. bestowed on him the title "Augustus" ("exalted" or "venerable" one). Augustus ruled as emperor until his death in A.D. 14, when he was replaced by Tiberius (see Luke 3:1). Demonstrating extraordinary skills as a leader and administrator, he inaugurated the *Pax Romana* ("Roman Peace"), an unprecedented period of peace and stability throughout the Mediterranean region. The freedom and relative safety of travel afforded by this peace would prove a major factor for the rapid expansion of the gospel message.

The main Roman emperors of the New Testament period following Augustus include:

Tiberius (A.D. 14–37). The emperor during Jesus' public ministry.

Caligula (A.D. 37–41). Provoked a crisis by demanding that his image be set up in the Jerusalem temple, but died before the order was carried out.

Claudius (A.D. 41–54). He expelled the Jews from Rome (Acts 18:2), probably because of conflicts with Christians (Seutonius, *Life of Claudius* 25:4).

Nero (A.D. 54–68). He persecuted the Christians after blaming them for a fire he was rumored to have set in Rome (Tacitus, *Annals* 15:44). Both Paul and Peter were probably martyred under Nero.

Vespasian (A.D. 69–79). He was declared emperor while in Palestine putting down the Jewish revolt. He returned to Rome, leaving his son Titus to complete the destruction of Jerusalem and the temple.

Domitian (A.D. 81–96). Initiated severe persecution of the church, the likely background to the book of Revelation.

ancient traditions have claimed),[40] or even (3) a feeding place under the open sky, perhaps in the town square. The present Church of the Nativity was built in the fourth century over a traditional cave site in Bethlehem. Whatever the precise location, the commonality and humility of the scene prepare the reader for the paradoxical story of the Messiah, who attains glory through suffering.

The Shepherds and the Angels (2:8–20)

The birth of Israel's king calls for recognition and acclaim, which is provided by the story of the shepherds and the angels. The account has two parts: *a heavenly response* in the angelic announcement and praise song (2:8–14), and *an earthly response* in the praise of the shepherds and the wonder of all who hear of these events (2:15–20). The theme is central to the birth narrative and to Luke-Acts as a whole: joy, rejoicing, and praise mark the arrival of God's great day of salvation.

Shepherds (2:8). Later rabbinic writings describe shepherds as dishonest and untrustworthy, and some commentators have suggested that here they represent the sinners Jesus came to save.[41] Yet the biblical portrait of shepherds is almost always positive, and nothing in this context suggests otherwise. David was a shepherd; the Lord is our shepherd (Ps. 23:1); Jesus is the good shepherd (see comments on 11:23).[42] What *is* clear is that shepherds were among the lower class in Israel and so represent the poor and humble for whom the message of salvation is indeed good news (Luke 1:52; 4:18).

It has also been suggested that, considering their proximity to Jerusalem, these sheep may have been raised for

right ▶

SHEPHERD

A shepherd tends his sheep near Bethlehem.

▶

MODERN BETHLEHEM

Near the Shepherd's Field Church.

temple sacrifices. Though speculative, if true this could point forward to Jesus' role as the sacrificial lamb of God.

Living out in the fields nearby, keeping watch over their flocks at night (2:8). Shepherds normally lived outside during warmer months, perhaps March-November, though there is some rabbinic evidence for year-round grazing. The actual time of Jesus' birth is unknown. The traditional December date for Christmas seems to have arisen in the time of Constantine (306–37) to coincide with the pagan feast of Saturnalia. The NIV's "keeping watch" is literally "keeping watches"; they take turns sleeping and guarding the flock against thieves and animals.

An angel of the Lord appeared to them (2:9). See comments on 1:11, 19.

The glory of the Lord (2:9). Glory (*doxa*) is used in the LXX to translate the Hebrew *kābôd*, often referring to God's visible presence.[43] In Exodus 24:16, 17 "the glory of the LORD"—the manifestation of his glorious presence—settles on Mount Sinai and remains there.

I bring you good news ... for all the people (2:10). The announcement of good news (*euangelizomai*) is a common verb for Luke[44] and has its roots in Isaiah's announcement of end-time salvation (Isa. 52:7; 61:1). There is also an interesting parallel in an inscription found at Priene celebrating the birth of Augustus. The inscription calls him a "savior" and says that "the birth date of our God has signaled the beginning of good news for the world."[45] Both of these backgrounds could have had significance for Luke, who has just referred to Caesar Augustus (2:1) and for whom Isaiah's portrait of salvation plays a leading role (2:32; 3:4–6; 4:18–19). Though Augustus is acclaimed by many as the world's god and savior, Jesus is the true deliverer.

"All the people" does not here refer to all nations (though this would fit well with Luke's overall theme), but rather to all Israel. Luke always uses the singular noun *laos* in this way.

The town of David (2:11). See comments on 2:4.

A Savior ... he is Christ the Lord (2:11). In the Old Testament, especially in the Psalms and Isaiah, God is frequently identified as the "Savior" of his people.[46] Jesus is Savior because through him God will redeem his people.[47]

"Christ" (*christos*) is a Greek translation of the Hebrew term *māšiaḥ*, meaning "anointed one" or "messiah." The title has its roots in the identification of Israel's king—especially David—as the Lord's anointed, his chosen vice-regent.[48] From this background the title "Messiah" came to be used in Judaism with reference to the coming king who would bring salvation to God's people. A manuscript fragment from the Dead Sea Scrolls says that the Messiah from David's line will "arise to save Israel"[49] (see further comments on 1:32–33; 9:20; also "Messianic Expectation in Jesus' Day).

A great company of the heavenly host ... praising God (2:13). The "hosts" or "armies" (*stratia*) of heaven reveal God's sovereign power and authority (cf. 2 Kings 6:17). A common Old Testament name of God is "LORD of Hosts" (*yhwh ṣᵉbnam'oftn*; NIV, "the Sovereign LORD"). Such praise by heaven's armies appears

REFLECTIONS

BORN TO PEASANT PARENTS, LAID in a feeding trough, visited by lowly shepherds. The commonness of Jesus' birth reminds us how Jesus, though Lord of the universe, stooped down to our humble level to bring us salvation. As John puts it, "The Word became flesh and made his dwelling among us" (John 1:14). Jesus now calls us to represent him—to live out his incarnation—for a lost world.

in Psalm 148:2: "Praise him, all his angels, praise him, all his heavenly hosts."

Glory to God in the highest (2:14). "In the highest" (2:14) means "in the heavenly realms," which reflects the present praise of the heavenly hosts. It finds its counterbalance "on earth" in the next line.

On earth peace to men on whom his favor rests (2:14). The difference between the NIV and the traditional "on earth peace, good will toward men" (KJV) is a textual one, with the better manuscripts reading *eudokias* ("of good will") rather than *eudokia* ("good will"). The phrase "people of good will" is a Hebrew idiom referring not to the good will of humans, but to *God's* favor bestowed on his people. The phrase "a people of his good pleasure" appears in the Qumran scrolls.[50]

Jesus Presented in the Temple (2:21–40)

The proclamation of Jesus' messianic identity continues as two prophetic heralds, Simeon and Anna, join the angels in announcing his arrival. The birth narrative theme of the righteous remnant permeates the narrative. Mary and Joseph are exemplary Jews who faithfully fulfill the Old Testament laws related to circumcision, purification, and the dedication of their firstborn to the Lord. Simeon and Anna represent faithful Israel, anxiously longing for the Messiah.

On the eighth day, when it was time to circumcise him (2:21). See comments on 1:59.

He was named Jesus (2:21). See comments on 1:31.

Their purification according to the Law of Moses (2:22). The Old Testament required a forty-day period of purification for the mother after the birth of a son: seven days before the circumcision and thirty-three days after (Lev. 12:1–8). During this time, "she must not touch anything sacred or go to the sanctuary until the days of her purification are over" (12:4). At the end of this time, a sacrifice was made for her purification (see Luke 2:24). The reference to "their" purification is odd, since the Old Testament set out requirements only for the mother. It is possible that Joseph was rendered unclean during the birth process or, more likely, Luke refers to the family's participation in both the purification and dedication ceremonies.

To present him to the Lord . . . as it is written . . . (2:22–23). The Old Testament law stipulated that every firstborn male, whether human or animal, was to be dedicated to the Lord. Firstborn animals were to be offered as a sacrifice. For humans the Lord took the Levites as his own tribe instead of the firstborn sons, but a redemption price of five shekels was to be paid.[51] Nehemiah 10:35–36 suggests that this dedication of sons was generally done in the temple. Luke

MODEL OF THE TEMPLE AND ITS COURTS

explains these requirements by alluding to Exodus 13:2, 12 in Luke 2:23: "Every firstborn male is to be consecrated to the Lord." Some scholars have suggested that since no mention is made of Jesus' redemption, he was not redeemed but wholly dedicated to the Lord, after the model of the child Samuel (1 Sam. 1–2). It is perhaps significant that there are echoes in this verse to 1 Samuel 1:24, 28 (cf. Luke 2:34, 40).

To offer a sacrifice . . . "a pair of doves or two young pigeons" (2:24). The quotation is from Leviticus 12:8, which concerns the sacrifice of purification for the woman, not the redemption of the firstborn. The woman was to offer a lamb and a pigeon or dove (12:6), or two doves or pigeons if she was poor (12:8). We have incidental evidence here that Joseph and Mary belonged to the lower economic classes.

Simeon. A common name among first-century Jews, derived from one of the sons of Jacob (Gen. 29:33; 35:23) and the tribe of Israel that came from him. It is the more Hebraic form of the name Simon. (Simon Peter is called Simeon [*symeōn*] in Acts 15:14 and 2 Peter 1:1.) Some have suggested that Simeon was a priest since he was in the temple, though the text does not say this.

He was waiting for the consolation of Israel (2:25). The "consolation of Israel" comes from Isaiah 40, where the prophet announces Israel's "comfort" (= salvation) after her exile.[52] The phrase represents the salvation, peace, and forgiveness Israel will receive in the messianic era. It finds a parallel in the "redemption of Jerusalem" in 2:38.

That he would not die (2:26). Literally "to see death," an Old Testament expression (Ps. 89:48). This suggests that Simeon was an old man, though the text does not specifically say so.

The Lord's Christ (2:26). This phrase is equivalent to the Old Testament expression "the LORD's Anointed" (see comments on 1:32; 2:11) and carries the sense, "Yahweh's chosen agent of redemption." Luke elsewhere uses similar expressions "Christ of God" (9:20; 23:35) and "his Christ" (Acts 3:18; 4:26).

He went into the temple courts (2:27). Luke uses *hieron* to refer to the general temple area (see comments on *naos* at 1:9–10). This encounter probably takes place in the Court of Women, since Mary is present and since Anna shortly appears.

Sovereign Lord . . . now dismiss your servant (1:29). The NIV's "Sovereign Lord" is a rare New Testament word, *despotēs* (used ten times). In parallel with *doulos* ("servant" or "slave"), it means "master," pointing to a master/servant relationship. Simeon has accomplished his task as a faithful servant and herald of his Master's salvation.

Your salvation, which you have prepared in the sight of all people (2:30–31). The reference to God's salvation being seen by all people captures the thought of Isaiah 52:10: "The LORD will lay bare his holy arm in the sight of all the nations, and all the ends of the earth will see the salvation of our God." The plural noun "people" (*laoi*) here means Jews and Gentiles (contrast the singular *laos* in Luke 2:10). See the following verses for more allusions to Isaiah's portrait of salvation.

HEROD'S TEMPLE FROM INSIDE THE COURT OF WOMEN

A light for revelation to the Gentiles (2:32). Not only will the nations see God's salvation, but Simeon now reveals that they will participate in it. He alludes to Isaiah 42:6 and 49:6, where Isaiah prophesies that the Servant-Messiah will bring salvation to the Gentiles as well as the Jews. This is the first indication in Luke's Gospel that Israel's salvation will extend to the Gentiles.

And for glory to your people Israel (2:32). The "light" for the Gentiles finds its parallel in "glory" for Israel. In Isaiah 46:13 Israel's glory is associated with her salvation: "I will grant salvation to Zion, my splendor to Israel." Israel's glorious salvation will serve as the attracting light that draws in the Gentiles.

This child is destined to cause the falling and rising of many in Israel (2:34). Though not a direct quotation, this phrase reflects a stone metaphor drawn from Isaiah 8:14–15 and 28:16. It refers to two responses to Jesus among those in Israel: To some, the Messiah will be "a stone that causes men to stumble and a rock that makes them fall" (8:14); to others, he becomes "a precious cornerstone for a sure foundation" (28:16; cf. Ps. 118:22), upon which they will rise. This dual stone metaphor was an important one for the early church, used both to explain the rejection of Israel (Rom. 9:32–33) and to express the foundation of the church (Eph. 2:20). Both images appear in 1 Peter 2:6–8, which cites all three Old Testament texts.[53] Luke uses this double stone image again in Luke 20:17–18.

A sign that will be spoken against (2:34). If the reference to "falling" in 2:34 is an allusion to Isaiah 8:14–15, the next phrase—that the child will be "a sign that will be spoken against"—may allude to the same context, where Isaiah and his children are said to be for "signs and symbols in Israel" (Isa. 8:18). Just as Isaiah's oracles divided Israel into a faithful remnant and an apostate majority, so the "sign" of Jesus will provoke similar opposition and division (cf. Luke 11:29–30).

A sword will pierce your own soul (2:35). This phrase sounds like Psalm 37:15: "But their swords will pierce their own hearts . . ." (cf. Ezek. 14:17), though that passage is in a context of judgment against the wicked. The idiom itself means to experience great pain and probably refers to the pain and sorrow Mary will experience because of Jesus' rejection and death.

A prophetess, Anna (2:36). Anna's prophetic office places her in a category with such Old Testament worthies as Miriam (Ex. 15:20), Deborah (Judg. 4:4), and Huldah (2 Kings 22:14). The Talmud identifies seven Old Testament women as prophetesses: Sarah, Miriam, Deborah, Hannah, Abigail, Huldah, and Esther (*b. Meg.* 14a). Prophetesses are mentioned in the New Testament in Acts 2:17–18; 21:9; 1 Corinthians 11:5. "Anna" is the Greek equivalent of the Hebrew "Hannah," Samuel's mother (1 Sam. 1–2). This is significant in light of various allusions to Samuel's dedication in the passage.

Of the tribe of Asher (2:36). Asher was one of the ten northern tribes of Israel, named after Jacob's eighth son Asher.[54] The reference to a northern tribe confirms that not all first-century Israelites were, strictly speaking, "Jews" (= from the tribe of Judah), and that members of other tribes had maintained their identity through the Babylonian exile. The designation Jew came to be used synonymously with "Israelite," encompassing those from other tribes as well (Paul was a Benjamite; Phil. 3:5). It is therefore not accurate to speak of the "lost (ten) tribes of Israel."

She was very old . . . a widow until she was eighty-four (2:36–37). In the ancient world being old was often associated with wisdom and piety. Similarly, the widow who remained single to be devoted to the Lord was a common image both in Judaism (Judith 8:4–8) and early Christianity.[55] Josephus describes Antonia, the widow of Drusus the great, as a "virtuous and chaste woman. For despite her youth she remained steadfast in her widowhood and refused to marry again. . . . She thus kept her life free from reproach."[56] Judith, the pious widow and heroine of the apocryphal work that bears her name, remained for years a widow after the death of her husband Manasseh. She "fasted all the days of her widowhood. . . . No one spoke ill of her, for she feared God with great devotion" (Judith 8:6–8). The Greek text is unclear as to whether Anna's eighty-four years refer to her present age (so NIV) or to the number of years she had been a widow after her seven-year marriage. If the latter, she would have been about 105 years old (assuming she was married at the age of fourteen: 14 + 7 + 84 = 105), the age attributed to Judith at her death.

She never left the temple but worshiped night and day, fasting and praying (2:37).

The statement that Anna never left the temple does not mean that she slept there (women would not normally live on temple grounds), but that she was wholly devoted to worship. This recalls Samuel's devotion to his temple service (1 Sam. 1:28; 2:11). "Night and day" follows the Jewish way of reckoning time from sunset to sunset. Fasting and prayer were common signs of deep piety in Judaism (see Judith 8:6, cited above). In the apocryphal book of 2 Esdras (*4 Ezra*) 9:44, a certain barren woman is said to have prayed for a child "every hour and every day . . . night and day" for thirty years until God answered her prayers.

Redemption of Jerusalem (2:38). The phrase "redemption [*lytrōsis*] of Jerusalem" is linked with the "consolation of Israel" in 2:25, both of which refer to the promised messianic salvation (cf. 1:68). The ideas of comfort and redemption appear together in Isaiah 52:9: "Burst into songs of joy together, you ruins of Jerusalem, for the LORD has comforted his people, he has redeemed Jerusalem." During the second Jewish revolt against Rome (A.D. 132–135), when messianic hopes centered on Simon Bar-Kochba, documents were sometimes dated to the years of the "Redemption of Israel."[57]

THEATER AT SEPPHORIS

Just a few miles from Nazareth, this city had a theater with a seating capacity of 4,500.

And the child grew and became stron[g] (2:40). This verse, like the description o[f] John in 1:80, echoes what is said abou[t] Samuel in 1 Samuel 2:21, 26. For a close[r] parallel, see Luke 2:52.

He was filled with wisdom (2:40). In Isa[iah] 11:2 the Messiah is said to have a spe[cial] endowment of wisdom from th[e] Spirit (see comments on Luke 2:52).

The Boy Jesus at the Temple (2:41–52)

The Passover Jerusalem visit of th[e] twelve-year-old Jesus is the only accoun[t] from Jesus' childhood found in th[e] canonical Gospels. Though other storie[s] appear in the so-called "infancy Gospels," these are late, fanciful, and historicall[y] unreliable. Luke includes this story not t[o] fill in details for the curious reader, but t[o] reveal Jesus' real human growth, both spiritual and physical.

Every year . . . to Jerusalem for the Feas[t] of the Passover (2:41). See "Passover an[d] the Feast of Unleavened Bread."

When he was twelve years old (2:42)[.] According to Jewish tradition, a Jewis[h] boy became responsible to observe th[e] law when he was thirteen years old— though the actual ceremony of *bar-mitzvah*, whereby a Jewish boy becomes a "so[n] of the covenant," is of later origin.[58] Though it is not specifically stated tha[t] this is Jesus' first trip, the identification o[f] his age as twelve probably suggests that hi[s] parents are taking steps to prepare him fo[r] his covenantal responsibility. The wisdo[m] and spiritual awareness he demonstrate[s] are intended to be all the more extraordinary since it takes place prior to his thirteenth year. Josephus similarly identifie[s]

Samuel's age as twelve when he received his call from the Lord and when he began to prophesy.[59] According to 1 Kings 2:12 in the LXX, Solomon's reign began when he was twelve.

Jesus stayed behind . . . but they were unaware of it (2:43). The journey from Nazareth to Jerusalem is about eighty miles (if they are traveling around, rather than through, Samaria); it would take approximately three days. The family is probably traveling in a caravan of relatives and friends for protection from bandits on the roads. This explains how Jesus' parents could have left without him, assuming he is elsewhere in the caravan.

After three days (2:46). The three days probably refers to the total time from their departure after the Feast to the discovery of Jesus (one day out, one day back, a day of searching).

In the temple courts, sitting among the teachers (2:46). For the temple courts (*hieros*) see comments on 2:27. Jesus is in the traditional position of a disciple, sitting at the feet of his teachers. This is the only place Luke uses the term "teacher" (*didaskalos*) for the rabbinic experts in the law. Elsewhere they are usually "lawyers" (*nomikos*) or "scribes" (*grammateus*). Luke probably seeks to retain a positive portrait here, since the other terms carry negative connotations in the Gospel.

Listening to them and asking them questions (2:46). Rabbis often taught in a question-and-answer format. The teachers are viewed as responding to Jesus' questions in rabbinic style with counter-questions, since it is both Jesus' "insight" (*synesis*) and his "answers" that provoke amazement among all who hear.

Amazed at his understanding and his answers (2:47). The motif of a hero who shows unusual intelligence as a child is common in both Greek and Jewish biography. There are similar stories told of Moses, Cyrus the Great, Alexander the Great, and Apollonius.[60] In his autobiography, Josephus describes himself in a similar manner:

bottom left

ISRAEL

The route from Galilee to Jerusaelm.

bottom right

CROWDED STREET IN OLD JERUSALEM

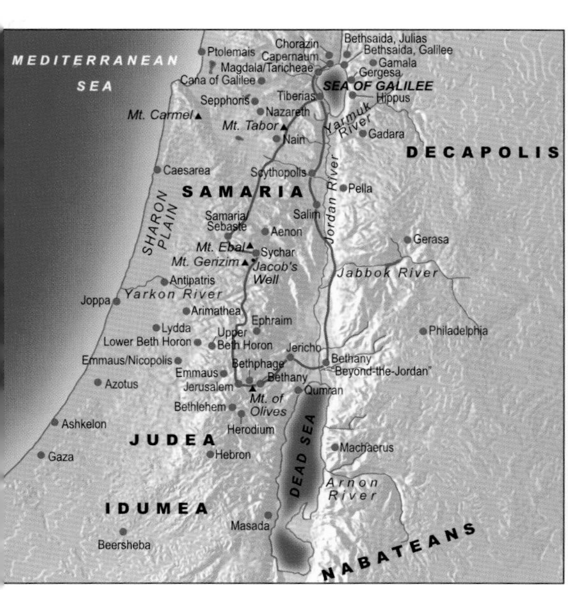

While still a mere boy, about fourteen years old, I won universal applause for my love of letters; insomuch that the chief priests and the leading men of the city used constantly to come to me for precise information on some particular in our ordinances.[61]

The most important background to this text, however, is the description of the coming Messiah in Isaiah 11:2: "The Spirit of the LORD will rest on him—the Spirit of wisdom and of understanding, the Spirit of counsel and of power, the Spirit of knowledge and of the fear of the LORD."

I had to be in my Father's house (2:49). Though the Greek phrase used here can be translated "about my Father's business," or even "among my Father's people," the NIV translation "in my Father's house" is probably the correct one. The idiom appears with this sense in both biblical and extrabiblical texts and fits the present context well.[62]

He . . . was obedient to them (2:51). Luke wants to avoid any suggestion that Jesus' priority to pursue his Father's purposes resulted in a failure to submit to his earthly parents. This statement of obedience confirms that Jesus was not the rebellious son so often condemned in Scripture.[63] The fifth commandment instructs us to honor our father and mother.[64]

And Jesus grew in wisdom and stature, and in favor with God and men (2:52). This verse echoes 1 Samuel 2:26: "And the boy Samuel continued to grow in stature and in favor with the LORD and with men" (cf. also Luke 1:80; 2:40). Isaiah 11:2–4 identifies the coming Messiah as one who will bear extraordinary wisdom.

John the Baptist Prepares the Way (3:1–20)

Like the other Gospel writers, Luke begins his account of Jesus' ministry with the appearance of John the Baptist. John is the forerunner of the Messiah predicted in Isaiah 40:3–5 and Malachi 3:1; 4:5–6. For Luke he is the last and the greatest of the Old Testament prophets,

Passover and the Feast of Unleavened Bread

Passover was the Jewish festival commemorating the deliverance of the Hebrews from slavery in Egypt. The angel of death spared the firstborn sons of the Hebrews, "passing over" those households that sacrificed a lamb and placed its blood on the doorframes (Ex. 12). It was celebrated on the 15th of Nisan (March/April), the first month in the Jewish calendar. Lambs were sacrificed in the temple on the afternoon of Nisan 14 and were roasted and eaten with unleavened bread that evening (Nisan 15 began after sunset). Family or larger units celebrated Passover together. Unleavened bread was then eaten for the next seven days—the Feast of Unleavened Bread.[A-11] The term "Passover" was sometimes used for both festivals. Extensive traditions and liturgy eventually became attached to Passover, though how much of this was practiced in Jesus' day is unknown.

Passover was one of three pilgrim feasts that Jewish males were expected to attend; the other two were Pentecost and the Feast of Tabernacles.[A-12] Because of the rigors of travel, it is a sign of the piety of Joseph's family that in 2:41 they make the journey "every year." This piety is also evident in the fact that Mary and Jesus join Joseph, since only males were required to attend (see comments on 22:1; 22:7).

a transitional figure forming a bridge between the age of promise and the age of fulfillment (Luke 7:24–28; 16:16). In light of impending judgment, John preaches a "baptism of repentance for the forgiveness of sins" (3:3), warning his hearers to produce fruit—a radical kingdom ethic—that is in accordance with their repentance.[65]

In the fifteenth year . . . the word of God came to John (3:1–2). The introduction to John's ministry is reminiscent of the call of Old Testament prophets, including the dating of John's career to the year of the king's reign, the establishment of his identity by his ancestry ("son of Zechariah"), and the reception of his prophetic message ("the word of God came to John"). For these elements see the opening verses of Jeremiah, Ezekiel, Hosea, Joel, Jonah, Micah, Zephaniah, Haggai, and Zechariah.

The reign of Tiberius Caesar (3:1). Tiberius Caesar became emperor in A.D. 14, at the death of his stepfather Augustus (cf. 2:1), and reigned until A.D. 37. A difficulty arises in establishing a firm date here, however, since Tiberius became coregent with Augustus in A.D. 11/12. Following this earlier date, some claim Jesus' ministry began in A.D. 25/26 or 26/27. Others take the later date and, depending on when the first year is reckoned to begin and end, arrive at A.D. 27/28 or 28/29.[66] A date of around A.D. 28 seems most likely. Either reckoning, A.D. 26 or 28 fits Luke's statement in 3:23 that Jesus is "about thirty" when his ministry begins.

Pontius Pilate . . . Herod . . . Philip . . . Lysanias (3:1). After the death of Herod the Great in 4 B.C., his kingdom was divided among his three sons. Archelaus received Judea, Samaria, and Idumea (cf. Matt. 2:21–23), Herod Antipas took over Galilee and Perea, and Philip inherited Iturea and Trachonitis, regions north and west of Galilee.[67] When Archelaus was removed from office in A.D. 6 by Augustus because of misrule (see comments on

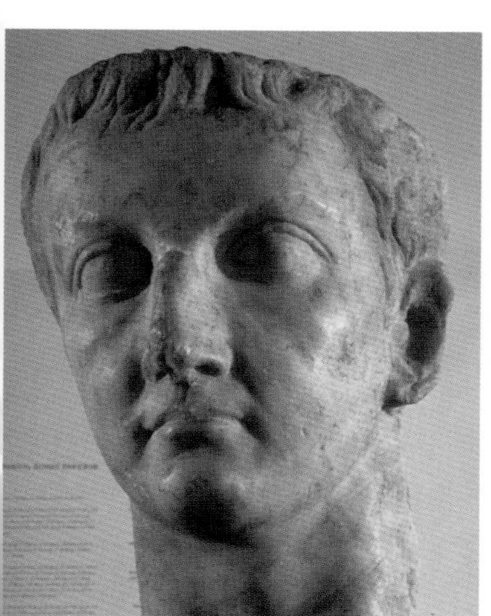

◀ *left*

MARBLE BUST OF THE EMPEROR TIBERIUS

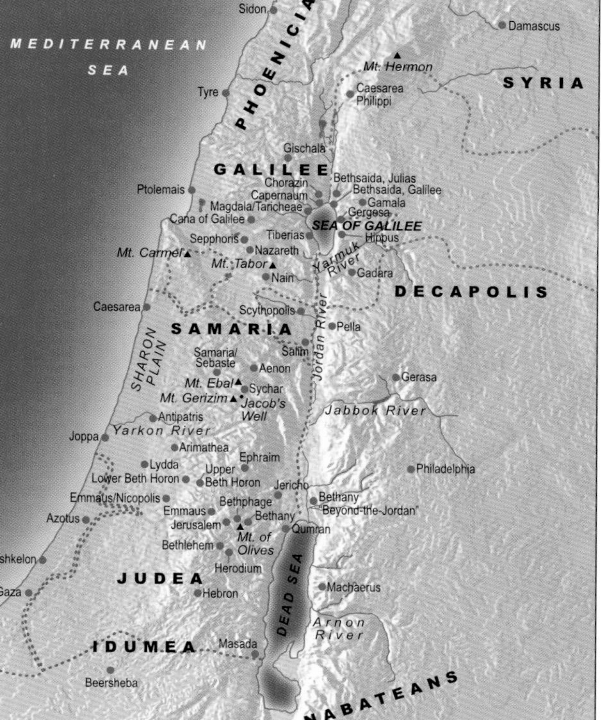

◀

THE KINGDOM OF HEROD

Showing the divisions of the kingdom among Herod's sons.

19:14), Judea and Samaria were transferred to the control of Roman governors, known as prefects and procurators. Pontius Pilate is one such prefect, governing Judea from A.D. 26–36. In presiding over Jesus' trial, Pilate will play a key role in Luke's Gospel.[68] For more on Pilate and his harsh rule, see comments on 13:1 and the sidebar at Mark 15:1.

Herod Antipas ruled over Galilee and Perea from his father's death until he was deposed by the emperor Caligula in A.D. 39. This is the Herod who imprisoned and eventually executed John the Baptist after John spoke out against his marriage to Herodias, his brother's wife.[69] It is also Antipas who wonders about Jesus' identity (9:7–9) and whom Jesus calls "that fox" (13:31–32). Only Luke records that Jesus stood before Herod during his trial (23:7–12; cf. Acts 4:27). The title "tetrarch" originally meant ruler of a fourth part of a region, but it came to be used of any minor ruler.

Philip, the half brother of Herod Antipas, ruled as tetrarch of Iturea and Traconitis from 4 B.C. until his death in A.D. 34. Generally recognized as the best of the Herodian rulers, he died without an heir, and his territory became part of the Roman province of Syria. He is mentioned in the New Testament only here. The Philip identified in Matthew 14:3 and Mark 6:17 as the husband of Herodias and half brother of Antipas is a different son of Herod the Great. He lived in Rome and did not rule after his father's death.

The region of Abilene, over which Lysanias ruled as tetrarch, is located northwest of Galilee in Syria. The identity of Lysanias is something of a problem since Josephus mentions an individual by this name who was executed by Mark Antony in 36 B.C.[70] While some conclude that Luke is in error, Josephus elsewhere refers to another Lysanias of Abila, who ruled at a later time; there is also inscriptional evidence for such an identification.[71]

During the high priesthood of Annas and Caiaphas (3:2). Luke's reference to two high priests at first seems odd, since Judaism had only one high priest. Annas, who came to office in A.D. 6, was deposed in A.D. 15 by Valerius Gratus. He was eventually succeeded by his son-in-law Caiaphas, who served from A.D. 18–37.[72] Annas continued to wield enormous influence, however, and was viewed popularly as continuing as high priest.[73] In this sense there were indeed two high priests: one who held the official office and one who wielded power behind the scenes. Luke thus demonstrates an astute historical sense by identifying not only the actual office holder, but also the political intrigues behind the office.

All the country around the Jordan (3:3). John's ministry most likely took place in the Judean desert around the Jordan River west and north of the Dead Sea.

A baptism of repentance for the forgiveness of sins (3:3). The Greek term *baptizō* means to dip or immerse. In non-Christian literature the term sometimes means to plunge, sink, drench, or overwhelm.[74] Rites of washing and immersion were common in Judaism and other religious traditions. In the Old Testament bathing and sprinkling were used to remove ceremonial uncleanness.[75] The high priest bathed before and after making atonement (Lev. 16:4, 24). At the Qumran community washings were associated with participation in the end-time community of God (see quotations below).[76] Some have identified John's baptism with Jewish proselyte (new convert) baptism. John would then be calling the apostate nation to become real Jews again. While this image fits John's message and milieu, the evidence from the Talmud for such proselyte baptism is late, rendering it questionable whether such a practice goes back to the first century.[77] Since none of these parallels is exact, John's baptism may best be viewed as a unique eschatological (i.e., end times) application, drawing conceptually from the cleansing and initiatory rites of first-century Judaism.

John's baptism is described as one "of repentance for the forgiveness of sins." The Old Testament often speaks of repentance, a turning to God from sin.[78] Spiritual cleansing is frequently associated with God's forgiveness.[79] At Qumran a close connection is drawn between ceremonial washings and turning from sin. 1QS 3:8–9 reads, "By the spirit of uprightness and of humility his sin is atoned. And by the compliance of his soul with all the laws of God his flesh is cleansed by being sprinkled with cleansing waters and being made holy with the waters of repentance." It is not the act of washing, but the repentance itself that results in forgiveness, "for they have not been cleansed unless they turn away from their wickedness."[80] In John's baptism too it is not the act of immersion but the repentant heart that results in forgiveness. Josephus notes that John's baptism itself did not accomplish remission of sins, but was rather "as a consecration of the body implying that the soul was already thoroughly cleansed by right behaviour."[81]

As is written in . . . Isaiah the prophet (3:4–6). John's prophetic ministry is confirmed with a quote from Isaiah 40:3–5. Isaiah's prophecy, which originally referred to the return of the Babylonian exiles, had subsequently been

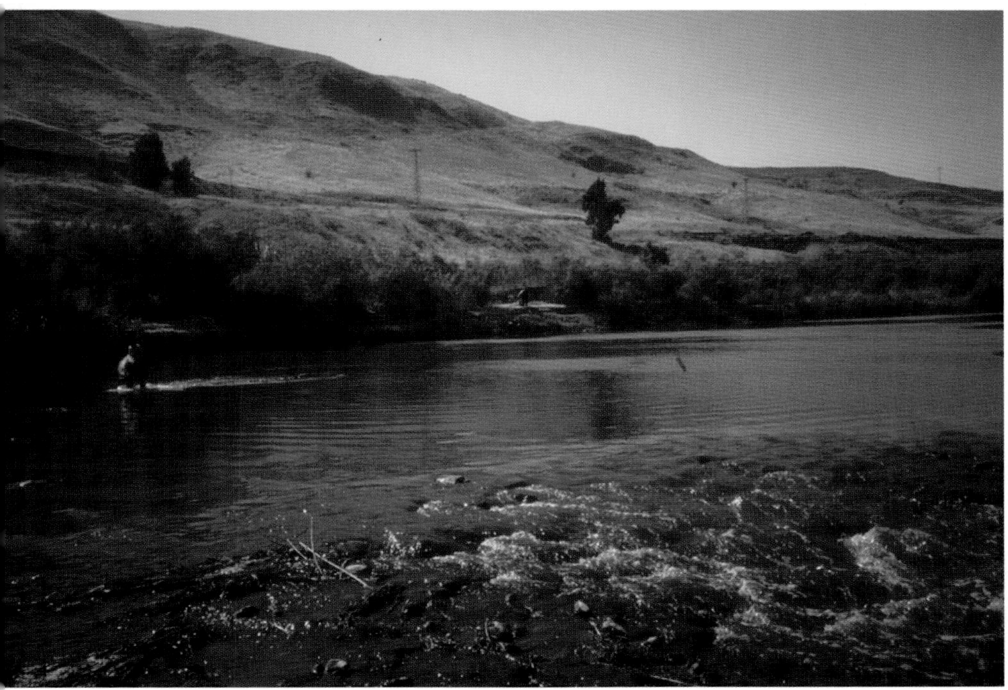

JORDAN RIVER

interpreted eschatologically in Judaism.[82] At Qumran the preparation of a way is identified with the community's withdrawal to their desert community to study the law.[83] Sirach too identifies Isaiah's prophecies with events of the last days: "By his [Isaiah's] dauntless spirit he saw the future, and comforted the mourners in Zion. He revealed what was to occur to the end of time, and the hidden things before they happened."[84] The prophetic announcement of deliverance from exile becomes for Luke a type or model for John's announcement of end-time restoration through the Messiah.

A voice of one calling in the desert (3:4). The reference to the desert presents the return from the Exile as a "new exodus," analogous to God's deliverance of his people from Egypt. In the Old Testament and in Judaism, God's final salvation is often presented as a second and greater exodus.[85]

Prepare the way for the Lord (3:4–5). The preparation of a way reflects Near Eastern imagery of clearing the path for a royal figure. Only a smooth, straight road is appropriate for a king. The imagery is metaphorical, referring to a people spiritually and morally prepared to welcome their Lord.

All mankind will see God's salvation (3:6). While Matthew and Mark cite only Isaiah 40:3, Luke continues the quotation with a confirmation of the universal application of God's message. Among the Old Testament prophets, Isaiah most stressed the universality of the gospel, that Gentiles as well as Jews will one day

Josephus on John the Baptist

In a short passage, the Jewish historian Josephus refers to John the Baptist. When the troops of Herod Antipas were defeated by Aretas, king of Arabia, rumors spread that God was punishing Herod for his arrest and execution of John. Josephus describes this rumor and then gives a brief description of John:

> For Herod had put him to death, though he was a good man and had exhorted the Jews to lead righteous lives, to practice justice towards their fellows and piety towards God, and so doing to join in baptism. In his view this was a necessary preliminary if baptism was to be acceptable to God. They must not employ it to gain pardon for whatever sins they committed, but as a consecration of the body implying that the soul was already thoroughly cleansed by right behavior.

While the Gospel writers attribute John's arrest to his criticism of Herod's divorce and remarriage, Josephus refers more generally to the Baptist's growing influence among the people. Josephus describes the place of John's imprisonment as the castle Machaerus, which was east of the Dead Sea.

> When others too joined the crowds about him, because they were aroused to the highest degree by his sermons, Herod became alarmed. Eloquence that had so great an effect on mankind might lead to some form of sedition, for it looked as if they would be guided by John in everything that they did. Herod decided therefore that it would be much better to strike first and be rid of him before his work led to an uprising, than to wait for an upheaval, get involved in a difficult situation and see his mistake.... John, because of Herod's suspicions, was brought in chains to Machaerus, the stronghold that we have previously mentioned, and there put to death.[A-13]

be welcomed into God's kingdom (see Isa. 42:6; 49:6).

You brood of vipers! (3:7). Whereas Israelites viewed themselves as the children of Abraham (see next verse), John identifies the apostate nation as the offspring of "vipers." The image points to the destructive power of poisonous snakes, a common metaphor for evil. Israel's apostasy is similarly described in Isaiah 59:4–5: "they conceive trouble and give birth to evil. They hatch the eggs of vipers and spin a spider's web" (cf. Isa. 14:29).[86] Although "vipers" in Luke 3:7 is plural, there may be an indirect allusion to Satan as the serpent of the Garden of Eden. Similar imagery appears in the Dead Sea Scrolls and in John's Gospel, where Jesus accuses his opponents of being children of Satan (John 8:44).[87]

We have Abraham as our father (3:8). Descent from Abraham was a source of great pride in Judaism.[88] In the *Psalms of Solomon* it is said that while God's compassionate judgments encompass the whole world, his "love is for the descendants of Abraham."[89] According to the intertestamental *Testament of the Twelve Patriarchs*, it is this alone that had protected Israel from more severe judgment for her sins: "Unless you had received mercy through Abraham, Isaac, and Jacob, our fathers, not a single one of your descendants would be left on the earth."[90]

Out of these stones God can raise up children for Abraham (3:8). There may have been a pun in John's original words, since the Aramaic words for "sons" (*bebnayyam*) and "stones" (*abnayyam*) are similar.

The ax is already at the root of the trees (3:9). Jeremiah 46:22–23, part of an oracle of judgment against Egypt, provides an interesting parallel to Luke 3:7–9 since it contains both images of fleeing serpents and an ax cutting down trees (cf. Isa. 10:33–34).

Every tree that does not produce good fruit (3:9). The image of Israel as a rebellious vine that God will judge appears in the Old Testament (Jer. 2:21–22; Hos. 10:1–2) and will be taken up by Jesus later in Luke 13:7–9. There are also clear conceptual parallels to Isaiah's Song of the Vineyard, where Israel's unfruitfulness results in her judgment (Isa. 5:1–7). This song will be adapted by Jesus and applied to his ministry in the parable of the tenant farmers (Luke 20:9–19).

Two tunics (3:11). The tunic (*chitōn*) was a garment worn against the skin, normally under a cloak (*himation*, cf. 6:29). One might wear two tunics for warmth or could simply own a spare. In either case the exhortation is to share even the smallest surplus with those in need.

Tax collectors (3:12). The Roman government together with local authorities imposed a range of taxes on its citizens, from direct poll and land taxes to indirect tolls or customs on goods in transit (cf. 5:27).[91] The Romans leased out the right to collect taxes to individuals, who then took a surcharge for their own expenses. Since this charge was seldom controlled, the system was open to great abuse and corruption.[92]

Tax collectors were despised in Israel, not only because of their reputation for extortion, but also for their complicity with the hated Romans. Jesus' association with them is an important part of his identification with the poor, the lowly, and the outcasts of Israel (for more on tax collectors see comments on 18:10; 19:2).

Soldiers (3:14). These are probably not Roman soldiers, but Jewish troops employed by Herod Antipas (cf. 23:11). Josephus refers to such troops.[93] Their mention beside the tax collectors may indicate they were assigned to assist and protect them in their duties. John tells them not to use violent intimidation or to falsely accuse others for monetary gain, but to be content with their wages (*opsōnion*, a military term for rations or provisions). Just as tax collectors were tempted to grow rich through excessive charges, soldiers were tempted to use their position of power to intimidate and control others for financial advantage.

If John might possibly be the Christ (3:15). For Jewish expectation for the "Christ" see comments on 1:33–34; 2:11.

One more powerful than I (3:16). See 11:21–22.

The thongs of whose sandals I am not worthy to untie (3:16). The untying of a sandal was the duty of a slave for his master. Although Jewish disciples were expected to perform a range of menial tasks for their masters—anything a slave would do—the rabbis specifically exempted them from this as too degrading. Even Hebrew slaves were exempted from this task.[94] Yet John says he is unworthy even to carry out this lowly duty.

Baptize you with the Holy Spirit and with fire (3:16). The Old Testament predicted that in the end times God would pour out his Spirit on his people.[95] This prophecy was at least partially fulfilled on the Day of Pentecost (Acts 2:1–4), when a rushing wind and "tongues of fire" accompanied the coming of the Spirit. In the Old Testament and intertestamental Judaism fire is a common symbol for God's judgment,[96] and this idea is present in the context.[97] While some view these Spirit and fire baptisms as distinct, the former for the righteous and the latter for the wicked, it seems more likely that we have here one Spirit-and-fire baptism, which purifies the righteous and judges the wicked (cf. 1 Cor. 3:10–15). Isaiah 4:4 speaks in an eschatological context of a "spirit of judgment and a spirit of fire" that will "cleanse the bloodstains from Jerusalem" (cf. Mal 3:2). Such imagery was common in apocalyptic Judaism of the first century.[98]

Winnowing fork (3:17). After being harvested, wheat was tossed into the air with a fork-like shovel or winnowing fork. The heavier grain fell back to the ground while the lighter chaff blew away. For the

right

WINNOWING FORK

A wooden pitchfork and a grain sifting net.

idea of winnowing out the wicked see Proverbs 20:26; Jeremiah 15:7.

Unquenchable fire (3:17). Judgment as unquenchable fire appears in Isaiah 34:10; 66:24 (cf. Mark 9:43–44, 48, where Isa. 66:24 is quoted).

Herod the tetrarch . . . Herodias (3:19). This is Herod Antipas, the son of Herod the Great (see comments on 3:1). Antipas had divorced his first wife, the daughter of the Arabian king Aretas, and had married Herodias, his niece and the former wife of his brother Phillip (see Mark 6:17). John, in typical prophetic fashion, rebukes Herod for taking his brother's wife (see Lev. 18:16) and for other "evil things." Herod responds by imprisoning and eventually executing John (Luke 9:9). For a fuller account of these events see Mark 6:14–29 and "Josephus on John the Baptist."

John here fulfills a common role of the prophets in the Old Testament, who suffered for boldly calling Israel's king to account for breaking God's law.[99] Jeremiah was similarly treated.[100] The rejection and persecution of the prophets is a common theme in Luke.[101]

The Baptism of Jesus (3:21–22)

Jesus' baptism marks the beginning of his public ministry. For Luke the descent of the Spirit on Jesus signifies his "anointing" as Messiah and his empowerment to accomplish the task God has set out for him (see 4:1, 14, 18). The voice from heaven provides divine confirmation that Jesus is the Messiah and Son of God (cf. Matt. 3:13–17; Mark 1:9–11).

As he was praying (3:21). Jesus' prayer life is an important theme in Luke's Gospel. Luke portrays Jesus praying at key points in his ministry: at his baptism (3:21), after cleansing a leper (5:16), before calling the Twelve (6:12), before Peter's confession (9:18), at the Transfiguration (9:28), before teaching the disciples to pray (11:1), for Peter that he would be restored (22:32), in the Garden of Gethsemane (22:41, 44), for his murderers from the cross (23:34), and with his last breath (23:46).

Heaven was opened (3:21). The opening of heaven is a common image in apocalyptic literature, often associated with the giving of revelation.[102]

The Holy Spirit descended . . . like a dove (3:22). The symbolism associated with the dove has been much debated. Some see an allusion to Genesis 1:2, where the Spirit "hovers" over the waters at creation. Later rabbinic works interpret this "hovering" as that of a bird, and even specifically as a dove.[103] In this case Jesus can here be identified with the new creation. Others suggest an allusion to Genesis 8:8–12, where Noah's dove represents God's gracious deliverance after judgment. Neither of these have strong verbal or conceptual parallels, however, and the image may be merely a visual description of the Spirit's descent.

You are my Son, whom I love; with you I am well pleased (3:22). The voice from heaven alludes to at least two, and perhaps three, Old Testament passages: Psalm 2:7; Isaiah 42:1; and perhaps Genesis 22:2, 12, 16. (1) In Psalm 2:7 the messianic king's divine sonship and legitimate rule from Mount Zion are announced by God: "You are my Son; today I have become your Father." (2) "With you I am well pleased" alludes to Isaiah 42:1, where the faithful Servant of the Lord is identified as God's chosen one, "in whom I delight." (3) The clause "whom I love," may also allude to Genesis 22:2, where Isaac is described as Abraham's only son, "whom you love." This suggests an Isaac-Jesus typology, with Abraham's willingness to offer his beloved son as analogous to God's offering of his Son. If all three allusions are present, this single announcement makes an extraordinary statement about Jesus' identity: He is the promised Messiah, who will fulfill the role of the Lord's suffering Servant through his sacrificial death.

The Genealogy of Jesus (3:23–38)

The genealogy that follows the baptism provides further confirmation that Jesus is the Christ. As in Matthew's genealogy, Jesus' ancestry is traced back through David and Abraham, confirming that he is the fulfillment of the Abrahamic and Davidic covenants. Jesus is the "seed" (NIV: "offspring") of Abraham, through whom "all nations on earth will be blessed," and the seed of David, who will reign forever on Israel's throne.[104] Yet while Matthew's genealogy begins with Abraham (in line with his Jewish emphasis), Luke's goes all the way back to Adam. This fits well his emphasis on the universal application of the gospel. Jesus is not just Israel's Messiah, he is the Savior of all humanity. For the importance of genealogies in Judaism, see comments on Matthew 1:2–16.

Jesus himself was about thirty years old (3:23). Thirty was viewed in both Jewish and Greco-Roman society as an appropriate age to enter public service. At thirty priests began their duties (Num. 4:3), Joseph entered Pharaoh's service (Gen. 41:46), and Ezekiel was called to his prophetic ministry (Ezek. 1:1). Most significantly, David's reign as king began at the age of thirty (2 Sam. 5:4). Jesus, the Davidic Messiah, follows in the steps of his father David. Since Luke does not give us an exact age, this reference cannot be used precisely to identify the year of Jesus' birth.

Zerubbabel (3:27). Zerubbabel was appointed governor of Judea by the Persian authorities when the Jews returned from Babylonian exile. He supervised the rebuilding of the temple (Ezra 3:2, 8) and was exhorted by the prophets Haggai and Zechariah to finish the task (Hag. 1:1–15; Zech. 4:6–10).

Nathan, the son of David (3:31). This was the third son of David, born to him in Jerusalem (2 Sam. 5:14). He should not be confused with Nathan the prophet.

The son of Adam, the son of God (3:38). That Adam is "the son of God" means that he came through direct creation of God rather than through human procreation. The designation "son of God" also provides an implicit comparison between Adam and Jesus. Whereas Adam, the first son of God, failed in his obedience to God, Jesus, the true Son of God, succeeds when tested (see Luke's temptation account in 4:1–13).

Philo, the first-century Jewish philosopher from Alexandria, writes similarly of Adam that his father "was no mortal, but the eternal God."[105] For Philo, however, this carried a sense of semidivinity not found in Luke. For Philo Adam lost this status at the Fall when he chose evil over good and was "condemned to change an immortal for a mortal existence . . . so as to descend into a laborious and miserable life."[106] For Luke, by contrast, all human beings, though fallen, remain God's offspring because he created them (Acts 17:28–29). Jesus shares in this sonship by virtue of his true humanity, but is also the unique Son of God by virtue of his unique relationship with the Father, his divine origin (Luke 1:35), and his unprecedented obedience to his Father (4:1–13).

The Temptation of Jesus (4:1–13)

The temptation narrative provides the last stage in Jesus' preparation for ministry. The theme of the temptation is the steadfast obedience of the Son to the will of the Father. Two typologies appear to be present, comparing and contrasting Jesus with Adam on the one hand and with the nation Israel on the other. (1) While Adam, the first son of God, failed in his test of obedience, Jesus, the true Son of God, resists temptation and so succeeds (see comments on 3:38). (2) Even more prominent, while God's son Israel (Ex. 4:22–23) failed when tested in the desert, Jesus, the true Son of God, succeeds. Jesus' forty days in the desert are analogous to Israel's forty years, and the three Old Testament passages Jesus cites all relate to Israel's failure.[107]

Israel was tested with hunger so that she would learn dependence on God, but failed to do so. Jesus depends wholly on God for his sustenance, quoting Deuteronomy 8:3: "Man does not live on bread alone" (Luke 4:4). Israel was commanded to worship God alone (Deut. 6:13–15), but turned to idolatry (Deut. 9:12; Judg. 3:5–7). Jesus rejects the devil's offer of the kingdoms of the world in exchange for his worship, quoting Deuteronomy 6:13: "Fear the LORD your God and serve him only" (Luke 4:8). Israel doubted God's power and put him to the test at Massah/Meribah (Ex. 17:1–7; Deut. 6:16). Jesus refuses to throw himself from the temple and so test the Lord God, citing Deuteronomy 6:16: "Do not put the Lord your God to the test" (Luke 4:12). As the messianic King and Son of God, Jesus represents the nation and fulfills the task of eschatological Israel in the desert (cf. Matt. 4:1–11).

By the devil (4:2). In the New Testament the tempter is sometimes called the "devil" and sometimes "Satan."[108] Satan, whose name in Hebrew means "adversary" or "accuser," appears in the Old Testament as the tester or accuser of God's people.[109] The LXX translates these passages with the Greek word *diabolos,* which means "accuser" or "slanderer." In the New Testament Satan appears as a

THE JUDEAN WILDERNESS

Between Jericho and Jebel Quruntul (the traditional "Mount of Temptation").

ROUND LOAVES

Woman making bread in the Middle East.

personal adversary, opposing God's purpose and his people.[110]

He ate nothing during those days (4:2). Moses spent forty days and nights without bread or water on Mount Sinai when writing the Ten Commandments (Ex. 34:28), and Elijah was sustained for a similar period during his journey to Mount Horeb (= Sinai; 1 Kings 19:8). In light of the Israel/Jesus typology developed in this passage, the most important allusion is Israel's forty-year sojourn in the desert.

Kingdoms of the world (4:5). While Matthew uses the more general word *kosmos* ("world"), Luke uses *oikoumenē* ("inhabited world"; cf. 2:1). This word, often used of the Roman empire, gives this temptation a stronger political flavor and so stresses Satan's offer of messianic rule over the nations (cf. Ps. 2:8).

For it has been given to me (4:6). The devil's power and authority in the world is a common theme in the New Testament. In the Johannine writings he is identified as the "prince of this world" (John 12:31; 14:30; 16:11), and the whole world is under his control (1 John 5:19). Paul calls him the "god of this age" (2 Cor. 4:4) and the "ruler of the kingdom of the air" (Eph. 2:2). Yet Satan's authority is mediated by God, who is sovereign over all things (Dan. 4:32). "It has been given" is a divine passive. As in the case of Job (Job 1:12), God allows Satan a measure of freedom to test believers in the present age.

I can give it to anyone I want (4:6). In light of the previous note, this must be seen as a half-truth, or perhaps Satan's own self-deception. Similar arrogant boasts were made by the Caesars. The emperor Nero once said, "I have the power to take away kingdoms and to bestow them."[111]

Highest point of the temple (4:9). The location of this "pinnacle" (lit., "winglet") is uncertain, but has been traditionally identified with the Royal Portico on the southeast corner of the temple, overlooking the Kidron Valley. Josephus speaks of the dizzying height of this location.[112] A later rabbinic tradition (which may or may not go back to the first century) says that "when the King, the Messiah, reveals himself, he will come and stand on the roof of the Temple."[113]

right ▶

HIGHEST POINT

The modern east wall of the old city of Jerusalem looking up at the southeast pinnacle.

He will command his angels (4:10). The devil responds to Jesus' Scripture quotations by quoting one himself (Ps. 91:11–12). The psalm promises divine protection for those who are faithful to God. Jesus refuses to misuse this passage by putting God to the test.

Jesus Rejected at Nazareth (4:14–30). The great Galilean ministry, often identified as the "period of popularity," is covered in 4:14–9:50. Throughout this period Jesus proclaims the message of the kingdom of God, calls disciples, and performs miracles demonstrating his kingdom authority. The Galilean ministry will climax in 9:20, where Peter as representative of the disciples confesses that Jesus is the Christ. From Peter's confession onward Jesus begins to clarify the nature of his messiahship by teaching his disciples that he must go to Jerusalem to suffer and die.

Jesus' public ministry begins for Luke with the sermon in Nazareth, the town where Jesus grew up (2:4, 39, 51; 4:16). Jesus enters the Nazareth synagogue and announces through a reading of Isaiah 61:1–2 that he is God's messianic herald of salvation. At first the townspeople welcome this "hometown boy made good" for his eloquent speech and his message of hope. They turn against him, however, when he points out that in the past God has sometimes chosen to favor Gentiles over his people Israel. Enraged at such heresy, the townspeople drive Jesus out of town and attempt to throw him off a cliff. Jesus walks through the crowd and escapes.

It seems likely that Luke has taken this episode from a later point in Mark's Gospel (Mark 6:1–6) and placed it first in order to introduce key themes in Jesus' ministry. Rejection by Jesus' own people in Nazareth foreshadows his coming rejection by his own nation, Israel. Jesus' announcement that "no prophet is accepted in his hometown" (Luke 4:24) becomes in turn a prediction of his own suffering fate. God's favor to Gentiles in the past—the widow of Zarephath and Naaman the Syrian—foreshadows the mission to the Gentiles in Acts.

Luke's description here and in Acts 13:14–48 represent the oldest written accounts of Jewish synagogue services. Agreements with later rabbinic sources suggest a relatively fixed order of service. This would include the recitation of the *Shema* (Deut. 6:4–9), various prayers (especially the *Shemoneh Esreh*, "Eighteen Benedictions," also known as the *Tephillah*, "the Prayer"), readings from the Law and (generally) the Prophets, an oral targum (an Aramaic paraphrase for those who could not understand Hebrew), a homily or sermon on the text or texts for the day, and a closing benediction. Psalms may also have been sung (cf. Mark 14:26). Any qualified male might be invited to read the Scripture and give instruction. Tasks were assigned and the service overseen by the synagogue ruler (*archisynagōgos*, Luke 8:49; 13:14; Acts 13:15; 18:8, 17), who would be assisted by an attendant (*hypēretēs*; see 4:20).[114]

Jesus returned to Galilee (4:14). Jesus' final preparation for his ministry—his baptism and temptation—took place in the Judean desert near the Jordan River (see 3:3). Jesus now returns north to his home region of Galilee to begin his preaching and healing ministry.

He taught in their synagogues (4:15). Visiting rabbis were normally invited to teach (cf. Acts 13:15). Jesus was earning a reputation as a respected rabbi and teacher.

Nazareth (4:16). See comments on 1:26 and "Inscription Bearing the Name of 'Nazareth.'"

The scroll of the prophet Isaiah was handed to him (4:17). Did Jesus choose this text from Isaiah or was it assigned to him? Later Judaism had a fixed three-year reading schedule from the Law, but it is uncertain whether this was established by this time and whether it would have included the Prophets. In any case, divine providence is clearly at work in the chosen text.

"The Spirit of the Lord is on me" (4:18). Jesus reads from Isaiah 61:1–2 with a line inserted from 58:6. The prophet Isaiah here uses language reminiscent of Israel's Year of Jubilee (see comments on Luke 4:19) to announce deliverance and release to those in Babylonian exile. Jesus takes this same announcement of release and applies it to his ministry of deliverance from sin and Satan. Jesus does not cite the last part of Isaiah 61:2, "the day of vengeance of our God," in order to highlight the positive message of salvation. Judgment will be announced only when Israel rejects her Messiah (see Luke 13:34–35).

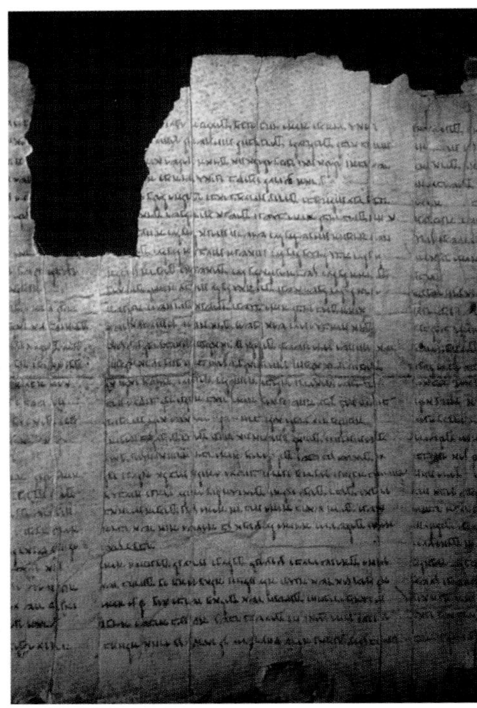

ISAIAH SCROLL

A portion of the famous Isaiah Scroll, the longest and oldest (c. 100 B.C.) of the "Dead Sea Scrolls" found at Qumran.

"Anointed . . . to preach good news" (4:18). Jesus is the Spirit-anointed prophet and Messiah, "proclaiming good news" (*euangelizomai*) to the poor (4:18). These images bring together Isaiah's related portraits of the messianic King (Isa. 11:1–2), the Servant of the Lord (42:1), and the prophetic herald of salvation (61:1–2). For the Old Testament background to *euangelizomai* see comments on Luke 2:10.

"The year of the Lord's favor" (4:19). Isaiah's language echoes the description of the Year of Jubilee in Leviticus 25, where every fiftieth year (after seven Sabbath years) property in Israel was to be returned to its original inheritors, debts were to be canceled, and slaves set free. In the Dead Sea Scrolls (DSS) and in later rabbinic literature, Isaiah 61 with its Jubilee imagery was interpreted with reference to God's end-time salvation. The DSS document 11QMelchizedek interprets Isaiah 61 with reference to Melchizedek, who appears as a heavenly redeemer.[115]

Gave it back to the attendant (4:20). The "attendant" here (Greek: *hypēretēs*) is probably equivalent to the Hebrew *ḥazzan*, an assistant to the synagogue ruler who took care of the scrolls and synagogue furnishings.

Sat down (4:20). While standing to read signified respect for the sacred Scripture, itting was the traditional (though not he only) posture for teaching (see Matt. ;:1–2; 26:55; Luke 5:3). Standing is ound in Acts 13:16.

This proverb . . . "Physician, heal your-elf!" (4:23). This proverb was a common one, appearing in both Jewish and Greek writers.[116] Here it may mean, Prove your worth as a physician." Or, the emphasis may be on "yourself," with the dea, "Heal your own people rather than outsiders from Capernaum." Both ideas nay be present.

tell you the truth (4:24). The Greek *amēn*, "in truth" or "truly," is from a Hebrew word traditionally used at the end of a saying to confirm its validity much as we use "Amen"; see Deut. 27:15; Ps. 41:13; etc.). Jesus uses it in a unique sense at the *beginning* of his sayings (both singularly and doubly) to demonstrate the authority with which he poke (lit., "Truly, truly, I say to you . . ."). Sometimes Luke leaves the term in this Hebrew form; sometimes he uses the Greek equivalent *alēthōs.*

No prophet is accepted in his hometown (4:24). "Acceptable" (*dektos*) is the same Greek word translated "favor" in 4:19 (the Jubilee "year of the Lord's favor"). Ironically, God's people refuse to show favor to the messenger announcing God's favor to them. For the theme of prophetic suffering see comments on 3:19–20. The following illustrations of Elijah and Elisha, two of Israel's greatest prophets, reinforce Jesus' prophetic identity.

In Elijah's time . . . the sky was shut . . . a widow in Zarephath (4:25–26). See 1 Kings 17–18. Elijah was God's prophet sent to announce to King Ahab judgment against Israel because of the people's unfaithfulness and worship of Baal. After hiding from Ahab and his wicked Queen Jezebel at the brook at Kerith Ravine,

MODERN NAZARETH

God sent him to a widow in Zarephath on the Phoenician coast north of Israel, between Tyre and Sidon. God's blessings came to the widow (a Gentile) in the form of the miraculous supply of flour and oil and subsequently in the raising of her son from the dead.

In the time of Elisha . . . Naaman the Syrian (4:27). See 2 Kings 5. Naaman was a commander in the Syrian army who came to Elisha to be cured of his leprosy. Elisha ordered Naaman to wash himself seven times in the Jordan River. Naaman reluctantly agreed and was healed. The key to both illustrations is that God has at times shown favor to Gentiles even over his people Israel. Such a statement is too much for the people of Nazareth, and they attempt to murder Jesus.

The brow of the hill on which the town was built (4:29). Though there is no obvious cliff just outside the city, Nazareth is in a hilly area and various plausible locations have been identified.

In order to throw him down the cliff (4:29). The crowd appears to be following the normal procedure for stoning, which was to cast the victim off an elevated spot so that large rocks could be thrown down on him.[117]

REFLECTIONS

IN HIS INAUGURAL SERMON IN Nazareth, Jesus announces that the message of salvation is "good news" to the outcasts of society: the poor, the oppressed, and those on the margins. If we are going to reflect the heart of Jesus to a lost world, we must demonstrate this same love for those most marginalized in our society. *To whom would God have you reach out today?*

Jesus Drives Out an Evil Spirit (4:31–37)

In the Nazareth sermon Luke presented Jesus' announcement of the nature of his ministry: good news to the poor and release to prisoners. Now he provides examples of this ministry (4:31–44) as Jesus casts out demons and heals the sick, demonstrating his authority over satanic forces and physical infirmity. The primary focus remains on Jesus' teaching and preaching of the good news of the kingdom of God (4:31–32, 43–44). The miracles are meant to confirm the message that in Jesus the power of God's kingdom is breaking into human history (cf. Mark 1:21–28).

He went down to Capernaum (4:31). Capernaum was a fishing village of some prominence on the northwestern shore of the Sea of Galilee. The name means "village of Nahum," though the identity of this Nahum is not known (most scholars identify Capernaum with a site known as Tell Hum). Jesus moves from Nazareth and establishes his base of operations here during his Galilean ministry (see Mark 2:1). The statement "he went down" reflects the geography of the city, since the Sea of Galilee lies almost seven hundred feet below sea level.

They were amazed at his teaching because his message had authority (4:32). Mark adds "not as the teachers of the law" (Mark 1:22). The Jewish teachers of Jesus' day taught with constant appeal to rabbis and traditions of the past. Jesus teaches with a sense of origi

CAPERNAUM

Remains at Capernaum with the Sea of Galilee in the foreground.

nality and personal authority that astonishes the people. For Luke this authority comes especially from the Spirit endowment that Jesus received at his baptism (Luke 3:22; 4:1, 14, 18).

In the synagogue (4:33). An impressive synagogue has been excavated in Capernaum (see photo). It dates from the second century and probably lies on top of the one in which Jesus taught.

A man possessed by a demon, an evil spirit (4:33). Literally, "having a spirit of an unclean demon." This is probably a genitive of apposition, meaning "a spirit, that is, an unclean demon." The word *daimonion* ("demon") was used in the Hellenistic world of various spirit beings, good or evil, so Luke clarifies for his readers that these are wicked forces standing in opposition to God. He refers to them elsewhere as "unclean spirits," "spirits," and "demons," and identifies them as Satan's allies in 11:17–18. For more on demonic possession and exorcism, see comments on 8:26–39.

Ha! . . . Have you come to destroy us? (4:34). The demon speaks in the plural ("us"), representing the demonic hordes who are aware of Jesus' coming and quake in fear at his authority to destroy them. The word "Ha!" (Gk. *ea*) may

AERIAL VIEW OF THE SYNAGOGUE RUINS AT CAPERNAUM

either be an interjection of surprise and displeasure (found in Classical Greek), or may be the imperative form of the verb *eaō*, meaning "let us alone!"[118]

I know who you are (4:34). Knowledge of the name of a spirit being was thought to be a way of gaining power over it. This may have been the demon's futile attempt to gain power over Jesus. In the pseudepigraphic Jewish-Christian work *Testament of Solomon*, Solomon uses a magic seal ring given to him by the archangel Michael to learn the names of various demons, and then to coerce their help in building the temple.[119]

The Holy One of God! (4:34). "Holy One of God" is not a traditional title for the Messiah. Its sense, however, is clear: Jesus is the Righteous and Holy One set apart to accomplish God's purpose and plan. While the demon is "unclean," Jesus is "holy." In the Old Testament, nothing unclean could come in contact with God's holy presence, so conflict is inevitable. The demon shudders at the awareness that his destruction is imminent.

"Be quiet!" Jesus said sternly (4:35). The word "rebuked" (NIV, "said sternly"; *epitimaō*) was used in Judaism as a technical term for a command that brought evil powers into submission.[120] Jesus' ability to silence demons (cf. 4:41) demonstrates his absolute authority over them.

All the people were amazed (4:36). Exorcists in the ancient world often used elaborate rituals or incantations to control demons.[121] Jesus' ability to cast out demons by merely commanding them brings amazement from the people. The demon's immediate response without injuring the man further demonstrates Jesus' extraordinary authority.

Jesus Heals Many (4:38–44)

The casting out of the demon in the synagogue is followed by further examples of Jesus' healing and exorcising ministry. Jesus heals Peter's mother-in-law and then ministers to the people in general, healing the sick and casting out demons. Once again demons recognize Jesus as the mighty Messiah and Son of God and cry out in fear. Jesus silences them with a word, demonstrating his supreme authority over them.

The home of Simon (4:38). Simon Peter evidently owned a home in Capernaum. John identifies Bethsaida as the town of Andrew and Peter (John 1:44), but this probably means their birthplace or the town where they grew up. Peter's present home and fishing business are in Capernaum.

Simon's mother-in-law (4:38). Simon's marriage is also attested by Paul in 1 Corinthians 9:5.

A high fever (4:38). Ancient medical writers distinguished between a "small" (*mikros*) and a "great" (*megalos*) fever. Luke clarifies that Peter's mother-in-law has the latter, thus emphasizing Jesus' healing power. Though such a clarification cannot *prove* that a physician wrote this Gospel (other educated writers might make such a distinction),[122] it provides one more piece of evidence for Luke's authorship of this Gospel.

Rebuked the fever (4:39). Just as Jesus "rebuked" the demon (see 4:35; cf. also 4:41), so now he "rebukes" (*epitimaō*) the fever. This does not mean that the fever is a demonic presence. Though illness was often associated with spiritual oppression in the ancient world and is sometimes so linked in Luke's Gospel (8:29; 9:39; 11:14; 13:11), elsewhere in Luke Jesus' healings are distinguished from his exorcisms (see 4:40–41; 7:21; 13:32). Jesus' "rebuke" is meant rather to demonstrate his authoritative power over all illness. Disease, like demonic oppression, is part of the evil fallen world that Jesus came to save.

She began to wait on them (4:39). Hospitality had great significance in this culture and the senior woman of the house would have been most responsible for it. That Peter's mother-in-law can fulfill this role demonstrates that she has been immediately and completely cured—again confirming Jesus' authority.

When the sun was setting (4:40). This marks the end of the Sabbath, when people could carry their sick without violating the Sabbath commandment.

Demons came out of many people, shouting, "You are the Son of God!" (4:41). "Son of God" is used coreferentially with the "Holy One of God" (4:34) as a title for the Messiah. This is clear from Luke's clarification that "they knew he was the Christ." For the Messiah as God's Son see 2 Samuel 7:14; Psalm 2:7; 89:26; 4QFlor (4Q174). Luke links the titles "Christ" and "Son of God" elsewhere.[123]

But he rebuked them (4:41). See comments on 4:35.

The good news of the kingdom of God (4:43). This is Luke's first explicit reference to the kingdom of God (but see 1:33). In Jewish thought God's kingdom could refer both to his sovereign reign over the whole universe and to the consummation of that reign through the establishment of a righteous kingdom on earth. To state that "God's kingdom" is near (cf. 10:9, 11) to most first-century Jews meant that God is about to intervene in human affairs to deliver the righteous, judge the wicked, and bring in an era of peace, justice, and righteousness. In some apocalyptic writings, God establishes his kingdom through a messianic agent. In others, the emphasis is on deliverance by God himself. The length of the kingdom is also debated: In some Jewish writings the kingdom is said to last for eternity[124]; in others it is an interim age or "messianic kingdom" prior to the eternal state. The rabbis speculated on the length of this interim kingdom, identifying it sometimes as four hundred years, and other times as a thousand years.[125] For more on the messianic reign see 17:20.

The Calling of the First Disciples (5:1–11)

The Galilean ministry is marked not only by Jesus' teaching and healing ministry, but also by his calling and training of disciples. After using Simon's boat as a teaching platform to keep back the overwhelming crowds, Jesus asks the fishermen to put out into deeper water and drop their nets. Simon, discouraged from a long night of unsuccessful fishing, only reluctantly agrees. His obedience pays off, however, when the net emerges overflowing with fish. Astonished, Simon recognizes God's awesome power in Jesus' actions and falls down in unworthiness before him. In an act of grace, Jesus lifts him up and calls him to a new life of "catching" people. Simon and his companions leave everything and follow Jesus. The continuing theme of the authority and power of Jesus merges here with that of authentic discipleship.

Lake of Gennesaret (5:1). The "lake" (*limnē*) of Gennesaret is another name for the "sea" (*thalassa*) of Galilee. Luke prefers *limnē* to Matthew and Mark's *thalassa*, perhaps because of his more precise historical sense. The Jewish historian Josephus also prefers "lake" to "sea" when referring to Gennesaret.[126]

Taught the people from the boat (5:3). This becomes Jesus' preferred method of crowd control in Galilee (see Mark 3:9; 4:1). The people can sit comfortably on the beach without pressing against Jesus, and the rising shoreline serves as an amphitheater with good acoustics. A magnificent example of a first-century Galilean fishing boat was recently discovered and excavated near Kibbutz Ginosar on the Sea of Galilee (see photo).

We've worked hard all night. . . . I will let down the nets (5:5). The "nets" (*diktyon*) here are probably long nets supported on floats used for night fishing in deep water. They are different from the round casting nets used for shallow water day fishing (Matt. 4:18, *amphiblēstron;* Mark 1:16, *amphiballō*). A third kind of net, a dragnet (*sagēnē;* Matt. 13:47), was dragged along between two boats.[127]

They caught such a large number of fish (5:6). The miraculous catch recalls Old Testament miracles of multiplying food related to Elijah (1 Kings 17:10–16) and Elisha (2 Kings 4:1–10, 42–44), as well as the provision of manna and quail for the Israelites in the desert (Ex. 16).

Their partners in the other boat (5:7). The term "partners" (*metochos*) is often used of partners in business and refers here to James and John, the sons of Zebedee (see 5:10). Fishermen often came together in cooperatives for more efficiency. Zebedee must have been a relatively successful businessman since Mark 1:20 refers to hired servants as well as his two sons.

Go away from me, Lord; I am a sinful man! (5:8). Peter's awe at the overwhelming presence of God recalls Isaiah's fear when he saw the awesome glory of the Lord at his prophetic call

GALILEAN FISHING BOAT

Remains of the first-century boat recently discovered near Gennesaret.

REFLECTIONS

WHEN JESUS CALLS ON PETER TO trust him for a seemingly foolish request, Peter reluctantly agrees. Peter's own faith is hardly magnificent, yet the awesome object of that faith—Jesus himself—produces a transforming miracle in Peter's life. A little faith in a big God can accomplish extraordinary things.

(Isa. 6:5). Whereas Peter had earlier referred to Jesus as *epistata* ("Master"), he now calls him *kyrios* ("Lord").

You will catch men (5:10). The participle *zōgrōn* means "catching alive." Some have suggested that this statement alludes to Jeremiah 16:16, a passage related to judgment, but this is unlikely. All the emphasis here is on salvation.

The Man With Leprosy (5:12–16)

Luke provides another example of Jesus' authority over illness with the healing of a man with leprosy. Lepers were social outcasts in first-century Palestine, living on the margins of society. Jesus thus continues his mission to the outcast and the oppressed that he announced in the Nazareth sermon (4:18–27). In 7:22 Jesus will identify the healing of leprosy together with other healings as evidence that the time of salvation has arrived and that he is "the one who was to come"—the Messiah.

The healing results in even greater popularity for Jesus and more and more people crowd to him for healing. Jesus, however, withdraws to a deserted place to pray. Prayerful communion with the Father is Jesus' source of strength and vitality. On the importance of this theme in Luke see comments on 3:21 (cf. Matt. 8:1–4; Mark 1:40–44).

Covered with leprosy (5:12). The biblical words traditionally translated "leprosy" (Heb. *ṣāraʾat;* Gk. *lepra*) do not refer to the same disease as modern day leprosy (i.e., Hansen's disease). The descriptions given in Leviticus 13–14 suggest rather a variety of skin disorders, including psoriasis, lupus, ringworm, and others. Because of the uncertainties of diagnosis and the difficulties in distinguishing highly contagious diseases from relatively harmless ones, the Old Testament set out strict guidelines for the examination and isolation of these skin disorders. If found to be "leprous" after examination by the priest, the diseased individual would be isolated from the rest of the congregation and was required to wear torn clothes, cover the lower part of his face, and cry out "Unclean! Unclean!" whenever he was approached.[128]

Jesus reached out his hand and touched the man (5:13). Because of fear of contagion, lepers were ostracized from society and repulsive to the common people. That Jesus is willing to touch this man shows not only his authority over the disease, but also his great compassion. There are no "untouchables" in Jesus' ministry.

Be clean (5:13). Leprosy results not only in social ostracism, but isolation from Israel's religious life. Jesus' words indicate spiritual as well as physical restoration.

Show yourself to the priest and offer the sacrifices (5:14). The Old Testament prescribed that lepers who were healed

Scribes

The scribes were experts in the interpretation and exposition of the law of Moses.[A-14] The scribes traced their origin back to the priest Ezra, who established postexilic Judaism based on the law (Ezra 7:6, 10). As the teaching of Torah gained a more central place in the life of Judaism, the scribal office took on greater importance and influence. Later known as rabbis, scribes would be found in every village in Israel, providing exposition of the Mosaic law for everyday life and education for children in rabbinic schools.

Most scribes were probably Pharisees (Mark 2:16), though there were likely also Sadducees among them (cf. Matt. 16:1–2; 21:15). Most New Testament references to scribes are negative, and they are condemned together with the Pharisees for their legalism and hypocrisy. Jesus speaks of the validity of the office however, in Matthew 13:52: "Every teacher of the law who has been instructed about the kingdom of heaven is like the owner of a house who brings out of his storeroom new treasures as well as old."

had to be reexamined by the priest and declared "clean," and that a sacrifice was to be offered on their behalf (Lev. 14:1–32). By ordering the leper to follow this procedure, Jesus demonstrates faithfulness to the requirements of the law.

Jesus Heals a Paralytic (5:17–26)

The account of the healing of a paralyzed man continues Luke's theme that Jesus' claims are confirmed through the power of God at work in him. Jesus' authority over disease is again evident as Luke notes that "the power of the Lord was present for him to heal the sick." Luke does not mean to suggest that such power was absent on other occasions, but that Jesus' God-given authority to heal *was obvious to all* on this occasion. No one should have missed it. This is important because this passage also presents the beginning of opposition to Jesus. The Pharisees and teachers of the law appear for the first time in Luke's Gospel, having come to observe Jesus "from every village of Galilee and from Judea and Jerusalem" (5:17). They see God's power at work but still reject Jesus' authority. When Jesus makes the extraordinary claim to forgive sins, these Jewish leaders accuse him of blasphemy by claiming it as a prerogative of God alone.

This passage is also a lesson in faith and the various human responses to Jesus' power and identity. On the negative side the religious leaders see God's power but reject the messenger. On the positive side the paralytic and his friends demonstrate extraordinary faith by tearing the roof apart to reach Jesus. The paralytic is rewarded with both spiritual and physical healing: forgiveness of sins and the ability to walk. The miracle has its intended result. The people stand in awe and give praise to God (cf. Matt. 9:1–8; Mark 2:1–12).

Pharisees (5:17). See "The Pharisees." This is Luke's first mention of the Pharisees.

Teachers of the law (5:17). The "teachers of the law" (*nomodidaskaloi*) were also called "scribes" (*grammateis;* 5:21; NIV, "teachers of the law") and "lawyers" (*nomikoi;* 7:30; NIV, "experts in the law"). See "Scribes."

Through the tiles (5:19). A Palestinian roof was normally flat, made of beams covered with reeds and a layer of clay. External stairs or a ladder could be used to reach the roof or upper floor. Mark speaks of the men (lit.) "digging through" the roof (Mark 2:4) while Luke refers to lowering the man down "through the tiles." Luke may be interpreting the passage for his Hellenistic readers, who were more familiar with tile roofs. The two accounts can be harmonized, however, since Mark does not specifically state the composition of the roof and tile roofs were in use in Palestine by this period.[129]

Your sins are forgiven (5:20). A connection between disease and forgiveness of sins is found in Psalm 103:3, where it is said that the Lord "forgives all your sins and heals all your diseases." Some Jews believed that all disease was the result of an individual's personal sin, a perspective that Jesus refutes in John 9:2–3. It is not clear in the present case, however, whether Jesus is suggesting that this man's paralysis is a result of specific sins, or whether his words merely stress the priority of the man's spiritual needs over his physical needs. The latter is more likely. Jesus' healing power is meant to confirm his authority to announce the kingdom of God and the eschatological forgiveness of sins.

Who is this fellow who speaks blasphemy? (5:21). In the Old Testament and Judaism "blasphemy" is sometimes defined narrowly as the misuse of the divine name "Yahweh," such as in using it in a curse (see Lev. 24:10–23). The penalty for such abuse was death. The Mishnah (c. A.D. 200) states that "the blasphemer is not culpable unless he pronounces 'the Name' [YHWH] itself."[130] Elsewhere blasphemy is identified more generally with anything that challenges or brings dishonor to God's name or authority.[131] Here the accusation is that Jesus is arrogantly usurping the authority of God.

Who can forgive sins but God alone? (5:21). While only God can forgive sins, he sometimes offers forgiveness through a human agent (2 Sam. 12:13). The teachers of the law and the Pharisees reject Jesus' claim to be acting with God's authority and so consider his statement to be blasphemous.

The Son of Man (5:24). This is the first use of Jesus' favorite self-designation in Luke's Gospel. The Greek phrase *ho huios tou anthrōpou* is a literal translation of the Hebrew *ben ʾādām* ("son of man"; Aramaic: *bar ʾenāš*), which means "a human being." It is often used in the Old Testament (especially in Ezekiel) to contrast the lowliness of humanity with the transcendence of God. A special use of

TILED ROOFS

Homes in the village of Dar Samet near Hebron.

the designation appears in Daniel 7:13, where an exalted messianic figure—one "like a son of man" (i.e., "having human form")—comes with the clouds of heaven and is given great glory and power. Jesus probably adopts the title because: (1) It stresses his true humanity; (2) it points to Daniel 7:13 and so reveals his messianic identity and the glory he will receive (see Luke 22:69); but (3) it does not carry as much political "baggage" as other titles, like "Messiah" or "Son of David." Jesus can define his messiahship on his own terms rather than on the basis of popular expectation. See also comments on 9:26.

The Calling of Levi (5:27–32)

The call of Levi plays out in miniature a central theme in Luke's Gospel: Jesus' ministry to sinners who will repent and follow him. The great physician has not come to heal the "righteous"—that is, the *self*-righteous—but sinners who recognize their desperate need of repentance and spiritual healing. This passage is parallel to the Zacchaeus episode at the end of Jesus' ministry, where Jesus declares, "The Son of Man came to seek and to save what was lost" (19:10).[132]

A tax collector . . . sitting at his tax booth (5:27). For more on tax collectors see comments on 3:12. This may have been not a tax office per se, but a toll booth, where customs would be collected on goods in transit. As a tax collector (*telōnēs*), Levi is probably an agent of a "chief tax collector" (*architelōnēs*), such as Zacchaeus (19:2).

Levi (5:27). Since in Matthew's Gospel this individual is named "Matthew"

▸ The Pharisees

The Pharisees, one of several religious parties within Judaism, probably arose from the *Hasidim,* the pious Jews who had fought with the Maccabees against the oppression of Antiochus Epiphanes (175–163 B.C.). The word "Pharisee" is probably derived from a Hebrew term meaning "separatists" and was applied to this group because they separated themselves from those who did not follow their rigid standards of righteousness.[A-15]

While the Sadducees were primarily upper-class aristocrats who dominated the Sanhedrin (the Jewish high court; see 22:66) and the temple worship, the Pharisees appear to have been primarily middle-class businessmen and merchants more involved in the synagogue communities. Josephus claims that the Pharisees numbered about six thousand.[A-16] The most distinctive characteristic of the Pharisees was their strict adherence to the Torah—not only the written law of the Old Testament, but also the "oral law," a body of traditions that expanded and elaborated on the Old Testament law. Their goal was to "build a hedge" around the Torah so as to guard against any possible infringement. Their expansions of the law were also intended to apply its mandates to the changing circumstances in life. The common people had much admiration for the pious Pharisees.

Despite sharing many common beliefs, Jesus comes into frequent conflict with the Pharisees. He condemns them for raising their traditions to the level of Scripture and for focusing on the outward requirements of the law, while ignoring matters of the heart (Luke 11:39–43). For their part, the separatist Pharisees attack Jesus' association with tax collectors and sinners (7:36–50; 15:1–2, etc.) and the way he places himself above Sabbath regulations (6:1–5). Most importantly perhaps, Jesus is seen as a threat to their leadership and influence over the people.

(Matt. 9:9), we may assume he is to be identified with the disciple by that name in Luke 6:15. Some have suggested that this is Matthew's second name, Matthew Levi, or perhaps that Matthew is a Levite from the tribe of Levi (see comments on 10:31–32). If the latter were the case, he would be especially hated by his countrymen as one who should have been pursuing a religious vocation, but instead chose a dishonest one.

Left everything and followed him (5:28). Though hated for their duplicity with the Romans, tax collectors made a good living. To leave such a lucrative career was a major sacrifice.

Held a great banquet (5:29). That Levi had the resources for such a banquet confirms his financial success. It was common in the ancient world to repay honor with honor, so Levi holds a banquet for Jesus in his home. He also wants to introduce his friends and former colleagues to Jesus.

The teachers of the law who belonged to their sect (5:30). Literally, "their scribes." This refers to those teachers of the law (or "scribes") who are also Pharisees (see comments on 5:17).

Why do you eat and drink with . . . sinners (5:30). Table fellowship had great significance in the ancient world, meaning acceptance of those with whom you dined (see comments on 14:8–9). In Judaism a scrupulous Pharisee would not eat at the home of a common Israelite (those known as *ʿam ha-'aretz*, "people of the land"), since he could not be sure that the food was ceremonially clean or that it had been properly tithed (*m. Dem.* 2:2). To avoid ceremonial defilement, a guest at the home of a Pharisee would be required to wear a ritually clean garment provided by the host (*m. Dem.* 2:3). The Pharisees expect Jesus, a respected rabbi, to act in the same exclusive manner.

I have not come to call the righteous, but sinners to repentance (5:32). Although a guest, Jesus now functions as the host of the banquet, inviting the outcasts to dine with him.[133]

Jesus Questioned About Fasting (5:33–39)

The religious leaders' dismay that Jesus dined with sinners provokes a further question as to why Jesus and his disciples do not fast like other good Jews. Jesus replies with an analogy about God's providing a joyful wedding banquet for his people (the time of salvation) where he himself is the bridegroom. Is it appropriate for his disciples, the guests at the wedding, to fast during such a celebration? Of course not. Now is the time to celebrate the great salvation God is accomplishing through Jesus.

But a time will come when the bridegroom will be taken away, and fasting will then be appropriate (5:35). Jesus thus hints for the first time at his rejection and "departure" (cf. 9:31, 51) and the sorrow this will cause to his followers.

Jesus' wedding feast analogy is followed by three metaphors that further elaborate the significance of his coming. The point of all three is the inevitable clash between old and new, which his ministry will provoke. The first two analogies (the patch and the wineskins) demonstrate the inevitable clash between traditional Jewish expectations and the new thing God is accomplishing in Jesus. Jesus' ministry is more than a reformation of Judaism; it is the dawn of God's final salvation. The old is gone (i.e., "fulfilled"), the new has arrived. The third analogy (unique to Luke) is about the power and resilience of traditional beliefs in Judaism. The traditions and exclusiveness of Judaism will provide strong opposition to the advance of the "new" and inclusive gospel proclaimed by the early church.

Fast and pray (5:33). Fasting was a common practice in Judaism, and pious Jews fasted twice a week, on Mondays and Thursdays.[134] Fasting is often associated with prayer. The point here is not that Jesus and his disciples do not pray, but that they do not fast as an essential part of their prayer life. In the Old Testament, fasting is associated with times of spiritual preparation and repentance.[135] Yet fasting as a means to self-righteousness is rejected by the prophets.[136] For more on fasting see comments on 18:12.

Can you make the guests of the bridegroom fast . . . ? (5:34). Weddings were times of extravagant festivities and celebration, lasting an entire week (Judg. 14:17) or even two (Tobit 8:20; 10:7). Though wedding customs of this day are not fully known, certain features seem clear. The bridegroom went out to receive his bride from her parent's home and bring her to his own, with friends and family joining in the joyful procession (Matt. 25:1–13). This was followed by the marriage feast, and eventually the consummation of the marriage in the bridal chamber. Mourning or fasting was unthinkable during such a joyful time of celebration.[137]

He told them this parable (5:36). Luke uses the term *parabolē* for various figures of speech, including proverbs (4:23), metaphors, and more extended stories. Here the term refers to three similitudes, or extended metaphors.

Wineskins (5:37). Skins of animals were scraped of their hair and sewn together to contain liquids. The process of wine fermentation would force the expansion of the skins.

Lord of the Sabbath (6:1–11)

The opposition to Jesus that began with the healing of the paralytic and the call of Levi continues in a series of controversies concerning the Sabbath. When the Pharisees accuse Jesus and his disciples of breaking the Sabbath commandment (Ex. 20:8–11; Deut. 5:14), he responds by defining the true meaning of keeping God's laws. It is not meticulously following a set of rules and regulations, but rather a life oriented towards loving others and pleasing God.

To pick some heads of grain, rub them in their hands (6:1). The Old Testament law allowed one to pluck ears of grain and eat them while walking through a field, so long as one did not use a sickle

right ▶

HEADS OF WHEAT

(Deut. 23:25). Rubbing the grain separated the kernel from the chaff.

What is unlawful on the Sabbath (6:2). The disciples are not being accused of stealing (see previous comment), but of working on the Sabbath by harvesting the grain. Exodus 34:21 forbade work on the Sabbath, noting that "even during the plowing season and harvest you must rest."[138] Later rabbinic tradition took this command and elaborated on it with detailed lists of what constituted work. The Mishnah lists not only activities like reaping, threshing, and winnowing, but even such minutia as tying a knot or sewing two stitches.[139]

What David did . . . consecrated bread (6:3–4). In 1 Samuel 21, while fleeing from Saul, David came to the sanctuary at Nob, a town northeast of Jerusalem. The tabernacle had apparently been set up at Nob after the destruction of Shiloh (1 Sam. 4:2–4; Jer. 7:12). There David requested and received from Ahimelech the priest the consecrated "bread of the Presence." This bread was set out weekly as a sacrifice to the Lord and was consumed by the priests when new bread was set out.[140] Later Jewish sources sought to downplay David's violation. Josephus mentions only that David received provisions, not that he took the consecrated bread.[141] Some rabbinic sources claim that it was not really the consecrated bread, or that it was old bread that had already been removed from the table.[142] Jesus treats it as a real violation of the law, but points out that the meeting of human needs constitutes a higher law, overriding the ceremonial requirement.

The Son of Man is Lord of the Sabbath (6:5). This statement probably represents a play on words. Since the Hebrew idiom "son of man" in the Old Testament means a "human being," the saying can be taken to mean that the Sabbath was made for people and so people have priority or authority over it. Yet in the context of Jesus' ministry and Luke's Gospel, "Son of Man" must here carry its full messianic sense as the exalted king and Lord of all (see Dan. 7:13 and comments on Luke 5:24; 9:26). If human beings have priority over the Sabbath, how much more is the Son of Man "Lord of the Sabbath." He instituted it, so he has the authority to abrogate it, redefine it, or reinterpret its significance.

A man was there whose right hand was shriveled (6:6). The Greek word translated "shriveled" (*xēros*) can mean "dried" or "withered." The hand may have been paralyzed and been suffering from atrophy.

A reason to accuse Jesus . . . if he would heal on the Sabbath (6:7). The rabbis debated whether it was justified to offer medical help to someone on the Sabbath. In general they concluded that it was allowed only in extreme emergencies or when a life was in danger. The Mishnah says that "whenever there is doubt whether life is in danger this overrides the Sabbath."[143] A midwife could work on the Sabbath, since birth could not be delayed. Circumcision could also be performed since this was a sacred act and did not profane the Sabbath.[144] In the present case, this man's life is not in immediate danger, so the teachers of the law and the Pharisees view his healing as a Sabbath violation (cf. 13:14).

They watched him closely (6:7). In contexts like this the Greek term *paratēreō* carries sinister connotations: to spy on, watch maliciously, lie in wait for.[145] The secretive and malicious motives of the Pharisees are contrasted with the sincerity of Jesus' public act, as he brings the man forward for all to see.

But they were furious (6:11). The Greek reads literally, "they were filled with madness [or, mindless fury, *anoia*]." The impression is that these Jewish leaders are at their wits' end and do not know what to do.[146] The reference to destroying a life in 6:9 takes on heavy irony here, as the Pharisees break the Sabbath by plotting against Jesus' life. The real Sabbath violation is not Jesus' healing, but the uncaring and hypocritical attitude of the Pharisees.

The Twelve Apostles (6:12–16)

Jesus knows that the shortness of his ministry means he will need to select others to take his message of salvation to the ends of the earth. Only Luke among the Synoptics notes that Jesus spends a full night in prayer before this crucial decision (see comments on 3:21).[147]

Jesus went out to a mountainside to pray (6:12). This is also the hill on which Jesus gives his great sermon (see 6:17). Luke's reference to "a mountainside" is vague and the location is uncertain. It has traditionally been identified with the "Mount of Beatitudes" at Tabgha, a mile and a half from Capernaum. Others identify the location as the Horns of Hattim near Tiberias.[148]

Designated apostles (6:13). The term *apostolos* means "one who is sent." In the New Testament this word takes on the technical sense of one commissioned by Jesus to preach the good news of salvation. The number twelve is also significant, modeled as it is after the twelve tribes of Israel. Jesus in some sense views this new community as the righteous remnant of Israel, the reconstitution of God's people. Later, at the Last Supper narrative Jesus will assign a place of authority for these twelve, sitting on thrones and judging the twelve tribes of Israel (22:30; cf. Matt. 19:28).

Matthew . . . Simon . . . the Zealot (6:15). Though Luke does not explicitly identify Matthew with Levi, this identification seems likely (see comments on 5:27). If this is the case, the contrast between Matthew the tax collector and Simon the Zealot is striking. While tax collectors were viewed as Roman sympathizers and traitors to the cause of Jewish independence, the Zealots were freedom fighters who actively worked to overthrow the Romans. The Zealots provoked the Jew

PALESTINE

Showing the distances people came to hear Jesus when he gave his sermon on the plain.

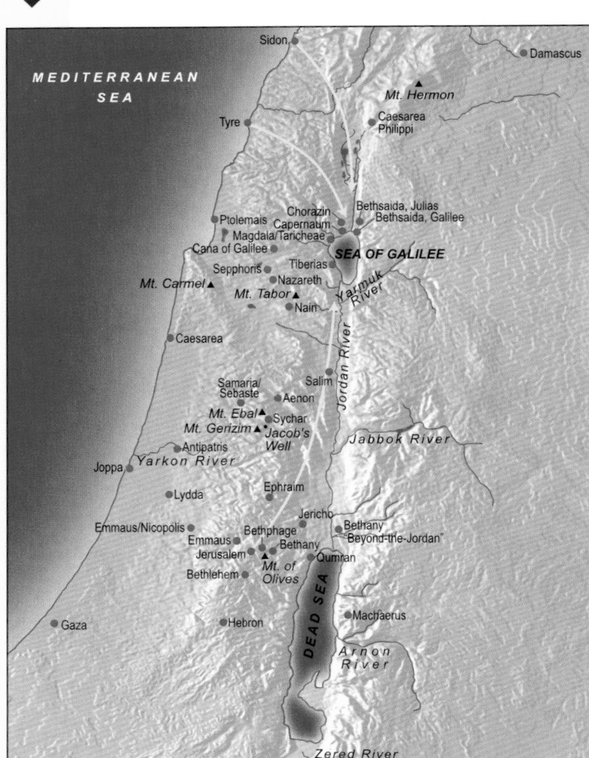

ish revolt against Rome in A.D. 66–74, which resulted in the destruction of Jerusalem.

Judas son of James (6:16). Sometimes called "Jude" to distinguish him from Judas Iscariot, this disciple is probably to be identified with Thaddaeus in the corresponding lists of disciples in Matthew 10:3 and Mark 3:18. He is also to be distinguished from Jude, the brother of James (and probably the half brother of Jesus), who authored the letter of Jude.

Judas Iscariot (6:16). The background to the name "Iscariot" is debated, but probably means "a man of Kerioth." Kerioth-Hezron was a village of Judea about twelve miles south of Hebron.[149]

The Great Sermon (6:17–49): Introduction (6:17–19)

Jesus has been proclaiming the message of the kingdom of God. Now in a sermon addressed especially to his disciples, he defines the radical values that should characterize those anticipating life in God's kingdom (6:20).

Is this sermon the same as Matthew's Sermon on the Mount (Matt. 5–7)? While there are many similarities, there are also many differences. Matthew's sermon is placed much earlier in the Galilean ministry and precedes the calling of the Twelve. In addition to the many differences in wording, Matthew's sermon is much longer and much of its material appears elsewhere in Luke's Gospel.[150] Despite these differences, the many agreements in content and order render it likely that these are two versions of the same sermon. Both begin with the Beatitudes and end with the account of wise and foolish builders. Both include Jesus' teaching on love for enemies, judging others, and a tree known by its fruit.

The timing of the sermon in Matthew's Gospel is not really a problem since Matthew frequently follows a topical rather than a chronological order. He appears to have moved the sermon forward to serve as Jesus' inaugural address. While some have contrasted the setting of the sermons—Matthew's Sermon on the *Mount* versus Luke's Sermon on the *Plain*—such a dichotomy is unnecessary. Luke does not speak of a plain but of a "level place" to which Jesus descends after a night of prayer on the mountain (6:12, 17). The implication is that Jesus is seeking a level place or plateau where he can teach.

KERIOTH-HEZRON

A village about twelve miles south of Hebron and the possible home of Judas. These are the remains of a Byzantine church.

REFLECTIONS

BECAUSE OF THE SHORTNESS OF his ministry Jesus knows he has to train others who can take forward his message of salvation to the ends of the earth. Jesus' example reminds us that disciples are made not by reading books or teaching the masses, but by investing ourselves in people and reproducing the life of Christ in them.

Blessings and Woes (6:20–26)

In the "Beatitudes" Jesus announces that God's values are often radically different from the world's. God will bless those who pursue the ethics of his kingdom and choose to put him first over the things of this world. While Matthew has nine beatitudes, Luke has four, balancing these with four "woes." These woes fit the common Lukan theme of indictment of the rich and powerful for their independence of God and their oppression of the poor. This "rich versus poor" theme also appears in Luke's blessings, which do not contain the spiritual qualifications found in Matthew. It is not "blessed are the poor *in spirit*" (Matt. 5:3, italics added), but simply "blessed are you who are poor" (Luke 6:20). This is not to suggest that Luke's beatitudes lack spiritual dimensions. It is because of their allegiance to the Son of Man that the "poor" are oppressed (6:23). But Luke realizes that social and economical realities go hand in hand with spiritual ones. The physically poor *are* spiritually advantaged because their poverty fosters reliance on God. The physically rich *are* spiritually disadvantaged, because their wealth represents a danger and a hindrance to putting God first (cf. 12:13–21; 16:19–31).

Poor (6:20). Like Matthew, Luke has more in mind than physical poverty. The Greek expression *hoi ptōchoi* ("the poor") probably has behind it the Hebrew term *ʿānāwîm*, which originally referred to the physical poor, but came to be used of the righteous remnant of Israel who suffer oppression and poverty because of their status as God's people. The "poor" are those who trust in God for their salvation. They stand over against the arrogant rich, who mock God's name and oppress his people (see comments on 1:46–55). Isaiah 49:13 says that "the LORD comforts his people and will have compassion on his afflicted ones [*ʾānāwîm*]."[151]

Who hunger . . . who weep (6:21). See the comments on 1:52–53. In the Old Testament God often promises to satisfy the hungry[152] and to bring comfort and joy to his people.[153] There may be an

POSSIBLE LOCATION OF THE SERMON ON THE MOUNT

The Sea of Galilee at Tabgha. The "Mount of Beatitudes" is in the background.

Blessings and Woes

There are few parallels in the Old Testament and Judaism for lists of beatitudes and woes. Somewhat parallel are the lists of blessings and cursings found in Deuteronomy 27–28, which were to be pronounced from Mount Gerizim and Mount Ebal after the Israelites crossed the Jordan into the Promised Land. In wisdom literature, blessings and woes mark out the way to a life oriented toward God.[A-17] Sirach pronounces three woes (*ouai*) on those who are timid and fainthearted in their commitment to God (Sir. 2:12–14) and sets out ten characteristics of the one who is "blessed" (*makarios;* Sir. 25:7–10). Blessing, he says, comes to those who rejoice in their children, who live with a sensible wife, who do not sin with the tongue, who find a friend, etc.

Closer similarities to the blessings and woes of Luke may be found in prophetic and eschatological contexts of the Old Testament and Judaism. Prophetic woes are pronounced against nations and individuals who oppress God's people and profane his name.[A-18] Blessings, by contrast, come to God's people when they wait patiently and expectantly for his salvation.[A-19] Perhaps the closest parallel to Jesus' beatitudes is found in Tobit 13:14: "Happy [*makarios*] also are all people who grieve with you because of your afflictions; for they will rejoice with you and witness all your glory forever" (NRSV).

allusion here to the messianic banquet, when "the LORD Almighty will prepare a feast of rich food for all peoples.... [He] will wipe away the tears from all faces ..." (Isa. 25:6–8). The eschatological banquet feast is a common theme in Luke (see comments on Luke 13:29; 14:15).

When men hate you ... because of the Son of Man (6:22). This verse echoes Isaiah 66:5, which speaks of those "who hate you, and exclude you because of my name." Some commentators have identified this exclusion with formal expulsion from the synagogue, which the early Jewish Christians often experienced (see comments on John 9:22). This is possible, but Jesus' words probably refer more generally to all kinds of rejection and slander.

When all men speak well of you (6:26). False prophets were often popular because they spoke what the people and the leaders wanted to hear.[154] Note especially Micah 2:11: "If a liar and deceiver comes and says, 'I will prophesy for you plenty of wine and beer,' he would be just the prophet for this people!"

Love for Enemies (6:27–36)

Jesus commands his followers to a radical new ethic: to love one's enemies. Though the advice to repay good for evil is not without precedent in the ancient world (see "Love Your Enemies"), Jesus sets this as the normative standard of behavior for his followers. Only in this way can they reflect the character of their Lord. Love here is not a feeling or an emotion, but a concrete action.

Strikes you on one cheek, turn to him the other (6:29). The blow here is probably an insulting slap with the back of the hand. Contrary to the Old Testament laws of retaliation (e.g., "life for life, eye for eye, tooth for tooth," Deut. 19:21), Christians are to seek no retribution.

If someone takes your cloak . . . your tunic (6:29). This next example goes beyond nonretaliation to radical self-giving. The "cloak" here is a *himation*, a robe-like outer garment, whereas the tunic (*chitōn*) is the garment worn next to the skin. The taking could be an act of theft or perhaps a legal action, where a creditor would take the debtor's cloak as a pledge.[155] Exodus 22:25–27 commands that a cloak taken for such a pledge be returned by sunset so that the poor will have protection against the cold. Jesus' exhortation thus calls not only for radical self-sacrifice towards one's enemies but also for complete reliance on God.

Do to others as you would have them do to you (6:31). The so-called Golden Rule is not unique to Jesus, for it appears in various forms in the ancient world. Leviticu 19:18 says to "love your neighbor as yourself." The philosopher Seneca wrote: "Le us show our generosity in the same manner that we would with to have i bestowed on us."[156] The negative versio appears in Tobit 4:15 ("And what yo hate, do not do to anyone," NRSV) and i also attributed to Rabbi Hillel, a near contemporary of Jesus: "What is hateful t you, do not do to anyone else; that is th whole Law, all else is commentary."[157]

If you love those who love you (6:32) The concept of reciprocity, or doing goo in order to receive something back, wa the norm in the ancient world.[158] A benefactor providing funds for a publi project, for example, expected to receiv appropriate honors in return. F. W Danker cites a decree passed by th people of Dionysopolis honoring a ma named Akornion for his beneficence t the city:

Love Your Enemies

Conventional wisdom tells us to love our friends and to hate our enemies. The Greek writer Lysias wrote: "I considered it established that one should do harm to one's enemies and be of service to one's friends."[A-20] Though this quotation represents the conventional wisdom of the day, advice to love one's enemies was not unheard of in the ancient world. Exodus 23:4–5 enjoins God's people to give help to an enemy whose ox or donkey has been lost or has stumbled under its load. According to Proverbs 25:21 we are to provide food or water to an enemy who is hungry or thirsty. In the Qumran scrolls we find similar advice: "I shall not repay anyone with an evil reward; with goodness I shall pursue the man. For to God belongs the judgment of every living being."[A-21]

Such ideas were sometimes expressed in the pagan world. A Babylonian wisdom text reads: "Do not return evil to the man who disputes with you; requite with kindness your evil-doer."[A-22] The Roman philosopher Seneca (c. 4 B.C.–A.D. 65) wrote: "If you wish to imitate the gods, do good deeds also to the ungrateful; for the sun also goes up upon the evil."[A-23] See also comments on Luke 10:29.

Yet only with Jesus does this command become the fundamental standard of behavior for God's people—the reflection of God's love for us. In the Greek world such commands are usually intended to gain power over one's enemies or to shame them. The same Dead Sea Scroll that calls the sectarians to withhold vengeance also enjoins them "to detest all the sons of darkness."[A-24] Withholding personal vengeance merely allows God time to exact a vengeance that is much better.[A-25]

> Therefore, in order that all might know that the People honor such wonderful human beings who prove to be their benefactors, be it resolved . . . that Akornion . . . be crowned annually at the Dionysia with a golden crown, and that the most advantageous place in the agora be allotted him for the erection of his statue.[159]

The theme of doing good in order to receive something in return is common both in Greco-Roman and Jewish thought. Sirach 12:1–2 reads: "If you do good, know to whom you do it, and you will be thanked for your good deeds. Do good to the devout, and you will be repaid—if not by them, certainly by the Most High." Jesus calls his followers to a higher standard of practicing good deeds without expecting anything in return.

Lend to them without expecting to get anything back (6:34–35). The Old Testament forbade charging interest to fellow Jews, so lending was viewed as an act of kindness and charity.[160] Yet for some it became a way to build "credit" for a time when you might be the one in need. Since the law required debts to be cancelled every seventh (Sabbath) year, the rich would be reluctant to loan to the poor as the Sabbath year drew near (see Deut. 15:9). Jesus says that such reciprocal or self-centered loans are no better than the dealings of "sinners." Christian "lending" should be equivalent to self-sacrificial giving, expecting nothing in return.

REFLECTIONS

CONVENTIONAL WISDOM TELLS us to love our friends and to hate our enemies. But in his great sermon Jesus calls on his followers to a radical new value: to love even their enemies, even those who hate, curse, and persecute them. It is this kind of love, demonstrated by God through his Son Jesus Christ, that is capable of breaking down the barriers of anger and hate in our world.

Judging Others (6:37–42)

Jesus elaborates on his command to do good to others by showing how it relates to forgiveness and judgment. We must not judge or condemn others, but rather forgive them just as we desire to be forgiven. Jesus' command not to judge or condemn does not mean that we never confront sin. Rather, what Jesus condemns is hypocritical judgment.

Good measure, pressed down . . . will be poured into your lap (6:38). The image here relates to the purchase of grain. A generous seller not only fills up the measuring container for the customer, but then presses down the grain and shakes the container to make room for even more. He then tops it off until it overflows into the customer's lap. The "lap" (*kolpos*) may refer to the folds of the garment at the waist, which could serve as a large pocket for the grain.[161]

For with the measure you use, it will be measured to you (6:38). The Mishnah provides similar advice: "With the measure a man metes, it shall be measured to him again."[162] Grain contracts sometime stipulated that the same instrument—that of the purchaser—must be used to measure both the grain and the payment.[163]

Can a blind man lead a blind man? (6:39). This is a common proverbial image found in both Greek and Jewish sources.[164]

A student is not above his teacher (6:40). Before the widespread availability of books, a teacher was the only resource for a student or disciple, so his knowledge could go no further than that which he was taught. The kind of forgiveness believers show will be picked up by those who follow them.

The speck . . . the plank in your own eye (6:41). Similar proverbs appear in Greek literature.[165] The "plank" (*dokos*) here probably refers to a large beam rather than a board or two-by-four, making the exaggerated image even more striking.

You hypocrite (6:42). The Greek term *hypocritēs* is a colorful one and was often used of a play-actor in a drama. Metaphorically it came to designate one who pretended to be something one was not. By New Testament times the term was often used of a deceiver or hypocrite.[166]

A Tree and Its Fruit (6:43–45)

The reference to hypocrisy in 6:42 is now developed with several illustrations from nature. Just as good trees produce good fruit and bad trees bad, so those whose hearts are right with God produce good deeds.

Bad tree . . . [bad] fruit (6:43). The term "bad" (*sapros*) originally meant "decayed" or "rotten" and so is an appropriate term for "bad" fruit. It could also mean anything of inferior quality, thus designating both the tree and its fruit.

Figs . . . grapes (6:44). Olives, figs, and grapes were the most common agricultural products in Palestine, so the image would have been a common one for Jesus' hearers.

The Wise and Foolish Builders (6:46–49)

Jesus' reference to the good deeds that flow from a good heart (6:45) transitions naturally into a saying about putting his words into practice (6:46) and an illustration of the consequences that will follow (6:47–49). Those who hear his words and practice them are like a man who builds his house on a firm foundation that will survive through life's storms. Those, however, who merely play lip-service to Jesus, calling him "Lord" but not doing what he says, are building on a weak spiritual foundation that will collapse when the storms of life strike.

Who hears my words and does not put them into practice (6:49). Jesus' saying is similar to Ezekiel 33:31–33: "With their mouths they express devotion. . . . For they hear your words but do not put them into practice."

He is like a man building a house (6:48–49). Ezekiel uses a similar image of a devastating storm to describe the fate of false prophets who deceive God's people (Ezek. 13:13–14).

The Faith of the Centurion (7:1–10)

Following his account of Jesus' sermon, Luke narrates a series of episodes illustrating responses to Jesus' person and message. In the first a group of Jewish elders come to Jesus with a request from a certain centurion to heal his dying servant. The story demonstrates not only the power and potential of faith, but also the inclusive nature of the gospel message. Though Jesus came especially for the "lost sheep of Israel" (Matt. 15:24), he often finds greater faith among those out-

◀ *left*

CENTURION

The typical dress of a Roman centurion.

side of Israel's fold. For Luke the episode foreshadows the mission to the Gentiles in Acts. Its parallel is the story of the centurion Cornelius, whose conversion confirms God's purpose and plan to bring salvation to the Gentiles (Acts 10).

A centurion's (7:2). The centurion was the mainstay of the Roman army, commanding a "century" of approximately one hundred soldiers. A Roman legion was made up of sixty centuries. As veteran soldiers, centurions maintained discipline and commanded great respect. They were paid about fifteen times as much as an ordinary soldier.

Since Roman troops were not stationed in Galilee until A.D. 44,[167] this individual may have served under Herod Antipas, tetrarch of Galilee (see 3:1), performing police or customs services. Conversely, he may have been a retired Roman soldier living in Galilee. In either case, his support for the Jewish community suggests he is a "God-fearer" like Cornelius (Acts 10:2), a Gentile who worships the God of Israel but has not undergone full conversion.

Some elders of the Jews (7:3). These are apparently local community leaders.[168] In Matthew's parallel account the centurion himself approaches Jesus. This can be explained from Matthew's tendency to abbreviate and telescope his narratives. It is indeed the centurion's request (see 7:3), even if it is brought by others.

He loves our nation and has built our synagogue (7:5). There is inscriptional evidence for Gentile support for synagogues,[169] and in at least one case, for the erection of a Jewish "place of prayer" (*proseuchē*) by a Gentile.[170] Gentiles who showed kindness toward Jewish communities were highly respected and honored.

This story has as its background the Roman system of patronage, whereby a patron provided protection or favors for a "client," who in turn pledged loyalty and service. The centurion has served as a patron for the Jewish community, providing his own resources and perhaps

GALILEE

Showing the location of Capernaum and the probable location of the village of Nain.

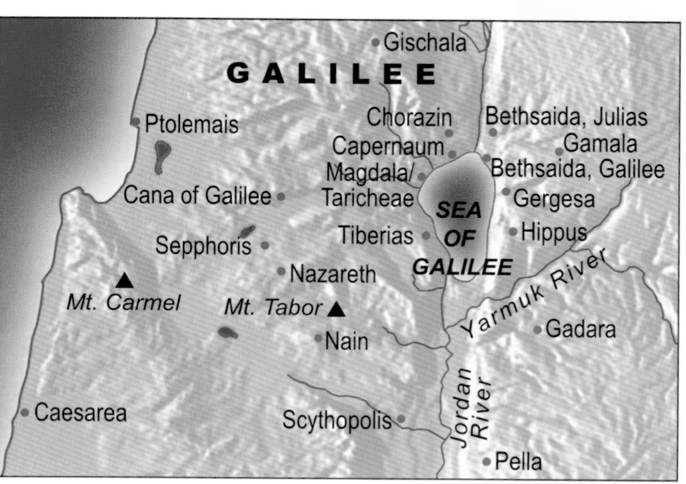

imperial influence for the building of a synagogue. The Jewish elders seek to repay him by serving as his brokers, approaching Jesus with his request.[171]

I do not deserve to have you come under my roof (7:6). According to Jewish tradition, entering the home of a Gentile rendered a Jew ceremonially unclean (see Acts 10:28; 11:12). The Mishnah says that "the dwelling places of Gentiles are unclean."[172] The centurion thus shows respect for Jewish sensibilities. Yet there is more to the statement than this. By recognizing Jesus' superiority, the centurion identifies himself as the subordinate "client" seeking a favor from Jesus, who now fulfills the role of the patron.

But say the word, and my servant will be healed (7:7). The Roman army was renowned for its discipline and organization. As a soldier commanding authority, this centurion recognizes in Jesus one with even greater authority. The authority of God's word to heal appears in Psalm 107:20.

I have not found such great faith even in Israel (7:9). This is not only extraordinary praise for a Gentile, but probably contains an implicit indictment of Israel for her lack of faith.

The men . . . returned . . . and found the servant well (7:10). An account of healing over distance appears in the Babylonian Talmud.[173] When the son of Rabbi Gamaliel falls ill, he sends two disciples to Rabbi Hanina ben Dosa to pray for him. Rabbi ben Dosa prays and tells Gamaliel's disciples, "Go, for his fever has left him." When the men return, they find the fever left the boy at the hour that ben Dosa prayed.

Jesus Raises a Widow's Son (7:11–17)

Jesus' extraordinary authority to heal over distance in the account of the centurion's servant (7:1–10) is now exceeded as he raises a young man from the dead. The story is important because it provides an illustrative example of Jesus' identity in response to the questions raised by John the Baptist. It not only demonstrates Jesus' messianic authority, but also shows his compassion for the grieving mother.

The story has important parallels in the accounts of Elijah, who raised the only son of the widow of Zarephath (1 Kings 17:17–24), and Elisha, who raised the Shunammite's son (2 Kings 4:18–37). The former account, to which Luke has already referred (4:25–26), has particularly close verbal parallels.

Though rare, similar accounts of miracles are not wholly absent from other ancient literature. Perhaps the closest parallel appears in an account from the life of Apollonius, a Neo-Platonic teacher and wonder-worker who lived about the time of Jesus. An account of his life was composed in the third century A.D. by Philostratos. In the story, Apollonius is in Rome when he comes across the funeral of a girl who has died on the day of her wedding. Apollonius stops the funeral procession, touches the girl, and whispers some "spell" over her. The girl awakens and is restored to the grieving bridegroom. Philostratos, describing the account almost two hundred years later, wonders whether the resuscitation was authentic or whether Apollonius saw some spark of life in the girl and revived her.[174]

A town called Nain (7:11). Though the location is uncertain, Nain was probably ıt the site of the modern town of Nein, ;ix miles southeast of Nazareth.

A dead person was being carried out (7:12). According to Jewish burial cus- oms a body was anointed with spices, vrapped in cloth, and laid on a plank or n a coffin. The funeral procession, ıccompanied by mourners, proceeded ɔutside the city gate to the family burial ;ite. Burial took place soon after death to ıvoid decomposition.[175]

She was a widow (7:12). Widows are viewed throughout Scripture as the most vulnerable members of society, those for whom God has special concern.[176] For a widow to lose the only son left to support ıer would be a terrible loss. In the Old Testament the death of an only son is the epitome of great sorrow.[177]

A large crowd from the town was with ıer (7:12). A large number of mourners revealed the great love for the deceased ınd the severity of the loss. Rabbinic writings said that if the procession was small, one should interrupt the study of Torah to participate (so as to supply a sufficient number of mourners), but if the procession was already large enough, one should continue studying.[178]

He went up and touched the coffin (7:14). The term *soros* (NIV "coffin") can refer to either a coffin or a bier (a funeral plank) on which the body was placed. The latter is probably intended here. Touching a bier or coffin would render a person ceremonially unclean (Num. 19:11, 16). Jesus' authority reverses the direction of defilement, "cleansing" the corpse through his power over death.

The dead man sat up (7:15). The episode is not a "resurrection," since in Jewish and Christian thought the resurrection occurs at the end of time, when believers receive glorified bodies. Jesus' own resurrection is the "firstfruits" of this end-time resurrection (1 Cor. 15:20). This and similar Gospel miracles are better termed "resuscitations," the restoration of mortal life to an individual who has died. True resurrection is to eternal life.

bottom left

NAIN

The modern village of Nein in the plain of Jezreel where the ancient town once stood.

bottom right

TOWN GATE

The city gate at the tel of Megiddo.

Jesus and John the Baptist (7:18–35)

As John the Baptist languished in prison (put there by Herod Antipas, see 3:19–20), he begins to have doubts about Jesus' identity. These are evidently brought on by reports concerning the nature of Jesus' ministry. Why is Jesus not fulfilling the messianic task of overthrowing the Roman oppressors and establishing God's kingdom? John sends his disciples to ask Jesus whether he is indeed the "one who was to come" (the Messiah).

Jesus' response is meant to redirect John's expectations. He points to his healing and preaching, alluding to passages in Isaiah that concern the messianic age. When Jesus turns and speaks to the crowd concerning John, he declares that John is the greatest of all the prophets—indeed, the greatest person who ever lived (7:28). This is because he is the messenger of God's end-time salvation, the forerunner of the Messiah (Mal. 3:1). Yet in an odd twist Jesus adds that the one who is *least* in the kingdom of God is greater than John. No one who came before, not even John, can compare with those who now have the privilege of living in the age of salvation, the age of the Spirit.

In a brief aside (7:29–35), Luke points out that while "all the people," even tax collectors, submitted to John's baptism of repentance and so were ready to accept Jesus' message of the kingdom, the religious leaders rejected John and so rejected God's purpose for them (7:29–30). Jesus likens the present situation to children playing make-believe games in the marketplace. One group plays a flute and calls the other to a game of joyful dance, probably a wedding feast. When the other children sulk and refuse to play, the first group switches to a dirge and calls on them to play a funeral game instead (appropriate for the sulkers!). Jesus compares the sulking children to the present generation. When John came with his solemn call for mourning and repentance (analogous to the dirge), the religious leaders accused him of being demon-possessed (i.e., of being a madman). When Jesus came with his joyful announcement of God's kingdom and free forgiveness for sinners (analogous to a joyful wedding ceremony), he is accused of partying with the wrong crowd. God's way, personified here as wisdom, is proven right or "justified" by her offspring, that is, those tax collectors and sinners who are joyfully receiving God's salvation.

John's disciples (7:18). See comments on 5:33.

The one who was to come (7:19). "The Coming One" is treated by John's disciples as a title for the Messiah. The same verb (*erchomai*) appears in Zechariah 9:9 (LXX): "See, your king *comes* to you, righteous and having salvation. . . ." The Qumran scrolls speak of the "coming" of the Messiah of righteousness, the shoot of David.[179] For more on the Messiah see comments on Luke 1:32–33; 2:11; see also "Messianic Expectation in Jesus' Day."

The blind receive sight . . . and the good news is preached to the poor (7:22). These phrases allude to various passages in Isaiah, which refer to God's end-time reversal of the effects of the Fall. The messianic age has arrived.[180] In his sermon at Nazareth Jesus has already cited Isaiah 61:1 and the preaching of "good news" to the poor to define the nature of his ministry. Jesus' present mission is not to conquer the Romans, but to conquer the forces of sin and Satan.

Leprosy (7:22). See comments on 5:12.

Blessed is the man who does not fall away on account of me (7:23). Jesus pronounces a blessing on those who are able to set aside their personal agendas and expectations in favor of God's greater plan. The Greek term *skandalizō* means "to cause to stumble or fall." A messiah who came with healing and reconciliation rather than with conquest over the Romans was a major obstacle to Jewish belief. Paul says elsewhere that a crucified Messiah is a "stumbling block" (*skandalon*) to Jews (1 Cor. 1:23). See Isaiah 8:14 for the Old Testament background to this image.

A reed swayed by the wind? (7:24). The image here is proverbial, referring to something fragile, undependable, and easily swayed. In 1 Kings 14:15 Israel is described as a reed that is easily uprooted. Isaiah 36:6 says that Egypt is like a "splintered reed" that pierces a man's hand when he tries to lean on it as a staff (cf. 2 Kings 18:21). John is a man of conviction, not a spineless "yes-man." He is in prison because he boldly spoke the truth against Herod Antipas.

"I will send my messenger ahead of you" (7:27). The quotation here combines language from Exodus 23:20 and Malachi 3:1. This latter text is linked to Malachi 4:5, where the "messenger" is identified as Elijah the prophet, who will be sent by God before the great Day of the Lord. These Malachi passages, together with Isaiah 40:3, are identified with John the Baptist throughout the Gospels.[181] Though John denied that he was Elijah incarnate (John 1:21–23), he came "in the spirit and power of Elijah" (Luke 1:17) to fulfill the task of forerunner of the Messiah. For more on Jewish expectations related to the coming of Elijah see 1:17; 3:4–5.

Among those born of women (7:28). This is an Old Testament expression meaning "among human beings."[182]

Even the tax collectors (7:29). On tax collectors see comments on 3:12.

Pharisees and experts in the law (7:30). For Pharisees see "The Pharisees" at 5:17. For the "experts in the law," see comments on 5:17 and "Scribes."

We played the flute for you (7:32). The children are probably playing a game of "wedding," where dancing and great celebration take place (see 5:34). The Greek historian Herodotus (5th cent. B.C.) recounts a similar proverb of obstinance and rejection. Fishes in the sea refuse to come to dry land to dance for a flute player. He then catches them in a net and scolds them for dancing (=wriggling) now rather than when he played for them.[183]

John the Baptist came neither eating bread nor drinking wine (7:33). "Bread" (*artos*) here probably means "food" and refers to an ascetic life of fasting and self-

ANCIENT FLUTE

A flute made of bone excavated in the City of David.

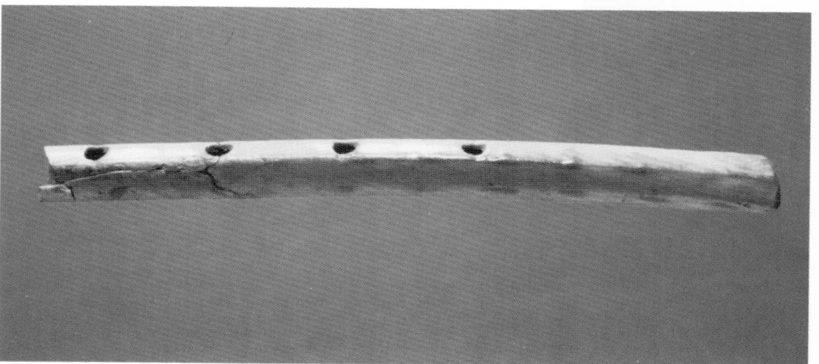

denial. In Luke's birth narrative John is described as a Nazirite from birth, who will not drink wine or other alcoholic beverages (see 1:15). According to Mark 1:6, John lived off the land, eating locusts and honey.

Here is a glutton and a drunkard (7:34). These accusations against Jesus are similar to the description of a rebellious son in Deuteronomy 21:20 (whose punishment was stoning!). While John lived a life of asceticism, Jesus spends time with tax collectors and sinners, even attending their banquets (Luke 5:27–32). The separatist Pharisees reject this behavior and accuse Jesus of being a sinner himself. Yet for Jesus these events represent God's celebration at the finding of lost sinners (see 15:23–25, 32). His arrival as the bridegroom means it is time to celebrate, not time to mourn (see 5:33–39).

Wisdom . . . all her children (7:35). In the Old Testament and in Judaism, "wisdom" is often personified as a woman, an agent of God who calls human beings to a life of wisdom and godliness.[184] Wisdom's "children" are those who follow her guidance (see Prov. 8:32; Sir. 4:11). The children here are the "sinners" and tax collectors who have responded to the calls of Jesus and John.

Jesus Anointed by a Sinful Woman (7:36–50)

Jesus' conclusion in the previous episode—that "wisdom is proved right by all her children"—is now illustrated with a touching story of a repentant sinner, one of the precious "children of wisdom" being transformed by the grace of God in Jesus' ministry. Jesus is dining at the home of a certain Pharisee named Simon when a notorious sinner enters and attempts to anoint him with expensive perfume. The Pharisee is aghast that a respected rabbi and supposed prophet like Jesus allows such a woman to touch him. Jesus turns the tables on Simon with a parable illustrating the appropriate response to the free gift of grace offered to sinners. Those, like this woman, who have been forgiven much, respond by loving much. The self-righteous Pharisees see no need to repent because they don't think they have done anything wrong. They respond not with love, but with indifference and rejection to God's offer of forgiveness through Jesus.

One of the Pharisees invited Jesus to have dinner with him (7:36). The invitation indicates that Simon views Jesus as a social equal, that is, a respected rabbi. Simon's attitude will change, however, when Jesus "defiles" himself by allowing this sinful woman to touch him.[185]

Reclined at the table (7:36). The reclining position indicates that this is a banquet.[186] Guests normally reclined on mats or couches around a short table, with their legs extended behind them (cf. John 13:23–25).

A woman who had lived a sinful life (7:37). Life was far more public in the first century than it is today, and at a dinner party such as this one, interested (but uninvited) observers were allowed to stand on the sidelines and listen to the conversation of influential guests. This woman, probably a prostitute, is despised not because she "crashes" the party, but because her sinful lifestyle brings defilement to the gathering. The religious elite would never socialize with or even touch such a person. This makes her actions toward Jesus particularly offensive to those present.

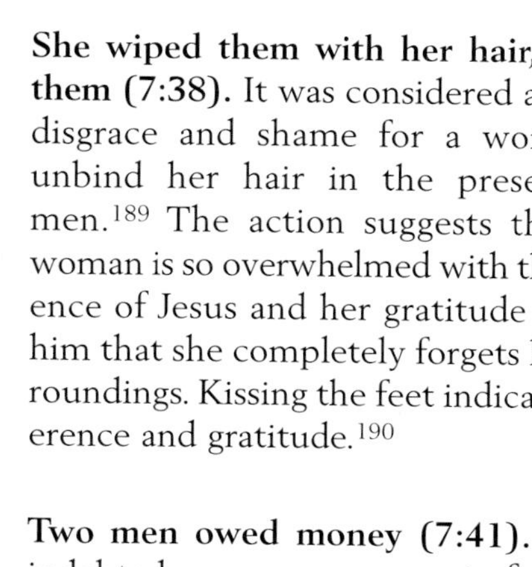

◀ *left*

ALABASTER JAR

An alabaster jar of perfume (7:37). The term *alabastros* probably refers to a flask carved from alabaster with a long neck that was broken off when the contents were used.[187] Such flasks were used for fine perfumes and ointments. The Greek *myron*, translated "perfume" in the NIV, is a general term that can mean "ointment" or "perfume." If this is nard, as in Mark 14:3 and John 12:3, it would have cost as much as three hundred denarii, a year's wages for a day laborer.[188] The purchase of such a gift represents an extraordinary sacrifice.

As she stood behind him at his feet weeping (7:38). The woman is probably trying to anoint Jesus' head, but she cannot reach him because of the manner in which the guests are reclining. Anointing the head was an act of respect given to an honored guest (cf. Ps. 23:5). She has brought no towel, so when her tears of gratitude fall on Jesus' feet, she wipes them with her hair. She then emotionally kisses and anoints his feet with the perfume she has brought for his head. The whole scene reveals a spontaneous and dramatic expression of gratitude.

She wiped them with her hair, kissed them (7:38). It was considered a sign of disgrace and shame for a woman to unbind her hair in the presence of men.[189] The action suggests that this woman is so overwhelmed with the presence of Jesus and her gratitude toward him that she completely forgets her surroundings. Kissing the feet indicates reverence and gratitude.[190]

Two men owed money (7:41). Heavy indebtedness was common in first-century Palestine, caused by several factors. Wealthy landowners leased land to poor peasants and then demanded a large percentage of the profits. This together with demands for tithes, taxes, and a variety of tolls kept constant pressure on farmers. It has been estimated that between 35 to 40 percent of total agricultural production went for taxes.[191] During times of drought or famine, a small farmer could easily lose everything to a rich overlord. (Major famines hit Palestine in 25 B.C. and again in A.D. 46.) The resentment provoked by such indebtedness is evident from an event described by Josephus, where, at the beginning of the Jewish War against Rome in A.D. 66–73, the rebels burned the debt archives.[192]

Five hundred denarii . . . fifty (7:41). A denarius was a Roman coin equivalent to about a day's wages for a laborer. The

◀

DENARIUS

A silver denarius depicting Alexander the Great.

REFLECTIONS

THE PEOPLE OF JESUS' DAY WOULD have assumed that the religious-minded Pharisees had the greatest love for God. Yet Jesus here praises not a pious Pharisee but a notorious sinner for her great love. The story reminds us that loving God does not mean "doing religious things" to earn our way to him, but gratefully accepting the free gift of salvation offered through his Son Jesus Christ.

borrowers' debts are therefore equivalent to about two year's versus two month's wages.

Which of them will love him more? (7:42). There is no specific verb "to thank" in Aramaic (the language Jesus usually spoke), so the verb love (*agapaō*) here expresses the manner in which gratitude is expressed.[193]

Water for my feet . . . a kiss . . . oil on my head (7:44–46). There is no evidence that these are actions a host was expected to perform. While Simon could have graciously had a servant wash Jesus' feet, this was not a requirement of hospitality.[194] He was certainly not expected to perform this action himself as host (cf. John 13). Similarly, while a kiss was a common form of greeting,[195] it was not a necessary social grace. The same can be said for anointing a guest's head with olive oil. The point is that Simon did nothing exceptional for Jesus, but acted with relative indifference. The woman, by contrast, went far beyond the norms of hospitality: washing his feet not with water and a towel, but with her tears and her hair; kissing him not on the cheek, but on his feet; and anointing his feet not with (inexpensive) olive oil, but with costly perfume.

A TYPICAL VILLAGE

The village of Yata, near Hebron, which preserves the appearance of typical villages in ancient Judea.

Jesus' Itinerant Ministry and the Women Who Supported Him (8:1–3)

In a short note, Luke summarizes Jesus' itinerant teaching ministry. He is traveling through the towns and villages of Galilee (cf. 4:43) proclaiming the "good news of the kingdom of God"—a message defined in the Nazareth sermon (4:18–21) and worked out in the episodes since. In addition to the twelve disciples, Luke mentions some women who travel with him and support his ministry financially. These references are significant. Jesus shatters the societal conception of the inferiority of women, raising them to the status of disciples (unheard of in Judaism) and to a place of spiritual equality.

Mary (called Magdalene) from whom seven demons had come out (8:2). Magdalene means an inhabitant of Magdala, a town on the western shore of the Sea of Galilee, a few miles north of Tiberias. Mary will play a prominent role as a witness to Jesus' burial and resurrection.[196] For more on multiple demonic possession and exorcism, see comments on 8:26–39.

Joanna the wife of Cuza, the manager of Herod's household (8:3). The Greek term *epitropos* can refer to a business manager (cf. Matt. 20:8, "foreman"), a child guardian (Gal. 4:2), or even a governor or procurator.[197] The sense here is probably the manager of Herod's estate. The reference confirms that Jesus' ministry is reaching even the upper echelons of society. This Herod is Herod Antipas, son of Herod the Great (see Luke 3:1).

Susanna (8:3). Nothing else is known about this woman.

These women were helping to support them (8:3). Literally, the text reads: "They were serving them from their possessions." These are women of some substance and means. It was not uncommon for wealthy patrons to support traveling teachers in the Greco-Roman world. What is uncommon is that these women travel with Jesus, a respected rabbi, and are treated as his disciples. Rabbis of this day did not have women disciples.

The Parable of the Sower (8:4–15)

In one of his most famous parables, Jesus uses a farming metaphor to describe various responses to his announcement of the kingdom of God. While traditionally called the parable of the sower, this is really the parable of the soils, since the emphasis is on the reception of the seed and the resulting crop that is produced. The parable is puzzling to Jesus' disciples, so they ask for an explanation. Jesus first responds by noting the twofold reason he tells parables. The first is *to reveal* the truth to those who have "ears to hear" (8:8), that is, those who are willing to respond to God's call. The second reason is just the opposite, *to conceal* the message from those who reject the message because of the hardness of their hearts. Jesus concludes by explaining the meaning of the parable in terms of the responses of different individuals to the "word of God," that is, Jesus' proclamation of the kingdom of God.

A farmer went out to sow his seed (8:5). Jesus here uses a common image immediately recognizable to people in an agrarian society. Sowing took place in the late fall or early winter, during the rainy season. A farmer walked along with a bag of seed over his shoulder, scattering the seed in the field. Though the evidence is debated, it seems that sowing was generally done prior to plowing.[198] The Jewish book of *Jubilees* (second century B.C.) speaks of crows stealing the grain "before they plowed in the seed."[199] The farmer scattered seed more or less indiscriminately, expecting to come back later to plow it in.

Some fell along the path (8:5). These are the right-of-ways, either alongside or

ROCKY SOIL

A modern Palestinian plowing in rocky soil.

through the midst of the field. People walking along crush the seed into the path, and the birds then devour it.

Some fell on rock (8:6). "Rock" (*petra*) here probably refers to bedrock covered by a thin layer of soil. Without sufficient soil, the plants cannot take in enough moisture.

A hundred times more than was sown (8:8). The average yield for grain in Palestine has been estimated at a seven to fifteenfold increase, although Genesis 26:12 speaks of Isaac receiving a hundredfold increase "because the LORD blessed him." The yields mentioned in this verse are therefore extraordinary, but not outlandish.[200]

He who has ears to hear, let him hear (8:8). The same phrase is used at 14:35. Ezekiel speaks of Israel as a rebellious people who have "eyes to see but do not see and ears to hear but do not hear" (Ezek. 12:2). Jesus' call for a response prepares the way for his quoting Isaiah 6:9 in verse 10 (cf. Ezek. 3:27).

The secrets of the kingdom of God (8:10). The "secret" or "mystery" (*mystērion*) refers here to the as-of-yet unrevealed plan of God in establishing his kingdom. In Daniel the Aramaic term *rāz* (LXX *mystērion*) refers to the "mystery" of Nebuchadnezzar's dream that Daniel reveals—a mystery concerning the coming kingdom of God that would crush all other kingdoms and would endure forever.[201] The Qumran scrolls sometimes use the expression "mysteries of God" to refer to God's secret purposes now being revealed to his chosen ones.[202] To the Teacher of Righteousness, the community's original leader, "the mysteries . . . of the prophets" have been revealed.[203]

"Though seeing, they may not see" (8:10). This is an abbreviated quotation from Isaiah 6:9, which Mark quotes more fully (Mark 4:12). In its Old Testament context the passage refers to the certainty of coming judgment on Israel. Israel's rebellion had reached the point that her fate was sealed. God would blind her eyes until his discipline was complete. The agent of judgment in Isaiah's day was the Assyrian army, which would bring devastation to Israel.

Isaiah 6:9 was an important proof text throughout the New Testament concerning Israel's rejection of the gospel: "Though seeing, they may not see; though hearing, they may not understand."[204] The text points to God's active blinding of the eyes and closing of the ears against those who obstinately refuse to repent and believe.

This is the meaning of the parable (8:11). The apocryphal book of 2 Esdras (*4 Ezra*; c. A.D. 100) has a similar parable, though its origin may be later than Jesus' words:

> For just as the farmer sows many seeds in the ground and plants a multitude of seedlings, and yet not all that have been sown will come up in due season, and not all that were planted will take root; so also those who have been sown in the world will not all be saved.[205]

The seed is the word of God (8:11). Similar imagery appears in 2 Esdras (*4 Ezra*) 9:31–32, where it is said that the law was "sown" in Israel, but those who received it perished because they did not keep it. Jesus proclaims God's message—the announcement of the kingdom of God—but many do not receive it.

The devil comes and takes away the word (8:12). Birds sometimes appear in

Judaism as symbols of evil.[206] In the *Apocalypse of Abraham* (first to second century A.D.), an unclean bird harassing Abraham is identified as Azazel, the chief of the fallen angels.[207]

But they have no root . . . they fall away (8:13). Not having root indicates a lack of spiritual depth and stability. Sirach 40:15 reads: "The children of the ungodly put out few branches; they are unhealthy roots on sheer rock." With no soil to support the plants and little moisture to utilize, this soil "falls away" in times of testing.

A noble and good heart (8:15). The Greek expression *kalos kai agathos* (the terms are near synonyms) is a common Greek expression for someone with an honorable character.[208] While Mark says simply that these individuals hear the word and accept it, Luke explains the nature of the good soil for his Hellenistic audience.

A Lamp on a Stand (8:16–18)

Jesus continues with a second parable or analogy, this one comparing the proclamation of the kingdom to a lamp that gives forth light. A lamp is of no use if its light is obscured. Similarly, the good news of the kingdom must be proclaimed for all to hear. The lamp serves two functions. (1) It provides light for those who enter the room (8:16). Jesus' proclamation illuminates the truth of the gospel for those who will hear it. (2) It reveals things that are previously concealed (8:17). The message of the gospel demands a response and so lays bare the thoughts and intentions of people's hearts (cf. 2:35).

Luke 8:18 summarizes the need for a response to both parables. Those who "have" are followers who respond to his kingdom announcement and are receiving the "secrets" of the kingdom. Those who "do not have" are the ones who reject his call and so lose not only future blessings, but also what they *think* they already have. The religious leaders opposing Jesus think they have a special status before God. Even this supposed status will be taken from them.

Lights a lamp (8:16). This is probably a small oval lamp filled with olive oil (see photo), which would be set in an alcove to give light to the room.

Hides it in a jar (8:16). The Greek verb *kalyptō* can mean "to cover up, hide." The "jar" is the general term *skeuos,* used of various kinds of containers. This is why some versions speak of covering the light with a container (NASB; NKJV; CEV) rather than placing it inside. Covering the light would snuff it out, while hiding it would obscure its light. Since the second image (placing it under a bed) suggests obscuring the light, this latter sense is probably intended.

Whoever has will be given more (8:18). Old Testament wisdom literature confirms that those who are already wise seek and receive even greater wisdom. Proverbs 9:9 says, "Instruct a wise man and he will be wiser still; teach a righteous man and he will add to his learning" (cf. 1:2–6).

Jesus' Mother and Brothers (8:19–21)

The issue of the spiritual "haves" and the "have-nots" in verse 18 leads directly to a statement by Jesus concerning his true spiritual family. Jesus' teaching is set up by the announcement that his mother and brothers have arrived and are waiting outside the house for him. He replies,

"My mother and brothers are those who hear God's word and put it into practice." Jesus' statement is not meant to repudiate or reject his physical family, but rather to demonstrate the priority of spiritual relationships over physical ones.

Your mother and brothers (8:20). See "The Family of Jesus."

Jesus Calms the Storm (8:22–25)

In the previous parables and teaching, Luke has been illustrating Jesus' call to hear and respond to his message. In a series of miracle stories, Luke now turns to address the issue of Jesus' identity, setting the stage for Peter's confession in 9:20 and the confession of the Father in 9:35.

While Jesus' authority over nature is the controlling theme of this episode, there is an important subtheme related to the disciples' lack of faith. Jesus' calm in the face of the storm (he remains asleep!) is starkly contrasted with the disciples' terror and panic as they cry out, "We're going to drown!" Jesus' response, "Where is your faith?" is a call to these

▸ The Family of Jesus

According to the Gospels, Jesus had four brothers, James, Joseph, Judas and Simon, and an undisclosed number of sisters.[A-26] His brothers did not believe in him during his public ministry (John 2:12; 7:3, 5), but appear with Mary among the first believers in Jerusalem following the resurrection (Acts 1:14). Since his earthly father, Joseph, is never mentioned during Jesus' public ministry, it is likely that he had died before Jesus began to preach. Jesus' brother James plays a central leadership role in the Jerusalem church.[A-27] Independent confirmation of the conversion and leadership role of Jesus' brothers is provided by Paul, who identifies them as itinerant preachers (1 Cor. 9:5), calls James one of the "pillars" of the Jerusalem church (Gal. 1:19; 2:9, 12), and refers to a resurrection appearance to James (1 Cor. 15:7). Two New Testament letters, James and Jude, have traditionally been ascribed to these brothers of Jesus.

There is a lively debate concerning the actual relationship of these "brothers" to Jesus. There are three main possibilities. (1) Roman Catholic theologians have traditionally followed the interpretation of Jerome that these are not Jesus' brothers, but rather his cousins. This is usually suggested to protect the perpetual virginity of Mary. This view is unlikely, since Greek has a distinct word for cousin (*anepsios*, Col. 4:10).[A-28] (2) A second view is that these are children from a previous marriage of Joseph.[A-29] One problem with this is that no mention of these children is made in the birth narratives of Matthew or Luke. (3) The most likely explanation is that these are the brothers of Jesus born to Mary and Joseph after the birth of Jesus. Matthew 1:25 suggests that Mary and Joseph had normal sexual relations after Jesus was born.

Little is known of Jesus' brothers from extra-biblical material. Josephus reports the stoning of James, Jesus' brother, under the high priest Ananias.[A-30] The early church father Julius Africanus is quoted by the church historian Eusebius as saying that the relatives of Jesus spread the gospel throughout Palestine, starting in Nazareth and Cochaba (in Transjordan).[A-31] Hegesippus, also cited by Eusebius, relates a story about the grandsons of Jude, who were summoned to Rome by the emperor Domitian. Domitian feared that as members of the royal line of David they might be politically dangerous. When Domitian found that they were merely poor farmers and were looking for a heavenly rather than earthly kingdom, he dismissed them and ordered the persecution of the church to stop.[A-32] The historical veracity of this account is uncertain.

disciples (and all disciples) to greater faith in his sovereign control through the great storms of life.

A squall came down on the lake (8:23). The Sea of Galilee, lying in a basin seven hundred feet below sea level and surrounded by mountains, is particularly susceptible to sudden violent storms. With two large valleys open on the west (Wadi Hamam and the Beit Netopha Valley), cold westerly winds can descend quickly, turning the placid lake into a raging sea, with waves up to seven feet. In the winter sudden easterly winds can blow up to six- or seven-foot waves.[209] Luke is not exaggerating when he says the disciples are in great danger.

He . . . rebuked the wind and the raging waters (8:24). The "rebuke" does not mean that the wind and the sea are represented as demonic forces, but rather that Jesus is able to command even the forces of nature. God is described in the Old Testament as "rebuking" the sea, a demonstration of his sovereign control over all of nature.[210]

The storm subsided (8:24). While the Hellenistic world of Jesus' day sometimes attributed authority over the sea and wind to kings and wise men,[211] there are no actual accounts where a human figure exercises such power to calm a storm. The closest parallels in Jewish sources relate to the calming of a storm in answer to prayer. The Jerusalem Talmud (fourth century A.D.) records a story with parallels to the Jonah account, where a young Jewish boy is traveling with a boatload of Gentiles when a great storm strikes. After their cries to their pagan idols fail, they call out to the Jewish boy to pray to his god. He prays to the Lord and the storm ceases.[212] Unlike the present account, there is no indication of personal authority and power over nature.

In fear and amazement (8:25). See the similar reaction to the calming of the storm in Jonah 1:16. Fear and awe is the natural reaction to the powerful presence and work of God (see comments on 1:12; 5:8).

Who is this? He commands even the winds and the water (8:25). In the Psalms, the Lord is celebrated as the master of the storm and sea.[213]

REFLECTIONS

JESUS' EXTRAORDINARY AUTHORITY to calm a storm with a word reminds us that he is sovereign over all of life's circumstances and that he cares for our every need. In what difficulties in life do you need to trust the Lord of life's storms?

The Healing of a Demon-Possessed Man (8:26–39)

As Jesus arrives on the other side of the lake with his disciples, a demonized man approaches him. The story illustrates Jesus' authority over the forces of evil and provides one more part of the answer to the disciple's question, "Who is this?" (8:25). Jesus, the powerful Son of God, enters and overwhelms the dominion of evil. The account also contrasts various responses to Jesus' authority: terror and destruction within the demonic realm, fear and rejection from the people of Gerasa, but salvation and proclamation for the healed man.

The closest Hellenistic parallel to the present story appears in the third century A.D. *Life of Apollonius of Tyana,* written by Philostratus.[214] Common features include a dialogue between Apollonius and the demon before the exorcism, an authoritative command by Apollonius to the demon (as opposed to a series of incantations or rituals), an obvious "return to his own self" by the man after the exorcism, and an attempt by the healed man to become a disciple after the exorcism.

GALILEE

The "region of the Gerasenes" was located on the eastern shore of the Sea of Galilee.

Gischala
GALILEE
Ptolemais
Chorazin
Capernaum
Magdala/
Taricheae
Bethsaida, Julias
Gamala
Bethsaida, Galilee
Gergesa
Hippus
SEA OF GALILEE
Cana of Galilee
Sepphoris
Tiberias
Nazareth
Mt. Carmel
Mt. Tabor
Nain
Yarmuk River
Gadara
Jordan River
Caesarea
Scythopolis
Pella

Region of the Gerasenes (8:26). While Luke identifies this place as "across the lake from Galilee," its specific location has presented problems for scholars. The Gerasenes were inhabitants of the city of Gerasa (modern Jerash), a city of Decapolis located over thirty miles southeast of Galilee. This is much too far away for the story.[215] Related to this is a major textual problem, with some ancient manuscripts reading either "Gadarenes" or "Gergesenes." Gadara was another city of Decapolis, but it was only six miles southeast of the lake. Matthew seems to identify this as the location of the events (Matt. 8:28). The third possibility, Gergesa, is identified by the early church writer Origen as an old city on the shores of Galilee. It has been identified by many as modern Khersa on the eastern side of the lake.

Though any conclusion must be tentative because of the many unknowns, there are various ways to resolve the issue without denying the historicity of the passage. (1) The original reading may have referred to Gergesa, but later scribes mistook this obscure location for either Gerasa or Gadara. (2) The reading may have been Gadarenes, but with reference

GERASENE?

Traditional site of the region of the Gerasenes.

to the broader "region" of the Gadarenes, which stretched to the shores of the lake. (3) The reading Gerasenes may be authentic, but it may refer not to the city of Decapolis, but to an otherwise unknown (similarly sounding?) location on the eastern shore of Galilee.

A demon-possessed man (8:27). See "Demonization and Exorcism in the First Century."

Lived in the tombs (8:27). Contact with the dead rendered a Jew ceremonially unclean (Num. 19:11, 14, 16; Ezek. 39:11–15). Apostate Israel is described in Isaiah 65:3–4 as a people "who sit among the graves and spend their nights keeping secret vigil; who eat the flesh of pigs." In the intertestamental Jewish book of *Jubilees* (second century B.C.), Gentiles are viewed as unclean because they "slaughter their sacrifices to the dead, and

Demonization and Exorcism in the First Century

Demonization and exorcism were not uncommon in the first century, appearing both in Judaism and in the greater Hellenistic world. The New Testament itself testifies to Jewish exorcists other than Jesus and the apostles. Jesus points out in Luke 11:19 that the disciples of the Pharisees practiced exorcism, and in Acts 19 seven sons of a Jewish priest named Sceva attempt to cast out demons in Jesus' name (but fail miserably!).[A-33] Luke 9:49 (par. Mark 9:38) speaks of a man outside the band of disciples who is casting out demons in Jesus' name. This last example is somewhat different since this man appears to be a true follower of Jesus.

Demonic oppression of sorts appears in the Old Testament account of King Saul, who was tormented by an "evil spirit from the LORD" (1 Sam. 16:14). Later Jewish traditions trace exorcist techniques back to King Solomon. Jewish writers evidently interpreted Old Testament statements about Solomon's great wisdom (cf. 1 Kings 4:29–34) to include knowledge of exorcist techniques and the magical arts. The first-century Jewish historian Josephus writes:

> Now so great was the prudence and wisdom which God granted Solomon that he surpassed the ancients.... And God granted him knowledge of the art used against demons for the benefit and healing of men. He also composed incantations by which illnesses are relieved, and left behind forms of exorcisms with which those possessed by demons drive them out, never to return.[A-34]

A whole body of literature arose around Solomon's exploits. The *Testament of Solomon* (first to third century A.D.) recounts how Solomon used a magic ring to control demons tormenting a young boy, even coercing them to help him build the temple. This document illustrates a growing syncretism between pagan magic and Jewish traditions.

First-century exorcists—both Hellenistic and Jewish—used a variety of techniques, including rituals, incantations and spells, potions or herbs of various kinds, and rings or other magical objects. The magical papyri are full of incantations to ward off evil spirits.[A-35] Following his statement about Solomon (cited above), Josephus describes an exorcism he witnessed in which a man named Eleazar used a ring containing a magical root to draw out a demon through the nostrils of a demonized man.

Jesus' exorcisms contrast sharply with these examples. No incantations or magical objects are used. There is no sense that the power is in the technique or the words that are used. Jesus rather commands the demons from his own authority and they immediately submit. The exorcisms are not meant as showy demonstrations of his magical arts, but to confirm the in-breaking of the kingdom of God in his words and deeds. When the Lord's Messiah arrives, the forces of Satan are confronted and overcome.

to demons they bow down. And they eat in tombs."[216]

Had not worn clothes (8:27). Demonization often resulted in wildness of appearance and lack of personal care. The Talmud describes features of demon-possession as going out alone at night, sleeping in a graveyard, ripping one's clothes, and losing what is given to them.[217]

Evil spirit (8:29). Literally, "unclean spirit." This fits the whole context of ceremonial defilement. The tombs, the pigs, and the evil spirits all bring uncleanness. Jesus' presence and power brings purification to this defiled scene.

What is your name? (8:30). It was popularly believed that the knowledge of a demon's name gave a person control over it (see comments on 4:34 and references there). This cannot be a factor here, however, since Jesus already demonstrates complete mastery over these demons.[218]

Legion (8:30). A legion of Roman soldiers consisted of approximately six thousand men. As Luke points out, the number is meant to signify "many."

The Abyss (8:31). The Greek word means "bottomless" or "very deep" and came to be used of the place of captivity of evil spirits or fallen angels.[219] In Revelation 20:1–3 Satan is seized and sealed up in the Abyss for a thousand years. Matthew 25:41 speaks of the place of "eternal fire prepared for the devil and his angels."

A large herd of pigs (8:32). According to the Old Testament law, pigs were unclean animals.[220] The transfer of demons or disease into animals appears elsewhere in Hellenistic literature.[221]

Sitting at Jesus' feet (8:35). This is the position of a disciple, a point made explicit by the man's desire to follow Jesus (8:38).

A Dead Girl and a Sick Woman (8:40–56)

This double miracle is the third in a series of extraordinary acts leading up to Peter's confession in 9:20. As Jesus has demonstrated power over nature (8:22–25) and over the demonic realm (8:26–37), so now he reveals his authority over disease and death. This episode once again emphasizes Jesus' authority, but also highlights his compassion. On the human side, this story commends the importance of a response of faith.

A ruler of the synagogue (8:41). This administrative officer maintained the synagogue and organized the worship services.[222] Acts 13:15 speaks of "synagogue rulers" in the plural at Pisidian Antioch, suggesting perhaps a committee of elders.

His only daughter (8:42). See comments on 7:11–17. The loss of an only child represents a special tragedy. The Old Testament often speaks of the tragedy of losing an only son who could have carried on the family name,[223] but Judges 11:30–40 speaks of the tragedy of the loss of an only daughter.

Subject to bleeding for twelve years (8:43). The nature of this condition is not specified, but it may have been some kind of menstrual disorder. Such a condition not only damaged her health but rendered her ceremonially unclean, limiting her participation in Israel's religious life.[224]

The edge of his cloak (8:44). The word for "edge" (*kraspedon*) is used in the LXX of the "tassels" Israelites were to wear on the four corners of their robes; this may be the sense here.[225] It could also mean simply "hem" or "edge" (see Deut. 22:12, LXX).

Daughter (8:48). This is the only time in the Gospels Jesus addresses someone with this affectionate term. It indicates the tenderness with which Jesus speaks to her.

Your faith has healed you. Go in peace (8:48). Jesus said the same thing to the sinful woman who anointed his feet (7:50). "Peace" indicates the state of spiritual wholeness captured in the Hebrew word *shalom*.

All the people were wailing and mourning for her (8:52). It was important in Jewish culture to have a large group of mourners to demonstrate the great sadness at the loss of a loved one. These would have included not only family and friends, but also professional mourners (see comments on 7:12).

"My child, get up!" (8:54). Mark records the actual Aramaic phrase that Jesus used, "Talitha koum!" The impact of those words must have forever resonated in the disciples' ears. Luke provides only the Greek since the Aramaic carried no meaning for his Hellenistic readers.

She is not dead but asleep (8:52). "Asleep" here indicates the temporary nature of her condition, since Jesus is about to reverse it. The fact that the girl is in fact dead and not comatose is clear from Luke's explanation of the mourners' laughter: "knowing that she was dead." "Sleep" is often used in the New Testament of the temporary nature of a believer's death.[226]

Her spirit returned (8:55). As in the case of the son of the widow of Nain, this is a resuscitation rather than a true resurrection (see comments on 7:15). The girl's spirit returns to her mortal body. "Spirit" here may mean merely "life force," or may refer to her immaterial spirit distinct from her body.[227] It is sometimes said that Hebraic thought was monist rather than dualist, and that life returned only at the resurrection of the body. Dualist perspectives, however, appear in some Jewish sources.[228]

Jesus Sends Out the Twelve (9:1–9)

A new phase of Jesus' ministry begins in chapter 9 as Jesus sends out the twelve "apostles" (6:13; 9:10) on a mission of their own. Up to this point, the disciples have been portrayed primarily as observers, accompanying Jesus as he preaches and heals. Now he gives them the authority and power to do just what he has been doing: casting out demons, healing the sick,

TUNIC

An Egyptian (Coptic) tunic.

and proclaiming the message of the kingdom of God. The mission of the Twelve foreshadows the apostolic mission in Acts, where the apostles continue Jesus' work through the presence and power of the Holy Spirit.[229]

The Twelve (9:1). This designation becomes a technical term for the twelve "apostles" Jesus chose from among his larger band of disciples (see comments on 6:12–16). The term *apostolos* (6:13; 9:10) means "one sent out" with a delegated task. As a preview of the apostolic mission in Acts, this passage illustrates the role these apostles will fulfill. The number twelve represents the twelve tribes of Israel. The apostles are not only the foundation of the church, but also represent the righteous remnant of Israel. In Luke 10:1–16 Jesus will send out seventy-two more, a number that probably signifies the evangelization of the Gentile nations.

Take nothing . . . no staff, no bag, no bread, no money, no extra tunic (9:3). A staff was used not only as a walking aid, but also to ward off attackers. The bag here could be a beggar's bag to receive alms, but more likely refers to a knapsack to carry one's meager possessions (see 10:4; 22:35). Since no possessions are carried, no bag is required. The tunic was a shirt or undergarment worn next to the skin (see 3:11; 6:29).

Various suggestions have been offered for the reason for these prohibitions. (1) The Mishnah prohibits a man going onto the temple Mount "with his staff or his sandal or his wallet, or with the dust upon his feet."[230] Jesus may be saying that the task of the disciples is a sacred one and so they must leave behind anything that could defile them. While the "dust off your feet" comment in 9:5 provides some circumstantial evidence for this view, Jesus gives no indication that these items are associated with ceremonial uncleanness. (2) Others have suggested that the commands are meant to distance the Christian missionaries from the wandering Hellenistic philosophers of the Cynic tradition, who carried a purse or wallet to receive financial support.[231] This explanation, however, fits better with the later missionary movement than the historical context of Jesus' ministry. The fact that the injunctions are later altered in light of changing circumstances (22:35–38) suggests that Luke does not see these as established guidelines for the church's (later) missionary activities. (3) The simplest explanation is probably the best. The injunctions are meant to encourage traveling light and without encumbrance, living in complete dependence on God. While the principle is universal, the details are meant specifically for this mission of the Twelve.

Shake the dust off your feet (9:5). (Cf. 10:11). This is a formal act of separation, leaving the town to the judgment it deserves for rejecting the gospel (see the judgment pronounced against Korazin, Bethsaida, and Capernaum in 10:13–15; cf. Acts 18:6). In rabbinic traditions, the action indicated that the place was heathen and had no status among God's people.[232] This appears to be the sense in Acts 13:51, where Paul and Barnabas "shook the dust from their feet" against the Jews of Pisidian Antioch.

Herod the tetrarch (9:7). This is Herod Antipas, one of the sons of Herod the Great (see comments on 3:1; 3:19–20).

That Elijah had appeared (9:8). For expectations related to Elijah, see comments on 1:17; 3:4–5; 7:27.

I beheaded John (9:9). See Mark 6:14–29 and "Josephus on John the Baptist" at Luke 3:19–20.

Jesus Feeds the Five Thousand (9:10–17)

The feeding of the five thousand is the only miracle that appears in all four Gospels. Like the calming of the sea (8:22–25), this dramatic nature miracle provides one more clue to the answer of the question posed by Herod, "Who . . . is this?" (9:9). The answer will come in the confession of Peter that follows (9:20).

Important to the background of the passage are (1) the miraculous feeding of the people of Israel with manna in the desert (Ex. 16; Num. 11; cf. John 6:14–40); (2) Elisha's feeding of a hundred men with barley loaves and grain (2 Kings 4:42–44); and, perhaps most important, (3) the "messianic banquet," God's eschatological promise to feed and shepherd his people (Isa. 25:6–8; 65:13–14). The messianic banquet is an important theme for Luke, which will recur again and again during his travel narrative.[233]

The miracle reveals not only Jesus' power over nature, but also his ability to care for and sustain his people. The extra food left over confirms the abundant nature of God's blessings and sustenance.

A town called Bethsaida (9:10). Bethsaida was located on the northern shore of the Sea of Galilee, east of the Jordan River. It was the hometown of Peter and Andrew (John 1:44) as well as the disciple Philip (12:21).

In groups of about fifty each (9:14). It has been suggested that the people are organized in ranks like an army and that some of the people present may have thought Jesus was organizing them as a messianic army.[234] John's version of the account, in which the people wish to make Jesus king after the miracle (John 6:15), may lend itself to this interpretation. But there is no indication of this in the Synoptic accounts, either in Jesus' actions or in the interpretation of the Gospel writers. The word for "group" (*klisia*) is used elsewhere with reference to people gathered for a meal, not for battle.[235]

Looking up to heaven, he gave thanks (9:16). The Mishnah provides an example of an ancient prayer of thanksgiving before a meal: "Blessed art thou . . . who bringest forth bread from the earth."[236] Jesus may have prayed something like this on this occasion. Lifting one's eyes to heaven was a common posture for prayer.[237]

Taking the five loaves . . . he gave thanks and broke them (9:16). This passage has clear verbal parallels with the institution of the Lord's Supper (22:19), which itself has strong links to the Old Testament imagery of the messianic banquet.

Twelve basketfuls . . . were left over (9:17). The reference to leftover provisions is another parallel to 2 Kings 4:43, where the Lord promises that "they will eat and have some left over." The number twelve may symbolically point to the twelve tribes of Israel. Food is provided for all God's people.

Peter's Confession of Christ (9:18–27)

Luke's Gospel reaches a climax in 9:20 when Peter, after witnessing the powerful words and deeds of Jesus, confesses

Jesus to be the Christ. The confession represents an important first stage in Jesus' self-revelation. What the angel Gabriel had prophesied about Jesus (1:33–35) and what his miracles have revealed is now recognized and proclaimed by Peter as representative of the disciples. The question by Herod, "Who . . . is this?" (9:7–9) now finds its answer.

The passage represents a key turning point in Luke's narrative, as Jesus radically clarifies the role of the Messiah. His present task is not to conquer the Roman legions, but to suffer and die for his people (9:21–22). In light of his own suffering role, Jesus calls his followers to cross-bearing discipleship (9:23–26). The path to true life comes not through self-preservation, but through a daily willingness to sacrifice one's life for Jesus. Those who are not ashamed of the Son of Man in the present age will be given life and glory in the age to come.

Some say John the Baptist; others say Elijah (9:19). For expectations related to Elijah in Judaism, see comments on 1:17; 3:4–5.

The Christ of God (9:20). The word "Christ" (*christos*) is a Greek translation of the Hebrew word "Messiah" (*māšiaḥ*), meaning "anointed one." Kings, priests, and prophets were anointed with oil as a sign that they were consecrated to God and set apart for his work.[238] Luke's phrase "the Christ of God" (i.e., "God's Anointed One") recalls the Old Testament phrase, the "LORD's Anointed"—a designation applied to Israel's king, especially David (cf. 2:26). It eventually became a title, the "Messiah," for the coming deliverer from David's line (see comments on 1:32–33; 2:11; see also "Messianic Expectation in Jesus' Day"). In Jesus' day the title had strong political connotations.

The Son of Man must suffer many things (9:22). The suffering role of the "Servant of the Lord" is set out in Isaiah 52:13–53:12. There is little evidence, however, that the Jews of Jesus' day recognized this passage as referring to the Messiah.[239] Their messianic expectations focused instead on a powerful and triumphant king who would overthrow the Romans and reign in righteousness on David's throne (see *Pss. Sol.* 17–18; see comments on Luke 1:32–33; 2:11).

The elders, chief priests and teachers of the law (9:22). Though Israel only had one "high priest" (*archiereus*, see comments on 3:2), the plural of this term—translated as "chief priests" in the NIV—was used of the upper echelons of the priestly class, especially those who served on the Sanhedrin, the Jewish high court.[240] "Elders" probably refers to the lay nobility who served together with them.[241] (For "teachers of the law," see comments on 5:17 and "Scribes.")

On the third day (9:22). "The third day" may allude to Hosea 6:2, a reference to Israel's national restoration by God. As the Messiah, Jesus both represents and brings restoration to God's people.

Take up his cross daily (9:23). This is not merely an image of self-denial, but of violent death by execution. The term *stauros* ("cross") originally meant a stake set in an upright position. Persians, Greeks, and Romans used stakes both as instruments of execution and as a means of exposing an executed body to shame and humiliation (and as a warning to others). The Romans raised crucifixion to an art form, and it became a favorite method of torture and capital punishment.[242] Roman prisoners bound for crucifixion were forced to carry the horizontal cross beam (the *patibulum*) to the place of execution (cf. 23:26). This cross beam would then be affixed to a permanent upright beam, while ropes or nails in the wrists and feet were used to fasten the victim to the wood (see "Crucifixion" at 23:33 [cf. 14:27]). Jesus is here referring to a life of total commitment to him, even to the point of suffering and martyrdom.

The Son of Man . . . when he comes in his glory (9:26). On the title "Son of Man," see comments on 5:24. The allusion here is to Daniel 7:13–14, where an exalted messianic figure is described as "one like a son of man" who comes on the clouds of heaven and is given authority, glory, and an eternal kingdom. In Daniel, this figure appears to be identified not only with the "saints of the Most High" (7:18, cf. v. 27), but also as an individual Messiah (7:13–14). This is similar to the "Servant of the LORD" in Isaiah 40–55, who is identified both with corporate Israel (Isa. 44:1; 49:3) and with an individual (Isa. 42:1). The key here is that the Messiah functions as representative head of his people Israel.

The Jewish apocalyptic work *1 Enoch* uses the title "Son of Man" for a messianic heavenly deliverer who saves his people and judges the wicked.[243] The portrait is clearly drawn from Daniel 7, but it is debated whether it is pre- or post-Christian and whether Jesus' hearers would have identified him with this figure.[244]

Some . . . will not taste death before they see the kingdom of God (9:27). This cannot refer to the *parousia* (second coming of Christ) since Jesus would have been wrong; he did not return to earth in the lifetime of the disciples. The statement refers instead to the Transfiguration, which immediately follows in Luke's narrative. The disciples are given a glimpse of the coming kingdom through the manifestation of Jesus' glory on the mountain.

The Transfiguration (9:28–36)

At the Transfiguration, the veil over Jesus' person is lifted and Peter, James, and John (the inner circle of disciples) are given a glimpse of his true glory. The term "transfiguration" means to change form or appearance and is taken from the Latin translation of the Greek verb used in Mark 9:2 (*metamorphoō*). Two great Old Testament saints, Moses and Elijah,

MOUNT HERMON

MOUNT TABOR

appear with Jesus in "glorious splendor," confirming that Jesus' message and mission are from God and fulfill the Old Testament.

While in Matthew and Mark the Transfiguration is usually seen as a preview of the glory Jesus will have at his second coming, for Luke the greater emphasis is on the heavenly glory he will receive at his exaltation to God's right hand. Only Luke among the Synoptic Gospels mentions that the topic of Jesus' conversation with Moses and Elijah was his "departure" (*exodos*), which he was going to fulfill in Jerusalem (9:31). This term probably refers to the whole event of Jesus' death, resurrection, and ascension to God's right hand (Acts 2:33). This gives us a clue as to why this event occurs at this point in Jesus' ministry. Following Peter's confession of Jesus' messiahship (Luke 9:18–20), Jesus instructs his disciples on the true suffering role of the Messiah (9:21–22) and calls them to cross-bearing discipleship (9:23–26). The glimpse of his exaltation glory serves as encouragement and hope for the disciples during the dark days that lie ahead.

About eight days after Jesus said this (9:28). This statement links the Transfiguration with Jesus' words about the kingdom in 9:27. "About eight days" probably means "about a week." Mark refers to six days.

Onto a mountain to pray (9:28). Mountains are places of revelation in biblical tradition. Moses received God's law from the Lord on Mount Sinai/Horeb and there saw his glory (Ex. 24; 33–34). Elijah defeated the prophets of Baal on Mount Carmel (1 Kings 18) and heard God's quiet voice on Mount Horeb (ch. 19). The actual site of the Transfiguration is not named, but has been traditionally identified as Mount Tabor in southern Galilee. Others have suggested Mount Hermon because of its proximity to Caesarea Philippi, the place of Peter's confession.

His face changed (9:29). This recalls the face of Moses, which glowed from God's glory when he came down from Mount Sinai (Ex. 34:29). Paul points out that while Moses' glory faded, the glory we will receive through Christ is eternal (2 Cor. 3:7–18).

His clothes became as bright as a flash of lightning (9:29). Angelic and other heavenly beings are often described in Jewish apocalyptic and early Christian literature in terms of brightness and white clothing.[245]

Moses and Elijah (9:30). Why these two? They may signify the Law and the Prophets respectively, and so confirm Jesus' fulfillment of the Old Testament Scriptures. Both men also received mountaintop revelations of God (see comments on 9:28) and were known for their powerful miracles. Jesus' miracles often recall their works (e.g., Moses recalled in the feeding of the five thousand; Elijah recalled in the raising of the widow's son). Both men's lives also ended unusually. Elijah did not die, but was taken to heaven in a fiery chariot (2 Kings 2). Moses died alone on Mount Nebo and was buried by God himself (Deut. 34:6).

They spoke about his departure (9:31). "Departure" is the Greek word *exodos*, a term that can refer euphemistically to death.[246] The same word is used in the

LXX of the exodus from Egypt.[247] As Moses led the first Exodus, so Jesus, the new Moses, will lead a second one. God's end-time salvation is often described in the Old Testament prophets as a new and greater exodus.[248]

Let us put up three shelters (9:33). Scholars have puzzled over the significance of Peter's statement. The Greek word for "shelter" is *skēnē,* the word used in the LXX for the tabernacle, Israel's portable place of worship in the desert (Ex. 25:9). It is also used of the temporary huts or booths assembled during the Old Testament Feast of Tabernacles.[249] Since the tabernacle represented God's presence with his people, Peter may be wishing to celebrate God's intervention in the events he is witnessing. Another possibility is that he is hoping to prolong the experience by providing shelters for Moses, Elijah, and Jesus.

A cloud appeared and enveloped them (9:34). Clouds are often symbols of God's presence in the Old Testament and Judaism.[250] The closest Old Testament parallel appears in Exodus 24:16, when God's voice calls to Moses "from within the cloud" at Mount Sinai (cf. 16:10; 19:9).

They were afraid as they entered the cloud (9:34). The fear of the disciples parallels the fear of the Israelites at Mount Sinai.[251] Fear is the common reaction to a heavenly visitation or an act of divine power.[252]

This is my Son, whom I have chosen (9:35). The phrase "This is my Son" alludes to Psalm 2:7, identifying Jesus not only as uniquely related to the Father, but also as the Messiah from David's line.[253] The phrase "whom I have chosen" reflects Isaiah 42:1, where the messianic Servant of the Lord is called "my chosen one."[254] As at his baptism, Jesus is identified here as both the Messiah and the suffering Servant. The title "Chosen One" will be used again of Jesus in Luke 23:35.

Listen to him (9:35). This probably alludes to Deuteronomy 18:15, where Moses prophesied that God would one day raise up a prophet like himself within Israel and warned, "You must listen to him" (cf. Acts 3:22; 7:37). Jesus is the "prophet like Moses," who speaks God's word for the dawning age of salvation.

REFLECTIONS

AT HIS TRANSFIGURATION JESUS reveals to his disciples the awesome glory that was his before he came to earth and the glory to which he will return after his death and resurrection. This glimpse of the real Jesus is intended to encourage the disciples during the dark days that lie ahead. Such a glimpse into Jesus' real glory should inspire us to live on a higher plane in the face of life's difficulties.

The Healing of a Boy With an Evil Spirit (9:37–45)

The episode that follows the Transfiguration presents further proof of the identity of Jesus revealed on the mountain. As Jesus and the three disciples are coming down the mountain, a crowd meets them. The disciples who remain behind have been unable to help a man whose son is suffering from epileptic-like symptoms caused by a demon. Jesus reacts strongly by rebuking this "unbelieving and perverse generation." The statement is probably directed not only at the disciples, but also at the crowd and the boy's father. All are lacking faith in the power of God to intervene. Jesus takes control of the situation by rebuking the demon and healing the boy. Characteristic of Luke, the crowd responds in amazement at the greatness of God manifested through Jesus' works.

As the crowd stands amazed at Jesus' power, he turns to his disciples and instructs them a second time on the suffering role of the Christ. Despite his acts of power, his present path is not one of conquest, but one of suffering and sacrifice. The disciples are unable to understand Jesus' words, however, not only because they are still looking for a conquering Messiah, but also because this understanding "was hidden from them" (9:45). The comprehension of the significance of the true role of the Messiah will come only through divine revelation (for this same theme see 24:16, 25–27, 30–32).

For he is my only child (9:38). The Old Testament often speaks of the tragedy of losing an only son who would receive the inheritance and carry on the family name.[255]

It throws him into convulsions so that he foams at the mouth (9:39). The symptoms here are similar to epilepsy, but this does not rule out demonization as the ultimate cause. Demons are often described as inflicting actual illnesses, including muteness (11:14), lameness (13:11), and madness (8:29). Nor are illnesses like epilepsy always considered demonic (see Matt. 4:24).

O unbelieving and perverse generation (9:41). This phrase echoes Deuteronomy 32:20, which refers to Israel's unfaithfulness and disobedience in the desert. Though the Israelites experienced the awesome power of God, they still demonstrated a lack of faith.

Who Will Be the Greatest? (9:46–50)

The disciples' failure to grasp the significance of Jesus' suffering role is now illustrated by a series of episodes revealing their pride and self-serving attitude. In the first, Jesus points out that true greatness is found in a humble heart of servanthood and love for others, which welcomes the most vulnerable members of society. Welcoming (or honoring) the weak and vulnerable is the same as welcoming Jesus, since they are special recipients of his grace. Welcoming Jesus, in turn, is the same as welcoming the Father, since Jesus is the Father's Son and representative (cf. 9:35). Jesus sums up by noting that "he who is least among you all . . . is the greatest" (9:48). "Least" here means not social inferiority, but those willing to take a lower place in order to lift up and encourage others.

In the second episode, the disciple John informs Jesus that he has tried to prevent a man from driving out demons in Jesus' name, since the man was not one of the Twelve. Jesus says not to stop the man, since "whoever is not against you is for you." The cause of advancing the kingdom takes precedence over individual status and privilege. The man casting out demons is viewed as no different from the disciples themselves, since all are merely servants and instruments to accomplish God's work.

Took a little child (9:47). Status and position were of supreme importance in first-century culture. Each member of family and society knew his or her position in this hierarchy. Though children were certainly loved and cared for by their parents, they had essentially no social status.[256]

Whoever welcomes this little child (9:48). People of position and status were "welcomed," that is, treated with honor and respect as social equals or superiors. Here Jesus, the disciple's honored master and teacher, shockingly places a child on the same social status as himself.

Driving out demons (9:49). See comments on 8:26–39 and "Demonization and Exorcism in the First Century."

We tried to stop him (9:49). This episode has an interesting parallel in the life of Moses. When two elders (Eldad and Medad) begin prophesying apart from the seventy elders appointed by Moses, Joshua calls on Moses to stop them. Moses replies, "I wish that all the LORD's people were prophets and that the LORD would put his Spirit on them!" (Num. 11:24–30).

Whoever is not against you is for you (9:50). This statement is proverbial, appearing in a similar form in Cicero.[257] There the philosopher pleads with Caesar on behalf of a client by pointing out that "while we considered all who were not on our side to be our opponents, you held all those who were not against you to be your adherents."[258] Since the statement is proverbial, we would expect it to be a general rather than an absolute truth; in fact, Jesus cites the inverse statement in 11:23: "He who is not with me is against me."

Samaritan Opposition (9:51–56)

At 9:51, Jesus' Galilean ministry comes to a close and a section begins that has been called Luke's "Travel Narrative" or "Journey to Jerusalem." Luke tells us at this point that "Jesus resolutely set out for Jerusalem" (lit., "set his face to go to Jerusalem") in order to fulfill the role of the suffering Messiah (see 13:31–35). Luke takes ten full chapters to treat a period that Mark covers in a single chapter.

The journey to Jerusalem begins with a story of opposition from a certain Samaritan village. It continues the theme of the disciples' pride and self-importance found in 9:46–50 and alludes to the theme of God's love for all people, regardless of ethnic or cultural background.

When Jesus sends messengers ahead to prepare a Samaritan village for his visit, the Samaritans refuse to welcome him (see 9:48) because he is traveling toward Jerusalem. When James and John ask whether they should call down fire from heaven to destroy the village, Jesus rebukes them. The episode forms a fitting introduction to a travel narrative in

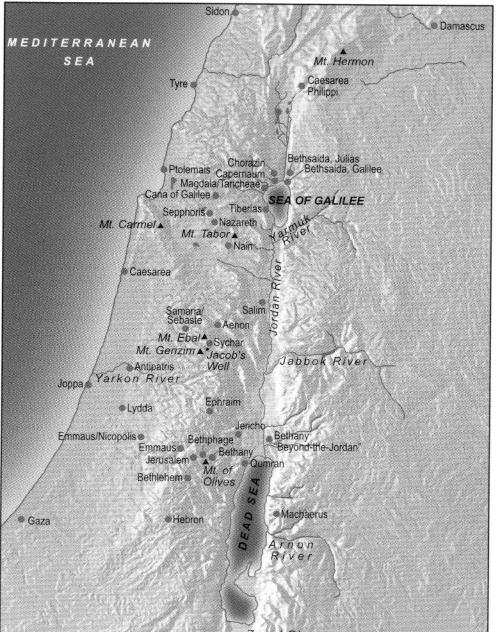

GALILEE, SAMARIA, AND JUDEA

The region around Mount Gerizim was the location of many Samaritan villages.

which God's love for the outcast is on center stage. Despite their past animosity toward God's people, even despised Samaritans are offered the free gift of salvation that Jesus brings (see Acts 8:4–25).

To be taken up to heaven (9:51). The Greek here is literally "for his taking up" or "his ascension" (*analēmpsis*), with no specific reference to "heaven." *Analēmpsis* is occasionally used of death in Jewish literature, and this sense may be present here.[259] More likely, however, the meaning is similar to the term *exodos* in 9:31 and refers to the whole event of Jesus' death, resurrection, and ascension to heaven.

To get things ready for him (9:52). Jesus is seeking hospitality or at least accommodations in this Samaritan village. While some pilgrims may have purchased provisions from the Samaritans, most probably carried sufficient supplies for their journey. Many pious Jews

SEBASTE

A Hellenistic tower is in the foreground and the Roman theater is in the background.

right

MODERN SAMARITANS

Men seated around a table at mealtime.

Samaria

Samaria was the region located between Judea and Galilee, west of the Jordan River. According to the Old Testament, the Samaritans arose as a race from the population of foreign colonists settled by the Assyrians following their conquest of the northern kingdom of Israel. Samaritan religion was syncretistic, with elements both of pagan and Israelite worship (2 Kings 17:24–41). There was much animosity between Jews and Samaritans, initially sparked when the Jews returning from Babylon resisted Samaritan attempts to aid in the construction of the temple (Ezra 4). The Samaritans eventually built their own temple on Mount Gerizim (see John 4:21), developed their own liturgy, and used as their Scriptures only the Pentateuch, the first five books of the Old Testament. The hatred between the two peoples became particularly intense during the period of the Maccabees, when the Hasmonean priest-king John Hyrcanus marched against Samaria and destroyed the temple on Mount Gerizim (c. 128 B.C.).[A-36]

It was a three-day journey through Samaria from Galilee to Jerusalem.[A-37] Contrary to the popular view that Jewish pilgrims commonly went *around* Samaria, Josephus says the usual custom was to pass *through* Samaria. (The route through Perea to bypass Samaria would mean passing through Gentile territory, which was equally distasteful to pious Jews.[A-38]) But Josephus also cites an example where Jewish pilgrims were attacked by a Samaritan village, and certainly some Jews would have bypassed Samaria.[A-39] Relations between Jews and Samaritans were always tense and often hostile.[A-40] viewed receiving hospitality from the Samaritans as scandalous.

Because he was heading for Jerusalem (9:53). From the Samaritan perspective, Jesus' intention is to worship at the temple in Jerusalem, a rival to their worship on Mount Gerizim.

To call fire down from heaven (9:54). Elijah had called down fire from heaven to consume two companies of troops sent against him by Ahaziah, the king of Samaria (2 Kings 1:1–17). Though "Samaria" in that case refers to the capital of the northern kingdom of Israel rather than the Samaritans of the New Testament, James and John may have connected the two. Elijah also called down fire from heaven to consume his sacrifice in the contest against the priests of Baal on Mount Carmel (1 Kings 18:38). The symbol is one of divine judgment against the enemies of God. In their misplaced zeal James and John seek divine retribution against those who oppose God's messenger.

The Cost of Following Jesus (9:57–62)

The key Christological theme of the Travel Narrative—that Jesus is heading to Jerusalem to suffer and die—has its corollary in the willingness of a disciple to suffer for the master. The present account introduces this prominent theme. Three men approach Jesus, all with aspirations of discipleship. All three of Jesus' responses point to the radical nature of commitment to him and the extreme cost a disciple must be willing to pay.

Foxes have holes and birds of the air have nests (9:58). A similar proverb appears in Plutarch, who cites Tiberius Gracchus: "The wild beasts roam over Italy and each one has his own hole and lair, but those who fight and die for Italy have only the light and the air as their portions."[260] Jesus' singular devotion to his task means that he has no permanent home to provide security.

First let me go and bury my father (9:59). Respect for parents was of utmost importance in Jewish society. To "honor your father and your mother" is among the greatest commandments.[261] Equally important was providing a proper burial for a loved one, a responsibility that took priority over even the study of the Law. The Talmud makes the surprising statement that "he who is confronted by a dead relative is freed from reciting the Shema, from the Eighteen Benedictions, and from all the commandments stated in the Torah."[262] Though this text is late, its spirit permeates earlier documents.[263] According to the Old Testament, even priests, who would normally be defiled by touching a dead body, could bury immediate family members (Lev. 21:1–3). It was especially the eldest son's responsibilities to make such arrangements (Tobit 6:15).

Let the dead bury their own dead (9:60). Jesus probably means to let those who are *spiritually* dead bury the *physically* dead. Some commentators have sought to soften Jesus' words by suggesting that the man is requesting a long delay until his father dies (which could take years), or that he is referring to the reburial of bones in a common family grave (a "gathering to the fathers") after the flesh has rotted off the bones (which could take a year).[264] It seems more likely, however, that the man's father has already died or is near death. Jesus' reply is meant to be truly radical and countercultural.

First let me go back and say good-by to my family (9:61). The statement echoes Elisha's request when he was called to be Elijah's successor (1 Kings 19:19–20). Jesus responds by playing off this same Old Testament text, since Elisha was plowing in his family's field when Elijah met him: "No one who puts his hand to the plow and looks back is fit for service in the kingdom of God" (Luke 9:62). The farmer must keep looking forward in order to plow a straight furrow. Likewise, a disciple constantly distracted by past associations cannot provide effective service for the kingdom of God. Jesus demands an even more rigorous commitment from his disciples than Elijah and an even more dramatic break with family.

No one who puts his hand to the plow (9:61–62). See comments above related to 1 Kings 19:19–20. A similar proverb appears in Hesiod, *Works and Days* 443, who speaks of "one who will attend to his work and drive a straight furrow and is past the age for gaping after his fellows, but will keep his mind on his work."[265]

PLOW

Jesus Sends Out the Seventy-Two (10:1–24)

Jesus had previously sent out his twelve apostles to preach and to heal (9:1–6). Now he sends out a larger group of seventy (or seventy-two) disciples. While the earlier mission of the Twelve represents the gospel going to Israel, this one points to the mission to the Gentiles (see comments on 10:1). The actual target of the mission, however, remains the towns of Israel.

Jesus first calls his followers to prayer (10:2). The potential abundance of the harvest, the paucity of workers, and the dangers of the task mean that God's power and help are essential for the task. He also warns of the dangers of the task.

After their return the disciples announce with joy that even the demons have submitted to them. Jesus responds by affirming that Satan is being defeated through their actions (10:18–20). By defeating Satan, the in-breaking power of the kingdom is providing free and unhindered access to God's presence.

Jesus' joy at the spiritual success of his disciples and at the reception of the message of the kingdom results in a prayer of praise to the Father (10:21–22), the theme of which is God's self-revelation through the Son. Finally, Jesus turns to the disciples and describes the blessing and privilege they have so as to see and hear God's revelation through the Son (10:23–24). For centuries prophets and kings longed to experience the fulfillment of God's promises (cf. 1 Peter 1:10–12). The disciples now have that privilege.

Seventy-two (10:1). The number probably symbolically represents the nations of the world. There are seventy names listed in the table of nations in the Hebrew text of Genesis 10, and seventy-two names listed in the Septuagint, the Greek Old Testament (LXX). This difference in numbers could account for the textual problem in Luke, where some manuscripts read "seventy" and others "seventy-two" (10:1, 17). Luke may have written "seventy-two" and later scribes altered his text to agree with the Hebrew text of Genesis 10.

Sent them two by two (10:1). Going out in twos provides support and security. It is also in line with the Old Testament need for two witnesses to provide valid testimony in court (Num. 35:30; Deut. 19:15).

The harvest is plentiful (10:2). The final gathering of God's people is described with harvest imagery in Isaiah 27:12, suggesting the eschatological significance of Jesus' words. This is the end-time gathering of God's people. The harvest image also conveys a sense of urgency, since crops must be gathered in a timely fashion when they are ripe. The disciples are participating in a unique window of opportunity.

Like lambs among wolves (10:3). This is an image of danger and vulnerability. In the Old Testament Israel's unrighteous leaders are described as ravenous wolves devouring the poor and helpless among God's people.[266] Israel is also described in Jewish literature as sheep living among wolves (*Pss. Sol.* 8:23, 30). A rabbinic conversation dated to the late first century reads, "Hadrian said to R. Jehoshua [c. A.D. 90]: 'There is something great about the sheep [Israel] that can persist among 70 wolves [the nations].' He replied: 'Great is the Shepherd who delivers it and watches over it and destroys them [the wolves] before them [Israel].' "[267]

Do not greet anyone (10:4). A similar command was given by Elisha to his servant Gehazi in 2 Kings 4:29, when he sent him to place his staff on the face of the Shunammite's dead son. The key there, as here, is the urgency of the task.

"Peace to this house" . . . a man of peace (10:5–6). The offer of peace here is more than a greeting. It suggests spiritual wholeness and so represents the offer of the kingdom of God (see 10:10–11). A "man of peace" (lit., "son of peace") is one whose heart is ready to welcome the kingdom.

For the worker deserves his wages (10:7). Paul quotes this proverb in 1 Timothy 5:18.[268] In the former Paul

GALILEE

The map shows the relative locations of Chorazin, Bethsaida, Tyre, and Sidon.

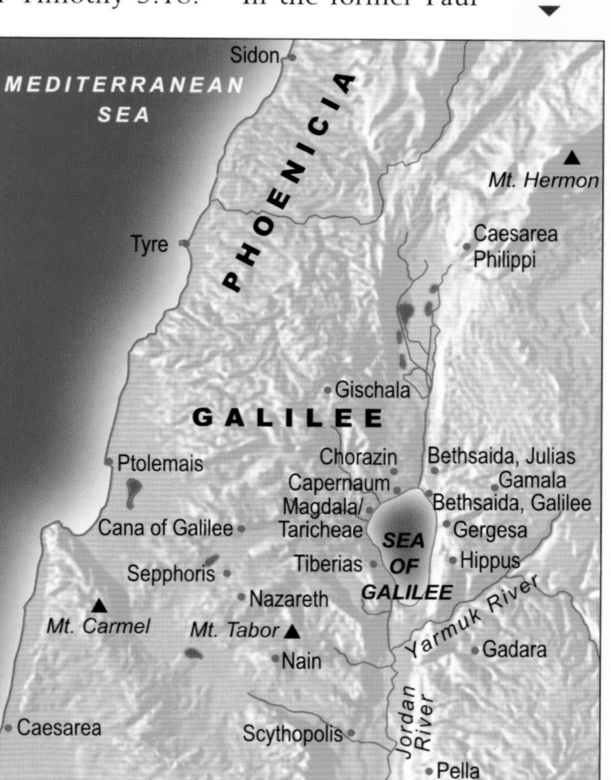

identifies this as the teaching of Jesus and in the latter as "Scripture." This may suggest that Jesus' recorded words were already being treated as authoritative Scripture in Paul's day.

Heal the sick. . . . The kingdom of God is near you (10:9). In Isaiah, the healing of the sick is a sign of the dawn of the new age, the arrival of the kingdom of God.[269] The phrase "is near you" can mean temporal or spatial nearness. Jesus may be saying that the kingdom is about to arrive or that it is already in some sense present in his own person, words, and deeds.

The dust . . . wipe off (10:11). See comments on 9:5.

More bearable on that day for Sodom (10:12). God destroyed Sodom and Gomorrah with fire and brimstone (NIV "burning sulfur") because of their grievous sin (Gen. 18:16–19:29). Their sin and destruction became proverbial already in the Old Testament[270] and are recalled repeatedly in later Jewish tradition. The Mishnah says, "The men of Sodom have no share in the world to come, for it is written, *Now the men of Sodom were wicked and sinners against the Lord exceedingly.*"[271] Yet the sin (and hence the judgment) is even greater for those who reject God's present offer of salvation (see 17:26–30).

Woe to you Korazin . . . Bethsaida (10:13). Korazin has been identified with Khirbet Korazim, three miles north of Tell Hum, the probable site of Capernaum. It is the northernmost city bordering the Sea of Galilee.[272] On Bethsaida see comments on 9:10.

Tyre and Sidon (10:13–14). These were Phoenician (and hence, pagan) cities located on the Mediterranean coast northwest of Galilee (see 6:17). Judgment oracles like those pronounced here are made against Tyre and Sidon in the Old Testament (Isa. 23; Ezek. 28).[273] As bad as Tyre and Sidon were, they would have repented if they had seen the miracles performed in Korazin and Bethsaida.

Sitting in sackcloth and ashes (10:13). "Sackcloth" (*sakkos*) was the material used to make sacks and was normally made of goats' hair. It is often identified in the Old Testament as a garment of mourning and is sometimes associated with ashes.[274] The symbolism of sitting in or being covered with ashes reflects one's utter devastation (Job 2:8), as though one's life were a burned-down house.

Capernaum . . . you will go down to the depths (10:15). Jesus made Capernaum his base of operations (see comments on 4:31; cf. Mark 2:1), yet many rejected him there. Jesus' statement alludes to the judgment against the prideful king of Babylon in Isaiah 14, a text traditionally associated with the fall of Lucifer, or Satan, from heaven (see next note).[275] Though the prideful king thinks he will "ascend to heaven," he will instead be "brought down to the grave [*sheol*]" (Isa. 14:13–15). Similarly, while prideful Capernaum thinks she will be "lifted up" because of Jesus' presence there, her disbelief and rejection of him means she will "go down to the depths." "Depths" here is *hadēs*, the equivalent of the Hebrew *Sheol* of Isaiah 14:14 (LXX *hadēs*). While Isaiah may be referring to physical death, both terms were increasingly used with reference to the place of punishment for the wicked dead (see Luke 16:23).

"I saw Satan fall like lightning from heaven" (10:18). Jesus again alludes to

Isaiah 14:12 (see previous note), linking it explicitly with Satan's fall from heaven (for "Satan" see Luke 4:2). Jesus may be referring to an original fall of Satan, which he saw in his preincarnate state. More likely, he is drawing on the traditional image of Satan's fall to describe his defeat in the present exorcisms of the disciples. Similar imagery related to Satan's defeat appears in John 12:31; Revelation 12:7–17; 20:1–3, 10.

Trample on snakes and scorpions (10:19). Snakes and scorpions were symbols of extreme danger in the Old Testament and Judaism.[276] "Trampling" snakes is evidence of divine protection in Psalm 91:13. The more difficult question is whether these snakes and scorpions represent natural dangers or are symbols for evil spirits. If the latter, a striking parallel appears in the pseudepigraphic *Testament of Levi* 18:12, where the messianic high priest is described as one who will "grant to his children the authority to trample on wicked spirits." Demonic forces are described like scorpions in Revelation 9:3–4, and Satan is the wicked serpent who will ultimately be crushed by the "seed" of the woman.[277] Both views are possible, but the force of the text seems to suggest victory over both natural dangers ("snakes and scorpions") and supernatural ones ("the power of the enemy" = Satan).

Your names are written in heaven (10:20). Jesus is here referring to the common image of a book in heaven that records the names of the righteous. It is found throughout the Old Testament, the New Testament, and Jewish literature.[278] The background is the common practice of ancient cities and kingdoms to keep lists of citizens' names.

Lord of heaven and earth (10:21). This is a Jewish way of addressing God, acknowledging him as the sole Creator of all things.[279]

Hidden . . . from the wise . . . revealed . . . to little children (10:21). In the Old Testament God's wisdom is said to confound the wise (Isa. 29:14). Paul cites this Isaiah text when he points out that in the cross God has made foolish the wisdom of the world.[280] The term *nēpios* ("little child") refers to a child older than an infant, but probably not more than three or four. The image conveys both spiritual need and simple faith in God. Small children are immature and in need of guidance, but their simple faith makes them open to such instruction (cf. Ps. 19:7; 116:6).

No one knows who the Son is except the Father (10:22). The intimacy of relationship between the Father and the Son has parallels to the personification of wisdom in the Old Testament and Judaism. Job 28:21, 23 says that while wisdom "is hidden from the eyes of every living thing . . . God understands the way to it and he alone knows where it dwells." The apocryphal book of Baruch similarly speaks of God's knowledge and revelation of wisdom: "But the one who knows all things knows her [Wisdom], he found her by his understanding . . . and gave her to his servant Jacob."[281]

Blessed (10:23). For beatitudes see comments on 6:20–22.

Blessed are the eyes that see. . . . For . . . many prophets and kings wanted to see what you see . . . (10:23–24). Jesus' statement carries a strong eschatological flavor, reflecting the messianic hopes of Judaism. In the *Psalms of Solomon* (first century B.C.), the psalmist beseeches God to raise up the "Son of David" Messiah to deliver Israel from her enemies, and then reflects: "Blessed are those born in those days to see the good fortune of Israel which God will bring to pass."[282]

The Parable of the Good Samaritan (10:25–37)

This famous parable of Jesus teaches that authentic spiritual life is defined not by ethnic or national heritage, but by love for God and for others. When a "lawyer," an expert in the Mosaic Law, asks Jesus, "And who is my neighbor?" whom he is commanded to love, the man probably intends to limit the scope of his neighborly love and so justify his antipathy toward his enemies. Jesus, however, shatters the common conception of a neighbor by telling a parable in which a despised Samaritan turns out to be the true neighbor because he reaches out in love and self-sacrifice to his enemy.

An expert in the law (10:25). The term here is *nomikos*, "lawyer," and is essentially the same office as a "scribe" (*grammateus*). These were experts in the Old Testament law (see comments on 5:17; 7:30).

"What must I do to inherit eternal life?" (10:25). The same question will be posed later by the rich ruler (18:18–23; cf. Mark 10:17–22). It appears to be a common one in rabbinic dialogue. Rabbi Eliezer (c. A.D. 90) is reported to have been asked by his pupils, "Rabbi, teach us the ways of life so that by them we may attain to the life of the future world."[283] Eternal life as the reward for God's people is promised in Daniel 12:2 and appears frequently in later Jewish literature.[284]

"Love the Lord your God . . ." and, "Love your neighbor as yourself" (10:27). The same two Old Testament texts (Deut. 6:5 and Lev. 19:18) are identified in Mark 12:28–34 as the first and second greatest commands. Both commandments occupied a prominent place in Jewish thought, and there is some evidence that they were linked together already before Jesus' time.[285] The command to love God was constantly before the Jews as they recited the daily prayer known as the *Shema*: "Hear, O Israel: The LORD our God, the LORD is one. Love the LORD your God with all your heart and with all your soul and with all your strength" (Deut. 6:4–5).

You have answered correctly (10:28). Jesus is not suggesting that salvation is by works. Rather, authentic acts of love arise from an attitude of faith. Through his parable, Jesus will expose the man's failure to truly love his neighbor. As in the case of David's sin, the parable will serve to catch the man in his shortcomings.[286]

And who is my neighbor? (10:29). A "neighbor" would normally have been identified as a fellow Israelite, though in Leviticus 19:34 this is extended to resident aliens living in Israel. It would not commonly include Samaritans or Gentiles. Indeed, the community at Qumran explicitly called for love for the "sons of light" (=members of the community) and hate for the "sons of darkness."[287] In the Wisdom of Jesus Ben Sirach, the author writes,

> *If you do good, know to whom you*
> *do it. . . .*
> *Give to the devout, but do not help*
> *the sinner.*
> *Do good to the humble, but do not*
> *give to the ungodly;*

hold back their bread, and do not give
it to them,
for by means of it they might
subdue you;
then you will receive twice as
much evil
for all the good you have done
to them.
For the Most High also hates sinners
and will inflict punishment on
the ungodly.
Give to the one who is good, but do
not help the sinner.[288]

While exhortations to love one's enemies were not unheard of in the ancient world (see Luke 6:27–28), conventional wisdom called for love for one's friends and hate for one's enemies. Sirach reveals Israel's distrust and hatred for the Samaritans and other surrounding nations when he writes: "Two nations my soul detests, and the third is not even a people: Those who live in Seir, and the Philistines, and the foolish people that live in Shechem" (Sir. 50:25–26). Seir is a designation for the Edomites (or Idumeans), the descendants of Esau southeast of Israel. The Philistines were the coastal peoples to the east. Shechem was the center of the northern kingdom of Israel and a euphemism for Samaria in Sirach's time. As a "half-breed" race with a perverted form of worship, the "foolish" Samaritans are not even to be reckoned as a real people (see comments on Luke 9:52).

Going down from Jerusalem to Jericho (10:30). This is a stark and desolate seventeen-mile road, dropping from over 2,500 feet above sea level in Jerusalem to approximately 800 feet below sea level at Jericho.[289] It was a dangerous place, and robbers often lay in wait for unprotected travelers.

A priest . . . a Levite . . . passed by on the other side (10:31–32). The Levites were the descendants of Levi, one of the twelve sons of Jacob (by Leah). Unlike the other tribes of Israel, they were not given a tribal allotment in the land (Num. 35:2–3; Deut. 18:1; Josh. 14:3), but were rather consecrated as

ROAD FROM JERUSALEM TO JERICHO

The road followed this gorge, known as the Wadi Kelt. St. George's Monastery is visible in this photo.

JERUSALEM TO JERICHO

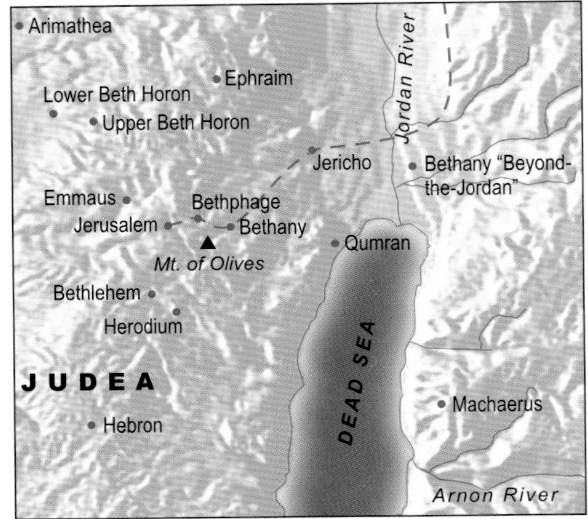

God's special tribe in place of the firstborn of all the Israelites (Num. 3:41, 45; 8:18). Their role was to assist the priests in the service of the tabernacle (Num. 18:4) and later the temple. Levites are mentioned only three times in the New Testament.[290]

The priests were also Levites, but were more specifically descendants of Aaron, the brother of Moses and first priest of Israel (Ex. 28:1–3). They were entrusted with the religious oversight of the nation, including teaching the law (Lev. 10:11; Deut. 17:18), administering the temple and the sacrificial system, and inspecting uncleanness, especially leprosy, in the people (Lev. 13–14).

Touching a dead body rendered priests and Levites ceremonially unclean and so unable to fulfill temple commitments (Lev. 21–22). The two who passed by may have suspected the man was dead. For the priest, however, this is a poor excuse, since he is specifically said to be "going down" the road and so presumably traveling *away* from Jerusalem after his temple service. Many priests were also members of the aristocratic elite and so would not associate with commoners. Jewish hearers may therefore have expected such snobbery from these two. Perhaps they would have expected a local rabbi or a respected Pharisee to come along next and help the man . . . .But a Samaritan?

Pouring on oil and wine (10:34). Both oil and wine had medicinal value (Isa. 1:6; *m. Šabb.* 19:2). The oil soothed and the wine served as a disinfectant.

Took him to an inn (10:34). The term *pandocheion* refers to a public lodging place, run by an "innkeeper" (*pandocheus*, 10:35), where a traveler might rent a room. See comments on 2:7 for the distinction between this and the so-called "inn" (*katalyma*) of the nativity story.

Two silver coins (10:35). The Greek says "two denarii." A denarius was equivalent to a day's wages for a laborer.

REFLECTIONS

LOVING GOD AND LOVING YOUR neighbor are the two greatest commandments. But who is your neighbor? When Jesus was asked this question, he told a story that shocked his hearers. A true neighbor is one who is willing to look past the differences that traditionally divide people and to love others unconditionally and without prejudice. Who would God have you to reach out to today?

At the Home of Martha and Mary (10:38–42)

The account of Jesus' visit to the home of Martha and Mary demonstrates the importance of learning from Jesus and being in relationship with him. Such a relationship takes priority even over service. When Martha complains to Jesus that her sister Mary is neglecting her household duties and leaving all the work to her, Jesus gently corrects her. While Martha is occupied with things, Mary is occupied with Jesus. She has chosen the better, which "will not be taken away from her." The "better" is the privilege of learning at Jesus' feet as a faithful disciple.

A village where a woman named Martha opened her home to him (10:38). We learn from John's Gospel that Mary, Martha, and their brother, Lazarus, are good friends of Jesus.[291] They live in Bethany, a few miles east of Jerusalem (see Luke 19:29). The invitation to Jesus is identified specifically with Martha, the matron of the home.

Mary, who sat at the Lord's feet (10:39). To sit at the feet of a respected rabbi was the position of a disciple. In Acts 22:3 Paul says he was instructed "at the feet of Gamaliel" (NRSV), a leading rabbi of Jerusalem (cf. Luke 8:35). The Mishnah speaks of a similar position: "Let thy house be a meeting-house for the Sages and sit amid the dust of their feet and drink in their words with thirst."[292] Mary's initiative in taking this position is particularly shocking, since rabbis did not have women disciples. Girls did not even receive a formal education; they were taught only in household duties like sewing and weaving.[293] In the Mishnah it is said that "if any man give his daughter a knowledge of the Law it is as though he taught her lechery."[294]

Martha was distracted by all the preparations (10:40). Literally, "distracted by much service [*diakonia*]." Jewish society placed a high value on hospitality, and a woman's honor and reputation depended on her ability to manage her household well.[295] Since service was a woman's highest calling, Martha's complaint against Mary would be seen as legitimate. Yet for Jesus all her hard work is a mere distraction compared to Mary's desire to sit at Jesus' feet as a disciple and learn from him. Jesus shatters cultural expectations by affirming the status of a woman as his disciple.

Jesus' Teaching on Prayer (11:1–13)

Luke here presents various teachings of Jesus on prayer, stressing dependence and trust in God. When his disciples ask him to teach them to pray, Jesus gives them a simple model prayer that sums up the essence of effective communication with God (11:1–4).

Jesus follows this model prayer with a parable about prayer (11:5–8). The parable of the persistent neighbor has been interpreted in two different ways. Some have argued that it is similar to the parable of the unjust judge (18:1–8), teaching God's desire for his people to be bold and persistent in prayer.

For others the parable is not about persistence (the borrower only asks once) or about boldness (what the man does is a cultural necessity, not a bold action), but about issues of honor and shame.[296] It must be understood in the context of Palestinian peasant society, where hospitality was the highest of values and the obligation of the entire community. The man who receives the traveler does not have enough food to provide the necessary level of hospitality, so he *must* go to a neighbor. This is expected behavior. While the sleeping neighbor has no *desire* to help because of the inconvenience involved, *not* helping would be unthinkable, an act of shame. Jesus concludes that while the sleeper may not get up because of friendship (notice he does not address the borrower as "friend"), he will get up to retain honor for himself and for the community. In this case, the parable teaches that God will surely answer prayers because it is a question of his honor and glory.

Whether the parable is about persistence in prayer or about God's honor, the proverb that follows turns to the petitioner's responsibility to pray and the certainty that God will answer (11:9–10). It is a natural transition from this proverb to Jesus' analogy of a father granting the request of a son. Fathers naturally desire to meet the needs of their children with good gifts. If this is true of sinful human beings, how much more will it be true of our loving heavenly Father, who gives us the greatest gift of all, the Holy Spirit (11:11–13).

Father (11:2). The Greek address *pater* almost certainly has behind it the Aramaic *Abba*, the term of intimacy that Jesus used to address God (Mark 14:36) and that he encouraged his disciples to use.[297] While it has been commonly said that *Abba* is a children's term meaning "daddy," this is not quite right, since Jewish adults also addressed their parents in this way. *Abba* was, however, a term of considerable intimacy. While Jews would sometimes refer to God as "our heavenly Father," they rarely if ever addressed him as "my father" or "father" (*Abba*).[298] Jesus calls his followers to a new intimacy with God through his unique relationship with the Father.

Hallowed be your name, your kingdom come (11:2). The petition means "cause your name to be honored." It points both to God's ultimate victory at the establishment of his kingdom, but also to the present, as God's people "hallow" his name through righteous living. "Your name" was a Jewish expression for "you" and a way of avoiding the holy name of God. There are interesting parallels to the Jewish prayer in Aramaic known as the *Qaddish* ("holy"), recited after the sermon in synagogue services:

Exalted and hallowed be his
great name
in the world which he created
according to his will.
May he let his kingdom rule
in your lifetime and in your days
and in the lifetime
of the whole house of Israel speedily
and soon.
Praised be his great name from
eternity to eternity.
And to this, say: Amen.[299]

Give us each day our daily bread (11:3). "Bread" here means "food" (cf. 7:33; 2 Thess. 3:8). The word translated "daily" (*epiousion*) is a rare Greek word with an uncertain meaning. It can mean (1) "necessary for existence," (2) "for today," or (3) "for the coming day." The reference recalls God's daily provision of manna for Israel in the desert (Ex. 16), as well as God's daily sustenance of his people (Prov. 30:8).

Forgive us our sins, for we also forgive (11:4). The idea that forgiven people should be willing to forgive was a common one in Judaism. Sirach 28:2 reads: "Forgive your neighbor the wrong he has done, and then your sins will be pardoned when you pray."

Lead us not into temptation (11:4). This phrase has caused difficulties since God does not tempt his people (James 1:13). One solution is that the word "temptation" (*peirasmos*) can also mean "trial" or "testing." Some have argued that this is a technical term for the eschatological "hour of trial" of the tribulation period (Rev. 3:10). Yet such a specific case would be odd in Jesus' general teaching on prayer. The term can mean testing in general, and there are certainly Old Testament examples where God tests his people.[300] Yet it would be unusual for Jesus to encourage prayer for the removal of all tests of faith. It seems best to retain the translation "temptation," not in the sense of "do not tempt us," but rather in terms of active protection from temptation (something like, "Protect us from the tempting power of sin"). Jesus says something similar in Luke 22:40, 46: "Pray that you will not fall into temptation." A prayer in the Babylonian Talmud reads, "Bring me not into the power of sin, nor into the power of guilt, nor into the power of temptation."[301]

At midnight . . . a friend of mine on a journey (11:5–6). While Bedouins in the desert often traveled by night to avoid the heat of the night, such travel was uncommon in Palestine. The friend's arrival is something unusual and inconvenient for those who must provide hospitality.[302]

Lend me three loaves of bread (11:5). It is debated among scholars whether bread was baked daily or less often in Palestinian villages. The latter seems more likely, with village women cooperating in the baking.[303] Everyone in the village knew who had baked most recently. Though some of the day's bread may have been left in the borrower's house, to feed a guest a broken loaf would have been an insult.

I have nothing to set before him (11:6). As in Middle Eastern culture today, hospitality was of critical importance in first-century Palestine and involved the whole community. Both the host who received a late night guest and the man already in bed would have been obligated to provide the best for the traveler. Jesus' hearers would have considered the "hassles" of getting up and unbolting the door a minor inconvenience compared to the scandal of not providing adequate hospitality.

The door is already locked, and my children are with me in bed (11:7). This is a peasant home where the whole family sleeps in a single room on mats on the floor. A wooden or iron bar through rings secures the door. To get up and unbolt it would disturb the whole family.

Because of the man's boldness (11:8). The Greek term *anaideia* normally carries the negative sense of "shamelessness." This is interpreted in the NIV positively in the sense of "boldness" or persistence and is applied to the borrower who is at the door. The Greek is ambiguous, however, and may refer to the sleeper, whose "shamelessness" would be revealed if he *failed* to provide bread for hospitality.[304] Bailey takes a similar approach, claiming that the term here means "avoidance of shame" and that the sleeper gets up so as to avoid the shame that would come to him if he did not provide hospitality.[305]

A fish . . . a snake . . . an egg . . . a scorpion (11:11–12). Fish bear a general resemblance to snakes in their slimy appearance. The parallel between eggs and scorpions may be because the latter roll themselves into balls[306] (see comments on 10:19 for snakes and scorpions as symbols of danger and evil).

If you then, though you are evil . . . how much more (11:13). This is a common rabbinic "lesser to greater" (*qal wāḥômer*) argument.

Jesus and Beelzebub (11:14–28)

This episode begins a series of controversies between Jesus and the religious leaders that will run through the rest of chapter 11. It will climax in 11:54 with their growing opposition and desire to trap him in his words.

The first controversy arises from Jesus' exorcism of a mute man. When some of Jesus' opponents accuse him of casting out demons by the power of Beelzebub, he answers with two arguments. (1) He points out how foolish it would be for Satan to cast out his own demonic forces, since a house or kingdom divided against itself cannot stand (11:17–18). (2) He notes that their accusation would indict their own followers, who also claim to perform exorcisms (11:19).

Jesus then goes on the offensive. Since his exorcisms are the work of God and not Satan, they reveal the presence and power of God's kingdom (11:20). Satan is like a strong man whose castle is being disarmed and overpowered by Jesus, the stronger man (11:20–23). Jesus then warns of the danger of exorcism without the inward spiritual renewal that comes with the kingdom of God (11:24–26).

Jesus' teaching on exorcism is followed by a short episode in which a woman in the crowd shouts an acclamation of praise for Jesus. Jesus, however, directs the praise away from himself and toward the message of the kingdom of God: "Blessed rather are those who hear the word of God and obey it" (11:27–28). True spiritual blessings come not through the acclamation of others, but through obedience to God's Word.

A demon that was mute (11:14). For the link between disease and demonic possession see comments on 4:39. In Isaiah

Beelzebub, the Prince of Demons

The Greek text actually reads *beelzeboul* (in some manuscripts) and *beezeboul* (other manuscripts). The spelling *beelzebub*, which appears in the NIV, comes from the Latin version (and the KJV), which has assimilated the text to 2 Kings 1:2, 3, 6. The historical background to the name is disputed. The prefix "Beel-" comes from the Canaanite god Baal (meaning "lord"), and Baal-Zebul probably means either "Baal, the Prince," or "Baal of the Exalted Abode."[A-41] The Israelites seem to have mocked this name, changing it to Baal-Zebub (Gk. *beelzeboub*), meaning "lord of the flies" (see Judg. 10:6; 2 Kings 1:2, 3, 6).[A-42]

Whatever its origin, the name Beelzeboul eventually came to be used in Judaism for the "prince of demons," the highest ranking angel in heaven prior to his fall.[A-43] The literature of Judaism contains a variety of names for the chief of demons. The book of *Jubilees* refers to the chief of the spirits as Mastema, a Hebrew term presumably meaning "hostility."[A-44] In the apocryphal book of Tobit the head of the demons is Asmodeus (Tobit 3:8, 17), and in *1 Enoch* 6:1 Semyaz is the leader of the fallen angels (cf. *1 Enoch* 8:7). Belial, or Beliar, meaning "the worthless one," is one of the most common names for Satan in the Dead Sea Scrolls and elsewhere in Judaism.[A-45] The New Testament refers to Satan by a variety of names, including the devil, the evil one (Matt. 6:13; 13:19), the father of lies (John 8:44), the god of this age (2 Cor. 4:4), the ruler of the kingdom of the air (Eph. 2:2), the dragon (Rev. 12:9), and the ancient serpent (12:9).

35:6, the healing of those who are mute is a sign of God's end-time salvation. For demons and demonization see comments on Luke 4:31–37; 8:26–39.

Asking for a sign from heaven (11:16). It is not clear what kind of a sign they are requesting. Signs from heaven in the Old Testament include the sun standing still (Josh. 10:13), the provision of manna from heaven (Ex. 16), and the turning back of the sun for Hezekiah.[307] There are also eschatological signs in the heavens predicted in the Old Testament.[308]

Any kingdom divided against itself will be ruined (11:17). Throughout history, civil war has weakened and destroyed nations from within. A first-century Jewish hearer would certainly think of the civil war that divided Israel and Judah (1 Kings 12), resulting in weakness and eventual destruction. More recently, the Roman occupation of Palestine took place during a period of division and conflict within the Hasmonean dynasty.

By whom do your followers (11:19). Lit., "your sons." The "sons" of the Pharisees, like the "sons of the prophets" (e.g., 2 Kings 2:3, RSV), were disciples or followers of the Pharisees. For Jewish exorcisms see the texts cited in "Demonization and Exorcism in the First Century" at Luke 8:26–39.

I drive out demons by the finger of God (11:20). While Matthew has "the Spirit of God," Luke has "the finger of God." The two expressions mean essentially the same thing—God's power—but Luke's reference alludes back to Exodus 8:19, where Pharaoh's magicians recognize the "finger of God" in Moses' miracles. The Ten Commandments are also said to have been inscribed by God's finger (Ex. 31:18; Deut. 9:10), and in Psalm 8:3 the heavens are said to be the work of God's fingers. Anthropomorphic images, especially the "hand" of God or the "arm" of God, are common in the Old Testament.

When a strong man, fully armed, guards his own house (11:21). While Mark's parallel presents an image of household robbery (Mark 3:27), the picture here is one of warfare, with two lords battling over a castle estate. Through his exorcisms, Jesus is disarming Satan and taking the spoils (=people bound by him) from his castle. The reference to "dividing the spoils" may be an allusion to Isaiah 53:12 and the ultimate victory of the Suffering Servant of the Lord.

He who is not with me is against me (11:23). This picks up the battle image of the previous verses. In Joshua 5:13, Joshua meets the commander of the Lord's army and, unaware of his identity, asks, "Are you for us or for our enemies?"

He who does not gather with me, scatters (11:23). This second image is probably related to the gathering of sheep. In the Old Testament, Israel is often identified as a flock and the Lord as their shepherd.[309]

Takes seven other spirits (11:26). The number "seven" may indicate completeness or may simply emphasize the greater power now controlling the man. There are verbal parallels in the "seven spirits" that are before the throne of God in Revelation 1:4; 3:1; 4:5; 5:6 and in the "seven angels" who stand before the glory of the Lord.[310]

Blessed is the mother who gave you birth (11:27). The Greek says literally, "Blessed is the womb that bore you and breasts at which you nursed," a figure of speech known as synecdoche, whereby a part of something is used for the whole. The NIV replaces "womb" and "breasts" with the thing signified, "mother." For a similar statement about Mary see 1:42.

It was common both in Greco-Roman and Jewish society to praise a child by congratulating the mother. The first-century Roman satirist Petronius writes, "How blessed is the mother who bore such an one as you."[311] The famous Rabbi Johannan ben Zakkai is said to have praised his student Joshua ben Hananiah with the statement, "Happy is she that bare him."[312]

The Sign of Jonah (11:29–32)

In 11:16 some responded to Jesus' miracles by asking for a sign from heaven. Jesus now answers by declaring that only one more sign will be given to this wicked generation, the "sign of Jonah" (11:29–30). In Matthew's Gospel this sign is identified with Jesus' resurrection (Matt. 12:40). For Luke, the stress seems to be on Jonah's preaching and call for repentance (see Luke 11:32). At the final judgment, those who *did* respond to God's word—the Queen of Sheba and the people of Nineveh—will condemn the present generation for rejecting a greater witness than Solomon or Jonah.

JONAH AND THE FISH

A Byzantine era pottery sherd.

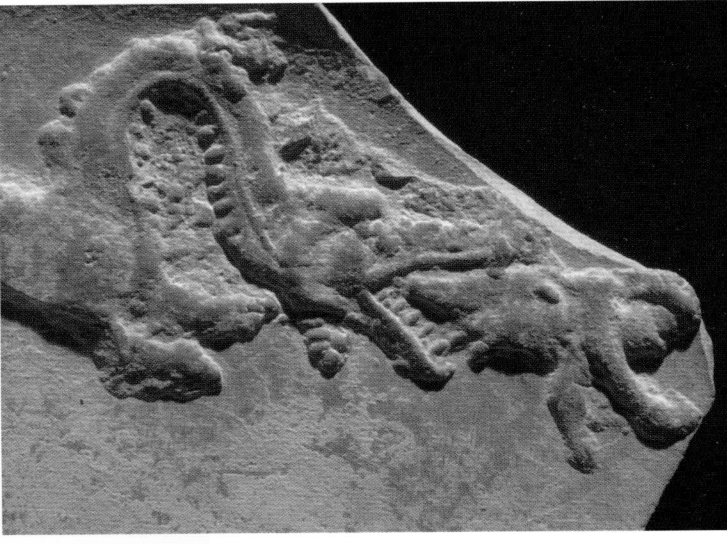

A wicked generation (11:29). See comments on 9:41.

Jonah (11:30). Jonah, the son of Amittai, is mentioned in 2 Kings 14:25 as well as the book of Jonah. He was from Gath Hepher in Zebulun and ministered from about 800–750 BC, predicting the restoration of Israel's borders during the reign of Jeroboam II. Jonah is best known, of course, from the book of Jonah, where he rejected God's call to preach his impending judgment against wicked Nineveh, the great city of the Assyrian empire (Jonah 1:1–2). When Jonah fled on a ship bound for Tarshish (probably a city in Spain), God pursued him with a storm. Jonah ended up in the belly of a great fish, where he repented and was spit up on dry land. Jonah finally fulfilled God's call to preach to Nineveh. When the city repented, however, Jonah was not pleased, for his hopes were placed on its destruction. The book ends with God's rebuke to Jonah (and implicitly, to the nation Israel) for his lack of compassion for a lost world.

The Queen of the South (11:31). This is the queen of Sheba, mentioned in 1 Kings 10:1–29 (cf. 2 Chron. 9:1–12), who traveled a great distance (the "ends of the earth" is hyperbole) to hear Solomon's wisdom. Sheba was located in southern Arabia.

Solomon's wisdom (11:31). In 1 Kings 3 Solomon asks for a discerning heart to rule God's people well. The Lord was pleased with this request and granted him not only wisdom, but also riches, power, and long life (1 Kings 3:10–15). Solomon's wisdom is said to be greater than all the kings of the earth (4:29–34; 10:23–24) and far surpassed the queen's expectations (10:6–9).

The men of Nineveh ... repented (11:32). Nineveh's notorious wickedness is identified in the book of Jonah as the reason for her impending judgment.[313] The city's extraordinary conversion through the preaching of Jonah stands in stark contrast to Israel's failure to respond to Jesus' even more powerful words and deeds.

The Lamp of the Body (11:33–36)

Jesus' teaching on hearing and responding to God's word continues with two analogies related to light and darkness. In the first, Jesus' kingdom proclamation is like light from a lamp that must shine forth for all to see. The second analogy takes this meaning forward with reference to the person receiving the light. Just as external light must be taken in by the eye in order to benefit the body, so Jesus' teaching must be appropriated by the person.

No one lights a lamp (11:33). See 8:16 for a similar lamp image.

In a place where it will be hidden (11:33). This phrase translates the Greek word *kryptē*, which indicates a dark and hidden place. It was commonly used of cellars, crypts, and vaults.[314] Since Palestinian homes did not usually have cellars, Luke may be referring to a hidden alcove or wall recess.

LAMP

Your eye is the lamp of your body (11:34). Some Greek writers considered the eye to be a source of light that shone outward to illuminate objects.[315] While this could be the sense intended here, more likely Jesus means that the eye is the lamp *for* the body, that is, it lets light *in* so that the person can see.

When your eyes are good ... when they are bad (11:34). The word translated "good" is the Greek word *haplous*, which means literally "single" or "simple." It can be used of eyes in the sense of "healthy" or "sound," but can also carry moral connotations of goodness or generosity. There is probably a play on words here, since *ponēros* can mean either "unhealthy" or "evil."

Light ... darkness (11:34). Light and darkness were common symbols for good and evil in both Greek and Hebrew literature.[316] The Qumran community, which produced the Dead Sea Scrolls, considered themselves to be the "sons of light" at spiritual war against the "sons of darkness" (cf. 16:8).

Six Woes (11:37–54)

The references to those who receive the light and those who reject it transitions naturally into an indictment by Jesus of the Pharisees, who are rejecting his message of the kingdom of God. The whole passage has the tone of the Old Testament prophets, who rebuked the nation of Israel for her wickedness and hypocrisy (e.g., Isa. 1). The context is a banquet setting with a Pharisee. When he is surprised that Jesus does not wash in the traditional manner, Jesus responds by noting the hypocrisy of the Pharisees. Though they "clean the outside of the cup"—an external show of religiosity—inside they are full of greed and wickedness. Jesus then launches into a series of six "woes" against the hypocrisy and pride of the Jewish religious leaders. They respond with fierce opposition, seeking to trap Jesus through his words.

A Pharisee (11:37). See comments on 5:17.

Reclined at the table (11:37). The reclining position may indicate a banquet setting or a Sabbath meal.[317] Jews normally ate two meals a day, a mid-morning and a mid-afternoon meal. Three meals were eaten on the Sabbath.[318] The word Luke uses in verse 38 (*ariston*) normally indicates the mid-morning meal.

TOMB OF THE PROPHETS

This tomb on the Mount of Olives contains over 30 burial shafts (*kokhim*). A medieval Jewish tradition claims this tomb was the burial place of Haggai, Zecharaiah, and Malachi.

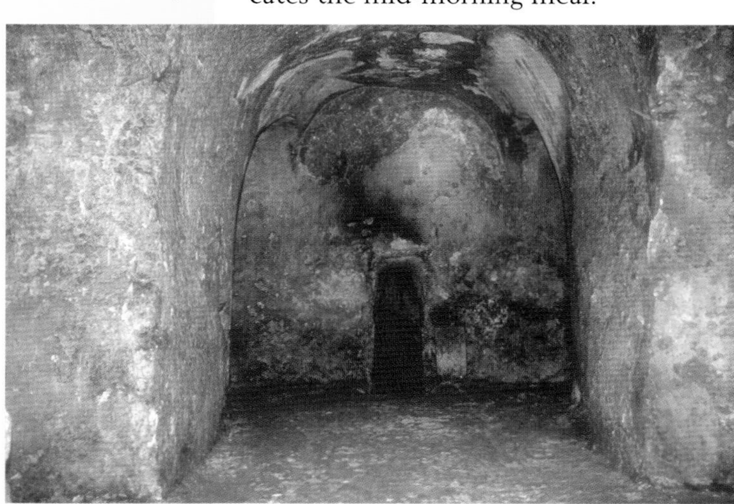

Jesus did not first wash (11:38). This is a ceremonial washing of the hands before the meal (see Mark 7:1–5 for a fuller description). The Pharisees had developed detailed regulations concerning the amount of water to be used, the kinds of vessels from which to pour, and the manner of pouring.[319] Such minutia was not commanded in the Old Testament.

You Pharisees clean the outside of the cup (11:39). The Old Testament law refers to occasions where a cup was to be cleaned or destroyed when something ceremonially unclean fell in it (Lev. 11:33) or if someone unclean touched it (Lev. 15:12). The Pharisees set out detailed regulations to govern the cleaning of vessels of various kinds.[320] Jesus' point is that the Pharisees are concerned with "externals" while ignoring the real matters of the heart.

Greed (11:39). This is a strong Greek word (*harpagē*), which can mean violent greed, robbery, extortion, or plunder.

Give what is inside the dish to the poor (11:41). The Greek literally says, "Give as alms what is inside. . . ." Giving alms to the poor was a sign of great piety in Judaism since it reflected God's mercy and care for the poor. The apocryphal book of Tobit says, "Prayer with fasting is good, but better than both is almsgiving with righteousness. . . . For almsgiving saves from death and purges away every sin. Those who give alms will enjoy a full life."[321]

Woe to you (11:42). For "woes" see comments on 6:20–26.

A tenth of your mint, rue . . . herbs (11:42). Tithing of crops and livestock was commanded in the Old Testament, and the Mishnah discusses tithing requirements in great detail.[322] Interestingly, *m. Šebiʿit* 9:1 lists "rue" as one of the herbs that is exempt from tithing. Jesus' point is that the Pharisees are meticulous in the small things, but then ignore the truly important things, like justice and love for God. God's demand for justice is a leading theme among the prophets.[323]

The most important seats in the synagogues (11:43). These are the places of honor near the front, where the leading elders sit.

Greetings in the marketplaces (11:43). These are not simple greetings, but honorary greetings of an inferior to a superior. Later Jewish literature speaks of the need to greet first a teacher of the Mosaic law.[324]

Unmarked graves (11:44). Touching a grave rendered a Jew ceremonially unclean because of the corpse inside (cf. Num. 5:2). If a grave was unmarked someone might accidentally touch it (cf. the "whitewashed tombs" of Matt. 23:27). Jesus' point is that while the Pharisees consider themselves to be pure, they are defiling everyone with whom they come in contact.

Experts in the law (11:45). Luke uses the term *nomikos* ("lawyer") here. See comments on 5:17 for their close association with the Pharisees.

Tombs for the prophets (11:47). It was common during this time to build tombs in honor of the prophets and other Old Testament figures. David's tomb is mentioned in Acts 2:29–30.

Your forefathers who killed them (11:47). Israel's persecution of the prophets is a common theme in the Old Testament.[325]

God in his wisdom said (11:49). The Greek says literally, "The wisdom of God said. . . ." Wisdom is often personified in the Old Testament and in Judaism, speaking God's word and imparting his wisdom to humanity.[326] The reference here could be to Jesus, who is God's wisdom incarnate, or to God himself (the NIV takes the latter interpretation). The quote that follows ("I will send them prophets . . .") is not from any known source.

This generation will be held responsible for the blood (11:50). The sense of corporate and accumulated guilt is a common theme in the Old Testament and in Judaism. Later generations suffer for the sins of their ancestors.[327] The language here echoes the Old Testament requirements for the death penalty for murder. Blood must be atoned for with blood.[328] In the Old Testament God promises to avenge the blood of his righteous servants.[329]

The blood of Abel to the blood of Zechariah (11:51). The murder of Abel by his brother Cain is recorded in Genesis 4:8. The stoning of Zechariah son of Jehoiada appears in 2 Chronicles 24:20–22 and was expanded upon in later Jewish tradition.[330] In the Hebrew canon, Chronicles is placed at the very end, as part of the section called the Writings. Jesus is thus saying, "from the first murder in the first book to the last murder in the last."

The key to knowledge (11:52). The "key" here may refer to access to the kingdom of God (see Matt. 16:19; 23:13) or perhaps to the "house of wisdom" of

Proverbs 9:1–4.[331] Though the scribes are to provide the people with access to God's Word, instead they are obscuring it from them.

Warnings and Encouragements (12:1–12)

After describing Jesus' confrontation with the religious leaders in chapter 11, Luke turns in chapter 12 to his instruction for the coming time of crisis. Jesus' popularity is high as a crowd of thousands gathers to hear him. Yet his teaching is directed primarily to his disciples (12:1), since his greatest focus now is to train them as he journeys to Jerusalem.

The yeast of the Pharisees (12:1). The background here is the Passover command to the Jews to remove all yeast from their homes and not to eat unleavened bread for seven days (Ex. 12:14–20). Yeast became a symbol in Judaism for the permeating power of sin (cf. 1 Cor. 5:6).[332]

There is nothing concealed that will not be disclosed (12:2). Proverbs 15:3 says, "The eyes of the LORD are everywhere, keeping watch on the wicked and the good." The reference here is to eschatological judgment. Since God sees and knows all things, every human deed will be righteously judged.[333]

HINNOM VALLEY

"Gehenna" was located along the west and south sides of Jerusalem.

Do not be afraid of those who kill the body (12:4). Such is the appropriate attitude for a martyr, whose focus is on heavenly realities. In *4 Maccabees*, a first-century Jewish text about the martyrdom of a man named Eleazar and his seven sons during the Maccabean period, the statement is made, "Let us not fear him who thinks he is killing us.... For if we so die, Abraham and Isaac and Jacob will welcome us, and all the fathers will praise us."[334]

To throw you into hell (12:5). The word "hell" is the Greek term *geenna*, a transliteration of the Hebrew Gehenna. It means "the Valley of (the son[s] of) Hinnom," a ravine running along the southwestern edge of Jerusalem (also called Topheth in the Old Testament). The valley became notorious as a place where the sons and daughters of Judah were offered as burnt sacrifices to the god Baal Molech.[335] Later it was used as a place to burn rubbish (Jer. 19:2, 10–13). The continually burning fire and stench provided an appropriate metaphor for the place of fiery judgment prepared for the wicked. God's judgment is already associated with fire in the Old Testament (Deut. 32:22), and a fiery place of torment for the wicked appears in Jewish and Christian literature.[336]

Five sparrows sold for two pennies (12:6). The word for penny here is *assarion*, a Roman copper coin worth only one-sixteenth of a denarius (see 7:41). The sparrow was one of the cheapest things sold in the marketplace and may have been eaten by the poor.[337] If God remembers even these "worthless" birds, how much more does he care for human beings.

The very hairs of your head are all numbered (12:7). Like the sparrow image in verse 6, this is a "from the lesser to the greater" (*qal wāḥômer*) style of Jewish argument. If God knows such insignificant details, how much more does he care for the important things. A similar image appears in the Old Testament, where "not a hair" being damaged means complete protection from harm.[338]

The Son of Man will also acknowledge him (12:8). The image here is of the throne room of God on the Day of Judgment. The reference to the Son of Man recalls the judgment scene in Daniel 7:7–14. For background on the Son of Man, see comments on Luke 5:24; 9:26.

Before the angels of God (12:8). When the throne room of God is described in Scripture, angelic attendants are present (see Isa. 6:1–4; Rev. 4:6–11). They are gathered here for the Day of Judgment.

Anyone who blasphemes against the Holy Spirit (12:10). Though blasphemy against the Spirit is not mentioned in the Old Testament, it does contain references to rebellion against and grieving the Spirit of God in the context of Israel's failure in the desert (Ps. 106:32–33; Isa. 63:10). The reference here (as in Mark 3:29) appears to be final rejection of the Spirit's revelation through Jesus, resulting in the certainty of judgment. This is because the Holy Spirit provides the authenticating evidence of the truth. It is turning to the darkness in the face of the greatest light.

Synagogues, rulers and authorities (12:11). Synagogues served as both administrative and worship centers in first-century Judaism, so the early Jewish Christians received trials and sentences there (cf. the disciples before the Sanhedrin in Acts 4:1–22; 5:17–42; 6:12–15). "Rulers and authorities" probably refer to Roman and other Gentile authorities (see Luke 21:12).

The Parable of the Rich Fool (12:13–21)

The parable of the rich fool demonstrates the dangers of covetousness and of not recognizing that our resources are merely gifts from God to be used for his service. A striking parallel appears in the book of Sirach:

> One becomes rich through diligence and self-denial, and the reward allotted to him is this: when he says, "I have found rest, and now I shall feast on my goods!" he does not know how long it will be until he leaves them to others and dies. (Sir. 11:18–19)

Teacher (12:13). Rabbis of that day often served as mediators for disputes, particularly those that involved the interpretation of the Mosaic law.

Divide the inheritance with me (12:13). The Old Testament laws of inheritance are set out in Numbers 27:1–11 and Deuteronomy 21:15–17. Rabbinic expansions of these laws appear in the Mishnah.[339] The firstborn son was to receive a double portion of the inheritance (Deut. 21:17). It is this "birthright" that Jacob purchased from Esau in Genesis 25:29–34. Since the man here assumes he is in the right (he does not ask Jesus to mediate, but rather tells him what to do!), he is probably a younger son asking for the share he deserves according to the law. Jesus' response concerning the insignificance of possessions would have been shocking in a society where inheritance and land rights were of great social importance.

Be on your guard against all kinds of greed (12:15). Commands and warnings against greed and covetousness are common in the Old Testament,[340] in Judaism,[341] and in the early church.[342] The *Testament of Judah* 19:1 (second century B.C.) reads, "My children, love of money leads to idolatry, because once they are led astray by money, they designate as gods those who are not gods. It makes anyone who has it go out of his mind."

The pseudepigraphic work *1 Enoch* speaks of the ultimate destruction of those who accumulate wealth:

> *Woe unto you who gain silver and*
> *gold by unjust means;*
> *you will then say, "We have grown*
> *rich and accumulated goods,*
> *we have acquired everything that we*
> *have desired.*
> *So now let us do whatever we like;*
> *for we have gathered silver,*
> *we have filled our treasuries (with*
> *money) like water.*
> *And many are the laborers in our*
> *houses."*
> *Your lies flow like water.*
> *For your wealth shall not endure*
> *but it shall take off from you quickly*
> *for you have acquired it all unjustly,*
> *and you shall be given over to a great*
> *curse.* (1 Enoch *97:8–10)*

GRAIN STORAGE BIN

The underground grain storage bin at Megiddo.

Take life easy; eat, drink and be merry (12:19). This was a common expression in both Jewish and Greek literature, indicating a carefree, sensuous lifestyle.[343] It was characteristic of the Greek Epicurean lifestyle, which sought comfort and pleasure above everything else in life.

You fool! (12:20). The Greek term for "fool" (*aphrōn*) is a strong one. In this context it indicates not only stupidity, but moral and spiritual deficiency. The term is used in the LXX in Psalm 14:1 (13:1 LXX): "The fool (*aphrōn*) said in his heart, 'There is no God'" (cf. Ps. 53:1 [52:2 LXX]).

Your life will be demanded from you (12:20). The term translated "life" here is *psychē*, which can mean life, soul, or self (cf. 12:19). The meaning here is the whole person—physical as well as spiritual destruction. There is an ironic play on words between 12:19 and 20. The man selfishly speaks to his "soul" (=himself), and it is this very soul that he loses. See 9:24: "For whoever wants to save his life (*psychē*) will lose it. . . ."

Then who will get what you have prepared for yourself? (12:20). The Old Testament speaks of the futility of storing up wealth that will only go to others who have not worked for it.[344]

Do Not Worry (12:22–34)

Jesus' negative illustration about the dangers of greed (12:13–21) is now balanced with positive instruction on how to live a life of trust and dependence on God, free from worry and anxiety. Using a rabbinic "from the lesser to the greater" style of argument, Jesus demonstrates that since God feeds the birds of the air and beautifully clothes the flowers of the field, he will surely care for his own children. Since God has already given us his eternal kingdom, the best one can do is to sell temporal earthly possessions and to give them to the poor.

Consider the ravens . . . God feeds them (12:24). In antiquity ravens were considered careless creatures that even failed to return to their own nests.[345] For the Israelites they were unclean birds, forbidden to be eaten and so of little value (Lev. 11:15; Deut. 14:14). Yet the Old Testament says that God cares for them and provides them with food: "He provides food for the cattle and for the young ravens when they call" (Ps. 147:9; cf. Job 38:41).

Add a single hour to his life (12:25). The Greek here is odd, reading literally "add a single cubit to his length." A cubit (*pēchys*) was a unit of measure of about eighteen inches (the length from the elbow to the end of the hand). The term for "length" (*hēlikia*) can mean either "life span" or "height." While the text could mean "add eighteen inches to his height," this would be odd, since the point is that this is a very little thing! More likely, a person's life is here portrayed as striding forward (in time). Jesus says, "By worrying you cannot add a single step on the road of life."

Consider how the lilies grow (12:27). The "lily" here has been identified with various flowers, including the white lily, the Easter daisy, the autumn crocus, and others.[346] Perhaps the most interesting suggestion is that it is the purple anemone, which is then contrasted with the royal purple of Solomon's robes.[347]

Even Solomon in all his splendor (12:27). Solomon's extraordinary riches are described in 1 Kings 10:4–23 and 2 Chronicles 9:13–21.

Here today, and tomorrow is thrown into the fire (12:28). The temporal and fleeting nature of plants is a common Old Testament image.[348] Dried grass was used to kindle fires.

The pagan world (12:30). The Greek here reads "the nations of the world," a reference to the Gentile world. Remember that Jesus is speaking to a Jewish

LILIES ON THE MOUNT OF BEATITUDES

audience, which viewed Gentiles as antagonistic to God's kingdom values.

But seek his kingdom (12:31). On the kingdom of God, see comments on 4:43; 17:20. Seeking God's kingdom means focusing one's life on things that have eternal value rather than on material things.

Do not be afraid, little flock (12:32). God's people are often identified as his flock in the Old Testament (see comments on 11:23).[349] Since God is a protecting shepherd, they have nothing to fear (on Old Testament commands not to fear, see comments on 1:12).

To give you the kingdom (12:32). On eschatological rulership by God's people, see comments on 22:30.

Give to the poor (12:33). Literally, "give as alms" (for the importance of almsgiving see Tobit 4:8–11 and comments on Luke 11:41). The command is not to make oneself destitute, but to recognize that all of our possessions are to be used for God's purposes.

A treasure in heaven (12:33). Various Jewish texts speak of good works (such as almsgiving) as a means of storing up true treasures.[350] Sirach says, "Lose your silver for the sake of a brother or a friend, and do not let it rust under a stone and be lost. Lay up your treasure according to the commandments of the Most High, and it will profit you more than gold" (Sir. 29:10–11).

REFLECTIONS

IN TODAY'S BUSY WORLD, IT'S EASY to let worry and anxiety control our lives and affect our relationships. Jesus calls on his followers to simple trust and dependence on their heavenly Father. The answer to anxiety is a deep-seated trust and dependence on God, and a focus on his kingdom and purpose in this world. In the end, this is all that really matters.

Watchfulness (12:35–48)

Jesus' call for an eternal perspective on material possessions in 12:22–34 now transitions naturally into a call for good stewardship and readiness for the return of the Son of Man. Jesus draws four analogies, all related to a Middle Eastern household where a master had many servants to manage his affairs.

Dressed ready for service (12:35). Literally, "let your waist be girded." The reference is to long garments that were drawn up around the waist and tucked in so that the servant could move around freely and quickly. In Exodus 12:11 the Passover was to be eaten with "your cloak tucked into your belt" (KJV, "your loins girded"), so that the Israelites could leave Egypt quickly.[351]

Keep your lamps burning (12:35). Having a lamp burning was a sign of vigilance, as with the continually burning lamp outside the curtain of the tabernacle (Ex. 27:20–21; Lev. 24:2).

A wedding banquet (12:36). Wedding banquets were times of extravagant festivities and celebration, lasting an entire week (Judg. 14:17) or even two (Tobit 8:20; 10:7). See comments on 5:34 for more details.

He will dress himself to serve (12:37). The image of a master putting on servants' clothes and serving is a shocking one; it recalls Jesus' washing the disciples' feet in John 13. The scene here is probably meant to represent the messianic banquet, when "the LORD Almighty will prepare a feast of rich food for all peoples" (Isa. 25:6; cf. 65:13–14), and when God's servants will receive their just reward (see comments on Luke 13:29; 14:15).

Second or third watch of the night (12:38). Jewish sources divide the night into three watches (6–10; 10–2; 2–6; see Judg. 7:19) and Roman sources into four (6–9; 9–12; 12–3; 3–6; see Mark 13:35).[352] In either case, this is meant to signify the dead of night.

Thief . . . broken into (12:39). The verb for "broken into" means to "dig through."[353] Thieves would dig through the sun-dried brick wall of a house to break into it.

The Son of Man will come (12:40). See comments on 5:24; 9:26.

Faithful and wise manager (12:42). The manager or steward (*oikonomos*) here is a chief servant who is left in charge of the household while the master is away. Such stewards often had significant authority over the master's business, household staff, and personal affairs.

He will put him in charge of all his possessions (12:44). Because of the servant's faithfulness, he is placed in an even greater position of authority, perhaps as second only to the master (cf. the role of Joseph in Gen. 39:8–9). Slaves in both Roman and Jewish society could rise to positions of great prestige and authority, managing their masters' large estates.

To eat and drink and get drunk (12:45). Gluttony, excessive revelry, and drunkenness are all viewed in Scripture as destructive and irresponsible behavior.[354] The same is true in Jewish literature.[355]

Cut him to pieces (12:46). The Greek term here (*dichotomeō*) is a strong one and means to cut in two or dismember.[356] Such horrible punishment was not uncommon in the ancient world,[357] but commentators are divided as to whether it is here to be taken literally or figuratively. The next phrase, "assign him a place with the unbelievers," does not solve the problem, since this can mean social ostracism or the lack of a proper burial among God's people. Whether a literal or figurative image, there is the further question of the intended application. Spiritually speaking, is this an allusion to hell or to being cut off from the community of faith? The former seems more likely in light of the previous parable of the rich fool.

Does not do what his master wants (12:47). Sins of ignorance are less severe and so deserving of less punishment than intentional sins. This is true in the Old Testament (Num. 15:22–26; Ps. 19:13), in Judaism (1QS 7.3; 8.22, 24; CD 10:3; *m. Šabb.* 78:1), and in the New Testament (Luke 23:34).

From everyone who has been given much, much will be demanded (12:48). Higher standards are demanded of those who have been given greater gifts and abilities. Wisdom of Solomon 6:6, 8 reads: "For the lowliest may be pardoned in mercy, but the mighty will be mightily tested. . . . A strict enquiry is in store for the mighty." See also James 3:1, where teachers "will be judged more strictly."

Not Peace but Division (12:49–53)

Jesus' instructions on the need for good stewardship before his return (12:35–48) now lead to a discussion of the profound seriousness of his present ministry. He is engaged in a cosmic war that will climax in his sacrificial death (his "baptism") and will ultimately bring fiery judgment on the earth (12:49–50). This war mentality means that sides must be taken. It will divide even family members, with parents and children standing on opposite sides of the spiritual battlefield. Wartime means wholehearted commitment to the cause, no matter what the price.

To bring fire on the earth (12:49). Fire is a common symbol of God's judgment in the Old Testament and Judaism[358] and is used this way by Luke elsewhere (3:16–17; 9:54; 17:29; see comments on 3:16). Here the image may be both judging the wicked and purifying the righteous.[359] Jesus' coming provokes a time of crisis and decision.

A baptism (12:50). "Baptism" here is not Christian baptism but rather the judgment of God that Jesus will receive at his crucifixion. In the Old Testament God's judgment is often described as an overwhelming deluge or flood.[360]

Family divided against each other (12:52). The division of close friends and families indicates great crisis in a nation, such as civil war. The passage recalls Micah's description of the social disintegration in Israel leading up to the Assyrian conquest, when "a man's enemies are the members of his own household" (Mic. 7:6). The rabbis interpreted this Old Testament passage with reference to the great time of crisis before the coming of the Messiah, when "children shall shame the elders, and the elders shall rise up before the children."[361] Similar images appear elsewhere in Jewish literature.[362]

Interpreting the Times (12:54–59)

Addressing the crowds again, Jesus continues the theme of eschatological crisis and preparation that runs through this section. He points out that although they know how to read the signs of the changing weather, they have failed to recognize the clear signs of the kingdom of God in his ministry. The second saying of Jesus may seem to have little connection to the first. He encourages his hearers to settle their disputes before going to court, thus avoiding debtor's prison. While the parable may concern the need for reconciliation in personal relationships, more likely it allegorically portrays the need to get right with God before the final judgment.

A cloud rising in the west (12:54). In Palestine a cloud from the west usually contained moisture from the Mediterranean Sea and so indicated rain (see 1 Kings 18:44).

The south wind blows (12:55). The sirocco or khamsin wind blowing in from the southern or southeastern desert meant hot weather.[363] Such a scorching wind could even wither crops (Gen. 41:6; Isa. 40:7).

The magistrate . . . the judge . . . turn you over to the officer (12:58). The scene envisioned is a civil case involving an unpaid debt. The "magistrate" (or ruler, *archōn*) is the same individual as the judge (*kritēs*) who hears the case. The "officer" (*praktōr*) refers to the constable or bailiff in charge of a debtor's prison. See James 2:6 for a similar image.

The last penny (12:59). The "penny" (*lepton*) was the smallest coin available, worth about half a quadrans (Mark 12:42), or 1/128th of a denarius. A denarius was a day's wages for a laborer (Luke 7:41; 12:6). Thus, the lepton was worth less than five minutes of a ten-hour work day (see 21:2 for the widow's *lepta*).

◀ *left*

PENNIES

A pile of copper *lepta*.

Repent or Perish (13:1–9)

Jesus' teaching on the need for eschatological preparation (12:54–59) continues with a call for repentance (13:1–5) and a parable on the need to produce the fruit of repentance (13:6–9). The teaching is evoked when some in the crowd ask Jesus to comment on a brutal police action taken by the governor Pilate against some Galileans in the temple precincts. Though the specific incident is unknown, it is in line with Pilate's character (see comments on 13:1). Evidently the questioners believed the popular misconception that personal tragedy was always the result of individual sins. Jesus rejects that idea and stresses that *all* people are sinners who need to repent before God.

Whose blood Pilate had mixed with their sacrifices (13:1). Though this incident is unknown, Josephus recounts several times when Pilate faced protests from the Jews and sometimes resorted to bloody oppression. In A.D. 26 Pilate brought effigies of Roman emperors into Jerusalem. Viewing these as idols (Ex. 20:4), a large number of Jews marched in protest to Pilate's headquarters in Caesarea. After they had petitioned him for six days, Pilate surrounded them with his soldiers and threatened a massacre. The Jews threw themselves on the ground and said they would rather accept death than let their law be broken. Pilate was moved by this action and removed the images from Jerusalem.[364] Such mercy was uncharacteristic of Pilate's later oppressive techniques. On one occasion popular demonstrations broke out when Pilate used money from the temple treasury to build an aqueduct for Jerusalem. Pilate sent soldiers to surround and attack the protestors, killing many.[365] Typical of the Romans, Pilate met protest with ruthless and overwhelming force. For more on Pilate see "Pilate" at Mark 15:1.

Were worse sinners . . . were more guilty . . . ? (13:2, 4). It was popularly held that tragedy was the result of personal sins. Job's friend Eliphaz asks rhetorically, "Who, being innocent, has ever perished?" (Job 4:7).[366]

Eighteen who died when the tower in Siloam (13:4). This incident is otherwise unattested. The pool of Siloam was a reservoir in the southeastern corner of Jerusalem.[367] This tower may have been part of the fortifications of the southern or eastern walls of Jerusalem, or perhaps was part of an aqueduct that Pilate built to improve Jerusalem's water supply.[368]

A fig tree (13:6). In the Old Testament Israel is sometimes compared to a fig tree or an unfruitful vine or vineyard.[369] Micah 7:1–2 presents an image similar to this one, where God seeks for figs (=righteous people) but finds none.[370]

Planted in his vineyard (13:6). It was common to plant figs and other kinds of trees in vineyards, though the law forbade planting two kinds of crops together (Lev. 19:19; Deut. 22:9). Healthy vineyards and fig trees are common images in the Old Testament for success and prosperity and their destruction serves as a symbol of judgment.[371]

For three years (13:7). Fig trees bear annually, so the farmer had already demonstrated great patience.

Cut it down! (13:7, 9). A cut-down tree or a stump was a common symbol of judgment (Isa. 6:13; 9:10).[372]

Leave it alone for one more year (13:8). There is an interesting parallel in an Aramaic rabbinic text. When an owner is about to dig up an unfruitful palm tree, the tree itself speaks and asks him to grant it one more year. The owner refuses saying, "You miserable tree! You did not bear your own fruit, so how could you bear other fruit?"[373]

Dig around it and fertilize it (13:8). Digging around the plant would allow more moisture to reach the roots and also provide space for fertilizer. The Greek for "fertilize" is to "throw manure" around it. For similar statements of God's care for his vineyard, see Isaiah 5:1–2; Mark 12:1.

A Crippled Woman Healed on the Sabbath (13:10–17)

Jesus' teaching that has occupied most of chapters 11–13 is now interrupted with a healing miracle, returning to the Sabbath-controversy theme developed earlier in Luke.[374] While teaching in a Sabbath synagogue service, Jesus heals a woman who has been crippled by an evil spirit for eighteen years. The ruler of the synagogue objects, citing the Old Testament prohibition against work on the Sabbath (Ex. 20:9–11; Deut. 5:13). Jesus responds by rebuking the religious leaders for their hypocrisy. They selfishly take care of the needs of their animals on the Sabbath, but then object to meeting the greater spiritual and physical needs of a human being.

Sabbath . . . teaching in one of the synagogues (13:10). Visiting rabbis were often asked to give the sermon or homily for the synagogue service. For the order of a Jewish synagogue service see the introduction to 4:14–30.

A woman was there (13:11). Though women were excluded from much of Israel's religious life, including access to the inner temple court, they participated in synagogue worship.[375]

Crippled by a spirit (13:11). The Greek says literally, "having a spirit of weakness." Luke explains that the condition caused her to be stooped over, a condition many commentators have identified as *spondylitis ankylopoietica*.[376] Verse 16 indicates that this was caused by demonic oppression of some sort. Demons are often described as inflicting actual illnesses, including epilepsy (9:39), muteness (11:14), lameness (here), and madness (8:29). Yet such illnesses are not always considered demonic (see Matt. 4:24). Elsewhere Luke distinguishes between Jesus' healings and his exorcisms.[377] For demons and demonization see comments on 4:31–37; 8:26–39.

Synagogue ruler (13:14). This administrative officer maintained the synagogue and organized the worship services.[378]

There are six days for work (13:14). This verse alludes to the prohibition to work on the Sabbath in Exodus 20:9–11 (cf. Deut. 5:13). Notice that the synagogue ruler does not address Jesus directly, perhaps to avoid a direct confrontation or to respect his position.

Be healed on those days, not on the Sabbath (13:14). The rabbis debated whether it was justified to offer medical help to someone on the Sabbath. It was generally concluded that it was allowed only in extreme emergencies or when a life was in danger.[379] Since this woman's life is not in immediate danger, the synagogue ruler considers this a Sabbath violation (see comments on 6:1–11).

Untie his ox or donkey . . . lead it out to give it water (13:15). The Mishnah allows that animals can go out on the Sabbath, but restricts the burdens they can carry.[380] While restricting the kinds of knots that could be tied on the Sabbath, the rabbis allowed animals to be tied to prevent straying.[381] They also found ways to water their animals without breaking the limits of Sabbath travel (Sabbath travel was limited to two thousand cubits, about six-tenths of a mile, from home; *m. ʿErub.* 4:3).[382] They would build a crude structure around a public well, converting it into a private residence. Since the well was now a "home," animals could be taken there for watering, provided "the greater part of a cow shall be within [the enclosure] when it drinks."[383] Jesus points out the hypocrisy of taking such measures to protect one's property while objecting to an act of human compassion.

Then should not this woman . . . be set free on the Sabbath. . . ? (13:16). This is a rabbinic "from the lesser to the greater" (*qal wāḥômer*) style argument. If an animal can be helped on the Sabbath, how much more a human being. The contrast is heightened by a Greek wordplay, since the verb for "set free" is the same word used for untying an animal in 13:15 (*luō*).

His opponents were humiliated (13:17). In both Greek and rabbinic rhetorical debate, a wise and skillful orator was one who could baffle and silence his opponents.[384] Luke makes it clear that Jesus has won this one.

The Parables of the Mustard Seed and the Yeast (13:18–21)

The reference to the defeat of Satan in the woman who was healed (13:10–17) recalls for the reader the in-breaking power of the kingdom of God in Jesus' ministry. Jesus now provides two short parables to reveal the nature of God's kingdom. While the traditional Jewish expectation envisioned a dramatic and cataclysmic event that would bring in the kingdom, these parables suggest a gradual but overwhelming growth, permeating and transforming the hearts of people throughout the world (see also comments on Mark 4:26–29).

The kingdom of God (13:18). See comments on 4:43; 17:20.

A mustard seed (13:19). The mustard seed was used proverbially in Judaism of something very small.[385] It normally grows into a bush of about four feet, but can reach ten feet or more.[386]

Planted in his garden (13:19). The Mishnah indicates that the mustard seed was not cultivated in gardens, but rather in fields (*m. Kil.* 3:2). It is uncertain whether this was true in first-century Palestine, however, so its effect on the parables' interpretation is doubtful.

Became a tree (13:19). This is a somewhat surprising image, since the mustard "tree" is really a bush (contrast the mighty cedars in the next note). This may be meant to give the parable an unexpected twist (the bush becomes a great tree!) in line with the theme of the "mysteries" of the kingdom in Matthew 13.[387] On the other hand, since mustard is a large bush, it may rightly be called a "tree." The Greek naturalist Theophrastus in fact notes that mustard grows into a "tree" (*dendron*).[388]

MUSTARD PLANTS

The birds of the air perched in its branches (13:19). The picture is one of peace and security that the tree provides for birds. Such an image appears repeatedly in the Old Testament.[389] While some have argued that the birds represent evil influence permeating the kingdom, there is nothing in the present context or the Old Testament background to suggest this.

Yeast (13:21). While yeast is often used in Scripture as a negative image (see comments on 12:1), here it probably functions positively. Yeast was used every day for baking bread, a staple of life, so it was certainly not universally viewed as something evil. As in the mustard seed parable, the sense is that the kingdom starts small and grows large. The additional sense here is that it quietly permeates the entire world.

A large amount of flour (13:21). The "large amount" here in the Greek is "three *sata*." A *saton* was a unit of dry measure equal to about three gallons (approx. twenty pounds).[390]

The Narrow Door (13:22–30)

After reminding his readers that Jesus is journeying to Jerusalem where God's salvation will be achieved, Luke records a question posed by one of Jesus' followers about whether many or few will be saved. Jesus responds with two related analogies, the first portraying salvation as a narrow door through which many will try but fail to enter, and the second about a banquet at the home of a wealthy owner. When the time for this banquet arrives, the owner shuts the door and late arrivals are refused entrance. The analogy is a transparent reference to Jesus' ministry. Jesus is issuing an urgent call to Israel to respond in repentance and enter the kingdom. Those who refuse will be shut out of the messianic banquet.

Are only a few people going to be saved? (13:23). This question was sometimes discussed in Jewish literature. 2 Esdras (*4 Ezra*) 8:1–3 reads: "The Most High made this world for the sake of many, but the world to come for the sake of only a few. . . . Many have been created, but only a few shall be saved."[391]

It was a common belief among the Jews that all Israelites would be saved. The Mishnah says, "All Israelites have a share in the world to come," citing Isaiah 60:21 as the proof text. The only exceptions are those who deny the resurrection, who deny the divine origin of the Law, who read heretical books, who utter charms, who pronounce the divine name YHWH, and Epicureans (*m. Sanh.* 10:1). "Epicureans" here does not refer to the Greek philosophy of Epicurus, but was a common designation for Jews and Gentiles who opposed the teachings of the rabbis.[392]

Enter through the narrow door (13:24). In Matthew 7:13 Jesus speaks of a narrow gate and a narrow road, images that are similar to the "way of life" and the "way of death" of Jeremiah 21:8 (cf. Deut. 30:15). Somewhat similar imagery appears in 2 Esdras (*4 Ezra*) 7:3–14, where a narrow strait to a vast sea and a narrow gate to a large city symbolize the difficulties the righteous suffer in life, which will ultimately open into a broad place of blessings and inheritance. The key difference is that in Jesus' words the narrow door does not symbolize life's difficulties but the exclusivity of salvation found in him.

Closes the door (13:25). The shutting of the door indicates both the authority of the owner and the lost opportunity for those shut out.[393]

I don't know you (13:25). In the Old Testament "knowing" often means God's sovereign choice to have a saving relationship with another. In Amos 3:2 God says to Israel: "You only have I chosen [lit., known] of all the families of the earth" (cf. Isa. 63:16; Jer. 1:5). Here the sense is a refusal to acknowledge a relationship (cf. Isa. 63:16). Some commentators have seen parallels here to Jewish texts on excommunication from the synagogue.[394]

Where you come from (13:25). A person's identity was closely associated with his or her place and people of origin. To

A NARROW DOOR

refuse to acknowledge origin was to refuse to acknowledge identity.[395]

Away from me, all you evildoers! (13:27). These words allude to Psalm 6:8, where a righteous sufferer cries out to his persecutors to depart from him.

Weeping there, and gnashing of teeth (13:28). This combination appears repeatedly in Matthew.[396] Weeping in this context is a symbol of both mourning and torment. Judith 16:17 reads: "Woe to the nations that rise up against my people! The Lord Almighty will take vengeance on them in the day of judgment; he will send fire and worms into their flesh; they shall weep in pain forever." In the Old Testament gnashing or grinding the teeth is a sign of anger (Ps. 35:16; 37:12)[397] and perhaps, as here, rejection and judgment (112:10).

Abraham, Isaac and Jacob (13:28). As the recipients of God's covenant, these three patriarchs symbolized Israel's national identity. God delivered the Israelites in the Exodus when he "remembered his covenant with Abraham, with Isaac and with Jacob."[398] Their names appear together throughout the Old Testament and Jewish literature.[399]

People will come from east and west and north and south (13:29). It is a common Old Testament image that when the kingdom is established, the Gentile nations will stream to Jerusalem to worship God (Isa. 2:2; 55:5).[400] Isaiah 25:6–9 provides the closest parallel since it combines this image with that of the messianic banquet (see next comment). While in Judaism the point is often the subjugation of the nations to Israel's authority (*Pss. Sol.* 17:30–31; cf. Isa. 45:14), here Jesus indicates that the Gentiles will be full participants in the blessings of the kingdom—even to the exclusion of many Israelites. For more on this theme see 14:15; 17:20.

The feast in the kingdom of God (13:29). This refers to the messianic banquet, a symbol of God's eschatological blessings for his people. The imagery has its roots in the promise of Isaiah 25:6: "On this mountain [Mount Zion] the LORD Almighty will prepare a feast of rich food for all peoples, a banquet of aged wine—the best of meats and the finest of wines."[401] The emphasis is on God's eternal and bountiful sustenance for his people (Ps. 22:26; 23:5).[402] The Qumran scrolls give detailed rules for seating and procedure at the banquet.[403] See also 14:15.

REFLECTIONS

IT IS OFTEN SAID THAT ALL ROADS lead to God and that everyone must find his or her own way. But Jesus teaches that the door to God's presence is a narrow one and that salvation belongs only to those who personally know him. Yet paradoxically, this "exclusive" gospel is also fully inclusive, and those from every corner of the earth will participate in it. Salvation does not come to those with an outward show of religiosity, but to all who lean wholly on God's saving grace.

Jesus' Sorrow for Jerusalem (13:31–35)

In this passage Jesus receives a warning from some Pharisees that Herod Antipas is seeking to kill him. Jesus takes the opportunity to reaffirm his resolve to complete his God-ordained mission in Jerusalem and to pronounce judgment against the nation.

Throughout his Gospel Luke stresses Jesus' role as a prophet. This passage brings out key aspects of his prophetic identity.[404] Jesus will suffer the fate of the prophets, that is, rejection and martyrdom in Jerusalem (13:33). As a prophet he speaks for God, expressing his heart of compassion for the nation. Though Jerusalem (representing Israel) rejects his messengers, God still loves her and longs to gather her under his wings as a hen gathers her chicks (13:34). Finally, he prophetically pronounces impending judgment against her (13:35).

Herod (13:31). This is Herod Antipas, one of Herod the Great's sons (see comments on 3:1, 19–20). Since Herod ruled over Galilee and Perea, this event probably takes place in one of these two regions.

Go tell that fox (13:32). Today the fox is viewed as clever and sly; this is one of the qualities attributed to it by the Greeks and in later rabbinic literature (often with negative connotations of deception and cunning).[405] In other Jewish contexts, however, the fox is viewed as an insignificant creature (Neh. 4:3) or as a destroyer. Ezekiel identifies false prophets as prowling "jackals among ruins."[406] Jesus' comment may contain a variety of these connotations. It was certainly not intended as a compliment. It is significant that while Herod is a fox who preys on chicks, Jesus is the hen who protects them (see comments on 13:34).[407]

left

COIN MINTED DURING THE REIGN OF HEROD ANTIPAS

Today and tomorrow, and on the third day (13:32). This is probably not a reference to three literal days, but rather to Jesus' continuing journey. The "third day" may perhaps be an allusion to Jesus' resurrection, when he will complete his messianic task.

No prophet can die outside Jerusalem (13:33). See 11:47 for this theme. Since Jerusalem was the center of Israel's religious life, this statement would have shocked Jesus' listeners.[408]

Stone those sent to you (13:34). Stoning was the prescribed method of capital punishment in the Old Testament law (Lev. 20:2; Num. 15:35), but here Israel stones God's messengers! The stoning of a prophet appears in 2 Chronicles 24:21, where Zechariah son of Jehoiada the priest is murdered in the courtyard of the temple (see comments on Luke 11:51).

Hen gathers her chicks (13:34). The Old Testament frequently speaks of the protection found in the shelter of God's wings (Deut. 32:11 [an eagle's wings]).[409]

Your house is left to you desolate (13:35). The "house" here may refer to the temple or more generally to Jerusalem. Jesus is no doubt speaking of the destruction of Jerusalem in A.D. 70 (see comments on 21:6). Jeremiah similarly prophesied the desolation of Jerusalem and the temple ("this house") in the Babylonian conquest.[410]

Blessed is he who comes in the name of the Lord (13:35). This comes from Psalm 118:26. Psalm 118 was one of the "Hallel" (praise) psalms (Ps. 113–118) used liturgically by pilgrims at various Jewish feasts (especially Tabernacles and Passover). There is some evidence that the psalm was interpreted with reference to the Messiah in later Judaism, though whether this was true of Jesus' day is uncertain.[411]

Jesus at a Pharisee's House (14:1–14)

In this passage and the next (14:15–24) a cluster of Jesus' teaching is set in the context of a meal at the home of a prominent Pharisee (cf. 7:36; 11:37). The key themes are criticism of the Pharisees for their pride and hypocrisy and affirmation of God's love for the lowly and outcast. Humility and love should characterize the people of the kingdom.

The house of a prominent Pharisee (14:1). Literally, "one of the leaders of the Pharisees." For Pharisees see comments on 5:17. Though the Jewish high court, the Sanhedrin, was made up mostly of Sadducees, some prominent Pharisees like Gamaliel were also members (Acts 5:34).

A man suffering from dropsy (14:2). Dropsy (Gk. *hydrōpikos*), medically known as edema, is an excessive accumulation of serous fluid in tissue spaces or a body cavity, causing excessive swelling.[412] It is not a disease but rather a symptom and usually points to a more serious condition. It is not clear whether the man was an invited guest, whether he was "planted" by the Pharisees to provoke Jesus to heal, or whether he was an uninvited guest who came in seeking Jesus (see comments on 7:37 for such uninvited observers).

Is it lawful to heal on the Sabbath . . . ? (14:3). The rabbis debated this question, generally concluding that it was allowed only in extreme emergencies or when a life was in danger (see comments on 6:7). Here they refuse to answer, perhaps because their traditions are unclear or because they realize that if they say "no," Jesus will attack their lack of compassion (as he did at 13:15–17; cf. 6:9).

A son or an ox that falls into a well on the Sabbath day (14:5). See Deuteronomy 5:14 for the Sabbath commandment related to household members and livestock. Rabbinic writings debate the kind of help that may be given to animals on the Sabbath.[413] The Qumran scrolls explicitly say that "no one should help an animal give birth on the sabbath day. And if he makes it fall into a well or a pit, he should not take it out on the sabbath" (CD 11:13–14). Human beings may be rescued, but one must not use a ladder, a rope, or other implement to save them (!) (CD 11:16–17; see comments on Luke 13:15 for the elaborate rabbinic means of circumventing the Sabbath prohibitions in order to care for animals).

A wedding feast (14:8). Weddings were major social events, lasting a week or more (see comments on 5:34).

Do not take the place of honor (14:8). Jesus' words here are a commentary on Proverbs 25:6–7: "Do not exalt yourself in the king's presence, and do not claim a place among great men; it is better for him to say to you, 'Come up here,' than for him to humiliate you before a nobleman." Similar advice appears in rabbinic writings.[414] The Greek writer Theophrastus (c. 372–287 B.C.), a pupil of Aristotle, gives as one of the traits of an arrogant man that he seeks the place of honor beside the host.[415]

Then, humiliated . . . the least important place (14:9). Honor and shame were pivotal values of the ancient Mediterranean world. A family's honor in the community determined whom they could marry, what functions they could attend, where they could live, and with whom they could do business.[416] The public shame of moving from the first seat to the last in front of one's colleagues would be a humiliation almost worse than death.

He who humbles himself will be exalted (14:11). Jesus encourages his followers not to seek honor but to serve others in humility. While similar proverbial wisdom appears in Sirach 3:18 ("The greater you are, the more you must humble yourself; so you will find favor in the sight of the Lord"), Jesus' words have more in common with the eschatological tone of Ezekiel, who predicted that in the wake of God's judgment, "The lowly will be exalted and the exalted will be brought low" (Ezek. 21:26).

A luncheon or dinner . . . a banquet (14:12–13). The terms in 14:12 refer to the two daily meals: the *ariston*, a late morning meal, and the *deipnon*, a late afternoon meal (see comments on 11:37). The "banquet" (*dochē*) in 14:13 is a more formal dinner party or reception. The use of this term with reference to the social outcasts makes Jesus' image even more striking.

They may invite you back (14:12). Since giving and receiving such invitations

Banquets, Meals, and Social Status

Meals were important social rituals in the ancient world, and one would normally eat only with those of his or her own social class. One's place at the table was determined by social status, and the places beside the host represented the highest status. This was true both in Greco-Roman and Jewish society. Roman sources describe meals where guests of different social status are seated in different rooms and are even served different food and wine depending on their social rank.[A-46] Various writers criticize such behavior as elitist. Martial describes an incident where a host alone eats choice food while his guests look on:

> Tell me, what madness is this? While the throng of invited guests looks on, you, Caecilianus, alone devour the mushrooms! What prayer shall I make suitable to such a belly and gorge? May you eat such a mushroom as Claudius ate [i.e., a poisonous one]![A-47]

In another humorous passage Martial criticizes the different quality of food served to guests:

> Since I am asked to dinner . . . why is not the same dinner served to me as to you? You take oysters fattened in the Lucrine lake, I suck a mussel through a hole in the shell; you get mushrooms, I take hog funguses; you tackle turbot, but I brill. Golden with fat, a turtle-dove gorges you with its bloated rump; there is set before me a magpie that has died in its cage. Why do I dine without you, although Ponticus, I am dining with you?[A-48]

While affirming the inclusive nature of the gospel, the early church still struggled against traditional and societal pressures to maintain such social distinctions (see 1 Cor. 11:17–34). See comments on Luke 5:30 for the exclusive table fellowship of the Pharisees.

determined one's social status, "accepting a dinner invitation normally obligated the guest to return the favor."[417]

Invite the poor, the crippled (14:13). It was uncommon to eat with someone of a lower social status. Such fraternization could risk one's social standing with friends and colleagues. See also comments on 14:15–24.

The resurrection of the righteous (14:14). The first clear reference to the resurrection of the righteous appears at Daniel 12:2, and it was a common theme in Jewish literature.[418] Josephus points out that the Pharisees believed that the righteous would be rewarded with the resurrection, while the wicked would be detained in everlasting prison.[419]

REFLECTIONS

WE TEND NATURALLY TO STRIVE for recognition and esteem from others. But Jesus says that those who seek self-glorification will ultimately find themselves humbled, while those who put others first will be exalted. The highest calling of a Christian is to look out for others first, encouraging them to be all that God would have them to be.

The Parable of the Great Banquet (14:15–24)

This parable is set in the same meal context as the previous passage. It reflects what is happening in Jesus' ministry. While the religious elite are refusing to accept Jesus' preaching of the kingdom (his invitation to the messianic banquet), spiritual outsiders—the poor, sinners, Samaritans, and (in Acts) the Gentiles—are responding with faith and repentance. This passage recalls Jesus' teaching on exclusion from the messianic banquet in 13:28–30 and once again plays out the theme of eschatological reversal.[420]

An interesting parallel to this story appears in the Jerusalem Talmud. When a village tax collector named Bar Ma'jan dies, the whole town comes out to mourn. A poor holy man, a teacher of the law, also dies, but he is not properly mourned. When the holy man's friend bemoans this injustice, he is informed in a dream that the tax collector's honor came because of a single good deed. He had invited the city officials to a banquet, and when they failed to come, he gave orders that the poor should be invited so that the food would not be wasted. The story has a very different moral, however, as Bar Ma'jan's fate in the afterlife is contrasted with that of the holy man. The holy man's friend has a dream in which he sees his friend in Paradise beside streams of flowing water, but Bar Ma'jan standing beside a river unable to reach the water. Though the banquet scene is similar to the present parable, Bar Ma'jan's fate is more like the rich man in the parable of the rich man and Lazarus (see comments on 16:19–31).[421]

The feast in the kingdom of God (14:15). This refers to the end-time messianic banquet predicted by Isaiah: "On this mountain [Zion] the LORD Almighty will prepare a feast of rich food for all peoples . . ." (Isa. 25:6; see comments on Luke 13:29). While Isaiah makes it clear that the messianic banquet is for "all peoples," there was a tendency in Judaism to reject the notion that Gentiles would be included. The Targum (an Aramaic paraphrase of Scripture) on Isaiah 25 dramatically alters the original meaning:

> Yahweh of Hosts will make for all the people in this mountain a meal; and though they suppose it is an honour, it will be a shame for them, and great plagues, plagues from which they will be unable to escape, plagues whereby they will come to their end.[422]

Isaiah spoke of the salvation of the Gentiles; the Targum now speaks of their destruction! Though the Targum is difficult to date, the tendency to emphasize the Gentiles' judgment over their salvation was common in Judaism. The first-century B.C. *Psalms of Solomon* offers a prayer that the Messiah will "purge Jerusalem from gentiles" and "will destroy the unlawful nations with the word of his mouth. At his warning the nations will flee from his presence."[423] Jesus is about to radically alter this exclusive view of messianic salvation.

Preparing a great banquet and invited many guests (14:16). This would be a major social event in the life of a Middle Eastern village, with all those of social status attending.

He sent his servant (14:17). It seems to have been common practice in both Hellenistic and Jewish society to issue an original invitation and then to send a servant to summon the guests when the banquet was prepared (see Est. 6:14).[424] This custom is still practiced today in traditional Middle Eastern contexts and is intended to allow the host to calculate the correct amount of (freshly butchered) meat to prepare.[425] Once the invitation has been accepted, not to show up is an insult as well as a financial burden to the host. The passage is not about a last minute invitation that is impossible to accept, but a shameful refusal to come after sending in an RSVP.

All alike began to make excuses (14:18). From a Middle Eastern perspective, none of the excuses is legitimate and all would be insulting to the host.

I have just bought a field, and I must go and see it (14:18). Bailey argues that this is a bold-faced lie since "no one buys a field in the Middle East without knowing every square foot of it like the palm of his hand," including things like anticipated rainfall, trees, paths, stone walls, and so forth.[426] Fertile land was scarce and of premium value. Its history of ownership and productive value would be known well before the sale. While Bailey's insistence that the man is lying may be an exaggeration (commentators have pointed to some late rabbinic evidence for post-purchase inspections of land[427]), there is no doubt that the excuse is a great insult to the host. In a culture where personal relationships are of supreme importance, the guest essentially says that a field is more important than their relationship.

I have just bought five yoke of oxen (14:19). A "yoke" is a pair or team of oxen. Like the previous excuse, this one is inadequate and insulting since oxen were tested before purchase rather than

YOKED OXEN

after. The prospective buyer needed to know the animals' strength and ability to work as a team before beginning negotiations. Bailey points out that teams of oxen are sold in the Middle East in two ways. Either a small field beside the marketplace is used by prospective buyers to test the team, or a farmer invites buyers to his farm on a given day to watch the animals work.[428] Again the invited guest has placed property above friendship.

I just got married, so I can't come (14:20). While some have seen more legitimacy in this excuse, it too is unnecessary and insulting. (1) The excuse cannot mean that the marriage is presently taking place, since no host would schedule a major banquet at the same time as a wedding. Everyone in the village would be at the latter event.[429] (2) While the language of the verse suggests a recent marriage, it does not say the wedding has *just* taken place (the word "just" is not in the Greek). After all, the invitee accepted the original invitation to the banquet (see 14:17), something he would not have done if his wedding were imminent. (3) While men were exempt from military service for their first year of marriage (Deut. 20:7; 24:5), this does not apply here, since this is not a distant war but a village social event. Though women were often excluded from such occasions (and that is the assumption here), the man would be absent from his new wife for only a few hours. (4) Bailey also points out that Middle Eastern men are reluctant to discuss their women in formal settings.[430] It was considered crude and unbecoming to use his sexual relationship as an excuse. (5) Finally, unlike the first two invitees, this man does not even ask to be excused, but rudely announces that he is not coming.

The poor, the crippled, the blind and the lame (14:21). The new invitation reflects Jesus' ministry to the outcasts of Israel. The Old Testament promised eschatological blessings to the poor and handicapped (see comments on 4:18; 7:22).[431] Just as "blemished" animals could not be offered as sacrifices in Israel (Lev. 22:19–22), so priests who were blind, lame, or crippled were excluded from full participation in Israel's worship (Lev. 21:17–23). The Qumran scrolls are particularly relevant to the present context since they explicitly exclude the "lame, blind, deaf, dumb or defiled in his flesh" from the messianic banquet.[432] Jesus came to heal the broken and to invite all to the banquet.

The roads and country lanes (14:23). While the poor and handicapped were from the host's community ("the streets and alleys of the town," 14:21), the call now goes to those outside the community. While the former represent the outcasts within Israel, the latter probably portrays the mission to the Gentiles in Acts.

The Cost of Being a Disciple (14:25–35)

Jesus sets out the extraordinarily high cost of discipleship. Commitment to him must far exceed devotion to family or to self (14:26–27). In light of such demands, everyone should weigh the cost carefully before making such a commitment (14:28–33). Just as salt is useless if it loses its saltiness, so a disciple without full commitment is useless to the kingdom of God (14:34).

Hate his father and mother (14:26). (Cf. Matthew 6:24; John 12:25.) This is obvious hyperbole since elsewhere Jesus says we must love even our enemies (Matt.

5:44; Luke 6:27, 35). The point is that love for family must seem like hate by comparison to devotion to Jesus. There are biblical examples where Hebrew or Greek words for "hate" mean to reject in favor of a greater love.[433]

Carry his cross (14:27). Roman prisoners bound for crucifixion were forced to carry the horizontal cross beam (the *patibulum*) to the place of execution (cf. 23:26). See comments on crucifixion at 9:23 and "Crucifixion" at 23:33. The image reflects not just self-denial, but humiliation and sacrificial death.

To build a tower (14:28). Towers were used as protective fortifications for cities as well as for private homes, land, or vineyards.[434] See 13:4 for the collapse of a poorly built tower, perhaps because financial corners were cut.

Everyone who sees it will ridicule him (14:29). In a society where honor and shame were pivotal values (see 11:5–8; 14:9), an uncompleted tower would serve as a monument of shame.

Estimate the cost (14:28). It is common sense to count the cost before a major project. Similar advice appears in Greek and Jewish literature. The Stoic philosopher Epictetus (A.D. 50–130) wrote: "Reckon, sir, first what the task is, then your own nature, what you are able to carry."[435]

A king is about to go to war (14:31). The phrase "go to war" means to engage an enemy on the battlefield (1 Macc. 4:34; 2 Macc. 8:23). History is full of examples of kings who lost battles because they miscalculated the strength of the opposition. Proverbs 20:18 reads: "Make plans by seeking advice; if you wage war, obtain guidance." The Jewish philosopher Philo draws on similar proverbial wisdom when he writes:

> Virtue's nature is most peaceable; she is careful, so they say, to test her own strength before the conflict, so if she is able to contend to the end she will take the field; but if she finds her strength too weak, she may shrink from entering the contest at all.[436]

Salt is good (14:34). Salt in the ancient world was used for various purposes: as flavoring, as a preservative, as a fertilizer, as weed killer, and as a catalyst in certain kinds of ovens.[437] The functions envisioned here are flavoring (14:34), fertilizing ("for the soil," 14:35), and weed-killing ("for the manure pile," 14:35).

Loses its saltiness (14:34). Sodium chloride (table salt) cannot actually lose its saltiness. Indeed, a later rabbinic story attributed to Rabbi Joshua ben Hananiah (c. A.D. 90) seems to intentionally refute Jesus' words when it points out that just as a mule (a sterile offspring of a donkey and a horse) cannot bear young, so salt cannot lose its saltiness.[438] There are several possible explanations for Jesus' words. He may be indicating an absurdity ("If salt were to lose its saltiness, which it obviously can't . . ."). More likely, however, his statement refers to the kind of salt found around the Dead Sea, which is a mixture of sodium chloride and other compounds. When water evaporates from this mixture, the sodium chloride crystallizes first and may be removed. What is left are gypsum and other impurities, that is, "salt" that has lost its saltiness.[439]

Fit neither for the soil nor for the manure pile (14:35). Though flavoring and preserving were the most important functions of salt, it was secondarily used to fertilize soil and to spread on manure piles. On the latter it killed weeds and slowed down the fermentation process.[440]

He who has ears to hear (14:35). See comments on 8:8.

The Parable of the Lost Sheep (15:1–7)

Luke 15 contains three parables that concern things that are lost and then found: a sheep, a coin, and a son. The parables symbolically depict the central theme of Luke's Gospel, God's love for his lost children and the joy he experiences when they return.

Tax collectors (15:1). See comments on 3:12.

Pharisees and the teachers of the law (15:2). See comments on 5:17.

Eats with them (15:2). Table fellowship with common people and especially "sinners" was frowned upon by the scrupulous Pharisees. A later rabbinic saying reads, "Let not a man associate with the wicked, even to bring him near to the law."[441] See comments on 5:30; 14:7.

One of you has a hundred sheep (15:4). On the social status of shepherds in the first century see comments on 2:8. In the Old Testament, Israel is often identified as a flock and the Lord as their shepherd; for references see 11:23. A hundred sheep was an average flock for a herdsman of modest means.[442]

Does he not leave the ninety-nine in the open country. . . ? (15:4). This is not an irresponsible act. Shepherds generally worked in teams, so this man likely left the flock with one of his companions.[443] "In the open country" (lit., "in the wilderness") means that the shepherd delayed taking the rest home until he found the lost sheep.

He joyfully puts it on his shoulders (15:5). God is portrayed as carrying his people as sheep in Psalm 28:9 and Isaiah 40:11. See comments on the Lord as a shepherd at Luke 2:8.

The Parable of the Lost Coin (15:8–10)

As with the previous parable, the key themes here are the intense effort to find what is lost and the joy experienced when it is found. God longs for his children to return to him.

Ten silver coins (15:8). The coin here is the Greek *drachmē*, approximately equivalent to a Roman denarius, worth about a day's wages. Some have suggested this is part of the woman's dowry and may have been worn as a headdress bedecked with coins or on a necklace (giving the coin special value to her).[444] This is speculative since the parable doesn't even mention her marriage. In any case, the woman's relative poverty makes the coin a major loss.

Sweep the house (15:8). The coin could have fallen in the many crevices on a stone floor. By sweeping, she may hope to hear the coin rattle.[445]

The Parable of the Lost Son (15:11–31)

The parable of the lost (or prodigal) son brings the three parables on things lost to a climax. The parable has two principal parts. The first concerns the departure and reconciliation of the prodigal (15:11–24). As with the previous two parables, the finding of the lost symbolizes Jesus' ministry to the outcasts and sinners in Israel. God longs for and rejoices at the restoration of his lost children. In the second part (15:25–32), the older brother represents the religious leaders in Israel, who refuse to join Jesus in welcoming sinners and rejoicing at their restoration to God's family.

Father, give me my share of the estate (15:12). An inheritance was not normally distributed until a father's death; thus, to ask for it early would be a great insult to the father. It would be like saying, "I wish you were dead."[446] Upon receiving such a disgraceful request a father would be expected to beat his son or perhaps cut off his inheritance. Ben Sirach warns against giving one's inheritance while still alive, lest you be left destitute: "For it is better that your children should ask from you than that you should look to the hand of your children." The appropriate time to distribute it is "in the hour of death" (Sir. 33:20–24). While the Mishnah allowed for a father to legally divide his property before his death, the right to dispose of it did not pass to the heirs until he died. Until that time, the father retained control and did with it as he wished.[447] What is extraordinary here is that the younger son demands and receives the actual property, which he squanders, canceling any further claims to inheritance. The older son receives his inheritance ("he divided his property between *them*"), but it appropriately remains under the control of the father.[448] Jesus' readers would have been horrified first that the younger son would ask for the division, but then that he would demand power over it immediately. They would be equally shocked that a father would allow himself to be treated in this way.

Got together all he had (15:13). The Greek verb here (*synagō*) has the sense "to turn into cash."[449] The son callously sells off the family inheritance.

A distant country . . . squandered his wealth in wild living (15:13). The verb translated "squandered" normally means to scatter; the image is of throwing one's possessions to the wind.[450] The adverb translated "wild living" (*asōtōs*) suggests both reckless and immoral behavior.[451] The Jews considered the loss of family property to Gentiles a particularly grievous offense and grounds for excommunication.[452]

To feed pigs (15:15). Pigs were unclean animals for Jews (Lev. 11:7; Deut. 14:8) and to tend them was viewed as despicable work. The Talmud says, "Cursed is the man who raises swine and cursed is the man who teaches his son Greek philosophy."[453]

The pods that the pigs were eating (15:16). Most commentators consider these to be carob pods (*ceratonia siliqua*), which were used for animal feed and eaten only by very poor people.[454] A rabbinic saying reads: "When the Israelites are reduced to carob pods, then they repent."[455] This young man has sunk to the lowest possible state, working for a Gentile, tending pigs, and longing to eat their slop.

When he came to his senses (15:17). A later rabbinic proverb reflects the sentiments of the son: "When a son abroad goes barefoot [becomes destitute], then he remembers the comfort of his father's house."[456]

I have sinned against heaven (15:18, 21). "Heaven" is a Jewish expression for God, a way to avoid using the divine name.

His father . . . ran to his son (15:20). The scene is striking since even today, a distinguished Middle Eastern patriarch in robes does not run, but always walks in a slow and dignified manner. Running was viewed as humiliating and degrading.[457] The man's unrestrained joy and affection—even to the point of humiliation before others—reveals God's overwhelming love and grace for the lost sinner and the joy experienced when a person repents.

The best robe . . . a ring . . . sandals (15:22). These items represent full reinstatement into the family. The best robe was probably the father's own, since the patriarch had the finest robe in the house.[458] For the robe as a symbol of honor and royal authority see Esther 6:6–11. There may also be eschatological significance here since glorified believers are said to receive white robes (Rev. 6:11; 7:9, 13). The ring may be a signet ring, indicating membership and authority in the family (cf. Gen. 41:42; Est. 3:10; 8:2). Sandals distinguished sons from servants.

Bring the fattened calf (15:23). A fattened calf was selected and fed for a special occasion such as a wedding feast. Bailey claims that the choice of a calf over a goat or a sheep indicates that the whole village is to be invited, confirming the father's desire to reconcile his son to the community.[459]

The older brother became angry (15:28). According to Middle Eastern custom, the oldest son should have been the key reconciler between the father and his rebellious sibling. Moreover, to refuse to join in a banquet given by his father would be viewed as a great public insult. Instead of confronting the father privately later, he dishonors him by arguing while the guests are present.[460] His failure to use an honorific title ("my father" or "sir") in 15:29 also demonstrates a disrespectful attitude.

This son of yours . . . squandered your property with prostitutes (15:30). The older brother attempts to represent his brother as the rebellious son of Deuteronomy 21:18–21, who should by law be stoned. He also refuses to identify him as "my brother."

REFLECTIONS

THE PARABLE OF THE PRODIGAL son illustrates God's grace and forgiveness for us as sinners. Though we have turned from God and squandered our inheritance, he is always ready to welcome us back with open arms. Since God has forgiven us in this way, we must reflect our Father's character and welcome those who return to him.

The Parable of the Shrewd Manager (16:1–15)

Whereas chapter 15 concerns parables about God's love for the lost, chapter 16 concerns the spiritual dangers of their counterparts, the wealthy and powerful. The parable of the shrewd manager is an encouragement to use worldly wealth shrewdly for eternal purposes (16:9). Though this general moral is clear, the parable itself is one of Jesus' most puzzling.

The primary problem facing interpreters is that Jesus appears to condone the steward's seemingly dishonest behavior. Various explanations have been suggested. (1) The traditional one is that though the manager acted dishonestly, Jesus' application relates only to the manager's shrewdness, not to his dishonesty. (2) Other interpretations seek to justify the manager's actions, claiming that while he originally acted dishonestly in squandering his master's resources (16:1), he is now acting justly in reducing the clients' debts (16:2–8). (a) Some suggest he is removing the master's interest charges, forbidden by the Old Testament law.[461] (b) Others think that he is removing his own exorbitant commission.[462]

Whichever interpretation is correct, Jesus' sayings that follow draw application from the parable. (1) God's people should act with discernment and shrewdness in the management of their resources (16:8b). (2) Worldly wealth (lit., "unrighteous mammon") should be used to make friends who will provide access to "eternal dwellings" (16:9). The plural "friends" here may refer to God the Father and Jesus or perhaps God and the angels. (3) Those who are faithful with a little will be entrusted with much (16:10). (4) No one can serve two masters (16:13). The manager appropriately chooses a secure future with his "friends" (=God) over his worldly wealth, which will be lost anyway when he loses his position. (5) Finally, the Pharisees—described by Luke as "lovers of money"—scoff at Jesus' criticism of worldly wealth. Jesus condemns their self-justification and pronounces their worldly value system detestable in God's sight (16:14–15).

A rich man whose manager (16:1). The rich man here may be an absentee landlord and the servant his estate manager (*oikonomos*). This situation was common in Galilee, with its large landed estates and many peasant tenant farmers (see 20:9–19). Managers of this kind had significant financial and administrative authority.

Give an account of your management (16:2). The owner is asking for a written statement of financial accounts, probably for the benefit of his successor.

To dig . . . to beg (16:3). Manual labor was viewed as a lower manner of life than that of a scholar or other "white-collar" worker.[463] Begging was considered a shameful life. Sirach says, "It is better to die than to beg."[464]

His master's debtors (16:5). These may be either independent merchants or perhaps the owner's tenant farmers. If the latter, their debts are the portions of the crops owed to the landlord. The former may be suggested by the large value of their debts and the fact that they are portrayed as capable of employing a manager (16:4).

Eight hundred gallons of olive oil . . . a thousand bushels of wheat (16:6–7). The large debt suggests relatively wealthy businessmen. The actual measurements are 100 "baths" (a bath was about 8 gallons of olive oil) and 100 "cors" (a cor was about 10 bushels) of wheat. The former would have been worth about 1,000 denarii or about three years' wages for a day laborer; the latter,

2,500 denarii or about eight years' wages.[465] The reduction of debt in each case (from 100 to 50 baths and from 100 to 80 cors, respectively) would have been roughly the same, worth about 500 denarii.

The master commended the dishonest manager (16:8). Since the owner is now in good graces with his clients (who assume the manager's actions were at the owner's command), he will not reverse the transactions, which would bring shame on himself and accusations of miserliness. Instead, he accepts the loss and wryly commends the manager's cleverness.[466] On the values of shame and honor see comments on 11:5–8; 14:9.

People of this world . . . people of the light (16:8). Lit., "sons of this age . . . sons of light." The children of the light are those who will enter God's glorious kingdom. The community at Qumran considered themselves the "sons of light," God's eschatological community opposing the forces of darkness[467] (see also John 12:36; 1 Thess. 5:5).

Worldly wealth (16:9, 11). This is a good translation for the literal "mammon of unrighteousness" (KJV), which does not mean "wealth gained dishonestly." Mammon is an Aramaic term that refers to possessions of all kinds. "Unrighteousness" (*adikia*) here carries the sense "of this world" in contrast to "of God's kingdom."[468]

When it is gone . . . you will be welcomed (16:9). An old Egyptian proverb says, "Satisfy thy clients with what has accrued to thee. . . . If misfortunes occur among those [now] favored, it is the clients who [still] say: 'Welcome!'"[469] Old Testament wisdom literature speaks of the fleeting nature of riches (Prov. 23:5; 27:24; cf. Isa. 10:3).

Whoever can be trusted with very little (16:10). There are rabbinic parallels to this principle. One notes that God "does not give a big thing to a man until He has tested him in a small matter; and afterwards He promotes him to a great thing." The illustration is then given of Moses and David, who were faithful with sheep and so were given leadership over the nation.[470]

No servant can serve two masters (16:13). Some have claimed that behind this verse is the fact that slaves in the ancient world could not be owned by more than one person. But this is not the case (see Acts 16:19).[471] The saying means rather that complete devotion to more than one master is impossible. The temptation will always be to love and serve one more than the other.

Pharisees, who loved money (16:14). While the Sadducees—the religious aristocracy—were especially known for their love of wealth,[472] the Pharisees are sometimes accused of greed and hypocrisy in Jewish literature.[473]

Additional Teachings (16:16–18)

This passage sums up the theme of promise and fulfillment that runs as a thread throughout Luke-Acts. Jesus affirms that John the Baptist stands at the crossroads of the two ages. Though the last of the old covenant prophets, he is also the herald of the Messiah and the dawning kingdom of God. John's relationship to the two covenants then sparks a statement about the continuing validity of the Old Testament law. This does not mean that each individual command must continue to be obeyed (many were unique for Israel), but that the Old Testament remains God's Word because it prophetically points to the Christ. Luke views the Old Testament primarily as "promise" rather than "law."

Jesus' statement about divorce seems at first sight unrelated to the context. Luke probably includes it here to show that in the new covenant age, Jesus' authoritative teaching sets the new standard, both explaining and fulfilling the Old Testament law.

The Law and the Prophets (16:16). This is a way of referring to the Old Testament, which in the Hebrew canon was divided into three sections, the Law (*Torah*), the Prophets (*Neviʾim*), and the Writings (*Ketuʾbim*). The Hebrew canon is known as the *Tanak,* from the first letter of each of these names (cf. 16:29; 24:27, 44).

John (16:16). See comments on 1:5–25; 7:18–35, especially verses 24–28, and "John the Baptist and the Community at Qumran" and "Josephus on John the Baptist."

Easier for heaven and earth to disappear (16:17). "Heaven and earth," conjoined like this, are symbols of permanence, but only temporal permanence. At the end of history, the present heavens and earth will be destroyed and replaced by a new heaven and earth (Job 14:12; Ps. 102:26).[474] God's Word, however, endures forever (Ps. 119:89, 160; cf. Luke 21:33).[475]

The least stroke of a pen (16:17). The Greek word *keraia* (lit., "horn") means a "hook" or "projection" and was used of a short stroke or a part of a letter of the alphabet.[476] In the Hebrew alphabet certain letters are distinguished by very short strokes, as with the difference between the *resh* (ר) and the *daleth* (ד).

Anyone who divorces his wife (16:18). The Old Testament recognized the reality of divorce, even if it did not explicitly sanction it (Deut. 24:1–4). The rabbis debated legitimate grounds. The conservative school of Shammai allowed a man to divorce his wife only in the case of unfaithfulness, while the more liberal school of Hillel accepted almost any reason, including the ruining of a meal. Rabbi Akiba is even cited as saying that divorce was allowed if the man "found another fairer than she" (*m. Gitt.* 9:10), giving as justification Deuteronomy 24:1, "[if she] becomes displeasing to him." Jesus reacts strongly against such a casual attitude toward the law and points to the inviolable nature of marriage: To break a marriage vow and marry another constitutes adultery. God hates divorce (Mal. 2:16).[477]

The Rich Man and Lazarus (16:19–31)

This parable repeats a theme found throughout Luke's Gospel, the great eschatological reversal that comes with the kingdom of God. Lazarus represents the humble and contrite poor who will be made rich, while the rich man represents the arrogant wealthy who will be left destitute. The twin morals of the story are: (1) Those who value riches more than God will be rejected (cf. 12:13–21); and (2) God demands a heart of love and justice for the poor and lowly (cf. 14:12–14). The final part of the parable introduces a third theme relating more directly to Jesus' ministry (16:27–31). When in Hades, the rich man's request for water is rejected, and he begs that Lazarus be sent to his five living brothers to spare them the same fate. Abraham denies the request, pointing out that they already have the Scriptures to show them the truth. Even if someone were to rise from the dead they would not believe. The statement is a veiled reference to the religious leaders, who are presently rejecting the scriptural prophecies concerning Jesus the Messiah and who will continue to reject him even when he rises from the dead.

Stories of justice attained in the afterlife appear occasionally in ancient literature. A Jewish parallel, the story of Bar Ma'jan, has been described in the introduction to the parable of the great banquet (14:15–24). In a first-century Egyptian parallel, a man named Setme views two burials, one of a very rich man and one of a poor man. While the rich man's is conducted with much pomp and a great crowd of mourners, the poor man is wrapped in a mat and carried out alone. When Setme announces how much more blessed it is to be rich, his son Si-osire says he hopes his father will have an afterlife like the poor man. Setme expresses dismay at this remark, so his son (who has been reincarnated) takes him to the underworld and shows him both men. Because of his good deeds, the poor man is living in royal splendor, while the rich man, whose evil deeds outweighed his good, is in gruesome torment.[478]

Dressed in purple and fine linen (16:19). Purple was the color of royalty. The term probably refers to an outer robe made of fine wool dyed with Phoenician purple, an expensive dye made from murex, a type of mollusk. Fine linen probably refers to his undergarments—the best underwear money could buy.

At his gate was laid a beggar named Lazarus (16:20). The reference to a "gate" suggests that the rich man owns a large estate. "Lazarus" is an abbreviated form of Eleazar and appropriately means "God helps."[479]

Covered with sores . . . longing to eat what fell (16:20–21). The picture is one of absolute degradation. A later rabbinic

RICH MAN'S HOUSE

Remains of a Herodian-era home discovered in Jerusalem.

proverb says, "There are three whose life is no life: he who depends on the table of another, he who is ruled by his wife, and he whose body is burdened with sufferings."[480] Lazarus has two out of three. From society's perspective, he has "no life" at all.

Even the dogs came and licked his sores (16:21). The Jews viewed dogs as detestable animals and dangerous scavengers, not lovable pets (1 Kings 14:11; 21:19, 23).[481]

Angels carried him to Abraham's side (16:22). Literally, "to Abraham's chest or bosom." The phrase probably alludes to a feast (perhaps even the messianic banquet, see comments on 13:28–29; 14:15), where guests reclined beside one another around a table (see John 13:23). The place beside the host was the position of highest honor (see 14:7). Pious Jews expected to join Abraham and the patriarchs at the messianic banquet (see 13:28).

In hell (16:23). See comments on 10:15; 12:5. The Greek here is *hadēs* (the parallel to the Hebrew *Sheol*), which can refer (1) to the grave or death itself (the place of both the righteous and unrighteous; see Acts 2:27); or (2) to the place of the wicked dead. Here it carries this second sense. *Hadēs* is sometimes viewed as an interim place of torment, ultimately to be thrown into the lake of fire (Rev. 20:13–14).

I am in agony in this fire (16:24). Torment and fire are associated with the judgment of the wicked both in Judaism and in early Christianity[482] (see comments on 12:5).

A great chasm has been fixed (16:26). The permanence of divine judgment and reward was commonly taught in Judaism. Second Esdras (*4 Ezra*) 7:104 reads, "The day of judgment is decisive and displays to all the seal of truth" (cf. Rev. 20:10).

Moses and the Prophets (16:29). This is the same as "the Law and the Prophets" (16:16), identifying the five books of the Law by their traditional author.[483] The Qumran scrolls use a similar designation.[484]

If they do not listen to Moses and the Prophets (16:31). Despite the Old Testament's repeated instruction to care for the poor and outcast, Israel's rich and powerful often oppressed them.[485]

Sin, Faith, Duty (17:1–10)

This section is directed to Jesus' disciples (17:1) and contains various teachings on the characteristics of true discipleship: forgiveness, faith, and servanthood.

A millstone tied around his neck (17:2). This would be a large round stone with a hole in its center, pulled by an animal

MILLSTONE

An olive press with a millstone in the center.

to grind grain. It would weigh hundreds of pounds and so would cause certain drowning.

If your brother sins, rebuke him . . . forgive him . . . seven times (17:3–4). "Seven times" is not an exact number, but means "many times" a day, as in Psalm 119:164. The principle of rebuke and forgiveness appears in Leviticus 19:17–18 as well as in Jewish texts.[486] Yet none emphasizes such unlimited forgiveness (cf. Matt. 18:21–22).

As small as a mustard seed (17:6). The mustard seed was used proverbially in Judaism of something very small (see comments on 13:19).[487]

Mulberry tree, "Be uprooted and planted in the sea" (17:6). This tree has been identified as the black mulberry, which has a vast root system enabling it to live up to six hundred years.[488] To uproot it required a major effort. To "plant it in the sea" is an odd and paradoxical image, since the roots could not be established in water. The point is that faith can do the impossible.

Would he say to the servant " . . . sit down to eat"? (17:7). "Servant" here is *doulos*, a bondservant or slave. A master would never think of eating with his slaves. For the shocking image of a master serving in this way see 12:37; for social status at meals see 14:7.

We have only done our duty (17:10). Similar expressions of humility and service owed to God appear in Jewish writings. Rabbi ben Zakkai is cited in the Mishnah as saying, "If you have wrought much in the Law claim not merit for yourself, for to this end you were created."[489] Similarly, Antigonus of Soko said, "Be not like slaves that minister to the master for the sake of receiving a bounty."[490] The believer owes all to God without expectations of reward.

Ten Healed of Leprosy (17:11–19)

When Jesus heals ten men with leprosy, only one returns to thank him, and this one is a hated Samaritan. The episode not only demonstrates Jesus' compassion, but also symbolizes what is happening in Jesus' ministry: The religious leaders reject the gospel while "outsiders" (sinners, tax collectors, and Samaritans) joyfully receive it with a heart of gratitude.

Samaria (17:11). On Samaria and the hatred and distrust between Jews and Samaritans see comments on 9:52; 10:29; John 4:4–42.

Ten men who had leprosy (17:12). Biblical leprosy was not the same as modern leprosy (Hansen's disease), but a variety of diseases that may have included psoriasis, lupus, ringworm, and others (see comments on 5:12). Lepers were required to keep their distance from people and to cry out "Unclean! Unclean!" when approached (Lev. 13:45–46). Because of this social ostracism, lepers sought out others with the disease, even those with whom they would not normally associate.

Go, show yourselves to the priests (17:14). The Old Testament set out strict guidelines in Leviticus 13–14 for the examination and isolation of leprosy (see Lev. 13–14). It was the job of the priests to diagnose leprosy and to declare healed lepers "clean" (see comments on 5:12, 14).

He was a Samaritan (17:16). It would have been shocking to Jesus' Jewish audience that only the despised Samaritan returned with a grateful heart. See 2 Kings 5 for an Old Testament account of a non-Jew healed of leprosy and Jesus' reference to this episode in Luke 4:27.

Your faith has made you well (17:19). The Greek says, "Your faith has saved you." While the Greek verb *sōzō* is often used by Luke of healings, here there is probably the added dimension of spiritual healing. While all ten were healed, only one was "saved."

REFLECTIONS

WHEN JESUS HEALED TEN MEN with leprosy, only one saw fit to come back and thank him. Astonishingly, he was a despised Samaritan, the least likely of the ten to return. From this story we learn that a grateful heart is one that recognizes God's undeserved favor poured out for us and responds with faith and obedience.

The Coming of the Kingdom of God (17:20–37)

Jesus' teaching here concerns the nature of the kingdom, both in its present and future manifestations. The first part is directed at the Pharisees (17:20–21) and responds to the traditional Jewish expectation of a dramatic and cataclysmic arrival of the kingdom of God. Jesus teaches that the kingdom of God will not come (at first) in a outward visible form, but rather through his healings, exorcisms, and authoritative teaching (see 4:18–19; 7:22–23).

Turning next to his disciples, Jesus affirms that the kingdom *will come* in a dramatic and cataclysmic manner, when he—the Son of Man—returns. But first he must be rejected by his own people, suffer, and die. During the interim period that follows, his disciples need not look for hidden signs or chase rumors of his coming, for his return will be evident to all (17:22–25). It will be a time of great judgment against those who have turned from God (17:26–29). In light of these coming events, God's people must stay focused on his priorities, forsaking all to follow him. Jesus gives additional teaching on the end times in the Olivet Discourse in chapter 21.

The Pharisees (17:20). For Pharisees see comments on 5:17 and next comment.

When the kingdom of God would come (17:20). The Pharisees had a strong expectation for the reestablishment of God's kingdom on earth through the Davidic Messiah. The *Psalms of Solomon,* a first-century B.C. document arising from Pharisaic circles, beseeches God to raise up his Messiah, the Son of David, to rule over Israel, to destroy her enemies, and to establish a glorious and righteous kingdom.[491] Jesus has been proclaiming the kingdom of God, and the Pharisees want to see a physical manifestation of its power and glory. For more on the kingdom of God see comments on 4:43.

With your careful observation (17:20). This Greek phrase is better translated "with premonitory signs" or "with signs predicting its arrival." Jesus is referring to the dramatic heavenly signs common in the apocalyptic literature of his day.[492] Jesus does not say these signs will not occur in the future (see 21:25; Acts

2:19–20), but that the Pharisees are missing the present manifestation of the kingdom in Jesus' ministry.

Days of the Son of Man (17:22). The "days of the Messiah" was a rabbinic way of referring to the time when the Messiah would come and establish his glorious kingdom on earth.[493] For more on the kingdom of God see comments on 4:43; for background to the Son of Man title see comments on 5:24; 9:26.

Men will tell you, "There he is!" (17:23). Jesus warns against following false messiahs. Messianic expectations were high in first-century Palestine, and at various times individuals arose claiming to be God's agent of deliverance, a prophet, or a messiah. In Acts 5, Rabbi Gamaliel speaks of two such messianic pretenders: Theudas, who "claimed to be somebody" (i.e., a messiah), and Judas the Galilean, who led a revolt against the Romans (Acts 5:36–37). Similarly, in 21:38 Paul is suspected by the commander of the Roman temple guard of being a certain Egyptian who led four thousand Jews to the Mount of Olives in a messianic action.

Josephus, with his pro-Roman sympathies, speaks of such prophets and messiahs as dangerous criminals bent on leading the nation to destruction.[494] In one episode a group of these "wicked" men deceived the people by claiming divine inspiration and leading them into the desert to await a sign of God's deliverance. The procurator Felix responded by sending troops to destroy and disperse them.[495] Such Roman police actions were not uncommon (cf. 13:1).

The Son of Man in his day (17:24, 30). The "day" of the Son of Man here and in 17:30 probably alludes to the Old Testament "day of the LORD," the great and final time of judgment for all the earth (Isa. 13:6).[496]

He must suffer many things (17:25). See comments on 9:22.

The days of Noah . . . the days of Lot (17:26–28). (Cf. Genesis 6–9 [Noah]; 18:16–19:29 [Lot].) The generations of Noah and Lot are often identified together in Judaism as symbols of great wickedness and examples of God's judgment.[497] Sirach 16:7–8 reads: "He did not forgive the ancient giants who revolted in their might. He did not spare the neighbors of Lot, whom he loathed on account of their arrogance." The Mishnah says neither the "generation of the Flood" nor "the men of Sodom" have any share in the world to come.[498] (Cf. comments on 10:12.)

The day the Son of Man is revealed (17:30). Some Jewish texts speak of the Messiah as hidden by God and waiting to be revealed at the end time.[499]

On the roof (17:31). The flat roofs of Palestine were used as living space and usually had external staircases. The idea is that there will be no time to go inside to retrieve possessions.

right ▶

SOD ROOF

A house in Beit Guvrin.

Remember Lot's wife (17:32). Lot's wife became a pillar of salt when she looked back at the destruction of Sodom (Gen. 19:26)—an example of unbelief in later Judaism. Wisdom of Solomon 10:7 speaks of "a pillar of salt standing as a monument to an unbelieving soul."

One will be taken and the other left (17:34–35). The image is of separation, one to salvation and one to judgment.

Where there is a dead body, there the vultures will gather (17:37). Jesus' puzzling response to the disciples' question, "Where, Lord?" seems to mean that the place of judgment will be as evident to all (and as gruesome) as a dead body around which vultures gather (17:37).

The Parable of the Persistent Widow (18:1–8)

Jesus' discussion of the end times and coming judgment (17:20–37) naturally raises the issue of trials and perseverance. Jesus tells a parable about a widow who through perseverance eventually receives justice from an uncaring and unjust judge. The theme develops through a rabbinic style "lesser to greater" (*qal wāḥômer*) argument. If this woman's persistence resulted in justice from an evil judge, how much more will our persistent prayers be answered by our loving heavenly Father.

A judge who neither feared God (18:2). Judges in Israel were supposed to be God's representatives, administering justice to those who most needed it. When King Jehoshaphat appointed judges in Judah, he instructed them: "Consider carefully what you do, because you are not judging for man but for the LORD . . . for with the LORD our God there is no injustice or partiality or bribery" (2 Chron. 19:6–7). The judge in the parable is the opposite of the model judge. Edersheim claims that judges in Jerusalem were so corrupt they were referred to as *Dayyaney Gezeloth* (Robber-Judges) rather than by their real title, *Dayyaney Gezeroth* (Judges of Prohibitions).[500]

A widow (18:3). Widows are viewed throughout Scripture as the most vulnerable and helpless members of society, for whom God has special concern. The Old Testament warns that God will avenge those who withhold justice from the widow and the fatherless.[501] The same is true later on in Judaism.[502]

Grant me justice against my adversary (18:3). The widow may be facing a creditor trying to take her land or property. The law is evidently on her side since she only asks for justice.[503]

Wear me out with her coming (18:5). "Wear me out" carries the literal sense of "strike the eye" or give someone a black eye. The figurative sense intended here is to "wear down with persistence," as one boxer wears down another.

Will not God bring about justice . . . who cry out to him (18:7). God's vindication of the widow and fatherless when they cry out to him is a common theme in the Old Testament and Judaism (see comments on 18:3). Sirach 35:17–21 says that God

> *will not ignore the supplication of*
> *the orphan,*
> *or the widow when she pours out*
> *her complaint. . . .*
> *The prayer of the humble pierces the*
> *clouds,*

and it will not rest until it reaches
its goal;
it will not desist until the Most High
responds.

Will he find faith on the earth? (18:8). Jewish writings often portray the time of distress before the dawn of the messianic age as one of lawlessness and apostasy (see comments on 21:23).[504] This verse connects the parable to the eschatological theme of 17:20–37.

REFLECTIONS

THE STORY OF THE PERSISTENT widow reminds us of the power and potential of prayer. If this woman's persistent requests to an unjust judge results in an answer, how much more will our prayers of faith to our loving heavenly Father be answered.

Parable of the Pharisee and the Tax Collector (18:9–14)

This parable illustrates the need for a humble and contrite heart before God. In the parable forgiveness comes not to the proud and self-righteous Pharisee, who thinks that his good deeds have earned him a right standing before God, but to the tax collector, who recognizes his own sinfulness and prays for mercy. The parable probably shocks Jesus' listeners, who consider the Pharisees' pious and upright, but the tax collectors wicked sinners.

A Pharisee (18:10). For background on the Pharisees see comments on 5:17. The Pharisees were admired by the common folk for their piety and devotion to the Mosaic Law. Our contemporary equation of Pharisaism with hypocrisy would not have been made by a first-century Jew.

A tax collector (18:10). See comments on 3:12. The tax collectors were among the most despised members of Jewish society because of their reputation for embezzlement and their complicity with the Roman oppressors. The Mishnah prohibits even receiving alms from a tax collector at his office, since the money is presumed to have been gained illegally.[505] If a tax collector entered a house, all that was in it became unclean.[506] The very presence of a tax collector in the temple, the house of God, was viewed as an act of defilement.

God, I thank you that I am not like other men (18:11). The Pharisee's prayer has an external air of humility since thanksgiving is given to God. Psalm 26 is conceptually similar, as David speaks of his "blameless" life and his separation from sinners. The difference is one of heart attitude. David had a pure heart (Ps. 26:2); this Pharisee has a heart of pride, praying "about himself" (Luke 18:11) and seeking self-glorification. Similar prayers of self-congratulation appear in later Jewish literature (though there are also examples reflecting greater humility). One, recorded in the Jerusalem Talmud (c. A.D. 400) and attributed to a first-century rabbi, reads:

> I give thanks before thee O Lord my God, and God of my fathers, that thou has appointed my portion with those who sit in the College and the Synagogue, and hast not appointed my lot in the theatres and circuses. . . . I labour to inherit Paradise and they labour to inherit the pit of destruction.[507]

I fast twice a week and give a tenth of all I get (18:12). Both fasting and tithing were signs of piety in Judaism. Fasting was required only on the Day of Atonement (Lev. 16:29–31), but pious Jews fasted twice a week, on Mondays and Thursdays.[508] For more on fasting see comments on Luke 5:33. On tithing and almsgiving see comments on 11:41–42. The problem here is not the man's accomplishments (which are impressive), but his self-righteousness and attitude of superiority.

Beat his breast (18:13). Beating the breast was a sign of mourning and/or repentance.[509]

God, have mercy on me, a sinner (18:13). Like the prayer of the Pharisee (see comments on 18:11), this one has conceptual parallels in the Psalms. In Psalm 51, David prays, "Have mercy on me, O God. . . . For I know my transgressions, and my sin is always before me."[510] God longs to forgive and welcome back the repentant sinner (see Luke 15:11–32).

Everyone who exalts himself (18:14). See comments on 14:11.

The Little Children and Jesus (18:15–17)

The reference to the humble who will be exalted (18:14) transitions naturally into a passage about people bringing their children to be blessed by Jesus. When the disciples try to turn them away, Jesus says not to hinder them because the kingdom of God belongs to "such as these." The point is that receiving the kingdom of God takes childlike faith and dependence on God.

Bringing babies . . . children (18:15–16). The word for "baby" (*brephos*) usually means an infant, but it can refer to a child old enough to understand Scripture (see 2 Tim. 3:15). The use of the more general term *paidia* ("children") in verse 16 confirms that various ages are present.

To have him touch them (18:15). The people are probably requesting a blessing from this respected rabbi.[511]

They rebuked them (18:15). Children had essentially no social status in the ancient world, so the disciples consider this an intrusion on Jesus' valuable time. For the status of children, see comments on 9:47–48.

The Rich Ruler (18:18–30)

This story illustrates the need for absolute commitment to Jesus and the impossibility of earning salvation through human achievement. Just as it is impossible for a camel to pass through a needle's eye, so *no one* can be saved through human effort or riches. Faith in God alone saves.

A certain ruler (18:18). Luke does not specify what kind of a ruler this is. He may have been a synagogue official or a secular city official. The latter is more likely since Luke does not identify him with the teachers of the law or the Pharisees.

What must I do to inherit eternal life? (18:18). The same question was posed earlier by a teacher of the law (10:27) and concerns immortal life in God's presence received at the final resurrection—a common topic in rabbinic discussions. On eternal life see comments on 10:27.

No one is good—except God alone (18:19). While the Old Testament frequently refers to God's goodness (Ps. 34:8; 106:1), the point here is moral perfection, a doctrine also taught in the Old Testament and Judaism.[512]

You know the commandments: "Do not commit adultery . . ." (18:20). Jesus cites, though not in biblical order, the fifth through the ninth of the Ten Commandments.[513] These are commands relate to relationships with other human beings.

All these I have kept since I was a boy (18:21). It was not uncommon for pious Jews to claim complete adherence to the Old Testament law.[514] Paul says he was "faultless" before his conversion (Phil. 3:6). Luke describes Zechariah and Elizabeth as upright, "observing all the Lord's commandments and regulations blamelessly" (Luke 1:6).

Treasure in heaven (18:22). See comments on 12:33.

How hard it is for the rich to enter the kingdom of God! (18:24). Since wealth is sometimes viewed in the Old Testament and Judaism as evidence of God's blessing, it was popularly believed that the rich were favored by God.[515] Yet the Old Testament and Judaism also repeatedly warn against the dangers of trusting in riches instead of God.[516]

A camel to go through the eye of a needle (18:25). Some commentators have tried to soften Jesus' hyperbole by claiming that there was a small gate in Jerusalem known as the "Needle's Eye." Camels could pass through it only by unloading and stooping down low. But there is no archaeological or literary evidence that such a gate existed in the first century. Others have claimed that the word *kamēlos* (camel) was originally *kamilos*, a ship's cable or rope, and that the idea was passing a rope through a needle's eye. Again this is unlikely since there is no manuscript evidence for this reading. In fact, both these "solutions" miss Jesus' point, which is the *impossibility* of a rich man being saved *by trusting in his riches.* It is only through faith in God that anyone can be saved. Jesus explicitly says, "What is *impossible* with men is possible with God" (18:27, italics added).

Jesus Again Predicts His Death (18:31–34)

Jesus has explicitly predicted his death three times in Luke's Gospel (9:22, 44–45; 17:25) and has alluded to it at least three other times (5:35; 12:49–50; 13:32–33). Now, as the Journey to Jerusalem draws to a close (see introductory comments to 9:51–19:44), Jesus again predicts the suffering, death, and resurrection that await him in Jerusalem. As before, the disciples fail to grasp its significance (cf. 9:45).

Everything that is written by the prophets (18:31). The premier passage on the suffering of the Messiah is Isaiah 52:13–53:12, where the Suffering Servant offers up his life for the sins of his people. Jesus may also be thinking of Old Testament passages like Psalm 16 (Acts 2:25–28), Psalm 2 (Acts 4:25–26), Psalm 118:22 (Luke 20:17), and Isaiah 50:4–9 (see comments on Luke 18:32). The Jews of Jesus' day did not interpret Isaiah 53 with reference to a suffering Messiah, focusing instead on the Old Testament portrait of a conquering, victorious king (Isa. 11, etc.; see comments on 9:22).

The Son of Man (18:31). See comments on 5:24; 9:26.

Mock him . . . spit on him, flog him (18:32). The verse probably alludes to the suffering of the Servant of the Lord in Isaiah 50:4–9, the third of Isaiah's Servant Songs: "I offered my back to those who beat me, my cheeks to those who pulled out my beard; I did not hide my face from mocking and spitting" (Isa. 50:6; cf. John 19:1).

A Blind Beggar Receives His Sight (18:35–43)

The account of the healing of the blind man outside Jericho functions on various levels in Luke's Gospel. While another example of Jesus' compassionate heart, it also sets the stage for the Messiah's entrance into Jerusalem. Healing the blind recalls Isaiah's promise of the signs of the new age and points back to Jesus' use of these texts to define his ministry.[517] The reader is reminded that in Jesus the age of salvation is dawning. Further, the blind man's cry to Jesus as "Son of David" recalls Gabriel's announcement to Mary that Jesus is the promised Messiah from David's line, who will reign forever on his throne (1:32–33; cf. 2:11). Israel's Savior and King is about to enter Jerusalem. Finally, the blind man's simple faith and subsequent healing pick up the Journey-to-Jerusalem theme that the humble outcasts of Israel are the recipients of God's mercy and salvation.

Begging (18:35). With little in the way of social welfare in the first century, those who could not work were forced to beg (see comments on 16:3 for the shamefulness of begging). Giving alms to a beggar was considered a righteous deed in Judaism (see comments on 11:41).

Son of David, have mercy on me! (18:38, 39). "Son of David" became a favorite title in Judaism for the Messiah from David's line, who would defeat Israel's enemies and reign forever in justice and righteousness on David's throne.[518] Its background is found in the Davidic covenant of 2 Samuel 7:12–16.[519] For the messianic hope in the first century see Luke 1:32–33; 9:20; see also "Messianic Expectation in Jesus' Day."

Zacchaeus the Tax Collector (19:1–10)

The story of Zacchaeus together with the parable of the ten minas (19:11–27) bring Luke's Journey to Jerusalem to a close (9:51–19:44). This episode is a fitting conclusion to a section that has sometimes been called "The Gospel to the Outcast." Zacchaeus is the ultimate of Israel's outcasts, not just a hated tax collector, but a *chief* tax collector, the worst among the worst. Yet manifesting God's grace, Jesus reaches out and offers salvation even to him. The "today" of salvation announced in the Nazareth sermon (4:21) now arrives in Zacchaeus's home (19:9). Many commentators consider 19:10 to be the best summarizing and epitomizing verse of Luke's Gospel: "For the Son of Man came to seek and to save what was lost."

Jericho (19:1). See "Jericho."

A chief tax collector (19:2). Both the Romans and local authorities imposed various taxes, tolls, and customs in Palestine. The Romans often leased the right to collect taxes to individuals, who then hired underlings to collect the taxes. Although the term "chief tax collector" (*architelōnēs*) is unique to this passage, it probably indicates that Zacchaeus is responsible for a broader region—perhaps the custom on goods passing between Perea and Judea—

JERICHO

(top) The Old Testament era tel is in the foreground. Jebel Quruntul (the Mount of Temptation) is in the background. *(bottom left)* Roman era Jericho: excavations at Herod's palace. *(bottom right)* Roman era Jericho: the remains of Herod's palace.

▸ Jericho

Jericho is located in an oasis in the Judean desert eighteen miles northwest of Jerusalem.[A-49] A winding desert road, familiar to Luke's readers from the parable of the good Samaritan (10:30), connects the two cities. In Jesus' day there were two Jerichos, the uninhabited city of the Old Testament and a new city located about a mile to the south. Since Mark says Jesus healed the man while leaving Jericho (10:46), some commentators think Jesus was between the two cities, leaving old Jericho (Mark) and approaching new Jericho (Luke). Another possibility is that Luke has rearranged the account to place the healing before the Zacchaeus episode in Jericho.

Archaeologists consider Jericho to be the oldest continuously inhabited city on earth, with settlements dating back to 8,000 B.C.[A-50] At 820 feet below sea level, it is also the world's lowest city.

with subordinates working for him.[520] It is not surprising, therefore, that Luke identifies him as a wealthy individual.

Tax collectors were despised in Israel because they were viewed as extortionists and Roman collaborators (see comments on 3:12; 18:10). The Jewish Mishnah goes so far as to say it is permissible to lie to tax collectors to protect one's property![521]

A sycamore-fig tree (19:4). This is evidently not the European sycamore, but the *ficus sycōorus,* also known as the "fig-mulberry." It is something like an oak with a short trunk and wide branches, making it easy to climb.[522]

The guest of a "sinner" (19:7). Table fellowship carried great social significance in the ancient world. For a religious-minded Pharisee to eat with a notorious sinner brought ceremonial defilement and social ostracism (see comments on 5:30; 14:7).

I give half of my possessions to the poor (19:8). Though almsgiving was a sign of great piety in Judaism (see comments on 11:41), later rabbis considered it unwise to give away more than twenty percent of one's goods, lest one become a burden to others.[523] Zacchaeus takes the radical step of giving away half.

REFLECTIONS

THOUGH THE STORY OF ZACCHAEUS is often viewed as a cute children's story, it is in fact one of the most important stories in the whole Bible, since it reveals the heart of Jesus' mission and God's purpose for the world. Jesus came quintessentially to "seek and to save what was lost." Those who love God will share his passion to bring his wondrous salvation to a lost world.

I will pay back four times the amount (19:8). Normal restitution in the Old Testament for a wrong committed was to add one-fifth or 20 percent to the value of the goods lost.[524] The penalty for outright theft of an animal was much more severe, requiring restitution of four (2 Sam. 12:6) or five times (Ex. 22:1) the value of the animal. Similar penalties appear in Roman sources and in the Qumran scrolls.[525] Later Judaism seems to have softened this penalty, and the Mishnah only requires restitution equivalent to the loss.[526] By contrast Zacchaeus treats his ill-gotten wealth as theft and promises a full fourfold restitution (see comments on Luke 3:12; 18:10 for the Jewish presumption that a tax collector's wealth was illegally gained).

A son of Abraham (19:9). The Jews were proud of their status as children of Abraham (see 3:8) and treated this as reason enough for God's blessing. But a tax collector was viewed as having forfeited his rights as Abraham's offspring.

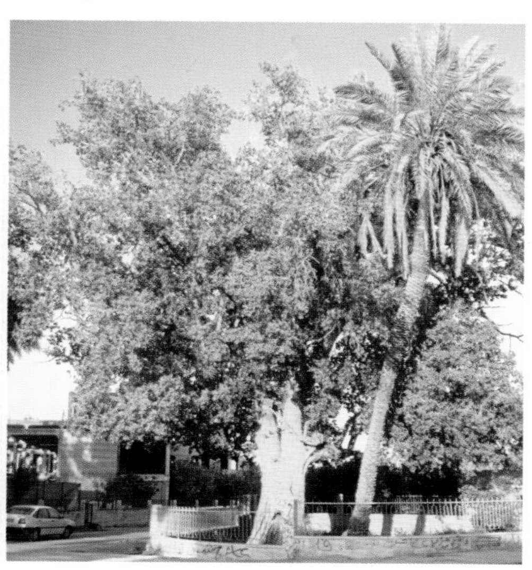

◀ *left*

SYCAMORE TREE IN THE JORDAN VALLEY

To seek and to save what was lost (19:10). This is a major theme in Luke's Gospel and reflects the image of a shepherd seeking his lost sheep (see comments on 11:23). It recalls especially the image in Ezekiel 34 of God as shepherd of his nation Israel.

The Parable of the Ten Minas (19:11–27)

The parable of the ten minas teaches the need for Jesus' disciples to practice good stewardship during his absence. Servants who are faithful with the resources Jesus has given them will be rewarded at his return with greater privilege and responsibility. Those who exercise poor stewardship will suffer loss (see 1 Cor. 3:14–15).

A second point of the parable (not found in Matthew's similar parable of the talents, see Matt. 25:14–30) is to explain why the kingdom of God does not appear physically on earth at Jesus' entrance into Jerusalem (Luke 19:28–40). In his narrative introduction Luke says Jesus told the parable "because he was near Jerusalem and the people thought that the kingdom of God was going to appear at once" (19:11). The nobleman in the parable goes away "to a distant country" to be appointed king, later to return with reward and judgment (19:12). The point is that Jesus will receive his royal authority not now in Jerusalem, but in heaven at his exaltation to God's right hand (see Acts 2:32–36). He will then return in the future to assume his throne, to reward his faithful stewards, and to judge those who rejected his kingship (19:14, 17, 27).

The kingdom of God was going to appear at once (19:11). Most Jewish expectations envisioned an earthly kingdom with Jerusalem as its center.[527] While not rejecting this expectation, Jesus makes it clear that the present manifestation of the kingdom will take on a different form (cf. Acts 1:6–8).

Went to a distant country to have himself appointed king (19:12). Since Rome ruled Palestine as a vassal kingdom, it was necessary to gain favor in the capital to consolidate one's kingship. Herod the Great, Archelaus (see 19:14), Herod Antipas, Herod Philip, and Herod Agrippa I all spent time in Rome to gain approval for their reigns.[528]

Ten minas (19:13). A mina was equivalent to one hundred drachmas; one drachma was approximately a day's wages. Each servant is thus given several month's wages and told to invest it appropriately to turn a profit.

But his subjects hated him and sent a delegation after him (19:14). This would recall for Jesus' hearers the story of Archelaus, the son of Herod the Great. When protests broke out after the death of Herod, Archelaus used his soldiers to violently restore order, killing over three thousand Jews at a Passover demonstration. The Jews responded by sending a fifty-man delegation to Rome to plead against his kingship. The emperor Caesar Augustus compromised by giving Archelaus half of Herod's kingdom (dividing the other half between his brothers Philip and Antipas; see comments on 3:1) and the title *ethnarch* instead of king. Augustus ruled that if Archelaus governed wisely, he would later appoint him king.[529] Instead, Archelaus ruled poorly and was deposed in A.D. 6.

Take charge of ten cities . . . five cities (19:17, 19). In the parable this refers to servants who have proven faithful in lesser administrative roles being appointed to regional governorships. A rabbinic proverb affirms the principle: "Run to fulfill the lightest duty even as the weightiest . . . for the reward of a duty [done] is a duty [to be done]."[530] In the application of the parable the authority given to the servants coincides with the eschatological rule promised to God's faithful servants. Such rule by the saints appears in both Jewish and early Christian literature.[531]

Laid away in a piece of cloth (19:20). The rabbis speak of this as a careless and irresponsible way to guard money.[532] The servant is not only unfaithful, he is also foolhardy. Even hiding money in the ground was considered safer (cf. Matt. 25:18, 25).

Put my money on deposit . . . collected it with interest (19:23). The servant is chastised for not bothering to (lit.) "put the money on the table," that is, to loan it to money lenders in order to receive interest. Because wealth in the ancient world tended to be concentrated in the hands of few, high interest rates could be charged and large profits made. The Mishnah says that an individual is not personally liable for money lost by a money lender.[533]

To everyone who has, more will be given (19:26). See comments on 8:18.

Those enemies . . . kill them in front of me (19:27). Jesus' hearers understood this image since it was a common practice in the ancient world for kings to eliminate their enemies and rivals when they ascended to the throne (see 1 Kings 2:13–46).[534] The application of the parable is the final judgment against those who ultimately reject Jesus as Savior and King.

The Triumphal Entry (19:28–44)

Jesus' approach to Jerusalem (19:28–40) and his lament over the city (19:41–44) together set the stage for the climactic events that will occur there. On the one side there is rejoicing as Jesus publicly reveals his messiahship. Yet there is also a tragic side as he weeps over the city and predicts her destruction. Jerusalem has refused to recognize and acknowledge her Messiah and so faces judgment.

Though Luke does not explicitly cite Zechariah 9:9–10 (cf. Matt. 21:5), there is little doubt that Jesus' actions point to the prophet's portrait of the humble and righteous king, bringing salvation and peace:

Rejoice greatly, O Daughter of Zion!
Shout, Daughter of Jerusalem!
See, your king comes to you,
righteous and having salvation,
gentle and riding on a donkey,
on a colt, the foal of a donkey. . . .
He will proclaim peace to the nations.
His rule will extend from sea to sea
and from the River to the ends of
the earth. (Zech. 9:9–10)

THE AREA AROUND JERUSALEM

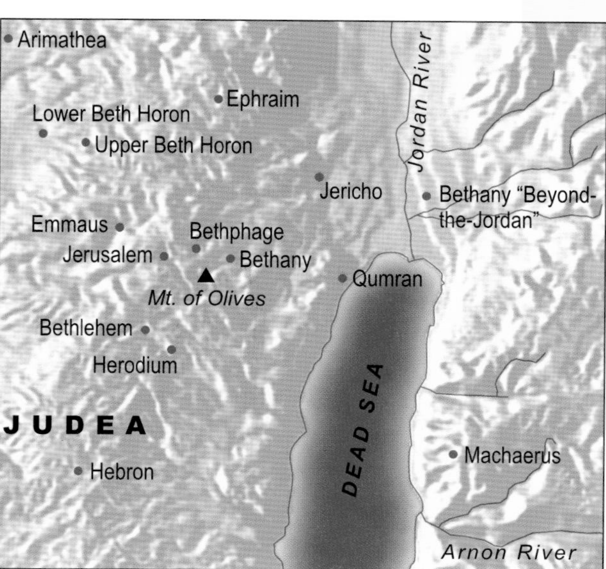

PASSION WEEK

Bethany, the Mount of Olives, and Jerusalem

4. Clearing of the temple
MONDAY
Mt 21:10—17
Mk 11:15—18
Lk 19:45—48

The next day he returned to the temple and found the court of the Gentiles full of traders and money changers making a large profit as they gave out Jewish coins in exchange for "pagan" money. Jesus drove them out and overturned their tables.

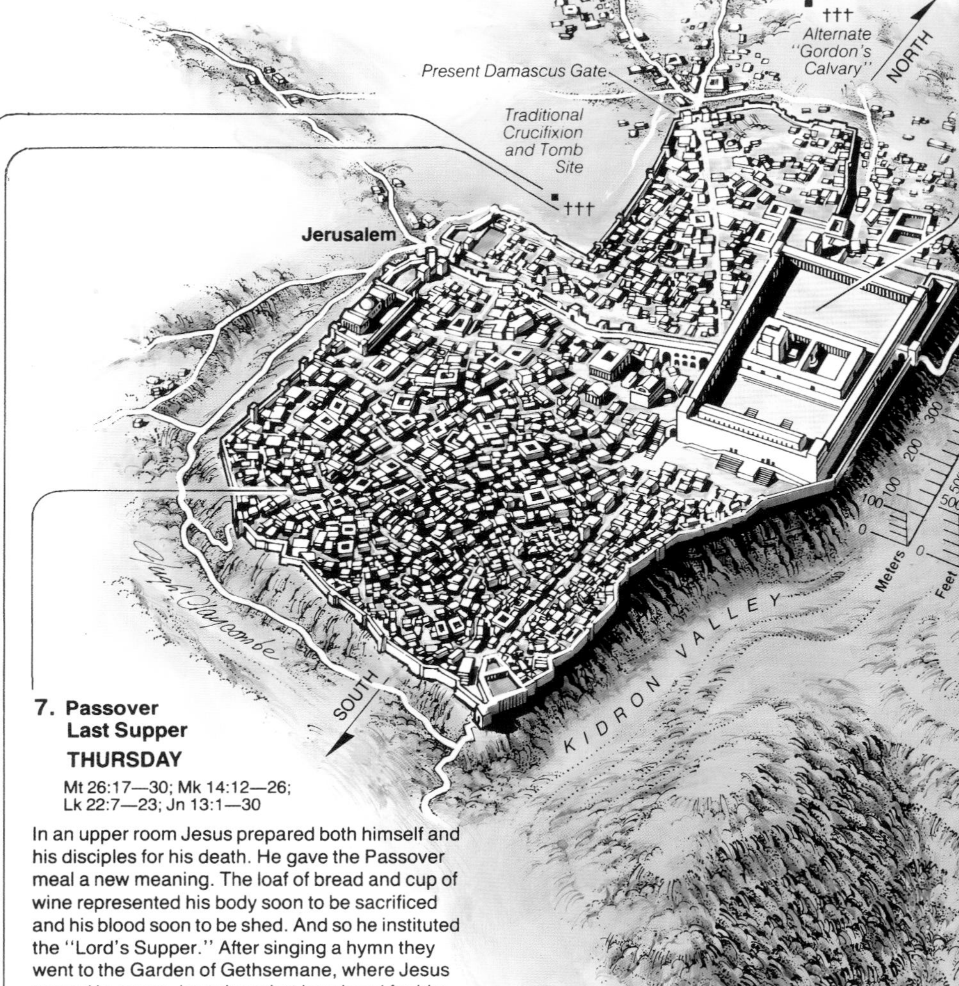

7. Passover Last Supper
THURSDAY
Mt 26:17—30; Mk 14:12—26; Lk 22:7—23; Jn 13:1—30

In an upper room Jesus prepared both himself and his disciples for his death. He gave the Passover meal a new meaning. The loaf of bread and cup of wine represented his body soon to be sacrificed and his blood soon to be shed. And so he instituted the "Lord's Supper." After singing a hymn they went to the Garden of Gethsemane, where Jesus prayed in agony, knowing what lay ahead for him.

8. Crucifixion—FRIDAY Mt 27:1—66; Mk 15:1—47; Lk 22:66—23:56; Jn 18:28—19:37
Following betrayal, arrest, desertion, false trials, denial, condemnation, beatings and mockery, Jesus was required to carry his cross to "The Place of the Skull," where he was crucified with two other prisoners.

9. In the tomb
Jesus' body was placed in the tomb before 6:00 P.M. Friday night, when the Sabbath began and all work stopped, and it lay in the tomb throughout the Sabbath.

10. Resurrection—SUNDAY Mt 28:1—13; Mk 16:1—20; Lk 24:1—49; Jn 20:1—31
Early in the morning, women went to the tomb and found that the stone closing the tomb's entrance had been rolled back. An angel told them Jesus was alive and gave them a message. Jesus appeared to Mary Magdalene in the garden, to Peter, to two disciples on the road to Emmaus, and later that day to all the disciples but Thomas. His resurrection was established as a fact.

5. Day of controversy and parables

TUESDAY Mt 21:23—24:51; Mk 11:27—13:37; Lk 20:1—21:36

IN JERUSALEM
Jesus evaded the traps set by the priests.

ON THE MOUNT OF OLIVES OVERLOOKING JERUSALEM
(Tuesday afternoon, exact location unknown)
He taught in parables and warned the people against the Pharisees. He predicted the destruction of Herod's great temple and told his disciples about future events, including his own return.

6. Day of rest

WEDNESDAY
Not mentioned in the Gospels

The Scriptures do not mention this day, but the counting of the days (Mk 14:1; Jn 12:1) seems to indicate that there was another day concerning which the Gospels record nothing.

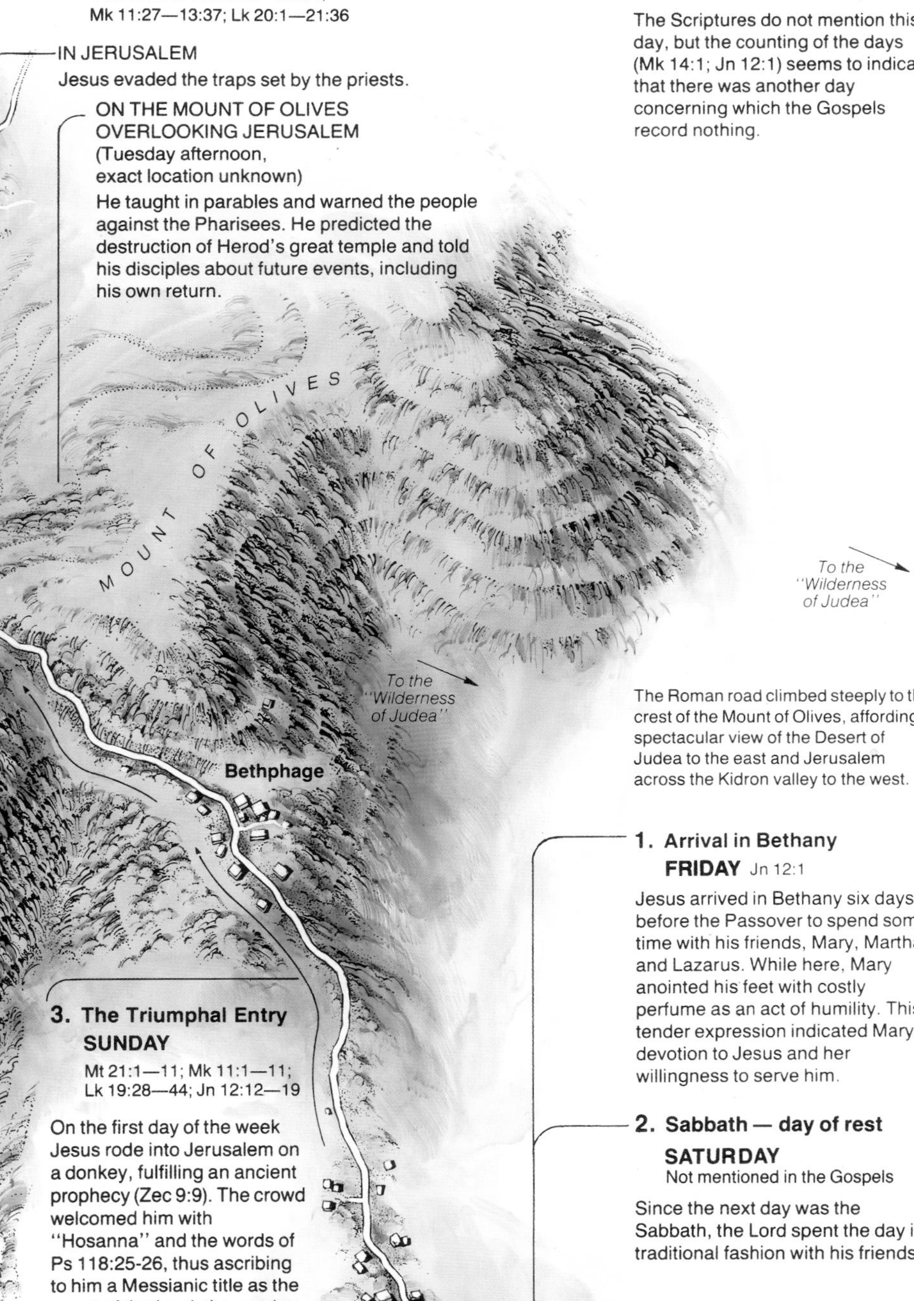

The Roman road climbed steeply to the crest of the Mount of Olives, affording a spectacular view of the Desert of Judea to the east and Jerusalem across the Kidron valley to the west.

1. Arrival in Bethany

FRIDAY Jn 12:1

Jesus arrived in Bethany six days before the Passover to spend some time with his friends, Mary, Martha and Lazarus. While here, Mary anointed his feet with costly perfume as an act of humility. This tender expression indicated Mary's devotion to Jesus and her willingness to serve him.

2. Sabbath — day of rest

SATURDAY
Not mentioned in the Gospels

Since the next day was the Sabbath, the Lord spent the day in traditional fashion with his friends.

3. The Triumphal Entry

SUNDAY
Mt 21:1—11; Mk 11:1—11; Lk 19:28—44; Jn 12:12—19

On the first day of the week Jesus rode into Jerusalem on a donkey, fulfilling an ancient prophecy (Zec 9:9). The crowd welcomed him with "Hosanna" and the words of Ps 118:25-26, thus ascribing to him a Messianic title as the agent of the Lord, the coming King of Israel.

Bethphage and Bethany (19:29). Bethany (meaning "House of Ananiah") was a village located on the road from Jericho about two miles east of Jerusalem, on the eastern slope of the Mount of Olives. It was the home of Lazarus and his sisters, Mary and Martha.[535] The location of Bethphage is uncertain, though it was probably near Bethany on the same road.

The Mount of Olives (19:29). The Mount of Olives (2,660 feet above sea level) overlooks Jerusalem and the temple mount from the east. The prophet Zechariah predicted that when Messiah came, he would appear on the Mount of Olives (Zech. 14:4). Though Zechariah describes a scene of cataclysmic judgment—a description of Jesus' second coming—the mountain's eschatological significance contributes to the messianic imagery found here. It is significant that Jesus ascends from the Mount of Olives in Acts 1 with the promise to return "in the same way" (Acts 1:11).

You will find a colt tied there (19:30). The "colt" here is the offspring of a donkey, not a horse (cf. Zech. 9:9; Matt. 21:2). The use of the colt certainly alludes to Zechariah 9:9–10, but may also relate to Solomon's coronation (1 Kings 1:32–40) and/or the messianic figure from Judah's line predicted in Genesis 49:9–11 (who tethers his colt to a vine). Together these background texts give the scene a strong royal and messianic flavor.

Some commentators point out that animals were often kept for the benefit of travelers who might borrow or hire them. While this may be the case, a more likely background is the right of a king or other person of authority to borrow an animal needed for immediate service.[536] While it is possible that Jesus arranged earlier to borrow the colt, the point here seems to be his divine knowledge and foresight (19:32).

Which no one has ever ridden (19:30). An unridden colt points to its purity—fitting for a king. The Old Testament sometimes demands animals that have never been worked or yoked to provide pure sacrifices (Num. 19:2; Deut. 21:3) or to carry the ark of the covenant (1 Sam. 6:7).

People spread their cloaks on the road (19:36). The spreading of garments indicates homage to a person of high rank and recalls the royal greeting to Jehu in 2 Kings 9:13.[537] Luke omits the reference to palm branches found in Matthew and Mark, probably because his Gentile audience would not have recognized these as symbols of Jewish nationalism. Palm branches, praise, hymns, and songs are associated with the entrance of Simon Maccabeus into Jerusalem after his victory over the Syrians.[538]

Blessed is the king who comes in the name of the Lord! (19:38). The phrase is drawn from Psalm 118:26, with the addi-

A ROAD ON THE MOUNT OF OLIVES

Jerusalem is visible in the distance.

tion of "the king" for "he." This links the psalm to Zechariah 9:9 and brings out its messianic significance. In its original context Psalm 118 probably celebrated the return of a Davidic king from victory in battle (Ps. 118:10–118) and his ascent to the temple to worship (118:19–29). In Judaism it became one of the Hallel Psalms (Ps. 113–18), used liturgically by pilgrims at the Feast of Tabernacles and Passover. For the disciples the psalm clearly carried messianic significance (cf. Luke 13:35).[539]

The stones will cry out (19:40). The personification of creation recalls Isaiah 55:12, where the mountains and hills "burst into song" and the trees of the field "clap their hands," rejoicing at God's deliverance. There may also be an allusion to Habakkuk 2:11, where the prophet announces that "the stones of the wall will cry out" in judgment against Babylon. Jesus will soon pronounce judgment against Jerusalem, predicting her destruction (Luke 19:43–44).

He wept over it (19:41). Jesus' judgment oracle and tears of lament recall the Old Testament prophets, who often wept over Israel's sins and impending judgment.[540] Jeremiah has been called the "weeping prophet."

Your enemies will build an embankment against you (19:43). Jesus predicts the destruction of Jerusalem by the Romans, which took place in A.D. 70. Josephus describes the walls and embankments built by the Roman general Titus (son of Emperor Vespasian) to besiege the city and prevent the escape of its inhabitants.[541]

Dash you to the ground, you and your children (19:44). Josephus portrays in great detail the terrible and gruesome suffering of the inhabitants of Jerusalem during the three-year siege of the city.[542] Many died by a terrible famine. Others were killed by desperate bandits within the city. Thousands were slaughtered by the Romans when they breached the walls.[543] Josephus claims that eleven hundred thousand perished during the siege and ninety-seven thousand were taken captive.[544] Though the number is almost certainly grossly exaggerated (it may have been between one-quarter and one-half million), these numbers reveal the horrible sufferings the city will experience (see 21:23 for more details).

Not leave one stone on another (19:44). See 21:6. This image is one of total devastation, but should not be taken too literally. According to Josephus, Titus demolished the entire city but left some of the important towers and part of the west wall standing to use as a garrison for his troops. The city as a whole was leveled to the ground, "as to leave future visitors to the spot no ground for believing that it had ever been inhabited."[545]

Jesus at the Temple (19:45–48)

Upon entering the temple, Jesus drives out those selling animals and other goods to pilgrims for sacrifices. By "cleansing" the temple, Jesus symbolically acts out the judgment he has just predicted (19:41–44). His actions provoke outrage among the leadership, who plot to kill him. Yet his popularity among the people prevents a public arrest.

Those who were selling (19:45). Pilgrims coming to Jerusalem had to purchase animals and other products for sacrifices (animals, birds, wine, oil, flour, etc.; *m. Šeqal.* 4:8).[546] These sellers were located

MODERN JERUSALEM FROM THE MOUNT OF OLIVES

in the Court of the Gentiles. Luke does not specifically mention the money changers (see Matt. 21:12; Mark 11:15), who exchanged local currencies for the Tyrian shekel required for the temple tax.[547] Jesus' actions against the temple would have been viewed as disruptive to the sacrificial system and thus blasphemous by the Jerusalem leadership.

"My house will be a house of prayer" . . . "a den of robbers" (19:46). This is a combination of Old Testament citations from Isaiah 56:7 and Jeremiah 7:11. The former speaks of a future restoration of the temple, when the Gentile nations will stream to Jerusalem and the temple will be called "a house of prayer for all nations." The latter is an indictment against Israel for her injustice and unrighteousness. The nation has turned God's temple, which bears his name, into "a den [or cave] of robbers." As in the present context (19:41–44), Jeremiah also includes an oracle of judgment, predicting the temple's destruction (Jer. 7:14).

THE JERUSALEM TEMPLE

The Court of the Gentiles is the spacious area surrounding the temple proper.

Chief priests, the teachers of the law and the leaders among the people (19:47). These probably represent the three groups comprising the Sanhedrin. The chief priests were the upper echelon of the Jewish priesthood (see comments on 9:22); the teachers of the law were "scribes" or experts in the Mosaic law—mostly Pharisees (see comments on 5:17). The "leaders among the people" were probably the lay nobility in Jerusalem, the "elders" of 9:22; 20:1.[548]

The Authority of Jesus Questioned (20:1–8)

In chapter 20 a series of controversies takes place between Jesus and the religious leaders in Jerusalem—controversies that will result in the plot to seize him.

The temple courts (20:1). For this term see comments on 2:27.

The chief priests and the teachers of the law, together with the elders (20:1). This was probably an official delegation from the Sanhedrin (see comments on 19:47).

John's baptism—was it from heaven (20:4). "From heaven" means "from God," a Jewish expression to avoid using the divine name. Counter-questions were a common rabbinic method of argumentation.

Jesus turns the question to one of *prophetic* authority. In the period of the united monarchy there was a separation of powers between the Davidic king, who oversaw secular affairs, and the Aaronic priests, who oversaw religious affairs. Yet everyone recognized that God could raise up a prophet as his mouthpiece to indict both king and priest of corruption and sin. First Maccabees 14:41 says that the Maccabean ruler Simon "should be their leader and high priest forever, until a trustworthy prophet should arise." If these leaders admit that John was a prophet—as the people believe (Luke 20:6)—they should submit to his indictment of their corrupt leadership.

The people will stone us (20:6). Stoning was the prescribed Old Testament punishment for blasphemy (Lev. 24:14), idolatry (Lev. 20:2; Deut. 13:10), and other sins of defiance against God. To knowingly reject God's prophet was surely a capital offence.

The Parable of the Tenants (20:9–19)

Jesus now tells a parable that allegorically depicts his controversy with Israel's leadership. The parable draws imagery from Isaiah's song of the vineyard (Isa. 5:1–7), where the vineyard represents Israel and the owner God. When the vineyard fails to produce fruit, the owner takes away its protection and allows invaders—the Assyrians in Isaiah's context—to overwhelm and destroy it. It is a parable of impending judgment. Here Jesus expands on Isaiah's imagery with a new parable. God is again the owner and the vineyard Israel, but the main characters are now tenant farmers, representing Israel's corrupt leadership. When the owner sends servants (=the prophets) to receive the produce of the vineyard, the tenants beat and abuse them, sending them away empty-handed. Finally, the owner sends his own son (=Jesus), whom the farmers murder, thinking they will now inherit the vineyard. Jesus concludes by asking, "What then will the owner . . . do to them?" The answer is obvious: "He will come and kill those tenants and give the vineyard to others" (Luke 20:16). Israel's rejection of her

VINEYARD

A vineyard near the tel of Lachish.

Messiah will result in her destruction, and Israel's salvation blessings will pass on to others.

The people, who certainly knew Isaiah's parable, gasp in response, "May this never be!" Jesus replies by pointing to the Old Testament prophecy of Psalm 118:22. Though the rejected stone, Jesus will be vindicated as the cornerstone of God's new building. The teachers of the law and the chief priests also understand the parable and look for a way to destroy Jesus. Again, however, his popularity prevents a public arrest.

Rented it to some farmers (20:9). Wealthy landowners often leased land to poor farmers, so the portrait here was familiar to Jesus' hearers. There were many such estates with absentee landlords in Palestine, especially in Galilee.

Some of the fruit of the vineyard (20:10). Rent to the landlord was normally paid through a percentage of the grapes produced.

He sent a servant . . . the tenants beat him (20:10). The Old Testament speaks of God's repeated sending of prophets to call Israel to repentance and Israel's frequent mistreatment and even murder of them (see comments on 3:19–20; 11:47).[549]

My son, whom I love (20:13). The Messiah was expected to have a unique father-son relationship with God (see comments on 1:32–33).[550] Though it is debated whether "Son of God" was a common messianic title in the first century, Jesus' hearers may have recognized a messianic allusion here.[551] As in the divine voice at Jesus' baptism (see comments on 3:22), there may also be an Isaac typology ("whom I love" = Gen. 22:2).

They threw him out of the vineyard and killed him (20:15). While Mark speaks of the tenants killing the master's son and throwing the body out of the vineyard—a reference to the shame associated with an unburied corpse (see Mark 12:8)—Luke emphasizes first his rejection ("they threw him out") and then his murder. The present rejection of the Messiah will result in his death.

The stone the builders rejected has become the capstone (20:17). The disciples shouted Psalm 118:25–26 as Jesus approached Jerusalem (Luke 19:38; cf. 13:35). Now Jesus cites Psalm 118:22 to refer to his rejection. The meaning of "capstone" (*kephalē gōnias;* lit., "head of the corner") is debated, but probably refers to the "cornerstone" used at the corner of a building to support two adjoining walls. Such stones were essential to maintain the integrity of the structure.[552] The stone metaphor was a common one among the early Christians, who used a catena of texts to explain Jesus' rejection and vindication (see also next comment).[553]

right ▶

CAPSTONE

A huge lintel stone at Nimrud.

Everyone who falls on that stone . . . but he on whom it falls (20:18). The second and third stone images are about judgment and allude respectively to Isaiah 8:14–15 and Daniel 2:34, 44–45. In the former text, the Lord Almighty identifies himself as a sanctuary for those who fear him, but a "stone that causes men to stumble" for unrepentant Israel. In the latter, God's kingdom is apocalyptically portrayed as a stone "[not made with] human hands," which crushes the other kingdoms of the world and endures forever. Jesus, the rejected stone, will triumph in judgment over those who have rejected him (see comments on 2:34).

Paying Taxes to Caesar (20:20–26)

Conflict and controversy continue as the religious leaders send spies to catch Jesus in a compromising statement. They ask him a clever "no-win" question: Should we pay taxes to Caesar? The beauty of Jesus' response is its disarming ambiguity. On the surface it affirms Roman authority, encouraging obedience to the government while maintaining spiritual allegiance to God. Yet for those most opposed to Rome, it could be interpreted to mean "since everything belongs to God, nothing belongs to Caesar." Jesus' opponents are astonished and silenced by his answer.

Spies, who pretended to be honest (20:20). The term "spy" (*enkathetos*) means someone hired to lie in wait and so indicates the desire of Jesus' enemies to trap him.[554] "Honest" (*dikaios*, "righteous, innocent") probably here means pious and sincere observers of the Mosaic law.

We know that you speak and teach what is right . . . the way of God (20:21). The spies seek to gain Jesus' confidence through flattery. The Old Testament repeatedly warns against the danger of flattering lips (Ps. 5:9; 12:2–3).[555] The spies affirm that Jesus teaches the "way of God," an expression that means obedience to God's law, living the righteous life he desires (Deut. 8:6; 10:12).[556]

Is it right . . . to pay taxes to Caesar . . . ? (20:22). This refers especially to the poll tax paid directly to Rome, not to local customs or property taxes. The Jews hated Roman rule with its heavy burden of taxation. Josephus describes how, under the governorship of Coponius (A.D. 6–10), the insurrectionist Judas of Galilee "incited his countrymen to revolt, upbraiding them as cowards for consenting to pay tribute to the Romans and tolerating mortal masters, after having God for their Lord."[557]

Show me a denarius. Whose portrait and inscription are on it? (20:24). While there were many coins in circulation in the Roman empire, Jesus requests a Roman denarius (worth about a day's wages). The coin bore the image of the emperor Tiberius (cf. 3:1), with the inscription "Tiberius Caesar, Augustus, son of the divine Augustus." Both the image and the acclamation of deity were abhorrent to the Jews (see Ex. 20:3–5, 23). There is great irony in the fact that Jesus' "pious" inquisitors themselves carry and trade Roman coins bearing idolatrous images and blasphemous inscriptions.

DENARIUS

A silver denarius with the image of the emperor Tiberius.

Give to Caesar what is Caesar's (20:25). Ecclesiastes 8:2 enjoins obedience to the king, and the New Testament repeatedly commands submission to governmental authorities.[558] God's establishment of and sovereignty over all the kings of the earth is also an important Old Testament theme.[559]

The Resurrection and Marriage (20:27–39)

Another attempt to discredit Jesus now comes from some Sadducees, who pose a question about levirate marriage (see comments on 20:28).[560]

Sadducees (20:27). See "The Sadducees."

Who say there is no resurrection (20:27). The clearest Old Testament reference to the resurrection is Daniel 12:2, but it is alluded to elsewhere.[561] Since the Sadducees viewed only the Torah (first five books of the Old Testament) as authoritative, they rejected any proof texts from the Writings and the Prophets.

Moses wrote . . . if a man's brother dies (20:28). The Old Testament law of levirate marriage required the brother of a deceased man to bear children with the dead man's wife in order to preserve the latter's genealogical line (Deut. 25:5–10). Old Testament examples appear in Genesis 38:8 and Ruth 4:1–12. Extensive rules relating to the practice are discussed in the Mishnaic tract *Yebamot* ("sisters-in-law").

Now there were seven brothers (20:29). An interesting parallel appears in the apocryphal book of Tobit (fourth or third century B.C.), where seven husbands of a young woman named Sarah die before giving her children (all killed by the evil demon Asmodeus). The grief-stricken woman eventually finds solace through her marriage to Tobit's son Tobias, the closest relative in a levirate marriage.[562]

For they are like the angels (20:36). Jesus did not say that believers become angels (a popular misconception), but that their glorified state will be like that of angels. Angels and human beings are distinct creations of God (Heb. 1–2).[563] The Jewish apocalyptic work *1 Enoch* develops a midrash around the account of the "sons of God" in Genesis 6. Though created not to marry, some of the angels sinned by taking wives for themselves from the daughters of man, producing giants as offspring.[564]

In the account of the bush, even Moses showed (20:37). Since the Sadducees viewed only the Pentateuch (Genesis to Deuteronomy) as authoritative, Jesus appeals to the account of the burning bush in Exodus 3 for proof of the resurrection. Jesus' argument may seem odd to modern ears, but it was a common rabbinic method. In a second-century rabbinic text, Rabbi Simeon ben Eleazar says:

> On the following basis I proved that the versions of Scripture of the Samaritans are forgeries, for they maintained that the dead do not live. I said to them, "Lo, Scripture says, ' . . . that person shall be utterly cut off; his iniquity shall be upon him.' "

The Samaritans had their own version of the Pentateuch, and they, like the Sadducees, did not believe in the resurrection. The rabbi here uses the future sense of the phrase "shall be upon him" (Num. 15:31, RSV) to prove that this person will face a future judgment, so there must be a resurrection.[565]

He is not the God of the dead (20:38). This expression of God's ongoing relationship with his people has an interesting parallel in *4 Maccabees*, where it is said of the Maccabean martyrs that "those who die for the sake of God live to God, as do Abraham and Isaac and Jacob and all the patriarchs" (*4 Macc.* 16:25; cf. 7:19).

Some of the teachers of the law responded, "Well said, teacher!" (20:39). Most teachers of the law were Pharisees (see 5:17), who, contrary to the Sadducees, agreed with Jesus' teaching on the resurrection.

No one dared to ask him any more questions (20:40). The ability to silence an opponent was viewed in Hellenistic culture as one of the marks of a wise man and a skilled orator (cf. Wisd. Sol. 8:12).

Whose Son Is the Christ? (20:41–44)

The controversies and debates in Jerusalem conclude with three episodes in which Jesus challenges or rebukes the religious leaders. These include the question about David's son (20:41–44), a rebuke of the teachers of the law (20:45–47), and the account of the widow's offering (21:1–4). In the first Jesus asks how the rabbis can call the Messiah the "Son of David," when David himself calls him "Lord" in Psalm 110. The title "son" implies subordination, so how can he be David's Lord? Jesus' point is that his messianic identity exceeds traditional Jewish expectations of an earthly, conquering king.

The Christ is the Son of David (20:41). The title "Son of David," which appears here and in 18:38–39, was a favorite title for the Messiah in rabbinic Judaism. It first appears in the first century B.C. *Psalms of Solomon* (17:21), where it carries strong political connotations (see "Messianic Expectation in Jesus' Day"). Its roots are to be found in the promise to David that God would raise up his offspring after him who would reign forever on his throne (2 Sam. 7:11–16). For more on traditional messianic expectations see comments on Luke 1:32–33; 9:20. For the related title "shoot of David," see comments on 1:78–79.

The Sadducees

The origin of the Sadducees is uncertain, but they appear to have arisen from the priestly families of the Jerusalem aristocracy who supported the Hasmonean dynasty during the period of Hebrew independence (c. 164–63 B.C.). In New Testament times, they controlled the priesthood and most political affairs, dominating the Sanhedrin (Acts 5:17). According to Josephus, they only considered the Pentateuch (the Torah) fully authoritative, denying the oral traditions of the Pharisees. As a result they denied the immortality of the soul and the resurrection of the body, no doubt claiming that these were later accretions to the Torah. They also emphasized human free will over divine predestination, in contrast to the Pharisees and (especially) the Essenes.[A-51] Luke further notes in Acts that the Sadducees did not believe in angels or spirits (Acts 23:8), which may mean the kinds of angelic orders and hierarchies characteristic of apocalyptic Judaism. Since the Sadducean power base was the priesthood and the temple, the destruction of Jerusalem in A.D. 70 ended their political influence, and the group disappeared from history.

David himself declares . . . "'The Lord said to my Lord . . .'" (20:42). Jesus identifies the speaker in Psalm 110 as David, who addresses the Messiah as "my Lord" and speaks of his enthronement at God's right hand. Surprisingly, first-century Judaism does not seem to have interpreted Psalm 110 messianically, though some have argued that the messianic interpretation was suppressed by later rabbis opposing its use as a messianic proof text by Christians. It is among the most frequently cited Old Testament texts in the New Testament.[566]

Denouncing the Teachers of the Law (20:45–47)

In this episode, Jesus warns his disciples against the hypocrisy of the teachers of the law. Though making an outward show of religiosity in the public arena, they act with injustice and exploit the poor. God will judge such hypocrisy. The passage is similar to the woes pronounced against the teachers of the law and the Pharisees in 11:37–54.

Teachers of the law (20:46). See comments on 5:17 and "Scribes."

THE "HOUSE OF DAVID" INSCRIPTION

A ninth-century B.C. Aramaic inscription found in Dan mentioning the battle of Ben Hadad, king of Aram, against "the house of David."

Flowing robes (20:46). This probably refers to long robes with tassels used to distinguish the office of the teacher of the law.

Greeted in the marketplaces . . . important seats in the synagogues (20:46). See comments on 11:43.

Places of honor at banquets (20:46). Meals carried great social significance in the ancient world, with guests seated according to their social status. See comments on 5:30; 14:7.

They devour widows' houses (20:47). This may refer to exploiting the estate of widows for whom they had been appointed guardians,[567] or perhaps the abuse of a widow's hospitality, a charge leveled at the Jerusalem aristocracy in the *Testament of Moses* 7:6.[568] Widows are viewed throughout Scripture as the most vulnerable and helpless members of society. God will judge those who oppress them. See comments on 18:3 for Old Testament and Jewish references.

The Widow's Offering (21:1–4)

The episode of the widow's sacrificial offering stands in contrast to the greed of the teachers of the law (see previous passage). While they exploit others for gain, she gives self-sacrificially from her poverty.

The temple treasury (21:1). The term *gazophylakion* refers either to one of various treasury rooms located in the temple[569] or to a chest or receptacle used to receive the money. The Mishnah speaks of thirteen shofar-chests (trumpet-shaped receptacles) located in the temple, which were used to collect various kinds of offerings.[570] Since people are "throwing" (*ballō*; NIV, "putting") money into the *gazophylakion*, this latter sense seems more likely. The former sense is evident in John 8:20, where Jesus is said to have been teaching in the *gazophylakion*.

A poor widow (21:2). Widows were often the poorest and most helpless members of society. See comments on 18:3.

Two very small copper coins (21:2). The copper coin here is a *lepton*, the smallest coin in circulation in Palestine (see 12:59). It was worth one-half a quadrans (Mark 12:42), or 1/128 of a denarius (the wage of a day laborer). A common laborer would earn one *lepton* in about four minutes of a ten-hour work day. Since this is "all [this widow] had to live on" (Luke 21:4), the woman is indeed very poor.

This poor widow has put in more (21:3). There are Jewish and Greek parallels to the maxim that generosity is relative to a person's wealth. Aristotle wrote that "one's generosity is to be evaluated in terms of one's resources. . . . People who are truly generous give in proportion to what they actually have. It is possible, therefore, that a person who gives but little out of small resources is more generous than another."[571]

Signs of the End of the Age (21:5–38)

With the time of his departure rapidly approaching, Jesus instructs his disciples on the cataclysmic events to come for Jerusalem and the signs that will accompany his return. In the first part of the discourse, Jesus speaks of signs that, though often interpreted eschatologically, are *not* indications of the imminent end (21:8–24). These include the appearance of false christs (21:8), catastrophic events like wars, earthquakes, and famines (21:9–11), widespread persecution of believers (21:12–19), and the horrific destruction of Jerusalem (21:20–24). For Luke Jerusalem's destruction serves as a preview and "type" of the final day of God's judgment; but it must be distinguished from it. A key transition occurs in 21:24, when Jesus predicts that "Jerusalem will be trampled on by the Gentiles *until the times of the Gentiles are fulfilled*" (italics added). The discourse then turns to the events that will follow the "times of the Gentiles" and will herald the end.[572]

The temple was adorned with beautiful stones and with gifts dedicated to God (21:5). Herod the Great's greatest building project was his restoration of the temple in Jerusalem. The extraordinary beauty of the place astounded everyone who saw it. A later rabbinic proverb reads, "He who has not seen the temple of Herod has never seen a beautiful building in his life."[573] Josephus gives a detailed description of the buildings and ornaments and remarks that the exterior of the building lacked nothing that could astound a person. The sun reflecting off the massive gold plates on the building "radiated so fiery a flash that persons straining to look at it were compelled to avert their eyes as from solar rays." Massive white stones twenty-five cubits long (37.5 feet), with some as much as forty-five cubits long (67.5 feet), were used in the construction. These gave the building a brilliant white appearance so that to approaching strangers the temple looked like a snow-covered mountain.[574] The

HERODʼS TEMPLE

A model of the Jerusalem temple.

“gifts dedicated to God” (*anathēma*) are probably offerings given by worshipers in fulfillment of vows.

Not one stone will be left on another (21:6). This image indicates total devastation, but should not be read over-literally (see comments on 19:44). Jesus was not the only one to predict the destruction of Jerusalem. Josephus describes a man named Jesus son of Ananus, who, for four years before the Jewish revolt and then for three years during it, wandered the city crying, “Woe to Jerusalem!” Though whipped first by the Jewish leadership and then by the Roman procurator Albinus, for seven years he continued his mournful cry. He was eventually killed during the siege of Jerusalem by a stone from a Roman catapult.[575]

Many will come in my name, claiming, “I am he” (21:8). Messianic and prophetic claims were not uncommon in the first century (see comments on 17:23). Josephus blames an incorrect interpretation of “an ambiguous oracle” from the sacred writings about one who would become “ruler of the world” (a reference to Isaiah 9?) for the disastrous Jewish revolt of A.D. 66–74. Josephus denies the messianic significance of this prophecy and claims it concerned the establishment of Vespasian as Roman emperor.[576]

Wars and revolutions ... great earthquakes, famines and pestilences (21:9–11). Cataclysmic events, whether human conflicts like war and revolution[577] or “natural” disasters like earthquakes are often associated in the Old Testament and Judaism with God’s judgment.[578] The judgments of the Day of the Lord are marked by earthquakes and other cosmic disturbances.[579] Apocalyptic Judaism drew strongly on this imagery. In the third vision of 2 Esdras (also *4 Ezra*), Ezra asks the Lord when the signs he has been showing him will take place. The Lord responds:

> Measure carefully in your mind, and when you see that some of the predicted signs have occurred, then you will know that it is the very time when the Most High is about to visit the world that he has made. So when

there shall appear in the world earthquakes, tumult of peoples, intrigues of nations, wavering of leaders, confusion of princes, then you will know that it was of these that the Most High spoke from the days that were of old, from the beginning.[580]

Jesus responds against overzealous apocalyptic fervor by pointing out that these events are typical of human history and should not be confused with the end.

Great signs from heaven (21:11). Cosmic signs are also common in prophetic and apocalyptic literature as portents of God's judgment (see comments on 21:25).

Deliver you to synagogues (21:12). (Cf. 12:10.) In first-century Judaism the elders of the synagogue were administrative as well as religious leaders, and the synagogue served not only as a place of worship, but also for public gatherings, including judicial hearings.[581] The judicial hearings and sentences that led to Paul's five lashings by the Jews (2 Cor. 11:24) probably took place in local synagogues.

I will give you words and wisdom (21:15). These words recall God's promise to Moses (Ex. 4:12, 15) and Jeremiah (Jer. 1:9) that he would put his words in their mouths.[582]

Betrayed even by parents, brothers, relatives and friends (21:16). (Cf. Micah 7:6.) In the tight-knit Diaspora Jewish communities, acceptance of Jesus as Messiah could result in excommunication and even stoning.[583] Such social disintegration was viewed by the rabbis as a sign of the end of the age (see comments on 12:52–53).[584]

Not a hair of your head will perish (21:18). This is an idiom meaning complete protection.[585] In light of the reference to martyrdom in 21:16 and to "gaining life" in 21:19, this probably means spiritual rather than physical deliverance.[586]

When you see Jerusalem being surrounded by armies (21:20). The horrific siege of Jerusalem by the Romans and its accompanying famine is described by Josephus in great detail in books 5–6 of

bottom left

ARCH OF TITUS

The arch depicts the captives of Jerusalem in the aftermath of the Jewish war in A.D. 70.

bottom right

JUDEA CAPTA COIN

An imperial bronze coin commemorating the Roman victory over the Jews in A.D. 70. It is inscribed with the words, "captive Judea" (*IVDEA CAPTA*).

his *Jewish War* (see comments on 19:44; 21:23).

Let those who are in Judea flee to the mountains (21:21). Normally, people in the countryside would flee to the fortified cities for protection. Yet Jerusalem will be the wrong place to be during this siege (see comments on 21:23). The early church historian Eusebius records that, in response to this oracle, Christians in Judea fled to the city of Pella in Decapolis during the Jewish revolt.[587]

Punishment in fulfillment of all that has been written (21:22). The Old Testament repeatedly speaks of judgment against Jerusalem for her sins.[588] While many of these prophecies speak of Jerusalem's destruction by the Babylonians in 586 B.C., Jesus saw them as prophetic previews for the destruction of A.D. 70.

How dreadful . . . for pregnant women and nursing mothers! (21:23). The siege and famine in Jerusalem were particularly traumatic for those with children. Josephus describes one gruesome episode where a starving woman, whose food was repeatedly stolen by certain city defenders, killed and cooked her own infant. She ate half and, when the guards arrived and demanded the food they smelled cooking, offered the other half to them. In horror they fled from the house. When this report went out to the city, "those who were starving longed for death, and considered blessed those who were already dead, because they had not lived long enough either to hear or to see such evils."[589]

STANDARD OF THE 10TH ROMAN LEGION

This was a key Roman army in the Jewish war.

Jerusalem will be trampled on by the Gentiles (21:24). Israel's darkest times were when foreign nations conquered and occupied the holy city of Jerusalem, whether at the Babylonian captivity (Jer. 25:10–11), during the Maccabean period, or now with the Romans.[590] The author of 1 Maccabees deplores the time when "Jerusalem was uninhabited like a wilderness. . . . The sanctuary was trampled down, and aliens held the citadel; it was a lodging place for the Gentiles. Joy was taken from Jacob" (1 Macc. 3:45).

The times of the Gentiles (21:24). This is a period of world domination by the Gentiles that precedes the return of the Messiah. Daniel's prophecies of a great statue (Dan. 2) and beasts from the sea (Dan. 7) envision a period of world domination by the Gentiles before the establishment of the kingdom of God (2:44; 7:27).

Signs in the sun, moon and stars . . . the heavenly bodies will be shaken (21:25–26). Cosmic signs and disturbances are common in prophetic and apocalyptic literature as evidence of God's judgment and the end of the age (Isa. 13:9–10; 34:4).[591] Ancient peoples viewed heavenly signs as omens of good or evil. Josephus describes a star shaped like a sword and a comet that appeared over Jerusalem as a sign of her coming destruction.[592] Heavenly armies were also seen running through the clouds and surrounding the city.[593]

Nations will be in anguish and perplexity. . . . Men will faint (21:25–26). It was widely held in Judaism that the time leading up to the end, sometimes called the "messianic woes" or the "birth pains of the Messiah," would be a period of great distress and tribulation.[594] The War Scroll at Qumran says, "It will be a time of suffering for all the people redeemed by God. Of all their sufferings, none will be like this, from its haste until eternal redemption is fulfilled" (see comments on 21:9–11).[595]

The Son of Man coming in a cloud with power and great glory (21:27). This image is taken from Daniel 7:13, 14, where an exalted messianic figure is described as "one like a son of man," who comes on the clouds of heaven and is given authority, glory, and an eternal kingdom. The apocalyptic work *1 Enoch* develops this image with reference to the Messiah (see comments on 5:24; 9:26).

Look at the fig tree and all the trees (21:29). The fig tree here represents a nature analogy and is not a symbol for Israel (contrast 13:6). Fig trees are bare in the winter, so the first signs of leaves are evidence that summer is near. The signs Jesus has been describing will herald the return of the Son of Man.

This generation (21:32). The Greek term *genea* normally means "generation," that is, people living at a particular time. Some have suggested that the word instead should be translated "race" and that the saying means the nation Israel will survive until the return of Christ.[596] Although possible, this is an unusual use of *genea*. If the reference is to the disciples' own generation, either Jesus' prediction was wrong (since he did not return in the first century) or else the events of A.D. 70 in some way fulfilled the prophecy (the Son of Man "came" in judgment). Perhaps the best explanation is that "this generation" refers not to the disciples' generation, but to a (later) generation alive when the signs begin to take place.

Heaven and earth will pass away (21:33). See comments on 16:17.

To stand before the Son of Man (21:36). To "stand before" in this context means to stand confident of approval and vindication. In *1 Enoch* 62:8–9 the "elect ones" stand before the Son of Man in glory, while the wicked fall on their faces and flee from his presence in shame.

Judas Agrees to Betray Jesus (22:1–6)

The climax of this Gospel is now reached with Luke's account of Jesus' Passion (chs. 22–23). It begins with Judas's agreement to betray Jesus (22:1–6) and includes the Last Supper (22:7–38), Jesus' arrest on the Mount of Olives (22:47–53), Peter's denial (22:54–62), Jesus' trials before the Sanhedrin, Pilate, and Herod (22:63–23:25), the crucifixion (23:26–49), and

REFLECTIONS

THE THEME THAT RECURS OVER AND OVER IN JESUS' great Olivet Discourse is the need to be ready and prepared for the Lord's return. While biblical scholars may debate the details of how end-time events will play out on the stage of human history, two themes permeate biblical prophecy. The first is that God is sovereign over world events. He will bring them to their appropriate conclusion. The second is that the Christian must persevere in righteousness, always ready for the Master's return.

the burial (23:50–56). The primary theme is Jesus as the innocent and righteous servant who remains faithful to God's calling.

The Feast of Unleavened Bread, called the Passover (22:1). Passover was celebrated on the fifteenth of Nisan (March/April) and was followed by the seven-day Feast of Unleavened Bread.[597] See "Passover and the Feast of Unleavened Bread" at 2:41. The two festivals were often linked together and called "Passover."[598] Large crowds of pilgrims gathered in Jerusalem for this festival season.

Chief priests and the teachers of the law (22:2). See comments on 9:22. Jesus is viewed as a threat to the power of both the chief priests, who administer the temple and control the Sanhedrin, and the teachers of the law, who lead the local synagogue communities.

Satan entered Judas, called Iscariot (22:3). For Old Testament and Jewish background on Satan see comments on 4:2; 10:18; cf. 11:15. A similar statement appears in the Jewish work *Martyrdom and Ascension of Isaiah* (second century B.C. to fourth century A.D.), where Beliar (=Satan) "dwelt in the heart of king Manasseh," prompting him to arrest and eventually execute Isaiah by sawing him in half (3:11; 5:1). For similar activity by Satan see comments on John 13:2; Acts 5:3. On the name "Iscariot" see comments on 6:16.

The Last Supper (22:7–38)

In the Last Supper narrative, Jesus interprets his death as the sacrifice that will establish the new covenant predicted in Jeremiah 31. Jesus calls on his disciples to take the bread and the cup together as a remembrance of what he will accomplish for them. In the discourse that follows the supper, Jesus predicts his betrayal and once again calls his disciples to true servant leadership. He also affirms their leadership role in the kingdom. Yet such leadership will not come easily. The crisis they are about to face will be far more severe than anything they have encountered.

The day of Unleavened Bread on which the Passover lamb had to be sacrificed (22:7). Passover lambs were sacrificed in the temple on the late afternoon of Nisan (March/April) 14. The Passover (Nisan 15) began at sunset. Each family was to have one lamb, though a small family could share one with neighbors. The lamb was to be roasted and eaten with bitter herbs and unleavened bread.[599] The bitter herbs symbolized the bitterness of their slavery in Egypt and the unleavened bread the haste with which they left Egypt (see "Passover and the Feast of Unleavened Bread" at 2:41).[600]

A man carrying a jar of water (22:10). This man—probably a servant of the household—would stand out since

right ▶

STORAGE JARS

These large jars were found in Ekron and could have been used for storing water, oil, or wine.

women normally carried water jars (Gen. 24:11; John 4:7).[601] Though it is possible that Jesus had prearranged for this room, the text seems to suggest divine foreknowledge (see 1 Sam. 10:2–8 for a similar Old Testament story).

The guest room (22:11). The word used here (*katalyma*) is the same one used for the crowded "inn" where Joseph and Mary could find no room (see 2:7). It here means a guest room in a private residence. In 22:12 it is described as a "large upper room, all furnished" (22:12). The furnishings would have included the couches or cushions on which the guests reclined.

Jesus and his apostles reclined at the table (22:14). The Passover was originally to be eaten standing in readiness to flee Egypt, "with your cloak tucked into your belt, your sandals on your feet and your staff in your hand" (Ex. 12:11). Yet by Jesus' day, "even the poorest in Israel must not eat unless he sits down to the table."[602] This was because standing was the position of a slave, an inappropriate posture for celebrating freedom from slavery in Egypt!

After taking the cup, he gave thanks (22:17). The traditional Passover celebration used four cups of wine: (1) the first with an opening benediction over the Passover day; (2) the second after the explanation of the Passover and the singing of the first part of the Hallel (Ps. 113–114); (3) the third following the meal of unleavened bread, lamb, and bitter herbs; (4) the fourth following the concluding portion of the Hallel.[603] Luke refers to two cups (22:17, 20), but it is debated by scholars which two these were. It seems likely that the second cup in 22:20 is the third Passover cup (see below). This one is probably the first since it accompanies Jesus' introduction to the meal.

He took bread . . . "This is my body . . ." (22:19). Jesus inaugurates a new Passover by confirming that his body, symbolized by the bread, is the fulfillment and replacement for the Passover lamb (see 1 Cor. 5:7). His death will provide deliverance for God's people.

This cup is the new covenant in my blood (22:20). This is probably the third Passover cup, after the meal (see comments on 22:17). Covenants in the Old Testament were ratified with a blood sacrifice (Gen. 15:9–10; Ex. 24:8). Jesus' death will inaugurate the new covenant predicted by Jeremiah (Jer. 31:31–34).

The hand of him who is going to betray me is with mine on the table (22:21). Sharing a meal indicated a relationship of friendship and trust, so the note of betrayal is shocking. Jesus' words recall Psalm 41:9: "Even my close friend, whom I trusted, he who shared my bread, has lifted up his heel against me" (cf. John 13:18).

Kings of the Gentiles lord it over them . . . call themselves Benefactors (22:25). Ancient Near Eastern kings usually exercised absolute authority over their subjects, taking exalted titles and even claiming to be gods. The Jews could relate well to Jesus' words, having suffered much under despots like Antiochus Epiphanes (see 1 Macc. 1–6). A "benefactor" (*euergetēs*) was one who bestowed gifts on his subjects to gain loyalty and praise.[604] The title was taken by many rulers, though often it "would conceal tyranny under extravagant expenditure."[605]

Who is greater, the one who is at the table (22:27). See comments on 12:37; 17:7.

Eat and drink at my table . . . sit on thrones, judging the twelve tribes of Israel (22:30). Eating and drinking here points to the messianic banquet (see comments on 13:29; 14:15).[606] The image of God's people reigning and judging appears in Daniel 7:9, 14, 27; Matthew 19:28; 1 Corinthians 6:2–3. On the foundational role of the apostles see Ephesians 2:20; Revelation 21:14.

Satan has asked to sift you as wheat (22:31). Satan is the "accuser" of God's people (see comments on 4:2; 10:18; 11:15). As he gained permission to test Job (Job 1:12; 2:6), so now he will test Peter and the other apostles (in the Greek "you" is plural in Luke 22:31, but singular in 22:32). Wheat was sifted through a sieve to separate the grain from chaff and other foreign matter (Isa. 30:28; Amos 9:9). Sirach 27:4 reads: "When a sieve is shaken, the refuse appears; so do a person's faults when he speaks."

I am ready to go with you to prison and to death (22:33). Peter will be jailed several times in Acts (Acts 4:3; 5:18; 12:1–19). According to church tradition he suffered martyrdom in Rome by being crucified upside down.[607]

Before the rooster crows today (22:34). Some have suggested that this does not refer to an actual rooster, but to the bugle call marking the third division of the Roman night, called *gallicinium* in Latin and *alektorophōnia* ("cockcrow") in Greek.[608] The context, however, suggests Jesus meant an actual rooster. Although the Mishnah says it was forbidden to raise chickens in the holy city of Jerusalem, this is likely a later idealization rather than a first-century reality.[609]

Purse, bag or sandals (22:35). See comments on 9:3; 10:3–4.

It is written: "And he was numbered with the transgressors" (22:37). Jesus quotes Isaiah 53:12, from Isaiah's fourth Servant Song, about the suffering of the Messiah (see comments on 9:22; 18:31). To be "numbered" with transgressors means to be considered a criminal and alludes to the two criminals crucified with Jesus (23:32–33).

See, Lord, here are two swords. . . . "That is enough" (22:38). It is perhaps not surprising that the disciples were carrying two swords since opposition was growing and since at least one of Jesus' disciples had a Zealot background (see 6:15). Josephus mentions that the Essenes commonly carried weapons for defense against thieves.[610] Jesus' response may mean, "Two swords is enough," but more likely his comment is negative, indicating the disciples have misunderstood his meaning: "Enough of this silly talk!"

REFLECTIONS

WHEN JESUS' DISCIPLES ARGUE among themselves as to who is the greatest, Jesus teaches them the true meaning of greatness. Greatness comes from a humble heart of servanthood. It is epitomized in Jesus' self-sacrificial death on the cross. If Jesus served us in this way, how ought we to serve others?

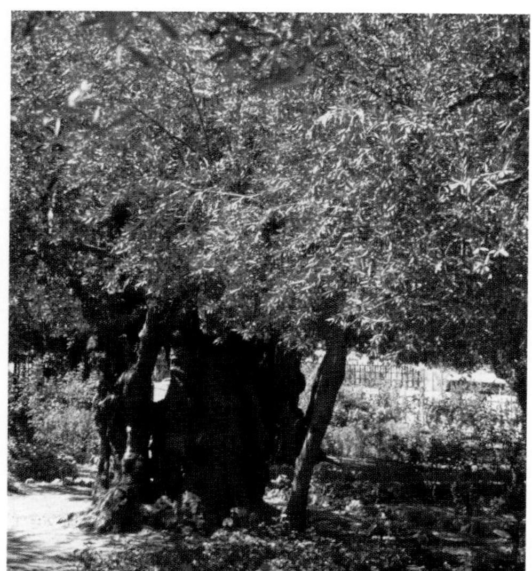

◀ *left*

GARDEN OF GETHSEMANE

Jesus Prays on the Mount of Olives (22:39–46)

Following the Last Supper, Jesus and his disciples go to the Mount of Olives. There Jesus agonizes in prayer over his coming ordeal. Both Jesus' true humanity and his willing obedience are evident as he prays, "Father, if you are willing, take this cup from me; yet not my will, but yours be done." By contrast, the weakness of the disciples is evident as they fall asleep, failing to obey Jesus' call to watchfulness and prayer.

The Mount of Olives (22:39). See comments on 19:29.

Take this cup from me (22:42). Drinking a cup was a common metaphor for experiencing a traumatic event (cf. Mark 10:38). In the Old Testament it is often associated with the outpouring of God's judgment.[611] This sense is probably present here since on the cross Jesus will receive God's judgment against humanity's sin.

An angel from heaven . . . strengthened him (22:43). Angels appear as servants for aid and encouragement in both the Old Testament and Judaism.[612]

Sweat was like drops of blood (22:44). Luke does not say that Jesus sweated blood, but that his sweat was *like* (*hōsei*) drops of blood—that is, it fell profusely. While there are references to blood-red sweat in ancient literature[613] and medical claims of this possibility,[614] it is not necessary to appeal to them here.

Jesus Arrested (22:47–53)

Judas, having arranged earlier to betray Jesus (see 21:37–22:6), suddenly appears with a crowd to arrest him. In a brief attempt to defend Jesus, one of the disciples (identified as Peter by John) strikes the servant of the high priest with a sword, cutting off his ear. Jesus' sovereign control is particularly evident in Luke, who alone recounts that Jesus heals the man's ear and prohibits further resistance. He then rebukes the leaders for treating him like an insurrectionist when they could have openly arrested him at any time. Yet the present time of darkness is a fitting metaphor for their sinister act.

He approached Jesus to kiss him (22:47). The kiss was (and is) a common Middle

COURTYARD

The church of St. Peter in Gallicantu. One tradition regards this as the area for the home of the high priest Caiaphas.

Eastern greeting between friends and those with a special bond (Gen. 29:13; 33:4).[615] It can also indicate homage and respect (Job 31:27; Ps. 2:12) and was probably the common greeting between disciple and rabbi. In 2 Samuel 20:9, as here, it is used in an act of treachery.

Should we strike with our swords? (22:49). See comments on 22:38.

The chief priests, the officers of the temple guard, and the elders (22:52). See comments on 22:2. The chief priests and the elders represent the religious and lay leadership of the Sanhedrin. The officers of the temple guard are the Sanhedrin's police force.

Am I leading a rebellion. . . ? (22:52). The Greek says literally, "as against a thief." Josephus uses the term *lēstēs* of revolutionaries opposing the Roman authorities.[616] To patriotic Jews they were freedom fighters; to the Romans they were common criminals.

Peter Disowns Jesus (22:54–62)

The house of the high priest (22:54). This may be either the house of Caiaphas, the actual high priest, or Annas, his father-in-law, whom Luke also calls high priest (see comments on 3:2). John reports that Jesus was first taken to Annas and then to Caiaphas (John 18:13, 24).

A fire in the middle of the courtyard (22:55). Large homes were built around an open courtyard. While the leaders go in the house, the servants and perhaps guards stay in the courtyard.

For he is a Galilean (22:59). Peter's accent must have given him away as a Galilean (see comments on Matt. 26:73). For an Old Testament example see Judges 12:6, where Ephraimites are identified because they pronounce "Shibboleth" as "Sibboleth."

The rooster crowed (22:60). See comments on 22:34.

The Guards Mock Jesus (22:63–65).

The men who were guarding Jesus (22:63). These are members of the Jewish temple guard used in the arrest of Jesus (see comments on 22:52).

Mocking and beating him . . . "Prophesy! Who hit you?" (22:63–64). See comments on 18:32. The abuse of Jesus recalls the suffering of the righteous servant in Isaiah 50:6; 53:3–5. That those considered false prophets were subject to such treatment by the Jewish authorities is clear in the case of Jesus son of Ananus (see comments on 21:6).

right ▶

HIGH PRIESTLY GARMENTS

An illustration of Aaron from a 16th century German manuscript.

Trial Before the Sanhedrin (22:66–71)

Jesus' hearing before the full Sanhedrin occurs at daybreak on Friday morning. The purpose is to gather evidence to bring charges of messianic claims against Jesus before the governor. Scholars have noted that Jesus' trial as reported in the Gospels violates various regulations concerning judicial protocol set forth in the Mishnah (*m. Sanh.*; for details see "The So-Called Illegalities of Jesus' Trial" at Mark 14). Some have used these "illegalities" to point out the gross disregard for justice of the Jewish authorities. Others use them to argue against the historicity of the Gospel accounts. Neither of these conclusions is warranted. The mishnaic regulations are from the late second century and present an idealized picture of the judicial system. They may not have been strictly followed, or even in force, in the first century. In the eyes of the Sanhedrin, Jesus is a false prophet and a dangerous threat to national stability. They must expedite this matter quickly to eliminate the threat to their position and authority.

The council of the elders (22:66). This refers to the Sanhedrin, the Jewish high court. See "The Sanhedrin."

From now on, the Son of Man will be seated at the right hand of the mighty God (22:69). This phrase combines the image of the Son of Man from Daniel 7 (see comments on 5:24; 9:26) with the exaltation of the Messiah in Psalm 110:1–2 (see comments on 20:42).

Are you then the Son of God? (22:70). The Sanhedrin is probably not asking whether Jesus is claiming deity, but whether he is the Messiah. The Old Testament promised that the Messiah would have a special father-son relationship with God.[617] It is debated whether "Son of God" was a common messianic title in first-century Judaism (see comments on 1:35; 4:41).

Trial Before Pilate and Herod (23:1–25)

Having affirmed Jesus' guilt in their eyes, the Sanhedrin now takes him to the Roman prefect, Pilate, to obtain a capital

▸ The Sanhedrin

Though later rabbis traced its origin to the appointment of seventy elders by Moses in Numbers 11:16 (*m. Sanh.* 1:6), there is little evidence for a formal council until the Greek period (third century B.C.).[A-52] The Sanhedrin was originally made up of the Jerusalem nobility, both lay leaders and priests, with the hereditary high priest as its head. In the time of Jesus the Sadducees (the party of the aristocracy and the priesthood) still controlled the Sanhedrin (see Acts 5:17), though leading Pharisees and scribes had also gained a prominent place (cf. Acts 23:7). Luke's reference to the "chief priests" and "teachers of the law" (Luke 22:66) probably refers respectively to these Sadducean and Pharisaic power blocks.

The authority and jurisdiction of the Sanhedrin waxed and waned depending on the political situation. Josephus reports that Herod the Great consolidated his reign by ordering the execution of the whole Sanhedrin, and he held the council in tight check during his reign. Under the Roman governors, the Sanhedrin exerted greater influence, with wide-ranging judicial and administrative jurisdiction.[A-53] sentence. The charges against Jesus here take a more political tone: misleading the nation, opposing Roman taxes (a blatantly false accusation; cf. 20:20–26), and claiming to be Christ, a king. Luke's central theme of this Roman phase of the trial is Jesus' innocence. Both Pilate and Herod find no guilt in Jesus (23:4, 14–15, 22). Later, the repentant criminal on the cross and the centurion on duty also affirm his innocence (23:41, 47). Jesus is the righteous and innocent suffering servant.

Led him off to Pilate (23:1). According to John 18:31, the Sanhedrin did not have the right to administer capital punishment, so they had to bring Jesus before Pilate. This judicial limitation is confirmed by later rabbinic tradition and by Josephus, who reports that the high priest Ananus was deposed for orchestrating the execution of Jesus' half-brother James during the interim period between the Roman governors Festus and Albinus.[618]

The seat of Roman government in Judea was at Caesarea on the Mediterranean coast, but Pilate was usually in Jerusalem to maintain order during the festival. He resided either at the fortress of Antonia overlooking the Temple Mount, or at the Herodian palace on the western wall in the upper city (see map of Jerusalem). For more on Pilate see comments on 13:1; also Mark 15:1.

THE PONTIUS PILATE INSCRIPTION

A Roman era stone slab discovered in Caesarea that names Pontius Pilate.

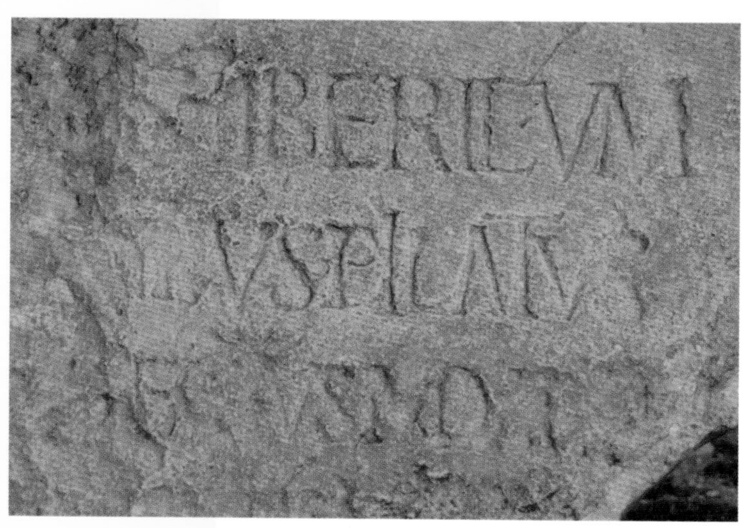

And they began to accuse him (23:2). The Romans had two main judicial systems, jury courts (which tried cases involving formal statutes of state law—the *ordo*) and more informal police courts (adjudicated by a magistrate). These latter were the norm in the Roman provinces, where local governors would hear charges, conduct examinations (*cognitio*), and pronounce sentences.[619] Jesus' trial before Pilate is a typical example of such a *cognitio.*[620]

Opposes payment of taxes to Caesar (23:2). This was a serious charge. Twenty-five years earlier Judas of Galilee provoked an insurrection in Judea over the issue of Roman taxation.[621]

Christ, a king . . . "Are you the king of the Jews?" (23:2–3). While the Jewish religious title "Christ" (Greek) or "Messiah" (Hebrew) would have carried little significance for Pilate, the claim of "king" would represent a threat to Roman authority.

Yes, it is as you say (23:3). The Greek here (lit., "You have said so") is more ambiguous than the NIV translation suggests, but probably indicates a qualified affirmation. In any case, Pilate looks at Jesus and judges that he is not a political threat.

Jesus was under Herod's jurisdiction (23:7). See comments on 3:1; 3:19–20. Herod Antipas ruled as tetrarch over

Galilee and Perea from the death of his father Herod the Great in A.D. 4 until A.D. 39. He appears in the Gospels as the executor of John the Baptist (3:19–20) and as a distant but curious spectator of Jesus' ministry (9:7–9; 13:31–32). Like his father, he sought to present himself as a faithful Jew. His coins, like those of Herod the Great, did not bear an image of the emperor,[622] and, as this passage shows, he faithfully attended Jewish festivals in Jerusalem.

He sent him to Herod (23:7). Pilate may have wanted to avoid personal liability for a difficult decision, or perhaps he was seeking expert Jewish advice from Herod. Herod was in Jerusalem for the Passover and was probably staying in the Hasmonean palace, to the west of the temple (see map of Jerusalem).

Jesus gave him no answer (23:9). Isaiah 53:7 predicts the silence of the Suffering Servant before his oppressors: "As a sheep before her shearers is silent, so he did not open his mouth." Ancient writers sometimes speak of the wisdom of silence before false and hypocritical accusations. Note Sirach 20:1: "There is a rebuke that is untimely, and there is the person who is wise enough to keep silent."[623]

Dressing him in an elegant robe (23:11). The Greek says "bright" (*lampros*) clothing, which may mean either "white" or "regal" (cf. the purple robe used by the Roman soldiers in Mark 15:17, 20). In either case, the point is mocking Jesus' kingship.

Herod and Pilate became friends—before this they had been enemies (23:12). Pilate and Herod Antipas had good reasons to be suspicious of each other, since Pilate was governing the land of Antipas's father, Herod the Great. Surely Antipas hoped one day to rule it for himself. The Jewish philosopher Philo reports an incident in which Pilate

FORTRESS OF ANTONIA

The four towers mark the location of this palace on the northwest corner of the Temple Mount.

offended Jewish sensibilities by setting up golden shields inscribed with patrons' names in the Herodian palace in Jerusalem. Four sons of Herod the Great—including Antipas—brought charges against him before the emperor Tiberius, who ordered Pilate to remove them (see comments on 13:1 for similar actions by Pilate).[624] Incidents like these had made Pilate and Antipas enemies and rivals.

I will punish him (23:16; cf. v. 22). The verb translated "punish" (*paideuō*) is a mild one which can mean "discipline" or even "instruct." Here it is a euphemism for a beating, something like the English idiom "to teach him a lesson." The Romans distinguished between three kinds of beatings: *fustes, flagella,* and *verbera*. The first was the lightest and was often used as a judicial warning against further infractions. The third was the most severe and was usually given as a prelude to a more severe punishment like execution.[625] Pilate intends to give Jesus a *fustigatio* and release him. As it turned out, Jesus certainly received the *verberatio* when Pilate conceded to his crucifixion (for a description of this kind of beating see Matt. 27:26; Mark 15:15).

PAVEMENT FROM THE FORTRESS OF ANTONIA

The "Lithostratos"—a Roman era pavement stone found near the location of the fortress where Jesus carried his cross.

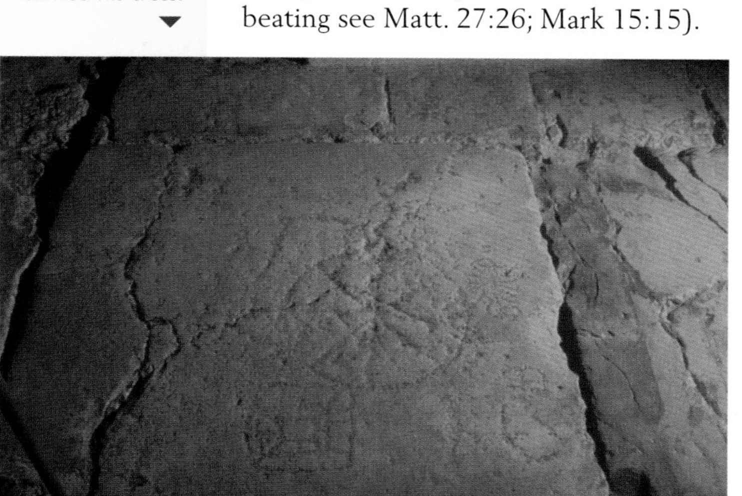

I will . . . release him (23:16). The other Gospels note that it was the custom of the day to release a prisoner at the Passover.[626] It is implied in Luke, since the crowd cries out to release Barabbas instead of Jesus. Though the custom is not explicitly described outside the Gospels, it fits well with the clemency practices of religious festivals in the Greco-Roman world.[627]

Barabbas . . . thrown into prison for an insurrection in the city, and for murder (23:19; cf. v. 25). First-century Palestine was a hotbed of revolutionary movements in the years leading up to the Jewish revolt of A.D. 66–74. Josephus describes a variety of such insurrectionists, which he calls "robbers" and "imposters."[628] Among the most vicious were the Sicarii, who would mingle with the crowds during the festivals and stab Roman sympathizers with small swords (*sicae*) hidden under their robes.[629] Josephus identifies the Zealots who occupied Masada during the Jewish War as Sicarii.[630] Though Barabbas is not explicitly called a Zealot or a Sicarii, his crimes of insurrection and murder are suggestive of this kind of revolutionary activity. Perhaps he was an associate of the two criminals crucified with Jesus (see comments on 17:23; 21:8).

"Crucify him! Crucify him!" (23:21). See "Crucifixion" at 23:33.

Pilate . . . surrendered Jesus to their will (23:24–25). Pilate was a pragmatist more interested in maintaining his own power than in justice for an individual. His tendency to capitulate under pressure is seen elsewhere in his withdrawal of Roman standards from Jerusalem and his removal of golden shields from the

Herodian palace (see comments on 13:1; 23:12).[631]

The Crucifixion (23:26–43)

Luke's crucifixion scene shows Jesus faithfully fulfilling his calling to suffer as the servant of God. Though a victim of injustice, he is in charge of his own fate. He continues to act as a prophet, calling on the grieving women to mourn for themselves because of their coming devastation (in the fall of Jerusalem; cf. 13:34–35; 19:41–44; 21:20–21). He continues to dispense God's grace, forgiving his enemies and offering salvation to the repentant criminal.

The earliest extant Roman record of Pilate's crucifixion of Jesus is from the historian Tacitus. Writing about the persecution of Christians by Nero, he describes their founder as a certain Christus, who "suffered the extreme penalty during the reign of Tiberius at the hands of one of our procurators, Pontius Pilatus."[632] In his famous *Testimonium*, Josephus also mentions Jesus' crucifixion by Pilate.[633] Although this passage has clearly been embellished by later Christians, a recently discovered Arabic version of the *Testimonium* appears to be closer to Josephus' original:

> At this time there was a wise man who was called Jesus. And his conduct was good, and (he) was known to be virtuous. And many people from among the Jews and other nations became his disciples. Pilate condemned him to be crucified and to die. And those who had become his disciples did not abandon his discipleship. They reported that he had appeared to them three days after his crucifixion and that he was alive; accordingly, he was perhaps the Messiah concerning whom the prophets have recounted wonders.[634]

Simon from Cyrene (23:26). Cyrene was located in north Africa, in the Roman province of Cyrenaica (modern Libya). Simon was probably a Jewish pilgrim visiting Jerusalem during the Passover.

Put the cross on him (23:26). This would be the *patibulum*, or crossbeam of the cross.

Blessed are the barren women (23:29). In a culture where childlessness was the cause of great shame (see comments on 1:7) Jesus' words represent a shocking reversal. It is the barren who are blessed because they will not watch their children suffer and die before their eyes. See comments on 21:23 for the horrors of the siege of Jerusalem, particularly on women and children.

They will say to the mountains, "Fall on us!" and to the hills, "Cover us!" (23:30). This alludes to Hosea 10:8, a judgment oracle against Israel (cf. Rev. 6:16, where the same verse is cited). The image probably indicates a desire for swift death over prolonged judgment. There may also be the sense that the painful crushing of creation is like "protection" when compared to the awful wrath of God.

For if men do these things when the tree is green . . . when it is dry (23:31). Dry wood is sparked to life and burns more easily than freshly cut green wood. The saying probably means that if the Romans crucify an innocent man during relatively peaceful times (the green wood), how much worse will they do during the coming days of revolution (the dry). Josephus records the crucifixion of thousands of

Jews by the Romans during the siege of Jerusalem:

The soldiers out of rage and hatred amused themselves by nailing their prisoners in different postures; and so great was their number, that space could not be found for the crosses nor crosses for the bodies.[635]

The place called the Skull (23:33). Luke gives only the Greek term *kranion* rather than the Aramaic "Golgotha" (Matt. 27:33; Mark 15:22). "Calvary" (*calvaria*) is the Latin word for skull. The location is uncertain. It would have been outside the city (Lev. 24:14; Heb. 13:12) and located near a major road, since crucifixion was intended to be a public spectacle and a warning to others.[636] The name could refer to an outcropping of rocks shaped like a skull, or perhaps to the presence of tombs in the area. The traditional site is in an upper section of the Church of the Holy Sepulchre on the west side of Jerusalem. More recent claims have been made for Gordon's Calvary, which has a skull-like appearance and is located near the Garden Tomb. Most contemporary scholars are inclined toward the former traditional site (or remain agnostic).

THE "WAY OF SORROWS"

The sign marks the location of the Via Dolorosa, the road Jesus walked to the place of his crucifixion.

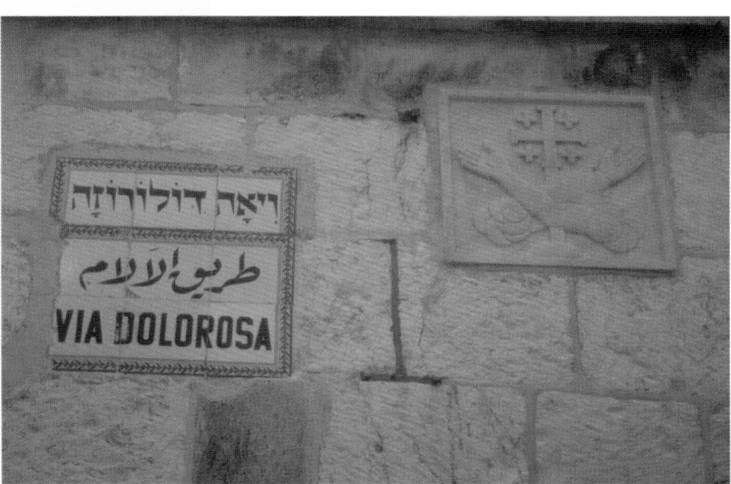

There they crucified him (23:33). See "Crucifixion."

"Father, forgive them, for they do not know what they are doing" (23:34). Jesus' prayer for the forgiveness of his executioners stands in contrast to the cries for vengeance of the Maccabean martyrs of 2 Maccabees 7:17, 19, 34–35 (cf. 7:14; *4 Macc.* 9:15):

> Keep on, and see how his mighty power will torture you and your descendants! . . . But do not think that you will go unpunished for having tried to fight against God! . . .
>
> But you, unholy wretch, you most defiled of all mortals, do not be elated in vain and puffed up by uncertain hopes, when you raise your hand against the children of heaven. You have not yet escaped the judgment of the almighty, all-seeing God.

And they divided up his clothes by casting lots (23:34). The language alludes to Psalm 22:18. It was a common Roman custom for executioners to divide the meager possessions of their victims. This arose from the practice of taking plunder from the battlefield.[637]

The rulers even sneered at him. . . . The soldiers . . . mocked him (23:35–36). The taunting and mocking, like the dividing of garments, recalls the treatment of the righteous sufferer in Psalm 22:7–8.

The Chosen One (23:35). See comments on 9:26, 35.

They offered him wine vinegar (23:36). This sour wine (*oxos*) was a favorite beverage of the lower classes and especially soldiers. It was cheaper than regular wine and relieved thirst better than water.[638]

An allusion to the righteous sufferer of Psalm 69:21 may be present.

A written notice above him, which read: THIS IS THE KING OF THE JEWS (23:38). It was evidently common for the Romans to hang a notice (in Latin, a *titulus*) on the cross with the name of the victim and the charge against him.[639] The title mocks Jesus' claim to messiahship.

Today you will be with me in paradise (23:43). "Paradise" is from a Persian word meaning "garden" and is used in the LXX and other Jewish writings for the Garden of Eden.[640] In apocalyptic Judaism it came to signify the eternal place of bliss for the righteous. 2 Esdras (*4 Ezra*) 8:52 reads:

> . . . it is for you that paradise is opened, the tree of life is planted, the age to come is prepared, plenty is provided, a city is built, rest is appointed, goodness is established and wisdom perfected beforehand.[641]

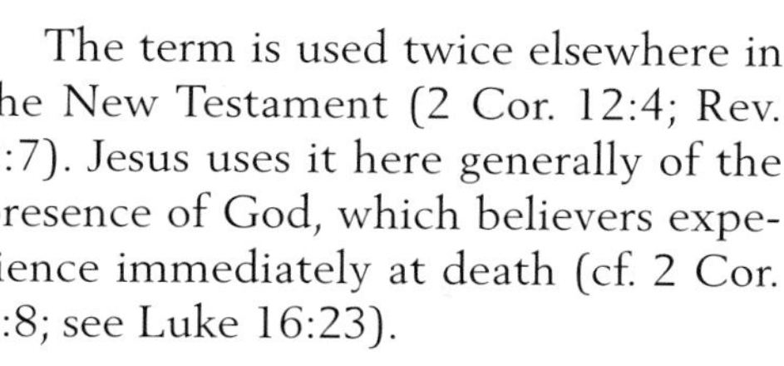

The term is used twice elsewhere in the New Testament (2 Cor. 12:4; Rev. 2:7). Jesus uses it here generally of the presence of God, which believers experience immediately at death (cf. 2 Cor. 5:8; see Luke 16:23).

▲ **GARDEN TOMB (GORDON'S CALVARY)**

An alternative (although unlikely) site of Jesus' tomb. The tomb is associated with the site that General Charles Gordon suggested as the location of Golgotha in 1883.

Crucifixion

Crucifixion was used both as a means of execution and for "exposing" an executed body to shame and humiliation.[A-54] The Romans practiced a variety of forms. The main stake or *palus* generally remained at the place of execution, while the victim would be forced to carry the crossbeam or *patibulum* (see 23:26). The crossbeam was placed either on top of the *palus* (like a "T") or in the more traditional cross shape (†). The victim would be affixed to the cross with ropes or, as in the case of Jesus, with nails (John 20:25). Various positions were used to maximize torture and humiliation (see comments from Josephus at 23:31). Seneca wrote that "some hang their victims with head toward the ground, some impale their private parts, others stretch out their arms on fork-shaped gibbet."[A-55] Death was caused by loss of blood, exposure, exhaustion, and/or suffocation, as the victim tried to lift himself to breathe. Victims sometimes lingered for days in agony. Crucifixion was viewed by ancient writers as the cruelest and most barbaric of punishments[A-56] (see comments on Luke 9:23).

The bones of a crucified man named Jehohanan were discovered in 1968 at *Giv'at ha Mivtar* in the Kidron Valley northeast of the Old City, dated between A.D. 7 and 70.[A-57] He was probably a victim of one of the various insurrectionist movements of the first century.

Jesus' Death (23:44–49)

Jesus' death in Luke picks up various themes of the Passion narrative. The nation's sin and God's coming judgment are indicated by the darkness, the tearing of the curtain, and the mourning of the people. Jesus, by contrast, stays faithful to the end, committing his spirit to God. Finally, his innocence is once again affirmed as the centurion declares him to be a "righteous" or "innocent" man (*dikaios*). Jesus dies as the faithful and righteous Servant of the Lord (Isa. 53:11).

The sixth hour darkness came . . . until the ninth hour (23:44). The sixth hour is twelve noon, so the darkness continued from 12:00 to 3:00 P.M. According to Mark 15:25, the crucifixion began at the third hour (9:00 A.M.). In the Old Testament darkness is related to the judgments of the Day of the Lord, and the motif of judgment is probably present here.[642] Darkness is also associated with the death of great men in both Greco-Roman and Jewish traditions.[643]

The curtain of the temple was torn in two (23:45). This could be either the curtain that separated the temple from the inner courtyard, or the curtain between the Holy Place and the Most Holy Place.[644] Josephus describes this latter as a magnificent Babylonian curtain of blue, scarlet, and purple, symbolically representing the universe.[645] The symbolism of tearing is probably threefold: judgment against the nation, the cessation of temple sacrifices, and a new way open for all into the presence of God (Heb. 10:19–20).

Josephus reports various signs that served as omens of the destruction of the temple (see comments on 21:25–26). One of these was the mysterious opening of the massive eastern gate of the inner court at midnight on a certain Passover. Though the gate normally took twenty men to open and shut, on this night it mysteriously opened of its own accord. While the ignorant considered this to be a positive sign—God's opening the door of happiness—the wiser men of learning recognized it as opening for the advantage of their enemies—an omen of the coming desolation.[646]

right ▶

THE CURTAIN IN THE TEMPLE

A reconstruction of the appearance of the temple veil.

REFLECTIONS

JESUS' WILLINGNESS TO FORGIVE EVEN HIS MURDERERS sets a new standard of forgiveness and epitomizes Jesus' teaching about loving your enemies. Just as God loved us "while we were still sinners" (Rom. 5:8), so we ought to reach out in love and forgiveness to those who have wronged us. We are not to be overcome by evil, but to overcome evil with good (Rom. 12:21).

Father, into your hands I commit my spirit (23:46). Jesus' final words allude to Psalm 31:5, a psalm of a righteous sufferer crying out for deliverance from enemies who are persecuting him. The psalm is here used typologically. Jesus is the righteous sufferer par excellence.

The centurion (23:47). A centurion commanded a "century" of about one hundred soldiers. This man was probably in charge of the crucifixion.

Surely this was a righteous man (23:47). The term *dikaios* can mean either "innocent" or "righteous." Both senses are significant for Luke. Throughout the trial and crucifixion Jesus is described as an innocent sufferer. This in turn points to Isaiah 53:11, where God's "righteous [LXX *dikaios*] servant will justify many" (cf. Acts 3:14; 7:52; 22:14).

They beat their breasts (23:48). Beating the breast is a sign of mourning and, perhaps, repentance (see comments on 18:13).[647] In context the point seems to be that the people recognize that a great injustice has been done.

Jesus' Burial (23:50–56)

Joseph, a member of the Council . . . asked for Jesus' body (23:50–52). On the basis of Deuteronomy 21:22–23, the Jews sought to bury a crucified body before nightfall, especially before the Sabbath began.[648] This sometimes clashed with the practice of the Romans, who used crucifixion as a public example to provoke fear. They often refused burial for their victims. It was probably Joseph's status as a respected member of the Sanhedrin that prompted Pilate to release Jesus' body so soon after death.

Arimathea (23:51). The location of Arimathea is uncertain, but may refer to Ramathaim, another name for Ramah, the birthplace of Samuel (1 Sam. 1:1, 19; 2:11). It was located east of Joppa, twenty miles northwest of Jerusalem.[649]

Placed it in a tomb cut in the rock, one in which no one had yet been laid (23:53). Family tombs of Jesus' day were usually caves carved into the sides of hills. In the first century the Jews practiced two-stage burial. In the first stage the corpse would be laid lengthwise in a niche cut in the wall or on a shelf carved alongside the wall. After the flesh decomposed, the bones would be either gathered together in a common pile with other family bones or placed in a small ossuary (burial box) about two feet long and one foot wide. In this way the tomb could be used for many family members over several generations.[650]

It was Preparation Day, and the Sabbath was about to begin (23:54). Preparation Day refers to the day before the Sabbath, which began on Friday evening at sunset. Preparations had to be completed quickly so that no work would be done on the Sabbath.

Then they went home and prepared spices and perfumes (23:56). Spices and oils were used to honor the dead and to keep down the stench of decomposition.

But they rested on the Sabbath in obedience to the commandment (23:56). The Mishnah allows the preparation of the body on the Sabbath but not its movement: "They may make ready [on the Sabbath] all that is needful for the dead, and anoint it and wash it, provided that they do not move any member of it."[651]

RECONSTRUCTING THE TOMB OF CHRIST

Based on "Reconstructing the Tomb of Christ from Archaeological and Literary Sources" by Eugenia L. Nitoviski, Ph.D., O.C.D., University of Notre Dame

All dimensions shown here are based on studies of actual rolling stone tombs. The original tomb of Christ was destroyed by the Roman Emperor Hadrian.

84″
CENTRAL CHAMBER
4″
24″
KOKH
KOKH
24″
60″ SQUARE
BENCH
36″
KOKH
12″
72″
FRONT WALL OF TOMB
14″
48″
ROLLING STONE
24″
36″
18″
ENTRANCE
PIT
STOPPING STONE
SLANTED ROLLING STONE TRACK
OUTER COURT
Body placed on BENCH for burial preparation
KOKH
KOKH
KOKH
LIVING ROCK shown in darker tone
Hugh Claycombe
METERS
FEET

After preparation for burial, bodies were placed in the kokh (niche) which was then sealed with a closure stone. Much later these dried bones were stored in ossuaries (stone boxes).

The original tomb belonging to Joseph of Arimathea was destroyed by the Roman Emperor Habrian after a.d. 135. This reconstruction is based on 61 other "rolling stone" tombs which have remained, particulary on a classic example found in Heshbon, Jordan in 1971. Joseph's tomb may not have been this extensive nor complete, being as yet unused. Affordable by wealthy familes only, these tombs were constructed according to Jewish law, the Mishnah, as follows:

> "If a man sold to his fellow a place to make a tomb (so, too, if a man received from his fellow a place in which to make hima tomb), he must make the inside of the vault four cubits by six, and open up within it eight niches, three on this side, and two oppisite [the doorway]. The niches must be four cubits long, seven handbreadths high and six wide. R. Simeon says: He must make the inside of the vault, four cubits by eight and open up within thirteen niches, four on this side, four on that side, three opposite [the doorway] and one to the right of the doorway and one to the left. He must make a courtyard at the opening of the vault, six cubits by six, space enough for the bier and its bearers; and he may open up within it two other vaults, one on either side. R. Simeon says: Four, one on each of its four sides. Rabban Simeon b. Gamaliel says: All depends on the nature of the rock." (Baba Bathra 6:8)

Tomb F.1 at Tell Hesban, Transjordan
Courtesy of the Heshbon Expedition Andrews University

These were emergency procedures to prevent the onset of decomposition before burial. Since Joseph had been able to complete burial before the Sabbath, the women appropriately rest on the Sabbath.

The Resurrection (24:1–12)

Luke provides three accounts of resurrection appearances: the women at the tomb (24:1–12), the appearance to two disciples on the road to Emmaus (24:13–35), and the appearance to the eleven disciples in Jerusalem (24:36–49). He then concludes his Gospel with a short account of Jesus' ascension (24:50–53).

All four Gospels agree that women first discovered the empty tomb on Sunday morning and that the resurrected Jesus first appeared to women. This is particularly striking since women were not considered reliable witnesses in first-century Judaism. Josephus claims to be reporting the law of Moses when he writes:

> Put not trust in a single witness, but let there be three or at the least two, whose evidence shall be accredited by their past lives. From women let no evidence be accepted, because of the levity and temerity of their sex.[652]

While the reference to two or three witnesses comes from Deuteronomy 17:6; 19:15, the statement about women is nowhere found in the Old Testament and must come from first-century rabbinic traditions. Philo, too, claims that women are "irrational" and should not be trusted.[653] Considering this background, it is unlikely that the followers of Jesus would have *created* stories in which women were the primary witnesses to the empty tomb. Few would have believed them. This is a strong argument for the essential historicity of these accounts.

They found the stone rolled away from the tomb (24:2). This stone would have been a disk-shaped stone placed in a track or groove and rolled in front of the opening.[654]

Two men in clothes that gleamed like lightning (24:4). In the Old Testament and Judaism angels are often called "men" because of their human appearance.[655] They often appear shining and in white clothing—signs of purity and holiness (Dan. 10:5–6; cf. Luke 9:29).[656]

In their fright the women bowed down (24:5). Fear is a common response to the appearance of an angelic presence (see comments on 1:12).[657]

On the third day be raised again (24:7). The "third day" does not refer to three twenty-four hour days, but inclusively to any part of three days: Friday, Saturday, and Sunday. The "third day" may be an allusion to Hosea 6:2, a reference to Israel's national restoration.

TOMB WITH A ROLLING STONE

The first-century A.D. tomb of Queen Helena of Adiabene.

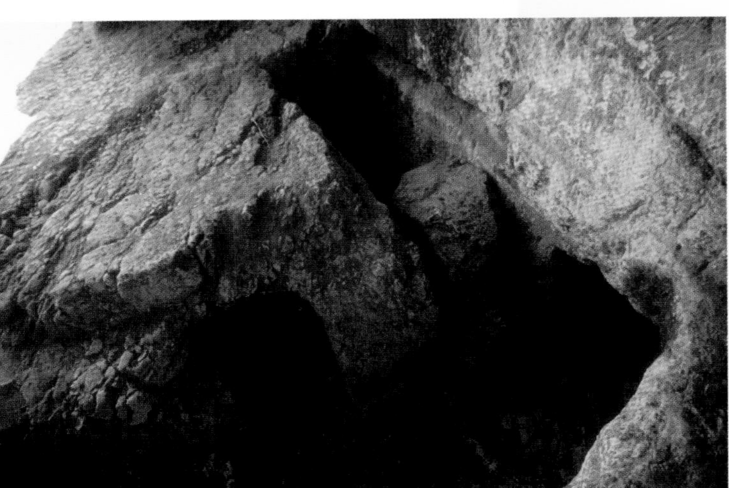

As the Messiah, Jesus both represents and brings restoration to God's people.

It was Mary Magdalene, Joanna, Mary the mother of James, and the others with them (24:10). For the first two women see comments on 8:2–3. The third name says literally "Mary of James," which could refer to James's wife, mother, or even sister. Mark 15:40 suggests "mother" is meant. This is not the mother of James and John, who appears beside this woman in Matthew 27:56. It may be the mother of James the son of Alphaeus (Luke 6:15) or of another unknown James.

But they did not believe the women, because their words seemed to them like nonsense (24:11). The disciples' unbelief may have been partly due to a first-century view of women (see comments on 24:1–12), but relates primarily to the strangeness of the report. In Jewish understanding the resurrection of the dead occurred not within history, but at the end of time (see comments on 8:55; 14:14; 20:27).

On the Road to Emmaus (24:13–35)

The account of two disciples on the road to Emmaus occurs only in Luke and represents his most theologically significant contribution to the resurrection narratives. Cleopas and his companion represent the discouragement and unbelief of Jesus' followers. When they meet Jesus on the road, his identity is hidden from them. They express their profound disappointment at the tragic events in Jerusalem. While Jesus of Nazareth was clearly a great prophet, they had hoped that he might be even more—the Messiah who would redeem Israel. Yet his crucifixion dashed all such hopes. Jesus responds by rebuking them for their hardness of heart. Did not the Scriptures predict the suffering of the Messiah?

GARDEN TOMB

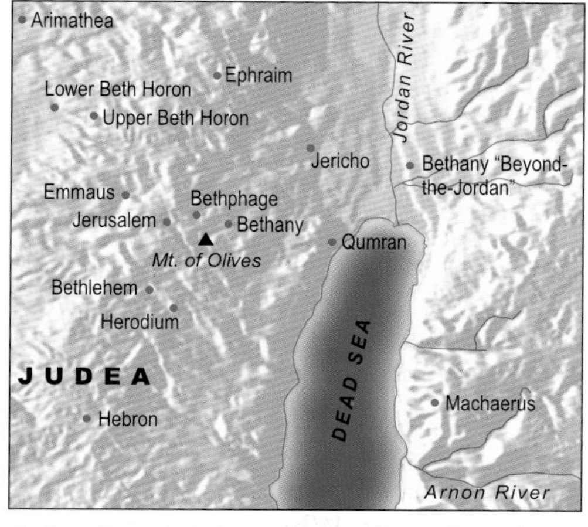

◀ *left*

JERUSALEM AND ITS VICINITY

Emmaus was located just northwest of Jerusalem.

School is in session as Jesus takes them through the Old Testament, showing them that all the Scriptures point to the coming of the Christ. He is the centerpoint of salvation history.

Though now equipped with the truth of Scripture, the disciples' recognition of Jesus does not occur until they invite him into their home and he breaks bread with them. Jesus meets them—as us—in personal fellowship and communion. When Jesus disappears from their presence, they joyfully rush back to Jerusalem to report their experience. There they find the apostles already announcing the same message: Jesus is risen indeed!

Two of them . . . Cleopas (24:13, 18). Nothing else is known about Cleopas or the identity of his companion. It may have been his wife. They are probably returning home after a Jerusalem Passover visit and probably assume the stranger walking with them is doing the same.

A village called Emmaus, about seven miles from Jerusalem (24:13). The location of Emmaus is uncertain, although two possible sites have been suggested.[658] (1) Josephus mentions an *Ammaous* thirty stadia (three and a half miles) from Jerusalem. In this case Luke could be describing a roundtrip distance. (2) There is an Arab village seven miles northwest of Jerusalem on the road to Lydda named El-Qubeibeh, where the Crusaders built a fort called Castellum Emmaus. While this village is the right distance from Jerusalem, no first-century evidence attaches the name "Emmaus" to it.

But they were kept from recognizing him (24:16). While this could have something to do with the differences in Jesus' resurrection body, the passive suggests that God intentionally prevents their recognition until the moment of revelation (see 2 Kings 6:17 for God's opening blind eyes to spiritual realities).

"Did not the Christ have to suffer these things. . . ?" And beginning with Moses and all the Prophets . . . (24:26–27). This is a surprising revelation since first-century Jews did not view the Messiah as a suffering figure (see comments on 9:22; 18:31).[659] "Moses and the Prophets" is a shorthand way of describing the Old Testament—the Law, the Prophets, and the Writings (see comments on 16:16, 19; 24:44). The whole Old Testament points forward to Jesus the Messiah. The early church recognized the suffering of the Messiah in passages like Psalms 2; 16; 22; 118; Isaiah 50:4–9; 52:13–53:12.[660]

But they urged him strongly, "Stay with us . . ." (24:29). Middle Eastern culture demanded such hospitality (see Gen. 18:3; 19:2; Judg. 19:5–9; also comments on Luke 11:1–13).

He took bread, gave thanks, broke it (24:30). Although in the home of these disciples, Jesus takes over the role of the host. As with so many meals in Luke, this one points forward to the messianic banquet over which the Messiah will preside (see comments on 13:29; 14:15). The breaking of bread recalls the feeding of the five thousand (9:16) and the Last Supper (22:19), both of which contain messianic-banquet imagery.

He disappeared from their sight (24:31). Jewish and Greco-Roman literature speaks of similar disappearances by angelic and divine figures.[661] Jesus' disappearance confirms he has received a unique and glorified resurrection body.

Were not our hearts burning within us (24:32). This idiom could mean that their hearts were grieved at Jesus' convicting words on the road (see Ps. 72:21 LXX), but more likely means they felt a strong urge to respond to Jesus' powerful words (see Ps. 38:4 LXX; Jer. 20:9).

The Lord has risen and has appeared to Simon (24:34). The Greek grammar makes it clear that this is a report coming from the Eleven, not the Emmaus disciples. A resurrection appearance to Peter is independently confirmed by Paul in 1 Corinthians 15:5.

Jesus Appears to the Disciples (24:36–49)

While the Emmaus disciples are giving their report to the Eleven, Jesus suddenly appears before them all. There is a strong emphasis in the scene on the real and bodily resurrection of Jesus, as he lets the disciples touch him and eats before them. Jesus reveals to them how his death and resurrection were in fulfillment of Scripture—a key theme throughout Luke-Acts. The salvation he has achieved means that repentance and forgiveness of sins can now be preached in his name to all nations. They will be his witnesses, going forth in the power of the Spirit from Jerusalem to the ends of the earth.

They were startled and frightened, thinking they saw a ghost (24:37). Although Jewish eschatology focused on the resurrection of the body at the end of time, there was also popular belief in disembodied spirits or ghosts. As today, spiritualists and mediums consulted with the dead.[662]

Look at my hands and my feet (24:39). This provides indirect evidence that Jesus was nailed rather than tied to the cross.

Touch me and see; a ghost does not have flesh and bones (24:39). Jesus' resurrection is neither the simple resuscitation of his body nor the appearance of a disembodied spirit, but rather a true resurrection into a new and glorified body (1 Cor. 15:20–23, 35–49). It is the beginning—the firstfruits and guarantee—of the end-time resurrection of all believers.[663]

Everything must be fulfilled that is written about me (24:44). See comments on 24:26.

Law of Moses, the Prophets and the Psalms (24:44). This is a reference to the threefold division of the Hebrew Scriptures: the Law (*Torah*), the Prophets (*Neviʾim*), and the Writings (*Ketuʾbim*). The Psalms stood at the head of the Writings and here represents them (see comments on 16:16, 29; 24:27).

This is what is written: The Christ will suffer and rise . . . repentance and forgiveness of sins will be preached in his name to all nations (24:46–47). For Old Testament texts related to the suffering of the Christ see comments on 24:26. The resurrection is defended by the apostles in Acts from Psalms 2:7; 16:9–10; 110:1–2; and the universal proclamation of the Gospel from Isaiah 42:6; 49:6; Joel 2:28–32; Amos 9:11–12.[664]

I am going to send you what my Father has promised (24:49). In the Old Testament God promised the outpouring of his Spirit on his people in the end times.[665]

The Ascension (24:50–53)

The Gospel ends with a brief account of Jesus' ascension, described in more detail in Acts 1:1–11. Luke here abbreviates events, giving the appearance that Jesus ascended on the day of his resurrection rather than forty days later, as Acts will clarify (see comments on Acts 1:3). This ascension gives closure to Luke's Gospel and sets the stage for Jesus' guidance over his church from his authoritative position at the right hand of God (cf. Acts 2:33–36).

The vicinity of Bethany (24:50). Bethany was located two miles east of Jerusalem on the eastern slope of the Mount of Olives. Acts 1:12 identifies the ascension with the Mount of Olives, the place where the Messiah will return in glory (Zech. 14:4).

He lifted up his hands and blessed them (24:50). Jesus' blessing provides closure of this Gospel and sends the disciples on their way to accomplish God's purposes. Sirach 50:20 describes a similar blessing by the high priest Simon II (219–196 B.C.) during worship at the Jerusalem temple: "Then Simon came down and raised his hands over the whole congregation of Israelites, to pronounce the blessing of the Lord with his lips, and to glory in his name." Jesus is portrayed as the authoritative mediator between God and his people.

He left them and was taken up into heaven (24:51). In the Old Testament Elijah ascended to heaven in a whirlwind with a fiery chariot (2 Kings 2:11; cf. 1 Macc. 2:58), and Enoch "was no more, because God took him away" (Gen. 5:24). In later Jewish traditions various Old Testament heroes ascend to heaven.[666] These are sometimes journeys to heaven to receive revelations and then return to earth (Enoch, Abraham, Isaiah, Baruch, Ezra). Other times they are permanent departures—a royal transport—at the end of life (Enoch, Moses, Elijah). Jesus' ascension is much more significant, establishing his exalted position of glory and power over all of creation.[667]

They stayed continually at the temple (24:53). The temple was a place of worship and prayer as well as a place of sacrifice.

ANNOTATED BIBLIOGRAPHY

Bailey, Kenneth E. *Poet and Peasant* and *Through Peasant Eyes: A Literary-Cultural Approach to the Parables of Luke.* Combined edition. Grand Rapids: Eerdmans, 1983.

This is a fascinating and informative work on the Lukan parables by a biblical scholar who has spent years studying contemporary Middle Eastern peasant culture. Many unique cultural insights into the parables may be found here.

Bock, Darrell L. *Luke.* 2 vols. BECNT. Grand Rapids: Eerdmans; *Volume 1: 1:1–9:50,* 1994; *Volume 2: 9:51–24:53,* 1996.

This massive two-volume commentary provides extensive discussion in all key aspects of Luke's Gospel, including background, historicity, and theology. Though written in a popular and accessible style, it is well documented, with extensive references to other commentaries and background material.

Boring, Eugene M., Klaus Berger, and Carsten Colpe, eds. *Hellenistic Commentary to the New Testament.* Nashville: Abingdon, 1995.

This volume gathers a wide range of Hellenistic texts related to the New Testament. An excellent resource for those without easy access to the more obscure primary sources.

Danker, Frederick W. *Jesus and the New Age: A Commentary on St. Luke's Gospel.* 2d ed. Philadelphia: Fortress, 1988.

This commentary provides a wealth of classical and Hellenistic background. While most commentaries focus on Jewish background, Danker keeps a constant eye on the wider literature of the Greco-Roman world.

Fitzmyer, Joseph A. *The Gospel According to Luke: A New Translation with Introduction and Commentary.* 2 vols. AB 28, 28A. New York: Doubleday; *Luke I-IX,* 1981; *Luke X-XXIV,* 1985.

Fitzmyer's expertise in New Testament background, and especially in Aramaic and the Dead Sea Scrolls, makes this two-volume commentary a wealth of information for background material on Luke's Gospel.

Jeremias, Joachim. *Jerusalem in the Time of Jesus.* Translated by F. H. Cave and C. H. Cave. Philadelphia: Fortress, 1969.

This classic work by one of the foremost New Testament scholars of the twentieth century is a wealth of background material on first-century Palestinian culture and society. Caution must be exercised, however, against uncritical acceptance of later rabbinic material as necessarily applicable to Jesus' day.

Malina, Bruce J. and Richard L. Rohrbaugh. *Social-Science Commentary on the Synoptic Gospels.* Minneapolis: Fortress, 1992.

This volume is a unique and helpful resource for the distinct sociological background to the New Testament, particularly with references to issues like social status, honor and shame, rich and poor, etc. Such issues, while often overlooked in the past, have profound significance for the interpretation of certain texts.

Manson, T. W. *The Sayings of Jesus.* London: SCM, 1949.

Manson's constant eye on the rabbinic literature makes this a helpful background resource for the sayings of Jesus common to Matthew and Luke.

Marshall, I. Howard. *The Gospel of Luke: A Commentary on the Greek Text.* NIGTC. Grand Rapids: Eerdmans, 1978.

Marshall's careful and erudite scholarship makes this a classic commentary not only for Lukan purpose and theology, but also for background and historical material.

Nolland, John L. *Luke.* 3 vols. WBC 35. Dallas: Word; : 1989 (a); 1993 (b, c).

This three-volume work provides extensive bibliographical material on individual passages. An excellent research tool.

Main Text Notes

1. Luke 2:32; 3:6; 4:25–27.
2. Col. 4:7–17; 2 Tim. 4:10–11; Philem. 23–24.
3. Josephus, *J.W.* 1.1 §§1–2.
4. For examples see J. A. Fitzmyer, *The Gospel According to Luke: A New Translation with Introduction and Commentary* (AB 28, 28A; New York: Doubleday, 1981, 1985), 1:292.
5. Cf. 1 Chron. 26:13–16; Neh. 11:1; Jonah 1:7.
6. *m. Tamid* 5:2–6:3.
7. Josephus, *Ant.* 13.10.3 §§282–3.
8. Cf. Sir. 48:10; 2 Esd. (*4 Ezra*) 6:26; Justin, *Dialogue with Trypho* 8, 49; Str-B 4:784–89, 792–98; J. Jeremias, "Ἠλίας," *TDNT*, 2:928–34.
9. Dan. 8:16; 9:21; the other is Michael: 10:13; 12:1; cf. *1 En.* 20:1–7.
10. *m. Yoma* 5.1.
11. See Jeremias, *Jerusalem*, 105–8, 206.
12. For more details see Jeremias, *Jerusalem*, 364–67.
13. See Isa. 9:6–7; 11:1–5; Jer. 23:5–6; 33:15–16; Ezek. 37:24–25.
14. Luke 1:69; 20:41–44; Acts 2:30–36; 13:23.
15. See also 4QFlor 1.11 (=4Q174); 1QSa 2.11.12 (=1Q28a); Ps. 2:7; 89:26; Isa. 7:14.
16. Matt. 16:16; 26:63; Luke 4:41; 22:70.
17. Cf. John 10:30 (and throughout John); Rom. 1:3; Gal. 4:4; Heb. 1:1–4.
18. Both cited by I. Howard Marshall, *The Gospel of Luke: A Commentary on the Greek Text* (NIGTC; Grand Rapids: Eerdmans, 1978), 80.
19. Ex. 6:6; Deut. 4:34; Ps. 44:3.
20. 1 Sam. 2:5, 7; cf. Ps. 147:6; Jer. 5:27–29.
21. Luke 1:73; 3:8; 16:24; Acts 3:25; 7:5–6.
22. See Marshall, *Gospel of Luke*, 88; John L. Nolland, *Luke* (WBC 35; Dallas: Word Books, 1989, 1993), 1:79.
23. Ezra 7:6, 28; Isa. 41:20; Ex. 9:3; Judg. 2:15; etc.
24. See Luke 1:46–55; 2:14; 2:29–32.
25. Cf. Ps. 2; 72; 89; 110; 132.
26. 1 Kings 1:48; 1 Chron. 16:36; Ps. 41:13; 68:19; 72:18; 106:48; etc.
27. Jer. 31:34; 33:8; 50:20.
28. See Isa. 11:1–5; Jer. 23:5–6; 33:15–16; Zech. 3:8; 6:12; 4QFlor 1.10–13; 4QPBless 1–5 (4Q252); 4QpIsa[a]; *Shemoneh Esreh* 14.
29. Isa. 9:2; 42:6–7; 49:6.
30. See, for example, 4QTestim 12; CD 7.18; 1QM 9.6; *T. Levi* 18.3; *T. Jud.* 24.1–6.
31. See Isa. 58:8–10; 60:1–3; Mal. 4:2.
32. Judg. 13:24–25; 1 Sam. 2:21, 26; 3:19; cf. Luke 2:40, 52.
33. See Jos. *Ant.* 18.1.1 §§3ff.; 18.2.1 §26.
34. See W. M. Ramsay, *The Bearing of Recent Discovery on the Trustworthiness of the New Testament* (4th ed.; London: Hodder & Stoughton, 1920), 275–300. Unfortunately the inscription is damaged (the name Quirinius does not appear on it), and so this proposal is highly speculative.
35. Nolland, *Luke*, 1.101.
36. 1 Sam. 17:12, 58; 20:6.
37. Ex. 13:2; Deut. 21:15–17.
38. Cf. the description of Solomon in the Wisd. Sol. 7:4.
39. See Ex. 4:24 LXX; 1 Kingdoms 1:18 LXX; Jer. 14:8 LXX.
40. The tradition that Jesus was born in a cave appears in the *Protevangelium of James* 18–19, Justin, *Dialogue with Trypho* 78:4; Origin, *Against Celsus* 1:15.
41. For the rabbinic evidence see Str-B 2:113–14.
42. John 10:11; Heb. 13:20; 1 Peter 2:25.
43. Ex. 16:7, 10; 33:18, 22; 40:34, etc.
44. See Luke 1:19; 2:10; 3:18; 4:18, 43; 7:22; 8:1; 9:6; 16:16; 20:1.
45. For the full text and references see Frederick W. Danker, *Jesus and the New Age: A Commentary on St. Luke's Gospel* (2d ed.; Philadelphia: Fortress, 1988), 54.
46. Ps. 18:46; 24:5; Isa. 17:10, etc.
47. Luke 1:47, 68–69, 71; cf. Acts 5:31; 13:23.
48. 2 Sam. 22:51; Ps. 2:2; 89:20, 38.
49. Cf. 4QFlor (4Q174) 1:13. Cf. *Pss. Sol.* 17:21–43; 18:5–9; 1QSb (1Q28b) 5:21–29; *4 Ezra* 11:1–12:39; etc.
50. For details see Marshall, *Gospel of Luke*, 112; Fitzmyer, *Luke*, 1:411, 412; Nolland, *Luke*, 1:109.
51. Ex. 13:1–15; 34:19–20; Num. 3:11–13, 40–51; 18:15–16.
52. Isa. 40:1–2; cf. 49:13; 57:18; 61:2.
53. Ps. 118:22; Isa. 8:14; 28:16.
54. Borne of Zilpah, Leah's maidservant; Gen. 30:12–13; cf. Num. 1:40, 41; Rev. 7:6.
55. 1 Cor. 7:8, 34; 1 Tim. 5:3–16; Titus 1:10.
56. Josephus, *Ant.* 18.6.6 §180.
57. Fitzmyer, *Luke*, 1:432.
58. Ibid., 1:440; *m. Nid.* 5:6; *m. ʾAbot* 5:21; *Gen. Rab.* 63:10.
59. Josephus, *Ant.* 5.10.4 §348; cf. 1 Sam. 3.
60. Moses (Josephus, *Ant.* 2.9.6 §§230–31; Philo, *Moses* 1:21); Cyrus the Great (Herodotus 1:114–15); Alexander the Great (Plutarch, *Alex.* 5); Apollonius (Philostratus, *Vita Apoll.* 1:7).
61. Josephus, *Life* 2 §9.

62. A similar neuter plural expression appears in the LXX at Gen. 41:51; Est. 7:9; Job 18:19; and in Josephus (*Ant.* 8.5.3 §145; 16.10.1 §302).
63. Deut. 21:18–21; Prov. 30:17; 2 Tim. 3:2.
64. Ex. 20:12; Deut. 5:16; Mark 7:10 pars.; 10:19 pars.; Eph. 6:2.
65. Luke 3:7–14; see also Matt. 3:1–12; Mark 1:2–8.
66. For details see Marshall, *Gospel of Luke,* 13. The other rulers mentioned here do not help to narrow the date further since their dates overlap with all of these.
67. Josephus, *Ant.* 17.11.4 §§317–20; *J.W.* 2.6.3 §§93–100.
68. Luke 23:1–24, 52; cf. Acts 3:13; 4:27; 13:28.
69. Luke 3:19–20; cf. Mark 6:17–29.
70. Josephus, *Ant.* 14.13.3 §330; 15.4.1 §92.
71. Josephus, *Ant.* 19.5.1 §275; 20.7.1 §138; *J.W.* 2.11.5 §215; 2.12.8 §247. The inscriptional evidence may be found in A. Böckh, *Corpus Inscriptionum Graecarum* (Berlin: Reimer, 1828–1877). See Fitzmyer, *Luke,* 1:457–58.
72. Josephus, *Ant.* 18.2.2 §§33–35.
73. Cf. John 18:13–14, 24; Acts 4:6.
74. BAGD, 131.
75. Ex. 30:19–20; Lev. 14:7–8, 51; 15:5–27; Num. 19:18.
76. 1QS 3:5–9; 1QS 5:13–14.
77. *b. Yebam.* 47ab.
78. 2 Chron. 7:14; Isa. 6:10; Jer. 36:3; Ezek. 18:21, 30, 32; 33:9, 14.
79. Jer. 33:8; Ezek. 34:25–26.
80. 1QS 5:13–14.
81. Josephus, *Ant.* 18.5.2 §117.
82. See K. R. Snodgrass, "Streams of Tradition Emerging from Isaiah 40:1–5 and Their Adaptation in the New Testament," *JSNT* 8 (1980): 24–45.
83. 1QS 8:12–15; 9:19–20.
84. Sir. 48:24–25.
85. See Isa. 11:15–16; 42:14–16; 43:1–3, 14–21; 48:20–21; 49:8–12; 52:11–12; 55:12–13; *Pss. Sol.* 11:2–5; 17:21–46; *4 Ezra* 13; *Tg. Lam.* 2:22.
86. The eventual destruction of evil will mean the harmlessness of snakes: "The young child [will] put his hand into the viper's nest" (Isa. 11:8).
87. 1QH 3:12–18.
88. See also John 8:33–39; Acts 7:2; Rom. 4:1.
89. *Pss. Sol.* 18:4.
90. Cf. Str-B 1.116–21; Fitzmyer, *Luke,* 1:468; *T. Levi* 15:4; cf. *m. ᵓAbot* 5:19.
91. Cf. O. Michel, "τελώνης," *TDNT* 8:88–105; J. R. Donahue, "Tax Collectors and Sinners: An Attempt at Identification," *CBQ* 33 (1971): 39–61.
92. For evidence of abuses see Josephus, *Ant.* 18.6.5 (§§172–78); *J.W.* 2.14.1 (§§272–76); Philo, *Embassy* 199.
93. Josephus, *Ant.* 17.8.3 §§198–99; 18.5.1 §113.
94. Cf. Str-B 1:121; 4:2, 712, 717–18; Darrell L. Bock, *Luke* (BECNT; Grand Rapids: Eerdmans, 1996), 1:320–21.
95. Isa. 32:15; Ezek. 36:26–27; Joel 2:28–32.
96. See Gen. 19:24; Isa. 29:6; Ezek. 38:22; Amos 7:4; Zeph. 1:18; 3:8; Mal. 4:1; *4 Ezra* 13:10–11, 27; *1 En.* 67:13; 90:24–27; 1QS 2:8; 4:13.
97. Luke 3:17; cf. Luke 9:54; 12:49; 17:29.
98. Cf. 1QH 8:20; 1QS 3:7–9; 4:21; *T. Isaac* 5:21–32; *T. Ab.* 12–13.
99. See 1 Kings 13:4; 18:13; 19:2; 22:26–27; 2 Kings 1:9; 6:31; 2 Chron. 24:21.
100. Jer. 18:18, 23; 26:11, 20–23; 36–38.
101. Luke 4:24; 11:47–51; 13:34; Acts 7:52.
102. Ezek. 1:1; John 1:51; Acts 7:56; 10:11; Rev. 19:11.
103. *b. Ḥag.* 15a.
104. Gen. 22:17–18; Luke 1:54–55, 72–73; 2 Sam. 7:12–16; Luke 1:32–33.
105. Philo, *Virtues* 204–5.
106. Philo, *Virtues* 205.
107. Deut. 8:3; 6:13, 16.
108. Cf. Mark 1:13; Luke 4:3, 5, 13; 8:12; 10:18; 11:18; 13:16; 22:3, 31.
109. 1 Chron. 21:1; Job 1–2; Zech. 3:1–2.
110. John 8:44; 2 Cor. 12:7; 1 Peter 5:8; Rev. 12:9; 20:2.
111. Dio Cassius, *Roman History* 62.5.3; cited by Danker, *Jesus and the New Age,* 102.
112. Josephus, *Ant.* 15.11.5 §415.
113. *Pesiq. Rab.* §36; cited by Fitzmyer, *Luke,* 1:517.
114. Cf. Matt. 4:12–17; Mark 1:14–15; 6:1–6.
115. See J. A. Sanders, "From Isaiah to Luke 4," in *Luke and Scripture: The Function of Sacred Tradition in Luke-Acts* (Minneapolis: Fortress, 1993), 46–69.
116. See J. L. Nolland, "Classical and Rabbinic Parallels to 'Physician, Heal Yourself' (Lk iv 23)," *NovT* 21 (1979):193–209.
117. See J. Blinzer, "The Jewish Punishment of Stoning in the New Testament Period," in *The Trial of Jesus* (FS C. F. D. Moule, ed. E. Bammel; London: SCM, 1970), 147–61.
118. Marshall, *Gospel of Luke,* 193.
119. Though this work postdates the New Testament, its traditions probably come from much earlier; cf. Josephus, *Ant.* 8.2.5, where Solomon's gifts of exorcism are described: *T. Sol.* 1:7.
120. H. C. Kee, "The Terminology of Mark's Exorcism Stories," *NTS* 14 (1967–1968): 232–46.
121. See, for example, the many rituals described in the *T. Sol.*

122. See H. J. Cadbury, "Lexical Notes on Luke-Acts: II. Recent Arguments for Medical Language," *JBL* 45 (1926): 190–209.
123. See Luke 9:35; 22:66–71; Acts 9:20, 22.
124. See Jer. 33:17, 22; Ezek. 37:25; Dan. 7:27; *Pss. Sol.* 17:4; *1 En.* 62:14; Str-B 2:552.
125. See *4 Ezra* 7:28–29 (400 yrs.); 12:34; *b. Sanh.* 97a, 99a; cf. Rev. 20:4–6. See Schürer, 2:536–37.
126. Josephus, *Ant.* 18.2.1 §28.
127. See E. F. Bishop, "Jesus and the Lake," *CBQ* 13 (1951): 398–414, esp. 401.
128. Lev. 13:45–46; cf. Luke 17:12, 14.
129. Marshall, *Gospel of Luke,* 213.
130. *m. Sanh.* 7:5.
131. For references see H. W. Beyer, "βλασφημέω," *TDNT,* 1:621–25.
132. Cf. Matt. 9:9–13; Mark 2:13–17.
133. Danker, *Jesus and the New Age,* 126.
134. See Luke 18:12; *Didache* 8:1; *b. Taʿan.* 12a.
135. Est. 4:16; 2 Sam. 12:23; Joel 1:14; Jonah 3:5.
136. Isa. 58:4–5; Jer. 14:12.
137. For more on first-century marriage customs see J. Jeremias, *The Parables of Jesus* (rev. ed.; trans. S. H. Hooke; New York: Scribner's, 1963), 171–75.
138. Cf. Ex. 20:8–11; Deut. 5:14.
139. Cf. *y. Šabb.* 7.9b; Str-B 1.617; *m. Šabb.* 7:2.
140. Ex. 25:30; 35:13; 40:23; Lev. 24:8–9.
141. Josephus, *Ant.* 6.12.1 §§242–243.
142. Fitzmyer, *Luke,* 1:609; Str-B 1.618–19.
143. *m. Yoma* 8:6.
144. *m. Šabb.* 18:3; 19:2.
145. BAGD, 622.
146. Marshall, *Gospel of Luke,* 236.
147. Cf. Mark 3:13–19.
148. George A. Turner, *Historical Geography of the Holy Land* (Grand Rapids: Baker, 1973), 104–6.
149. Fitzmyer, *Luke,* 1:620.
150. For a good discussion of the similarities and differences, and a general introduction to the sermon, see Bock, *Luke,* 1:931–49.
151. Cf. Ps. 149:4; Isa. 66:5.
152. See Ps. 22:26; 107:9, 36–41; 132:15; Isa. 49:10–13; 65:13; Jer. 31:12, 25; Ezek. 34:29; 36:29.
153. See Ps. 126; Isa. 40:1; 51:3; 57:18; 61:2; 66:13.
154. 1 Kings 22:12–13; Isa. 30:9–11; Jer. 5:31; 6:14; 23:16–17.
155. Cf. Deut. 24:10–17; Amos 2:8.
156. For other texts see Danker, *Jesus and the New Age,* 146–47; Fitzmyer, *Luke,* 1:639–40; Seneca, *De Beneficiis* 2.1.1.
157. *b. Šabb.* 31a.
158. See the sources cited by Marshall, *Gospel of Luke,* 262.
159. F. W. Danker, *Benefactor: Epigraphic Study of a Graeco-Roman and New Testament Semantic Field* (St. Louis: Clayton, 1982), 78; idem, *Jesus and the New Age,* 147.
160. Ex. 22:25; Lev. 25:35–37; Deut. 23:20; Ps. 112:5; Sir. 29:1–2.
161. Cf. Ruth 3:15; Isa. 65:6.
162. *m. Soṭah* 1:7.
163. Nolland, *Luke,* 1:301.
164. See examples in W. Schrage, "τυφλός," *TDNT,* 8:275–76, 286. The image of the blind leading the blind appears in Sextus Empiricus, *Pyrrhonic Elements* 3.259.
165. Cf. Plutarch, *De curios* 515d; Horace, *Satires* 1.3.25. The Jewish example often cited (*b. ʿArak.* 16b) is probably anti-Christian polemic dependent on Jesus' saying. It is attributed to Rabbi Tarphon (c. A.D. 100), a strong opponent of Palestinian Christians; it criticizes those (Christians?) who will not accept correction: "If one says to a man, 'Remove the spelk [*sic*] from your eye,' he will reply, 'Remove the beam from yours.'" See T. W. Manson, *The Sayings of Jesus* (London: SCM, 1949), 58.
166. U. Wilckens, "ὑποκρίνομαι, κ.τ.λ.," *TDNT,* 8:559–71.
167. A. N. Sherwin-White, *Roman Society and Roman Law in the New Testament* (Oxford: Clarendon, 1963), 123–24.
168. Cf. Luke 9:22; 20:1; 22:52; Acts 4:5, 8, 23.
169. W. Schrage, "συναγωγή," *TDNT,* 7:813.
170. W. Dittenberger, *Orientis graeci inscriptiones selectae* (Leipzig: Hirzel, 1903–5), §96; cited by Fitzmyer, *Luke* 1:652; Creed, *St. Luke,* 101.
171. For these terms and a description of Roman patronage see Bruce J. Malina and Richard L. Rohrbaugh, *SSCSG,* 326–29.
172. *m. ʾOhal.* 18:7.
173. *b. Ber.* 34b.
174. Philostratos, *Life of Apollonius of Tyana* 4.45; for other parallels see *Hellenistic Commentary to the New Testament,* 203–5; Marshall, *Gospel of Luke,* 283. A somewhat similar account of resuscitation at a funeral can be found in Apuleius of Madaura, *Florida* 9:2–6.
175. Burial customs are referred to in various rabbinic tracts, especially in the tractate *Ṣemaḥot.* See D. Zlotnick, *The Tractate "Mourning" (Ṣemaḥot): Regulations Relating to Death, Burial, and Mourning* (YJS 17. New Haven: Yale Univ. Press, 1966). Cf. *m. Ber.* 3.1–2; *m. Šabb.* 23.4–5; *m. Sanh.* 6:5; *t. Neg.* 6:2.
176. Ex. 22:22; Deut. 10:18; 27:19.
177. Jer. 6:26; Amos 8:10; Zech. 12:10.
178. Cf. Str-B 1:1047–48; *m. Ber.* 3:1–2; *b. Ketub.* 17a.

179. 4QPBless (4Q252) 1–5; cf. 1QS 9:11.
180. Isa. 26:19; 29:18–19; 35:5–6; 61:1–2.
181. See Matt. 3:3; 11:10, 14; 17:10–13; Mark 1:2–4; Luke 1:17, 76; 3:4–6.
182. Job 14:1; 15:14; 25:4.
183. *HCNT,* 207; Herodotus, *Histories* 1.141; cf. Aesop, *Fables,* 27b.
184. See Prov. 1:20–33; 8:1–9:6; Sir. 1; 24; *1 En.* 42; Wisd. Sol., *passim;* Marshall, *Gospel of Luke,* 303; G. Fohrer and U. Wilckens, "σοφία," *TDNT,* 7:465–526.
185. See Malina and Rohrbaugh, *SSCSG,* 331.
186. J. Jeremias, *The Eucharistic Words of Jesus* (trans. Norman Perrin; London: SCM, 1966), 20–21; Fitzmyer, *Luke,* 1:688.
187. BAGD, 34.
188. BAGD, 534; Bock, *Luke,* 1:696.
189. Jeremias, *Parables,* 126. Jeremias cites *t. Soṭah* 5.9; *y. Giṭ.* 9.50d.
190. See Marshall, *Gospel of Luke,* 309.
191. Malina and Rohrbaugh, *SSCSG,* 332–33.
192. Josephus, *J.W.* 2.17.6 §§426–27 (LCL, 491).
193. Marshall, *Gospel of Luke,* 311.
194. See L. Goppelt, "ὕδωρ," *TDNT,* 8:324 n.63; Str-B 4.615.
195. See 2 Sam. 15:5; Job 31:27; Luke 22:47; Rom. 16:16; 1 Peter 5:14; Cant 8:1.
196. Mark 15:40, 47; Luke 24:10; John 19:25; 20:1, 18.
197. BAGD, 303.
198. See especially Jeremias, *Parables,* 11–12, 149–51; Fitzmyer, *Luke,* 1:703.
199. Cf. *m. Šabb.* 7.2, where sowing is listed before plowing in a list of agricultural work that appears to be in chronological order; *Jub.* 11:11.
200. Nolland, *Luke,* 1:371, citing G. Dalman for typical crop yields.
201. Dan. 2:18, 19, 27–30, 47.
202. Cf. 1QpHab 7:4–5, 8; 1QS 3:23; 1 QM 3:9; 1QH 4:23–24.
203. 1QpHab 7:4–5.
204. Luke 8:10; cf. John 12:40; Acts 28:26–27; Rom. 11:8.
205. 2 Esd. 8:41; cf. 9:31.
206. Cf. *Jub.* 11:11 (see comments on 11:5); *1 En.* 90:2–4, 8–13; *Apoc. Ab.* 13:3–7.
207. *Apoc. Ab.* 13:3–7.
208. Marshall, *Gospel of Luke,* 327; citing W. Grundmann, "ἀγαθός," *TDNT,* 1:11–12; 3:538–44. See Tobit 5:14; 2 Macc. 15:12 for its use in Hellenistic Judaism.
209. J. Rousseau and R. Arav, *Jesus and His World* (Minneapolis: Fortress, 1995), 246; Fitzmyer, *Luke,* 1:729.
210. See 2 Sam. 22:16; Ps. 18:15; 104:7; 106:9; Isa. 50:2; Nah. 1:4.
211. Nolland, *Luke,* 1:398. Nolland notes that such attribution was given to, among others, Caesar, Caligula, Xerxes, Apollonius of Tyana, and Empedocles. The closest parallel is that of Apollonius, where people press to travel in the same boat because he is reportedly more powerful than storm, fire, or other dangers (Philostratus, *Life of Apollonius* 4:13).
212. Cf. *y. Ber.* 9.1; cf. the account of R. Gamaliel in *b. B. Meṣiʿa* 59b. These and other parallels are conveniently surveyed in *HCNT,* 66–68.
213. Ps. 65:7; 89:9; 104:6–7; 107:23–32.
214. Philostratus, *Life of Apollonius* 4:20 (LCL); cf. *HCNT,* 71–72.
215. Fitzmyer, *Luke,* 1:736, wryly notes that if this were the location, it would have been the most energetic herd of pigs in history.
216. *Jub.* 22:16–17.
217. *y. Ter. 1.1* [40b]; cited in *HCNT,* 72. Cf. Str-B 1:491.
218. Nolland, *Luke,* 1:409.
219. 2 Peter 2:4; Rev. 9:1–2, 11; 11:7; 17:8; 20:1, 3.
220. Lev. 11:7; Deut. 14:8.
221. See *HCNT,* 72–73, where examples are provided of the banishment of disease (epilepsy?) into wild goats and of a demon into the head of a bull.
222. See Schrage, "συναγωγή," *TDNT,* 7:847; see 8:49; 13:14; Acts 13:15; 18:8, 17.
223. See Gen. 22:16; 1 Kings 17:17–24; Jer. 6:26; Amos 8:10; Zech. 12:10.
224. Lev. 15:19–31; Ezek. 36:17.
225. Num. 15:38–39; Deut. 22:12.
226. See John 11:11; Acts 7:60; 13:36; 1 Cor. 11:30; 15:6, 18, 20, 51; 1 Thess. 4:14–15; 5:10.
227. Cf. Luke 23:46; Acts 7:59.
228. Cf. *1 En.* 22; 39:4–8.
229. Luke 24:46–48; Acts 1:1–2, 8; 2:33.
230. Manson, *Sayings,* 181, 182; *m. Ber.* 9.5.
231. See Nolland, *Luke,* 1:427.
232. Cf. Str-B 1:571.
233. Luke 12:35–40; 13:24–30; 14:15–24; cf. 22:30; see comments on 13:29; 14:15.
234. Keener, *BBC,* 213.
235. BAGD, 436.
236. *m. Ber.* 6:1.
237. Job 22:26–27 LXX; Ps. 121:1; 123:1.
238. Priests: Lev. 4:3, 5, 16; 8:12. Prophets: 1 Kings 19:16; CD 2:12; 6:1; 1QM 11:7. Kings: 1 Sam. 10:1; 16:13; 1 Kings 19:16.
239. See Sydney H. T. Page, "The Suffering Servant Between the Testaments," *NTS* 31 (1985): 481–97.
240. See Luke 20:1; 22:52; Acts 23:14; 25:15. See Nolland, *Luke* 2:466; G. Schenk, "ἀρχιερεύς," *TDNT,* 3:268–72; J. Jeremias, *Jerusalem,* 160–81; Schürer 2:213, 233–36.
241. See Jeremias, *Jerusalem,* 222–32.

242. On crucifixion see especially M. Hengel, *Crucifixion in the Ancient World and the Folly of the Message of the Cross* (tr. J. Bowden; Philadelphia: Fortress, 1977); Fitzmyer, *Luke*, 1:787.
243. *1 En*. 37–71.
244. There is a growing consensus that the *Similitudes* of Enoch (*1 En*. 37–71) are Jewish Palestinian and that they are pre-A.D. 70. See J. H. Charlesworth, *The Old Testament Pseudepigrapha and the New Testament* (SNTSMS 54; Cambridge: Cambridge Univ. Press, 1985), 89.
245. See the descriptions of angels and heavenly beings at Dan. 10:5–6; Matt. 28:3; Mark 16:5; Luke 24:4; John 20:12; Acts 1:10; Rev. 4:4; 19:14; *1 En*. 71:1, and of glorified saints at Dan. 12:3; Rev. 3:4–5, 18; 6:11; 7:9, 13; *1 En*. 62:15–16; 38:4; 104:2; *4 Ezra* 7:97.
246. See Wisd. Sol. 3:2; 7:6; Josephus, *Ant*. 4.189; cf. 2 Peter 1:15; BAGD, 276.
247. See Ex. 19:1; Num. 33:38; 1 Kings 6:1; 10:29 (cf. Judg. 5:4; Ps. 104:38; 113:1).
248. Isa. 11:11–16; 40–55; Jer. 23:7–8.
249. See Lev. 23:42; Neh. 8:14–17.
250. See Ex. 16:10; 19:9; 33:9; 40:34–35; Lev. 16:2; Num. 11:25; 1 Kings 8:10–11; 2 Chron. 5:13–14; Ps. 18:11–12; 97:2; Isa. 4:5; Ezek. 1:4, 28; 10:3–4; Zech. 2:17 (LXX); 2 Macc. 2:8. See Oepke, "νεφέλη," *TDNT*, 4:905.
251. Ex. 19:16; 20:18; 34:30; Deut. 5:5, 23–27.
252. See Wanke, "φοβέω," *TDNT*, 9:200–203; Balz, "φοβέω," *TDNT*, 9:209–12; see Luke 1:12; 2:9; 5:26; 7:16; 8:25, 35–37; Acts 5:5, 11.
253. See 2 Sam. 7:14; comments on Luke 3:22.
254. Many Old Testament persons are described as being "chosen" by God, including Abraham (Neh. 9:7; cf. *4 Ezra* 3:13; *Apoc. Ab*. 14), Moses (Ps. 105:26; Sir. 45:4), Levi and Aaron (Num. 17:5; Ps. 105:26; Sir. 45:16), Saul (1 Sam. 10:24; 12:13), David (Ps. 89:20; cf. Sir. 45:4), Solomon (1 Chron. 28:5, 6), Zerubbabel (Hag. 2:23), and others. The Teacher of Righteousness, the leader of the Dead Sea sect, is called "his elect" in 1QpHab 9:12. Throughout the intertestamental book of *1 En*., the Messiah is called the "Elect One."
255. Gen. 22:16; 1 Kings 17:17–24; Jer. 6:26; Amos 8:10; Zech. 12:10; see comments on Luke 7:12; 8:42.
256. For the status of children in the ancient world see A. Oepke, "παῖς," *TDNT*, 5:639–52.
257. Cicero, *Pro Ligario* 33.
258. Cited by Danker, *Jesus and the New Age*, 206. For other references see Fitzmyer, *Luke*, 1:821.
259. See Nolland, *Luke* 2:534–35 for references.
260. Plutarch, *Lives* 828c; cited by Danker, *Jesus and the New Age*, 210.
261. Ex. 20:12; Deut. 5:16.
262. Cited by Nolland, *Luke*, 2:542. See also M. Hengel, *The Charismatic Leader and His Followers* (trans. J. C. G. Greig; New York: Crossroad, 1981), 8–10; Str-B 1:487–89; 4:1, 578–92; *b. Ber. 31a*.
263. Cf. Gen. 50:5; Tobit 4:3; 6:15.
264. This latter is suggested by Keener, *BBC*, 215.
265. See Marshall, *Gospel of Luke*, 412, for this and other parallels.
266. Jer. 5:6; Ezek. 22:27; Zeph. 3:3; cf. the Babylonians in Hab. 1:8.
267. Tanchuma, *Toledoth*, 32b; cited by J. Jeremias, "ἀρνός," *TDNT*, 1:340.
268. Cf. 1 Cor. 9:14; *Did*. 13:1–2.
269. Isa. 29:18–19; 35:5; see comments on Luke 7:22; 4:43.
270. See Deut. 29:23; 32:32; Isa. 1:9–10; 3:9; 13:19; Jer. 23:14; 49:18; 50:40; Lam. 4:6; Ezek. 16:46–56; Amos 4:11; Zeph. 2:9.
271. See also Str-B 1:574; 4:2; 4:1188; *m. Sanh*. 10:3.
272. Turner, *Hist. Geog*. 96.
273. Nolland, *Luke* 2:555–56.
274. E.g., Gen. 37:34; 2 Sam. 3:31; 1 Kings 21:27; Est. 4:1, 3; Isa. 58:5; Dan. 9:3.
275. See *Life of Adam and Eve* 12–16; Wisd. Sol. 2:24.
276. See Num. 21:6–9; Deut. 8:15; 1 Kings 12:14; Isa. 11:8; Ezek. 2:6; Sir. 21:2; 39:30.
277. Gen. 3:15; Rom. 16:20; Rev. 12:9; 20:2.
278. Old Testament: Ex. 32:32–33; Ps. 69:28; Isa. 4:3; Dan. 12:1; Mal. 3:16–17; Jewish Literature: *Jub*. 19:19; 30:19–23; *1 En*. 47:3; 104:1, 7; 108:3, 7; 1 QM 12:2; New Testament: Phil. 4:3; Heb. 12:23; Rev. 3:5; 13:8; 17:8; 20:12, 15; 21:27.
279. See Tobit 7:17; Judith 9:12; 1QapGen. 22:16, 21; cf. Gen. 14:19, 22.
280. 1 Cor. 1:18–31; cf. 2:6–13; 3:18–20.
281. Bar. 3:32, 36; cf. Wisd. Sol. 8:4.
282. *Pss. Sol*. 17:21, 44; 18:6.
283. Marshall, *Gospel of Luke*, 442, citing *b. Ber*. 28b; Str-B 1:808.
284. See 2 Macc. 7:9; *4 Macc*. 15:31; 17:18; *1 En*. 37:4; 40:9; 58:3; *Pss. Sol*. 3:12; 13:11; 14:10; 1QS 4:7; 4Q181 1:4; cf. R. Bultmann, "ζάω," *TDNT*, 2:855–61.
285. The command to love one's neighbor appears in *Jub*. 7:20; 36:7–8; CD 6:20–21; Sir. 7:21; 34:15; *T. Benj*. 3:3–4; *T. Dan* 5:3. The two are linked in *T. Iss*. 5:2; 7:6; *T. Dan* 5:3; cf. Philo, *Spec. Laws* 2.63.
286. 2 Sam. 12:7; cf. 2 Esd. 4:20; 1 Kings 20:40–42.
287. 1QS 1:9–10.

288. Sir. 12:1–7.
289. Josephus, *J.W.* 4.8.3 §474.
290. Luke 10:32; John 1:19; Acts 4:36.
291. See John 11:1–44; 12:1–11.
292. *m. ʾAbot* 1:4.
293. Jeremias, *Jerusalem*, 363. For the role of women in Jewish society see Jeremias, *Jerusalem*, ch. 18; Malina and Rohrbaugh, *SSCSG*, 348–49.
294. *m. Soṭah* 3:4.
295. Malina and Rohrbaugh, *SSCSG*, 348.
296. See especially Kenneth E. Bailey, *Poet and Peasant* and *Through Peasant Eyes: A Literary-Cultural Approach to the Parables of Luke* (combined ed.; Grand Rapids: Eerdmans, 1983), 119–41.
297. Cf. Rom. 8:15–16; Gal. 4:6.
298. See J. Jeremias, *The Prayers of Jesus* (Philadelphia: Fortress, 1978); idem, *New Testament Theology* (London: SCM, 1971), 63–68.
299. Cited in Jeremias, *New Testament Theology*, 198.
300. Ex. 16:4; 20:20; Deut. 8:2, 16; Judg. 2:22.
301. Cf. *b. Ber.* 60b; cited by Bock, *Luke*, 2:1056.
302. Bailey, *Poet and Peasant*, 121.
303. Ibid., 122; Jeremias, *Parables*, 157, claims bread was baked daily.
304. Jeremias, *Parables*, 158, citing A. Fridrichsen.
305. Bailey, *Poet and Peasant*, 130–33.
306. Nolland, *Luke*, 2:631.
307. 2 Kings 20:8–11; Isa. 38:7–8.
308. E.g., Isa. 13:10; 34:4; Joel 2:30–31.
309. See Ps. 23; Isa. 53:6; Jer. 13:17; Ezek. 34; Zech. 10:3; 13:7; cf. comments on 10:3; 12:32; 15:4.
310. Tobit 12:15.
311. *Satyricon* 4:1; cited by Danker, *Jesus and the New Age*, 234; cf. Ovid, *Metamorphoses* 4.320–24.
312. *m. ʾAbot* 2:8.
313. Jonah 1:2; cf. Nah. 1:11; 2:12–13; 3:1, 19.
314. Nolland, *Luke*, 2:657.
315. See D. C. Allison Jr., "The Eye Is the Lamp of the Body (Matthew 6.22–23 = Luke 11.34–36)," *NTS* 33 (1987): 61–83.
316. For the literature see H. Conzelmann, "σκότος, κ.τ.λ.," *TDNT*, 7:423–45; cf. 9:310–58.
317. See 7:36; 11:37; 14:1, 10; 22:14.
318. Marshall, *Gospel of Luke*, 493–94.
319. *m. Yad.* 1:1–5.
320. See *m. Kelim* 25; Str-B 1:934–35.
321. Tobit 12:8–9; cf. 4:8–11; 14:10–11; Sir. 3:30; 7:10; 29:12.
322. Lev. 27:30–33; Num. 18:21–32; Deut. 14:22–29; 2 Chron. 31:5–12; see the tractates *m. Maʿaś.* ("Tithes"); *m. Maʿaś. Š.* ("Second Tithe"), and *m. Demai* ("Produce not certainly tithed").
323. E.g., Isa. 1:17, 21; 5:7; Mic. 6:8.
324. Cf. *y. Ber.* 4b [2.1]; Str.-B 1:382; H. Windisch, "ἀσπάζομαι," *TDNT*, 1:498.
325. 1 Kings 19:10, 14; Neh. 9:26; Jer. 2:30; 26:20–24; cf. Matt. 5:12; 23:34–36; Luke 4:24; 6:23, 26; 13:34; Acts 7:52.
326. See Prov. 1:20–33; 8:1–9:6; Sir. 1; 24; *1 En.* 42; Wisd. Sol., *passim*; Bar. 3–4.
327. Ex. 20:5; Isa. 65:7; Jer. 32:18.
328. See Gen. 9:5–6; 2 Sam. 4:11.
329. Deut. 32:43; 2 Kings 9:7; Ps. 79:10; cf. *1 En.* 47; Rev. 6:10.
330. Cf. Str-B 1:940–943; Keener, *BBC*, 222.
331. Fitzmyer, *Luke*, 2:951.
332. Cf. Str-B 1:128–29; H. Windisch, "ζύμη," *TDNT*, 2:905–6.
333. Job 10:4–7; 11:11; Ps. 11:4; 33:15; 139:2.
334. *4 Macc.* 13:14–17, NRSV.
335. 2 Kings 16:3; 21:6; 23:10; Jer. 7:32; 19:4–6; 32:34–35.
336. Judith 16:17; *4 Ezra* 7:36; *1 En.* 10:13; 18:11–16; 27:1–3; *Jub.* 9:15; Mark 9:45–48; Rev. 20:10–15.
337. Manson, *Sayings*, 108.
338. 1 Sam. 14:45; 2 Sam. 14:11; 1 Kings 1:52; Dan. 3:27; cf. Luke 21:18; Acts 27:34.
339. Cf. Str-B 3:545–49; *m. B. Bat.* 8–9.
340. See Ex. 20:17; Deut. 5:21; Job 31:24–25; Ps. 49; Eccl. 2:1–11.
341. *T. Jud.* 18–19; Sir. 11:18–19; *1 En.* 97:8–10.
342. Mark 7:22; Col. 3:5; 1 Tim. 6:10; 2 Peter 2:3.
343. Old Testament and Jewish: Eccl. 2:24; 3:13; 5:18; 8:15; Isa. 22:13; Tobit 7:10; Sir. 11:19; cf. 1 Cor. 15:32 (citing Isa. 22:13). Greek parallels include Euripides, *Alcestis* 788–89; Menander, *Fragment* 301 (Fitzmyer, *Luke*, 2:973).
344. Ps. 39:6; 49:10; Eccl. 2:18.
345. See references in Fitzmyer, *Luke*, 2:978.
346. See ibid., 2:979.
347. Manson, *Sayings*, 112.
348. See Job 8:12; Ps. 37:2; 90:5–6; 102:11; 103:15–16; Isa. 37:27; 40:6–8.
349. See Jer. 13:17; Ezek. 34; Zech. 10:3; 13:7.
350. Sir. 29:8–17; Tobit 4:7–11; *Pss. Sol.* 9:5.
351. See 1 Kings 18:46; 2 Kings 4:29; 9:1; Job 38:3; Jer. 1:17; 1 Peter 1:13.
352. Fitzmyer, *Luke*, 2:988.
353. BAGD, 199.
354. Prov. 23:2; Zech. 7:6; Rom. 14:17; Ex. 32:6; Isa. 22:2; 1 Cor. 10:7; Prov. 20:1; Isa. 28:7; 56:12; Luke 21:34; Rom. 13:13; 1 Cor. 11:21; Gal. 5:21; 1 Peter 4:3.
355. Sir. 23:6; 31:29–30; 37:30–31; Tobit 4:15; *4 Macc.* 1:3.
356. Ibid., 200.
357. Homer, *Odyssey* 18.339; Herodotus 2.139; Judith 5:22; Sus. 55; 2 Macc. 1:13; Heb. 11:37.

358. See Gen. 19:24; Isa. 29:6; Ezek. 38:22; Amos 7:4; Zeph. 1:18; 3:8; Mal. 4:1; *4 Ezra* 13:10–11, 27; *1 En.* 67:13; 90:24–27; 102:1; *Pss. Sol.* 15:4–5; *Jub.* 9:15; 36:10; 1QS 2:8; 4:13; *T. Isaac* 5:21–25; *T. Ab.* 12–13.
359. Isa. 4:4; Mal. 3:2; 1 Cor. 3:10–15.
360. Ps. 18:4; 42:7; 69:1–2; Isa. 8:7–8; 30:27–28; Jonah 2:5; see also Mark 10:38.
361. *m. Soṭah* 9:15.
362. *Jub.* 23:16, 19; *4 Ezra* 6:24.
363. Job 15:2; 37:17; Jer. 4:11; Ezek. 17:10; Sir. 43:16.
364. Josephus, *Ant.* 18.3.1 §§55–59.
365. Ibid., 18.3.2 §§60–62; *J.W.* 2.9.4 §§175–77. For other incidents see Marshall, *Gospel of Luke,* 553; Fitzmyer, *Luke* 2:1006–7.
366. See also Job 8:4, 20; 22:5; Ps. 34:21; 75:10; Prov. 3:33; 10:3, 6–7, 16, 24–25; John 9:2–3.
367. Josephus, *J.W.* 5.4.2 §145; John 9:7, 11.
368. Marshall, *Gospel of Luke,* 554.
369. Jer. 8:13; 24:1–10; Hos. 9:10; Mic. 7:1; Isa. 5:1–7.
370. See Matt. 21:19–21; Mark 11:12–14, 20–21.
371. 1 Kings 4:25; 2 Kings 18:31; Isa. 36:16; Joel 2:22; Isa. 5:5; 9:10; Jer. 5:17; Hos. 2:12; Joel 1:7.
372. See also Isa. 10:34; 11:1; Jer. 46:22; Dan. 4:23; Matt. 3:10; 7:19; Luke 3:9.
373. Syriac *Ahikar* 8:35; cited in *HCNT,* 218. Cf. other parallels in Str-B 4:1, 474; Armenian Philo, *De Jona* §52.
374. Luke 4:31–41; 6:6–11; cf. 14:1–6.
375. Jeremias, *Jerusalem,* 373; Bock, *Luke,* 2:1215; *m. Ber.* 3:3; Acts 16:13; 17:4.
376. Marshall, *Gospel of Luke,* 557; Bock, *Luke,* 2:1215; Fitzmyer, *Luke,* 2:1012.
377. Luke 4:40, 41; 7:21; 13:32.
378. See Luke 8:41, 49; Acts 13:15; 18:8, 17.
379. *m. Yoma* 8:6; *m. Šabb.* 18:3; 19:2.
380. *m. Šabb.* 5:1–4.
381. Ibid., 15:1–2; 7:2.
382. CD 11:5–6 forbids taking an animal beyond 1000 cubits (1500 feet) for pasturing. The Qumran sectarians appeared to be stricter than the Pharisees, forbidding help for an animal giving birth or pulling it out of a well on the Sabbath (CD 11:13–14).
383. *m. ʿErub.* 2:1–4.
384. Keener, *BBC,* 227.
385. *m. Nid.* 5:2.
386. Marshall, *Gospel of Luke,* 561; cf. Str-B 1:669; O. Michel, "κόκκος, κόκκινος," *TDNT,* 3:810 n.1.
387. Bock, *Luke,* 2:1227.
388. *Hist. Plant.* 7.1, 2–3; noted by Fitzmyer, *Luke,* 2:1016–17.
389. Ps. 104:12; Ezek. 17:22–24; Dan. 4:10–15.
390. BAGD, 745 ("a peck and a half"); Bock, *Luke,* 2:1228.
391. Cf. 2 Esd. (*4 Ezra*) 7:47; 9:15; *2 Bar.* 44:15; 48:45–50; Str-B 1:883.
392. Danby, *The Mishnah,* 397 n.4.
393. Isa. 22:22; Rev. 3:7–8, 20; cf. Matt. 7:7; 25:10; Luke 11:9.
394. Nolland, *Luke,* 2:734; Str-B 1:469; 4:293.
395. Cf. John 7:27–28; 9:29–30.
396. Matt. 8:12; 13:42, 50; 22:13; 24:51; 25:30.
397. See also Job 16:9; Ps. 112:10; Lam. 2:16; cf. Sir. 51:3; Acts 7:54.
398. Ex. 2:24; cf. Gen. 50:24; Ex. 3:6, 15.
399. See Tobit 4:12; Judith 8:26; Sir. 51:12; Bar. 2:34; 2 Macc. 1:2; *4 Macc.* 13:17.
400. See also Isa. 6:7; Mic. 4:1–2; Mal. 1:11; cf. Isa. 51:4; 52:10; 59:19; Zech. 2:13. For the eschatological regathering of Israelites see Ps. 107:3; Isa. 43:5–6; 49:12; 66:19–20.
401. Cf. *2 En.* 42:5; *m. ʾAbot* 3:17; also the "wedding supper of the Lamb," Rev. 19:9.
402. See also Isa. 55:1–2; 65:13–14; *1 En.* 62:14; *2 Bar.* 29:1–8.
403. 1QSa (1Q28a) 2:1ff.
404. Cf. Luke 4:24; 7:16; 11:47–51; 24:19.
405. For Greek literature Fitzmyer (*Luke,* 2:1031) cites Pindar, *Pyth. Od.* 2.77.78; Plato, *Resp.* 2.8 §365c; Plutarch, *Life of Solon* 30.2; Epictetus, *Diatr.* 1.3.7–8. For the rabbinic writings see Str-B 2.200–1.
406. Ezek. 13:4; cf. Lam. 5:18; *1 En.* 89:42–50.
407. Keener, *BBC,* 228.
408. Ibid., 228.
409. See also Ruth 2:12; Ps. 17:8; 36:7; 57:1; 61:4; 63:7; 91:4.
410. The close parallel in 2 Esd. 1:33 is probably dependent on the Gospel text (see previous note); Jer. 26:9; 12:7; 22:5; cf. Isa. 24:10.
411. Cf. Str-B 1:849–50, 876.
412. *American Heritage Electronic Dictionary* (New York: Houghton and Mifflin, 1992).
413. Cf. Str-B 1:629. See Marshall, *Gospel of Luke,* 580.
414. *Lev. Rab.* 11.5 on 1:1 (commenting on Prov. 25:7); cited by Manson, *Sayings,* 278; Str-B 1:916.
415. Theophrastus, *Characteres* 21.2; noted by Manson, *Sayings,* 278.
416. See B. J. Malina and J. H. Neyrey, "Honor and Shame in Luke-Acts: Pivotal Values of the Mediterranean World," pp. 25–65 in *The Social World of Luke-Acts: Models for Interpretations* (ed. J. H. Neyrey; Peabody, Mass.: Hendrickson, 1991); Malina and Rohrbaugh, *SSCSG,* 76–77, 213–14, 309–11.
417. Malina and Rohrbaugh, *SSCSG,* 365.
418. E.g., 2 Macc. 7:9, 14; *1 En.* 103:4.
419. Josephus, *Ant.* 18.1.3 §14.
420. cf. Luke 1:52–53; 6:21, 25; 10:15; 18:14.

421. Cf. *y. Sanh.* 6:23c, 30–43. The text is reproduced in *HCNT,* 228–9 §338.
422. Cited by G. B. Gray, *The Book of Isaiah* (ICC; New York: Scribner's Sons, 1912), 1:429–30.
423. *Pss. Sol.* 17:22–25; cf. 17:30–31; *1 En.* 62:9–13.
424. The Hellenistic Jewish philosopher Philo notes that "givers of a banquet. . .do not send out the summonses to supper till they have put everything in readiness for the feast" (*Creation* 25 §78). For additional Greek and Jewish references see Marshall, *Gospel of Luke,* 587–88; Nolland *Luke,* 2:755.
425. Bailey, *Through Peasant Eyes,* 94–95.
426. Ibid., 95–96.
427. Marshall, *Gospel of Luke,* 589.
428. Bailey, *Through Peasant Eyes,* 97–98.
429. Ibid., 98–99.
430. Ibid., 99.
431. Isa. 29:18–19; 35:5–6; 61:1–2.
432. 1QSa (1Q28a) 2:2–7.
433. Gen. 29:31, 33; Deut. 21:15; Rom. 9:13.
434. See Josephus, *J.W.* 5.4.3 §§156–71 for towers in Jerusalem. For a vineyard watchtower see Isaiah 5:2; Mark 12:1.
435. Epictetus, *Dissertationes* 3.15.8; cited by Fitzmyer, *Luke,* 2:1065.
436. Philo, *Abraham* 21 §105.
437. Nolland, *Luke,* 2:765.
438. Cf. *m. Bek.* 8b; cited by Marshall, *Gospel of Luke,* 596, and Fitzmyer, *Luke,* 2:1069.
439. Marshall, *Gospel of Luke,* 596. A less likely solution noted by Marshall involves the use of salt in ovens, where it gradually loses its catalytic power.
440. Ibid., 597.
441. *Mekilta de Rabbi Ishmael,* tractate *Amalek* 3.55–57 on Ex. 18:1; cited by Bock, *Luke,* 2:1299.
442. Jeremias, *Parables,* 133.
443. Bailey, *Poet and Peasant,* 149–50 n.34.
444. Jeremias, *Jerusalem,* 100; idem, *Parables,* 134–35; Bailey, *Poet and Peasant,* 157, points out the headdress would be a Bedouin custom, while the necklace would be characteristic of a village woman.
445. Keener, *BBC,* 232.
446. Bailey, *Poet and Peasant,* 161–65.
447. *m. B. Bat.* 8:7.
448. Bailey, *Poet and Peasant,* 162–66; Manson, *Sayings,* 286–87.
449. BAGD, 782; Marshall, *Gospel of Luke,* 607.
450. Bock, *Luke,* 2:1310.
451. Marshall, *Gospel of Luke,* 608.
452. Bailey, *Poet and Peasant,* 167–68.
453. Cf. *b. B. Qam.* 82b. Cf. Str-B 1:492–93.
454. Bailey, however, claims that this is not Syrian carob (*ceratonia siliqua*), which is sweet, but a bitter variety of wild carob (*Poet and Peasant,* 171–73).
455. Rabbi Acha (c. A.D. 320) in *Lev. Rab.* 35.6 on 26.3; cited by Marshall, *Gospel of Luke,* 609.
456. *Lam. Rab.* 1.34 on 1:7; Str-B 2:215–16.
457. See references in Bailey, *Poet and Peasant,* 181–82.
458. Ibid., 185.
459. Ibid., 186–87.
460. Ibid., 168, 195–96.
461. J. D. M. Derrett, *Law in the New Testament* (London: Darman, Longman and Todd, 1970), 48–77; Ex. 22:25; Lev. 25:35–37; Deut. 15:7–8; 23:20–21.
462. Fitzmyer, *Luke,* 2:1098.
463. Cf. Sir. 38:24–34; Aristophanes, *The Birds* 1430–33.
464. Sir. 40:28.
465. Jeremias, *Parables,* 181; Marshall, *Gospel of Luke,* 618–19.
466. See Bailey, *Poet and Peasant,* 86–110.
467. See 1QM 1:3, 11, 13; 1QS 1:9; 3:13, 24–26; cf. *1 En.* 108:11. For additional references see Fitzmyer, *Luke,* 2:1108.
468. See Marshall, *Gospel of Luke,* 621 for details.
469. Cited in James B. Pritchard, ed., *Ancient Near Eastern Texts Relating to the Old Testament* (3rd ed., Princeton, N.J.: Princeton University Press, 1969), 413; cf. *HCNT,* 226–7 §335.
470. *Ex. Rab.* on Ex. 3:1; cited by Manson, *Sayings,* 293–94. For other parallels see Bock, *Luke,* 2:1335 n.27.
471. See Marshall, *Gospel of Luke,* 624 for other examples.
472. Josephus, *Ant.* 13.10.6 §298. The *Pss. Sol.* (a Pharisaic document from the first century B.C.) repeatedly condemns the unrighteous aristocracy of Jerusalem.
473. Cf. Str-B 1:937; Jeremias, *Jerusalem,* 114; Marshall, *Gospel of Luke,* 625.
474. See also Isa. 51:6; 65:17; 66:22; 2 Peter 3:7, 10; Rev. 21:1.
475. See also Isa. 40:8; 55:10–11; Bar. 4:1; 2 Esd. (*4 Ezra*) 9:36–37.
476. BAGD, 428.
477. Cf. Matt. 5:32; 19:9; Mark 10:11–12.
478. *Demotic Narrative about Setme Chamois,* in *HCNT,* 227–28 §338.
479. Marshall, *Gospel of Luke,* 635.
480. Cf. *b. Beṣah* 32b; cited by Manson, *Sayings,* 299.
481. See also Ps. 22:16, 20; 59:6, 14; Jer. 15:3.
482. See Sir. 21:9–10; *1 En.* 10:13; 2 Esd. (*4 Ezra*) 8:59; Matt. 25:41; Rev. 20:10, 14–15.
483. See Luke 16:31; 24:27, 44; Acts 26:22; 28:23.
484. 1QS 1:3.
485. See also Isa. 10:1–3; Jer. 5:26–28; Ezek. 18:12–18; Amos 5:11–12; Mal. 3:5; Deut. 15:7; 24:14, 19–21; Isa. 58:10; Isa. 3:14–15; 5:7–8.

486. See Sir. 28:2; 1QS 5:24–6:1; CD 9:3–4; *T. Gad* 6:1–7; Str-B 1:795–99. The *Testament of Gad* text is closest, but it may have undergone Christian redaction.
487. *m. Nid.* 5:2.
488. Bock, *Luke*, 2:1391.
489. *m. ᵓAbot* 2:8.
490. *m. ᵓAbot* 1:3.
491. *Pss. Sol.* 17:21–46; 18:5–9.
492. See 2 Esd. (*4 Ezra*) 5:4–10; *1 En.* 91, 93; *2 Bar.* 25–27, 53. These passages have their background in the apocalyptic passages of the Old Testament (see Isa. 24–27; Ezek.; Dan. 7–12; Joel 2; etc.).
493. Cf. *m. Ber.* 1:5; 2 Esd. (*4 Ezra*) 13:52; Str-B 2:237; 4:826–27.
494. See Josephus, *Ant.* 17.10.5 §§271–72 (Judas the Galilean); *Ant.* 17.10.6 §§273–77 (Simon); *Ant.* 17.10.7 §§278–81 (Anthronges); *Ant.* 20.5.1 §§97–99 (Theudas); *Ant.* 20.8.6 §§169–72; *J.W.* 2.13.5 §§261–63 (the Egyptian); *Ant.* 18.4.1 §§85–87 (a Samaritan).
495. Josephus, *J.W.* 2.13.4–6 §§258–65; cf. 6.5.4 §§312–13.
496. See also Ezek. 30:3; Joel 1:15; 2:1, 11, 31; Amos 5:18; Obad. 15; Zeph. 1:14; Mal. 4:5.
497. See Wisd. Sol. 10:4–6; 14:6; *3 Macc.* 2:4–5; *T. Naph.* 3:4–5; Philo, *Moses* 2:10–12 §§52–65; *Gen. Rab.* 27 on 6:5–6; Str-B 1:564. Cf. 2 Peter 2:5–7.
498. *m. Sanh.* 10:3.
499. See 2 Esd. (*4 Ezra*) 14:9, 52; *1 En.* 48:6; 62:7; Str-B 2:334.
500. A. Edersheim, *The Life and Times of Jesus the Messiah* (Grand Rapids: Eerdmans, 1971), 2:287.
501. See also Deut. 24:17; 27:19; Ps. 68:5; Isa. 1:23; 10:2; Jer. 22:3; Ezek. 22:7; Amos 5:10–13; Zech. 7:10; Mal. 3:5; Ex. 22:22; Deut. 10:18.
502. 2 Esd. 2:20; Sir. 35:17–21; Wis. 2:10.
503. Bailey, *Through Peasant Eyes*, 134–35, recounts a similar story witnessed by a Western traveler in Iraq.
504. See *m. Soṭah* 9:15; 2 Esd. 6:24; 9:1–12; 13:29–31; Matt. 24:10–12; 2 Thess. 2:3; 1 Tim. 4:1.
505. *m. B. Qam.* 10:1.
506. *m. Ṭehar.* 7:6.
507. Cf. *y. Ber.* 2.7d; cited by Manson, *Sayings*, 311. Cf. *b. Ber.* 28b; *b. Sukkah* 45b; Jeremias, *Parables*, 142; Bock, *Luke*, 2:1463 n.7.
508. This is attested in later Judaism (*b. Ta'an.* 12a) and is implied in the *Did.* 8:1, where Christians are instructed not to fast on these two days "with the hypocrites" (Fitzmyer, *Luke*, 2:1187).
509. Isa. 32:12; Jer. 31:19; Ezek. 21:12; Nah. 2:7; Luke 23:48.
510. Psalm 51:1, 3; cf. Ps. 6; 32; 38; 102; 130; 143.
511. For such blessings in Judaism see Marshall, *Gospel of Luke*, 682; Str-B 2:138.
512. Deut. 32:4; 2 Sam. 22:31; Job 36:4; cf. Matt. 5:48.
513. Ex. 20:12–16; Deut. 5:16–20.
514. Cf. Str-B 1:814; *b. Sanh.* 101a; Marshall, *Gospel of Luke*, 684.
515. 2 Chron. 1:11–12; Ps. 112:3; 128:2; Prov. 8:18; Isa. 61:6; Wisd. Sol. 8:18.
516. Ps. 62:10; Prov. 11:28; Jer. 9:23–24; 49:4–5; Sir. 5:1, 8; 40:13.
517. Isa. 29:18–19; 35:5–6; 61:1–2; Luke 4:18; 7:22.
518. *Pss. Sol.* 17:21.
519. Cf. Isa. 9:6–7; 11:1–5; Jer. 23:5–6; 33:15–16; Ezek. 37:24–25.
520. O. Michel, "τελώνης," *TDNT*, 8:97–99; Marshall, *Gospel of Luke*, 696.
521. *m. Ned.* 3:4.
522. Marshall, *Gospel of Luke*, 696; C.–H. Hunzinger, "συκάμινο, συκομορέα, συκοφαντέω," *TDNT*, 7:758–59.
523. Cf. Str-B. 4:546–47; *b. Ketub.* 50a; S. T. Lachs, *A Rabbinic Commentary on the New Testament: The Gospels of Matthew, Mark and Luke* (New York: Ktav, 1987), 331 n.6; Bock, *Luke*, 2:1482.
524. Lev. 5:16; Num. 5:7.
525. For references see Michel, "τελώνης," *TDNT*, 8:105 n.154; Marshall, *Gospel of Luke*, 698; Bock, *Luke*, 2:1520.
526. *m. Ketub.* 3:9.
527. See, e.g., Isa. 2:2–4; 35:1–10; 65:17–25; Jer. 30–31; Ezek. 37, 40–48; Mic. 4:1–5; *Pss. Sol.* 17–18; *1 En.* 45, 51; *2 Bar.* 71–74.
528. Josephus, *Ant.* 14.14.1–4 §§370–85 (Herod the Great); idem, *J.W.* 2 §§20–22; idem, *Ant.* 17.9.4 §§224–27 (Antipas); *Ant.* 17.11.1 §303 (Philip); *Ant.* 18.6.1–11 §§143–239 (Agrippa I).
529. Josephus, *Ant.* 17.8.1 §188; 17.9.3 §§213–18; 17.11.1–4 §§299–320; idem, *J.W.* 2.6.1–3 §§80–100; 2.1.3 §§8–13.
530. *m. ᵓAbot* 4:2.
531. See also *1 En.* 62:15; 96:1; Dan. 7:18, 22; Luke 12:32; 22:30; 1 Cor. 6:2–3.
532. Cf. *m. B. Meṣiᶜa* 3:10–11; Str-B 1:970–71; 2:252.
533. *m. B. Meṣiᶜa* 3:11.
534. There are many examples of this in the ancient world. See Josephus, *Ant.* 13.14.2 §380 (Alexander Jannaeus); idem, *Ant.* 14.9.4 §175; 14.16.4 §489 (Herod the Great).
535. John 11:1, 18; 12:1; cf. Luke 10:38.
536. See J. D. M. Derrett, "Law in the New Testament: The Palm Sunday Colt," *NovT* 13 (1971): 241–58; esp. 243–49.
537. Cf. Josephus, *Ant.* 9.6.2 §111.

538. *1 Macc.* 13:51.
539. Later rabbis interpreted the psalm messianically, but it is uncertain whether this interpretation goes back to Jesus' day. See Str-B 1:849–50, 876.
540. See also Jer. 13:17; 14:17; Lam. 1:1–4, 16; 3:48; Mic. 1:8; Isa. 22:4; Jer. 9:1–2, 10.
541. Josephus, *J.W.* 5.11.4–6 §§466–490; 5.12.1–4 §§491–526.
542. Ibid., 5–6.
543. Ibid., 6.3.3 §§193–195; 6.8.5 §§403–406.
544. Ibid., 6.9.3 §§420–21.
545. Ibid., 6.9.4 §434; 7.1.1 §§1–3; 7.8.7 §§375–77.
546. Cf. Str-B 1:850–52.
547. Ex. 30:11–16; *m. Šeqal.* 1:3; 2:1, 4; 4:7–8.
548. See Luke 20:1; 22:52; Acts 23:14; 25:15. See Nolland, Luke, 2:466; G. Schenk, "ἀρχιερεύς," *TDNT,* 3:268–72; J. Jeremias, *Jerusalem,* 160–81.
549. See also 2 Chron. 24:21; 36:16; Neh. 9:26; Jer. 2:30; 26:20–24; 37:15; 2 Chron. 24:19; 36:15–16; Jer. 7:25–26; 1 Kings 19:10, 14.
550. Ps. 2:7; 89:26–29; Isa. 7:14.
551. Cf. 4QFlor 1:11 (= 4Q174).
552. Fitzmyer, *Luke,* 2:1282.
553. Esp. Ps. 118:22–23; Isa. 8:14; 28:16; Rom. 9:32–33; Eph. 2:20; 1 Peter 2:6–8; 2:34.
554. BAGD, 215.
555. See also Ps. 78:36; Prov. 26:28; 28:23; 29:5; Ezek. 12:24.
556. See also Job 23:11; Ps. 27:11; 119:15; 1QS 3:8–11; CD 20:18–19.
557. Josephus, *J.W.* 2.8.1 §118. For tribute to Rome in general see *J.W.* 1.7.6 §154; idem, *Ant.* 14.10.6 §§202–3.
558. Rom. 13:1–7; Titus 3:1; 1 Peter 2:13–17.
559. Isa. 40:23; Dan. 2:21; 4:17.
560. Cf. Matt. 22:23–33; Mark 12:18–27.
561. Job 19:26; Ps. 16:9–11; Isa. 25:7–8; 26:19; Hos. 13:14.
562. Tobit 3:7–17; 6:10–8:18.
563. The same concept prevailed in Judaism, where saints receive glory and immortality *like* that of the angels; see Wisd. Sol. 5:5; *2 Bar.* 51:10; *1 En.* 104:5–6; 1QSb (1Q28b) 4:28.
564. *1 En.* 15:7; 6–10.
565. *Midrash Sifre* on Numbers 112; cited in *HCNT,* 127. Cf. *m. Meg.* 3:3; *Sifre* on Deut. 32:2.
566. See Mark 14:62; Acts 2:34; 7:56; Rom. 8:34; 1 Cor. 15:25; Eph. 1:20; Col. 3:1; Heb. 1:3, 13; 5:6; 7:17, 21; 8:1; 10:12–13; 1 Peter 3:22; Rev. 3:21.
567. Cf. *b. Giṭ.* 52a-b.
568. Cf. *Pss. Sol.* 4:1–13.
569. Josephus, *J.W.* 6.5.2 §282; 5.5.2 §200; idem, *Ant.* 19.6.1 §294; 1 Macc. 14:49; 2 Macc. 3:4–40.
570. Cf. *m. Šeqal.* 6:1, 5; cf. Neh. 12:44.
571. Aristotle, *Nikomachean Ethics* 4.1.19; cited by Danker, *Jesus and the New Age,* 328. Cf. Euripides, *Danaë* frg. 319. For a later Jewish parallel involving a widow see *Lev. Rab.* 3.5 on 1:7 (see comments on Mark 12:42).
572. Cf. Matthew 24:1–35; Mark 13:1–37.
573. Cf. *b. B. Bat.* 4a; *b. Sukkah* 41b.
574. Josephus, *J.W.* 5.5.6 §§ 222–24; idem, *Ant.* 15.11.3–7 §§ 391–425; cf. *m. Mid.*
575. Josephus, *J.W.* 6.5.3 §300–309.
576. Ibid., 6.5.4 §§312–13; cf. Tacitus, *Hist.* 5.13.
577. See 2 Chron. 15:6; Isa. 19:2; Jer. 4:20; Dan. 11:44; Joel 3:9–14; cf. Rev. 6:4, 8.
578. Earthquakes: 1 Sam. 14:15; Ps. 18:7–8; Isa. 5:25; 13:13; 29:6; Amos 1:1; Hag. 2:6, 21; Zech. 14:4; famines and plagues: Jer. 14:12; 21:6–7; Ezek. 14:21.
579. See Isa. 2:19, 21; 13:13; 24:18; 29:5–6; Ezek. 38:19; Joel 2:10.
580. See also 2 Esd. 13:31; *2 Bar.* 27:7; 70:2–8; Josephus, *J.W.* 6.5.3 § 299; cf. Rev. 6:12; 8:5; 11:13, 19; 16:18; 2 Esd. 9:1–5.
581. See Schürer, 2:427–33.
582. See also Num. 23:5; Deut. 18:18; Isa. 50:4; 51:16; Ezek. 29:21; Acts 6:10.
583. On excommunication in Judaism see Schürer, 2:431–33.
584. *m. Soṭah* 9:15; *4 Ezra* 6:24; *Jub.* 23:16, 19.
585. 1 Sam. 14:45; 2 Sam. 14:11; 1 Kings 1:52; Dan. 3:27.
586. Cf. 9:24; 17:33; John 12:25.
587. Eusebius, *Eccl. Hist.* 3.5.3.
588. 1 Kings 9:6–9; Jer. 6:1–30; 32:24–25; Ezek. 14:12–23; Dan. 9:26; Mic. 3:12.
589. Josephus, *J.W.* 6.3.4 §§201–13 (my translation).
590. 1 Macc. 3:45, 51; 4:60; 2 Macc. 8:2; *Pss. Sol.* 2:19–21; 8:14–22; 17:7–18, 22–24, 30.
591. See also Jer. 4:23, 28; Ezek. 32:7–8; Joel 2:10, 30–31; 2 Esd. 5:4–5; 7:39; *T. Mos.* 10:5.
592. Josephus, *J.W.* 6.5.3 §289; cf. *Sib. Or.* 3.797.
593. Josephus, *J.W.* 6.5.3 §§297–98; Tacitus, *History* 5:13; cf. 2 Macc. 5:2–3; *Sib. Or.* 3:795–807; 1QM 12:9; 19:1–2.
594. See 2 Esd. (*4 Ezra*) 6:24; 9:1–12; 13:29–31; *2 Bar.* 27:1–15; 70:2–8; *m. Soṭah* 9:15; 1QM *passim*; cf. 1 Cor. 7:26.
595. 1QM 1:11–12.
596. BAGD, 154.
597. Nissan 15–21; see Ex. 12:1–20; 23:15; 34:18; Deut. 16:1–8.
598. Josephus, *Ant.* 14.2.1 §21; 17.9.3 §213; idem, *J.W.* 2.1.3 §10.
599. Ex. 12:1–11; Num. 9:11–12; Deut. 16:1–8.
600. Deut. 16:3; *m. Pesaḥ.* 10:5.
601. Marshall, *Gospel of Luke,* 791.
602. *m. Pesaḥ.* 10:1.

603. J. Jeremias, *The Eucharistic Words of Jesus* (trans. Norman Perrin; London: SCM, 1966), 84–88; Fitzmyer, *Luke*, 2:1390. The use of the fourth cup in first-century Palestine is disputed; Ps. 115–118; see *m. Pesaḥ*. 10:2, 4, 7.
604. See 2 Macc. 4:2; *3 Macc.* 3:19; prologue to Sirach; Josephus, *J.W.* 3.9.8 §459 (Vespasian). See Fitzmyer, *Luke*, 2:1417 for inscriptions of Caesar Augustus and Nero using the title.
605. Danker, *Jesus and the New Age*, 348.
606. Cf. *1 En.* 62:14.
607. *Acts Pet.*, 37–38.
608. Fitzmyer, *Luke*, 2:1426.
609. *m. B. Qam.* 7:7.
610. Josephus, *J.W.* 2.8.4 §125.
611. See Ps. 11:6; 60:3; 75:8; Isa. 51:17, 21–23; Jer. 25:15–29; 49:12; 51:57; Lam. 4:21; Ezek. 23:31–34; Hab. 2:16; Zech. 12:2.
612. See also Prayer of Azariah 26; Tobit 5:17, 22; Bar. [Letter of Jeremiah] 6:7; 2 Esd. (*4 Ezra*) 5:15, 31; 7:1; 1 Kings 19:5–8; Ps. 91:11–12; Dan. 3:28; 10:16–19; cf. Heb. 1:14.
613. *Jos. and Asen.* 4:11; see Marshall, *Gospel of Luke*, 832, for additional sources.
614. See Bock, *Luke*, 2:1761.
615. See also 2 Sam. 15:5; Song 8:1; 1 Esd. (3 Ezra) 4:47; Rom. 16:16; 1 Cor. 16:20; 2 Cor. 13:12; 1 Peter 5:14.
616. Josephus, *J.W.* 2.13.2–3 §253–54.
617. Ps. 2:7; 89:26; Isa. 7:14.
618. Cf. *y. Sanh.* 1.1, 18a; Josephus, *Ant.* 20.9.1 §§ 200–203.
619. See Sherwin-White, *Roman Society and Roman Law*, 12–23.
620. Ibid., 24–27.
621. Josephus, *J.W.* 2.8.1 §118.
622. Schürer 1:343. See sidebar on *Herod the Great* at 1:5.
623. For individuals staying silent at their trials see Josephus, *Ant.* 15.7.5 §235 (Mariamne, the wife of Herod the Great); Diogenes Laertius 3:19 (Plato); 9.115 (the sophist philosopher Timon). Cf. Danker, *Jesus and the New Age*, 365.
624. Philo, *Embassy* 38. It is not certain whether this episode was before or after Jesus' crucifixion.
625. Sherwin-White, *Roman Society and Roman Law*, 27.
626. Luke 23:17 does not occur in the best Greek manuscripts and is probably a later scribal harmonization; Matt. 27:15; Mark 15:6; John 18:39.
627. R. L. Merritt, "Jesus Barabbas and the Paschal Pardon," *JBL* 104 (1988): 57–68.
628. Josephus, *Ant.* 17.10.5 §§271–72; idem, *J.W.* 2.8.1 §118 (Judas the Galilean); idem, *Ant.* 17.10.6 §§273–77 (Simon); *Ant.* 17.10.7 §§278–81 (Anthronges); *Ant.* 20.5.1 §§97–99 (Theudas); *Ant.* 20.8.6 §§169–72; idem, *J.W.* 2.13.5 §§261–63 (the Egyptian); idem, *Ant.* 18.4.1 §§85–87 (a Samaritan).
629. See Josephus, *Ant.* 20.8.10 §186–88; idem, *J.W.* 2.13.3 §254; 2.17.6 §425; 4.7.2 §400.
630. Josephus, *J.W.* 7.8.1 §253–54.
631. See Josephus, *Ant.* 18.3.1 §55–59; Philo, *Embassy* 38.
632. Tacitus, *Ann.* 15.44.
633. Josephus, *Ant.* 18.3.3 §§63–64.
634. Shlomo Pines, *An Arabic Version of the Testimonium Flavianum and Its Implications* (Jerusalem: Israel Academy of Sciences and Humanities, 1971), 16.
635. Josephus, *J.W.* 5.11.1 §451.
636. *Digesta iuris Romani* 48.19.28.15, cited in Hengel, *Crucifixion*, 50. Cf. Quintilian, *Training in Oratory* 274.
637. Brown, *Death*, 853–958; Sherwin-White, *Roman Society and Roman Law*, 46.
638. BAGD, 574.
639. Eusebius, *Eccl. Hist.* 5.1; Suetonius, *Caligula* 32; *Domitian* 10; Dio Cassius, *Roman History* 54.3; BAGD, 291; Marshall, *Gospel of Luke*, 870.
640. Gen. 2:8–10, 15; Josephus, *Ant.* 1.1.3 §37; *1 En.* 20:7; 60:8.
641. See also *4 Ezra* 4:7; 6:2; 7:36, 123; *1 En.* 32:3; *T. Dan* 5:12; *T. Levi* 18:11.
642. Isa. 13:9–13; Joel 2:10; 3:14–15; Amos 5:18, 20; 8:9; cf. Ex. 10:21–23.
643. Darkness is reported with reference to the deaths of Alexander the Great (Ps-Callisthenes 3.3.26); Caesar (Virgil, *Georgics* 1.463ff.), Aeschylus (Aristophanes, *Ael. Aristid.* 32.32), and others (see BAGD, 757; H. Conzelmann, "σκότος," *TDNT*, 7:439; for rabbinic parallels see Str-B 1:1040–41).
644. Ex. 26:33–37; 27:16.
645. Josephus, *J.W.* 5.5.4 §212.
646. Josephus, *J.W.* 6.5.3 §293–96.
647. Isa. 32:12; Jer. 31:19; Ezek. 21:12; Nah. 2:7.
648. See Josephus, *J.W.* 4.5.2 § 317; *Ag. Ap.* 2.29 §211; Philo, *Flaccus* 83–84; Tobit 1:17–18.
649. Marshall, *Gospel of Luke*, 879; Rathamin (1 Macc. 11:34) and Ramathain (Josephus, *Ant.* 13.4.9 §127) may designate the same location.
650. Finegan, *Archaeology*, 166–68; 181–219; Rachel Hachlili, "Burials, Ancient Jewish," *ABD* 1:789–91; Rousseau and Arav, *Jesus and His World*, 164–69.
651. *m. Šabb.* 23:5.
652. Josephus, *Ant.* 4.8.15 §219.
653. Philo, QG 4:15.
654. See J. Finegan, *Archaeology*, 198, 202.

655. Gen. 18:2; 19:1, 10; Josh. 5:13; Judg. 13:6–11; Tobit 5:4–5; cf. Heb. 13:2.
656. See also *1 En.* 71:1; 2 Macc. 11:8; Acts 1:10; Rev. 4:4; 19:14.
657. Judg. 6:22–23; 13:22; Dan. 8:16–17; 10:10–11.
658. Fitzmyer, *Luke*, 2:1561–2; Marshall, *Gospel of Luke*, 892.
659. See Sydney H. T. Page, "The Suffering Servant Between the Testaments," *NTS* 31 (1985): 481–97.
660. Cf. Luke 18:32; 20:17; 23:47; Acts 2:25ff.; 4:25–26.
661. See 2 Macc. 3:34; Euripides, *Orestes* 1496; idem, *Helen* 605–6; Virgil, *Aeneid* 9.656–58.
662. 1 Sam. 28:3–19; Isa. 8:19; 19:3.
663. Dan. 12:2; 2 Macc. 7:9, 14; *1 En.* 103:4; see also Luke 8:55; 14:14; 20:27.
664. Acts 2:25–28, 34; 13:33–35; 2:17–21; 13:47; 15:16–18.
665. Isa. 32:15; Ezek. 36:26–27; Joel 2:28–32; cf. Jer. 31:33; see Acts 2:14–21.
666. Enoch: Gen. 5:24; Heb. 11:5; Sir. 44:16; 49:14; *1 En.* 17–36; 39:3; Elijah: Sir. 48:9, 12; *1 En.* 89:52; 93:8; Jos. *Ant.* 9 §28; Bar.: *3 Apoc. Bar.*10–17; Moses: *As. Moses.* In Greco-Roman traditions too, heroes and gods sometimes ascend. Dio Cassius, *Roman History* 56.46 describes the ascent of Caesar Augustus, supposedly witnessed by the senator Numerius Atticus. For this and other examples see *HCNT*, 309 §485.
667. Acts 2:32–36; 5:31; Eph. 1:19–23; Phil. 2:9–11; Heb.

Sidebar and Chart Notes

A-1. Cf. A. W. Mosley, "Historical Reporting in the Ancient World," *NTS* 12 (1965–66): 10–26; and C. J. Hemer, *The Book of Acts in the Setting of Hellenistic History*, ed. C. H. Gempf (WUNT 2.49; Tübingen: Mohr, 1989), 43–44, 75–79.
A-2. On Luke's value as a historian see the above-mentioned works; also M. Hengel, *Acts and the History of Earliest Christianity* (Philadelphia: Fortress, 1979).
A-3. Josephus, *Ag. Ap.* 1.1 §§1–4.
A-4. Josephus, *Ag. Ap.* 2.1 §§1–2.
A-5. The fascinating story of Herod the Great is given in great detail by the Jewish historian Josephus in his *Antiquities of the Jews*. See *Ant.* 14.15.2 §403 (Edomite or "1/2 Jewish" heritage); 15.7.3 §§215–17 (allegiance switched to Caesar); 15.7.4–6 §§230–39 (execution of Miriamme); 15.10.4 §365 (Jewish taxes relieved); 15.11 §§380–425 (building the temple); 17.7.1. §§182–87 (execution of sons); 17.6.5 §§174–78 (death of key Jews ordered); 17.8.1 §§188–92 (death of Herod).
A-6. See especially J. Neusner, W. C. Green, and E. S. Frerichs, eds., *Judaisms and Their Messiahs at the Turn of the Christian Era* (Cambridge: Cambridge Univ. Press, 1987).
A-7. See 2 Esd. (*4 Ezra*) 12:32; 13:3–11, 26–38; *1 En.* 48:10; 49:3; 62:2.
A-8. See 4QFlor (4Q174); 4QPBless (4Q252); 4QpIsa[a] (4Q161); 4Q504; 4Q285.
A-9. Cf. 1QS 9:11; 1Qsa 2:11–21; 1QSb; 4QTestim. For a survey of this material see M. L. Strauss, *The Davidic Messiah in Luke-Acts* (JSNTSup 110; Sheffield: Sheffield Academic Press, 1995), ch. 2.
A-10. Josephus, *J.W.* 2.8.2 §§120–121.
A-11. Ex. 12:17–20; 34:18; Lev. 23:6.
A-12. Ex. 23:14–17; Deut. 16:16; cf. *m. Ḥag.* 1:1, which provides exceptions.
A-13. Josephus, *Ant.* 18.5.2 §§116–119.
A-14. See Jeremias, *Jerusalem*, 233–45; idem, "γραμματεύς," *TDNT*, 1:740–42.
A-15. Recent research has challenged traditional views of the Pharisees. See the bibliography and history of interpretation in A. J. Saldarini, "Pharisees," *ABD*, 5:303.
A-16. Important references to the Pharisees in Josephus include *J.W.* 1.5.2 §110; 2.8.14 §§162–65; idem, *Ant.* 13.5.9 §§171–72; 13.10.6 §§297–98; 17.2.4 §§41–45; 18.1.4 §16.
A-17. Prov. 3:13; 8:34; 14:21; 16:20; 28:20; Sir. 31:8.
A-18. Isa. 3:11; 5:8; Jer. 48:1; 50:27; Zech. 11:17.
A-19. Nolland, *Luke*, 1:280; Isa. 30:18; Dan. 12:12; *Pss. Sol.* 17:44; 18:6–7.
A-20. Lysias, *Pro Milite* 20.
A-21. 1QS 10:18–19.
A-22. *Counsels of Wisdom*, lines 41–45; from the translation by W. G. Lambert, *Babylonian Wisdom Literature* (Oxford: Clarendon, 1960), 101.
A-23. For other texts see Fitzmyer, *Luke*, 1:637–38; Nolland, *Luke*, 1:294–96; Seneca, *De Beneficiis*, 4.26.1.
A-24. 1QS 1:9–10.
A-25. Cf. 1QS 10:19.
A-26. Matt. 13:55–56; Mark 6:3; cf. Matt. 12:46; Mark 3:31.
A-27. Acts 12:17; 15:13; 21:18.
A-28. Cf. Fitzmyer, *Luke*, 1:723–24 who rejects the "cousin" view, but suggests that "brothers" could refer to a more distant relationship than a physical brother.
A-29. See R. J. Bauckham, *Jude and the Relatives of Jesus in the Early Church* (Edinburgh: T. & T. Clark, 1990).
A-30. Josephus, *Ant.* 20.9.1 §§ 200–203; ca. A.D. 61.

A-31. Eusebius, *Eccl. Hist.* 1.7.14.
A-32. Ibid., 3.19.1–3.20.8.
A-33. For other Jewish parallels see Str-B 4:1, 527–35.
A-34. Josephus, *Ant.*8.2.5 §§42–45.
A-35. For examples of such incantations see H. D. Betz, ed., *The Greek Magical Papyri in Translation* (Chicago: Univ. of Chicago Press, 1986).
A-36. On the Samaritans, see Jeremias, *Jerusalem*, 352–58; idem, "ὁδός," TDNT, 7:88–94; R. J. Coggins, *Samaritans and Jews: The Origins of the Samaritans Reconsidered* (Oxford: Blackwell, 1975); R. Pummer, *The Samaritans* (Leiden: Brill, 1987).
A-37. Josephus, *Life* 269.
A-38. *HCNT,* 262–63.
A-39. Josephus, *Ant.* 20.6.1 §118.
A-40. See Luke 10:25–37; 17:16; John 4:4–42.
A-41. Fitzmyer, *Luke*, 2:920.
A-42. There are many other suggestions related to the meaning. See Marshall, *Gospel of Luke*, 472–73; Fitzmyer, *Luke*, 2:920.
A-43. *T. Sol.* 3:2–5; 4:2; 6:1–3.
A-44. *Jub.* 10:8; 11:5; 19:28; cf. Hos. 9:7.
A-45. 1QS 1:18, 24; 2:5, 19; *Jub.* 1:20; *T. Dan* 5:10; see 2 Cor. 6:15.
A-46. Malina and Rohrbaugh, SSCSG, 136, 191.
A-47. Martial, *Epigrams* 1.20 (LCL, 43); Juvenal, *Satires* 5 (LCL, 69–83); Pliny, *Letters* 2.6 (LCL, 109–13).
A-48. Martial, *Epigram* 3.60 (LCL, 201).
A-49. See Josephus, *J.W.* 4.8.3 §§459–75.
A-50. Turner, *Hist. Geog.* 234, citing Kathleen M. Kenyon, *Archaeology of the Holy Land* (New York: Praeger, 1960), 42ff.
A-51. Josephus, *Ant.* 13.5.9 §171–73; 13.10.6 §297–98; 18.1.4 §16; idem, *J.W.* 2.8.14 §§164–65. For rabbinic views of the Sadducees see Str-B 1:885–86.
A-52. See Josephus, *Ant.* 12.3.3. §138. But cf. also *Ant.* 11.4.7 §105.
A-53. Josephus, *Ant.* 14.9.4 §175.
A-54. On crucifixion see especially Hengel, *Crucifixion.*
A-55. Seneca, *Dialogue* 6 (*To Marcia On Consolation*) 20.3.
A-56. See Hengel, *Crucifixion*, 29–32.
A-57. On the original excavation findings see N. Haas, "Anthropological Observations on the Skeletal Remains from Giv'at ha-Mivtar," *IEJ* 20 (1970): 38–59. On a reassessment of the evidence see J. Zias and E. Sekeles, "The Crucified Man from Giv'at ha-Mivtar—A Reappraisal," *IEJ* 35 (1985): 22–27; and J. Zias and J. H. Charlesworth, "Crucifixion: Archaeology, Jesus, and the Dead Sea Scrolls," in *Jesus and the Dead Sea Scrolls*, ed. J. H. Charlesworth (New York: Doubleday, 1992), 273–89.

CREDITS FOR PHOTOS AND MAPS

Arnold, Clinton E. . . . . p. 274
Claycombe, Hugh. . . . . pp. 6, 78, 186, 278, 306, 329, 466–467, 496
Dunn, Cheryl (for Talbot Bible Lands) . . . . pp. 223, 236, 267, 288
Franz, Gordon . . . . pp. 111, 232, 377, 456
Haradine, Jane (public domain photos) . . . . . pp. 26, 86, 87, 147, 151, 224(2), 269
Isachar, Hanan . . . . pp. 31, 58, 157(2), 166, 168, 170(3), 182, 214, 232, 233, 286, 349, 368, 385, 408, 485
King, Jay . . . . pp. 340, 383, 443
Kohlenberger, John R. III . . . . pp. 14, 19, 29, 32, 62, 67, 71, 73, 88, 89, 92, 97, 99, 101, 118, 125, 207, 218, 226, 234, 236, 238, 242, 244, 251, 253, 258, 266, 267, 325, 331, 334, 349, 351, 376, 383, 396, 407, 411, 416, 465, 499
Konstas, Ioannis . . . . pp. 70, 167
Radovan, Zev. . . . . pp. 2–3, 17(2), 20, 26, 31, 36(2), 39, 41(2), 44(2), 47, 49, 50(2), 57(3), 61, 65, 66, 72, 75(2), 84(2), 87, 88(2), 89, 92, 93, 95(2), 98, 100, 103(2), 107, 109(2), 111, 115, 117, 120, 126, 128, 130(2), 132(2), 133, 135, 140, 144, 152(2), 160, 161, 162, 171, 174, 176, 185, 189, 218, 221, 240, 241, 251, 262(2), 267, 270, 273, 274, 276, 283, 285, 294, 300, 342, 351, 356, 362, 365, 371, 374, 387, 389, 390, 399, 410, 422, 433, 436, 437, 439, 452(2), 462, 470, 473, 476, 479, 480, 482, 485, 486, 490
Rigsby, Richard . . . . p. 2
Ritmeyer, Leen . . . . . . pp. 8, 39, 176, 206, 271, 277, 285, 292, 320, 327, 346, 494
University of Michigan . . . . p. 5
Zondervan Image Archive (Neal Bierling) . . . . pp. 10, 15, 21, 22(4), 23(2), 24, 27, 29(2), 33, 37, 39, 43, 49, 52, 60, 75(3), 83, 91, 101(2), 107, 113, 122, 126(2), 128, 129, 131, 144, 146(2), 148, 155, 159, 163, 166, 168(2), 172, 177(2), 179, 182, 204–205, 209(2), 214, 231, 242, 246, 255, 257, 261, 273, 279, 280, 282, 286, 297(2), 305(2), 318–319, 334, 338(3), 340, 342, 345, 348, 353, 359, 360(2), 365, 378, 385, 389, 391, 396, 403(2), 408, 415, 423, 424, 426, 428, 429, 453, 462(2), 463, 468, 470, 471, 472, 478, 479, 488, 489, 492, 493, 497, 498

We want to hear from you. Please send your comments about this book to us in care of the address below. Thank you.

GRAND RAPIDS, MICHIGAN 49530

WWW.ZONDERVAN.COM